Patent Litigation Through the Unified Patent Court and German Courts

Patent Litigation Through the Unified Patent Court and German Courts

An International Handbook

Alexander Harguth
Konstantin Schallmoser
Steven C. Carlson

Wolters Kluwer

Published by:
Kluwer Law International B.V.
PO Box 316
2400 AH Alphen aan den Rijn
The Netherlands
E-mail: lrs-sales@wolterskluwer.com
Website: www.wolterskluwer.com/en/solutions/kluwerlawinternational

Sold and distributed by:
Wolters Kluwer Legal & Regulatory U.S.
920 Links Avenue
Landisville, PA 17538
United States of America
E-mail: customer.service@wolterskluwer.com

ISBN 978-90-411-9106-9

e-Book: 978-90-411-9130-4
web-PDF: 978-90-411-9131-1

Table of Contents

List of Figures

List of Figures

List of Tables

CHAPTER 1
Preamble

§1.01 INTRODUCTION

Europe has instituted the most dramatic changes to its patent enforcement system ever. Through the enactment of the unitary patent (UP) system, and launch of the Unified Patent Court (UPC), Europe has established the ability to achieve pan-European enforcement of patents.

The new system provides innovators with the ability to obtain a UP that can have effect across the Contracting Member States of the Agreement on a Unified Patent Court (UPCA). These are almost all Member States of the European Union (EU). Enforcement can proceed through the UPC, rather than on a country-by-country basis. These reforms, with reach across Europe's lucrative market of more than four hundred million citizens, provide innovators powerful new tools for establishing and enforcing their patents. This book is designed to help innovative businesses around the world appreciate the opportunities and pitfalls posed by Europe's new system.

National patent systems continue to coexist with the new European patent system. For a transitional period of at least seven years, ordinary European patents either can be enforced in national courts, as they have been previously, or may be enforced in the new UPC. Furthermore, innovators can obtain protections through national patent offices (like the German Patent and Trademark Office (GPTO)) and enforce those national rights exclusively through national court systems. Thus, the range of options for procuring patent rights, and advancing an enforcement campaign, is ballooning. Smart companies are restructuring their patent portfolios and their enforcement strategies to take advantage of these multiple tiers of protection.

With the upsides of pan-European protection, there are pitfalls as well. While there are undeniable advantages to obtaining UPs and enforcing them across Europe in a single litigation at the UPC, the flip side is that a single adverse ruling can invalidate patents for all of Europe. Would-be infringers might take advantage of this structure and preemptively challenge European patents in the UPC, seeking to clear away troublesome patents in a single litigation. Therefore, companies are wise to pursue a mix of rights, with national patents, "ordinary" European patents, as well as patents with unitary effect. Part of this calculus, which companies must now evaluate, is to decide whether to "opt out" of the jurisdiction of the UPC.

The courts in Europe are faced with three distinct means of patent protection—UPs, ordinary European patents and national patents. These systems will intersect, interweave and interfere with one another in new and unpredictable ways. The savvy practitioner and the educated client will appreciate the nuances in the different tiers of protection and will know how to exploit the advantages offered by each. This handbook is aimed at unmasking that complexity to promote good strategies for decision-makers around the world.

§1.02 UPC VERSUS GERMAN "SPLIT SYSTEM"

In recent years, the jurisdiction of choice for enforcing patents in Europe has been Germany. Still today, there are sound reasons for litigants to choose Germany as their preferred jurisdiction: the German "split system"; the expertise and reputation of German infringement courts; and the speed and low costs of the proceedings. The German system is embedded in a new context with the UPC being operational alongside the German system. This provides additional tools to enforce and invalidate patents.

A defining characteristic of the German patent enforcement system is the split between infringement and invalidity rulings. Infringement and invalidity ("nullity") claims are tried in different courts, on different schedules. In most cases, an enforceable ruling can be expected in around one year, or, with the District Courts of Mannheim and Munich, even earlier. Almost all infringement cases track ahead of counterpart invalidity proceedings, thus presenting the opportunity to have infringement resolved before invalidity is tried. While the infringement court may suspend its proceedings to allow a corresponding nullity action to resolve validity first, frequently it does not.[1] This may lead to the so-called injunction gap, which is one of the reasons why German patent enforcement is considered to be particularly patentee-friendly in comparison to other jurisdictions.

The UPC will normally not follow a "split system" along the model of Germany's court structure. Infringement and invalidity ("nullity") claims are tried through one proceeding in one single division of the UPC, on the same schedule. At first blush, it appears that this procedural distinction would render the UPC to be less patentee-friendly than the German system. However, this assumption paints an incomplete picture. There are reasons, such as the benefits of harmonizing patent enforcement in Europe, that favor enforcing patents through the UPC.

Enforcement through the UPC also provides other advantages in comparison to national enforcement. The UPC has authority to grant injunctions and damages

1. Appeal Court Düsseldorf, 2 W 47/07, GRUR-RR 2008, 329, Olanzapine.

through one single proceeding for the contracting Member States. This unified proceeding contrasts with a costly country-by-country enforcement through national courts, which may result in diverging results among jurisdictions. The UPC has exclusive jurisdiction to adjudicate over infringement and revocation of UPs. UPs, which are an element of the so-called Patent Package,[2] necessarily fall under the exclusive jurisdiction of the UPC.

This handbook illustrates in detail the different advantages and downsides of the respective judicial tracks.

§1.03 SPECIAL REGIME FOR ORDINARY EUROPEAN PATENTS: OPT-OUT

A special regime applies to ordinary European patents (as opposed to European patents with unitary effect). For these patents, the jurisdiction of the UPC is not exclusive during a transitional period of seven years. Instead, the UPC's jurisdiction coexists alongside the jurisdiction of national courts. During the transitional period, actions based on ordinary European patents can thus be filed with either the UPC or national courts.

Companies that wish to invalidate patents may file revocation actions preemptively at the UPC. However, the opportunity for such a strategic attack is lost if the patent owner has already filed an "opt-out" for the patent to remove that patent from the UPC's jurisdiction. Thus, companies must actively decide whether to file such "opt-outs." Once a competitor sues in the UPC to challenge the patent, the ability to file such an opt-out is lost forever. Thus, innovators should not miss the opportunity to consider filing these opt-outs preemptively in order to preserve the ability to litigate in the national court systems. From the day of the entry into force of the UPCA, cases can be lodged at the UPC. Prior to that date, a so-called Sunrise Period of three months is/was running. That period starts/started to run with Germany's deposit of the UPCA ratification. During that period, applications to opt out European patents and European patent applications can/could be lodged (Rule 5 of the Rules of Procedure of the UPC). To be effective, an opt-out must be registered prior a revocation action or any other action has been filed with the UPC against the patent (Article 83(3) UPCA). Hence, a patentee who fears that a competitor could block through a UPC action the opt-out possibility shall file an opt-out during the Sunrise Period; this is a time when UPC actions are/were not yet possible. This handbook illustrates in detail the mechanism of opting-out. An outline of the mechanism of the opt-out system is illustrated in Table 1.1.

2. The EU Patent Package (the Patent Package) consists of two related but independent parts: a European Patent with Unitary Effect (the Unitary Patent or UP) and a UPC.

Table 1.1 Concept of the "Opt-Out": System

	Jurisdiction of the UPC	Jurisdiction of National Courts
No Opt-Out declared:	Yes	Yes
Opt-Out declared:	No	Yes
"Opt-in"*:	Yes	Yes
Unavailable:	Yes	No

*Opt-Out declared with later withdrawal of Opt-Out.

§1.04 EXPERTISE AND REPUTATION OF THE COURTS

The UPC is new and has not yet developed its own jurisprudence. Nevertheless, the incoming judges at the UPC convey a promising prospect that the court will quickly gain an extraordinary reputation. The undefined jurisprudence of the UPC stands in contrast to the well-developed bodies of law through the national court systems of Europe, particularly in Germany. Deciding which system to invoke for patent enforcement is an important choice, which requires foresight and preparation.

In Germany, infringement actions are filed in district courts, with the courts in Mannheim, Munich and Düsseldorf accounting for more than 75% of Germany's infringement cases. Due to the large number of cases handled each year by these courts, they have significant expertise in patent matters. This expertise is recognized in Europe and across the world. Among European national jurisdictions, Germany leads with around thousand cases handled by its patent infringement courts, followed by France with around three hundred cases, and the United Kingdom (UK) and the Netherlands with less than hundred cases.[3]

This handbook explains how and to what extent the established body of law in Germany may be used to shape the jurisprudence of the UPC, and whether one jurisdiction may be favored over the other in various situations.

§1.05 COSTS OF PROCEEDINGS

Litigating through the UPC is not expected to be more expensive than such proceedings in national courts, such as Germany. Because the UPC allows for pan-European enforcement, litigants can avoid the cost of having to litigate in multiple jurisdictions and avoid the risk of conflicting decisions. Thus, the broad territorial reach of the UPC is a primary advantage of the system, which reduces the cost and uncertainty of patent litigation in Europe, and provides greater relief than litigation through national courts. Moreover, in contrast to United States (US) litigation, the UPC will be less expensive, as costly pretrial proceedings typical of US litigation are not part of UPC proceedings. This is not to suggest that discovery is unavailable.[4] Finally, there are no jury trials in patent infringement cases handled by the UPC.

3. JUVE, Nachrichten vom 30.06.2018 "Weitere Patentgerichte legen Fallzahlen vor."
4. *See* Ch. 13.

Comparable features are available in national proceedings. However, the impact of such proceedings is limited to the national borders. As an example, the costs of German patent enforcement are usually ranging from Euro (EUR) 60,000 for less complex cases to EUR 240,000 for more complex cases.

This book provides a strategic framework for maximizing the benefit, and guarding against the downsides, of this new pan-European enforcement regime.

CHAPTER 2
Sources of Law

§2.01 INTRODUCTION

Patent enforcement in Europe is based on a complex interplay between international treaties, the European Patent Convention (EPC), the so-called EU Patent Package, national codes and the jurisprudence of national courts, the European Patent Office (EPO), its Boards of Appeal and the UPC. This chapter provides a high-level overview of these different sources of law. It is also aimed at providing the reader with tips on how to perform research into these various bodies of law.

§2.02 EUROPEAN LAWS

European laws either result from treaties concluded between countries of Europe or they represent legislation of the EU.

The EU promulgates two bases of laws governing intellectual property (IP): directives and regulations. The main difference between these two types of legislation is that a directive is not self-executing and requires Member States of the EU to enact legislation to achieve the results sought by the directive, without dictating the particular manner of doing so. Directives typically afford the Member States discretion as to the rules to be adopted, often just setting minimum standards, and generally requiring that provisions be enacted into national law. An important directive in the area of IP is the Enforcement Directive of April 29, 2004, setting forth common minimum standards for procedures for enforcing IP among the EU Member States.[1] This includes procedures for the preservation of evidence, including the physical seizure of infringing goods, and, in appropriate cases, the seizure of materials and tools

1. Enforcement Directive 2004/48/EC of the European Parliament and of the Council of Apr. 29, 2004 on the enforcement of intellectual property rights (the text can be found on the website: http://eur-lex.europa.eu/).

used in the production and/or distribution of such goods and documents relating thereto.[2] The Enforcement Directive also addresses damages, requiring that Members ensure that infringers must pay the patentee "damages appropriate to the actual prejudice suffered by him or her as a result of the infringement."[3] The Enforcement Directive has been implemented by the Member States of the EU, each with a somewhat different effect, depending on the unique procedural rules of each country. Germany implemented the Directive on July 7, 2008.[4]

On the contrary, EU regulations are self-executing and accordingly do not require any implementing measures at the national level. Examples of such regulations include regulation No. 1257/2012 of December 17, 2012, concerning the creation of a UP[5] and No. 1260/2012 of December 17, 2012, implementing the translation requirements for the UP.[6]

Chief among the European laws governing patents is the EPC, which is the treaty among European countries that established the ("EPO") and which provides a centralized system for granting (and opposing) patents in Europe. A further set of patent-related provisions are contained in what is referred to as the "EU Patent Package." The EU Patent Package, which is now being fully implemented, consists of two related but independent parts: a European Patent with Unitary Effect (the UP) and the UPC. In addition, there are border control laws derived from national and European laws that provide mechanisms for seizing infringing goods through customs authorities.

[A] European Patent Convention

The EPC was originally signed in Munich on October 5, 1973, and has been in force in Germany since October 7, 1977. The EPC is periodically revised, and the current version is the seventeenth edition of the EPC, which was published in 2020, and contains the revised texts of the Convention from November 29, 2000 (EPC 2000).

The primary focus of the EPC is to establish and regulate the procedures for the EPO, which is a central authority for examining patent applications. Upon grant, patents issuing from the EPO are either converted into a bundle of national patents for European Member States, such as Germany (so-called ordinary European patents), or become European patents with unitary effect in those Member States of the EPC adhering to the EU Patent Package. Both types of European patents are granted by the EPO under the same rules. The EPC is available in English and accessible through the EPO website www.epo.org. A selection of the most important provisions of the EPC can be found in §18.01 of Chapter 18 of this book.

---

2. Enforcement Directive, Art. 7.
3. Enforcement Directive, Art. 13.
4. Federal Law Gazette (BGBl.) I 1191, BlPMZ 08, 274.
5. Regulation (EU) No. 1257/2012 of the European Parliament and of the Council of Dec. 17, 2012 implementing enhanced cooperation in the area of the creation of unitary patent protection.
6. Regulation (EU) No. 1260/2012 of Dec. 17, 2012 implementing enhanced cooperation in the area of the creation of unitary patent protection with regard to the applicable translation arrangements.

Ordinary European patents carry the same rights as would be conferred by a national patent granted in each individual country of the EU. Such rights are established on the date of publication of the grant of the patent in the European Patent Bulletin.[7] For example, an applicant may obtain a patent through the EPO and designate Germany as a country for which a national stage patent shall issue. Enforcement of that patent proceeds either through the German national court system or through the unified court system, as discussed in subsequent chapters. Alternatively, the applicant may take the route of UP protection (referred to as "UP"), in which case the patent can be enforced exclusively through the UPC system. An applicant may validate a European patent in countries not adhering to the EU Patent Package (e.g., Spain, Switzerland and Turkey) and at the same time apply for UP protection in Member States adhering to the EU Patent Package.

The EPC also provides substantive laws governing patents, which include standards for patent validity and for establishing the scope of protection. Many of these standards have analogs in US patent law—for example, the concept of "novelty" in US law is roughly the same as in Europe (*see* Article 54 EPC), and the US concept of "non-obviousness" roughly corresponds to the concept of "inventive step" (*see* Article 56 EPC). The EPC also provides standards for patentable subject matter, including requirements for protecting computer programs, medical treatments and diagnostic methods. These matters are discussed in more detail in the following chapters.[8] The EPC comprises the texts of the Convention, its Implementing Regulations[9] and a set of protocols[10] and rules relating to fees and rules of procedure of the Boards of Appeal (RPBA) and the Enlarged Board of Appeal. In addition, special rules for the Unitary Patent (UPR) and relating to fees (RFeesUPP[11]) have been issued by the EPO's Select Committee of the Administrative Council.[12]

[B] London Agreement

On October 17, 2000, a number of Contracting States to the EPC adopted the so-called London Agreement,[13] which came into force on May 1, 2008, following lengthy ratification and accession procedures in national parliaments. This Agreement is aimed at reducing costs through a post-grant translation regime for ordinary European patents. The Contracting States are Albania, Belgium, Croatia, Denmark, Finland,

7. Article 64(1) EPC.
8. *See* Ch. 5.
9. Implementing Regulations to the Convention on the Grant of European Patents as last amended by decision of the Administrative Council of the European Patent Organization of Mar. 27, 2020.
10. Protocol on the Interpretation of Art. 69 EPC; Protocol on Jurisdiction and the Recognition of Decisions in respect of the Right to the Grant of a European Patent; Protocol on Centralization; Protocol on Privileges and Immunities of the European Patent Organization; Protocol on Staff Complement.
11. Rules relating to Fees for Unitary Patent Protection.
12. Rules relating to Unitary Patent Protection, Official Journal EPO, 2016, A39, A40.
13. The London Agreement can be consulted on the website of the EPO: www.epo.org.

Latvia, Lithuania, the Netherlands, France, Liechtenstein, Sweden, Slovenia, Germany, Luxembourg, Switzerland, Iceland, Ireland, the Republic of Macedonia, Monaco, Norway and the UK. The Agreement distinguishes between Contracting States having an official language in common with one of the official languages of the EPO (i.e., English, French or German) and States which do not have an official language in common with one of the official EPO languages. The first group, namely those States having a national language in common with one of the official languages of the EPO, have dispensed entirely with translation requirements. These States are France, Germany, Liechtenstein, Luxembourg, Monaco, Switzerland and the UK. States of the other group apply a less severe translation regime than was previously required. For instance, the Netherlands, Sweden and Denmark require that the claims of the European patent be supplied in Dutch, Swedish and Danish, respectively, for patentees who want protection in those countries. In addition, these States require that the European patent specification be available or supplied in English. Other EPC States, such as Italy, Spain, Portugal and Greece, have not ratified the London Agreement, and thus the normal translation regime is applicable. Complete translations of the patent are still required for patentees seeking protection in those countries. A different translation regime applies to UPs. That regime will be described in more detail in the following sections, which is an important element for the strategic and budgetary decision to apply either for an ordinary or a unitary European patent.

[C] EU Patent Package

The EU Patent Package establishes a major shift in patent law in Europe.

The EU Patent Package is based on two pillars: the UP and the UPC. The rules governing the UP system are founded in two European regulations, which have a direct effect across the participating EU Member States, and which provide for the issuance of patents to be enforceable across all those Member States. Furthermore, the EU Patent Package provides for the formation of a UPC, based on the UPCA. The UPC Agreement establishes the UPC through statute and provides a procedure for setting procedural rules.

The Patent Package excludes non-EU States from participation. Thus, UPs have no force in certain countries such as Switzerland,[14] even if those countries follow the EPC. In addition, a few EU Member States, such as Poland and Spain, have chosen—at least for the time being—to decline adopting the system to varying degrees.[15] Thus a UP cannot be enforced across all countries in Europe.

14. Also: Albania, Iceland, Liechtenstein, Macedonia, Monaco, Norway, Serbia, San Marino, Turkey.
15. The partial absence of these EU Members limits the territorial scope of the UP and UPC. The related effects will be illustrated in detail in the following chapters.

[1] *Regulations Relating to the UP*

UPs have "unitary effect" across participating EU Member States. In March 2011 the Council of Ministers of the EU authorized a group of EU Member States to participate in a so-called enhanced cooperation for the purpose of UP Protection. Currently, all EU Member States except Croatia and Spain are participating in that enhanced cooperation. Among these 25 EU Member States, 17 states have already ratified the Agreements and thus effectively participate in the UP System. UPs can be enforced in those countries through a single proceeding.

The UP System is founded on two European regulations that were passed on December 17, 2012. The first regulation concerns the general framework of the UP (the UP Regulation),[16] and the second relates to translation requirements (the Translation Regulation).[17] The issuance of two separate regulations was required because higher voting thresholds are needed for changes to translation arrangements. Both Regulations have direct effect on all participating EU Member States and accordingly do not require any further national implementing measures to be taken by the States. The procedures for granting UPs and ordinary European patents are essentially the same. Both are governed by the EPC.

According to Article 1(2) of the UP Regulation, the UP Regulation is considered to be a "Special Agreement" under Article 142(2) EPC. This provision can be found in Part IX of the EPC, entitled "Special Agreements." The only "Special Agreement" in force was concluded between Switzerland and Liechtenstein to form the basis of a patent having unitary character over the territories of both countries.[18] According to Article 142(2) EPC, the granting proceedings are essentially the same for an ordinary European patent and a UP. To both, the EPC is applicable.

[2] *Rules of the UPC*

The legal foundation for the UPC is based on the following laws.

UPCA: The UPCA is a treaty that has been signed by twenty-five of the twenty-eight Member States of the EU. It is the main legal foundation of the UPC. It was endorsed by the EU ministers in the Competitiveness Council on December 10, 2012, and by the European Parliament on December 11, 2012.[19] It was signed by the participating EU Member States on February 19, 2013. An excerpt of the UPCA can be found in Chapter 18.

16. Regulation (EU) No. 1257/2012 of the European Parliament and of the Council of Dec. 17, 2012 implementing enhanced cooperation in the area of the creation of unitary patent protection.
17. Regulation (EU) No. 1260/2012 of the European Parliament and of the Council Dec. 17, 2012 implementing enhanced cooperation in the area of the creation of unitary patent protection with regard to the applicable translation arrangements.
18. Agreement of Dec. 22, 1978.
19. Document 16351/12, of Jan. 11, 2013.

Statute of the Court: The Statute of the Court (the Statute) is an integral part of the UPCA[20] and is included in Annex I of the UPCA. The Statute determines the institutional and financial arrangements of the UPC, including the conditions for appointing the Court's judges and electing the President of the Court of First Instance[21] and of the Court of Appeal.[22]

Rules of Procedure (RoP): The procedural framework of the UPC is established in a set of rules that have been adopted by the Administrative Committee of the Court.[23] The rules address the different stages of proceedings, general case management, proportionality and fairness (such as the right to be heard). They also contain general provisions on languages of the proceeding, parties, representation, means of evidence, and experts and define the powers of the UPC to order provisional remedies (e.g., preliminary injunctions) and measures for preserving evidence (e.g., *saisie contrefaçon*).

Practical Guidance and Templates: This is content issued by the UPC containing non-binding recommendations helping to develop a harmonized format for decisions and orders.

[D] Border Measures Regulations

Customs authorities provide powerful means for enforcing patent rights. National border enforcement proceedings provide an analog to the US International Trade Commission (ITC) proceedings for excluding infringing goods from importation. National customs systems derive their authority in large part from EU Regulation 608/2013.[24] This Regulation provides measures to prohibit import or export of counterfeits and infringing goods. This Regulation applies directly to the EU Member States, such as Germany. These border control measures are discussed in detail in Chapter 16.

§2.03 OTHER INTERNATIONAL TREATIES

International treaties governing IP are usually not self-implementing. Rather the legislature of each country must separately enact national laws to be in compliance with such international agreements and obligations. The major patent-related treaties to which European countries, are signatories are discussed in brief below.

20. Article 2(i) of the UPCA.
21. Article 14 of the Statute.
22. Article 13 of the Statute.
23. Article 41(2) of the UPCA.
24. Regulation (EU) No. 608/2013 of the European Parliament and of the Council of Jun. 12, 2013 concerning customs enforcement of intellectual property rights and repealing Council Regulation (EC) No. 1383/2003 (OJ L 181, Jun. 29, 2013, p. 15); an excerpt of the most important provisions of the Regulation can be found in Ch. 18. The complete text (in English) can be found on the website http://eur-lex.europa.eu.

[A] Paris Convention

All Contracting Member States of the EPC as well as the UPCA have ratified the Paris Convention. Germany joined the Paris Convention on May 1, 1903. The Paris Convention establishes international standards for the protection of industrial property. A particularly important effect of the Paris Convention is the priority right embedded in the provisions of Article 4.[25] In particular, the Paris Convention provides that the filing of an application in one signatory country provides a right of priority, such that the applicant may later file applications in other member jurisdictions without loss of right due to activities occurring in the interval between the filings, such as publication or exploitation of the invention.[26] This period of priority is twelve months for patents and utility models.[27] The protections of the Paris Convention are codified in Article 87 of the EPC, for patents prosecuted through the EPO, and in section 41 of the GPA, for patents prosecuted through the GPTO.

[B] Patent Cooperation Treaty

The Patent Cooperation Treaty (PCT) was ratified by all Contracting Member States of the EPC and the UPCA. It was ratified by Germany in 1977,[28] and its provisions were implemented into the national law the following year.[29] This Treaty allows patent applicants to initiate multinational protection by filing a single international application. This Treaty centralizes application proceedings and provides a prior art search, including the possibility of a nonbinding, preliminary opinion on novelty and inventive step. In contrast to the EPC, the PCT does not provide centralized grant proceedings.[30]

[C] Trade-Related Aspects of Intellectual Property Rights

The Agreement on Trade-Related Aspects of Intellectual Property Rights (TRIPS) is an international treaty setting forth general guidelines for the structuring of patent systems and the enforcement of patent rights. The EU, all Contracting Member States of the UPCA and almost all Contracting Member States of the EPC signed TRIPS. Germany signed TRIPS in 1995.[31] Because the German legislature considered the German patent system already compatible with TRIPS, the provisions of this Treaty were not directly enacted into national law.[32] The national laws of Germany must be applied in

25. The text of the Paris Convention can be found on www.wipo.int.
26. *See* Paris Convention, Art. 4.
27. Six months for industrial designs and trademarks (Art. 4 of the Paris Convention for the Protection of Industrial Property).
28. Federal Law Gazette (BGBl.) II, 1978, 11.
29. *Ibid.*, 484.
30. The PCT can be found on www.wipo.org.
31. Federal Law Gazette (BGBl.) 1995, II, 456.
32. Gazette of the Federal Parliament (BT-Drucksache), 12/7655, 345.

conformity with the provisions of TRIPS, and accordingly German courts must ensure that the standards mandated by TRIPS are satisfied.[33]

A particularly significant application of TRIPS[34] to patent law in Germany concerns its standards for patent enforcement. Article 42 of TRIPS provides standards for procedural assertion of patents and other IP rights. In particular, Article 43 of TRIPS provides minimum standards for evidence taking. These articles prompted German courts to expand discovery under national law, allowing patentees to gather evidence in support of their enforcement activities.

In 2002, Germany's Federal Supreme Court issued a ruling reaffirming that the provisions of the relevant German evidentiary laws must be construed in such a way that they satisfy the requirements of TRIPS, thereby broadening the previously limited discovery available to patentees under German law.[35] And more recently, the German legislature has enacted into national law the provisions of the European Enforcement Directive, discussed above, which further expands the availability of discovery to patentees.[36] The Enforcement Directive is viewed as providing remedies beyond the minimum requirements of TRIPS, and so is sometimes referred to as "TRIPS-plus." This view is espoused particularly by developing countries and other entities that contend that European patent enforcement has gone too far in terms of the seizure of goods accused of infringement, including goods in transit to other countries.

It is still undecided as to what extent the UPC will be subject to the mandates of TRIPS. However, the patent system underlying the UPC does not manifest any incompatibility with the provisions of TRIPS. Accordingly, the question of whether TRIPS shall directly or indirectly govern the UPC appears to remain a largely academic concern.

§2.04 NATIONAL LAWS

[A] Germany

[1] Patent Act (**Patentgesetz**: *PatG)*

The primary source of substantive patent law in Germany is the GPA (Patent Act). This Act deals with the grant and enforcement of German patents. The Patent Act was first enacted in Germany in 1980 and has been periodically revised. The most recent amendments to the Patent Act were enacted by the German legislature on August 20, 2021.[37] A translation of the Patent Act can be found on the World Intellectual Property Organization (WIPO) website (www.wipo.org); however, this translation does not contain the most recent amendments. Accordingly, an unofficial translation of an

33. Federal Supreme Court, GRUR 2002, 1046, IIC 2003, 331, "Faxkarte."
34. The text of TRIPS can be found on www.wto.org.
35. Federal Supreme Court, GRUR 2002, 1046, IIC 2003, 331, "Faxkarte"; Federal Supreme Court, Aug. 1, 2006, X ZR 114/03 IIC 2007, 97 "Restschadstoffentfernung."
36. *See, for instance*, s. 140c Patent Act in Ch. 18, §18.03.
37. Federal Law Gazette (BGBl.) I, 2021, 4074.

excerpt of the Patent Act with the latest amendments can be found in §18.03 of Chapter 18 of this book.

[2] Code of Civil Procedure (**Zivilprozessordnung:** ***ZPO)***

While the substantive rules of patent law are provided for in the Patent Act, the procedural rules for carrying out patent enforcement in Germany are provided by the German Code of Civil Procedure.[38] This Code, which governs the course of judicial proceedings, is analogous to the Federal Rules of Civil Procedure in the US. An English translation of the complete Code of Civil Procedure is available online.[39]

[3] Utility Model Act (**Gebrauchsmustergesetz:** ***GebrMG)***

The Utility Model Act (GebrMG) is distinct from the Patent Act and provides a separate, enforceable IP right known as a utility model. A translation of that Act can be found on the WIPO website, but it does not contain the most recent amendments of the GebrMG, at least as of the printing of this book.

An unofficial translation of an excerpt of the GebrMG with the latest amendments can be found in §18.04 of Chapter 18 of this book. The registration system for acquiring utility models does not provide for a substantive examination over the technology for which protection is sought. Nonetheless, the resulting utility model is an enforceable right, whereby infringement proceedings can be prosecuted and injunctions over infringing goods can be obtained. These utility models do not have an analogous right under US law and can be powerful tools in a patent enforcement strategy. They are discussed in the following chapters.[40]

[4] Act on Employees' Inventions (**Arbeitnehmererfindergesetz:** ***ArbEG)***

Germany has enacted the Employee Invention Act (ArbEG), the goal of which is to solve the conflicting interests of the employed inventor and his or her employer. The Employee Invention Act was first enacted in 1957 and considerably amended in 2009.[41] There is an English language translation of the Act available in book form, although the most recent amendments are not yet reflected in it. Chapter 15, §15.05 discusses the most important aspects of the Act as recently amended.

[B] Overview: Other Jurisdictions

A complete overview of patent enforcement in Europe would require a description of the different patent laws of all European States. Each State possesses its own national

38. The latest version of the Code of Civil Procedure can be found on www.gesetze-im-internet.de (website of the Federal Ministry of Justice).
39. *See* http://www.gesetze-im-internet.de.
40. For more details on German Utility Models, *see* Ch. 4, §4.03[C].
41. Federal Law Gazette (BGBl.) I, 2009, 2521.

patent law. These laws govern the protection and enforcement systems of national patent rights having effect within the boundaries of the State in which they are granted (such as in France, Italy, Spain, etc.). Such national patent rights (i.e., patents and utility models where applicable) are enforceable through national courts. National patent rights are not affected by the EU Patent Package. They are not enforceable through the UPC. The national patent systems coexist with the EU Patent Package. In certain States, national patent rights and European patents may coexist, even with the same scope of protection. Patent owners may thus enhance their patent portfolio by splitting up the rights into national and European rights.

CHAPTER 3
Structure of Legal System

§3.01 INTRODUCTION

Patent disputes are resolved through a complex and evolving interplay of proceedings at both the European and national levels, including at the following tribunals:

- EPO, including its Boards of Appeal;
- UPC; and
- national courts.

The EPO has jurisdiction over challenges to the validity of newly issued European patents. These EPO opposition proceedings apply equally to UPs as well as to ordinary European patents. There is a hard deadline of nine months from patent issuance to file opposition proceedings. Once that nine-month period expires, only the UPC and, during the transitional regime according to Article 83 UPCA, the various national court systems have jurisdiction to hear patent validity challenges.

The UPC has a key role relating to litigation based on ordinary European patents and European patents with unitary effect (UPs). The UPC has jurisdiction over cases for both infringement and invalidity (revocation) of European patents. Also, at the European level, on rare occasions, the Court of Justice of the European Union[1] (CJEU) is invoked to rule on particular matters concerning the interpretation of EU law arising through the UPC or the local national court systems.[2]

The German court system has been the predominant court system in Europe for resolving infringement disputes. The German system is remarkable for having a "split system," with infringement disputes resolved in the district courts, on the one hand,

1. The Court of Justice of the European Union is situated in Luxembourg.
2. National courts in each EU country including the UPC are responsible for ensuring that EU law is correctly applied. To prevent different views on the interpretation and application of EU law, national courts may, and sometimes must, refer to the European Court of Justice and ask it to clarify a point concerning the interpretation of EU law.

and validity challenges resolved through a separate court, the Federal Patent Court. The German court system has exclusive jurisdiction over disputes arising from patent rights granted by the German national system, including German patents and German utility models. Patents granted through the German Patent Office, and likewise German utility models, cannot be litigated through the UPC. During a transitional period of (at least) seven years, an action for infringement of an ordinary European patent may still be brought before a German court.[3] The challenges and opportunities presented by this split system are discussed in this chapter, as well as in further detail in Chapters 9 and 10.

The proceedings at the UPC are grounded in the rules of the UPCA and the Rules of Procedure (RoP).[4] Within this legal framework, the UPC has the authority to develop its own body of case law based on the provisions of the UPCA and RoP. The UPCA is an international treaty. Guidance on how to interpret such a treaty is given by the Vienna Convention on the Law of Treaties.[5] In addition, other relevant European Laws provide sources of law that impact the UPC's jurisprudence, such as Directive 2004/48/EC on the enforcement of IP rights.[6] The terms of the UPCA will control when its own provisions are explicit, such as rules relating to the effects and limits of a patent, as provided in Articles 25 et seq. These explicit rules will trump the case law that has developed until now through the Members States. That is, preexisting national case laws will not have any binding effect on the UPC's interpretation and understanding of the provisions of the UPCA and the RoP.

A characteristic of the German system—as a civil law system—is that laws are codified in written principles as rules of law and not determined, as in common law, by judges. Accordingly, legislative acts are the primary source of law in Germany, and the court system is usually inquisitorial, unbound by precedent. However, German courts do carefully review previous rulings of other courts, in particular of appellate courts[7] and, of course, of the Federal Supreme Court. Due to the high volume of patent litigation, Germany has a well-developed body of precedent that can lend additional predictability to the patent litigation process.

3. Article 83(1) UPCA.
4. Excerpts of the UPCA can be found in Ch. 18.
5. Vienna Convention on the Law of Treaties stipulates in its Art. 31 that a treaty shall be interpreted in good faith in accordance with ordinary meaning to be given to the terms of the treaty in their context and in the light of its object and purpose. Its Art. 32 states that supplementary means of interpretation, including the preparatory work of the treaty and the circumstances of its conclusion, may be used in order to confirm the meaning resulting from the application of Art. 31, or to determine the meaning when the interpretation according to Art. 31: (a) leaves the meaning ambiguous or obscure, or (b) leads to a result which is manifestly absurd or unreasonably. Although not all Contracting Member States have ratified the Vienna Convention, these rules likely apply. They reflect what the common understanding of international laws is.
6. Article 24(1) UPCA.
7. Court instances: District Courts, the Appeal Courts and the Federal Supreme Court are three levels or instances of the civil court system. Rulings of a court may be appealed to a higher instance. Such higher instance may either uphold or reverse the ruling from the lower instance. Patent cases typically begin at a district court level with the possibility of appeal to an appeal court. In exceptional situations, the case might be brought before a third instance, namely the Federal Supreme Court.

Searching judicial precedent in Germany can be challenging. A few online databases collect German court decisions, but the decisions are usually not translated into English. A few German courts post their rulings on websites, but the lack of a central reporting agency requires the researcher to conduct a court-by-court search of opinions.[8] This is a time-consuming exercise that is fraught with the risk of missing important rulings. Accordingly, there is a premium on selecting counsel with expertise in the subject matter and extensive local litigation experience. The identification of relevant EPO decisions, in particular decisions of the Boards of Appeal, is less problematic, in light of a publicly available database on the website of the EPO.[9] Likewise, proceedings at the UPC can be investigated through a publicly accessible register containing filed pleadings, written evidence and decisions rendered by the UPC (unless certain information has been kept confidential).[10]

§3.02 GENERAL OUTLINE OF PATENT DISPUTES

There are different ways to invalidate patents in Europe: The EPO provides a time-limited window for filing oppositions against European patents. National patent offices offer similar proceedings for opposing patents issuing through those national offices. Furthermore, revocation actions are available at the UPC against European patents (with jurisdictional limitations discussed herein). During the transitional regime of Article 83 UPCA, nullity actions can also be filed with the Federal Patent Court in Munich against the German parts of European patents. The Federal Patent Court will continue to have irrespective of the transitional period of Article 83 UPCA the exclusive jurisdiction over German patents granted by the GPTO. National patent rights are unaffected by the UPC system. An outline of the jurisdiction over national and European patent rights in the context of Europe's court system during the transitional period of Article 83 UPCA is illustrated in Figure 3.1.

Figure 3.1 National and European Patent Rights During the Transitional Period of Article 83 UPCA

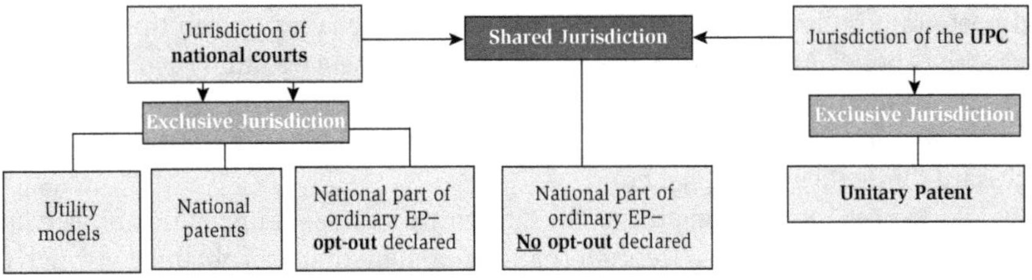

8. For instance, www.duesseldorfer-archiv.de: This website contains decisions, mainly of the district and appeal courts Düsseldorf; decisions of the Federal Supreme Court can be found on the official website: www.bundesgerichtshof.de; *see also* www.justizportal-bw.de.
9. *See* www.epo.org.
10. Articles 23 and 24 of the Statute of the UPC; Rule 262 RoP.

[A] Invalidity Challenges

[1] Oppositions

Within nine months after the publication of the grant of a European patent, anyone other than the patentee may file opposition proceedings with the EPO (*see* Article 99 EPC).[11] This narrow window is the only time during which the validity of a European patent can be challenged through EPO proceedings. This remedy is available regardless of whether the patent is an ordinary European Patent or a UP.

There are reasons not to miss that deadline. EPO oppositions tend to be less expensive than proceedings at the UPC or revocation proceedings handled by national courts. After the nine-month period, parties seeking to invalidate European patents must either resort to national nullity proceedings on a country-by-country basis or, if there are no legal grounds to the contrary, such as a properly executed opt-out, initiate revocation proceedings at the UPC.

Any person except the patentee may institute an opposition proceeding.[12] An entity which does not want to be identified in these proceedings may involve a so-called straw man. This is someone who acts in his own name, but on behalf of a third party. This is a common strategy of companies that do not want to appear as a party in the proceedings. It is acceptable and legally unobjectionable as long as the straw man is not used by the patentee to file an opposition against his own patents (which could be a plausible strategy for patentees that believe that opposition proceedings might be more favorable than national or UPC invalidation proceedings, for either budgetary or merits-based reasons).

Opposition proceedings are held in the first instance before the EPO's Opposition Divisions, which are distinct from the Examining Divisions. An opposition is adjudicated before three technical examiners, at least two of whom have not taken part in the proceedings for the underlying patent.[13] Given this makeup of the Opposition Divisions, different opponents get a fair chance to have the patent reexamined even if the opposition is based on documents that were already considered during the examination proceedings. Furthermore, a challenger in opposition proceedings is not estopped from reasserting the same arguments later in court. Unlike *inter partes* review (IPR) and post-grant review (PGR) proceedings in the US, a challenger can thus have "two bites at the apple." A challenger can subsequently commence a nullity action and assert the same art that was brought before the EPO. The fact that particular arguments had been raised and lost in EPO opposition proceedings would have weight but would not necessarily influence a national court.

Like the EPO opposition proceedings, there are analogous opposition proceedings that may be brought against a German (national) patent that was obtained through the GPTO. The window for bringing such opposition proceedings in Germany is also nine

11. Chapter 6 is devoted to the topic "Opposition Proceedings."
12. *See* Art. 99(1) EPC.
13. Article 19(2) EPC.

months from the publication of the German patent (section 59(1) GPA). The proceedings are handled by the opposition divisions of the GPTO, and their decisions can be appealed to the Federal Patent Court. Opposition proceedings against national patents are available in many other EU states, such as Austria[14] and France.[15] In France, they may be filed within nine months with the National Institute of Industrial Property (INPI) against French patents granted as of April 1, 2020. French opposition proceedings are similar to the EPO proceedings. A French opposition may also be filed by a strawman.

[2] Revocation Actions at the UPC

Revocation actions to invalidate a European patent can be asserted at the UPC. If the action is a stand-alone[16] revocation challenge, it can be filed with the Central Division of the UPC, pursuant to Articles 32(1)(d) and 33(4) of the UPCA. Such revocation actions must be directed against the patentee. However, if the patentee (or a license holder) has earlier filed an infringement action against the plaintiff of the revocation action before a local or a regional division of the UPC, then the revocation claim needs to be filed in that same division.

The Central Division has jurisdiction over matters involving the validity of European patents with unitary effect. The jurisdiction of the Central Division also extends to validity challenges against ordinary European patents as long as the patentee has not "opted out" of the jurisdiction of the UPC pursuant to Article 83(3) of the UPCA.

The challenger does not have to await the end of the opposition period (or the end of pending EPO opposition proceedings) to initiate the revocation action at the UPC.[17] Thus, a revocation action with the UPC may properly be filed even during the opposition period. For the German nullity proceedings, the rules are different. There, a nullity action may not be brought as long as an opposition may still be filed or if opposition proceedings remain pending.[18]

Depending on the technical nature of the patent-in-suit (using the classification of the International Patent Classification of the WIPO), a revocation action shall be assigned to UPC's main seat in Paris or to one of its branches, such as Munich. Previously, a second branch was supposed to be seated in London. This was abandoned following UK's withdrawal from the UPC system. The second branch will most likely be seated in Milan (Italy). *See* Table 3.1 which illustrates this allocation.

14. Austrian Patent Act, §102.
15. Law No. 2019-486 of May 22, 2019 known as the "PACTE Law."
16. This means that the revocation action is not related to an infringement action.
17. Article 33(8) UPCA.
18. §83(2) German Patent Act (GPA).

Table 3.1 Distribution of Cases Across the Branches of the Central Division

Paris (Seat)	*Munich*	*Second Branch*
(B) performing operations, transporting; (D) textiles; paper; (E) fixed constructions; (G) physics; (H) electricity	(F) mechanical engineering, lighting, heating, weapons, blasting	(A) human necessities; (C) chemistry, metallurgy

One branch of UPC's Central Division is responsible for adjudicating disputes involving chemistry, human necessities and metallurgy (sections A and C; around 20%); the branch in Munich handles cases concerning mechanical engineering (section F; around 15%); and the UPC's main seat in Paris will take cases over all other technical areas (around 65%). Essentially, the local and regional divisions of the Court of First Instance of the UPC decide infringement-related issues including revocation matters raised in response to an infringement claim, whereas the Central Division has jurisdiction over stand-alone validity-related issues.

As illustrated in the previous section of this chapter, in EPO opposition proceedings, the opponent does not need to demonstrate a legal or economic interest in the revocation of the patent as a standing requirement. It is thus acceptable for interested parties to use a straw man to file the notice of opposition. The same principles apply to German nullity proceedings filed with the Federal Patent Court.[19]

In contrast to the open standing rules for opposition proceedings, the ability to file revocation challenges at the UPC appears to be more tightly limited. According to Article 47(6) of the UPCA, "any other natural or legal person, or anybody entitled to bring actions in accordance with its national law, who is concerned by a patent, may bring actions in accordance with the Rules of Procedure." The term "who is concerned by a patent" could be understood to mean that not "any" claimant is entitled to file a revocation action. In fact, the UPCA could be interpreted to require at least some showing of an individual concern or legal interest for standing to proceed with a revocation action. Such an interpretation could exclude straw man actions, i.e., actions filed by someone who acts on behalf of the (interested) party who does not want to appear. The plaintiff would have to indicate why he is interested in filing the revocation action. Accordingly, the economic and strategic context of the revocation claim would become visible, potentially entailing the risk of a dispute escalating beyond the revocation claim. Against this background, an interested party might be inclined to refrain from filing such an action. This may impact the willingness of parties to advance the general public interest in reducing the number of invalid patents. It remains to be seen whether or not this view of standing under Article 47(6) of the UPCA will be enforced. It is noteworthy that Rule 44 of the RoP does not mandate that the statement for revocation must indicate a legal or economical interest. The risk of frivolous actions appears to be limited because the claimant has to pay a fee when filing the action. The

19. *See* Ch. 8.

development of standing rules at the UPC will be an important matter, involving a balancing between Article 47(6) UPCA, on the one hand, and Rule 44 of the RoP, on the other hand, taken in view of general public interest in reducing the number of invalid patents. Also noteworthy is that in most national patent revocation systems, a more open standing requirement is in force, which does not require the challenger to state its interest in invalidating the patent.

Nevertheless, some restrictions on standing might be appropriate given the purpose and special nature of revocation procedures, such as to restrict actions filed by the patent proprietor against his own patent. The same policy applies in the case of a straw man acting on behalf of the patent proprietor. Such restrictions have been upheld in the context of opposition proceedings.[20]

A different approach is justified in relation to a revocation action filed against an expired patent. It does no longer confer exclusivity. Competitors do no longer need to respect an expired patent. A public interest in invalidating an (invalid) patent has thus ceased to exist. Only those parties continue to have an interest in its invalidation against whom claims due to past infringements—i.e., unauthorized use during the life of the patent—are asserted. A more limited standing requirement may thus be applied under Article 47(6) of the UPCA.

[3] National Nullity Actions

Each European State provides for its own legal structure including its court(s) for asserting and invalidating issued national patents and national parts of ordinary European patents.[21]

In Germany, to invalidate a patent (separate and apart from EPO opposition proceedings), a "nullity action" may be brought. Only one court in Germany, namely the Federal Patent Court, has jurisdiction to adjudicate nullity actions aimed at invalidating a German national patent or—during a transitional period of seven years[22]—the German part of ordinary European patents. In situations where a European patent has been opted out from the jurisdiction of the UPC, a national revocation action can be brought against the German part of this patent even after the sunset of the transitional period.

The Federal Patent Court has no jurisdiction over UPs. It cannot adjudicate the validity of such patent. Such proceedings exclusively lie in the hands of the UPC.

The Federal Patent Court is headed by the Federal Supreme Court in Karlsruhe.

In addition to its first instance jurisdiction over patent nullity actions, the Federal Patent Court acts as a court for appeals against decisions of the GPTO such as decisions of an opposition division concerning German national patents or decisions in cancelation proceedings concerning German utility models, as well as against decisions by the boards of appeal of the Federal Office of Plant Varieties concerning plant variety rights.

20. G 9/93 (OJ 1994, 891).
21. Nullity actions are addressed in Ch. 8.
22. Article 83(1) UPCA.

Contrary to UPC revocation actions, a German nullity action may be brought only after the opposition window has closed, thus not earlier than nine months after the publication of the grant of a German patent, or of an ordinary European patent. As already indicated, the Federal Patent Court has no jurisdiction over UPs, which can only be limited at the UPC. If an opposition against a patent is filed, a nullity action with the Federal Patent Court is barred until the opposition proceedings are finally terminated. Nullity actions are subsidiary to opposition proceedings in order to avoid contradictory decisions of the EPO or GPTO and the Federal Patent Court.

UPC revocation proceedings and EPO opposition do not have to follow that chronological order. UPC revocation proceedings can be sought at any time after grant, even in parallel to EPO opposition proceedings.[23] The relationship between both routes is explained in the following chapters.

The Federal Patent Court has no jurisdiction over disputes concerning infringements of patents. This jurisdiction lies with special civil courts, namely twelve district courts and twelve appeal courts, which are headed by the Federal Supreme Court.

[B] Infringement Disputes

[1] UPC

The UPC has a Court of First Instance composed of Local Divisions, Regional Divisions and a Central Division. The Central Division is based in Paris. The Court of Appeal has its seat in Luxembourg (Figure 3.2).

[a] Court of First Instance

Local and Regional Divisions: Local and Regional Divisions have been established in the Contracting Member States. In many Contracting Member States, one local division has been set up.[24] However, States with more than hundred cases per calendar year are entitled to establish up to four local divisions per State.[25] Due to the high quantity of patent cases handled by German courts, Germany has opened four local divisions. These divisions have their seats in Munich, Mannheim, Düsseldorf and Hamburg. France has one local division in Paris; Belgium has one in Brussels; Austria has one in Vienna; Denmark established its local division in Copenhagen, Italy in Milan, the Netherlands in The Hague and Finland in Helsinki. Regional divisions may be established on request by two or more States. Sweden, Estonia, Latvia and Lithuania have established one regional division situated in Stockholm.

The choice of venue for filing an infringement action will be governed by the following criteria:

23. Article 33(8) UPCA.
24. Article 7(3) UPCA.
25. Article 7(4) UPCA.

(1) Where the actual or threatened infringement has occurred or may occur (forum of *actus in tort*).
(2) Where the defendant or, in the case of multiple defendants,[26] where one of the defendants has its residence, or principal place of business, or in the absence of residence or principal place of business, its place of business.
(3) Furthermore, the parties may agree on a venue.

Accordingly, a local division will have jurisdiction if the infringement occurs in the Contracting State hosting that division or if the residence or principal place of business of the defendant (or one of the defendants) is located there. A regional division will have jurisdiction if the alleged infringement takes place in at least one of its Contracting States, or if one of the defendants has its seat there. In a situation where the actual or threatened infringement takes place in a country that does not have a local division and does not participate in a regional cluster, the patentee may file his action with the Central Division.

The *actus in tort*[27] prong for the venue will be of particular importance for patentees if the accused infringer does not have a residence or place of business in the EU. According to Article 33(1) of the UPCA, the patentee may file the case in such a situation either with a division acting pursuant to the first option (i.e., at the forum of *actus in tort*) or he can file the case directly with the Central Division.

Forum shopping is a consequence of the *actus in tort* standard for venue. Infringing activities may take place in multiple states, so if, for example, a product that infringes the patent is sold all over Europe, then the patent owner has a wide range of venues to select for suit. A claimant can file a lawsuit at any local division of a Contracting State in which an infringement has been committed by the accused infringer. Likewise, the claimant can sue at a regional division if the alleged infringement takes place in at least one of the Contracting States which have set up the regional division. These are the locations where the allegedly infringing product has been produced, offered or placed on the market.[28]

Central Division: Local and regional divisions of the UPC's Court of First Instance will mainly decide infringement-related matters, whereas the Central Division will have jurisdiction over validity-related issues, such as stand-alone revocation actions and counterclaims for revocation if referred by a local or regional division to the Central Division. Nevertheless, the Central Division may also have jurisdiction over infringement-related matters if the actual or threatened infringement takes place in a Contracting State which neither hosts a local division nor participates in a regional cluster. The patentee will have then the option to file the action at the forum of *actus in tort* or to directly file his action with the Central Division. In addition, apart from cases arising through its *actus in tort* jurisdiction, the Central Division may also

26. An action may be brought against multiple defendants only where the defendants have a commercial relationship and where the action relates to the same alleged infringement (Art. 33(1)(b)).
27. Article 33(1)(a) UPCA.
28. Article 25(a) UPCA.

exercise jurisdiction if the accused infringer does not have a residence or place of business in one of the Contracting Member States. According to Article 33(1) UPCA, the patentee may file the case either with a division in compliance with the first option, at the forum of *actus in tort*, or file the case directly with the Central Division.

[b] Second Instance: Court of Appeal

As shown in Figure 3.2, an appeal against a decision of the Court of First Instance may be brought before the Court of Appeal in Luxembourg by any party that has been unsuccessful, in whole or in part, in its submissions, within two months of the date of the notification of the decision.[29] An appeal can be based on both points of law and matters of fact.[30] Nevertheless, new facts and new evidence may, in principle, only be introduced where the submission of them by the party concerned could not reasonably have been expected during proceedings before the Court of First Instance.

Figure 3.2 Structure of the UPC

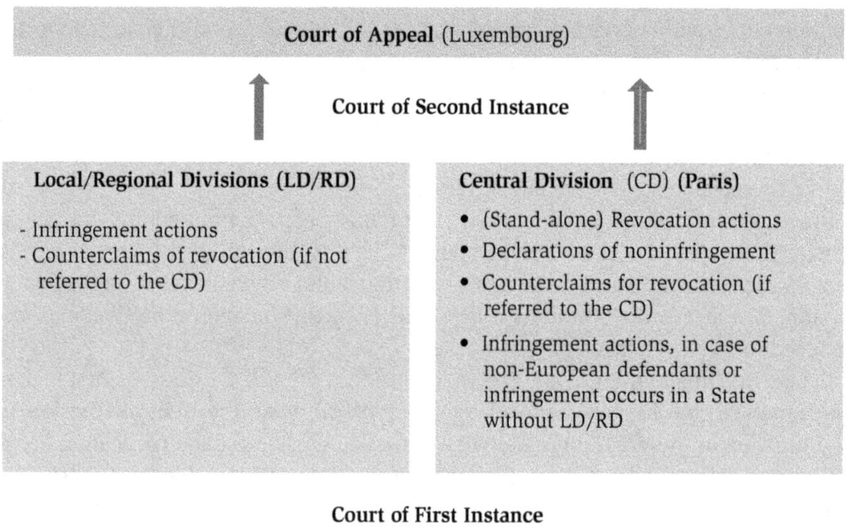

[2] National Infringement Proceedings

[a] Introduction

National enforcement systems continue to proceed, notwithstanding the institution of the UPC. The national systems continue to fulfill important tasks alongside the UPC.

29. Article 73(1) UPCA.
30. Article 73(3) UPCA.

For German patents and utility models, nothing has changed—those rights can be enforced in German's national court system. Likewise, national patent rights granted in other States which are signatories of the UPCA can similarly be enforced in the court systems of those countries. These rights do not fall within the jurisdiction of the UPC. Also, ordinary European patents may still be asserted before national courts, at least during the seven-year transitional period.[31]

There are two main approaches regarding how patent infringement and the related defense of revocation are litigated in Europe. A few States follow a bifurcated or split approach such as Germany and Austria. In those countries, patent infringement and invalidity proceedings are adjudicated in different judicial forums. The infringement courts do not have jurisdiction to rule on the validity of the asserted patent, and contrarily, the tribunal assessing validity cannot rule on infringement. Other countries such as France have systems where infringement and invalidity of the patent may be adjudicated at the same time through one proceeding in the same court. Each system has its own downsides and advantages.

[b] German Proceedings

A characteristic feature of patent litigation in Germany is that patent infringement and validity are by law adjudicated on separate tracks. The split system between nullity proceedings and infringement proceedings is illustrated in Figure 3.3. A particular challenge of the split system is to fairly balance the interests of the patentee to quickly enforce the patent rights, countered with the interests of the accused infringer to not be enjoined from commercial activities under an invalid patent. Of course, the proceedings are not completely disconnected from each other, and there are mechanisms that guarantee a fair resolution of the conflicting interests. These mechanisms are discussed in more detail in subsequent chapters.

31. *See* Ch. 4.

Figure 3.3 Split System

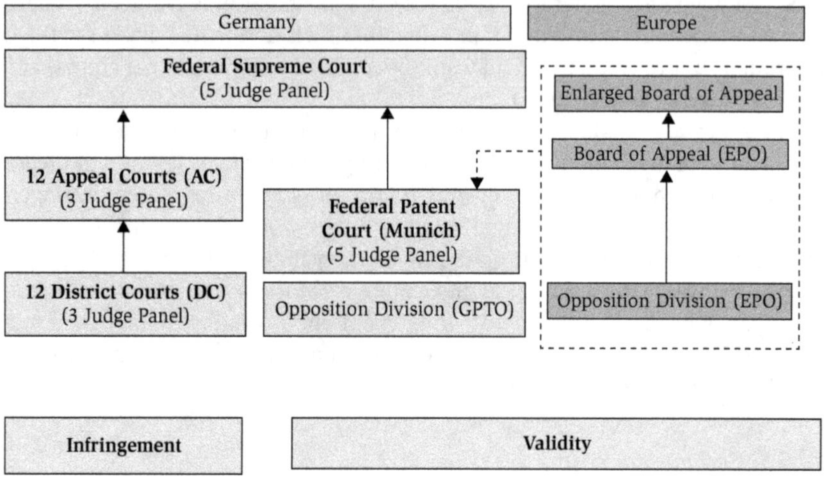

First Instance: The German government has vested twelve courts with jurisdiction over patent infringement cases. The most active German infringement court is the District Court Düsseldorf, followed by the District Court Mannheim, District Court Munich and District Court Hamburg. These district courts conform to one or more territories of a political subdivision of the Federal Republic of Germany and are uniformly distributed across the country, as can be seen in Table 3.2.

Table 3.2 Patent Infringement Courts (Twelve Districts)

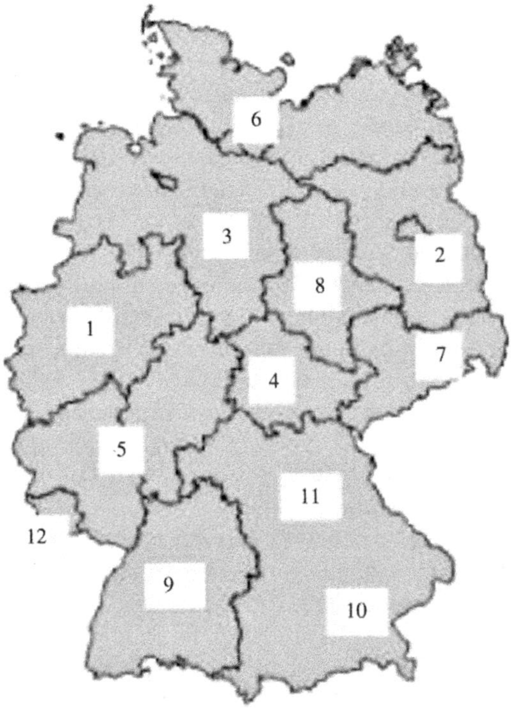

(1) DC Düsseldorf for *North Rhine-Westphalia*
(2) DC Berlin for *Berlin* and *Brandenburg*
(3) DC Braunschweig for *Lower Saxony*
(4) DC Erfurt for *Thuringia*
(5) DC Frankfort/Main for *Hesse* and *Rhineland-Palatinate*
(6) DC Hamburg for *Bremen, Hamburg, Mecklenburg-Western Pomerania* and *Schleswig-Holstein*
(7) DC Leipzig for *Saxony*
(8) DC Magdeburg for *Saxony-Anhalt*
(9) DC Mannheim for *Baden-Württemberg*
(10) DC Munich I for the *District of the Appeal Court Munich (Bavaria)*
(11) DC Nürnberg-Fürth for *Nürnberg* and *Bamberg (Bavaria)*
(12) DC Saarbrucken for *Saarland*

In the German system, there is flexibility when it comes to questions of jurisdiction and venue.[32] A court has jurisdiction to hear a case if either the defendant has his residence or principal place of business within its district or the infringing

32. Details concerning venue can be found in Ch. 10.

activities were committed in the court's district. A simple offer for sale of the accused product via the defendant's website might be sufficient to establish jurisdiction in any of the twelve district courts. The selection of the court is often based on strategic considerations of the patentee. This is a main reason that patent matters are concentrated in a few German district courts.[33] Defendants generally cannot influence the forum selection made by the plaintiff. Even an earlier-filed declaratory judgment action has no effect on that selection.[34]

The panels of the district courts are composed of three judges who are trained in patent law and have several years of practical experience with patent cases. Patent matters are assigned to dedicated chambers of the court. The district courts of Düsseldorf, Mannheim and Munich, which have especially high numbers of patent cases, have two or three chambers dedicated to patent infringement matters.

Second Instance: Appeals are heard by twelve appeal courts, with one appeal court corresponding to and taking appeals from each of the first instance district courts. The panels of these appeal courts are also composed of three judges who are trained in patent law and have several years of practical experience with patent cases. For instance, decisions rendered by the District Court Düsseldorf are appealed before the Appeal Court Düsseldorf, and decisions of the District Court Mannheim are heard before the Appeal Court Karlsruhe.

In appeals, the admission of new facts is restricted. The submission of new facts in the second instance proceeding might be rejected as belated if their consideration would lead to a delay of the proceedings. To avoid such a rejection, the late submission must be sufficiently excused. The excuse might be accepted if the newly brought facts were previously unknown to the submitting party through no fault of his own. Accordingly, it is important that all relevant and favorable facts be raised in the first instance proceedings to avoid being precluded from raising such facts at a later proceeding.

Third Instance: An appeal to the Federal Supreme Court in Karlsruhe represents a purely legal appeal in cases of general legal interest to the public, i.e., if the decision would contribute to the development of case law or if the consistency of German case law is in question. Submissions of new facts are not allowed. The facts established by the appeal courts are binding for the Federal Supreme Court, unless such findings are affected by a procedural error, and this error is adequately demonstrated in the grounds for appeal. Thus, generally, no evidence is heard at the Federal Supreme Court. The panel of the Supreme Court is composed of five judges.

33. *See* Ch. 10.
34. Details concerning the Declaratory Judgment Actions can be found in Ch. 10.

Table 3.3 Basic Overview

	District Courts	*EPO/GPTO Opposition*	*Federal Patent Court*
Proceedings	Bench Trial Without Jury	*Inter Partes* Proceedings	*Inter Partes* Proceedings/Subsidiary Character vis-à-vis Opposition
Remedy	Injunction/ Rendering of Accounts/ Damages	Cancelation/Modification	Cancelation/Modification
Duration (approx.)	One year	Two years	Two years

Presently the Federal Supreme Court has one panel handling patent cases. This panel is identified by "X," which is also reflected in the case docket number. The panel is in charge of patent infringement cases and validity cases.

The most important Federal Supreme Court decisions are contained in a compilation that is known by the abbreviation BGHZ.[35] This compilation is edited by the members of the Court and includes those decisions that the judges believe are of basic importance. All important decisions of the Federal Supreme Court can be obtained from its website.[36]

The basic characteristics of the judicial implementation of infringement and revocation claims in Germany are illustrated in Table 3.3.

§3.03 COURT OF JUSTICE OF THE EUROPEAN UNION

National proceedings are influenced, directly and indirectly, by laws of the EU. The same applies to the proceedings of the UPC. Due to the European unification process, the European Court of Justice (ECJ) situated in Luxembourg is gaining more and more importance. Under Article 267 Treaty of the Functioning of the European Union (TFEU), all courts of the EU, including German courts, as well as the UPC, may refer questions concerning the interpretation of EU law to the ECJ. These are not appeal proceedings that can be filed by a party who is dissatisfied with the court's judgment. Instead, these proceedings are invoked pursuant to the request of a national court. This has happened with respect to the question of admissibility of the so-called transborder decisions in patent cases. It also occurred in cases concerning supplementary protection certificates (SPC). SPCs are sui generis patent extensions available for medicinal products, such as drugs, and plant protection products, to compensate for the time needed to obtain regulatory approval for putting those products on the market. Another

35. BGHZ, Entscheidungen des Bundesgerichtshofs in Zivilsachen, Carl Heymanns Verlag.
36. *See* www.bundesgerichtshof.de. These decisions are published only in German. A few of these important decisions are translated and can be consulted in the legal review *IIC—International Review of Intellectual Property and Competition Law*, published by the Max Planck Institute for Intellectual Property, Competition and Tax Law.

example: In 2013, the DC Düsseldorf raised concerns as to Germany's FRAND case law. The Court asked the CJEU to consider a set of questions concerning the understanding of how patent monopolies and standard-essential proprietary technologies can be incorporated into EU's rules on competition and antitrust. This matter led to the well-known CJEU judgment of July 16, 2015, about FRAND, which is dealt with in more detail in Chapter 10.[37]

§3.04 ROLE OF JUDICIAL PRECEDENT

In civil law jurisdictions, such as Germany, judicial precedent is less authoritative than in common law countries such as the US. The same applies to the UPC. Accordingly, the code as issued by the legislator is the ultimate authority on substantive questions of patent law. However, many important questions are left unanswered by the code, and accordingly, judicial precedent plays an important role in patent litigation.

Due to the high volume of patent litigation in Germany, a substantial body of judicial precedent has developed over the years. German courts tend to follow judicial precedent in order to promote uniformity in the law. Thus, judicial precedent is an important source of authority in Germany, notwithstanding its civil law system. In particular, decisions of the Federal Supreme Court are rigorously respected by lower courts. Even though lower courts are not legally obliged to follow higher court opinions,[38] this body of case law is the persuasive authority, and courts are generally reluctant to break from precedent. Accordingly, the body of judicial patent law precedent may provide a further reason for potential litigants to select Germany as a patent forum to give a greater degree of predictability over the outcome.

Thus, in practice, Germany's court system functions in many respects in the same manner as in common law systems. The structure of Germany's court system and the manner in which judicial precedent is handled is discussed at length in subsequent chapters.

37. *See* Ch. 10, §10.03.

38. In the decision "Kreuzgestänge" (X ZR 103/13) as of Jun. 2, 2015, the Federal Supreme Court even ruled that lower courts have to find their own interpretation of a patent, even if it differs from the previous Federal Supreme Court decision.

CHAPTER 4

Forms of Patent Protection

§4.01 INTRODUCTION

Patent protection in Europe comes in different forms. Most commonly, inventors file their applications initially through the EPO and designate Germany among the countries in which they will pursue national stage patents ("ordinary European patents"). In addition, inventors may request that their European patents have "unitary effect" across the Participating Member States (UPs), rather than having a bundle of national patents, as is the case for ordinary European patents. UPs are exclusively litigated through the UPC. This contrasts with ordinary European patents which are subject to a complex transitional regime[1] that provides for jurisdiction in the UPC and in national courts while offering the patentee the option to "opt out" (i.e., to exclude) the patent from litigation in the UPC system.

Alternatively, inventors may directly file their applications with national patent offices, such as the GPTO. These filings may result in national patents. These German patents are not subject to the jurisdiction of the UPC. They are litigated exclusively through national court systems—for example, patents issued by the GPTO are enforced only through the German court system. Strategically, parties that wish to avoid the UPC can do so by obtaining their patents through the national patent offices.

A third type of protection arises from a separate type of IP called "utility model," which functions in many respects like a patent. Utility models are available under German law. These utility models are not subject to the jurisdiction of the UPC and are litigated exclusively through the German court system.

This chapter aims to identify the key characteristics of each of these types of protection, so that companies may strategically protect their inventions with the most advantageous forms of property rights. This strategy commonly requires balancing the often-competing considerations of speed, cost, enforceability, scope of protection and

1. *See* Ch. 4, §4.02[A][1][b] (below).

the appropriate litigation forum, be it the UPC or national courts. A company may elect to pursue a combination of these IP rights to develop a portfolio tailored to its needs, including a combination of the following, as shown in Table 4.1:

- ordinary European patents, having a twenty-year duration;
- UPs, having a twenty-year duration;
- national patents such as German patents, also with a twenty-year patent term;
- German utility models, which may be obtained immediately through Germany's registration system, providing ten-year protection.

What follows is a background discussion of these kinds of patent protection, with a discussion of how to obtain these rights. Because existing literature already explains the procedures for obtaining patents in Europe, the following sections will thus provide a high-level description of the patent prosecution process. For more detailed information on European Patents, refer to the regularly updated "Guidelines for Examination in the European Patent Office" published on the EPO Website (www.epo.org).

Table 4.1 Key Aspects of the Various Forms of Protection

	Ordinary European Patents/UPs	*National Patents (Example: German Patents)*	*German Utility Models*
Proceedings	Formal and substantive examination	Formal and substantive examination	Only examination of formalities
Subject Matter	Inventions	Inventions	Inventions excluding process and use claims
Grace Period	No	No	Yes (six months)
Prior Art	Every public description and public prior use	Every public description and public prior use	Every public written description, and public prior use only occurring in Germany
Term	Twenty years	Twenty years	Ten years
Enforceability	Publication of the mention of grant	Publication of the mention of grant	Immediately after registration (two to three months from filing)

§4.02 EUROPEAN PATENTS

The dominant channel for obtaining patents in Europe is by filing an application through the EPO. Prosecution through the EPO can be done through an initial filing at the EPO ("direct European route"), in which case the entire granting procedure is handled at the EPO. Alternatively, the applicant may file initially outside Europe, including by filing an application through the PCT, for which the EPO is a designated office (Euro-PCT application).[2] The application contains a request for grant of a European patent, a written description of the invention including any drawings, one or more claims, and an abstract.

[A] Categories

There are ordinary European patents and UPs. The granting proceedings follow basically the same rules regardless of whether the proprietor seeks a UP or an ordinary European patent. The differences between these two types of patents become pronounced once the patent rights are granted, as explained below. The applicant can defer the decision until the end of the prosecution process as to whether the resulting patent shall be an ordinary European patent or whether it shall have unitary effect.

[1] Ordinary European Patents

[a] General Remarks

An ordinary European patent must be validated country by country. Followed by a communication under Rule 71(3), the EPO issues a "Decision to Grant"[3] informing the proprietor that the EPO will soon issue a "Certificate of Grant." This notification specifies the date on which the publication will occur in the European Bulletin, which is the effective date of grant. At that stage the proprietor needs to decide whether to seek unitary protection or an ordinary European patent. In the latter case, the applicant needs, within three months of the date of the grant, to start the country-by-country validation process by implementing measures in the selected designated countries to give effect to the patent in those countries. At least one country must be selected for the patent to have an enforceable effect. In some countries, the European patent can still be validated for an extra fee within a timeframe of additional three to six months. The London Agreement, which establishes translation requirements, governs ordinary European patents. In addition, the fee regime for ordinary European patents applies, which requires a yearly maintenance fee to be paid in each validation country.[4]

[b] Opt-Out and Opt-In

[i] Introduction

During a transition period, owners of an ordinary European patent may "opt out" from the jurisdiction of the UPC. The opt-out provisions apply to existing European patents

2. Article 153(2) EPC.
3. Rule 71a(1) EPC: "The decision to grant the European patent shall be issued if all fees have been paid, a translation of the claims in the two official languages of the European Patent Office other than the language of the proceedings has been filed and there is agreement as to the text to be granted."
4. Chapter 4, §4.02[B][3].

that are still valid in one or more Contracting Member States, and also apply to newly granted European patents. Owners of published patent applications may also opt out of the jurisdiction of the UPC. If an owner does not affirmatively file an "opt-out" declaration, then the patent will be subject to the UPC. Patent owners who have opted out of the UPC may elect to subsequently opt back into the UPC regime.

[ii] Transitional Period

During a seven-year transitional period, a proprietor of an ordinary European patent may opt out of the jurisdiction of the UPC and thus permanently remove that patent from the jurisdiction of the UPC. The transitional period will last seven years from the date of entry into force of the UPCA. The Administrative Committee has the authority to prolong the transitional period for another seven years.[5] Before doing this the Administrative Committee will consult with the users of the system to identify advantages and disadvantages of the concurrent jurisdiction over ordinary European patents.

When the seven-year transitional period expires (absent any prolongation), the UPC will have jurisdiction over each new action arising from a patent issuing from the EPO. National courts will then lose the jurisdiction over European patents. Nevertheless, they will retain jurisdiction over actions based on ordinary European patents filed prior to the expiration term.[6] Also, the effects of an opt-out declared for a European patent will not cease at the end of the transitional period. That is, if an opt-out is filed for a European patent prior to the expiration of the transition period, that patent will remain outside the jurisdiction of the UPC.[7]

[iii] Applicable Law

The provisions governing the seven-year transitional period do not specify the applicable substantive law,[8] leaving open important questions of which substantive law should be applicable to a matter related to an ordinary European Patent.

There are substantial differences among the provisions of the UPCA and the terms of national law. Such differences exist in the area of indirect infringement,[9] limitations on the effects of patents (such as through experimental use exceptions),[10] and the statute of limitation period.[11] On January 29, 2014, the Preparatory Committee published an interpretation note, opining that national courts, within the jurisdiction pursuant to Article 83(1) and (3) UPCA, shall apply national law. Because this Committee has no authority to influence or clarify substantive law related to the UPCA,

5. Article 83(5) UPCA.
6. Article 83(2) UPCA.
7. This can be concluded from the wording of Art. 83(3) sentence 2 UPCA, which allows opt-outs to be registered until one month before expiry of the transitional period.
8. In dispute: *see* Statement of the Preparatory Committee from Jan. 29, 2014.
9. Article 26 UPCA.
10. Article 27 UPCA.
11. Article 72 UPCA.

this note has no binding effect. In the author's view, the interpretation of the UPCA proposed in that note should be disregarded. It would have unacceptable consequences. For instance, the patentee's choice of forum, or its decision to opt out, would unilaterally and retroactively change the substantive law applicable to an act committed in the past. This consequence is critical under the principles of private international law. The interpretation proposed in the note would even allow the applicable law governing past actions to revert if the patentee files an opt-in after filing an opt-out. The Committee's interpretation also neglects the wording of Article 83(1) UPCA, which only refers to the jurisdiction of the UPC and national courts. Accordingly, in an action filed pursuant to Article 83 UPCA, the alleged infringement act shall be subject to the substantive rules of the UPCA. The applicability of the UPCA to ordinary European patents does not depend on whether an opt-out has been declared or not. Not only the UPC but also national courts must apply the UPCA to ordinary European patents. The binding effect of the UPCA on ordinary European patents will lead to noticeable changes in national case law, for instance, in the area of direct and indirect patent infringement pursuant to Articles 25 and 26 UPCA.

[iv] Shared Jurisdiction (Article 83(1) UPCA)

During the transitional period, the national courts and the UPC have concurrent jurisdiction over ordinary European patents. Accordingly, an infringement action or an action for revocation may be brought either before the UPC or before any otherwise competent national court. The jurisdiction of the UPC thus exists concurrently with the continuing jurisdiction of the national courts. Upon expiration of the transitional period (seven years if not extended), then the UPC will have exclusive jurisdiction over such actions.

Article 83(1) UPCA specifies that national courts shall have jurisdiction over actions for infringement or for revocation of an ordinary European patent or a SPC issued for a product protected by a European patent. The wording of Article 83(1) UPCA leaves doubts as to whether national courts shall have jurisdiction also over the other categories of actions listed in Article 32 of the UPCA, such as actions for negative declaration, counterclaims for revocation, preliminary injunctions, and corrective measures, actions for compensations, damages and communication of information. These action types are not explicitly listed in Article 83(1) UPCA. A narrow interpretation of the provision would lead to problematic results. For example, if the scope of an "infringement action" under Article 83(1) UPCA were limited to the mere cease-and-desist request, the patent holder would in theory be excluded from making other requests related to the infringement of the patent, such as requests for damages and compensation. Thus, there are sound reasons that the scope of Article 83(1) UPCA should be interpreted expansively to encompass the broader list of actions of Article 32(1) UPCA.

If a patent holder invokes the jurisdiction of a national court, a question is the territory over which the court's jurisdiction shall have effect. The national court does not step into the legal position of the UPC. Rather, the jurisdiction of national courts follows from the general rules (such as the Brussels Ia Regulation). A first-filed national action does not preclude an additional UPC action relating to the same patent. In case of a first-filed national infringement action, the defendant may[12] file a counterclaim for revocation in the same national court, or, as it is the case in Germany, in a separate court having jurisdiction over revocation claims.[13] In addition, the defendant may file an action for revocation before the UPC with respect to all other national counterparts of the European patent, which are not yet subject to national proceedings, and/or a negative declaratory action with respect to all other national counterparts of the European patent. Also, in case of a first-filed national revocation action or a counterclaim for revocation, the claimant may still file a negative declaratory action at the UPC or a revocation action at the UPC for all other states of protection.

With respect to infringement actions that are first filed at the UPC, the accused infringer would be able to file revocation or nullity actions before national courts. If the accused infringer does bring a revocation action in national courts, then no counterclaim for revocation can be made in the UPC proceedings.

[v] Mechanism and Effects of Opting-Out

When a patent owner opts out of the jurisdiction of the UPC, as a consequence the entire European patent is removed from the jurisdiction of the UPC. It is not possible to limit the scope of the opt-out to only some national parts of the European bundle patent. This section explains the mechanism of opting-out of the UPC's jurisdiction.
Geographical scope: An application to opt out shall be made with respect to all states for which the European patent has been granted or which have been designated in the application.[14] Opting-out cannot be restricted to some selected states only.

Procedural Aspects and Costs: To opt out of the jurisdiction of the UPC, the patent owner must file a declaration with the Registry of the UPC. No fee is charged for the notification. The opt-out takes effect upon registration in the public register, provided that all conditions have been fulfilled. Patentees or applicants have to treat this procedure very carefully because the Registrar of the Court does not check whether the conditions for an opt-out are fulfilled. Therefore, it may be possible that the registered opt-out might not be valid. Failure to properly opt out might lead to the undesired consequence of a permissible UPC action against that European patent (e.g., a revocation action or a declaration of noninfringement action) notwithstanding the patent owner's filed registration. Furthermore, there is a potential for a timing problem: because the Registry of the UPC must process many declarations, there is a risk that the entry will not immediately occur, and meanwhile a revocation action with blocking effects may be filed in the intervening time period. For that reason, the *Protocol on Provisional Application* allows patent owners to register an opt-out declaration prior to the time that the jurisdiction of the UPC becomes effective. The opt-out declaration cannot be limited to a selected set of countries or claims; rather, the opt-out necessarily

12. Article 29 Brussels Ia Regulation.
13. Federal Patent Court: Bundespatentgericht.
14. Rule 5.1(b) RoP.

relates to the European patent as a whole. For Member States that join the UPC system at a later date, there is no need to refile the declaration.

Legal Effects of the Opt-Out: As soon as the opt-out becomes effective, any action in relation to a European patent must be brought before an appropriate national court. That is, after the opt-out declaration is properly registered, the UPC no longer has jurisdiction over the type of actions listed in Article 32(1) of the UPCA. At that point, the patent owner has the ability to choose the jurisdiction for enforcing his European patents. Third parties lose the ability to challenge the patent at the UPC. For instance, after a valid opt-out is registered, challengers may only file revocation actions in national courts. Again, this ability of the patent owner to preclude the jurisdiction of the UPC applies only to ordinary European patents and applications, not to UPs. An opt-out registered for a European patent covers all SPCs subsequently granted for it. European patents subject to a valid opt-out are excluded from the jurisdiction of the UPC and may only be litigated before the competent national courts or authorities, typically on a country-by-country basis.[15]

Joint Ownership: If the patent is jointly owned, the owners must jointly file the opt-out declaration. An opt-out could thus be blocked by a co-owner of the patent. This does not only refer to a classical co-ownership but also applies in cases where one or more national parts of the European bundle patent are held by a different entity (e.g., affiliates of a company group hold the national parts in accordance with their national seats).

Proving Standing for an Opt-Out: The true owner of the patent must declare the opt-out. Therefore, in order to ensure a proper filing, all documents proving that the person who registers the opt-out is entitled to do so should be filed along with the declaration. In case of doubt about whether a patent was validly transferred, it is preferable that all possible owners file the opt-out. Often the owners or applicants are legal entities. It is then crucial to file proof of power of representation for the entity signing the opt-out declaration. This also applies to power of attorneys for the attorney-at-law or the patent attorney responsible for the opt-out, and these papers must be signed by a duly authorized person. According to Rule 5A(1) RoP, the proprietor of a European patent may lodge an application to remove the entry of an unauthorized opt-out application. The same applies to an unauthorized application to withdraw an opt-out. The request will be marked in the Registry, and the Registrar shall decide on it as soon as practicable. The decision may be subject to an application for review to the President of the Court of Appeal.

Blocking Effect: If an action is filed at the UPC on a patent prior to the patent owner having filed an opt-out, then the owner is forever blocked from seeking an opt-out thereafter. This is not a question of lis pendens. That is, patentees may not file

15. Despite the somewhat misleading wording of Art. 83(3) UPCA, it seems that an opt-out takes away every jurisdiction from the UPC, not only the "exclusive competence." The UPC will not have a "non-exclusive competence" after an opt-out. This can be followed from the wording of Art. 32(1) and (2) UPCA. The UPC is either exclusively competent (Art. 32(1) UPCA) or has no competence at all (Art. 32(2) UPCA). By taking away the "exclusive competence," no competence remains, and the parties have to litigate on a national basis.

an opt-out for a European patent if it is already subject to UPC proceedings.[16] An opt-out is simply no longer possible, even after the proceedings causing the blocking effect are terminated. Even if the UPC action has been withdrawn or otherwise ended, the patent is no longer eligible for being opted out of UPC jurisdiction. The blocking effect can be triggered not only by an action of the patent proprietor but also by third parties, such as a licensee. The blocking effect will thus also take place if a third party started an action for revocation or a declaration judgment. Accordingly, patent owners should proactively determine if they want to opt out of the UPC's jurisdiction. Nevertheless, an action filed before a national court does not have such a blocking effect.

Sunrise Period: During the "sunrise period,"[17] which runs at least three months prior to the time actions can be filed with the UPC, patent owners are already enabled to declare opt-outs in relation to their European patents. Since no actions can be filed with the UPC during that time, there is not yet a risk to be preempted by a third party's UPC action. This means that the Registry exists prior to the entry into force of the UPCA and proprietors of European patents or applications may file applications to opt out without running the risk to be blocked to do so by a third party. An application to opt out that was registered during the sunrise period is deemed of being entered into the register on the date of the entry into force of the UPCA.[18]

[vi] Opt-In (Article 83(4) UPCA)

Scope: After having filed an "opt-out," a patent owner may later decide to "opt in" to the UPC's jurisdiction, thus restoring the ability to enforce the patent in the UPC. A patent owner who is skeptical of the benefits of the UPC, and opts out of that jurisdiction, may nonetheless choose to opt back into the UPC system. If enforcement through the UPC is subsequently deemed advantageous, the patent owner may withdraw a previously filed opt-out, and thus "opt-in" to regain the right to file an enforcement action in the UPC. The patent owner can do this at any time unless an action has been filed with a national court (blocking effect of an action). The opt-in declaration retroactively revokes the opt-out declaration. This applies to the entire European patent. Once an opt-in has been declared, no further opt-out can be declared for that patent.

Blocking Effect: An opt-in could be blocked! Any action brought by any claimant before a national court of a participating Member State precludes a subsequent return into the UPC system. An opt-in is no longer possible, even after the proceedings causing the blocking effect are terminated. The provision is aimed at avoiding divergent interpretations of the patent by the UPC on the one hand and national courts on the

16. Article 83(3) UPCA.
17. From the deposit of the last necessary ratification certificate until the entry into force of the UPCA (Art. 89(1), first sentence, UPCA), the so-called sunrise period is running. During that time period, patent owners may remove their European patents from the jurisdiction of the UPC by a so-called opt-out.
18. Rule 5.12 RoP.

other hand. This effect is of particular significance since any third party may start a revocation action in a country where this is very inexpensive (e.g., France), with no possibility for the patentee to restore the patent to the UPC jurisdiction.

Numerous publications about "opt-out" and "opt-in" rules under the UPC system may give the mistaken impression that patentees can file an "opt-in" to have their European patents litigated in the UPC system and preclude the ability of challengers from litigating the patent before the national courts on a country-by-country basis. This is false. In fact, there is no possibility for the owner of a European patent to prevent jurisdiction from being shared among the national courts and the UPC, pursuant to Article 83(1) of the UPCA. Despite some unclear wording in Article 83(1) of the UPCA, during the transitional period, the national courts have jurisdiction for all possible actions with respect to ordinary European patents. Possible conflicts of jurisdiction are governed by the Brussels-I-Regulation (EU 1215/2012), as amended by Regulation EU 542/2014. Accordingly, the UPC is deemed to be an ordinary court like any court of an EU Member State.[19] If a case is pending with a court of an EU Member State, any lawsuit filed with another court with the same parties and having the same subject matter must await the decision of the court in the first-filed action.[20] However, the question of validity and the question of infringement of a European patent are not the same subject matter.[21]

[vii] Strategic Aspects

The owner of European patent application may consider several strategic options:

- The patent application may be converted latest within one month after the publication of the grant into a UP: A UP confers upon the patent proprietor a broad territorial protection for relatively low renewal fees, as compared to the fees for an ordinary patent having the same territorial coverage. However, there is no possibility of reducing the costs (renewal fees) of a UP by reducing its territorial reach. This is, it is not possible to save renewal fees by dropping states. The scope of a UP is fixed throughout the patent life. This is a potential downside of the UP. "Dropping states" and thus reducing the quantity of renewal fees is possible in the case of ordinary European patents. Also, UPs must be translated into another EPC language,[22] which adds costs. A UP creates a risk of complete revocation through one UPC decision.
- If the European patent application is not converted into a UP, the patent is subject to the transitional provisions of Article 83 of the UPCA, in particular its opt-out mechanism. Opting-out removes the patent from the UPC and thus excludes the possibility of a single UPC ruling invalidating the patent across

19. Article 71a(2)(a) Reg. 1215/2012 as amended by Reg. 542/2014.
20. Article 29 Reg. 1215/2012 as amended by Reg. 542/2014.
21. This question has not finally been decided by the CJEU, but their explanations under paras. 16ff. of the *GAT/LUK* case (C-4/03, decision as of Jul. 13, 2006) can only be interpreted in that direction.
22. Cf. below section "Language Regime."

the Contracting Member States. Restated, if the patent owner does not file an opt-out for a European patent, then there is a risk of losing the patent for all protection states. A potential infringer may seize the opportunity to file a revocation claim through the UPC in order to invalidate the patent across all Contracting Member States. Patents with low invalidation risks are thus more appropriate for proceedings at the UPC.

Whether or not to opt out of the UPC's jurisdiction is a strategic decision, which must be assessed on a case-by-case analysis. The right strategy depends on many factors. These factors may relate to the nature of the owner, the particularities of the industry sector, the type of the patent portfolio, the breadth of the patent portfolio, etc. This list is not exhaustive. Many other criteria may play a role, such as:

- Does the patent at issue cover the core of the owner's business? Under a conservative view, because the UPC is untested, it may be advisable to opt out of the UPC's jurisdiction for core patents until the UPC's jurisprudence becomes more established.
- If an important product is covered by many patents in a portfolio, the owner has the choice to accordingly divide the portfolio into patents which are opted out and those which are not opted out to be later litigated through the UPC.
- As long as divisional patent applications are possible, the proprietor may branch off divisional applications for the purpose of forming categories of patents. One category might be converted into UPs. Another category could be used as ordinary European patents.

This is a sensitive decision which needs a case-by-case analysis as shown in Table 4.2.

Table 4.2 Simplified Overview: Jurisdiction—"Opt-Out" or "Opt-In"

State of the Ordinary European Patent	*UPC*	*National Courts*
No "Opt-out" has been declared.	**"Shared jurisdiction"**: UPC **and** National courts **have jurisdiction. Conflicts to be solved by** Brussels Ia Reg.	
Opt-out was duly declared.	UPC lacks jurisdiction.	National courts have jurisdiction.
"Opt-in" was declared; i.e., opt-out has been duly "withdrawn."	**"Shared jurisdiction"**: UPC **and** National courts **have jurisdiction. Conflicts to be solved by** Brussels Ia Reg.	

[viii] Weighing Criteria for Opt-Out Decision

Opt-out requests can be filed during the transitional period[23] which starts prior to the entry into force of the UPCA, namely within the three-month *sunrise period*. The patent owner is thus given time to assess the situation before third parties may create *faits accompli*. However, three months is a short time period to decide on whether to declare an opt-out for each patent. The decision depends on many different parameters, which often cannot be clearly determined. The patent owner who has (possibly prematurely) opted out still has the option of withdrawing the opt-out request. However, this is not possible at any time. As soon as national proceedings have been initiated, that option is gone. Thus, if the patent owner opts the patent out, competitors may block him from accessing the UPC system by filing a national nullity action or a national negative declaratory (noninfringement) action. By opting out, the patent owner therefore puts at risk his ability to take advantage of the UPC. He must weigh this risk against the risks that a *stay-in* may entail. The primary risk of a *stay-in* is that all national parts of his European patent may be invalidated by one central revocation action before the UPC. The decision-making process will have to be based on a number of factors. The most important—without being exhaustive—are listed here:

(i) **Risk of invalidation:** How great/low is the risk that the patent will be invalidated? A low-cost revocation action before the UPC may result in a total loss of the patent in all UPCA States. The owner of a patent (presumingly) facing high invalidation risks might be inclined to declare an opt-out. National courts may only invalidate the respective national parts of the European patent. The total loss of a patent may also be achieved through national invalidation proceedings, but this is associated with much higher costs. Competitors might be dissuaded from starting multinational revocation proceedings. Accordingly, the lower the invalidation risk is, the more the patent owner is inclined to adhere to the UPC system.

(ii) **Economic value of the patent:** The economic value is shaped by various factors that interact with the risk of invalidation:
   - **Importance for the business operations:** How important is the patent for the owner's business operations? Is the patent one of the crown jewels of the company? The more important the patent is, the more inclined the owner might be to take a conservative stance and declare an opt-out.
   - **Scope of protection:** How large is the scope of protection? How easily patent infringement can be proven? If the proof is difficult (e.g., process patents), the special procedures provided for in the UPCA, such as inspection procedures, could be advantageous. The latter favors a stay-in. Are indirect/contributory patent infringements conceivable? How great is the inclination to rely on established case law of national

23. §4.02[A][1][b][ii].

courts. The clearer patent infringement can be determined and proven, the lower is the importance to rely on established case law.

- **Competition:** What impact does the patent have on competitors? Where are the patent owner's most important markets located? In which UPCA States are infringement acts to be expected? Are cross-border infringement cases expected? Shall the patent be enforced in UPCA States with high/low reliability and efficiency of their judicial systems? For patents, e.g., from the telecom sector, which shall preferably be enforced in many or all UPCA States, it might be of interest to stay in the UPC system, especially, when it comes to the recovery of damages. The more foreseeable patent infringement possesses a pan-European character, the more inclined the owner is to favor the UPC system.
- **Costs:** Compared to several national infringement and revocation proceedings, central proceedings before the UPC are less expensive. How sure is it that judicial enforcement will be necessary? What might be the territorial breadth of such enforcement?

(iii) **Parallel protection:** Are there divisional applications or national rights with similar scope of protection in the portfolio in addition to the patent? Such fallback positions allow to form groups of patents, of which some are opted out and others stay in.

[2] European Patents with Unitary Effect (UP)

Two European regulations adopted on December 17, 2012, establish the primary framework governing UPs. The first deals with the general framework for the unitary effect of UPs (the UP Regulation),[24] and the second specifically relates to the translation requirements (the Translation Regulation).[25] Two regulations were necessary because higher voting thresholds are required for changes to translation arrangements. Both Regulations have direct effect in the Participating EU Member States. Accordingly, no further national transposition measures are necessary for these to take effect.

[a] General Remarks

The ability to apply for a UP pertains only to European patents granted after the effective date of the UPCA. This is in contrast to the ability to "opt in" or "opt out" of the UPC's jurisdiction, as discussed above, which applies also to European patents that are granted before and valid at the date of entry into force of the UPCA. For patents granted after the effective date of the UPCA, the applicants may request that their

24. Regulation (EU) No. 1257/2012 of the European Parliament and of the Council of Dec. 17, 2012 implementing enhanced cooperation in the area of the creation of unitary patent protection.
25. Regulation (EU) No. 1260/2012 of the European Parliament and of the Council Dec. 17, 2012 implementing enhanced cooperation in the area of the creation of unitary patent protection with regard to the applicable translation arrangements.

European patents have "unitary effect" across the Participating EU Member States, rather than having a bundle of national patents followed by a country-by-country validation, as is the case for ordinary European patents. The regulations adopted on December 17, 2012, are accompanied by secondary law, in particular the Rules relating to UP protection adopted by the EPO ("UPR").[26] The UPR establishes the procedures by which the EPO shall administer the UP Regulation and the Translation Regulation. The UPR contain provisions relating to the request to obtain unitary effect, provisions on the compensation scheme for translation costs, provisions on how to enter a statement on the willingness to grant licenses, and provisions about renewal fees and expiration. In addition, the UPR provides the foundation of a centralized Register for Unitary Patent Protection at the EPO and specifies the entries to be made in it.

The EPO has authority over UPs. According to Article 18 of the UP Regulation, UP protection may be requested for any European patent granted on or after the date of application of the Regulation. The request for unitary effect must be filed at the EPO no later than one month after the publication of the mention of the grant of the European patent.[27] The granting proceedings through the EPO are the same for ordinary European and UPs. Likewise, opposition proceedings under Article 99 EPC and limitation and revocation proceedings are available for UPs, pursuant to Articles 105a et seq. EPC.

The goal of establishing UP protection in Europe stretches back for decades. Article 1(2) and Recitals 6 and 16 of the UP Regulation classify the UP Regulation itself as a "special agreement" within the meaning of Article 142 EPC and implement the UP under Part IX of the EPC. This section of the EPC contains provisions that were originally conceived in the 1970s in connection with the Community Patent Convention, which was never ratified. In the past, such a "special agreement" was concluded between Switzerland and Liechtenstein.[28] The basic idea underlying Part IX of the EPC is aimed at establishing a European patent to which unitary character is given in the post-grant stage (Table 4.3).

Table 4.3 Comparison: UP/Ordinary European Patent

<table>
<tr><th></th><th>UP</th><th>Ordinary European Patent</th></tr>
<tr><td>Pre-grant</td><td colspan="2">Prosecution in compliance with the EPC</td></tr>
<tr><td rowspan="3">Post-grant</td><td colspan="2">Opposition proceedings in compliance with the EPC</td></tr>
<tr><td colspan="2">Limitation and revocation proceedings under Articles 105a et seq. EPC</td></tr>
<tr><td>Language Regime: Regulation (EU) No. 1260/2012</td><td>Language Regime: London Agreement</td></tr>
</table>

26. Decision of the Select Committee of the Administrative Council of Dec. 15, 2015 adopting the Rules relating to Unitary Patent Protection (SC/D 1/15), Official Journal EPO, 2016, A39.
27. Article 9(1)(g) UP Regulation; Rule 6 of the UPR.
28. Treaty between the Swiss Confederation and the Principality of Liechtenstein on Patent Protection of Dec. 22, 1978.

	UP	*Ordinary European Patent*
	Renewal Fees: Corresponds to the total of fees due in the four countries where European patents were most often validated in 2015[29]	**Renewal Fees:** Per validated country and as long as the patent has not been abandoned in that country
	Territorial Coverage: Unitary protection in all Participating Member States	**Territorial Coverage**: Country-by-country validation, i.e., protection in individually designated EPC Member States (bundle of national patents)
	Jurisdiction: UPC (exclusive)	**Jurisdiction**: During the transitional period, UPC or national courts, if opted out: only national courts; after transitional period: UPC (unless already opted out)

[b] Territorial Scope

The owner of a European patent will have, within a one-month deadline after grant, the opportunity to file a formal request for unitary effect (Article 3(1) UP Regulation, Article 6 Rules relating to UP Protection). Thus, until the deadline of one month after the patent grant, the patent owner may postpone a decision on whether to choose unitary protection or whether to validate the patent on a country-by-country basis. If a patent's owner request for unitary protection complies with all formalities, the European patent then will benefit from unitary effect in those Participating Member States in which the UPC is operating (Article 18(2) UP Regulation). The range of the patentee's protection through the UP is limited to the Participating Member States, which have already ratified the UPC Agreement, at the time the patentee makes its request for unitary effect. For all other states, the owner of a European patent must validate the patent on a country-by-country basis if protection is desired there. This particularly applies to EPC States which do not belong to the group of the EU States of the enhanced cooperation, such as Switzerland, Spain, UK or Turkey, and those States which are members of the enhanced cooperation but have not yet ratified the UPC Agreement. The territorial scope of the UP thus depends on how many Participating States have ratified the UPC Agreement when the proprietor of the European patent files the request for unitary effect. The unitary effect will not extend to future Participating States that ratify the UPCA during the lifetime of the UP. Subsequent ratification of the UPCA by other EU countries does not extend the territory of unitary effect into those jurisdictions. Nevertheless, a hybrid coverage is possible, i.e., by obtaining a UP as well as an ordinary European Patent (EP) to have effect in those EPC states to which UP protection is unavailable.

29. Rules relating to Fees for Unitary Patent Protection (SC/D 2/15); Official Journal EPO, 2016, A40; hereinafter "RFeesUPP."

[c] "Malta Problem"

An interesting wrinkle may arise for patents filed prior to March 1, 2007, due to Malta's entry into the EPC. The fundamental premise of the UPC is that the patent must apply equally across all participating Member States; i.e., a European patent with unitary effect must be granted with the "same set of claims in respect of all Member States participating in the unitary system."[30] Under that premise, a patent having different sets of claims effective in different participating states would appear to be ineligible for the unitary protection. The concern in this regard arises from Malta's entry into the EPC which occurred on March 1, 2007. For patent applications filed prior to that date, the resulting European patents had no effect in Malta. Thus, applications having an effective filing date prior to March 1, 2007, cannot literally satisfy Article 3(1) of UP Regulation. The practical effect of this "Malta problem" remains to be determined.
A problem analogous to the "Malta problem" similarly arises for European patent applications that were filed prior to April 1, 2009, and for international applications entering the regional phase before that date. For such applications, an old system of individual designation fees for each designated Contracting State was in force. For such applications that did not designate all EPC Member States, in particular, if the designation fees were paid for less than seven States,[31] such application is not deemed to be issued for all Participating Member States. Thus, the "Malta problem" appears to apply to those patent applications, as well, and may prevent those applications from qualifying for unitary protection. This framework changed on April 1, 2009, when a new designation system was instituted. Now, all the Contracting States to the EPC at the time of filing of a European patent application are deemed to be designated in the request for grant of a European patent, i.e., upon filing of the application and a timely paid flat designation fee. Thus, the "Malta problem" should not apply to patent applications filed after April 1, 2009.

[B] Ordinary EPs Versus UPs

[1] *Introduction*

A main difference between ordinary European patents and UPs arises from the rule that the UPC has exclusive jurisdiction over a UP, whereas the proprietor of an ordinary European patent may sue in either a national court or the UPC during a transitional period of seven years (which may be prolonged by a time period of up to further seven years).[32] During the transitional period, the owner of the ordinary European patent is entitled to "opt out" of the jurisdiction of the UPC, as set forth above.

30. Article 3(1) UP Regulation.
31. Only the payment of seven designation fees was sufficient for designating all EPC Member States.
32. Article 83(5) UPCA.

[2] Language Regime

Translation costs are an important aspect of patent portfolio management. Translations are required in order to obtain protection in certain states. Numerous efforts have been made in the past to reduce these costs. The result of such efforts is, for example, the London Agreement of October 17, 2000,[33] which is applicable to ordinary European patents, and to which many EPC Member States have been acceded. For those states that have not acceded to that Agreement, the rule still applies that the entire patent specification including the claims must be translated into the state's national language. This is the case for Spain and Italy, for example. The UP may imply lower translation costs. This is one of the factors for consideration when deciding to pursue unitary protection. Nevertheless, in many of the key countries, translation requirements have been eliminated for ordinary European patents by the grace of the London Agreement.

[a] Translations of Claims

Article 3(1) of the Translation Regulation provides that the UP, if published according to Article 14(6) EPC, does not require any further translation (at least in principle). This means that the specifications of the patent will be published in the language of the proceedings (English, French or German) including a translation of the claims in the other two official languages of the EPO. However, even the UP system does not function without translations. As is the case for ordinary European patents, the publication must include a translation of the claims into the other two official languages of the EPO. For example, if the UP has been prosecuted in English, its claims must be translated into French and German. The same applies to ordinary European patents. A communication under Rule 71(3) usually invites the applicant to file a translation of the claims in the two official languages of the EPO other than the language of the proceedings.

[b] London Agreement (Ordinary EPs)

The London Agreement[34] is applicable to ordinary European patents. It provides a financially attractive post-grant translation regime for ordinary European patents. States that are party to the Agreement waive, either entirely or largely, the requirement for translations. Under the London Agreement:

- a State that has an official language in common with one of the official EPO languages will dispense entirely with the translation requirements provided for in Article 65(1) EPC;[35]

33. OJ EPO 2001, 549.
34. OJ EPO 2001, 549.
35. FR, DE, LI, LU, MC, CH, UK.

- a State that does not have an official language in common with one of the official EPO languages will dispense with the translation requirements provided for in Article 65(1) EPC if the European patent has been granted in the official language of the EPO prescribed by that State, or translated into that language and supplied under the conditions provided for in Article 65(1) EPC. These States may, however, require that a translation of the claims into one of their official languages be supplied.

There are patent applicants, especially small- and medium-sized businesses, for which the broad territorial coverage of a UP is unnecessary. Such applicants do not necessarily benefit from a UP due to related translation costs. In particular, during a transitional phase[36] at least one translation of the UP must be provided. If the applicant only needs protection in the center of Europe (such as in France or Germany), the London Agreement would not require any translation of the specification. In addition, it must be taken into account that a UP will not be available in all EPC states. A patent applicant seeking protection in such states must therefore make an individual request for a conventional patent, i.e., a national patent or an ordinary European patent. Table 4.4 provides an overview of the translation modalities applicable to ordinary EPs.

Table 4.4 Language Regime of Ordinary EPs

Language of the proceedings		English, German or French.
Article 14(6) EPC		Translation of the claims in the other two official languages of the EPO is necessary. Claims of EP are always available in all three languages of the EPO.
Post-grant Translation Regime		**London Agreement and Article 65 EPC:** Not all EPC contracting states have acceded to the London Agreement. Those states which have acceded to the Agreement undertake to waive, entirely or largely, the requirement for translations of ordinary EP.
Parties to the EU and EPC		
AT	Austria	(a) **FR, DE, BE, LI, LU, MC, CH, UK**: Beyond Article 14(6) EPC no translation necessary!
BE	Belgium	
BG	Bulgaria	(b) States with a national language which does not correspond to EPO's official languages (i.e., **HR, MK, DK, FI, HU, IS, LV, LT, NL SE, SK)**:
CY	Cyprus	
CZ	The Czech Republic	
DE	Germany	- translation of **claims;** and
DK	Denmark	- translation of the **description** if the patent is not published in English in HR, DK, FI, HU, IS, NL SE;
EE	Estonia	
ES	Spain	
FI	Finland	- no translation of description in MK, LV, LT, SK, but claims.
FR	France	

36. Article 6 of the Translation Regulation.

GR	Greece
HU	Hungary
HR	Croatia
IE	Ireland
IT	Italy
LT	Lithuania
LU	Luxembourg
LV	Latvia
MT	Malta
NL	The Netherlands
PL	Poland
PT	Portugal
RO	Romania
SE	Sweden
SI	Slovenia
SK	Slovakia
Party only to EPC	
AL	Albania
CH	Switzerland
GB	United Kingdom
IS	Iceland
LI	Liechtenstein
MC	Monaco
NO	Norway
RS	Serbia
SM	San Marino
TR	Turkey

(2) **In case of dispute**—at patentee's expenses:
- on request of an alleged infringer, a full translation into an official language of the State in which the alleged infringement took place; or
- at the request of the competent court or quasi-judicial authority in the course of legal proceedings, a full translation into an official language of the State concerned.

(3) States not (yet) party to the London Agreement: AL, **AT (EU)**, **BG (EU)**, **CY (EU)**, **CZ (EU)**, **EE (EU)**, **ES (EU)**, **GR (EU)**, **IE (EU)**, **IT (EU)**, **MT (EU)**, NO, **PL (EU)**, **PT (EU)**, **RO (EU)**, RS, **SI (EU)**, SM, TR = full translation necessary.

[c] *Translation Requirements for UPs*

Currently, the request for a UP must be submitted together with a full translation of the specification. If the EPO prosecution was held in French or German, the translation of the specification must be provided in English. If the EPO prosecution was held in English, a translation must be provided into one other official EU language to be selected by the patentee. This translation requirement is applicable during a transitional period and is scheduled to lapse twelve years from the commencement of the new system. This twelve-year period may be terminated earlier by an expert committee finding that "high quality machine translations" are available for all official EU languages.[37]

In the event of a patent dispute, additional translation requirements may apply. According to the Translation Regulation,[38] a translation of the UP must be provided in case of a dispute—at the patentee's expenses—at the request and the choice of an alleged infringer either into the language of the State in which the alleged infringement

37. *See* Recital (11) of the Preamble to the Translation Regulation.
38. Article 4 Translation Regulation.

took place or in which the alleged infringer is domiciled. Also, a UPC division may ask in the course of legal proceedings for a translation of the patent-in-dispute into the language of the division's proceedings. Thus, even the UP System does not function without translations. Assuming that the patent has been prosecuted in English, it will be necessary to translate the patent into one other official EU language. There are twenty-three different official languages in the EU,[39] and the patentee is likely to select a language that could later be helpful in case of a dispute, mainly where it is most likely that the infringement will occur and where the patent will be litigated. The choice is limited if the prosecution proceedings at the EPO were held in French or German, in which case the patentee must translate the patent specification into English.

[3] Fees

[a] Pre-grant Fees

In addition to costs due to the preparation of the patent application and translation costs (*see* above), the applicant needs to pay fees to the appropriate patent offices, in particular to the EPOs and national patent offices. Fees are charged for filing, search and designation of contracting States, claims (if more than fifteen), examination, grant and printing. Renewal fees are also due from the third year and each subsequent year after the date of filing. Irrespective of whether the patent application becomes later an ordinary European patent or UP, the fees until grant are the same.[40] The filing and search fees are due at the beginning of the proceeding (presently about EUR 1,500). The remaining fees are payable later. At any stage the applicant may discontinue the prosecution and thus avoid the payment of further fees. On average, the fees to be paid for a patent application that is prosecuted through to the grant stage range from EUR 6,000 to EUR 6,500.

[b] Post-grant Fees

For the post-grant situation different fee regimes apply. With respect to ordinary European patents, at the post-grant stage, authority over such patents shifts from the EPO to the designated Contracting States. In most Contracting States, costs may be incurred for validating the European patent there, in addition to regular maintenance fees. The amount of the maintenance fees varies from State to State. Also, local counsel fees become necessary to oversee the maintenance process.

The situation is different for UPs. The "Select Committee" of the EPO's Administrative Council endorsed on June 24, 2015, the so-called True Top 4 proposal for post-grant renewal fees to be paid for a UP. It corresponds to the total sum of the maintenance fees currently paid for the four countries in which ordinary European

39. Bulgarian, Czech, Danish, Dutch, English, Estonian, Finnish, French, German, Greek, Hungarian, Irish, Italian, Latvian, Lithuanian, Maltese, Polish, Portuguese, Romanian, Slovak, Slovene, Spanish, Swedish.
40. Article 86 EPC.

patents are most frequently validated. It is a fee to be paid to one office, namely the EPO, under one legal regime governing deadlines and admissible means of payment. This is an important streamlining over the situation governing ordinary European patents, for which the maintenance fees, in varying amounts, must be paid according to different legal regimes to different national patent offices. The administrative burden is thus lower in the case of a UP. Nevertheless, European patents could be cheaper if they are validated only in three or fewer of these countries. In addition, the owner of ordinary European patent may reduce the costs by abandoning patent protection for selected EPC States in which the patent was previously validated. Such country-by-country abandonment in view of reducing costs is not possible in the case of UPs. Table 4.5 compares the annual fees (left column) and accumulated fees (right column) for maintaining UPs, in comparison to maintaining ordinary European patents that are either validated in German and France only or validated in 25 Member States.

The table shows that the annual fees of ordinary European patents are lower than UPs in case they are to be validated in two or three. The annual fees, however, vary depending on the EPC state. Obtaining an ordinary patent stays meaningful for companies whose market is limited to a few states and who do not expect any international expansion in the future. Nevertheless, as soon as protection is desired in more than three EPC states, the patent owner must consider whether it is more reasonable to pursue protection through the UP system. By means of a UP, protection can be obtained for all UP states at a price that is already achieved with an ordinary European patent with validations in four states. However, the owner of a UP cannot later waive protection in individual EPC states in order to save costs, which is possible in the case of ordinary European patents.

Table 4.5 Comparison: Costs of UP/Ordinary EP

Year	*UP (EUR)*		*Ordinary EP: Germany and France (EUR)*		*Ordinary EP for 25 Member States of the EU*	
	Fee	*Accumulated*	*Fee (Germany + France)*	*Accumulated*	*Fee*	*Accumulated*
2	35	**35**	38	**38**	220	**220**
3	105	**140**	70 + 38	**142**	1.452	**1.672**
4	145	**285**	70 + 38	**250**	1.857	**3.309**
5	315	**600**	100 + 38	**388**	2.506	**5.815**
6	475	**1.075**	150 + 76	**614**	3.250	**9.065**
7	630	**1.705**	210 + 96	**920**	3.861	**12.926**
8	815	**2.520**	280 + 136	**1.336**	4.615	**17.541**
9	990	**3.510**	350 + 180	**1.866**	5.554	**23.095**
10	1.175	**4.685**	430 + 220	**2.516**	6.463	**29.558**
11	1.460	**6.145**	540 + 260	**3.316**	7.526	**37.084**
12	1.775	**7.920**	680 + 300	**4.296**	8.655	**45.739**

Year	*UP (EUR)*		*Ordinary EP: Germany and France (EUR)*		*Ordinary EP for 25 Member States of the EU*	
	Fee	*Accumulated*	*Fee (Germany + France)*	*Accumulated*	*Fee*	*Accumulated*
13	2.105	**10.025**	830 + 350	**5.476**	9.854	**55.593**
14	2.455	**12.480**	980 + 400	**6.856**	11.028	**66.621**
15	2.830	**15.310**	1.130 + 460	**8.446**	12.189	**78.810**
16	3.240	**18.550**	1.310 + 520	**10.276**	13.569	**92.379**
17	3.640	**22.190**	1.490 + 580	**12.346**	14.912	**107.291**
18	4.055	**26.245**	1.670 + 650	**14.666**	16.166	**123.457**
19	4.455	**30.700**	1.840 + 730	**17.236**	17.729	**141.186**
20	4.855	**35.555**	2.030 + 800	**20.066**	19.227	**160.413**

[C] Granting Procedure

The procedures for filing applications in the EPO, whether for obtaining an ordinary European patent or a UP, are governed by the EPC, and a subset of its regulations entitled the Implementing Regulations to the Convention on the Grant of European Patents.[41] The provisions of these Regulations are referred to herein as "Rules of the EPC." The contents of patent applications are governed by Part III, Chapter II of the Implementing Regulations and shall include a description of the invention (Rule 42 EPC), one or more claims (Rule 43 EPC), the drawings (Rule 46 EPC) and an abstract (Rule 47 EPC).

The filing of a European patent application can be implemented by means of a direct filing (direct European Patent Application) or through an application under the PCT (so-called Euro-PCT Application). According to Article 153 EPC (Rule 159 EPC), a PCT application for which the EPO is a designated or elected office, and which has been accorded an international date of filing, is equivalent to a regular European application. There are however a few procedural differences depending upon which type of application (direct EP Application or Euro-PCT Application) is under consideration.[42]

The granting procedure for European patents can be divided into different parts. During the first part, a formalities examination and a mandatory search will be performed (Articles 90, 92 EPC). That part is completed with the publication of the application and the search report (Article 93, Rule 68 EPC). If the search report is available in time, it will be included in the publication; otherwise, it will be published

41. Implementing Regulations to the Convention on the Grant of European Patents of Oct. 5, 1973 as adopted by decision of the Administrative Council of the European Patent Organization of Dec. 7, 2006 and as last amended by decision of the Administrative Council of the European Patent Organization of Oct. 15, 2014 (*see* website of the EPO).
42. Euro-PCT Guide: PCT procedure at the EPO: 14th ed., January 2021.

separately. Then the substantive examination upon the applicant's request proceeds (Article 94(1) EPC).

Figure 4.1 General Overview of the Granting Procedure

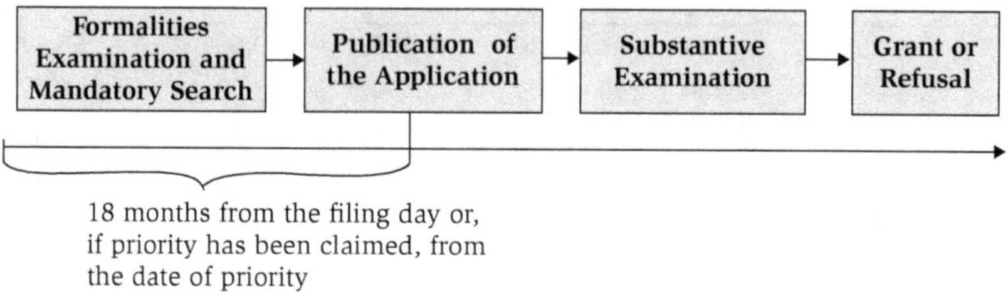

[1] The EPO's Initial Formality Review and Search Report

[a] General Remarks

Once the application is filed, the EPO checks whether the application meets the formal requirements, as shown in Figure 4.1. It also determines whether the application can be accorded a date of filing (Articles 90(1) and 80 EPC). While the formalities review is in progress, the EPO's search division prepares a search report that is drawn up on the basis of the claims, with due regard to the description and any drawings (Article 92 EPC).[43] The search includes prior art documents such as patents, patent applications and non-patent literature. It can also cover internet sources, including online technical journals, online databases or other websites (non-patent literature).[44] It is an essential element of the grant procedure and is designed to identify prior art relevant to the application to make it possible to determine, on the basis of the documents mentioned in the search report, whether and to what extent the invention is patentable. In addition, after the search report is published, the public may have a better understanding of the scope of protection that might be granted.[45] Upon the applicant's request[46] or if the patent application is a first filing, the EPO tries to deliver the search report to the applicant within about six months from the request or filing date. The EPO also draws up a nonbinding opinion on patentability to accompany the search report for European applications and international applications that enter the European phase and for which a supplementary search report is needed (Rule 62(1) EPC).[47]

43. Guidelines for Examination, ed. 2022, B-IV, 1.2.
44. *See* OJ EPO 2009, 456.
45. EPO—T 1242/04.
46. The accelerated drawing up of the search report is available under the program for accelerated prosecution of European patent applications "PACE" (Program for Accelerated Prosecution of European Patent Applications): EPO—OJ, Nov. 30, 2015: PACE enables applications to be processed rapidly to obtain the European search report plus opinion under Rule 62(1) EPC, the first examination report and any communication under Rule 71(3) EPC within tight deadlines.
47. Inserted by decision of the Administrative Council of Dec. 9, 2004, and entered into force on Jul. 1, 2005 (OJ EPO 2005, 5).

[b] Possible Events During the Search Phase

In the case of a European patent application filed directly at the EPO,[48] it is not possible to amend the application prior to receiving the search report (Rule 137(1) EPC). This prohibition avoids changes in the scope of the search. Nevertheless, the EPO may invite the applicant during the search phase to specify those independent claims on the basis of which the search shall be carried out if the application does not comply with Rule 43(2) EPC (*see* Rule 62a EPC).[49] The purpose of this invitation is to define the invention more clearly at the beginning of the search phase. According to Rule 43(2) EPC, the number of independent claims is limited to one of each category (i.e., product, process, apparatus or use). Even though Rule 43(2) EPC defines categories as "*product, process, apparatus or use*," there are only two basic categories of claims. One refers to a physical entity (i.e., product or apparatus); the other relates to an activity (i.e., process or use). A first category "product claim" may relate to substances or compositions, such as chemical compounds or any physical entities such as objects, apparatus, machines, or systems of components. The second basic category, the "process claim," includes all kinds of activities in which the use of some material product for effecting a process could be implied or is exercised upon material products, upon energy, upon other processes. Thus, the number of independent claims is limited to one independent claim in each category.

Exceptions to this rule are permitted in case of: "(a) a plurality of interrelated products," such as transmitter-receiver, intermediate components; or "(b) different uses of a product or apparatus," or "(c) alternative solutions to a same problem, where it is inappropriate to cover these alternatives by a single claim" (*see* Rule 43(2)(a), (b) and (c)).

If the search examiner opines that an application containing multiple independent claims does not comply with this rule, he invites the applicant to indicate the claims on which the search shall be based. If the applicant does not respond to the EPO's invitation within a two-month deadline, the search is carried out on the basis of the first claim in each category.[50]

Furthermore, if the EPO determines that it is impossible to carry out a meaningful search, it may invite the applicant to specify the subject matter to be searched (Rule 63 EPC). This invitation generally improves the quality of the search. The EPO does not search claims that are improperly drafted or that relate to unsearchable subject matter. If the applicant does not respond, the EPO may draw up a partial search report or give a reasoned statement of non-search if it concludes that the application is defective (e.g., missing clarity, conciseness or support).

48. Specific rules are applicable to Euro-PCT applications.
49. Inserted by decision of the Administrative Council of Mar. 25, 2009, and entered into force on Apr. 1, 2010 (OJ EPO 2009, 299).
50. Rule 62(a)(1) EPC.

[c] *Mandatory Reaction on Search Opinion*

Receipt of the EPO's search report provides a good opportunity for reassessing the patent prosecution strategy. Along with the search report, the EPO provides a search opinion on whether the application and the invention to which it relates may meet the requirements of the EPC. The search report and search opinion are aimed at streamlining the granting procedure and may encourage an early withdrawal of the application. This opinion along with the search report represents the so-called Extended European Search Report (EESR: Rule 62(1) EPC).[51]

Under Rule 70(a)(1) EPC, the applicant must reply to the search opinion within six months after the date on which the European Patent Bulletin mentions the publication of the European Search Report (Rule 70(1) EPC). That is, the EPO gives the applicant the opportunity to comment on the opinion and, where appropriate, invites correction of deficiencies by amending the description, claims and drawings. If no objections are raised in the opinion, i.e., no invitation to remedy the defects is issued, the applicant does not need to file a reply and will be informed accordingly.

In the case of a Euro-PCT application where the EPO was responsible for preparing the International Search Report (ISR), the applicant is also required to respond to an ISR and a related negative written opinion (WO-ISA) within a period of six months from the date of the notification of the invitation.[52] If the EPO has also prepared the International Preliminary Examination Report (IPER), the invitation will instead relate to the IPER (Rule 161(1) EPC).

If a Supplementary European Search Report is drawn up on a Euro-PCT-application (Rule 70(a)(2) EPC), the applicant will likewise be invited by the EPO to respond to a search opinion within a period of six months from the notification of the invitation. A Supplementary European Search Report is provided by the EPO in case of a Euro-PCT Application for which the EPO has not prepared the ISR. No such invitation will be made, however, where the search opinion is entirely positive.

[2] *Unity of the Invention*

The EPO imposes "unity" requirements for pending claims, somewhat akin to the restriction requirements employed in the US, whereby Patent and Trademark Office (PTO) examiners may require an applicant to restrict the claims within a single application to a more limited set drawn to an independent and distinct invention. Likewise, under Article 82 EPC, the claims must "relate to one invention only, or to a group of inventions linked so as to form a single general inventive concept."[53] The unity requirement is typically satisfied if the invention only relates to one independent

51. Inserted by decision of the Administrative Council of Dec. 9, 2004, and entered into force on Jul. 1, 2005 (OJ EPO 2005, 5).
52. Decision of the Administrative Council of Oct. 26, 2010 amending the Implementing Regulations to the EPC (CA/D 12/10). The deadline is only one month in Rule 161(1) EPC, which is applicable until May 1, 2011.
53. *See also* Rule 44 EPC.

claim of each category, except in case of: "(a) a plurality of interrelated products," such as transmitter-receiver, intermediate components; or "(b) different uses of a product or apparatus," or "(c) alternative solutions to a same problem, where it is inappropriate to cover these alternatives by a single claim."[54] If this is not the case, the search division of the EPO will usually restrict the search to the invention or the linked group of inventions first mentioned in the claims (Rule 64(1) EPC). If the search report covers additional inventions, further search fees will have to be paid.

If a "lack-of-unity" objection is raised by the searching examiner, the applicant can either pay one or more of the further search fees or simply not respond, in which case the search division assumes that the application should be prosecuted on the basis of the invention that has already been searched.[55] The applicant does not waive the unsearched subject matter by not paying the additional search fees. The unsearched subject matter can be prosecuted later through a divisional application.[56]

[3] Publication of the European Patent Application

The European patent application is published eighteen months after the filing date or the earliest priority date (Article 93 EPC). The applicant may also request an earlier publication (Article 93(1)(b) EPC). The publication contains the description, the claims, any drawings, all as filed and the abstract. Once the application is published, the public can inspect the files through the register and can access the information about the state of the proceedings including the application's biographic data. This can be accessed via the EPO website. If the European search report is available, it is annexed; if not, it is published separately. Amended claims filed after receiving the European search report but before completion of the technical preparations for publication will be published in addition to the claims as filed (Rule 68(4) EPC).

Even though an earlier publication of the European patent application can be requested, there are no provisions in the EPC which would permit any delaying of the publication. The public has a prevailing interest in a timely publication of the application.[57] Of course, the applicant can withdraw the application to avoid publication if, for instance, he decides to keep the invention secret.[58] But the withdrawal abandons the application without the possibility of revival.[59]

A European patent application may confer provisional protection from the date of its publication. According to Article 67 EPC, it is left to the Contracting States of the EPC to prescribe the content and requirements of the provisional protection for the time period between publication of the application and grant of the patent. Accordingly, there are differences from country to country. For instance, in Germany, the existence

54. *See* Rule 43(2)(a), (b) and (c) EPC.
55. *See* EPO—G 2/92, OJ 10/1993, 591.
56. *See* Ch. 4, §4.02[D], "Divisional Applications (Article 76 EPC)."
57. EPO—J 2/02.
58. Rule 67(2) EPC: "The application shall not be published if it has been finally refused or withdrawn or is deemed to be withdrawn before the termination of the technical preparations for publication."
59. EPO—J 4/04 of Sep. 9, 2004.

of such provisional protection necessarily requires, if the application is not already published in German, that a translation of the claims be made available to the public by the GPTO or communicated to the user of the claimed invention.[60] The German provisional protection only confers a financial compensation to the applicant. Content and the special requirements of this provisional protection and the related strategic considerations are described in detail in Chapter 14, §14.03[E][1][b], "Published Patent Applications."

[4] Examination Proceedings

The substantive examination and the grant decision lie in the hands of the examining divisions, which are composed of three technically qualified examiners, who may be joined, if necessary, by a legally qualified examiner.[61] Until a grant or the refusal of the application occurs, the examination is entrusted to one of the examiners, the so-called primary examiner. He or she is in charge of the communications and discussions with the applicant, which are mostly held in writing, but can also be in person, or by phone.[62] If oral proceedings are requested by the applicant or (in the rare instance) initiated by the examining division, they take place before the complete examining division. The final decision, that is to say, the grant or refusal of a patent, is also rendered by the full examining division.

Unless the application is directly ready for grant, communications under Article 94(3) EPC are issued by the Examining Division, inviting the applicant to file observations and, if necessary, to submit amendments to the description, claims and drawings (Rule 71(1) EPC). Even though the applicant is required to substantively respond to any objections raised in a (negative) opinion to the search report (Rule 70(a)(1), (2) or 161 EPC), the applicant is free to amend the application, in particular the claims (Rule 137(2) EPC) once he has received the search report and within the time limit for filing an examination request or confirming that request (i.e., in reply to the search report). This is the time period during which voluntary amendments are possible. Later, further amendments are subject to the consent of the examining division (Rule 137(3) EPC—*see* Figure 4.2).

Figure 4.2 Amending Applications During Grant Procedure

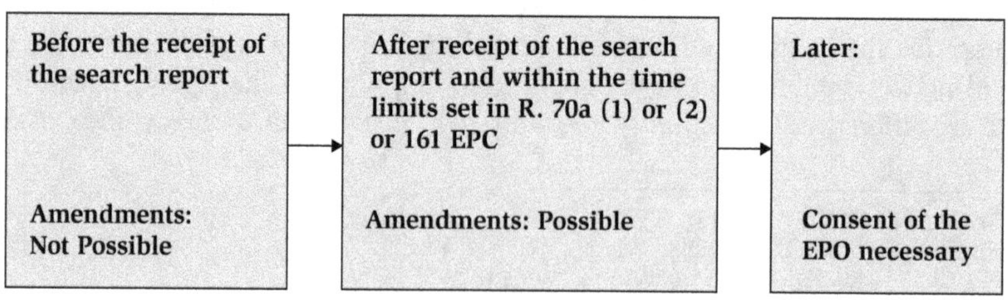

60. Article II, s. 1(2) IntPatÜG.
61. Article 18(1) EPC.
62. Article 18 EPC.

If after examining the response to the communications according to Article 94(3) EPC, the examiner considers the application not yet in condition for grant, he or she will continue the examination procedure by issuing written communications or talking to the applicant in person or by phone. If the examining division is of the opinion that a patent cannot be granted, the application will be refused (Article 97(2) EPC). Otherwise, if the application meets the requirements of the EPC, the division will grant a European patent, insofar as the requisite fees have been paid in due time and a translation of the claims into the other two official languages of the EPO has been provided (Rule 71(3) EPC). The EPO then publishes the specification of the European patent as soon as possible after the mention of its grant has been published in the European Patent Bulletin (Article 98 EPC).

[D] Divisional Applications (Article 76 EPC)

[1] Timing

Like other patent systems, the EPC allows the filing of divisional applications relating to any pending earlier European patent application ("parent application"). The earlier parent application may itself be a divisional application.

A European patent application remains pending until the application is granted, or more precisely until the date that the European Patent Bulletin mentions its grant.[63] An amendment of the EPC in 2010 introduced a controversial twenty-four months' time limit from the Examining Division's first communication for filing divisional applications. That time restriction was removed by the EPO effective April 1, 2014.[64] Accordingly, a divisional application only requires a pending parent patent application and can thus be filed until one day prior to the publication of the grant of the parent application.

When a communication is issued confirming the EPO's intention to grant a (parent) patent, the patentee should consider whether or not divisional applications are to be filed (in other words: branched off from the parent patent). In case of a refusal to grant a patent by the Examining Division, the application is still pending for the purpose of filing a divisional until expiration of the time limit for filing a notice of appeal, regardless of whether an appeal is filed or not.[65] When an appeal against a refusal by the Examining Division has been filed, the divisional application can still be filed during the ongoing appeal proceedings. However, it is impossible to file a divisional application when the parent application has been finally refused, withdrawn or is deemed to be withdrawn.

63. OJ EPO 2002, 112.
64. Amended Rule 36 EPC introduced in 2010 restrictions as to when a divisional application may be filed. These restrictions have been removed with effect from Apr. 1, 2014, by decision of the Administrative Council CA/D 15/13 of Oct. 16, 2013 (OJ EPO 2013, 501).
65. EPO—G1/09.

[2] Subject Matter and Claims

A divisional application may be filed only for subject matter that does not extend beyond the content of the original (parent) application.[66] That is, the subject matter of the divisional application must be *clearly and unambiguously* derivable from the parent application.[67] The divisional application is entitled to the application date of the parent application and thereby enjoys the parent application's priority date. The divisional application shall be deemed to have been filed on the date of the earlier application (*see* Article 76(1) EPC). Hence, the term of the divisional application shall be twenty years from the date of filing of the parent application,[68] not the filing date of the divisional application.

To prevent "double patenting," parent and divisional application shall not claim the same subject matter. There is no legitimate interest in proceedings that give rise to the grant of patents with identical claims.[69] Refiling the same subject matter comprised in an earlier application is thus an abuse of procedure.[70] Accordingly, the claims of the divisional application must be confined to subject matter that is not already claimed in the parent application. Nevertheless, the claimed subject matter could more or less overlap.[71] Even a mere (partial) overlap does not prejudice the grant of a patent.[72] Accordingly, it might be acceptable if an independent claim in the parent application includes all the features of an independent claim of the divisional application which is combined with an additional feature.[73] In particular, the lack of legitimate interest in obtaining two patents for the same subject matter cannot be invoked when the scopes of protection conferred by the respective subject matters overlap only partially with each other. A small difference in the scope of protection between the two patents may overcome in most cases the prohibition of double patenting.

[3] Strategic Use of Divisional Applications

Divisional applications may be filed for various reasons. One reason could be that the claims of the parent application relate to more than one invention and were thus considered by the EPO to lack unity. The applicant could be interested in quickly obtaining protection for a preferred embodiment and pursue other claims through a divisional application.[74] Alternatively, a divisional application could form a fallback position to face the potential risk of a refusal of the parent application or possible risks of opposition against it.

66. EPO—T 441/92.
67. EPO—T 423/03, T 687/05, T 549/09, T 2175/09.
68. Article 63(1) EPC: "The term of the European patent shall be 20 years from the date of filing of the application."
69. EPO—G 1/05, G 1/06, and G 4/19.
70. EPO—T 1287/07; EPO—G 4/19.
71. EPO—T 1391/07.
72. EPO—T 587/98, OJ 2000, 497; T 877/06; T 1491/06; T 1391/07; T 2402/10; T 2461/10; T 1780/12; T 621/15.
73. EPO—T 587/98, OJ 2000, 497.
74. EPO—G 2/10.

Furthermore, it must be taken into account that ordinary European patents (and national patents) may coexist with UPs. The jurisdiction of the UPC exclusively governs European patents with unitary effect. These patents may thus only be litigated through the UPC. The same does not apply to ordinary European patents. During a transitional period (currently set to seven years), proprietors of ordinary European patents may opt out of the jurisdiction of the UPC in which case these patents may only be litigated through national courts. The opt-out completely removes an ordinary European patent from the jurisdiction of the UPC. Without such opt-out a "shared jurisdiction" regime is applicable to ordinary European patents. This is, they may be litigated in the UPC, and through the national courts of the Contracting Member States. The complexity of that "shared jurisdiction" regime in connection with ordinary European patents is illustrated in the chapters of the book.[75]

It is thus possible to strategically divide a patent portfolio into two groups: one group that shall be subject to the UPC, and a second group supposed to be handled (only) by national court systems. For that purpose, divisional applications could be branched off from parent applications insofar as the requirements of Article 76(1) EPC are fulfilled, and it does not fall under the prohibition of "double patenting."[76] That strategic approach may suggest adding appropriate disclosure to the underlying parent patent application when drafting it in a way to legitimately circumvent the prohibition of double patenting if one or several divisional applications shall be (later) branched off from that parent application. This can be done in particular for the purpose of generating patents within the same patent family which may be enforced through either the UPC or national courts against the same or similar products. In addition to strategic considerations of dividing enforcement among the UPC and national courts for patents procured through the EPO, it is also possible to seek protection and enforcement by filing national patents (e.g., German patents and the utility models through the GPTO). According to the new rules, double protection of a European patent and a German national patent is possible, unless the applicant or proprietor—in the case of an ordinary European patent—has opted out from UPC jurisdiction. This is, under German law (Article II §8 IntPatÜbkG[77] (new version)), the prohibition against double patenting only applies to ordinary European patents for which an opt-out has been validly declared. A parallel German patent with the same claimed subject matter therefore only loses its effect in such a case. European patents with unitary effect can also be prosecuted in parallel to a national German patent with identical scope of protection. It is also permissible to subsequently file a German application, claiming priority of an EP application which was earlier filed. These tactics allow an inventor to retain the option of filing suit at the UPC against acts of infringement occurring throughout Europe without losing the option of suing the infringer in Germany by means of a German patent. Having a German patent, issued from the GPTO, gives the patentee a fallback position in case the UPC invalidates the UP. Under German law, this accommodating application of the rule against double patenting does not, however,

75. *See* Ch. 4, §4.02[A][1][b] (above).
76. *See* Ch. 4, §4.03[B][2][d] (above).
77. IntPatÜbkG: Act on International Patent Conventions, *see* Ch. 18, §18.04.

mean that the same alleged infringer may be sued before different courts under patents with identical claims. According to Article II §18 IntPatÜbkG (new version)), the alleged infringer may object to such parallel and duplicative actions.[78]

Moreover, if the invention has been the subject of European or German patents, an applicant may also receive a utility model without prohibition from double patenting.[79]

[E] Right of Priority (Articles 87 and 88 EPC)

[1] General Remarks

The right of priority is usually not analyzed during examination proceedings by the Examining Division unless prior art under Article 54(3) EPC is uncovered.[80] According to Article 87(1) EPC, a party who has filed an application to the "same invention" in another Paris Convention jurisdiction may apply for a European patent and claim priority back to that earlier-filed application, for a period of twelve months from the first-filed application.

Because of the strict requirements of Article 88 EPC, applicants should carefully consider proper drafting of their first-filed applications if they want to enjoy the benefit of the priority claim in Europe. For determining whether there is the "same invention," the EPO usually relies on the principles of the "novelty test,"[81] i.e., whether the subject matter of the subsequent application would theoretically be novel vis-à-vis the disclosure of the first filing. The priority claim can thus be asserted for those features or combination of features of the subsequent application which are directly and unambiguously disclosed in the earlier application.[82] That is, the requirement for claiming priority of "the same invention" means that priority of a previous application in respect of a claim in a European patent application is to be acknowledged only if the skilled person can derive the subject matter of the claim *directly and unambiguously*, using common general knowledge, from the previous application as a whole.[83]

When litigating a patent that claims priority to a previous application, the priority claim is often in dispute. This question arises in particular if the applicant of the priority application and the applicant of the subsequent application are not the same. The answer to this question may be of extraordinary importance. It determines the cutoff for prior art analysis for the novelty and inventive step assessment. In principle, the state of the art is the body of knowledge which has been made available to the public

78. *See* Ch. 18, §18.04.
79. *Ibid.*
80. *See* Ch. 5, §5.02[F].
81. EPO—T 18/87, OJ 1990, 250.
82. EPO—G2/98, OJ 2001, 431: "The requirement for claiming priority of 'the same invention,' referred to in Article 87(1) EPC, means that priority of a previous application in respect of a claim in a European patent application in accordance with Article 88 EPC is to be acknowledged only if the skilled person can derive the subject-matter of the claim directly and unambiguously, using common general knowledge, from the previous application as a whole."
83. EPO—T 18/87, OJ 1990, 250; T 136/95, OJ 1998, 198.

before the filing of the patent application (Article 54 EPC). However, the relevant date for determining the state of the art against a patent application could be up to one year earlier if a proper priority claim is established. If the priority claim is legitimate, then the subsequent patent application is accorded the priority date of the parent application. The protection of the applicant in terms of priority is one of the most important mechanisms under the Paris Convention for the Protection of Industrial Property (Paris Convention). It was introduced in 1883 and has been in force ever since.

For European patent applications, this mechanism is set out in Articles 87 et seq. of the EPC. Within one year from filing a parent application, its filing date could be claimed for a subsequently filed European patent application. This is of great benefit for the applicant because it protects any intervening prior art made available to the public between the filing date of the priority application and the subsequent European application. However, the priority right must be actively claimed by the applicant under Article 88(1) EPC. The effects of the priority right will not materialize without declaring to the patent office that the priority of a previous application is claimed. That is, if the priority of the first application has not been claimed properly in due time, the effects of the priority become void. The ineffectiveness of the priority is often discovered when the patent is enforced, i.e., at a time when a correction of the defect is no longer possible.

[2] Risks Associated with the Transfer of the Priority Right

The risks associated with transferring a priority right are often underestimated. The transfer of the priority right must occur within the priority year and a later transfer is in vain.[84]

The priority right emerges from the act of filing. Consequently, the filer of the priority application acquires the priority right due to the act of filing. For instance, if the applicant of the priority application is a trustee, he would acquire the priority right due to the act of filing the priority application. The trustor who is the owner of the subject matter of the application would however not acquire that right. The right to the invention and the priority right are thus independent rights.[85] Article 87 EPC assumes that the priority right is transferable by legal transaction. The priority right can thus be transferred to third parties as an asset isolated from the rights to the invention. The separation of the rights to the inventions, on the one hand, and the priority rights, on the other hand, becomes an issue in case of a written agreement concerning the transfer of the rights to the invention, in which the transfer of the priority rights is not explicitly mentioned. One could usually assume that the priority right has tacitly been transferred together with the rights to the invention.[86] The latter, however, is only one possible

84. Federal Court of Justice, Sep. 4, 2018, X ZR 14/17, "Drahtloses Kommunikationsnetz," online database of the Federal Court of Justice.
85. Grabinski, in Benkard EPC, 3rd ed. 2018, Art. 87 Rn. 3; Keukenschrijver, Mitt. 2001, 233 f.
86. *See, e.g.*, Federal Court of Justice, GRUR 2013, 712 marginal nos. 14 ff., "Fahrzeugscheibe."

interpretation.[87] Also, the requirements for the transfer of the priority right may vary depending on the applicable law. It has to be taken note that on January 28, 2022, legal questions as to the formal requirements of the transfer of priority rights were referred to the Enlarged Board of Appeal.[88] Answers to the legal questions by the Enlarged Board of Appeal are not expected shortly. Even if the answers are then available, likely not all questions relevant to the formal claiming of priority rights will have been clarified.

[a] Applicable Law

In transnational cases, complex questions of choice of law may arise that govern the priority claim. In evaluating whether the priority claim is adequately supported, there is an open question governing what source of law to apply. Essentially, there are three possibilities:

(1) the law of the subsequent application, i.e., the application of the law of the State, where the subsequent application is filed; or
(2) the law of the State, where the first/priority application is filed; or
(3) the law applicable to the legal relationship between the assignee and the assignor of the priority right, i.e., the law of the contract.

A recourse to the law of the state of the subsequent filing (possibility (1)) might result in a fragmentation into a plurality of national laws governing the transaction, depending on the country in which the subsequent application is made. This leads to legal uncertainty, as the applicable law to an existing right would have to be established retrospectively. Thus, the predominant view does not refer to the law of the State of the subsequent application. According to the Board of Appeal,[89] the law of the contract (possibility (3)) shall serve as reference because the parties are familiar with the law of their legal relationship.

The approach of the Board of Appeal seems, at least at a first glance, to be inconsistent with the German case law. In the decision *Fahrzeugscheibe*, the Federal Court of Justice[90] takes the view that the law of the State in which the first filing was made shall be used as the point of reference (possibility (2)). In the decision *Drahtloses Kommunikationsrecht* of September 4, 2018 (X ZR 14/17), the Federal Court of Justice clarifies this view to the effect that, although the laws of the State of the first application shall apply to the "assignability and the formal and other provisions on the effectiveness of the transaction," the transaction itself shall be assessed in accordance with the

87. OLG Düsseldorf, I-2 U 46/17, Urt. V. 06.12.2012, para. 45: "the distinction between the right to the invention and the formal position resulting from the application represents the cause that the claiming of an employee-invention by the employer (section 7 ArbEG) leads to a transfer of the right to the invention, but not of the protection rights based on it"; Federal Court of Justice, X ZR 72/10, p. 17, "Initialidee."
88. The referrals (G1/22 and G2/22) are based on the appeals T 2719/19 and T 1513/17.
89. EPA—T 205/14.
90. Federal Court of Justice, GRUR 2013, 712, "Fahrzeugscheibe."

law of the contract, including the employment statute in case of employer-employee relationships. This view is consistent with Article 14 of Regulation No. 593/2008.[91]

[b] Temporal Aspects

According to Article 87(1) EPC, a subsequent application may benefit from a priority right within twelve months from the date of the first application (priority year). If the subsequent filing is a European application, a priority right arising from the first application must be claimed by a corresponding declaration (Article 88(1) EPC). Complications commonly arise when the applicant of the first application and the applicant of the subsequent application are not the same person or entity, in which case it is necessary to have a valid transfer of the priority right among these entities. The burden of proof lies with the patentee.

The effective exercise of the propriety right requires that the transfer of the priority right has taken place within the priority year. The transfer is only possible from the date when the priority right emerges, i.e., the date of filing of the first application. Before that date, a right that could be transferred did not yet exist. The priority right expires irretrievably at the end of the priority year. There is no way to restore this right by agreement after the priority year has expired.[92]

According to the EPC rules, the declaration of priority can be made even after the priority year. That is, the EPC rules allow a sixteen-month period from the date of the first-filed application for filing the declaration of priority. However, this time limit concerns the formal procedure of filing the declaration of claiming the priority right. It does not apply to the substantive rule governing the transfer of the priority right within twelve months. The priority year is the period during which the priority right must be transferred. The transfer of the priority right could also take place after the filing date of the subsequent application, but only on the condition that the transfer is still effectuated in the current priority year. It should be noted, however, that there is some authority requiring that the substantive transfer be effected before the subsequent application is on file.[93] Even though a transfer of the priority right, which is completed during the priority year, seems to be sufficient to cure a missing entitlement when filing the subsequent application, it is recommended to have completed the written assignment signed and dated, before the filing date of the subsequent application.

There is one case from Germany's Federal Patent Court which allowed a transfer of the priority right after the one-year deadline as long as the declaration of priority was made prior to the deadline.[94] This case appears to be an outlier and is contrary to the clear wording of Article 87 EPC.

91. Pahlov, GRUR Int. 2017, p. 394.
92. EPA—T 62/05; EPA—T 788/05; Federal Court of Justice, GRUR 2013, 711, "Fahrzeugscheibe."
93. Benkard/Grabinski, EPC, 3rd ed. (2018), Art. 87 Rn. 4 with further references.
94. Federal Patent Court, Decision of Oct. 28, 2010, Mitt. 2011, 259.

[c] Content of the Transfer

The effectiveness of the transfer of the priority right depends on the applicable law. In situations where German law applies to the underlying legal relationship in accordance with the above criteria, the priority right is freely transferable, even without the application establishing the priority. The provisions of sections 398 and 413 of the German Civil Code can be applied to such transfer. The transfer must have taken place within the priority year. This is not questioned in literature and jurisprudence,[95] except in the abovementioned single decision of the Federal Patent Court.[96] The priority right must be proven by the patent owner if the priority becomes an issue in the course of opposition or invalidation proceedings, for instance, if relevant prior art is found in the priority interval. According to general principles of procedural law, this burden falls on the patent owner.[97] It is true that the priority right can also be transferred in an implicit manner.[98] The possibility of an implicit transfer supports the so-called PCT joint applicants approach[99] which allows the establishment of a valid transfer of the priority right in cases where a US priority application names one or more inventors as applicants, and those inventors are then later named as applicants only for the US designation on the PCT case, whereas a corporate applicant is named for the EP. This raises the question whether the priority claim has been validly made. As the PCT applicants have the right to priority, it is argued that this also applies to the EP designation and later EP application since the priority right in the PCT application has a unitary character for all designated states. This argumentation essentially circumvents any showing that the corporate applicant in the EP application is a successor in title to the inventors. The "joint applicants approach" is under dispute. Hopefully, the abovementioned pending referrals (G1/22 and G2/22) will provide clarification on the application of that approach. Even though the case law appears to be patentee-friendly, it is advisable to document the transfer of the priority right in a written document.

In *Drahtloses Kommunikationsrecht*, the Federal Court of Justice does not question that a transfer contract must be proven by the patentee. This case concerned the transfer of a priority right from an employee to the employer with subsequent transfer to a third party. In a rather lenient ruling, the court allowed the priority right to be established. The court found that a reference to a first US application could be sufficient for an offer (declaration of intent) to transfer the priority right. If one considers the principles of the German civil law applicable to declarations of intent, which presuppose the presence of a will to enter into a legal obligation, one can see that, in this case, rather the overall circumstances and interests may have played the

95. Federal Court of Justice, Decision of Sep. 4, 2018, X ZR 14/17 "Drahtloses Kommunikationsnetz"; OLG Düsseldorf, Decision of Dec. 6, 2012, 2 U 46/12, juris recital 44; Benkard/Grabinski, EPC, 3rd ed. (2018), Art. 87, marginal no. 3.
96. Federal Patent Court, Decision of Oct. 28, 2010, Mitt. 2011, 259.
97. Benkard/Grabinski, Art. 87, para. 25; OLG Düsseldorf, judgment of Dec. 6, 2012, 2 U 46/12, juris para. 56; Singer/Stauder/Spangenberg, EPC, 6th ed., Art. 87, para. 51; EPO-J 19/87.
98. Federal Patent Court, Aug. 4, 2021, 4 Ni 8/20 (EP) and 4 Ni 9/20 (EP); Appeal Düsseldorf GRUR-RR, 2021, 249—Cinacalcet I.
99. EPO—T 844/18.

decisive role for the acceptance of a valid transfer. The mere reference to a first US application is nothing other than a report of knowledge. However, the overall circumstances and interests of the parties, including the special situation following the German Employee Invention Act, were decisive for the court's conclusion. Even if the facts on which this decision is based have turned out well for the patent owner, one should never neglect the contractual side of the transfer to avoid the creation of an irreparable defect in the application procedure which cannot be cured in subsequent infringement proceedings. In fact, even in the light of the last decision of the Federal Court of Justice, the patentee has the duty to prove the existence of transfer of the priority right by means of a duly concluded contract.

In most cases, German law will not apply to the priority right and its transfer. If a US application serves as priority for a subsequent application, US law will apply in most cases. In such cases, US law has to be applied by German courts. If, therefore, the transfer of the inventor's rights from the employee to the employer takes place, special care is required. While an employment agreement falling under US law may often be interpreted as meaning that the employee assigns all rights to his employer, this does not necessarily mean that the assignment automatically takes place. In practice, often such agreements are unclear and only relate to the US situation. This opens the door for challenging the priority right.

Even though the German case law might be generous in view of proving the existence of a transfer agreement, it is not always so accommodating. Many European patents suffer from irreparable defects, which cannot be retroactively restored by agreements. Concerns often arise in the context of European patents that are derived from PCT applications filed with US priorities. The US priority is usually filed in the name(s) of the inventor(s), whereas the subsequent European application is filed by the corporation which employs or employed the inventors. Thus, the right to claim priority from the US application must have been assigned from the inventors to the corporation in a timely and appropriate manner, which often did not take place or took place but cannot be proven in German patent infringement proceedings.

[F] Duty to Disclose

An important question from the outset of filing a patent application in Europe is how much prior art to disclose. Rule 42(1)(b) of the Implementing Regulation provides:

> The description shall:
>
> ...
>
> indicate the background art which, as far as is known to the applicant, can be regarded as useful to understand the invention, draw up the European search report and examine the European patent application, and, preferably, cite the documents reflecting such art;

The description of the patent application must of course disclose the invention, but—as a rule—shall also indicate the background art that can be regarded as useful to understand the invention, to draw up the European search report, and to examine the

European patent application. Unlike in the US, in Europe, there is in principle no mandatory "duty to disclose." That is, under the EPC, there is no rule comparable to the 37 C.F.R. section 1.56 that imposes on the applicant the duty to disclose prior art that may be material to patentability. This means that a lengthy US-style Information Disclosure Statement (IDS) is usually not necessary under the European rules.

Nevertheless, according to Rule 141(1) EPC, an applicant claiming priority within the meaning of Article 87 EPC is obliged to file a copy of the search results carried out by the authority with which the previous (priority) application was filed. Other prior art that the applicant is aware of or subsequently becomes aware of is not covered by this rule. The rule only concerns prior art that has been identified by the authority of the priority application. In the case of Euro-PCT applications, this search result needs to be filed upon entry into the European phase, or without delay after the results have been made available to the applicant. If the EPO notes that this has not been done, it can invite the applicant to catch up or, at least, ask the applicant to state that these results are not available to him (Rule 70b(1) EPC). A failure to respond to this invitation may lead to a lapse of the application (Rule 70b(2) EPC).[100] Aside from the lapse caused by a missing response to the EPO's invitation, the EPC does not provide for any other legal effects arising from an incomplete, incorrect or even missing IDS. If the applicant fails to provide search results for the authority of priority applications after they have been made available to him, and the EPO does not realize this, there is no ill effect (Rule 141(1) EPC). Even though this could be considered a failure to comply with an EPC rule, it would not be regarded as a ground for revocation of the granted patent. The same seems to be applicable to the enforceability of the patent, which is then governed by national law.

The literature has discussed a theory for finding patents unenforceable for failure to disclose known material art in a case where the patent has been obtained by a fraudulent misguidance of the patent office.[101] This theory refers, however, to an exceptional situation which requires clearly false suggestions or misrepresentation. It thus does not play a role in practice. Accordingly, the question of whether the applicant has withheld information when filing the application or during the prosecution proceedings is not a litigated issue. Of course, the undisclosed prior art, to the extent it becomes available later, could be used to invalidate the patent for novelty or inventive step reasons.

[G] Opposition, Revocation and Limitation Proceedings

After grant, ordinary European patents or UPs may be subject to opposition, revocation and limitation proceedings. Opposition proceedings are discussed in detail below in

100. *See* OJ EPO 2010, 600 on the filing of copies of search results under Rule 141(1) EPC and decisions of the EPO's President exempting applicants claiming the priority of a first filing made in Austria, Japan, UK, the USA, the Republic of Korea, Denmark or in Spain from filing a copy of the search results under Rule 141(1) EPC: OJ EPO 2011, 62; OJ EPO 2012, 540; OJ EPO 2013, 216; OJ EPO 2015, A2, OJ EPO 2016, A18. *See also* notices from the EPO, OJ EPO 2010, 410 and OJ EPO 2016, A19.
101. RGZ 140, 184.

Chapter 6, "Opposition Proceedings." A revocation request according to Article 105a(1) EPC is a request which can only be filed by the proprietor and is aimed at abandoning his patent *ab initio*.

Limitation proceedings are ex parte proceedings used by the proprietor to narrow the scope of claims after the patent has been issued (Article 105a–105c EPC). The strategic role of the EPO's centralized limitation proceedings in patent litigation may be significant, as it can be used *inter alia* to present new claims during the course of national litigation or proceedings at the UPC, whether before or after a first instance decision on infringement and validity has been rendered.[102]

[1] Nature of Limitation Proceedings

Limitation proceedings may be initiated by the patent holder at any time after grant of the patent as a way to narrow the patent scope to avoid prior art. There is no time limit as to when the request for limitation can be made. However, the request may not be filed while opposition proceedings are pending (Article 105a(2) EPC). Pending limitation proceedings will be terminated as soon as an opposition is filed against the European patent-in-suit (Rule 93(2) EPC). These rules guarantee the principle of precedence of opposition proceedings. Proceedings initiated by the patentee for limitation of European patents fall into the jurisdiction of the examining divisions (Rule 91 EPC). Oppositions are handled by a different division within the EPO.

Limitation proceedings focus on the European patent as granted, or on the amended patent if it was previously subject to opposition or earlier limitation proceedings. Limitations are directed at amendments of the claims. Accordingly, the request shall include a complete set of the (newly) amended claims (and, if necessary, an amended description and drawings). Limitation proceedings do not provide an opportunity to reexamine the patent. Only the proposed amended claims are examined, namely (Rule 95(2) EPC):

- whether the amended claims constitute a limitation with respect to the claims as granted or amended;
- whether the amended claims are clear and concise according to Article 84 EPC; and
- whether the amended claims are disclosed in the originally filed application and do not contain subject matter extending beyond the application as filed according to Article 123(3) EPC.[103]

[2] Strategic Use of Limitation Proceedings

Limitation proceedings could be useful if a particular limitation seems to be necessary due to problematic prior art, in particular, prior art that was not subject to the grant

102. *Samsung Electronics Co Ltd v. Apple Retail UK & Apple Sales International* [2014] EWCA Civ 250.
103. Guidelines for Examination in the EPO, Part H, IV-4.4.

proceedings and that anticipates an independent claim or challenges the inventiveness of the teaching as claimed. The limitation might be beneficial for a later enforcement of the patent in national courts or at the UPC. Also, it could prevent competitors from filing national nullity or revocation actions at the UPC.

Limitation proceedings have proven their usefulness on the national track. The patent owner may preemptively seek to initiate them, for example, after receiving a ruling rendered by a national court finding the claims of a national stage patent invalid or maintaining them with a limited scope in view of prior art. The patentee can then invoke limitation proceedings at the EPO to obtain narrower claims harmonizing with the national court's decision. This would then have a pan-European effect. If the German Federal Patent Court renders a decision maintaining the claims of the German part of an ordinary European patent with a limited scope, that decision would have no effect on other national parts of the same patent and, accordingly, its German part would have claims of different scope than those in force in other countries. By then instituting limitation proceedings, the patentee could adapt the claim sets of the other national parts of the ordinary European patent to the decision of the Federal Patent Court in order to obtain harmonized claims across all countries.

This centralized ex parte procedure reduces costs and contentious issues when enforcing a European patent on a European scale.

[H] Observations by Third Parties

Upon the publication of a European patent application, any person may file observations regarding the patentability of the invention (Article 115 EPC). Although lack of novelty and/or inventive step are the most common observations, third-party observations may also be directed to clarity (Article 84 EPC), sufficiency of disclosure (Article 83 EPC), patentability (Articles 52(2) and (3), 53 or 57 EPC) and unallowable amendments (Articles 76(1), 123(2) EPC).[104] The observations can be filed anonymously and are entered into the prosecution file and considered by the EPO. It is a form of public participation in the EPO proceedings. However, the filing person does not become a party to the proceedings and is thus excluded from the oral proceedings before the examining division, which are not public. This contrasts with post-grant opposition proceedings, wherein the opponent is a party to the proceedings and obtains thereby the right to be heard before any decision is taken. If someone wants to stay anonymous or if he cannot file his own opposition because the opposition period has lapsed, this party can at least file observations during pending opposition proceedings.[105]

104. Guidelines for Examination in the EPO, Part E, V-3.
105. EPO—G 9/91.

§4.03 NATIONAL PATENTS

[A] National Routes

An inventor who intends to apply for patent rights in just a few European countries may—rather than applying for a European patent—use national proceedings and file patent applications with national patent offices in countries for which he seeks protection. Also, someone who wants to circumvent the jurisdiction of the UPC may do so. Again, national patent rights stay in the hands of the national courts.

Each jurisdiction in and outside Europe thus provides for additional tools for protection which might be used by the owner as additional fallback positions alongside European patents. The different national systems vary significantly as to costs and how the patents are prosecuted. Some national systems do not undertake substantive examinations in the manner of the EPO. These States only operate patent registration systems where the patent offices do not perform an examination of the application as to inventive step and novelty of the claimed teaching,[106] whereas other national patent offices,[107] such as the German patent office, provide for examination systems.

For instance, the French patent law defines two different types of protection tools, namely a patent of invention with a lifetime of twenty years and a utility certificate with a shorter duration of only six years from filing. The French Patent Office (INPI) examines all applications for patents and certificates of utility and may reject the application for formal reasons, such as lack of adequate support for the claims in the specification, in case the claims are not sufficiently clear, or do not cover only one invention. The patent office also examines whether the claimed invention contains patentable subject matter. In order to obtain a patent of invention, the applicant has to request the establishment of a search report and to pay the corresponding fee at the filing of the application. Under the so-called PACTE Act adopted by Parliament on April 11, 2019,[108] the INPI is allowed to reject a patent application for lack of novelty, lack of inventive step and/or lack of industrial application, among other things. In addition, any third party with an interest will be able to question the validity of a granted patent through opposition proceedings before the INPI. Prior to the entry into force of the PACTE Act, the only way to invalidate patents in France was to file a nullity action with a civil court. Since April 1, 2020, all French national patents may be subject to an opposition within a time limit of nine months of the date of publication of the notice of grant of the patent.[109] The proceedings of the French oppositions are similar to EPO oppositions, but cheaper, and there is no provision that allows an alleged infringer to intervene in pending opposition proceedings in contrast to the EPO proceedings.

Of particular importance for the parallel use of national tools is the question to which extent the national systems allow for double protection. According to a recently presented bill in France, the prohibition against double patenting shall be dropped in

106. Such as Belgium, France, Italy, and the Netherlands.
107. Such as Austria, Germany, and UK.
108. No. 2019-486. Art. L612-2 CPI.
109. Article L613-23, 24 CPI.

France. The current French law does not permit double patenting. That is, currently, a French patent may not cover an invention for which a European patent has been granted. As in Germany, that double patenting ban shall no longer apply to European patents with unitary effect and ordinary European patents for which no opt-out has been declared. This makes it also attractive in France to obtain a national patent.

[B] German Patents

[1] General Remarks

German patents are granted by the GPTO. Because they are enforceable only in Germany, patents originated through prosecution proceedings at the GPTO have been of lesser importance for international applicants than have been patents obtained through the EPO. Even though the European and national patent laws are broadly harmonized, there are a few differences between proceedings at the EPO and the GPTO.

German (and other national) patents are important strategic assets. One reason for this is that German patents are excluded from the jurisdiction of the UPC. Thus, while potential infringers may find it advantageous to attempt to invalidate patent rights on a pan-European basis through the UPC, this option is not available for attacking patents issued through the German Patent Office. This exclusion for German patents is and will be permanent, unlike the limited "transitional" period of time for patents issued from the EPO, for which an "opt-out" period is available. Ordinary European patents can be opted out from the UPC's jurisdiction during the transitional period of Article 83 UPCA.[110] At least during the transitional period the owner of an ordinary European is thus entitled to exclude it from the jurisdiction of the UPC and would not be required to use national patents in order to be sheltered from the UPC. The situation changes as soon as the transitional period expires and opt-outs are no longer permissible. At that point, ordinary European patents will fall under the jurisdiction of the UPC. In addition, any uncertainty as to whether an opt-out of a European patent has been validly declared may be avoided with a German national patent.

[2] Procedure in General

The language of the patent prosecution proceedings through the GPTO is necessarily German. Nevertheless, a German patent application can be filed in any other language provided a translation is submitted within three months from its filing date (section 35a Patent Act). If the application was filed in English or French, the applicant has twelve months to provide the translation. This allows applicants to obtain a filing date that is not delayed due to the time necessary for translating the application into German.

---

110. *See* Ch. 4, §4.02[A][1][b] (above).

In contrast to some other European countries, the granting proceedings at the GPTO include a substantive examination of the application. This does not apply to German utility models, which are not examined as to their substance. German utility models are discussed further below.[111]

During the first phase of the grant proceedings, the GPTO carries out an examination as to whether the application displays obvious deficiencies. In contrast to the proceedings at the EPO, the subsequent substantive examination of the application can be delayed by the applicant's filing of an examination request up to seven years after the filing date (section 44(2) German Patent Act (GPA)). This is an advantage particularly for small- and medium-sized companies and also an interesting option for larger companies if it is not known how the invention will be implemented in practice. In compliance with general standards, the application is published after the expiry of eighteen months from the filing date or the earliest priority date. However, interested third parties may file an examination request on behalf of the applicant.[112] Decisions rendered by examination sections of the GPTO during the examination proceedings can be appealed to the Federal Patent Court in Munich (section 73(1) GPA).

[a] Amendments

Amendments to the application are possible after filing the examination request (section 38 Patent Act). As is the case with European patent applications, applicants are not permitted to add new subject matter when amending a patent application ("inadmissible extensions").[113] However, although the legal standards are the same, in practice, German case law tended to be more lenient, so that it was often easier to introduce amendments in German proceedings. According to recent decisions of the Federal Supreme Court,[114] it seems however that Germany is aligning its case law with the case law of the EPO's Boards of Appeal.[115] The question of what is added subject matter depends on the content of the original disclosure. To determine the informative content of the original disclosure, it is crucial to determine those statements belonging to the same technical teaching. Accordingly, it is prohibited to regroup features from different parts of the disclosure if they do not belong to the same technical concept. There must be a sufficient relationship between these features; otherwise, the amendment would be considered to be a new subject matter that would jeopardize the grant of the patent and could later lead to its revocation.[116] The Federal Supreme Court[117]

111. *See* Ch. 4, §4.03[C].
112. Federal Patent Court, BPatGE 15, 134, GRUR 1974, 80: "The third party must not demonstrate a reason for the application. However, the third party does not become a party to the proceedings."
113. Article 123(2) EPC: "The European patent application or European patent may not be amended in such a way that it contains subject-matter which extends beyond the content of the application as filed."
114. Federal Supreme Court, Decision of Jul. 8, 2010, Xa ZR 124/07, GRUR 2010, 910, "Fälschungssicheres Dokument"; Federal Supreme Court, BGHZ 179, 168, GRUR 2009, 382, "Olanzapin."
115. Cf. EPO—T 0687/05.
116. BPatGE 3, 48, 52.
117. Federal Supreme Court, Decision of Jul. 8, 2010, Xa ZR 124/07, GRUR 2010, 910, "Fälschungssicheres Dokument"; Federal Supreme Court, BGHZ 179, 168, GRUR 2009, 382, "Olanzapin."

ruled that the original disclosure only comprises information which is "clearly and unambiguously" derivable for a person skilled in the art. Information resulting from far-reaching conclusions, which the skilled person might only draw on the basis of his technical knowledge or through modifications of the technical teaching disclosed, constitutes, by contrast, subject matter which extends beyond the original disclosure.

[b] Divisional Applications

During all stages of the grant procedure, divisional applications may be filed (section 39 GPA). The only requirement is that the parent application remains pending and that the grant procedure be not yet finally concluded. The divisional application enters the same procedural stages as the related parent application, meaning that if the parent application is already examined, the divisional application will be considered to be in the examination phase. The divisional application is entitled to the filing date and applicable priority dates of the parent application (section 39(1) GPA). Hence, the expiration term of a divisional application will be calculated from the date of filing of the parent application and not from the filing date of the divisional application. Of course, it is not possible to add new subject matter to a divisional application. Similar to European divisional applications, the parent and divisional application shall not claim the same subject matter to avoid double patenting.[118] Nevertheless, it is acceptable if the independent claim in the parent application includes all the features of an independent claim of the divisional application which is combined with an additional feature.

[c] Opposition Proceedings

Opposition proceedings against a German Patent may be filed by third parties within nine months[119] after the publication of the grant of the patent (section 59 GPA). After expiration of the opposition period, a nullity action can be filed.[120] In comparison to opposition proceedings, a nullity action is more expensive. Decisions in opposition proceedings are rendered by so-called Patent Divisions of the GPTO and can be appealed to the Federal Patent Court in Munich. As indicated, the same applies to decisions against the Examination Sections (section 73(1) GPA).

[d] Double Protection by German and EPs

The Act on International Patent Conventions (IntPatÜbkG)[121] adopts international patent laws, such as the EPC, the PCT and the UP System, into the German system.[122] The IntPatÜbkG also regulates the coexistence of ordinary European patents and UPs

118. *See* Ch. 4, §4.03[B][2][d] (below).
119. The opposition period has been extended from three to nine months by law amendment of Oct. 19, 2013, with effect from Apr. 1, 2014.
120. *See* Ch. 8, "Nullity Actions."
121. Gesetz über internationale Patentübereinkommen.
122. Sections 19 and 20 IntPatÜG.

on the one hand and German patents on the other hand. An excerpt of the most important provisions of the IntPatÜbkG can be found in Chapter 18 (§18.04).

Patenting the same invention through German and European patents was prohibited by German law until the UPCA took effect. Previously, upon expiration of the EPO opposition period or after conclusion of EPO opposition proceedings, the German part of the European patent rendered the German national patent permanently lapsed within the scope of the granted European patent. This situation often occurred where the German application forms the priority application of the subsequent European application. The policy behind this rule was to avoid a multiplicity of overlapping monopolies for the same invention contained in two (or more) coexisting patents with the same content.

[i] Ordinary EPs Not Opted Out and UPs

The current system allows double protection of a European patent and a German national patent, unless the applicant or owner of the European patent has opted out from UPC jurisdiction. In the event of an opt-out, the previous rules prohibiting double protection continue to apply.[123] Thus in principle an applicant is allowed to seek double protection conferred by non-opted-out ordinary European patents or UPs on the one hand and German national patents on the other hand. This is possible for all German national patents that were granted after the date of the entry into force of the UPCA. An important aspect of such allowed double patenting consists in that an applicant gets a larger radius of maneuver: Ownership of a German patent and a (non-opted-out) European patent or UP with the same scope of protection is possible. If the owner loses that European patent in proceedings at the UPC, he stays entitled to assert the German patent through German national proceedings. Thus, a German patent remains available for enforcement, even if the European patent or UP with the same scope of protection has been previously invalidated through proceedings at UPC.

However, the parallel enforcement of coexisting patents with the same scope of protection is limited by law. The defendant may raise a litigation estoppel objection in German proceedings. According to section 18 IntPatÜbkG, an action based on infringement or imminent threat of infringement pending at a German national patent could be dismissed or the German court may stay the proceedings until conclusion of the UPC proceedings[124] if:

1. the subject-matter of the German national patent is an invention for which the same inventor, or his successor in title, was granted an ordinary European Patent or a Unitary patent with the same priority date, and
2. there is a pending action before the UPC against the same party based on infringement or imminent threat of infringement of ordinary European Patent or a Unitary patent with respect to the same embodiment, or the UPC has finally decided on such request and

123. Article II, s. 8 IntPatÜG.
124. Section 18(2) IntPatÜG.

3. the defendant brings an objection at the first hearing after the above grounds have occurred before the oral hearing of the main proceedings starts.[125]

Section 18 IntPatÜbkG gives rise to strategic considerations. The litigation estoppel only applies to proceedings involving the same accused infringer. For instance, the patentee may attack different infringers out of the supply chain. He may sue one infringer on the basis of the German patent in a German court and other infringers at the UPC on the basis of the European patent. The litigation estoppel objection according to section 18 IntPatÜbkG would fail in such scenario because the party in the German infringement proceedings must equally be sued in proceedings at the UPC. Also, the litigation estoppel objection requires that the actions are directed at the same embodiment. However, the litigation estoppel objection may likely not be jeopardized by an assignment of one of the patents to a third party which then acts as the plaintiff in one of the proceedings. Similar considerations apply in relation to patentee and licensee. Finally, according to section 18(4) IntPatÜG, the litigation estoppel is not applicable for interim or protective measures, in particular preliminary injunction proceedings. If the UPC is considered too slow or unfavorable, the parallel German patent could be used in Germany as a relief.

It could thus be advantageous to obtain protection both through a European patent application and a national German patent application in parallel, for example, by entering the European and national German phase in parallel from an international application under the PCT. Another option is to use a German application as priority application of the subsequent EP application, which can be kept alive as fallback position.

[ii] Opted-Out Ordinary EPs

As indicated above, in the event of an ordinary EP for which a valid "opt out" from the UPC's jurisdiction has been declared, the rule forbidding double protection continues to apply (Article II §8 IntPatÜbkG). This is, a parallel German patent loses its effect on the day on which the opt-out has become effective, assuming no earlier loss applies. Article II §8 IntPatÜbkG refers to four possible points in time for the loss of the protection conferred by the German patent:

(1) expiry of the nine-month period after grant of the EP if no opposition has been filed against the EP;
(2) final termination of EPO opposition proceedings, should such proceedings be initiated against the EP;
(3) effective date of the opt-out if this date is later than no. 1 or no. 2;
(4) grant of the German patent if this occurs after the point in time according to no. 1 to 3.

125. Unofficial translation of Art. II, s. 18(1) IntPatÜG.

A later withdrawal of the opt-out under Article 83(4) EPC (so-called opt-in) would not restore the loss of the German patent. It will continue to have no effect.

Nevertheless, the situation is different if the corresponding (parallel) German patent application has not yet been granted. The prohibition of double protection may be overcome through a valid withdrawal of the opt-out (so-called opt-in) according to Article 83(4) UPCA occurring prior to a loss of the German patent. Accordingly, even if the patentee opts out of the UPC jurisdiction for a European patent (e.g., to adopt a "wait and see" strategy as the UPC jurisprudence develops), it may be advantageous to pursue an identical German patent application. The grant of a German patent application can be efficiently delayed by withholding a request to proceed with the examination of the German patent application for up to seven years.

[e] Costs

Aside from the costs for the professional work to prepare the application, which depends on the complexity of the invented technology, the filing of a German patent application is inexpensive. If the filing includes a request for search and examination, including preparing and filing the designation of inventors, depending on the number of claims, the official fees commonly are less than EUR 1,000. Subsequently, annual maintenance fees have to be paid starting from the third year of the patent.[126] The annual maintenance fees for Germany and France can be found in the middle column of Table 4.5 (*see* above §4.02[B][3]).

[C] German Utility Models (*Gebrauchsmuster*)

[1] Main Characteristics of German Utility Models

German utility models are a unique form of IP protection. They function through a swift and inexpensive registration process. Like German patents, German utility models are and will be forever excluded from the future UPC jurisdiction. They confer rights similar to a patent, i.e., cease-and-desist claims, damage claims, claims to render account and even destruction claims. Used in tandem with other forms of IP, utility models can be a powerful part of a patent portfolio.

Utility models provide protection only for product claims, including claims that are focused on substances, such as pharmaceuticals. Utility models cannot be used to protect method or use claims (section 2 No. 3 Utility Model Act), but the case law of the Federal Supreme Court seems to be rather flexible with this exception, which is detailed below.[127]

The process of obtaining a German utility model is uncomplicated. The GPTO registers these rights within two to three months without examination as to novelty or

126. *See* "Information Concerning Costs, Fees and Expenses of the German Patent and Trade Mark Office and of the Federal Patent Court" www.dpma.de.
127. Chapter 4, §4.03[C][4] "Protectable Subject Matter."

inventive step. Similar to a German patent application, a utility mode can be filed in any language provided a German translation is submitted within a three-month period from its filing date (section 4(b) Utility Model Act). The validity of a German utility model can later be challenged by cancelation proceedings filed with the GPTO (section 15 Utility Model Act). A special utility model division has jurisdiction to decide on the validity of the utility model in *inter partes* proceedings. Its decisions can be appealed to the Federal Patent Court (section 18(1) Utility Model Act), and in exceptional circumstances, a further appeal is possible to the Federal Supreme Court.

[2] Different Protection Standards

A particular advantage of utility models is that the novelty standards are different compared with patents.

Of particular interest is a six-month grace period from the disclosure of the invention (section 3(1) of German Utility Act), which would ordinarily preclude filing of patent applications. Publications or use within six months preceding the date relevant for the priority of the application shall not be taken into consideration if it is based on the conception of the applicant or his predecessor in title. Thus, where there has already been a barring disclosure for patent applications, an applicant may still be eligible to receive a German utility model.

Furthermore, prior public use of an invention is not a barring act for purposes of utility models if the prior public use occurred outside Germany, as provided in section 3(1) of the German Utility Act. However, written publications made in and outside Germany represent relevant prior art.

Moreover, even if the invention has been the subject of European or German patents, an applicant may still receive a utility model without prohibition from double patenting rules. Thus, in some circumstances, utility models may be the best, or only, option for protecting inventions in Germany.

Up until recently, the main hurdle in utility models was novelty rather than inventiveness. This has been changed by a landmark decision of the German Federal Supreme Court, in which the court ruled that an invention protected by a utility model needed, like a regular patent, to feature an inventive step.[128]

[3] Registration of a German Utility Model

A utility model application may be filed like any regular patent application, either without claiming a priority or within the priority year by claiming priority of a previously filed application (section 6 of the German Utility Model Act). The GPTO registers a utility model without examining its novelty or inventive step, and without examination of whether or not the application documents are supported by, or originally disclosed in, the parent application documents as filed.

128. Federal Supreme Court, Decision of Jun. 20, 2006, X ZB 27/05, "Demonstrationsschrank."

[4] *Protectable Subject Matter*

Utility model protection is possible for all product claims including claims that are directed to substances or pharmaceuticals. According to sections 1(2) and 2 of the German Utility Model Act, the following subject matter is excluded from utility model protection:

- discoveries, scientific theories and mathematical methods;
- aesthetic creations;
- schemes, rules and methods for performing mental acts, games, business methods and programs for computers;
- presentations of information;
- inventions which violate public policy or public order;
- plant species and animal species; and
- methods.

Although no examination is carried out by the GPTO with regard to novelty and inventive step, a formal examination is indeed carried out prior to registration to make sure that no subject matter is registered that falls under the abovementioned exclusions.

With respect to method claims that generally cannot be the subject matter of a German utility model, a few important decisions of the Federal Supreme Court illustrate that "use" or "method" elements in claims may be permissible in certain circumstances. First, the Federal Supreme Court ruled that utility model protection could be sought for the use of a substance for the treatment of a disease insofar as claims would at least contain elements of a product claim, namely a drug.[129] Accordingly, the use of a known substance for a medical indication can be subject to a utility model. The Federal Supreme Court referred in its ruling to the conclusions of the German legislature when enacting the German Utility Model Act in 1986 and concluded that the legislature did not exclude from the Act use of claims in the context of medical indications. Furthermore, product claims containing method features may be permitted insofar as the involved method features give an indication to the skilled person whether and how structural features of a product have to be implemented according to the teaching of the invention.[130] Accordingly, product-by-process claims are not excluded from being protected by a utility model.

[5] *Reasons for Filing a Utility Model*

[a] *Low Fees and Prosecution Costs*

The fees for applying for a utility model are very low. Currently, the fees are as follows:

- Filing fee: EUR 40
- First renewal fee after three years: EUR 210

129. Federal Supreme Court, X ZB 7/03, GRUR 2006, 135, "Arzneimittelgebrauchsmuster."
130. Federal Supreme Court, X ZR 188/01, GRUR 2005, 749, "Aufzeichnungsträger."

- Second renewal fee after six years: EUR 350
- Last renewal fee after eight years: EUR 530.

Accordingly, the fees for a utility model until the end of its life are slightly above EUR 1,000. Because the utility model is registered without examination, there are no prosecution costs. Furthermore, a utility model application provides a priority right under the Paris Convention that can be used for subsequent applications in the Member States of the Paris Convention. That is, the financial investment for the prosecution of full patents in signatory countries to the Paris Convention can be postponed by means of a utility model application.

[b] *Early Publication of the Invention*

In a few circumstances, the inventor may be interested in having his invention published as soon as possible so that the application documents become part of the relevant prior art under German and European standards. A German utility model is an inexpensive and fairly uncomplicated way to make the invention available to the public on the date of registration with the benefit of a priority right. This usually occurs two to three months after the filing of the application. Accordingly, the content of a utility model constitutes prior art relevant to novelty and inventive step from the date of its registration. This publication occurs earlier than the publication of a patent which is usually published eighteen months after the date of filing or, if priority has been claimed, from the date of priority.[131]

[c] *Enforceability*

The utility model applicant obtains an enforceable right from the day of its registration. He can sue the accused infringer on the basis of the utility model and may achieve the goal of stopping the infringer more quickly, even though it may still take considerable time until a parallel patent is granted. Thus, utility models can provide a powerful mechanism for blocking the early entrance of infringing products into the market while awaiting issuance of patents through the EPO or GPTO.

In principle, a utility model can be asserted against any infringer by way of a lawsuit in the same way as a granted patent. However, special characteristics apply because, unlike a patent, a utility model is not an examined property right. It is registered without substantive examination. To counterbalance the missing substantive examination, the law provides that utility model protection lapses insofar as a claim for cancelation of the utility model can be successfully brought forward against the utility model. Contrary to a patent, the infringement court can thus decide on the validity of the utility model and declare it invalid with effect between plaintiff and defendant (*inter partes*). In infringement proceedings, the defendant is free to raise an

131. Article 93(1)(a) EPC.

objection against the validity of the utility model without instituting separate cancelation proceedings at the GPTO. If cancelation proceedings have been instituted, the infringement court may order that the hearing (on the infringement dispute) be stayed until the cancelation proceedings have been settled (§19 first sentence, GebrMG). As a rule, reasonable doubts about the validity of the utility model are sufficient to stay a utility model infringement action under §19, first sentence, GebrMG.[132] If the infringement court is convinced of the invalidity of the utility model registration (§19 sentence 2, GebrMG), it must stay the proceedings, so-called mandatory stay.

A defendant who is convinced of the invalidity of the utility model and wishes to obtain a judgment dismissing the action for that reason may opt to refrain from initiating cancelation proceedings and only assert the objection of lack of validity of the utility model in the infringement proceedings. A dismissal of an action for lack of validity establishes *"inter partes"* that the utility model is invalid. The defendant does not have to observe it any further, but the utility model continues to have effect on third parties. This is different regarding decisions in cancelation proceedings. They have effect for and against everyone (*"erga omnes"*). If the utility model is canceled in cancelation proceedings, the action must therefore be dismissed. If, on the contrary, the cancelation request is rejected, the court is bound by this decision if it was made between the same parties (§19, third sentence, GebrMG).

Nevertheless, it is not impossible to base a preliminary injunction on a utility model. But, infringement courts will only issue injunctions if the validity of the utility model protection is sufficiently assured. This might be the case, for example, if a utility model has successfully survived cancelation proceedings. This is, if the utility model division of the GPTO has already decided positively on the legal validity of the utility model in suit, there is a presumption in favor of its legal validity.

In infringement proceedings based on utility models, the plaintiff is thus required to present corresponding evidence for the validity of the asserted right in the complaint brief, for instance, by submitting a prior art search made by a patent office or a qualified searcher. Often it is advantageous to refer to developments in parallel grant proceedings at the EPO or national offices. If, for example, the EPO has granted a parallel patent whose scope of protection corresponds to that of the utility model, its validity can be assumed.[133]

[d] Damages

The utility model applicant can claim damages as soon as the utility model has been registered. The registration of the utility model can thus trigger the accrual of damages without having to wait for issuance of a patent or the publication of a pending application. Moreover, the damages accruing based on the registered utility model may be higher than the provisional remedies that would pertain based on publication of a

---

132. Federal Supreme Court, GRUR 2014, pp. 1237, 1238—"Kurznachrichten"; Appeal Court Karlsruhe, 2.12.2013—6 W 69/13.
133. Appeal Court Düsseldorf, Jun. 11, 2018, Ref.: I-15 W 30/18, GRUR-RS 2019; Appeal Court Karlsruhe, GRUR 2014, p. 352.

pending patent application. The heightened damages based on registration of a utility model are illustrated below, as compared with the compensation that would be due based only on the publication of a pending patent application (*see* Figure 4.3).

Figure 4.3 Early Damage Claim due to Utility Model Protection

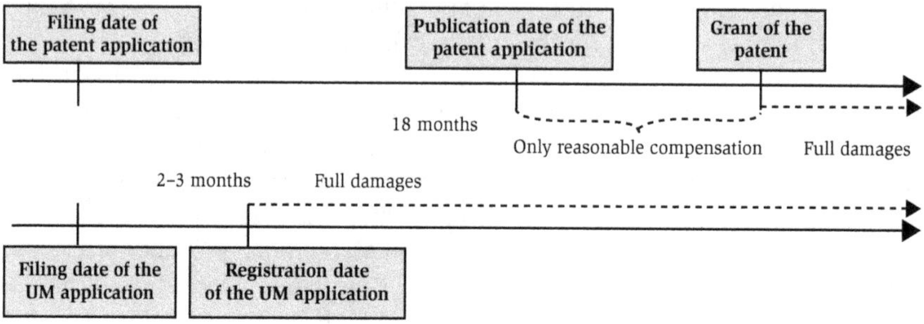

[e] Strategic "Branching Off"

[i] General Remarks

A strategic benefit of utility models is that they may be "branched off" from an earlier German, European or PCT application (section 5 of the German Utility Model Act). Such branching off is permissible up to the expiration of two months from the end of the month in which processing of the patent application or any opposition procedure is terminated. Because of the shortened ten-year term of utility models, filing the "branched-off" utility model must occur by the end of the tenth year from the date of filing of the earlier patent application, as shown in Figure 4.4. Normally, there must be a pending patent application to branch off a utility model because it cannot be branched off from a granted patent. An exception to this rule occurs if an opposition proceeding is commenced (under either the EPO or GPTO), at which point the patentee regains the opportunity to branch off a utility model during the pendency of the opposition.

The branched-off utility model is accorded the priority and filing date of the parent patent application insofar as the claims are supported by the earlier patent application.

[ii] Tailoring Claims in View of the Infringing Embodiment

An applicant may recognize that the claim language of an existing patent application could be improved with regard to infringing embodiments of a competitor. Utility models can be a powerful tool in this situation. By branching off a German utility model with refined claim language to more closely track a competitor's products, a patentee can continue to adapt to developments in the market.

[iii] Claim Sets for German Utility Models in Case of an Infringement

The applicant may even branch off several utility models and assert them against a competitor. The only requirement is that the claims of these applications be somehow different when compared with each other. It might be possible to claim different aspects of an invention, or to define the same invention from different perspectives. The patentee can assert the granted patent and additionally one or more utility models against the competitor. Thus, utility models can help build a thicket of IP rights to bolster an enforcement strategy.

When drafting claim sets for utility models, the following considerations should be noted:

- The claims must be supported by the parent patent application, although the related standards of the GPTO and the Federal Patent Court appear to be more flexible than the formalistic approach of the EPO.
- The subject matter of the utility model claims should be novel and inventive in view of the known prior art.
- Principles of claim construction, discussed below in Chapter 10, should be taken into account.

The main characteristics of utility models are provided in Table 4.6.

Figure 4.4 Branching Off

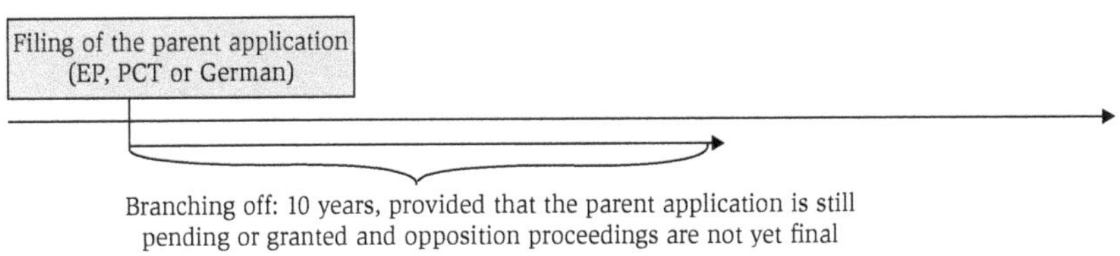

Table 4.6 Main Characteristics of Utility Models

Registration proceedings	No substantive examination. Can be branched off from a PCT, EP or German patent application. Early publication and enforceability of the invention through registration.
Protectable subject matter	Product claims are possible. Use and method claims are in principle not allowed.
Prior art	Grace period of six months; public prior use only relevant if occurred within German territory.
Judicial Enforcement	Immediately after registration possible. Utility Model gives almost the same rights as a granted patent. Utility Model can be used to tailor claims to the accused embodiment.

Damages	Relevant calculation period begins as soon as the Utility Model is registered.
Official fees	Very low, about EUR 1,000 for the life of the Utility Model.

CHAPTER 5
Patentability Standards

Patentability standards across Europe are largely harmonized under the EPC. Germany and the other national Member States have adopted patentability standards into their own laws that track the requirements of the EPC. At the European level, the patentability standards are codified in the EPC, specifically in Article 52, which applies to all European patents regardless of whether they are ordinary European patents or those with unitary effect. Thus, the present chapter does not need to differentiate between these categories.

For national German patents, the provisions of sections 1 et seq. of the GPA[1] are applicable. Both sets of provisions are substantively identical. Nonetheless, even though the laws are harmonized, there are practical differences in the application of these laws by the various tribunals charged with their implementation, including the EPO, national patent offices, such as the GPTO and national courts, such as the German courts. The laws define non-patentable subject matter and moreover require that to be patentable a claimed invention must be novel, must involve an inventive step (similar to the concept of nonobviousness under US law) and must be amenable to industrial application (Article 52(1) EPC, section 1(1) of the GPA). Moreover, like the US requirements under 35 U.S.C. section 112, European laws require that the patent specification be sufficient to enable the patented invention (although there is no "best mode" requirement). These patentability requirements are discussed in turn below.

§5.01 PATENTABLE SUBJECT MATTER

[A] Classes of Non-inventions

European law defines patentable subject matter in the negative by specifying classes of technologies for which no patent may be granted. Article 52(2) of the EPC and the

1. An excerpt of the GPA can be found in Ch. 18, §18.03.

corresponding section 1(3) of the GPA roughly correspond to the concept of unpatentable subject matter under US law, with important differences that have emerged in the wake of the US Supreme Court's ruling in *Alice v. CLS Bank*[2] and its progeny. European law defines classes of abstract theories, mental acts, business methods, computer programs, etc., which are basically ineligible for patent protection. Article 53 of the EPC recites classes of inventions that may not be patented for other reasons of public policy.

The classes of non-inventions specified by Article 52(2) EPC[3] are as follows:

> (2) The following in particular shall not be regarded as inventions within the meaning of paragraph 1:
> (a) discoveries, scientific theories and mathematical methods;
> (b) aesthetic creations;
> (c) schemes, rules and methods for performing mental acts, playing games or doing business, and programs for computers;
> (d) presentations of information.

This list is not exhaustive.[4] The carve-out of these subject matters from patentability is itself limited. Article 52(3) EPC clarifies that such non-inventions are only excluded from patentability to the extent that the patent or patent application relates to the excluded categories "*as such*":

> (3) Paragraph 2 shall exclude the patentability of the subject matter or activities referred to therein only to the extent to which a European patent application or European patent relates to such subject matter or activities as such.[5]

Accordingly, the exclusion from patentability applies if the subject matter of the claimed invention does not extend beyond an activity as mentioned in the negative list. Subject matter falling squarely within the list does not qualify as patentable invention. The claimed invention must contain subject matter apart from such unpatentable subject matter to overcome the "*as such*" threshold.[6] Neither national laws nor the EPC defines the term "invention." Generally, to be patentable an invention must at least have a technical character;[7] more precisely, it must provide a technical teaching based on concrete instructions utilizing forces of nature with a practical usefulness which can be repeatedly reproduced.[8] This European approach is more accommodating than the *Alice* standard in the US which has been widely applied to invalidate patents that may have a technical character, but which do not exceed the bounds of conventional technology. In Europe, as in the US, defining the contours of this allowable subject matter is a task that has been left to the patent offices and the courts, to allow flexibility

2. *Alice Corp. v. CLS Bank International*, US Supreme Court slip opinion, Jun. 19, 2014.
3. Section 1(3) of the GPA contains the same list.
4. Federal Supreme Court, GRUR 1969, 672, "Rote Taube."
5. Section 1(4) of the GPA.
6. EPO—T 154/04, "Duns."
7. EPO—T 1173/97; Federal Supreme Court, GRUR 2000, 1007, "Sprachanalyseeinrichtung."
8. EPO—G 2/07 (Broccoli/PLANT BIOSCIENCE) of Dec. 9, 2010; Federal Supreme Court, GRUR 1969, 672, "Rote Taube."

in adapting to new technologies.[9] Section 5.01[B][2] contains a list of examples of patent claims that have either survived or failed this patentability test.

For instance, a mathematical method is not patentable, but an electrical filter designed in compliance with such a method would not be excluded from patentability. It is therefore generally acceptable to have a mix of technical and "non-technical" features appearing in a claim.[10] Because nontechnical features "as such" do not provide a technical contribution to the prior art, they are essentially ignored in assessing novelty and inventive step.[11]

European law imposes further limits on patentable subject matter, whose purposes are rooted in matters of public policy and morality. Article 53 and Rule 28 of the EPC (section 2 GPA) recite these additional classes of invention excluded from patentability, namely *inter alia*:

(a) inventions, the commercial exploitation of which would be contrary to "ordre public" or morality; such exploitation shall not be deemed to be so contrary merely because it is prohibited by law or regulation in some or all of the Contracting States;
(b) plant or animal varieties or essentially biological processes for the production of plants or animals; this provision shall not apply to microbiological processes or the products thereof;
(c) methods for treatment of the human or animal body by surgery or therapy and diagnostic methods practiced on the human or animal body; this provision shall not apply to products, in particular substances or compositions, for use in any of these methods.

The exclusion of inventions being contrary to the "ordre public" or morality is limited to extreme cases. The patent granting system is not equipped to easily determine whether a particular exploitation is prohibited by law or regulation in some or all Member States. Article 53(a) is not aimed at preventing illegal activities. The provision rather expresses a general consideration, namely that those inventions that can only be used for purposes that the legal order disapproves[12]—that specifically endanger fundamental rules of the legal order—are excluded from patentability. Accordingly, a violation of the "ordre public" requires the violation of a "fundamental provision of the legal order,"[13] such as the UN Charter or the European Convention for the Protection of Human Rights and Fundamental Freedoms.[14] Furthermore, the exclusion may also apply to violations of more general legal prohibitions, such as crimes with a minimum custodial sentence of one year according to the Penal Code. Nevertheless, the exclusion from patentability requires that all conceivable exploitation possibilities would lead to the indicated violation. One possible disapproved exploitation (for instance, weapons, toxic substances, abortion means) is not sufficient to exclude the patentability as long as there are other possibilities to exploit the

9. Federal Supreme Court, GRUR 1969, 672, "Rote Taube."
10. EPO—T 154/04, "Duns."
11. *Ibid.*; EPO—G 0003/08.
12. Federal Supreme Court, X ZB 22/71, GRUR 1973, 585 "IUP."
13. Federal Supreme Court BlPMZ, 2003, 291, "Euro-Bauklötze."
14. Rome, Nov. 4, 1950.

invention in a legal manner, even if it requires a regulatory authorization. Accordingly, case law concerning the exclusion for reasons of "ordre public" is rare. The same applies to violations of morality, which are also limited to extreme cases. A violation has been affirmed by the Federal Patent Court for a coffin evacuating oxygen to avoid the awakening of an apparently dead person.[15] Such exceptional situations could also arise in the case of very dangerous, cruel or insidious weapons, as well as dangerous or medically disapproved agents. The same applies if the only purpose of the invention is a criminal offense aimed at the protection of elementary rights, such as an invention concerning the construction of a letter bomb.

Further exclusions can be found in Rule 28 of the EPC (and its corresponding section 2(2) Patent Act, i.e., Rule 28): (a) *cloning human beings*, Rule 28; (b) *modifying the germ line genetic identity of human beings*, Rule 28; (c) the *use of human embryos* and Rule 28; (d) *torture breeding of animals*.

[B] Computer-Implemented Inventions

The EPC does not contain a positive definition of the term "invention." Instead, it provides a list of subject matter that is not considered to qualify for an "invention." These non-inventions are listed in Article 52(2) EPC. The subject matters of these excluded categories do not, according to an established judicial practice of the EPO and national courts, have a "technical character" or, more precisely, do not involve a "technical teaching" which instructs a skilled person to solve a particular technical problem using particular (technical) means. According to that established judicial practice, technical character is a basic criterion for an invention. Computer programs are listed among these non-inventions (Article 52(2) EPC),[16] as are "methods for doing business" and the "presentation of information." However, Article 52(3) EPC clarifies that this only counts to the extent that the patent claims such subject matter "as such." Accordingly, subject matter which includes a computer program is not necessarily excluded from patentability.[17]

Patent claims typically consist of a plurality of features, of which some features describe nontechnical aspects and others have a technical character. The computer program might be loaded on a computer or data carrier. The storage means, or any other hardware component on which a computer program runs, may have a technical character. The assessment requires first an understanding of what is and what is not subject matter with technical character (§5.01[B][2]). The presence of only one technical feature within a feature combination might be sufficient to conclude that there is an invention. Of course, the invention must additionally be amenable to industrial application, and novel and inventive. The presence of both nontechnical and technical features impacts the assessment of novelty and inventive step. As described below, the assessment requires a factual separation of technical and nontechnical

15. Federal Patent Court, Decision of Jan. 15, 1971, 23W (pat) 248/70.
16. Section 1(3) of the GPA contains the same list.
17. Federal Supreme Court, X ZB 16/00, GRUR 2002, 143 "Suche fehlerhafte Zeichenkette"; EPO—T 1173/97 (no. 5-7), "Computerprogrammprodukt I."

aspects in order to determine whether the invention is novel and inventive (§5.01[B][2]).

[1] Technical Character

Whether the subject matter is patentable first depends upon the question whether the requirement of technicality is fulfilled—i.e., on whether the subject matter provides a technical solution to a technical problem based on technical considerations.[18] All features together are determinative of whether the claimed subject matter has a technical effect. The presence of a technical character is *sine qua non* for an invention.[19] The technical character must be determined without considering the prior art.[20] An invention in the meaning of Article 52(1) EPC simply requires "subject-matter having technical character" without regard to the prior art.[21] This determination of whether there is an invention is essentially separate from the three other requirements—novelty, inventive step and industrial application. The requirement of a "technical character" is usually fulfilled, and there is an "invention" as soon as the subject matter involves a physical entity such as a computer, network or another programmable apparatus, such as a mobile phone, or employs technical means.

Claimed subject matter which exclusively addresses a computer program is not excluded from patentability if, when executed by or loaded into a computer, it provides, or is capable of providing, a technical effect which goes beyond the normal physical interaction between software and hardware. The technical character must thus go beyond that self-evident effect—otherwise, the exclusion in Article 52 EPC for computer programs would be meaningless.[22] Nevertheless, allowable subject matter could be entirely resident within a computer. For instance, subject matter sufficient to provide a technical effect to overcome the exclusion of Article 52 EPC may include, for example:

- making a computer run faster (processing speed) or work more efficiently,
- making the computer easier to use,[23]
- reducing memory access time,[24]
- improving availability or scalability,
- reducing network traffic,
- better control of a robotic arm,

18. Federal Supreme Court, GRUR 2004, 667, "Elektronischer Zahlungsverkehr"; EPO—T 0931/95, "Steuerung eines Pensionssystems"; Federal Supreme Court, Xa ZB 20/08, GRUR 2010, 613, "Dynamische Dokumentengenerierung."
19. EPO—T 641/00, "Two entities/COMVIK," OJ 7/2004, 356; Federal Supreme Court, Decision of Dec. 18, 2012, X ZR 3/12, GRUR 2013, 275, n. 41, "Routenplanung"; Federal Supreme Court, Decision of Jun. 30, 2015, X ZB 1/15, "Flugzeugzustand"; EPO—G 3/08.
20. EPO—T 154/04, "Duns Licensing"; EPO—T 1173/97; EPO—G 3/08.
21. EPO—T 258/03, "Hitachi."
22. *Ibid.*
23. EPO—T 928/03, "Konami, Video"; Federal Supreme Court, GRUR 2002, 143, "Suche fehlerhafte Zeichenkette."
24. EPO—T 817/16.

- improved reception and/or decoding of a radio signal,
- a compression algorithm may contribute to the technical character of the claimed compression method if it is used to reduce the amount of data to be stored or transmitted.[25]

Hence, the technical effect does not necessarily have to be external to the computer on which the program runs;[26] reduced hard disk access time or an enhanced user interface could also be sufficient.[27] For instance, giving visual indications automatically about conditions prevailing in an apparatus or system might be sufficient as well.[28]

A physical product or an apparatus consisting of a physical entity has per se a technical character. This applies in particular to computer-implemented inventions. They involve the use of a computer, computer network or other programmable apparatus. If the subject matter refers, in addition, to such physical entities, usually the technical character cannot be denied. For instance, "a computer readable data storage medium" has the technical effect of being computer readable and of being capable of storing data. Also, features such as "server computer" or a "network" have a technical character. The same applies to methods and processes as long as they employ technical means explicitly set out in the claims. For instance, a method which is performed by means of a data storage system including a display would be an invention within the meaning of Article 52(1) EPC.[29] Accordingly, any claimed subject matter with any explicit technical bearing is sufficient[30] to satisfy the first threshold of patentability for computer-implemented inventions.

Non-inventions "as such" typically are directed to purely abstract concepts devoid of any technical implications. Overcoming this barrier is possible if only a partial aspect of the subject matter has a technical effect. The invention can thus consist of a mixture of technical and nontechnical features, even if the nontechnical features form a dominating part of the subject matter.[31] Often at least a part of the claimed subject matter, which can even be of secondary importance, has technical character, and there is consequently an invention.[32] Nevertheless, as previously indicated, the distinction between nontechnical and technical aspects of an invention is particularly important for the assessment of the other technical patentability requirements (§5.01[B][2]). Figure 5.1 contains an overview of the main steps when assessing patentability.

25. EPO—T 650/13.
26. Federal Supreme Court, Xa ZB 20/08, GRUR 2010, 613, "Dynamische Dokumentengenerierung." EPO—T 697/17.
27. EPO—T 877/92, p. 11, Reasons 4, p. 13, Reasons 5.
28. EPO—T 115/85 (OJ EPO 1990, 30), headnote 1.
29. EPO—T 1143/06 "Data selection System."
30. Federal Supreme Court, Decision of Oct. 26, 2010, X ZR 47/07, Mitt. 2/2011, p. 61, "Wiedergabe topographischer Informationen."
31. EPO—T 641/00, "Two identities/COMIVIK."; EPO—G1/19.
32. Federal Supreme Court, Decision of Feb. 24, 2011, X ZR 121/09, "Webseitenanzeige."

Figure 5.1 Simplified Patentability Test

Step (1) - Identify those features of the claim with technical character (= features achieving technical effect(s) in the context of the claimed teaching). Features which do not contribute to the solution of a technical problem shall be ignored when assessing novelty and inventive step (**COMVIK Approach**).

Step (2) - Determine the "**closest prior art.**"

Step (3) - Establish the "**objective technical problem**" to be solved.

Step (4) - Determine whether the closest prior art would (not simply could) have prompted the skilled person faced by the objective technical problem to modify/adapt the closest prior art to arrive at something falling within the scope of the claim (**Could-Would Approach**).

[2] Other Patentability Requirements

The assessment of whether the subject matter has a technical character is only the first step toward patentability. Article 52(2, 3) EPC and section 1(3, 4) of the GPA require that computer programs and computer-implemented inventions be susceptible of industrial application, and be novel, and need to represent a nonobvious technical solution to a technical problem.[33]

As indicated in section 5.01[A], nontechnical features, i.e., features from a field excluded from patentability, in principle shall not be taken into account for the assessment of inventive step, unless they interact with the technical subject matter to solve a technical problem.[34] Nontechnical features "as such" do not provide a technical contribution to the prior art and are thus ignored for the assessment of novelty and inventive step. In light of the negative list, it cannot be the application of the computer program itself on which the patentability is based, but rather the solution of a technical problem by means of a programed computer.[35] Consequently, when assessing novelty and inventive step, the technical problem and its solution need to be correctly identified with regard to the negative list of non-inventions.

It is often a difficult task to correctly separate the technical and nontechnical aspects of the invention, in particular, if they are hidden in a largely nontechnical context. Even a nontechnical feature may sometimes interact with technical elements

33. EPO—T 258/03.
34. Federal Supreme Court, BGHZ 159, 197, 205, "elektronischer Zahlungsverkehr"; Federal Supreme Court, X ZB 34/03, GRUR 2005, 143, 144, "Rentabilitätsermittlung"; Federal Supreme Court, X ZB 22/07, GRUR 2009, 479, "Steuerungseinrichtung für Untersuchungsmodalitäten"; Federal Supreme Court, Decision of Dec. 18, 2012, X ZR 3/12, GRUR 2013, 275, n. 41, "Routenplanung"; Federal Supreme Court, Decision of Jun. 30, 2015, X ZB 1/15, "Flugzeugzustand"; EPO—G 3/08.
35. Federal Supreme Court, Xa ZB 20/08, 8 "Dynamische Dokumentengenerierung."

and thus produce a technical effect, for instance, if its application is relevant for the technical solution of a technical problem. To such extent, it contributes to a technical effect and is thus not disregarded for the assessment of inventive step. In a landmark decision,[36] the EPO describes the assessment as follows:

> An invention consisting of a mixture of technical and non-technical features and having technical character as a whole is to be assessed with respect to the requirement of inventive step by taking account of all those features which contribute to said technical character whereas features making no such contribution cannot support the presence of inventive step.

In addition, the EPO explained in the same decision:

> Although the technical problem to be solved should not be formulated to contain pointers to the solution or partially anticipate it, merely because some feature appears in the claim does not automatically exclude it from appearing in the formulation of the problem. In particular, where the claim refers to an aim to be achieved in a non-technical field, this aim may legitimately appear in the formulation of the problem as part of the framework of the technical problem that is to be solved, in particular as a constraint that has to be met.

Accordingly, the assessment requires first the identification of the technical aspects of the invention in order to adequately formulate a technical problem, to apply the so-called problem-solution approach.[37] An aim to be achieved in a nontechnical field may appear in the formulation of the problem. This has the additional effect that nontechnical aspects are consequently disregarded when assessing inventive step. Even though this approach looks simple, it often encounters the difficulty of correctly separating nontechnical and technical aspects of the subject matter.

Subject matter which might be excluded from the assessment of novelty and inventive step may relate to features which are limited to abstract schemes for organizing commercial or administrative operations, business concepts, financial transactions or features which have only an aesthetic or cognitive effect.

The following list contains a few important cases concerning patentable or non-patentable subject matter. The full texts of the decisions rendered in these cases are available on the website of the EPO (www.epo.com):

Examples of patentable Subject Matter:

- **EPO—T 1194/97 (Philips/Data Structure Product):** Picture retrieval system comprising a record carrier on which functional data is recorded for synchronization of coded picture lines, line numbers and addresses.
- **EPO—T 1351/04 (Fujitsu/File search method):** Files search method by means of creating an index file containing management information to be used for searching a file.
- **EPO—T887/92 (HELP Facility):** User-friendly arrangement of the help facility of a computer program.

36. EPO—T 641/00, "Two identities/COMIVIK," Approved in EPO—G1/19.
37. *See* Ch. 5, §5.04[B].

- **EPO—T 110/90**: Control items (e.g., printer control items) included in a text represented in the form of digital data which are characteristic for the text-processing systems in which they occur in that they are characteristic for the internal technical working of that system.
- **EPO—T 424/03 (MICROSOFT/Clipboard formats I):** Method in a computer system having a clipboard for performing data transfer of data in a clipboard format.
- **EPO—T 1028/14 (Nontechnical features):** Reputation-based method and system for determining a likelihood that a message is undesired.
- **Federal Supreme Court,** decision of April 22, 2010 **(Dynamic Document Generation) Xa ZB 20/08)**: A method for dynamically generating structured documents on at least one host computer which communicates with a client.

Examples of non-patentable Subject Matter

- **EPO—T 22/12 (Spam classification/MICROSOFT):** Method for classifying undesired and desired emails by means of a supervised learning algorithm for assigning objects to different classes; it does not involve a technical contribution because the focus of the classification is content-based.
- **EPO—T 258/03 (HITACHI/Auction method):** Method steps consisting of modifications to a business scheme (here: auction method) aimed at circumventing a technical problem.
- **EPO—T 154/04** (Estimating sales activity/DUNS LICENSING ASSOCIATES): Method for estimating sales activity of a product at sales outlets.
- **EPO—T 0204/93:** Creation of concrete software written in a particular programer language.
- **EPO—T 931/95** (PBS PARTNERSHIP/Controlling pension benefits system): Methods involving economic concepts and practices of doing business even though technical means are used for that purely nontechnical purpose and/or for processing purely nontechnical information.
- **Federal Supreme Court,** decision of February 24, 2011, X ZR 121/09, *Webseitenanzeige*: Method for generating a presentation for relocating a webpage that has already been accessed, and which has been closed in the meantime.

Of course, different patentability standards apply in the US, and thus a successful patent portfolio should account for the standards in these various jurisdictions.

[C] Biotechnological Inventions

Biotechnology inventions represent another difficult aspect of defining patentable subject matter. According to Rule 26 EPC, these "are inventions which concern a product consisting of or containing biological material or a process by means of which biological material is produced, processed or used."

On July 30, 1998, the European Parliament and the Council of the EU promulgated the Biotechnology Directive on the legal protection of biotechnological inventions,[38] aimed at a consistent application of patent provisions and exclusions across the whole of the EU. On September 1, 1999, the Directive was adapted into the EPC through Rules 26–34 EPC.[39] On January 21, 2005, the Biotechnology Directive was transposed into German law.[40] The belated transposition to German law was caused by many years of public debate in Germany. A main point of that debate concerned the absolute product protection of genes of human origin. As a result of the implementation of the Biotechnology Directive in German Law, a number of provisions of the GPA have been amended or inserted. These provisions can be found in the Appendix of the present book.[41] The amendments to the existing Act are mainly aimed at making the patent provisions clearer and more specific. The wording has been largely copied directly from the Biotechnology Directive into the GPA and mainly matches the provisions of the EPC.

Nevertheless, the German law on the patenting of human gene sequences or partial sequences and the respective provisions of the EPC law are not completely identical. Whereas the EU Biotechnology Directive has been integrated into the EPC with the result that its provisions in principle allow absolute substance protection for human gene sequences, the GPA limits such protection for the same subject matter. Section 1a(4) GPA, without counterpart in the EPC, reads: If the object of the invention concerns a sequence or partial sequence of a gene, the structure of which is identical to the structure of a natural sequence or partial sequence of a human gene, its use, for which the industrial application is specifically described under subsection (3) must be included in the patent claim."[42] Thus, according to section 1a(3) of the Patent Act, the industrial application of a sequence or a partial sequence of a gene must be disclosed in the patent application, together with an indication of the function performed by the sequence or a partial sequence. The quoted subsection 4 of the same provision further provides a mandatory requirement that the use of the sequence or partial sequence of the gene must not only be disclosed, but has also to be incorporated into the patent claim. Thus, under German law, patent protection for human gene sequences needs to be limited to that particular use. The EPC does not require such limitation to a particular use in the claim and may consequently provide a broader scope of protection, which seems to be more advantageous compared to the German situation.

The general allowability of biotechnology patents is provided in section 1(2) GPA and Rule 26(2) EPC.[43] However, an exclusion from patentability applies to "the human body at the various stages of its formation and development" (section 1a(1) GPA and Rule 29 EPC). This provision of the German provision expressly includes "germ cells." On the contrary, "isolated elements" of the human body can be patented (section 1a(2) GPA and Rule 29(2) EPC). Furthermore, patents on human embryos, processes to clone

38. Directive 98/44/EC, *see* OJ EPO 1999, 101, the text can be found on: http://eur-lex.europa.eu.
39. *See* www.epo.org.
40. BioPatG, Federal Gazette (BGBl. I 2005, 146).
41. *See* Ch. 17, §17.02 and §17.03.
42. Unofficial translation.
43. The provision is contained in Ch. 17, §17.02.

human beings and the use of human embryos for industrial purposes are prohibited (section 2 GPA and Rule 28 EPC). The term "embryo" means any human ovum after fertilization, any non-fertilized human ovum into which the cell nucleus from a mature human cell has been transplanted and any non-fertilized human ovum whose division and further development have been stimulated by parthenogenesis constitute a "human embryo."[44] However, stem cell-related inventions based on methods which do not destroy human embryos are not excluded from patentability under these provisions.[45] This complex body of law is beyond the scope of this book, and the reader is referred to other excellent texts tracking this developing subject.[46]

§5.02 NOVELTY

While the novelty requirement for patentability is common to the US and Europe, important differences govern its application. Europe's "first-to-file" rules and its lack of a grace period for an inventor to seek patent protection after publicly disclosing his or her own invention are quite strict. But unlike the US, Europe private disclosures, such as confidential commercial sales, do not bar patentability. The novelty requirement in Europe, set forth in Article 54(2) of the EPC, provides that the prior art for assessing novelty encompasses "everything made available to the public by means of a written or oral description, by use, or in any other way, before the date of filing of the European patent application." An identical provision is contained in the GPA, namely section 3(1). Key issues relating to this requirement are discussed below.

[A] The Absolute Novelty Rule and the First-to-File Principle

Patentability in Europe follows the "absolute novelty" rule. That is, everything that was made publicly available before the priority date of a patent application is relevant for assessing the novelty of an invention. It makes no difference where in the world the disclosure was made or in which language. It is also irrelevant who made the disclosure. Even the applicant can destroy the novelty of his invention if he previously disclosed it to the public, in whatever form, in writing, orally, or over the Internet. This rule is a frequent trap for scientists at universities who seek prompt disclosure of their discoveries to ensure scientific credit for being first. Unfortunately, such a presentation of their achievements at conferences or in scientific journals renders this information public. It becomes prior art and can be invoked by anybody against a patent application

44. European Court of Justice, Decision of Oct. 18, 2011, C-34/10.
45. Federal Supreme Court, Decision of Nov. 27, 2012, X ZR 58/07, "Neurale Vorläuferzellen II."
46. English literature (for example): Amanda Warren-Jones, *Finding a "Common Morality Codex" for Biotech—A Question of Substance*, IIC 2008, 638; Dieter R. Schneider, *Patenting of Pharmaceuticals—Still a Challenge?*, IIC 2008, 511; Rob J. Aerts, *Biotechnological Patents in Europe—Functions of Recombinant DNA and Expressed Protein and Satisfaction of the Industrial Applicability Requirement*, IIC 2008, 282; Tine Sommer, *The Scope of Gene Patent Protection and the TRIPS Agreement—An Exclusively Nondiscriminatory Approach?*, IIC 2007, 30; Eva Willnegger, Michael A. Kock & Susann Porzig, *The Legal Protection of Plant-Biotechnological Inventions and Plant Varieties in Light of the EC Biopatent Directive*, IIC 2006, 135.

filed later by the scientist. There is generally no grace period that could help secure a patent in such a situation.

As a corollary to the absolute novelty rule, there is no exception for showing that a late applicant had nonetheless invented the subject matter before the barring disclosure. That is, Europe is a "first-to-file" not "first-to-invent," jurisdiction. In view of harmonizing its patent law system with other jurisdictions, in 2013,[47] the US changed its patent law from a first-to-invent to a first-to-file system.

Even if the inventor had conceived an invention, and reduced it to practice, prior to a novelty-destroying disclosure, that prior work cannot save a patent. The right to a particular invention is, accordingly, with the person who filed the application first, regardless of when the invention was made or that the invention has been made earlier by someone else. The decisive date is the filing date or the priority date of the application.

There are two exceptions to the absolute novelty rule, which may in exceptional circumstances allow a patent filing after a novelty-destroying disclosure. In these rare situations, there is a grace period of six months to file the application (*see* the following section).

[B] Non-prejudicial Disclosure

There are two exceptions to the general rule that there is no grace period. The first exception pertains if the disclosure has been made in one of the rare international exhibitions according to the Convention on International Exhibitions of 1928 (Article 55(1)(b) EPC = section 3(5) no. 2 GPA). The short list of such exhibitions is publicly announced.

The second exception pertains in cases of "an evident abuse in relation to the applicant or his legal predecessor." Article 55(1) EPC or section 3(5) provides that "a disclosure of the invention shall not be taken into consideration if it occurred no earlier than six months preceding the filing of the European patent application and if it was due to, or in consequence of an evident abuse in relation to the applicant or his legal predecessor." Such evident abuse concerns, for instance, cases in which the public obtained knowledge about the invention in violation of a legal or contractual duty vis-à-vis the inventor or his successors.[48] This is usually the case if the disclosure follows an illegal usurpation or represents a breach of contract, in particular if it occurs in violation of a Nondisclosure Agreement (NDA), or if the disclosure is intentionally made to harm the inventor or his successor.[49]

Because there is only a six-month grace period in this circumstance, the inventor should react as soon as he becomes aware of the wrongful disclosure in order to benefit from the provision. The circumstance of the abusive disclosure must be proven by the

47. The Leahy-Smith America Invents Act (AIA) signed on Sep. 16, 2011. Its central provisions went into effect on Mar. 16, 2013.
48. Report of the legal committee as to the IntPatÜG V 4 (para. 4), BlPMZ 76, 350.
49. EPO—T 0173/83, OJ 87, 465; EPO—T 0041/02.

party that relies on it, which is usually the inventor.[50] Given that the risk of wrongful disclosures is likely to increase along with the number of people with access to confidential information and the passage of time, a prior patent application could potentially avoid this issue altogether.

In addition to these rare grace periods for seeking patent protection, the inventor may also obtain a German utility model in the event of a premature disclosure. The German Utility Model Act allows a six-month grace period for filing the utility model after the otherwise-barring disclosure (section 3(1) Utility Model Act).[51] While the protection of a normal patent would be unavailable, the ability to nonetheless obtain a utility model is a way to salvage some protections for an invention that was prematurely disclosed. Utility models are discussed in detail in Chapter 4.

[C] Availability to the Public

A novelty-destroying disclosure requires "availability" to the public. It is sufficient if an unlimited group of people (not bound by confidentiality agreements) is objectively in a position to take notice of the disclosure.[52] In order to prove whether a disclosure was available to the public it is thus not necessary to prove that someone from the public actually took notice of the disclosure or the invention.

In case of a written disclosure with no publication date, it is necessary to show when the disclosure was made available to the public. If the publication date of a written disclosure, such as a printed document, book, magazine or manual cannot be proven, it would not be considered as prior art. Accordingly, it is sufficient to show when a book or scientific journal, for example, was entered into a library database.[53] It would not be necessary to show in addition that a visitor to the library indeed took notice of the concerned book or scientific journal. As soon as a visitor would have been able to look into the book or journal, the whole content of it is available to the public.[54] From a copyright or editor notice showing a date on the document, it is usually deduced in the form of a prima facie proof that it was subsequently circulated and available from the indicated date to the public. The prima facie proof can however be refuted if facts are demonstrated suggesting that there are doubts that the general assumption of such subsequent publication of the document indeed occurs.[55]

Regarding the publication of documents made available on the Internet, the EPO has not accepted that the mere existence of the document on the Internet is sufficient to establish a publication. That is, the mere theoretical possibility of having access to it at a particular time was found insufficient.[56] Rather, a direct and unambiguous access to it for at least one member of the public must be shown. If the disclosure can be found by using one or more keywords related to the essence of its content by means of a

50. Federal Patent Court, Decision of Mar. 17, 1987, Mitt. 88, 207.
51. *See* Ch. 18, §18.04.
52. Federal Supreme Court, X ZR 32/69, BlPMZ, 71, 230, "customer prints."
53. EPO—T 0834/09.
54. EPO—T 0381/87, OJ 90, 213.
55. EPO—T 1384/05.
56. EPO—T 1553/06.

search engine before the priority or filing date, it would not necessarily be sufficient to conclude that it was available to public. In addition, it is necessary to show that it remained accessible at that URL for a period of time long enough for a member of the public to get access to the document.[57]

The state of the art is held to comprise everything made available to the public; this is not limited to written or oral descriptions, but also includes a public use of the invention, so-called public prior use. For instance, an invention contained in a machine which is exhibited at a trade show, becomes state of the art provided it was possible for a skilled person to recognize—or to infer on the basis of further information—the technical features and the functions of the exhibited machine to an extent which would have enabled him to reproduce the inventive teaching.[58] Commercial sales of an invention to the public will generally amount to a prior art disclosure, which will bar the patentability of that invention. However, if the invention is so hidden within the object being sold that a skilled person would not be able to recognize the invention then there may be a good argument that no barring act has occurred. But in general an object that has been made available to the public also discloses those features that are derivable from routine analytical measures without undue burden for the skilled person in the art (such as through dismantling of a machine if the invention is hidden within a complex apparatus or by routine analytical test).[59] An incentive to carry out such tests is not required to be established.[60] The likelihood of analyzing such a prior sold product, and the degree of burden (i.e., the amount of work and time involved in carrying out such an analysis), is in principle irrelevant to the determination of what constitutes the state of the art. However, hidden features of a substance which might be identified through tests, but require the selection of specific test parameters, would principally not be considered public. To amount to a prior art disclosure, there must be a showing that a skilled person would be in a position to obtain reliable knowledge from the commercialization of the invention.

Furthermore, if an invention is a manufacturing method that could not be understood by a publicly available product, then the inventive method is not made available to the public by virtue of the product. The same may apply to computer-implemented inventions, namely where a computer program was publicly available, but it is not apparent to a skilled person how the program works by using it, assuming he has no access to the program itself and is unable to perform any reverse engineering.[61] Likewise, if the invention is hidden in a complex assembly, so that the skilled person in the art would not expect the presence of it within the assembly, it is not a public disclosure. However, if the object shows interesting particularities, such as clear

57. *Ibid.*
58. EPO—T 363/90.
59. EPO—G 1/92; EPO—T 2/09; Federal Supreme Court, X ZR 120/11, Decision of Oct. 23, 2012, "Gelomyrtol."
60. Federal Supreme Court, X ZR 3/10, GRUR 2012, 1133, "UV-unempfindliche Druckplatte."
61. EPO—T 0461/88, OJ 93, 295; Federal Supreme Court, Xa ZR 149/07, GRUR 2011, 129, "Fentanyl-TTS"; Federal Supreme Court, X ZR 120/11, "Gelomyrtol."

advantages vis-à-vis the prior art, it should be expected that a person skilled in the art would be motivated to investigate the reasons for these advantages.[62]

Of course, the question of when a disclosure was made available to the public is subject to many disputes and requires an investigation of the specific circumstances. The party challenging the validity of a patent needs to prove the disclosure. According to the Boards of Appeal, a "balance of probabilities" should suffice to prove that a document has been made accessible to the public. Accordingly, the question of when a document was first made available to the public is to be decided on the basis of what probably happened.[63] However, in cases of a prior use, where the evidence is entirely within the opponent's sphere, a stricter standard of proof of "almost certainly" (or "up to the hilt") applies.[64]

[D] Determination of What Is "Public"

To qualify as prior art, a disclosure must be made to the public. This is an important distinction from US law, where confidential sales may amount to prior art disclosures. Under European law, disclosures made to a defined group of people would generally not render its content public if the group feels at least implicitly[65] obligated to keep the material secret and provided the material will not later be disseminated outside that group. Missing such implicit secrecy agreement, a technical description sent to clients renders its content typically public.[66] However, a tacit obligation to maintain secrecy may result from commercial relationships or interests, such as where business partners have common interests in keeping information confidential.[67] This applies, for instance, to the communication between licensee and licensor or the exchange between scientific colleagues as long as it can objectively be expected that the disclosed information will stay within that defined group (for instance, in the case of a consultation). Thus, confidentiality agreements are extremely valuable in preventing an information exchange from rising to the level of a prior art disclosure. Such agreements do not require a particular form and can even be implicitly and tacitly concluded, although a formal written agreement is best.[68]

62. Federal Supreme Court, X ZR 53/83, GRUR 86, 372, "Thrombozyten-Zählung"; EPO—T 0270/90 EPOR 92, 365.
63. EPA—T 2451/13; EPA—T 545/08; EPA—T 842/14.
64. EPA—T 472/92,
65. Federal Supreme Court, Decision of Jan. 15, 2013, X ZR 81/11, "Messelektronik für Coriolis-durchflussmesser."
66. Federal Supreme Court, Decision of Oct. 15, 2013, X ZR 41/11, "Bildanzeigegerät."
67. EPO—T 1168/09.
68. Federal Supreme Court, I ZR 9/61, GRUR 62, 518, 521, "Blitzgerät"; Federal Supreme Court, GRUR 66, 484, 487, "Pfennigabsatz"; EPO—T 0830/90 OJ 94, 713, 722, "konkludentes Verhalten."

[E] Novelty Assessment

[1] Introduction

The EPO applies strict standards for the assessment of novelty. A prior art document is novelty-anticipating for a claimed feature combination only if each feature is *clearly and unambiguously disclosed* in the prior art document, and only if all the respective features are clearly and unambiguously disclosed in the claimed combination.[69] Under EPO rules, the skilled person shall only read the text and look at the drawings but is not allowed to read "between the lines." A so-called implicit disclosure of a feature, i.e., a feature which is not explicitly disclosed, is only accepted if it is *directly and unambiguously* derivable from the document. But this is rarely the case. The EPO standards on implicit disclosure are thus stricter than the US standards on "inherent disclosure." Rather, the EPO is inclined to evaluate these matters under the doctrine of obviousness.[70] These standards concerning the novelty assessment are also applied by the EPO when assessing the original disclosure requirements[71] (Article 123 EPC) and when checking the validity of a priority (Article 87 EPC).

In contrast to the EPO, the German courts have been more willing to read "between the lines" of the prior art to identify novelty-destroying disclosures. According to decisions of the Federal Supreme Court,[72] the prior art content of a disclosure includes not only its explicit statements but also the self-explanatory teachings that would be recognized from the document by a person of skill.[73] Accordingly, the German approach has historically accorded more leeway than the EPO when assessing the informative content of the disclosure of a prior art document. In recent decisions, however, the Federal Supreme Court has adopted the more restrictive case law of the EPO.[74] In these decisions, the court held that the original disclosure shall only comprise information which is "clearly and unambiguously" derivable for a person skilled in the art. Information resulting from far-reaching conclusions, which the skilled person might only draw on the basis of his technical knowledge or through modifications of the technical teaching disclosed, constitutes, by contrast, subject matter which extends beyond the original disclosure.[75] Thus, at least these decisions follow a more restrictive approach, and it seems that this case law tends to close the gap between EPO and German law.

69. Guidelines C IV 9.2; EPO—T 0465/92 OJ 96, 32 (No. 8.4); EPO—T 701/09.
70. EPO—T 0071/93.
71. *See* Ch. 5, §5.05.
72. Federal Supreme Court, GRUR 1995, 303, 332, "Elektrische Steckverbindung."
73. *Ibid.*; Federal Supreme Court, Decision of Mar. 18, 2014, X ZR 77/12; GRUR 2014, 758, "Proteintrennung."
74. Federal Supreme Court, Decision of Jul. 8, 2010, Xa ZR 124/07, "Fälschungssicheres Dokument"; Federal Supreme Court, Decision of Dec. 16, 2009, X ZR 89/07, BGHZ 179, 168, "Olanzapine"; Federal Supreme Court, Decision of Apr. 6, 2021—X ZR 54/19—"Cerdioxid."
75. Federal Supreme Court, Decision of Jul. 8, 2010, Xa ZR 124/07, "Fälschungssicheres Dokument." Federal Supreme Court, Decision of Mar. 18, 2014, X ZR 77/12; GRUR 2014, 758, "Proteintrennung"; Federal Supreme Court, Decision of Apr. 6, 2021—X ZR 54/19—"Cerdioxid."

The strict interpretive approach of the EPO has advantages and disadvantages when prosecuting claims. The applicant may generally favor the EPO approach when attempting to overcome prior art references, given the stringent standard applied for finding a prior art reference to be novelty-destroying. A contrary consideration, however, is that the EPO can be quite rigid when considering an applicant's attempt to amend pending claims. This process is governed by Article 123 of the EPC which provides that: "[a] European patent application or a European patent may not be amended in such a way that it contains subject matter which extends beyond the content of the application as filed." Under a more restrictive European approach, compared to the national standards, the EPO may be unwilling to allow claims when there is not *in haec verba* support in the originally filed specification, which could be a disadvantage for the applicant. These are strategic considerations which must be discussed between the inventor and his representative on a case-by-case basis.

[2] Combination of Features

A prior art document is only novelty-anticipating if all features of a claim are disclosed in it. Novelty can thus only be denied if all features of the patent claim are deducible from one single reference.[76] In addition, the combination of the features as claimed must be disclosed therein within the same context. Accordingly, an intermingling of features of different embodiments described in the specification of the prior art reference is generally not allowed. It would thus not represent a novelty-destroying disclosure. Features which are separately described within the same document only belong to the same disclosed subject matter if the document either explicitly states that they can be combined or if the person skilled in the art would learn such combination *directly and unambiguously* from the document.[77]

[3] Meaning of Terms

It is a commonly accepted standard that the assessment of novelty and inventive step must be carried out from the perspective of a skilled person at the priority date.[78] The question is which meaning the person skilled in the art would have objectively given at the priority date to a term used in the prior art document. This assessment may be performed both by reference to the particular documents being analyzed (i.e., the pending claims and the prior art of issue) and further by reference to extrinsic evidence which may give an understanding to the meaning of terms at issue. Much like in the US, a patentee may act as his or her own lexicographer, and provide definitions in the patent that are broader or narrower than the ordinary meaning of those terms.

76. Federal Supreme Court, Decision of Feb. 3, 2015—X ZR 76/13—"Stabilisierung der Wasserqualität."
77. EPO—T 0931/92 OJ 94, Special ed., 23, similar Federal Supreme Court, I ZR 73/52, GRUR, 54, 107, "Mehrfachschelle."
78. Federal Supreme Court, Decision of Jan. 14, 2014—X ZR 169/12.

[4] Incorporations by Reference

When performing a novelty assessment, only one single prior art reference is to be considered and compared with the disclosure in the patent application in which the invention is allegedly described.[79] The scope of a prior art reference must generally be assessed without having regard to other documents when assessing novelty. The novelty assessment needs to be done on a document-by-document basis. A lack of novelty may not be deduced from a combination of documents. A prior art document that refers to another prior art document normally does not incorporate it by such reference. When analyzing the novelty of a claim in such a circumstance, both documents would still be considered as separate disclosures. Only in the exceptional case of a reference to specific passages of a second document for a clearly recognizable purpose of incorporating it (such as citing a document to specify a testing method therein) may two documents or parts of it be combined.[80] A mere statement of "incorporated by reference" is thus not sufficient to extend the disclosure of a document to a second document.[81]

[F] Article 54(3) Documents (Section 3(2) GPA)

[1] Main Aspects

The content of a European patent application or a PCT application (EP1) that has entered the EP phase may be considered prior art for purposes of assessing the novelty of a second patent application (EP2), even if the application (EP1) was published after the priority or filing date of a second European patent or patent application (EP2) to be examined if the first application (EP1) has an earlier priority or filing date. That situation is demonstrated in the illustration of Figure 5.1. Article 54(3) EPC provides "the content of European patent applications as filed, the dates of filing of which are prior to the date referred to in paragraph 2 and which were published on or after that date, shall be considered as comprised in the state of the art." The GPA contains an equivalent provision namely section 3(2) of the GPA.

Both provisions seek to resolve the problem of conflicting patent applications. A patent application is kept secret during the period between filing and publication. Therefore, the contents of an application before publication do not belong to the state of the art. This raises the potential for a conflict with a later application for the same or a similar technology. Patent applications that fall under these provisions are considered for assessing the novelty, but not for inventive step. That is, the entire disclosure[82] of the prior application (EP1) becomes part of the art for EP2. The otherwise harsh effect of the approach to consider the whole content of the prior application is mitigated by considering it only for the novelty assessment and disregarding it in relation to

79. EPO—T 153/85.
80. Federal Supreme Court, X ZB 4/79, GRUR 80, 283, "Terephtalsäure"; EPO—T 0153/85, OJ 88, 1.
81. EPO—T 2477/12.
82. So-called whole contents approach; EPO—G 1/03, OJ 04, 413.

inventive step. In the case of European patent applications, these applications are so-called Article 54(3) Documents. That situation is demonstrated in the following illustration: The content of EP1 is prior art for EP2 (even though it is post-published) and will have to be considered when assessing novelty of EP2 (*see* Figure 5.2).

Figure 5.2 Article 54(3) Documents

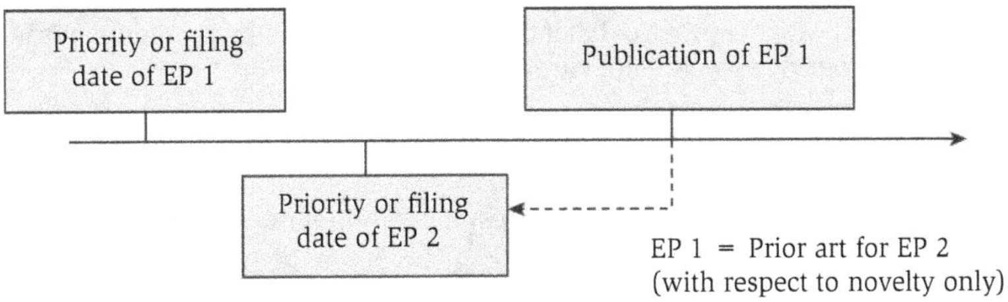

In practice, the hurdles are not too high for an applicant to overcome a so-called Article 54(3) Document (EP 1). As indicated, the claimed subject matter (of EP 2) must only be new in the face of such a document (EP 1). The applicant (of EP 2) may either:

- add a feature (which is not disclosed in the Article 54(3) Document) to the independent claim(s) that (insignificantly) limit the scope of protection (which is just sufficient to satisfy the requirement of novelty); or
- add a "disclaimer" to the independent claim(s). It represents one of the few circumstances under which the introduction of a disclaimer in a patent application is allowable to restore novelty over an Article 54(3) Document.[83]

As commonly accepted when assessing novelty, the disclosure of a prior art reference does not extend to well-known equivalents not disclosed in that document. As a gold standard, subject matter which is not *directly and unambiguously* derivable from a document is irrelevant for the novelty test. Thus, for overcoming an Article 54(3) Document, it would be sufficient to add one or more distinguishing features to the independent claim(s) of the patent application under consideration. Even if such feature(s) is/are almost implicitly disclosed in the Article 54(3) Document, they would sufficiently distinguish the claimed teaching of the patent application from it. It could be a self-evident feature which is necessary for implementing the claimed invention. When adding such a feature to overcome an Article 54(3) Document, however, it is of course important to avoid adding limitations that might frustrate claims of infringement against competitors. Of course, the added feature must *directly and unambiguously* be derivable from the application under consideration.

The "disclaimer" solution is supported by a decision of the Enlarged Board of Appeal[84] of the EPO. Limiting the scope of a claim by using a "disclaimer" to exclude a technical feature where the exclusion is not disclosed in the application as filed does

83. Enlarged Board of Appeal, EPO—G 1/16.
84. Enlarged Board of Appeal, EPO—G 1/03, OJ 8-9/2004.

not necessarily violate Article 123(2) in that case.[85] Illustrating the use of disclaimers, reference is made to claim 1 which was subject to the indicated decision of the Enlarged Board of Appeal (G 1/03)[86] which reads as follows:

1. A heat processable, metallic appearing coated article comprising:
   (a) ...
   (c) a protective layer comprising a ... metal ... selected from the group consisting of chromium, titanium, and nitrides and oxynitrides of silicon-metal alloys with the exception of silicon-zirconium nitride and silicon-tin nitride; with the proviso that if the metal compound film is titanium nitride the protective layer is not chromium.

The terms "with the proviso" and "not" in that claim indicate what is excluded from its scope of protection.

Note that special conditions must be respected when making an amendment that involves a disclaimer. A disclaimer is a negative claim feature aimed at excluding specific subject matter from the scope of a claim. Nevertheless, like any other amendment, the introduction of a disclaimer must not add subject matter to the claimed teaching. Usually, the disclaimer to be added is not disclosed in the original application (so-called *undisclosed disclaimer*). Rarely, the disclaimer is originally disclosed as an embodiment of the invention (so-called *disclosed disclaimer*). The quoted decision G1/03 of the Enlarged Board concerned the situation of a so-called undisclosed disclaimer. The Enlarged Board ruled that such disclaimer may be allowed in the following limited circumstances:

(1) to restore novelty over Article 54(3) EPC prior art;
(2) to restore novelty over an "accidental anticipation"[87] in a prior art document;
(3) to disclaim unpatentable subject matter.

In a recent decision,[88] the Enlarged Board of Appeal provided further clarification on how disclaimers should be treated. With respect to so-called **undisclosed disclaimers,** the Enlarged Board of Appeal endorsed the four-step questionnaire as defined in the earlier decision G 1/03. An allowable disclaimer requires that each of the questions of the questionnaire is answered affirmatively:

(1) Is there a suitable reason for a disclaimer? This question can be affirmed if one of the three suitable circumstances of a disclaimer mentioned in G 1/03 (*see* above) is given.

85. *See also* Enlarged Board of Appeal, EPO—G 2/03, OJ 8-9/2004, 448: This case law refers to undisclosed disclaimers, i.e., disclaimers without basis in the application as filed. The question whether a disclaimer violates Art. 123(2) EPC if its subject matter was disclosed as an embodiment of the invention in the application as filed is not yet settled and has been referred to the Enlarged Board of Appeal, where the case is pending under the docket G 2/10.
86. Decision of Technical Board of Appeal dated Dec. 20, 2002, EPO—T 507/99.
87. An anticipation is considered accidental when the disclosure of the document in question is "so unrelated and remote that the person skilled in the art would never have taken it into consideration when working on the invention" (EPO—G 2/03, OJ 2004, 413).
88. Enlarged Board of Appeal, EPO—G 1/16.

(2) Does the disclaimer remove no more than is necessary? This question can be affirmed if the disclaimer is not broader than is required to remove the subject matter excluded from patentability.
(3) Is the disclaimer unrelated to inventive step and sufficiency? This question can be affirmed if the disclaimer does not impact on inventive step or sufficiency. The undisclosed disclaimer shall, for instance, not improve the applicant's position on inventive step in relation to another piece of prior art.
(4) Is the disclaimer clear and concise?

In contrast hereto, so-called **disclosed disclaimers** shall comply with the "gold standard."[89] This means a disclosed disclaimer is allowable if the subject matter remaining in the claim after introducing the disclaimer is *directly and unambiguously* disclosed to the skilled person using common general knowledge of the field. Determining whether or not an amendment meets the gold standard requires a technical assessment of the overall circumstances of the case under consideration, taking into account the nature and extent of the disclosure in the application, the nature and extent of the disclaimed subject matter and its relationship with the subject matter remaining in the claim after the amendment.

The decision G 2/10 suggests that the gold standard test is applicable not only to disclosed disclaimers but also to undisclosed disclaimers. However, in G 1/16, the Enlarged Board of Appeal decided that undisclosed disclaimers only need to satisfy the four-step questionnaire of G 1/03. The gold standard test of G 2/10 does not apply to undisclosed disclaimers. The main reason for this decision was that applying G 2/10 to undisclosed disclaimers would leave "virtually no chance of an undisclosed disclaimer being allowable." This is because "where an undisclosed disclaimer is introduced into the claim it (almost) automatically follows that the subject matter remaining in the claim after the introduction ... can hardly be considered to have been explicitly or implicitly, and directly and unambiguously, disclosed in the application as filed."[90]

[2] Scope of Article 54(3)

Article 54(3) EPC does not apply to post-published (prior) national patent rights issued by national patent offices of EPC Member States. Article 54(3) EPC explicitly refers to "European patent applications" only. That is, prior national rights were filed (or validly claiming a priority date) earlier than—but published on or after—the date of filing (or date of priority) of the European patent application being examined. Unlike European applications, such prior national rights are not considered prior art for the purpose of the European substantive examination of patentability. Accordingly, prior German patent applications do not fall under Article 54(3) EPC.[91] However, prior national rights can be invoked in national proceedings as grounds for revocation after the European patent has been granted (Article 139(2) EPC). The effect of a prior national right upon

89. Enlarged Board of Appeal, EPO—G 2/10.
90. Enlarged Board of Appeal, EPO—G 1/16.
91. EPO—T 0550/88 OJ 92, 117; EPO—T 0361/06.

a European patent is thus a matter of national law, whereas the effect of a prior European application upon a European patent is specifically provided for in Article 54(3) EPC. Only the latter is an admissible ground for revocation in EPO opposition proceedings.

From Article 139(2) EPC follows that post-published national patent applications[92] issued in EPC Member States may well support actions filed with national courts, including the UPC. Accordingly, despite the wording of Article 54(3) EPC, prior national patent applications issued in EPC Member States may have novelty depriving effect as to the concerned national counterpart of the European patent. The effects of the prior national right are limited to the national part of the ordinary European patent. This is, it can invalidate or limit the scope of protection of that national part of the ordinary European patent, without affecting the other national parts of the patent. This is uncritical in the case of ordinary European patents because they could be invalidated country by country. An ordinary European patent must not have the same scope of protection in all EPC Member States. It may be pursued with narrower claims or abandoned in individual EPC Member States. However, due to its unitary character, a central question is what effect may have a prior national prior right vis-à-vis a UP (cf. next chapter).

[3] UPs and Prior National Rights

The UPC did not yet decide on the relationship of prior national rights and European patents with unitary effect. Contrary to an ordinary European patent, a European patent with unitary effect is a unitary title. Article 3(2) UP Regulation stipulates that a UP "*may only be limited, transferred or revoked, or lapse, in respect of all the participating Member States.*" This provision raises the question whether a prior national right may endanger a UP over its whole territory regardless of the limited territorial reach of the prior national right. In contrast hereto, a prior national right may only affect the concerned national part of an ordinary European patent causing a territorially fragmented scope of protection. Since Article 3(2) UP Regulation does not provide for such territorial fragmentation of UPs, this could mean that a prior national right may limit or even destroy a UP over the whole territory of application.

This solution is undesired from a policy point of view. It contains a significant drawback in comparison to ordinary European patents. It keeps applicants away from applying for unitary effect. It is thus not acceptable if a right holder of a UP is forced—due to the national prior right—to limit or even loses his UP for all states, without having a right to reestablish an ordinary European patent (without unitary effect) for the same invention. A system to transform a UP into an ordinary European patent in such cases does not exist.

92. A national application filed or validly claiming a priority date earlier than—but published on or after—the date of filing or valid date of priority of the application being examined.

It seems to be in line with Article 65(2) UPCA[93] that the UPC may revoke or limit UPs with respect to a Contracting Member State where a conflicting prior national right emerges. The unitary character of the right shall not prevent such territorial restrictions. The approach may also be reconciled with the Regulation. First, it does not contradict Article 3(1) UP Regulation, which generally refers to the phase of obtaining unitary effect in all Member States. Whereas Article 3(3) UP Regulation, on the contrary, specifically allows to apply all grounds of revocation of the EPC, including those following from Article 139(2) EPC to UPs. This includes challenges based on the novelty depriving effect of prior national rights. Such challenges are limited to the Member State for whose territory protection by a prior national right has been applied.

Since September 1, 2022, the EPO has been conducting so-called top-up searches to find older national patent rights and assess their prima facie relevance. This service is performed automatically by the EPO and is free of charge for all applicants.

[G] First Medical Use/Second Medical Use

When assessing the novelty of a product claim, the structural features must be compared with the disclosure of a prior art document, while a purpose or intended use of the product mentioned in the claim is normally irrelevant for that assessment.

However, under the provisions of Article 54(4)/(5) EPC and section 3(3)/(4) GPA, a substance or composition can be distinguished from the prior art by virtue of its use for a specific medical purpose, resulting in a "purpose-linked product claim." These provisions thus provide for an exception from the principle that product claims can only be obtained for (absolutely) novel products.

[1] First Medical Use

Thus, although the substance or composition may already be known in the prior art, it can nonetheless be the subject of a patent claim for a medical use, provided that the particular medical use is new and inventive. The novelty and the nonobviousness are thus not derived from the substance or composition as such but from the claimed purpose, namely from its intended use.[94] If that substance or compound is used for the first time for a medical use, its claims may be referred to as "first medical use claims" (Article 54(4) EPC and section 3(3) GPA). Thus, the requirements for such purpose-linked product claim are:

- the substance or composition is already known, and accordingly, the substance or composition itself is not patentable anymore;
- the substance or composition is intended for use in a medical method according to Article 53(c) EPC (section 2a(1) GPA);
- the use of the substance or composition in that method is new and inventive.

93. Article 65(2) "The Court may revoke a patent, either entirely or partly, only on the grounds referred to in Articles 138(1) and 139(2) of the EPC."
94. Enlarged Board of Appeal, EPO—G 2/08 of Feb. 19, 2010.

A first medical use claim may be worded "Compound A for use in the treatment … ."

[2] Second Medical Use

There are also "second medical use claims" (Article 54(5) EPC and section 3(4) GPA). "Second" means that the substance or compound is already known for one medical purpose, but can also be used for another purpose that was not previously known. Before the EPC 2000 entered into force, so-called Swiss-type claims were used to claim a second medical use, typically worded as: "Use of compound A for preparing a drug/medicament for treatment of disease B." Swiss-type claims were instituted by a decision of the Enlarged Board of Appeal of 1984.[95] The new provision of Article 54(5) EPC 2000, which corresponds to section 3(4) of the GPA, now explicitly allows claims to subsequent medical indications of a known medicament. Since the new legal framework allows for such patent protection, Swiss-type claims are no longer needed and, in fact, no longer permitted.[96] This means a simplified claim format can be used namely: "[Known substance or composition] for use in [new therapeutic application]." This has been confirmed by the Enlarged Board of Appeal[97] which pointed to that main change in law and stated "where the subject matter of a claim is rendered novel only by a new therapeutic use of a medicament, such claim may no longer have the format of a so-called Swiss-type claim as instituted by decision G 5/83." The Enlarged Board of Appeal[98] of the EPO also clarified that even when a medicament is already known to treat an illness, it may nevertheless be subject to a patent claim for use in a new and different treatment for the same illness. Accordingly, second medical use claims must not necessarily concern treatments for different diseases. Additionally, the Enlarged Board of Appeal clarified in the same decision that there may be novelty even if the only novel feature is the dosage regime, provided that the novel dosage gives rise to new effects.[99] A different treatment could also consist in a new administration method, such as the route of administration (e.g., orally, in a transdermal manner or by injection), the nature of the substance (solid, liquid or gaseous), the patient group or other parameters relevant as to the therapeutic effect of the substance. It could also consist in the immobilization of a patient after medication, provided that such treatment-related instructions are objectively aimed at influencing the effectiveness of the substance.[100] Accordingly, there must be a synergistic effect between such treatment-related instructions and the improved efficacy of the substance.

95. Enlarged Board of Appeal, EPO—G 5/83 of 1984.
96. Notice from the EPO in OJ EPO 2010, 514.
97. Enlarged Board of Appeal, EPO—G 2/08 of Feb. 19, 2010.
98. *Ibid.*
99. Similar: Federal Supreme Court, Decision of Jun. 9, 2011, X ZR 68/08, GRUR 2011, 999, "Memantin."
100. Federal Supreme Court, Decision of Feb. 24, 2014, GRUR 2014, 461 "Collagenase I"; Federal Supreme Court, Decision of Feb. 25, 2014, GRUR 2014, 462 "Collagenase II."

§5.03 PATENTABILITY STANDARDS APPLICABLE TO GERMAN UTILITY MODELS

In contrast to European and German patent applications, when filing a German "utility model," the inventor can benefit from a grace period of six months (section 3(1) of the Utility Model Act).[101] That is, previous publication of the invention is unobjectionable, provided that the previous publications occurred within the six-month period prior to the application and were made by the applicant or his legal predecessor. Furthermore, a public prior use may not be asserted against the utility model unless it occurred within German territory (section 3(1) of the Utility Model Act). The utility model thus provides inventors with patent protection in one of the biggest markets in the world despite having the traditional patent application path barred due to a disclosure of the invention to the public.

§5.04 STANDARDS ON INVENTIVE STEP: "NON-OBVIOUSNESS"

[A] Introduction

The European analog of the US "non-obviousness" requirement is called "inventive step." The requirement to have an inventive step is provided in Article 56 EPC and the corresponding section 4 of the GPA, which both state that "an invention shall be considered as involving an inventive step if, having regard to the state of the art, it is not obvious to a skilled person in the art."

The determination of an inventive step first requires the definition of the skilled person of the art. For the objective assessment, the skilled person, who is a fictitious person[102] with average and ordinary skills in the area of the invention, is set in the position of the inventor at the priority date of the patent application. The question is whether this person would have arrived at the invention with the knowledge of the state of the art by applying his skills.

[B] Problem and Solution Approach

To evaluate the inventive step, reference is usually made to the so-called problem and solution approach, which is an analytical framework commonly employed by the EPO. It is a guideline for an objective assessment of inventive step. Subjective considerations such as the individual performance of the inventor, the story of the invention, and whether it was coincidence or the result of intensive research are thus irrelevant. The vigorous application of that approach has proven to render the case law of the EPO relatively predicable.

The entire state of the art is relevant. In contrast to the novelty test, multiple prior art references may be combined, provided that such combination is obvious to the

101. Further information about the Utility Model can also be found in Ch. 4, §4.03.
102. Federal Supreme Court, X ZR 213/01, GRUR 2006, 663, "Vorausbezahlte Telefongespräche."

skilled person in the art. This basically means combining documents with contradictory teachings[103] might not be obvious (similar to the concept of "teaching away" under US law). The reference might be combined, in particular, if one document suggests the combination with another document, or at least if it does not prevent the person skilled in the art from doing so.[104] Of particular importance is that the skilled person is set in the position of the inventor at the date of the patent application to avoid an "ex post analysis" which is inadmissible, but a frequently contested mistake.[105] This is akin to the forbidden concept of "hindsight" under US law.

The problem and solution approach is based on three main steps, which are illustrated in Figure 5.3.

Figure 5.3 Problem and Solution Approach

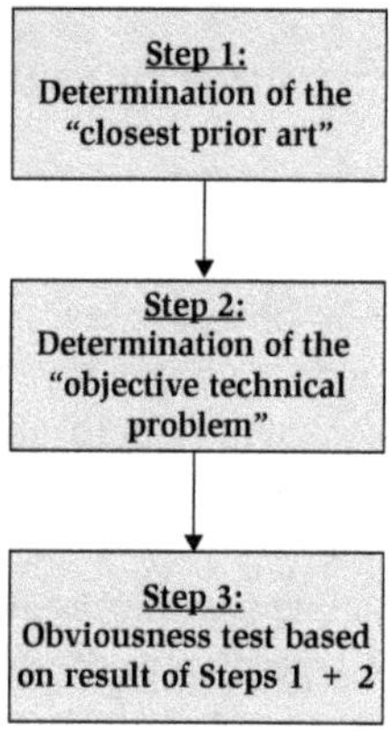

The basic question thus is: would the claimed invention, starting from the closest prior art and the objective problem, have been obvious to the skilled person?

[1] Step 1: Determination of the "Closest Prior Art"

The skilled person is deemed to choose, as a starting point for his or her analysis, the springboard to achieve the technical result of the invention.[106] This "most promising starting"[107] point is the "closest prior art." The closest prior art is usually a document that is the most pertinent for challenging the inventive step. In many cases, it addresses the same technical problems as the claimed invention, discloses most of the features of a claimed feature combination and requires the minimum of structural and functional

103. EPO—T 0176/89, OJ 91 Special ed., 24.
104. EPO—T 0095/90, OJ 93 Special ed., 26.
105. Federal Supreme Court, X ZR 95/87, GRUR 89, 899, 902, "Sauerteig"; EPO—T 0229/85, OJ 87, 237.
106. EPO—T 0644/97, OJ 00, 21.
107. Guidelines for Examination in the EPO, Part C, Ch. 5, s. 4.2.

modifications to arrive at the claimed invention. It typically belongs to the same technical field, or it is at least closely connected to it. A document disclosing a laryngeal catheter, for example, is not necessarily the closest prior art for a claim directed to a vascular catheter, even if the document discloses most of the claimed feature combination. Each claim feature must be evaluated in view of its importance for carrying out the invention. The function and effect of each specific feature may also have to be considered to determine its importance in order to correctly identify which document is the closest prior art. In practice, especially in EPO opposition cases, it may be wise to concurrently point to different documents as the closest prior art. In some cases, there might be several equally valid starting points for the assessment of inventive step.[108] Also, it is not always predictable which line of argument will later be taken by the opposition division or the Boards of Appeal.

During examination proceedings, the Examiner usually prefers that all features known from the closest prior art document are contained in the preamble to an independent claim, and that all distinguishing features appear in the characterizing portion of the claim. This is the so-called two-part form. In method claims, this is not observed so strictly as it is usually more difficult to arrange the method steps in two-part form rather than in a logical order.

The so-called closest prior art is only a starting point of the assessment. It does not mean that the subsequent assessment of inventive step is limited to a single document. It particularly helps to formulate the objective technical problem.[109]

[2] Step 2: Determination of the "Objective Technical Problem"

Prior to the formulation of the "objective technical problem," two sub-steps must be carried out:

> First, it is necessary to objectively determine the distinguishing features representing the difference between the closest prior art and the claimed invention. Second, it is then essential to identify the particular functions and effects achieved by these distinguishing features. As indicated in previous section 1.1, non-technical features, i.e., features from a field excluded from patentability, in principle shall not be taken into account for the assessment of inventive step, unless they interact with the technical subject matter to solve a technical problem.[110] This particularly counts for so-called non-patentable subject matter, such as pure data processing,[111]

108. EPO—T 1289/09.
109. EPO—T 0939/92, OJ 96, 309 (No. 2.34).
110. Federal Supreme Court, BGHZ 159, 197, 205, "elektronischer Zahlungsverkehr"; Federal Supreme Court, X ZB 34/03, GRUR 2005, 143, 144, "Rentabilitätsermittlung"; Federal Supreme Court, X ZB 22/07, GRUR 2009, 479, "Steuerungseinrichtung für Untersuchungsmodalitäten"; Federal Supreme Court, Decision of Dec. 18, 2012, X ZR 3/12, GRUR 2013, 275, n. 41, "Routenplanung"; Federal Supreme Court, Decision of Jun. 30, 2015, X ZB 1/15, "Flugzeugzustand"; EPO—G 3/08.
111. Federal Supreme Court, Decision of Dec. 18, 2012, X ZR 3/12, GRUR 2013, 275 N. 42, "Routenplanung."

the reproduction of information,[112] economical activities such as the organization of a pension.[113]

The objective technical problem can then be formulated, precisely in view of the functions and effects derivable from the distinguishing feature(s). The claimed invention should provide a desired technical effect or function by modifying or adapting the closest prior. In principle, any technical effect or function provided by the invention may be used as a basis for that reformulation so long as that effect is derivable from the application as filed. New effects submitted subsequently during the proceedings by the applicant may also be taken into account, provided that the skilled person would recognize these effects as implied by or related to the technical problem initially suggested.[114]

A common challenge when formulating the objective technical problem is that the more specifically the problem is formulated, the more obvious the solution provided by the claimed teaching might appear. Thus, it is frequently desirable for the applicant to formulate the problem as generically as possible, which may be satisfied by a simple statement such as "to improve a particular device." As a general rule, the objective problem should be formulated in view of the functions and effects achieved by the invention and should not contain hints to the technical solution of the invention. However, features which do not, either independently or in combination with other features of the claim, contribute to the technical character of the invention cannot be weighed in that assessment. This particularly applies to subject matter that is excluded from patentability.[115]

The inventor is usually not aware of the closest prior art when drafting the original application. New prior art is often revealed later, namely during the granting, opposition or judicial proceedings. Accordingly, often a reformulation of the problem is necessary.

[3] Step 3: Obviousness Test—"Could-Would-Approach"

The third step of the obviousness test starts from the question: "Would the claimed invention, starting from the closest prior art and the objective problem, have been obvious to the skilled person?" In practice, an opponent in opposition proceedings usually tries to establish that the distinguishing features are disclosed in a second prior art document, and that it would have been obvious for the skilled person at the priority date to combine both teachings. It must be shown that the skilled person would have come to the claimed solution. It is not sufficient that the skilled person *could* have come to the solution. The following questions are regularly discussed when determining whether a combination of prior art documents is obvious or not:

112. Federal Supreme Court, Decision of Oct. 26, 2010, X ZR 47/07, GRUR 2011, 125 Rn. 39—"Wiedergabe topographischer Informationen."
113. EPO—T 931/95, OJ 2001, 441.
114. EPO—T 184/82, OJ 6/1984, 261.
115. EPO—T 641/00, OJ 7/2003, 352.

- Does the second document belong to the same technical field? It is usually less obvious to combine documents of different technical fields. This also depends on who is the skilled person in the art.
- Does the second document give any hint as to whether the effects, on which the objective problem is based, can be achieved by the features of the characterizing portion of the claim?
- Does the closest prior art give any hint that points to the claimed solution?
- To what extent does it motivate the skilled person in the art to develop or investigate in view of the claimed solution? Are there any reasons that prevent the person skilled in the art from investigating in view of the claimed solution? Does the person skilled in the art need to overcome a technical prejudice?
- Is there an unexpected technical effect?

The so-called secondary indicators may also be taken into account, such as a "longfelt need" which is solved by the invention, i.e., a need that satisfies prior unsuccessful attempts to solve the objective technical problem. Commercial success will generally not be taken into consideration for the assessment of the inventive step unless this commercial success is linked to a specific technical effect or function of the claimed teaching. This is principally the same under US law, where secondary indicators such as long-felt needs, unexpected results, failure of others, skepticism, commercial success and copying may all help to overcome case of "obviousness."

[C] National Particularities: Germany

The doctrine of "inventive step" represents a general patentability requirement known in almost all national patent laws. However, its assessment may vary from one country to another.

While in most cases the arguments for inventiveness brought forward by the parties in proceedings before the EPO or Germany's Federal Patent Court have the same weight and lead to identical results, Germany's Federal Patent Court seems to apply slightly different and more flexible rules. This has been emphasized in a decision of the Federal Supreme Court.[116] The highest court ruled that, for assessing the inventive step, the "closest prior art" shall not necessarily represent the sole starting point. According to the Court, selecting one starting point (or several starting points) rather requires a particular justification that principally derives from the motivation of the skilled person who tries to find a better, or at least different, solution over the available prior art. This represents a deviation from the problem-solution approach used by the EPO and apparently leaves more flexibility when assessing the inventive step. The skilled person may, accordingly, combine documents if he is sufficiently motivated to do so. He might even combine the teachings of two distinct areas of the same technical field, if at the priority date appliances or methods were already known that crossed the boundaries between the technical areas, and if the technical problem to be solved is

116. Federal Supreme Court, Jun. 18, 2009, GRUR Int 2009, 1041, Xa ZR 138/05, "Fischbissanzeiger."

pertinent to both areas.[117] In addition, as can be taken from another decision rendered by the Federal Supreme Court,[118] the courts shall not solely rely on secondary indicia. Such secondary indicia are not suited to replace or exclusively justify the actual assessment that an invention involves an inventive step. Even though the formalistic problem-solution approach is not a guarantee for the best decision, it does however provide considerable legal security which might not be provided by a system where the assessment follows more flexible and thus less predictable ways.

§5.05 STANDARDS ON ORIGINAL DISCLOSURE

A further important aspect of patentability is the question of whether there is any undue broadening of the original disclosure. Article 123(2) EPC provides that a European patent application, or a European patent, may not be amended in such a way that it contains subject matter which extends beyond the content of the application as filed. An applicant is thus prevented from adding subject matter to claims, which is not disclosed in the application as originally filed. Such additions would give an unjustified advantage in conflict with the public notice function of the content of the original application.[119] The amendment is not allowable if the overall change in the content of the application, through an addition, alteration or omission, results in claimed subject matter which is not *directly and unambiguously* derivable from the application as originally filed.[120] Accordingly, an applicant usually cannot delete features from independent claims. Essentially, claim amendments must be literally supported by a dependent claim or by the specification as originally filed, unless the language is implicitly contained in it. Such "implicit disclosure," however, must represent a direct and unambiguous conclusion by the skilled person based on his common general knowledge of what is explicitly mentioned in the application as filed.[121]

For instance, a combination of two items, each taken from two lists of features, typically is not found to be sufficiently disclosed unless this combination is specifically mentioned in the original disclosure.[122] It would not be sufficient to satisfy Article 123(2) EPC if the application merely conceptually comprises that combination from the two lists.

[A] Removing a Feature from an Independent Claim as Originally Filed

An undue broadening may happen if non-European applicants amend the patent application during the international search or during the international preliminary examination of the PCT application. For applicants starting from an original US

117. Federal Supreme Court, Apr. 15, 2010, GRUR 2010, 712, Xa ZR 69/06, "Telekommunikationseinrichtung."
118. Federal Supreme Court, Jul. 30, 2009, GRUR 2010, 44 and in IIC 2010, 468, Xa ZR 22/06, "Dreinahtschlauchfolienbeutel."
119. EPO—G 1/93.
120. EPO—G 2/10.
121. EPO—T 823/96.
122. EPO—T 727/00.

document, it is likely that the amendment will be based on US rules, which are not necessarily in conformity with the EPC standards. When entering the regional phase, the PCT application will serve as the reference document for applying the standards of Article 123(2) EPC. It is important that applicants verify under the standards of Article 123(2) EPC that the claims are not broadened during that process beyond the scope of the original application. Removing claim limitations may be problematic in that the applicant needs to take due account that the replacement or removal of a feature from a claim is only permissible according to the Guidelines for Examination in the EPO[123] if the "skilled person would directly and unambiguously recognize that:

(i) the feature is not essential for the invention;
(ii) the feature is not, as such, indispensable for the function of the invention in the light of the technical problem the invention serves to solve; and
(iii) the feature's replacement or removal requires no real modification of other features to compensate for the change."

These requirements are handled very strictly and formalistically by the EPO. It is generally assumed that a feature is essential for the invention if the feature is contained in an originally filed independent claim. Exchanging or deleting features from independent claims during the prosecution proceedings is often problematic. The best strategy for the EPO is often to draft very broad independent claims which can be amended during prosecution by adding features from the dependent claims or from the specification.

[B] The So-Called Inescapable Trap of Article 123(2)/(3) EPC

The so-called inescapable trap, as shown in Figure 5.4, may occur due to a conflict between the requirements of Article 123(2) and 123(3) EPC.[124]

As previously mentioned, on the one hand, Article 123(2) EPC provides that a European patent application, or a European patent, shall not be amended in such a way that it contains subject matter which extends beyond the content of the application as originally filed. On the other hand, Article 123(3) EPC prohibits amendments to granted claims in such a way that it extends the scope of protection conferred by it. Article 123(3) EPC equally protects the interests of third parties. That is, a broadening of a claim of a granted European patent, even if there is support for such broadening in the specification, is prohibited. Accordingly, in opposition proceedings, the EPO will principally revoke a European patent if the claim contains subject matter which was not disclosed in the originally filed patent application.[125] Thus, Article 123(2) EPC is typically invoked to force applicants to remove subject matter which is not originally disclosed, whereas Article 123(3) EPC prohibits the applicant from removing the added subject matter because it would broaden the scope of protection of the claim. This is

123. Guidelines for Examination: Part H, Ch. V, 3.1.
124. The equivalent German provisions are §21(1) No. 4 and §22(1) Patent Act.
125. Enlarged Board of Appeal, decision G 1/93 confirmed recently by EPO—T 1180/05.

referred to as the "inescapable trap." A fundamental decision of the Enlarged Board of Appeal (G1/93) states the following:

> If a European patent as granted contains subject-matter which extends beyond the content of the application as filed within the meaning of Art. 123(2) EPC and which also limits the scope of protection conferred by the patent, such patent cannot be maintained in opposition proceedings unamended, because the ground for opposition under Art. 100(c) EPC prejudices the maintenance of the patent. Nor can it be amended by deleting such limiting subject-matter from the claims, because such amendment would extend the protection conferred, which is prohibited by Art. 123(3) EPC. Such a patent can, therefore, only be maintained if there is a basis in the application as filed for replacing such subject-matter without violating Art. 123(3) EPC.

The EPO would likewise revoke the patent if a removal of a feature from the claim extends the protection conferred by that claim. This prohibition would apply, for example, in the situation of a feature that has been added to a claim or a feature that has been replaced by a more generic term during prosecution proceedings. This prohibition would particularly be triggered if the added or replaced feature is accidentally taken from a part of the description describing a preferred embodiment which does not sufficiently disclose all other features mentioned in the independent claim. This would represent a violation of Article 123(2) EPC.

Sometimes, these kinds of "traps" are caused by the initiative of the Examining Division. For instance, the Examining Division may be of the opinion that the claimed combination is disclosed in the context of that embodiment and may allow an amendment to include the combination. However, what is and what is not originally disclosed is sometimes not clear. The applicant needs to know that simply relying on the view of the Examining Division may be fatal if the Opposition Division sees it differently later during opposition proceedings, landing the applicant in the "inescapable trap." Such traps may also arise from cases where the amendment was added prior to the entry into the regional phase of the PCT application process, leading to an impermissibly amended claim. The result can then be a granted patent containing an independent claim with such new subject matter.

During opposition proceedings, the Opposition Division may conclude that the added or replaced feature is not allowed under Article 123(2) EPC. Unfortunately, at that stage—with the patent already granted—it is no longer possible to simply remove that feature. That removal needs to comply with Article 123(3) EPC, which bars any deletion of a feature if this broadens the scope of protection conferred by the patent.

Because the removal of a feature usually leads to a broader scope of protection, the applicant is "trapped," and the patent will be revoked. In only a very exceptional situation can this trap be cured, namely if the feature in question can be replaced by a feature which does not broaden the protection and for which there is support in the application as originally filed.

An example of the so-called inescapable trap can be found in a decision of the Boards of Appeal,[126] where the EPO concluded that a feature of a claim concerning a

126. EPO—T 1180/05.

collecting bag for human body waste was not disclosed in the original filed documents. This led to a revocation of the patent. The EPO confirmed the prior case law and pointed out that a granted patent which contains subject matter which extends beyond the content of the application can only be maintained if there is a basis in the application as filed for replacing such subject matter without violating Article 123(3) EPC. It is also emphasized in that decision that a disclaimer may be permitted in order to restore novelty or to disclaim subject matter under Articles 52–57 EPC, but not for resolving a potential conflict between Article 123(2) and (3) EPC.

In contrast to the EPO, the German practice is more flexible and tends to solve the dilemma by a so-called disclaimer solution.[127] This approach has explicitly been rejected by the EPO in a decision[128] wherein it is stated: "There is no basis ... for allowing a disclaimer for resolving the potential conflict between Article 123(2) and (3) EPC."

A statement such as: "feature X is not disclosed in the originally filed application and, therefore, constitutes an inadmissible extension from which the patentee cannot derive any rights" would not solve the dilemma in EPO proceedings. German courts apply a different approach: On the one hand, the claim would be limited in its scope by the nondisclosed feature, which is thus considered when determining the scope of protection by the claim, and, on the other hand, the patentee may not use it to distinguish the claim over the prior art. This would be sufficient for German courts.[129] In a decision, the Federal Supreme Court[130] has ruled the following:

> A patent is not to be revoked if the insertion of a feature, which is not disclosed in the originally filed application, leads to a limitation of the claimed subject matter. In such a case, the interests of the public are sufficiently protected, if the inserted feature stays in the claim, provided it is assured ... that it is not used for supporting the patentability ... .[131]

According to this decision, a disclaimer to be inserted in the patent is not even necessary for solving the dilemma as long as it is assured that the added and nondisclosed feature is not used to distinguish the claim over the prior art. The German approach thus allows for the added feature to stay in the claim, without revoking the patent, provided that the insertion forms a limitation and does not constitute a new inventive aspect outside the originally filed documents ("aliud").[132] This is, the German approach only applies if the added, nondisclosed feature limits the subject matter of the patent but does not provide an inventive teaching ("aliud") reaching beyond what is disclosed in the original filed documents. Such patent claim would endanger legal certainty for third parties who rely on the content of the patent

127. Schulte, *Patentgesetz*, 10th ed., 2017, s. 21, No. 69-75.
128. EPO, Decision of Feb. 2, 1994, G 1/93.
129. Federal Supreme Court, Decision of Oct. 5, 2000, X ZR 184/98, GRUR 2001, 140 "Zeittelegramm."
130. Federal Supreme Court, Decision of Oct. 21, 2010, X a ZB 14/09, GRUR 2011, 40, "Winkelmesseinrichtung."
131. Unofficial translation.
132. Federal Supreme Court, Decision of Oct. 21, 2010, X a ZB 14/09, GRUR 2011, 40, "Winkelmesseinrichtung."

application as filed and published. Whether there is a solvable limitation in that sense or an "aliud" shall not be decided on the basis of formal criteria alone. Rather, it is decisive to distinguish whether the added feature merely implements an instruction for a technical teaching disclosed in the originally filed documents as belonging to the inventive teaching, or whether it addresses a technical aspect which cannot be inferred from the originally filed documents either in its concrete form or even in abstract form as belonging to the invention.

Thus, the German approach does not allow resolution to this dilemma if the adding of the subject matter leads to a different inventive teaching than is disclosed in the application as previously filed.[133] The German flexible approach, which deviates from the case law of the EPO, is applicable not only to national German patents but also to the German parts of European patents.[134] Indeed, the German approach finds a better balance between, on the one hand, the fundamental right to protection conferred by a patent and, on the other hand, the aim to avoid adverse effects for the public.

Figure 5.4 Inescapable Trap of Article 123(2)/(3)

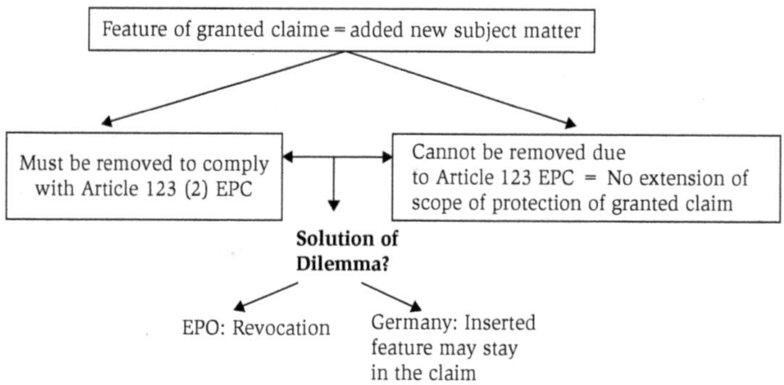

133. Federal Supreme Court, Decision of Feb. 17, 2015, X ZR 161/12, "Wundbehandlungsvorrichtung."
134. *Ibid.*

CHAPTER 6
Opposition Proceedings

§6.01 INTRODUCTION

After a patent issues from either the EPO or the GPTO, any person may challenge the patent's validity in an "opposition proceeding" at the granting agency. Opposition proceedings offer an independent *inter partes* procedure at the post-grant stage. Opposition proceedings in the GPTO are applicable to German national patents, whereas opposition proceedings at the EPO are applicable to European patents. This chapter will focus on opposition proceedings at the EPO, which are the most common. There is no need to distinguish between ordinary EPs and EPs with unitary effect. For both types of patents, the same EPC rules are applicable.

Opposition proceedings in the GPTO as well as in the EPO must be brought within nine months after publication of the patent grant (Articles 99(1) EPC, section 59(1) GPA). Thus, a good defense strategy is to monitor both the EPO and GPTO for the issuance of potentially problematic patents. There is only a short window for bringing an opposition.

§6.02 PATENT MONITORING PROGRAMS

Companies that may be subject to patent liability in Europe should establish programs to monitor patents issuing from the EPO and GPTO (and other national patent agencies). Particularly with respect to the EPO, an opposition proceeding represents an inexpensive opportunity to challenge the patent on a pan-European basis with *ex tunc* effect in all designated Contracting States, in the case of traditional European patents or for the whole territory in which European patents with unitary character have effect. Therefore, prudent companies will implement programs to monitor patents issuing from the EPO (and national-level patent offices), to take advantage of the limited opportunity to bring opposition proceedings.

Monitoring programs may use the online service of the EPO (www.epoline.com). The EPO online service provides free and convenient access to the public data published during the granting procedure. In addition to legal status information and search and examination reports, this database also contains all the documents exchanged between the applicant and the EPO. Documents of opposition proceedings are also available, including briefs, writs and related communications. The claims are published in all three languages used by the EPO, and the proceedings are often—although not always—in English.

This monitoring can be efficiently completed with an alert service system with automatic monitoring of selected patents. As soon as a particular event (such as a communication with the EPO, a submitted brief, the grant) is entered in the register, the interested party is informed by email.

§6.03 GROUNDS FOR OPPOSITION

Oppositions may only be filed on particular grounds mentioned in Article 100 EPC. The list of grounds for opposition as indicated in Article 100 EPC is exhaustive (*numerus clausus*). Accordingly, an opposition may only be filed on the grounds that:

(a) the subject matter of the European patent is not patentable under Articles 52–57;
(b) the European patent does not disclose the invention in a manner sufficiently clear and complete for it to be carried out by a person skilled in the art;
(c) the subject matter of the European patent extends beyond the content of the application as filed, or, if the patent was granted on a divisional application or on a new application filed under Article 61, beyond the content of the earlier application as filed.

Other deficiencies of the patent or the granting procedure are not considered in opposition proceedings. The most important ground for an opposition is if the patent's subject matter is not patentable within the terms of Articles 52–57 EPC, in particular, because the subject matter is not novel or lacks an inventive step (Article 100(a) EPC: Missing Patentability). Ground (b) is non-enablement (Article 100(b) EPC: Insufficiency of Disclosure).[1] Finally, an opposition could also assert that the patent's subject matter extends beyond the content of the application as originally filed, which would violate Article 123(2) EPC (Article 100(c): Added Subject Matter).[2]

All available grounds should be raised when filing the notice of opposition. Introducing a new ground for opposition after the opposition period has lapsed is, in principle, not permitted. Accordingly, it is not possible to open the proceedings on the basis of a lack of patentability (Article 100(a) EPC) and later, after the expiry of the

1. Article 100(b) refers to Art. 83 EPC: "The European patent application shall disclose the invention in a manner sufficiently clear and complete for it to be carried out by a person skilled in the art."
2. *See* Ch. 5, §5.05.

nine-month period, to add the new ground of added subject matter (Article 100(c) EPC).

However, the Opposition Division can raise objections on its own motion, which might, possibly, be triggered by a belated introduction of a ground for opposition (Rule 81(1) EPC, Article 114(1) EPC). So-called ex officio examinations may, in principle, occur in all procedures before the EPO. But, it has to be taken note that this flexibility is restricted in first—and even more in second[3]—instance opposition proceedings due to the contentious character of the proceedings between parties having adverse interests and a right to be treated in an equal and fair manner.[4] Thus, in principle, only those grounds are examined, which have been properly submitted in the originally filed petition.[5] Only in exceptional cases may the Opposition Division consider other or late-filed grounds for opposition. This situation is much more limited in appellate proceedings. On June 26, 2019, new Rules of Procedure of the Boards of Appeal (so-called RPBA 2020) of the EPO were adopted. These rules entered into force on January 1, 2020. These new rules have a significant impact on the management of both first instance and appeal examination and opposition proceedings because they apply, in general, to any appeal pending on, or filed after, the date of their entry into force (Article 25 RPBA 2020). The RPBA 2020 makes it more difficult—if not impossible—to get new documents, new lines of attack or defenses or claim requests admitted into the appeal proceedings.

In weighing whether to bring an opposition proceeding, potential challengers should be aware of the issues that tend to attract heavy scrutiny by the EPO. For instance, the EPO rigidly enforces the requirements of Article 123 EPC[6] to ensure that the claims do not contain subject matter extending beyond the application as filed. If the issuing patent is not clearly and unambiguously supported by the originally filed documents, potential opponents might be inclined to file an EPO opposition, rather than bringing a revocation claim with the UPC or a national court which may be less insistent on enforcing this requirement.[7] On the contrary, the EPO generally seems to have a more accommodating stance than invalidation courts in assessing inventive step.[8] Potential opponents should therefore carefully consider if a European opposition proceeding is the best strategy if the only available ground is lack of an inventive step. Likewise, the patentee also should assess these strategic considerations in deciding whether to commence enforcement measures against third parties prior to, or after, the lapse of the nine-month opposition period. A warning letter sent to an accused infringer may trigger the filing of an opposition. Accordingly, a patentee may choose to wait until the opposition period lapses.

3. EPO—G 1/99: "Article 114(1) EPC, which already has a restricted application in the opposition proceedings, is to be applied in an even more restrictive manner in appeal proceedings. This was essentially because, in the Enlarged Board's view, the appeal procedure is to be considered as a judicial procedure" (*see also* G 9/91).
4. EPO—G 1/99.
5. EPO—G 10/91.
6. The provision can be found in Ch. 19, §19.01.
7. *See* Ch. 5, §5.05 "Standards on Original Disclosure."
8. *See* Ch. 5, §5.04 "Standards on Inventive Step."

§6.04 ANY PERSON MAY OPPOSE

"Any person," with the exception of the patentee,[9] may initiate opposition proceedings. Article 99 EPC explicitly states that "any person may give notice" of opposition. The opponent need not demonstrate any legal or economic interest in the revocation when filing the notice.[10] There is no standing requirement. This is because the opposition procedure is designed as a legal remedy in the public interest.[11]

Accordingly, it is acceptable[12] and common for interested parties to set up a "straw man" to file the notice of opposition. Indeed, competitors often prefer to stay in the background and involve a straw man for oppositions against disagreeable and uncomfortable patents of competing companies. In many of these cases, it may be preferable to act anonymously through a straw man in order to avoid friction in relations with the patentee, or to be silent as to business intentions. There is no disadvantage to using a straw man even if the backer's identity incidentally becomes known during the proceedings. This tactic is prohibited only in rare cases, such as where the straw man is used to bypass a contractual promise not to challenge the validity of the patent,[13] or where the straw man is acting on behalf of the patentee.[14] Also, the repeated filing of an opposition with a similar focus by the same person could be objected to for lack of legitimate interest.[15]

§6.05 MAIN STEPS OF OPPOSITION PROCEEDINGS

The main steps of opposition proceedings are illustrated in Figure 6.1.

Figure 6.1 Steps of Opposition Proceedings (EPO)

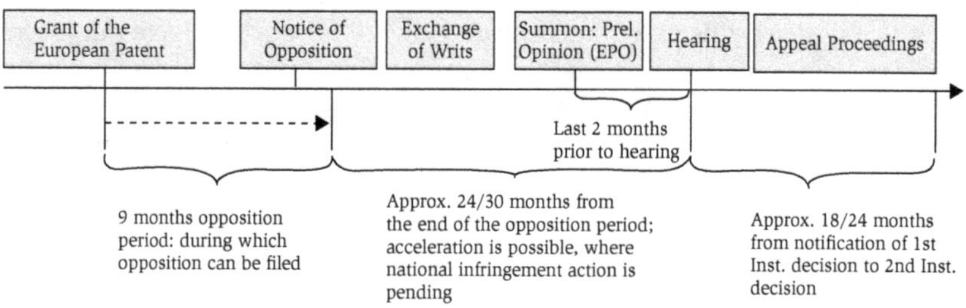

9. EPO—G 9/93, OJ 1994, 89: A patentee cannot oppose his own patent. Oppositions are *inter partes* procedures. Accordingly, the patentee and opponent must be different persons.
10. EPO—T 289/91, OJ 1994, 649.
11. EPO—G 3/97 and EPO—G 4/97, OJ 1999, 245, 270.
12. EPO—G 3/97, OJ 1999, 245.
13. EPO—G 03/97.
14. EPO—G 9/93, OJ 1994, 891.
15. EPO—T 9/00, OJ 2002, 275.

[A] Notice of Opposition

The notice of opposition must include a reasoned statement and must be filed within the nine-month period after the grant's publication. The opposition must state at least one ground for opposition under Article 100 EPC. For the opposition to be properly filed, it must fulfill the requirements of Rule 76(2)(c) EPC. Accordingly, the notice of opposition must contain three elements: a statement of: (i) the extent to which the European patent is opposed, (ii) the grounds on which the opposition is based, and (iii) the facts, evidence and arguments presented in support of those grounds. If a ground for opposition is alleged in the notice of opposition but not substantiated in that manner within the nine-month period for opposition, the opposition is flawed in that respect, and the failure cannot be cured thereafter.[16] Requirement (iii) is of particular importance because it is only satisfied if the contents of the notice of opposition are sufficient to be properly understood on an objective basis[17] to properly put the patent owner on notice of the basis of the opposition. The criteria of "when, where and what" needs thus to be set out in detail.[18] Otherwise, the notice of opposition will be rejected. The EPO provides a form (Form 2300)[19] that sets forth all the information needed to ensure that an opposition is properly filed. Notice of opposition may be filed either electronically using the EPO opposition filing software, by fax or by mail.

The notice of opposition must be complete and contain all available evidentiary support that might be used against the patent as well as possible attempts of the patentee to obtain a patent in an amended form. The reason for this is that evidence and facts submitted after the expiration of the opposition period may potentially be rejected as late filed. This evidentiary support should include prior art references, witness declarations, test reports, etc., which may be used to argue against the patentability of claims.

A notice of opposition is not deemed to have been filed until the opposition fee (presently: EUR 785) has been paid.[20] The payment must occur within the nine-month opposition period.[21] The failure to pay it within that period leads to the rejection of the opposition.[22]

[B] Amendments During the Proceedings

Shortly after expiration of the opposition period or the period provided for remedying deficiencies or presenting evidence, the patentee is allowed to file observations and, where appropriate, amendments within a period specified by the EPO (usually four months). Opposition proceedings do not represent a continuation of the examination

16. EPO—T 182/89, OJ 1991, 391.
17. EPO—T 222/85, OJ 1988, 128.
18. EPO—T 522/94, OJ 1998, 421.
19. The form can be downloaded from the EPO website and used as checklist for the information which is necessary for the notice: www.epo.org.
20. Schedule of fees and expenses of the EPO, applicable as from Apr. 1, 2018.
21. Article 99(1) EPC.
22. EPO—T 152/85, OJ 1987, 191.

proceedings. Any amendments must be occasioned by a ground for opposition even if that ground has not been raised by an opponent (Rule 80 EPC). For instance, the patentee is allowed to remove improperly added subject matter in opposition proceedings in relation to the ground of lack of patentability. However, the patentee is normally not allowed to file amendments, which are unrelated to the notice of opposition or to correct errors in the description. It would be an abuse of opposition if the patentee were allowed merely to improve the disclosure by amendments not specifically necessitated by the grounds advanced for the opposition.[23]

The patentee may request that the patent be maintained in its granted or amended form, and he may file a main request and one or more auxiliary requests. The main request is typically aimed at a confirmation of the claims of the patent as granted or in a slightly amended more narrow form, whereas auxiliary requests typically relate to sets of claims which are filed as fallback positions with a further narrowed scope of protection than the main request. Auxiliary requests are made in case the Division does not grant the main request. Auxiliary requests are considered in the sequence chosen by the patentee.

It is a general principle of the EPC that opposition proceedings are held in the interest of the public and not for the benefit of the patentee. Therefore, it is improper to amend the patent in any way other than to overcome a ground of opposition. Thus, the patentee is not allowed to introduce amendments meant solely to clarify the claims, to amend dependent claims, or to correct errors in the description unless these amendments are directly triggered by amendments to the independent claims.

If an amendment responds to an attack, then combining granted claims is an appropriate reply to an opposition, even if this generates two independent claims in the same category.[24] The requirement of unity does not apply in opposition proceedings. The patentee may also base amendments on the patent specification, as long as they are clearly and unambiguously supported therein. Dependent claims should represent the primary source for amendments in opposition proceedings. If the request represents a simple combination of granted claims, the risk of unity and clarity objections is lower and the Opposition Division is also more indulgent if the request is late filed.

During the proceedings, the Opposition Division invites, within fixed time periods, the parties to file observations on their own or other parties' communications by the Opposition Division. Upon receipt of such a communication, the patentee may amend the description or claims and drawings to respond to the grounds raised by the opposition(s). Of particular importance is the deadline which is typically set in the summons for filing written submissions or amendments in preparation for the oral proceedings (*see* next Chapters). New facts and evidence presented after that date will most likely not be considered by the Opposition Division, except that there are good reasons for such late submission. The division has discretion to consider such

23. EPO—T 127/85.
24. EPO—T 263/05, OJ 2008, 329: Pursuant to Rule 43(2) EPC, a plurality of independent claims in the same claim category are allowable in only exceptional circumstances, which are listed in Rule 43(2)(a), (b) and (c). The Boards of Appeal of the EPO held that Rule 43(2) was not applicable in opposition proceedings, but such amendment must be occasioned by a necessary and meaningful reaction on a ground of opposition.

amendments, whereby the common standard is that any amendment must be made in the most expedient manner, taking into due account the interests of all parties. Also undesirable delays should be avoided.[25]

[C] Summons

Oral proceedings take place either upon the order of the Opposition Division or on request by a party to the proceedings (Article 116(1) EPC). Typically, oral proceedings are requested by the parties. Summons are issued by the Division, normally about three to six months, but at least two months before the date of the final hearing.[26] The oral proceedings will take place at a specified date, time and place (Munich, The Hague or Berlin).

In a note annexed to the summons, the Opposition Division usually lists and explains the points that it believes need to be discussed. This note normally also includes the Division's nonbinding provisional opinion on the positions adopted by the parties, and specifically on amendments to the patent filed by the patentee. This opinion is called the "Preliminary Opinion." Even though this opinion is not binding, it challenges the parties to carefully review its points and objections in order to better focus their arguments.

At the same time, the Opposition Division fixes a final date, which is generally one or two months before the hearing, for filing written submissions or amendments in preparation for the oral proceedings.

[D] Late-Filed Requests by the Patentee

Any request to amend the claims filed after the deadline set in the summons is considered untimely and may be rejected on that basis (Rule 116(1) EPC). Normally, the EPO sets the final deadline for submissions one month before the date of the oral hearing. Untimely filed amendments must be based on good cause.[27] This is the case if they represent a reaction on a change of the proceeding, which might be caused by the submission of a relevant new prior art document.

In general, the Boards of Appeal admit amendments filed in response to comments and objections made by the EPO or the other party.[28] An untimely request is more likely to be accepted if it proposes a combination of granted claims submitted in order to overcome objections raised by an opponent during the proceedings.[29] Accordingly, opponents should be prepared for requests possibly being filed during the oral proceedings.

25. EPO—T 648/96.
26. Rule 115(1) EPC.
27. EPO—T 382/97.
28. EPO—T 648/96.
29. *Ibid.*

Late-filed requests should also contain prima facie allowable subject matter.[30] That is, they must be manifestly clear, they should not contain subject matter that extends beyond the content of the application as filed (Article 123(2) EPC),[31] and must be responsive to the objections raised up to then. Any doubts as to those issues may result in the request being rejected. The Boards of Appeal are much more restrictive than the Opposition Divisions with regard to late evidence, submissions or requests. In that respect, the RPBA provide a legal framework under which such late submissions or requests might be refused, as relevance is no longer the sole criterion.

The new RPBA 2020 have introduced stricter standards for amendments in the appeal proceedings. Previously, at least some degree of flexibility was given in bringing new requests, facts, objections, arguments and evidence on appeal. According to the new Article 12(4) of the RPBA 2020, it is left to the discretion of the Boards to admit amendments unrelated to the requests, facts, objections, arguments and evidence already discussed in the first instance decision. The new rule also requires that reasons are provided for justifying such belated amendment on appeal. In later stages of the proceedings, after the grounds of appeal and the response have been filed, the allowance of amendments is even more difficult. In the new Article 13(1) RPBA, the discretion to be exercised by the Boards is subject to the provision of a justification of the amendment. In addition, the burden is placed on the proprietor or applicant to demonstrate not only that the amendment of the claims or description prima facie overcomes the objections on file but also that it does not give rise to new objections. According to the new Article 13(2) RPBA, in the final stage of the proceedings which starts with the notification of the summons or the deadline set by the Board, amendments shall not be taken into account unless there are exceptional circumstances. The RPBA 2020 thus raises the bar for making amendments on appeal.

[E] Late-Filed Facts or Evidence by the Opponent

The EPO may disregard late-filed facts or evidence pursuant to Article 114(2) EPC. Their filing could be deemed untimely if a careful preparation would have given rise to an earlier submission.[32] This is the reason why the opponent is required to submit all facts and evidence during the nine-month opposition period.[33] Belated filings may, in exceptional circumstances, be accepted, provided that they are manifestly relevant to the matter, particularly if the evidence or facts are more relevant than what is already on file.[34] An untimely document might also be accepted if it is filed in response to another party's submission[35] or if it is an appropriate and immediate reaction to developments in the previous proceedings.[36] Usually, the division disregards late-filed

30. EPO—T 382/97.
31. *See* Ch. 5, §5.05 "Standards on Original Disclosure."
32. EPO—T 156/84.
33. EPO—T 117/89, OJ 1989, 401.
34. EPO—T 1557/05.
35. EPO—T 951/97.
36. EPO—T 855/96.

evidence, and/or states that the newly submitted evidence is cumulative.[37] Accordingly, late-filed evidence, documents and other matters could be rejected on the ground of their irrelevance, i.e., on the basis that they were no more "weighty"[38] than documents which were already on file. Of course, if a submission is considered abusive, it shall not be permitted.[39]

The new RPBA 2020 have introduced stricter standards for amendments in the appeal proceedings. The RPBA 2020 thus raises the bar for making amendments on appeal.[40]

[F] The Hearing

The chairman of the Division identifies the issues to be investigated and their order of treatment. Each party is then invited to present its case in the order of the issues as determined by the chairman. The opponent usually begins, and then the patentee has an opportunity to reply. Each party is given a second or further opportunity to speak on the same issue in question. Once a decision on a given issue has been reached and then announced by the chairman, the issue is considered to be settled and cannot be subject to further discussions.

During the COVID pandemic, most oral proceedings at the EPO were conducted as video conferences. The question arose as to whether the conduct of oral proceedings in the form of a videoconference was compatible with the right to oral proceedings enshrined in Article 116(1) EPC, especially if not all parties to the proceedings had consented thereto. On July 16, 2021, the Enlarged Board of Appeal of the EPO issued a decision on this (G 1/21). The Board is of the opinion that, in any case, in a general emergency situation during which the possibility for parties to participate in oral proceedings on the premises of the EPO is impaired, conducting them in the form of a video conference is compatible with the EPC, even if the parties to the proceedings have not given their consent. Oral proceedings by videoconference are also conceivable outside the exceptional situation of a pandemic. This applies in any case if the parties to the proceedings give their consent. Article 15a RPBA 2020 even allows the Boards of Appeal to convene oral proceedings by videoconference if the Board deems it appropriate, either at the request of a party or of its own motion. It remains to be seen in which cases oral proceedings by videoconference can take place outside of exceptional situations.

[G] Decision of the Opposition Division

It takes an average of two to three years from the end of the nine-month opposition period before a hearing takes place, and a first instance decision is then rendered by the Opposition Division.

37. EPO—T 237/03.
38. EPO—T 611/90, OJ 1993, 50.
39. EPO—T 273/84, OJ 1986, 346.
40. *See* Ch. 6, §6.05, last paragraph.

The proceedings can be accelerated if a party to the proceedings files a request containing legitimate interests for acceleration. For instance, in cases where an infringement action in respect of the European patent is pending before a national court, a party may request an accelerated processing of the opposition.[41] The EPO will then endeavor to issue the next procedural action (for instance, summons to the oral proceedings) within three months from the receipt of the request, or where the request is filed within the opposition period, within three months after the patentee's response to the notice of opposition.[42]

The decision is usually announced at the end of the hearing. A written decision follows several weeks later. The Opposition Division may reject the opposition and uphold the patent, may revoke the patent completely, or as a middle ground may maintain the patent in an amended form, as described in Table 6.1.

Table 6.1 Possible Result of Opposition Proceedings

Revocation	*Limitation by Amendment of the Claims*	*Maintenance of the Patent as Granted*
- **Scope of Decision**: It applies in all Contracting States in respect of which it has been granted. - **Costs**: Each party to the opposition proceedings shall bear the costs it has incurred, unless the Opposition Division, for reasons of equity, orders a different apportionment of costs.		

[H] Appeal

[1] Outline

Decisions of the Opposition Division can be appealed to the Board of Appeals (Article 106 EPC).[43] Note that according to Article 111 EPC, the Board of Appeals may itself exercise any power of the opposition division (such as revocation, maintenance or limitation of the patent), or it may remit the case to the opposition division. Under the present rules, the Boards have broad discretion to remit cases to the first instance and do so frequently. However, the new RPBA 2020 raises the bar for remittals. Article 11 RPBA 2020 stipulates that the Board shall not remit the case unless special circumstances are given.

A notice of appeal must be filed within two months of the notification of the decision of the Opposition Division, along with payment of the fee for appeal. The appellant has four months from the notification of the decision to make the statement setting forth the grounds for appeal (Article 108 EPC).

41. *See* Notice of the EPO dated Mar. 17, 2008, OJ EPO 2008, 221.
42. *Ibid.*
43. The provisions governing the appeal procedure are set out in Arts. 106–111 EPC and Rules 99–103 EPC and in the Rules of Procedure of the Boards of Appeal (OJ EPO 2007, 536).

Any opponents then have four months from notification of the grounds for filing a written reply to it.[44]

The Board of Appeal is normally the forum of last resort in opposition procedures before the EPO. Only on exceptional grounds (Article 112(a) EPC), such as in a case of a "fundamental violation of Article 113 EPC," which guarantees the right to be heard, can a further appeal for review of a decision rendered by the Board of Appeals be filed with the Enlarged Board of Appeal. Accordingly, the EPO opposition proceedings end with the decision of the Boards of Appeal in the vast majority of cases.

If the decision represents a full revocation of the patent, the patentee will lose the patent forever. The situation is different if an amended patent emerges after the end of opposition proceedings. The resulting patent might be subject to UPC revocation proceedings. During the seven-year transitional period according to Article 83 UPCA, the resulting patent might also be subject to national invalidation proceedings, which are limited to national territorial boundaries and the respective national part of the European patent. If the patentee has opted out from the jurisdiction of the UPC, the patent may be subject to national invalidation proceedings, even after the transitional period as set forth in Article 83 UPCA.

[2] Convergence Procedure

The primary objective of the RPBA 2020 is to streamline the appeal proceedings. This goal shall be achieved through a three-stage convergence procedure aimed at making new submissions more difficult the further the appeal proceedings have progressed. The first stage concerns the period until the reply to the grounds of appeal has been filed. Here the RPBA 2020 provides that the grounds of appeal and the reply must fully contain the position of the parties and clearly and concisely state the bases for reversing, amending, or confirming the appealed decision. Appeal arguments of a party that do not meet these requirements, i.e., that do not directly relate to a factual or legal argument made in the first instance shall be considered as an amendment. The board then has discretion to allow such amendments (Article 12(4) RPBA 2020).[45]

---

44. *See* Art. 12 of the Rules of Procedure of the Boards of Appeal: An extension of this time limit may exceptionally be allowed at the board's discretion following receipt of a written and reasoned request. Reasons lying entirely within the control of the party, such as holiday related absences, would however not be considered as exceptional.

45. "Any part of a party's appeal case which does not meet the requirements in paragraph 2 is to be regarded as an amendment, unless the party demonstrates that this part was admissibly raised and maintained in the proceedings leading to the decision under appeal. Any such amendment may be admitted only at the discretion of the Board. The party shall clearly identify each amendment and provide reasons for submitting it in the appeal proceedings. In the case of an amendment to a patent application or patent, the party shall also indicate the basis for the amendment in the application as filed and provide reasons why the amendment overcomes the objections raised. The Board shall exercise its discretion in view of, inter alia, the complexity of the amendment, the suitability of the amendment to address the issues which led to the decision under appeal, and the need for procedural economy."

Article 13(1) RPBA 2020[46] concerns the second convergence step during the period following the first step and up to the service of the summons to oral proceedings or up to the time limit indicated in the communication under Rule 100(2) EPC. Even more restrictive criteria apply for the second convergence step than in the first step. The parties must justify why amendments should exceptionally be allowed at this stage of the appeal proceedings. Admission of the amendments is also at the discretion of the Board. For example, in decision T 1004/18, the Board, referring to the criteria of Article 13(1) RPBA 2020, had not included auxiliary requests filed shortly before the oral proceedings. The Board held that the respondent had justified neither why the new auxiliary requests had been filed so late nor why these amendments were suitable to overcome the objections contained in the statement of grounds of appeal.

Article 13(2) RPBA 2020[47] regulates the third convergence step. It relates to the period after service of the summons until the oral hearing or until expiry of the time limit specified in the communication under Rule 100(2) EPC. During this stage, amendments are in principle not possible unless there are exceptional circumstances which are substantiated by the party concerned. In decision T 1482/17, the Board concluded that the auxiliary requests filed at the oral proceedings were admitted into the proceedings under Article 13(2) RPBA 2020 because the amendments were a direct response to an argument raised by the Board for the first time at the oral proceedings. Thus, the Board concluded that the patentee should still have the opportunity to rebut a newly raised objection at this late stage of the proceedings. Nevertheless, the Boards are normally reluctant to do this. In decision T 0752/16, the Board ruled that a change of the Board's preliminary opinion on a particular ground of opposition does not represent an exceptional circumstance within the meaning of Article 13(2) RPBA 2020. One should not wait to make amendments to an opponent's objections until confronted with a negative preliminary opinion of a Board.

In practice, the new RPBA has also a significant impact on first instance proceedings because there is essentially no opportunity for amendments in appeal proceedings.

46. "Any amendment to a party's appeal case after it has filed its grounds of appeal or reply is subject to the party's justification for its amendment and may be admitted only at the discretion of the Board. (...). The party shall provide reasons for submitting the amendment at this stage of the appeal proceedings. The Board shall exercise its discretion in view of, inter alia, the current state of the proceedings, the suitability of the amendment to resolve the issues which were admissibly raised by another party in the appeal proceedings or which were raised by the Board, whether the amendment is detrimental to procedural economy, and, in the case of an amendment to a patent application or patent, whether the party has demonstrated that any such amendment, prima facie, overcomes the issues raised by another party in the appeal proceedings or by the Board and does not give rise to new objections."

47. "Any amendment to a party's appeal case made after the expiry of a period specified by the Board in a communication under Rule 100, paragraph 2, EPC or, where such a communication is not issued, after notification of a summons to oral proceedings shall, in principle, not be taken into account unless there are exceptional circumstances, which have been justified with cogent reasons by the party concerned."

§6.06 WITHDRAWAL OF OPPOSITIONS

Opposition proceedings may be continued by the EPO on its own motion if the opposition is withdrawn (Rule 84(2) EPC). The Opposition Division has discretion to continue the proceedings after a withdrawal. For instance, the proceedings may be continued if the proceedings are in an advanced stage, and it is likely that they will result in a limitation or revocation of the patent.[48] The situation is different if the withdrawal of the opposition occurs during appellate proceedings. If the opponent is the sole appellant, then his withdrawal would immediately and automatically terminate the appeal proceedings, irrespective of the patentee's consent.[49] In such circumstances, the Board of Appeal cannot continue the appeal proceedings on its own motion. If, however, the opponent is the respondent, withdrawal of the opposition does not affect the appeal proceedings.[50]

§6.07 INTERVENTION AFTER THE NINE-MONTH OPPOSITION PERIOD

After the nine-month opposition period has passed, a party may intervene in an ongoing opposition proceeding if it has been sued for patent infringement (Article 105 EPC). Likewise, a party may intervene in an opposition if the party has received a request from the patentee to cease infringement of the patent, and the party has instituted proceedings for a court ruling of noninfringement. The accused infringer may intervene in the opposition proceedings within three months of the date on which infringement proceedings were instituted against the party, or on which the party instituted proceedings for a court ruling of noninfringement. Intervention is permissible as long as opposition or appeal proceedings are pending.

§6.08 STATISTICS

Approximately 6% of all granted European patents are subject to opposition proceedings.[51] Of those, about one-third are revoked, about one-third are maintained in an amended form, which generally means that the scope of protection is reduced, and about one-third are maintained as granted. This is a rough estimation, and there are significant differences among the various technical sectors.

§6.09 INTERACTION OF REVOCATION PROCEEDINGS

EPO opposition proceedings may lead to the revocation of the entire patent, its maintenance with the originally granted scope or the allowance of a more limited scope.

48. EPO—T 197/88, OJ 1989, 412.
49. EPO—G 8/93, OJ 1994, 887.
50. EPO—T 340/05.
51. *See* www.epo.org.

In several European jurisdictions, opposition proceedings at the EPO and national revocation actions cannot be implemented simultaneously. For example, in Germany, a national revocation action cannot be instituted against a patent from the EPO if there are opposition proceedings against the patent pending, and until the time period for filing an opposition against the patent has passed.[52] This requirement is designed to avoid contradictory decisions. Once that window has closed, a German nullity action against the German part of a traditional European patent can be filed by any person,[53] including the previous opponents from the opposition proceedings and irrespective of the fact that an opposition has been previously conducted.

There is no estoppel in Europe preventing relitigation of arguments that failed in opposition proceedings, unlike the US. This is an important difference in comparison to proceedings in the US through the Patent Trial and Appeal Board (PTAB), from which a losing challenger would be estopped from making the same invalidity arguments in district court (including arguments that could reasonably have been raised). Thus, challengers in Europe may get "two bites at the apple" in attempting to invalidate a patent first through opposition proceedings, and then through a nullity action in the national courts.

Decisions rendered by the EPO are not binding on Germany's Federal Patent Court and Supreme Court.[54] However, a European patent that has been finally revoked by the EPO (for instance, after appeal) cannot be "revived" by national courts. Similarly, as soon as a European patent gets a particular (limited) scope of protection through EPO opposition proceedings, national courts are prevented from reinstating a previously applied broader scope of protection.

Revocation actions filed with the UPC can be sought after the grant of a European patent.[55] The UPC thus offers third parties an opportunity, in addition to the EPO opposition route, to centrally revoke a European patent with pan-European effect. There is no requirement to pursue EPO opposition proceedings prior to seeking revocation actions through the UPC.[56] Both proceedings could be pending in parallel, or the claimant may directly file a revocation action with the UPC.[57] Article 33(8) of the UPCA explicitly states that the claimant in UPC revocation proceedings does not have to file first a notice of opposition with the EPO. Although it is not expressly stated, it follows from the rationale of the UPCA that the ability to pursue an action for revocation at the UPC does not depend upon whether the nine-month opposition period has already expired. This is different from the German situation, in which a nullity action cannot be filed with the Federal Patent Court against the German part of a European bundle patent if an opposition is still possible or opposition proceedings are pending.[58] This restriction in Germany even applies if the ground of revocation is only

52. Federal Supreme Court, Decision of Apr. 19, 2011, X 124/10, "Mautberechnung"; s. 81(2) GPA.
53. *See* Ch. 8, §8.03[B].
54. Federal Patent Court, Decision of Oct. 8, 1992, 3 Ni 50/91.
55. This necessarily applies not only to European patents with unitary effect but also to all other European Patents for which an opt-out has not been declared.
56. Article 33(8) UPCA.
57. Article 33(8) and (10) UPCA.
58. Article II s. 6 IntPatÜG, s. 81(2) Patent Act.

admissible in German proceedings but not in EPO opposition proceedings.[59] For instance, the effect of a prior national right upon a European patent is a matter for national law. Article 54(3) EPC only refers to "European patent applications," for which reason a prior national right is only relevant in national proceedings and thus cannot be asserted in EPO opposition proceedings.

During the transitional phase provided by Article 83(1) UPCA, the claimant may choose, in the case of a European bundle patent, to either file a national nullity action or file a revocation action with the UPC. A nullity action filed with the German Federal Patent Court would only be allowable after expiration of the opposition period or after the end of the opposition proceedings. If a revocation action is already pending before the UPC, a parallel nullity action before a national court, such as the German Federal Patent Court between the same parties would be blocked due to Articles 71(c)(2), 29 of Regulation (EU) No. 1215/2012. If the parties are not the same, the national nullity action may likely be suspended under Article 30 of that Regulation (EU).

§6.10 PARALLEL EPO OPPOSITION AND UPC REVOCATION ACTION

EPO opposition proceedings and UPC revocation proceedings against the same patent can be conducted in parallel. This is, a UPC revocation action can be initiated prior to the beginning, during the course and after the conclusion of opposition proceedings. UPC revocation actions thus do not depend on the plaintiff having previously filed an opposition at the EPO.[60] It is even possible for the same party to proceed with an opposition and a revocation action against a particular European patent. Since both proceedings, on the one hand at the UPC and on the other hand at the EPO, are basically not dependent on each other, and both judicial entities can take decisions on the validity of a European patent at different times and with different outcomes, the question arises as to the relationship between these decisions.

The plaintiff in UPC revocation proceedings has to "inform the Court of any pending revocation, limitation or opposition proceedings before the European Patent Office."[61] Furthermore, the provision stipulates that "the Court may stay its proceedings when a rapid decision may be expected from the European Patent Office."[62]

The UPC may—but must not necessarily—stay proceedings relating to patents that are the subject of parallel EPO opposition proceedings or limitation proceedings. The interplay between parallel EPO oppositions and UPC revocation proceedings is not detailed in the UPCA or the RoP. Determining standards for such stays is thus crucial.

The UPC is empowered to exercise its authority within the scope of protection determined by the EPO. This is, a European patent that has been finally revoked by the EPO (for instance, after an appeal) cannot be "revived" by the UPC. Also, as soon as the European patent receives a limited scope of protection through EPO opposition proceedings, the UPC does not have jurisdiction to reinstate a broader scope of

59. Federal Supreme Court, Decision of Apr. 19, 2011, X 124/10, "Mautberechnung."
60. Article 33(8) UPCA.
61. Article 33(10) UPCA.
62. Rule 295 RoP.

protection previously sought by the patentee. If the UPC upholds the patent while a parallel opposition is running against that patent, the EPO may render a judgment in the aftermath of such UPC decision. The EPO may even revoke—fully or partially—the European patent under the same arguments that were already discussed within the UPC proceedings. The EPO's revocation would prevail.

In case the UPC revokes an ordinary European patent, the EPO may still—fully or partially—uphold that patent however only with effect for those countries where the UPC has no jurisdiction (such as Spain, Poland, Turkey, Switzerland). With respect to the Contracting Member States of the UPC, the UPC decision revoking the patent would prevail, and the EPO cannot revive the patent with effect for those countries. Thus, one has to distinguish between countries in which UPC and EPO have overlapping jurisdiction, on the one hand, and, on the other hand, those countries over which the UPC has no jurisdiction. In all countries where UPC and EPO have common jurisdiction, the European patent must survive both attacks, i.e., EPO opposition and UPC revocation action, in order to stay in force.

§6.11 COSTS OF EPO OPPOSITIONS

Opposition proceedings are inexpensive. Besides a moderate opposition filing fee of less than EUR 1,000 and an appeal fee of about EUR 2,000, no other fees must be paid to the EPO for opposition proceedings. Parties to opposition proceedings normally cannot claim reimbursement of these costs. According to Article 104 EPC, each party to the opposition proceedings shall bear the costs it has incurred, unless the Opposition Division, for reasons of equity, orders a different apportionment. Such orders occur only in exceptional situations, such as when the opponent files a highly relevant document late, without any valid justification, and this renders both the oral proceedings and the patent proprietor's preparation useless.[63]

63. EPO—T 1306/05.

CHAPTER 7
Revocation Actions at the UPC

§7.01 MAIN CHARACTERISTICS

All divisions of the UPC have jurisdiction to adjudicate infringement and revocation actions, as well as counterclaims for revocation. A division handling an infringement action has the authority to contemporaneously adjudicate a counterclaim for revocation. It is possible, nevertheless, there is no compelling requirement for that UPC division to refer a counterclaim for revocation to a different division. In this manner, the UPC system differs from the German "split system."

§7.02 TYPES OF REVOCATION CHALLENGES

The UPC system distinguishes among two main situations: "Stand-alone" revocation actions and counterclaims for revocation. The term "stand-alone" commonly refers to a situation where an invalidation of the patent is sought without that a patent infringement action has been filed by the right holder. A stand-alone revocation action could be brought, for example, by a competitor who does not yet offer its own product but plans to come to the market with a product soon. The counterclaim for revocation, on the contrary, represents a reaction of the defendant to an infringement action.

[A] Stand-Alone Revocation Actions

[1] Parties

Stand-alone revocation actions shall be directed against the patent owner, pursuant to Rule 42 RoP. The challenger will typically identify the patent owner through the patent registry records. Nonetheless, there may be a mismatch between the listed owner and the "true" owner of the patent if those public registry records are outdated (such as following a sale of the patent). If there is such mismatch, then the registered owner, who is not the "true" owner, shall apply for his or her substitution in the proceedings (Rule 305.1(c) RoP).

Standing to proceed with a revocation action in the UPC is broad. According to Article 47(6) UPCA, "any other natural or legal person, or anybody entitled to bring actions in accordance with its national law, who is concerned by a patent, may bring actions in accordance with the Rules of Procedure." The term "who is concerned by a patent" could be understood to mean that not "any" claimant is entitled to file a revocation action. This could be understood as meaning that at least some showing of an individual concern or interest is necessary to establish the admissibility of the action. Rule 44 of the RoP, however, does not expressly mandate that the statement for revocation must contain a statement of interest. The public interest in reducing the number of invalid patents favors the indicated flexible approach of the EPO in opposition proceedings. There, anyone may file an opposition without indicating a particular interest (Article 99(1) EPC), unless the opponent is the proprietor.[1] Frivolous actions are discouraged because the claimant must pay a fee when filing the action.

[2] Allocation of Matters

The Central Division has its main seat in Paris with—at present—a branch in Munich. Depending on the technical nature of the patent-in-suit, the revocation action is heard either at the UPC's main seat in Paris or at its branch in Munich. Previously, a second branch was supposed to be seated in London. However, due to Brexit, the UK no longer hosts any branch of the Central Division. It is not yet decided if the workload will be shared between Paris and Munich. Also, consideration is currently being given to opening another branch in Milan, Italy. *See* Table 7.1 which illustrates the allocation of the cases which follows the main section of WIPO's International Patent Classification in compliance with Annex II of the UPCA.

Table 7.1 Allocation of Matters Within the Central Division

Paris (Seat)	*Munich*	*Second Branch*
(B) performing operations, transporting. (D) textiles; paper. (E) fixed constructions; (G) physics. (H) electricity.	(F) mechanical engineering, lighting, heating, weapons, blasting.	(A) human necessities. (C) chemistry, metallurgy.

Consistent with the importance of the technology classes, about 75% of stand-alone revocation actions are heard at the Central Division's main seat in Paris.

Where an action for revocation comprises a plurality of patents, the Court may order that the proceedings be heard in separate proceedings.[2] Parallel proceedings

1. EPO—G 9/93.
2. Rule 302(1) RoP.

relating to the same patent may be heard together when it is in the interest of justice to do so.[3]

[3] Jurisdiction

Stand-alone revocation actions must be filed with the Central Division of the UPC, Article 33(4) UPCA, absent a stipulation by the parties to adjudicate such action elsewhere. Parties may agree to bring a revocation action at any local or regional division of the Court of First Instance.[4] For example, a licensing agreement may provide that disputes be resolved at a particular division of the UPC. This choice may influence the language of the proceedings (*see below* §7.04). The revocation action will then be heard in one of the official languages of the local or regional division upon which the parties have agreed.[5]

[4] Clash of Revocation and Infringement Actions

Stand-alone revocation actions are not independent of other actions relating to the same patent. Where an action for infringement, based on the same patent and between the same parties, is already pending with a local or regional division, the revocation action must be filed (as a counterclaim) with the same local or regional division.[6] A defendant of an infringement action cannot split revocation from infringement. It is the choice of the patentee where to bring the infringement action without being threatened of having to litigate the revocation action in separate proceedings. Thus, as long as the same parties are facing each other, Article 34(4) UPCA prevents invalidity proceedings and infringement proceedings concerning the same patent from being allocated to different divisions of the court. However, the provision of Article 33(4) UPCA cannot prevent third parties from filing nullity actions with the central division or any other appropriate division against the patent during ongoing infringement proceedings pending at a local or regional division.

According to Article 33(5) UPCA, an infringement action may be filed with any division having jurisdiction, even after a stand-alone revocation action had been initiated at the central division between the same parties and relating to the same patent. Such "same party" includes any licensee entitled to bring an infringement action.[7] It is then within the discretion of the division handling the infringement action to decide whether it wants to hear both the infringement and the revocation action, whether it wants to separate the proceedings and continue only with the infringement action, or whether it wants to refer the infringement case to the central division. That decision shall be made after having heard the parties. The division handling the

3. Rule 302(3) RoP.
4. Article 33(7) UPCA.
5. Rule 45(2) RoP.
6. Article 33(4) UPCA.
7. Rule 75(1) RoP.

infringement action shall take into account how far the revocation action has advanced when exercising its discretion.[8]

[B] Counterclaims for Revocation

[1] Introduction

The UPC may also decide on the validity of a patent based on a counterclaim for revocation. Such counterclaim for revocation must be directed against the proprietor of the patent. It must be filed together with the defendant's statement of defense, which means within three months after the service of the infringement action.[9]

The counterclaim for revocation must be filed with the division hearing the infringement case.

[2] Split of Infringement and Revocation

The court has the possibility to split the infringement from revocation in exceptional cases. According to Article 33(3) UPCA, the division seized may (exceptionally) refer a counterclaim for revocation to the central division. This results in a split of infringement and revocation being pending then before two different divisions of the UPC. Such "split" may occur in the following situations:

- Article 33(10) UPCA: Infringement action with pending EPO opposition proceedings: According to Article 33(1) a) UPCA, infringement actions may be filed during EPO opposition proceedings. An opposition can even be filed after the infringement action has been initiated (if the opposition period is met). In both cases, opposition proceedings before the EPO and infringement proceedings before the UPC are pending simultaneously. If a rapid decision of the EPO is expected, the infringement proceedings may be suspended by the UPC.
- Article 33(5) UPCA: If a revocation action is already pending before the central division and an infringement action is subsequently brought between the same parties (Article 32(1)(a) UPCA), it is at the discretion of the local or regional division entrusted with the infringement matter to continue the case, to stay it (Article 33(5) UPCA) or to refer it to the central division.
- The second sentence of Article 33(3) UPCA refers to a situation where the counterclaim for revocation follows the infringement action between the same parties in which case the division has a choice: it may refer the counterclaim for revocation as such to the central division or it may refer the revocation together with the infringement action to the central division (transfer decision, Article 33(3)(b) and (c)). If it refers only the counterclaim to the central division, it must decide whether to stay the proceedings pending a decision on

8. Rule 75(4) RoP; Art. 33(3) UPCA.
9. Chapter 10, §10.01[B].

revocation or to continue the infringement proceedings. If the division refuses to stay the proceedings, the consequence is that the counterclaim before the central decision, which has now become a revocation action, and the infringement action before the (infringement) division are pending simultaneously.

According to Article 33(3) UPCA, the seized division has "discretion" to decide on these possibilities. In doing so, it must primarily consider the UPCA, such as the requirement that the procedure be "flexible" and "balanced" (Article 52(1) UPCA). Basically, the traditions applicable in Europe are not decisive, such as Germany's bifurcation or the uniform treatment of infringement and invalidity by the same panel. Rather, the division must determine and select the best solution for the induvial case. In most cases, this results in a uniform treatment of infringement and nullity being the better solution. It is also significant that the central division is not better equipped than the regional or local divisions. Accordingly, almost all infringement actions and counterclaims for revocation are therefore heard by the same panel, within the frame of one single action. Hence, the court organizes one oral hearing where both validity and infringement arguments shall be discussed and renders one judgment dealing with both aspects.[10] This is a major change from the way that infringement proceedings have traditionally been litigated in Germany, where infringement claims are heard in district court, and validity challenges are separately litigated in the Federal Patent Court.

§7.03 APPEAL PROCEEDINGS

Appeals of decisions of the Court of First Instance arising from actions having revocation and infringement claims will also encompass both aspects of the action. They may be brought before the Court of Appeal by any party which has been unsuccessful, in whole or in part, in its submissions, within two months of the date of the notification of the decision (Article 73(1) UPCA). In other words, an appeal may be filed if the party is adversely affected by the decision of the Court of First Instance. The extent to which the decision is reviewed by the Court of Appeal basically depends on the submissions, requests, and objections of the appellant. The court is bound by the requests and submissions of the parties (Article 76 UPCA, Rules 222 and 226(a) UPCA). It may review the findings of fact of the Court of First Instance. However, new factual allegations and evidence submitted for the first time at second instance will only be considered (Article 73(4) UPCA) if the Rules of Procedure allow it, in particular if the submission could not reasonably have been made at first instance. Because of this limitation, facts and evidence should be brought into the proceedings as early as possible. If they are presented later, the appeal court may disregard them under Rules 9.2, 239.1, 110, 103, and 104. Of course, a full review of the legal reasoning used by the court is possible (Article 73(3) UPCA).

10. Chapter 10, §10.01[E][3][b].

Even where separate decisions have been rendered by the Court of First Instance, the Court of Appeal may hear appeals together, where appropriate, according to Rule 220(5) RoP.

Contrary to the German case law, the UPC's Court of Appeal does—in principle—not remand a case back to the first instance tribunal in a situation where questions of facts or law that were not raised below subsequently become decisive during the appeal proceedings.[11] A referral back may occur in exceptional cases where the Court of Appeal would be burdened with duties that have not been satisfied through first instance proceedings and typically belong to main areas of responsibility of the first instance.[12] The mere fact that the Court of Appeal would be required to take evidence to render a final decision does not require remanding the case back to the first instance tribunal. Restricting such remands to exceptional cases promotes the goal of providing swift resolution of litigations, typically with a final and binding decision (through appeal) resulting usually within two and a half years.

§7.04 LANGUAGE REGIME

A stand-alone revocation action is heard in the language of the patent, which is the language of the EPO prosecution proceedings. This could be English, German or French. If parties agree to bring the revocation action before a local or regional division, the revocation action shall be heard in one of the official languages of the local or regional division.[13] A counterclaim for revocation shall be heard in the same language as the infringement action already pending with the same division.

§7.05 COMPOSITION OF THE PANELS

A stand-alone revocation action brought to the central division shall be heard by a multinational panel of judges, with two legally qualified judges and one technically qualified judge. The technically qualified judge will be experienced in the field of technology concerned.

§7.06 GROUNDS FOR REVOCATION

[A] Reference to Articles 138(1) and 139(2) EPC

According to Article 65(2) UPCA, a patent may only be revoked, either entirely or partly, on the grounds referred to in Articles 138(1)[14] and 139(2)[15] of the EPC. A

11. Rule 242(2)(b) RoP.
12. Rule 243 RoP.
13. Rule 45(2) RoP.
14. Article 138 Revocation of European patents:

> (1) Subject to Article 139, a European patent may be revoked with effect for a Contracting State only on the grounds that

primary challenge concerns the patentability of the claims for lack of novelty or inventive step, pursuant to Articles 52–57.[16] Another important ground is non-enablement (insufficiency of disclosure), when the patent does not disclose the invention in a manner sufficiently clear and complete for it to be carried out by a person skilled in the art. Another challenge that may be raised in revocation proceedings is that the patent's subject matter extends beyond the content of the application as originally filed, in violation of Article 123(2) EPC (added subject matter). The patent may also be revoked if the asserted proprietor of the European patent is improper under Article 60(1) EPC, i.e., if the right to the European patent does not belong to him or her. All available grounds should be contained in the written statement for revocation.[17] If the grounds for revocation challenge only portions of the patent, then the patent will be limited by a corresponding amendment of the claims.

The UPC is not legally bound by the EPO's case law. Nonetheless, because the grounds for revocation are primarily governed by the provisions of the EPC, the preexisting case law of the EPO will have a decisive influence on the UPC's jurisprudence. The UPC will have authority to develop its own case law regarding the grounds for revocation, taking also into account the different national approaches, which do not necessarily comply with the EPO case law. For example, German law takes a different approach when it comes to the so-called inescapable trap under Article 123 EPC, which is different from the approach taken by the EPO.[18] National courts, when applying the EPC, do not necessarily follow the case law arising from the EPO. Especially when assessing patentability, the UPC will most probably develop its case law on its own, taking into account not only the EPO case law but also the law of national courts, which sometimes diverges from EPO standards.

(a) The subject matter of the European patent is not patentable under Articles 52 to 57
(b) The European patent does not disclose the invention in a manner sufficiently clear and complete for it to be carried out by a person skilled in the art
(c) The subject matter of the European patent extends beyond the content of the application as filed or, if the patent was granted on a divisional application or on a new application filed under Article 61, beyond the content of the earlier application as filed
(d) The protection conferred by the European patent has been extended
(e) The proprietor of the European patent is not entitled under Article 60, paragraph 1.

15. Article 139 EPC Prior rights and rights arising on the same date:

(1) ...
(2) A national patent application and a national patent in a Contracting State shall have with regard to a European patent designating that Contracting State the same prior right effect as if the European patent were a national patent.
(3) ...

16. The Patentability Standards are explained in Ch. 5.
17. Rule 44(1)(e) RoP.
18. Chapter 5, §5.05[B].

[B] National Prior Rights

A national prior right is a national patent application or a national patent that was applied for prior to the priority date of the European patent-in-question but published afterward (so-called national prior right). Such national prior rights cannot serve as the basis of novelty challenges in opposition proceedings at the EPO. This is because they do not represent prior art under Article 54(3) EPC. By contrast, at the UPC a challenger can assert lack of novelty of a European patent in view of a national prior right.[19] But, the national prior right will only impact the national part of the ordinary European patent with respect to the Contracting Member State for which the national prior right was applied for. It may lead to a revocation or limitation of the ordinary European patent for that Contracting Member State.

It is still undecided what consequences such national prior right may have on a European patent with unitary effect (UP). In contrast to an ordinary European patent, a UP shall have the same unitary character over all Contracting Member States. That unitary character might be jeopardized if the UP is restricted or invalidated only for one country and not for all Contracting Member States. On the contrary, it would be unfair if a prior national right forces the holder of a UP to limit the scope of his patent for all countries where the unitary effect takes place or—even worse—be the reason for a complete revocation of the UP, without having the possibility to reestablish a European patent (without unitary effect) for the same invention. Therefore, it is likely that Article 65(2) UPCA will be applied to European patents with unitary effect in such a manner that the UP shall be revoked or limited only in the Contracting Member State where the prior national rights exist.[20]

Having this in mind, it is important for patent holders to have a safeguard position until the UPC has established its view on this question. Such s safeguard position could be to file national patent rights along with the European patent with unitary effect, for example, in Germany and France, because there, double protection is no longer prohibited. Parallel national patents are also available in Austria, Denmark, Finland, Hungary and Sweden.[21] Furthermore, owners of European patents with unitary effect should also carry out prior art searches focusing on national prior rights, to avoid negative surprises. Due to this problem, the EPO conducts searches to identify prior national rights. Such searches at the end of substantive examination constitute an additional quality control in the EPO grant procedure. It enables the applicant to assess the relevance of such documents.

19. Article 65(2) UPCA, Art. 139(2) EPC.
20. For more detail: Ch. 5, §5.02[F].
21. *See* "National law relating to the EPC—European patent applications and patents: law and practice of the EPC contracting states, extension and validation states" under X. Miscellaneous published by the EPO (current 18th ed.) and available under www.epo.org.

§7.07 FINANCIAL ASPECTS

[A] Overview

As for actions taken on a national level, both court fees and attorney fees need to be considered when budgeting the case. When filing the nullity action, the plaintiff has to advance the court fees.[22] At the end of the proceedings, reasonable and proportionate legal costs and other expenses have to be paid by the party who has lost the case, unless equity requires otherwise.[23] However, a party should bear any unnecessary costs it has caused the court or another party.[24] It is therefore necessary that parties undertake measures to minimize both court costs and costs of the parties.

If there is no fully prevailing party, then the costs are shared among the parties.

[B] Court Fees

The court fee for a stand-alone revocation action is a fixed amount of EUR 20,000 per instance independent upon the value in dispute. The court fees for a counterclaim for revocation are the same as the infringement action, subject to a fee limit of EUR 20,000. Court fees for the appeal are the same amount as the respective court fees in first instance.

Compared to German nullity proceedings, this fee structure is more attractive for plaintiffs of revocation actions filed with the UPC (*see* Table 7.2).

Table 7.2 Comparison of Court Fees for Revocation Actions in Germany and Counterclaim for Revocation at the UPC

Value in Dispute (EUR)	*Court Fees (Germany) (EUR)*		*Court Fees UPC (EUR)*	
	1st Instance	*2nd Instance*	*1st Instance*	*2nd Instance*
500,000	17,554.50	23,406	11,000	11,000
1.0 million	26,464.50	35,286	15,000	15,000
2.5 million	53,194.50	70,926	20,000	20,000
5 million	97,744.50	130,326	20,000	20,000
10 million	186,844.50	249,126	20,000	20,000
25 million	454,144.50	605,526	20,000	20,000
30 million	543,244.50	724,326	20,000	20,000
50 million	543,244.50	724,326	20,000	20,000

This should be considered as an advantage for both parties since it reduces significantly their overall cost risk.

22. Article 70(2) UPCA, Rule 371 RoP.
23. Article 69(1) UPCA.
24. Article 69(3) UPCA.

Consistent with the German system, the plaintiff shall provide a preliminary estimate of the litigation value at the beginning of the revocation proceedings. With respect to a counterclaim for revocation, the defendant of the infringement action shall at the same time declare if he accepts the indication of the value in dispute by the claimant of the infringement action.[25]

The litigation value is often difficult to determine. If the defendant does not object to the plaintiff's estimation, the court shall fix the litigation value based on this estimated litigation value.[26] Due to the public nature of nullity proceedings, the value of the infringement proceedings may be increased by up to 50%.

[C] Reimbursable Fees

Reimbursable fees are in principle all fees of one party's attorneys, patent attorneys, as well as reasonable disbursements. The court may order in advance of the decision on the merits that the parties submit a preliminary estimate of legal costs that they will seek to recover.[27] The successful party seeking a cost decision of the court has to lodge an application for cost decision within one month of service of the decision.[28] In case of a revocation action or counterclaim, the party shall indicate the value of the proceedings in order to assess the applicable ceiling.[29] Where an infringement action and a counterclaim for revocation are pending before the same division, the values of the infringement action and the value of the revocation action should be added for determining the level of recoverable costs.

Table 7.3 shows the ceiling for recoverable costs, for infringement actions (or stand-alone revocation actions) and infringement actions with counterclaims for revocation. Only reasonable and proportionate costs are recoverable. This is basically independent of the ceiling which is only an upper limit. In many cases, therefore, the upper limit will not be reached at all.

Table 7.3 Ceiling of Recoverable Costs for Infringement Action and Counterclaim for Revocation (UPC)

Value in Dispute (EUR)	*Infringement Action or Stand-Alone Revocation Action (EUR)*	*Infringement + Counterclaim for Revocation (EUR)*
500,000	56,000	112,000
1.0 million	112,000	200,000
2.5 million	400,000	600,000
5 million	600,000	800,000

25. Rule 24(i) RoP with respect to a counterclaim for revocation.
26. *See also* Guidelines for the determination of Court fees and the ceiling of recoverable costs of the successful party, as published by the Preparatory Committee.
27. Rule 118.5 RoP.
28. Rule 151 RoP.
29. Rule 152.3 RoP.

Value in Dispute (EUR)	*Infringement Action or Stand-Alone Revocation Action (EUR)*	*Infringement + Counterclaim for Revocation (EUR)*
10 million	800,000	1.2 million
25 million	1.2 million	1.5 million
30 million	1.2 million	1.5 million
50 million	1.5 million	1.5 million

The value shall be determined by applying a royalty rate based on the sales revenues of the allegedly infringing product through the expiration of the patent (for an injunction claim), including the past sales (for a damage claim). The royalty rate to be applied shall either be an existing royalty rate for the same invention, a generally accepted industry rate or a royalty rate determined by the court after hearing the parties.[30]

[D] Security for Costs

The rules on security for costs follow a different approach than the ones known in German proceedings. According to the German provision of section 110(1) of the Code of Civil Procedure, plaintiffs who do not have their habitual residence in a Member State of the EU or in a State party to the Agreement on the European Economic Area (EEA) must, at the request of the defendant, provide security in respect of the costs of the proceedings. This is different under the UPCA, where domestic parties and foreign entities are treated equally when assessing security for costs through the UPC. Thus, also domestic plaintiffs have to provide a security for the eventual reimbursement claim of the defendant.

Upon a reasoned request by one party, the court may order the other party to provide adequate security for the legal costs and other expenses that have been incurred or are likely to be incurred by the requesting party.[31] The court shall give the parties an opportunity to be heard. The court will either fix a security by deposit or by bank guarantee. The decision of the court may be appealed. It shall be enforceable under the same rules as all other decisions and orders of the court.[32]

30. *See* Guidelines for the determination of court fees and the ceiling of recoverable costs of the successful party, as published by the Preparatory Committee.
31. Rule 158.1.
32. Rule 354.

CHAPTER 8

National Nullity Actions: Germany

§8.01 INTRODUCTION

Germany is one of the few countries in the world where infringement proceedings are tried separately from validity challenges. This is different than in most of the European jurisdictions where infringement and invalidity may be dealt with in a combined manner within the same proceedings.

Patent validity in German must be attacked through "nullity" proceedings in the Federal Patent Court, after the limited time window for challenging patents in opposition proceedings has closed. This split system, with infringement tried in the District Courts of general jurisdiction, and nullity proceedings tried in the Federal Patent Court, is a defining characteristic of German patent litigation.

The separation of infringement and nullity proceedings is pursued even up to the Federal Supreme Court, where both sets of proceedings could be ultimately litigated. An infringement case started with one of the district courts will not be heard together with a parallel invalidation case filed with the Federal Patent Court. Even in the last instance, these cases are heard as separate cases and run independently with regard to timing.

The Federal Patent Court continues to play an important role in Europe's patent system. As a national court, it has not lost its importance due to the inauguration of the UPC. For instance, it continues to have the sole jurisdiction for revoking national German patents. Also, during the transitional period of seven years under Article 83 UPCA, the revocation of German parts of (traditional) European patents may still be asserted there.

Most commonly, nullity actions trail behind the associated infringement proceedings. This results from the fact that the first phase in a patent dispute is frequently the filing of an infringement complaint, and also from the fact that infringement proceedings are typically faster than nullity actions. The "head start" of infringement cases over the corresponding nullity action, and the district court's presumption that patents are valid, can put enormous pressure on the accused infringer. Frequently, the district court will impose injunctive relief before a nullity challenge can be heard.

Figure 8.1 illustrates the split system. Nullity proceedings in the Federal Patent Court are described in the left side of the table. Infringement proceedings (the focus of Chapters 9 and 10), which are tried in the district courts of general jurisdiction, are shown on the right.

Figure 8.1 Split System

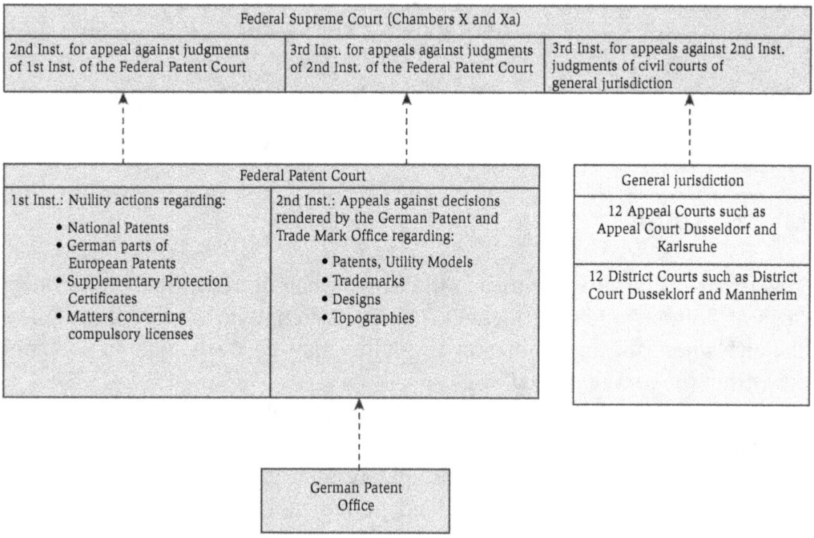

§8.02 COURT STRUCTURE

The Federal Patent Court in Munich was established on July 1, 1961. Until that date, the main tasks of today's Federal Patent Court were handled by the GPTO. Because this was considered to represent a conflict with the constitutional principle of separation of powers,[1] the tasks had to be handed over to a judicial authority that was independent of the GPTO. This is today the Federal Patent Court, with its independent judges appointed by the Federal President of Germany.

[A] Federal Patent Court

The Federal Patent Court is a Court of First Instance for nullity actions (shown in the left box of the table "Split System"). The Federal Patent Court also has second instance (i.e., appellate) jurisdiction over decisions rendered by the examining sections and

1. Federal Administrative Tribunal, Decision of Jun. 13, 1959, NJW 1959, 1507 or BVerwGE 8, 350.

patent departments of the German Patent Office (middle box of Figure 8.1). An appeal to the Federal Supreme Court may be lodged based on questions of law, without further review of facts. This applies likewise to judgments rendered in utility model matters (cancelation proceedings according to sections 17 and 18(4) Utility Model Act).

In contrast to the courts of general jurisdiction, the composition of the Federal Patent Court is not limited to legal judges. This court includes technically trained judges, who have the same duties as legally trained judges, and whose role is not limited to assisting the legally trained judges. These technical judges are appointed by the Federal President of Germany[2] only after they have typically worked for many years in a technical profession and have completed a degree in one of the sciences at a German university. Many of the technically trained judges previously served as examiners at the patent office.

[B] Federal Supreme Court

The court of last resort is the Federal Supreme Court in Karlsruhe. Until October 2009, appeals on judgments rendered by the Federal Patent Court on nullity actions could be focused on a review of points of law and on facts. Thus, the Federal Supreme Court had to take evidence and appointed a court expert in almost all cases. Since the enactment of the Patent Law Modernization Act on October 1, 2009, the role of the Federal Supreme Court has been significantly changed. According to section 111(1) of the GPA, the Supreme Court's role is now principally limited to a review of questions of law. This change was intended to concentrate the burden of the factual assessment, including the related evidence taking, on the first instance proceedings.[3] Accordingly, the assessment of the factual aspects of the case is on the shoulders of the Federal Patent Court.

The Federal Supreme Court has one chamber dealing with nullity actions in second instance proceedings, namely Chamber X. The chamber is composed of five judges. Even though these judges do not have a technical background, and tend to fall within the category of traditional judges, they are highly qualified and well regarded in the area of patent law. Many of them previously served as judges at the Federal Patent Court or were promoted from prominent infringement courts such as the District Court Düsseldorf. Chamber X is presided over by Justice Klaus Bacher.

§8.03 MAIN PROCEDURAL ASPECTS OF NULLITY ACTIONS

[A] Priority of Opposition Proceedings over Nullity Actions

Opposition proceedings and nullity actions must follow in chronological order. Figure 8.2 illustrates this. They may not be implemented simultaneously.[4] Section 81(2) of the Patent Act sets a timeline for the filing of a nullity action. A nullity action requires that

2. Section 65(3) of the Patent Act.
3. BlPMZ 2009, 307.
4. Federal Supreme Court, X ZR 29/05, GRUR 2005, 967, "Strahlungssteuerung."

no opposition proceedings against the patent be pending and that the time period for filing an opposition against the patent has passed. If a nullity action is filed too early, the Federal Patent Court would dismiss it on that basis. This rule is applicable to oppositions at the German Patent Office and the EPO. This requirement is aimed at avoiding contradictory decisions (Figure 8.2).[5]

Even if the Board of Appeals of the EPO remands the case for further prosecution to the Opposition Division (Article 111(2) EPC), a nullity action is not permissible as long as the opposition proceedings have not been closed. A third party which cannot file an opposition due to the lapsed opposition period may join pending opposition proceedings provided that an infringement lawsuit has been filed against this party (section 59(2) Patent Act, Article 105 EPC).[6] A nullity action cannot proceed while there is an opposition pending with the EPO even if the challenge is exclusively based on a national patent application with prior-right effect under Article 139(2) EPC, which can only be alleged in national revocation proceedings (national prior rights).[7]

After the opposition window has closed, a nullity action may be filed at any time. Nullity actions may even be brought after patent expiration, in the limited case where the challenger can show a special legal interest in the invalidation of the patent, such as where the patentee has sought damages for infringement that arose during the life of the patent.

[B] Different Approach under the UPCA

Unlike German nullify actions, which cannot be filed during a pending EPO opposition proceeding, there is a different set of rules governing revocation actions before the UPC. Revocation actions at the UPC may be filed prior to or during pending opposition proceedings (Article 33(8) UPCA). The UPC does not contain a provision, as in Germany or Austria, precluding the assertion of an invalidity action during the pendency of opposition proceedings or during the window in which opposition proceedings could be filed. Instead, the UPC decides on a case-by-case basis which course of action is appropriate in the event of parallel opposition proceedings. Thus, it may suspend the proceedings, for instance, if the opposition proceedings are already at an advanced stage. The alleged infringer thus has more options. He can file a revocation action at the UPC instead of an opposition. Filing an action for revocation may be the most expedient strategy after an infringement action has been brought against him since the seized division of the UPC could then decide on both validity and infringement. Whether it makes sense to file an opposition in addition to a revocation action before the UPC, provided that the opposition period has not yet expired, is primarily a question of cost. Opposition proceedings are less expensive (lower fees for proceedings before the EPO) compared to nullity proceedings before the UPC. Therefore, filing an isolated UPC revocation action instead of opposition proceedings often

5. *Ibid.*
6. *See* Ch. 6, §6.07.
7. Federal Supreme Court, Decision of Apr. 19, 2011, X ZR 124/10, GRUR 2011, 848, points 8 et seq. = IIC 2012, 475 "Mautberechnung." *See* Ch. 7, §7.06[B] and Ch. 5, §5.02[F].

does not seem to make sense for cost reasons, unless there are other reasons for initiating a UPC revocation action, for instance, because an infringement action by the patent proprietor is imminent. If the opposition does not lead to success, a subsequent revocation action at the UPC is possible at any time.

[C] Parties to the Nullity Action

Nullity actions may be filed by any person or legal entity.[8] When filing a lawsuit against a patent with the Federal Patent Court, the plaintiff is not required to demonstrate a particular interest. He or she can file the nullity action without being sued or otherwise threatened by the patentee. A party who filed an unsuccessful opposition proceeding is not precluded from bringing a second attack against the same patent through a subsequently introduced nullity action (i.e., two bites at the apple are permitted). The nullity action can even be based on the same arguments used in the opposition proceedings.[9] Furthermore, a final and non-appealable decision rendered in a previous nullity action does not hinder a subsequent nullity action. The filing of a subsequent nullity action is however impermissible if the same party files it based on the same ground for revocation, even if this action is based on new facts and evidence.[10] It is however acceptable if the same plaintiff subsequently files a nullity action based on a different ground for revocation. Thus, it would be possible for the same party to file a first nullity action based on the ground of missing patentability and a second based on lack of enabling disclosure.

Figure 8.2 Priority of Opposition over Nullity

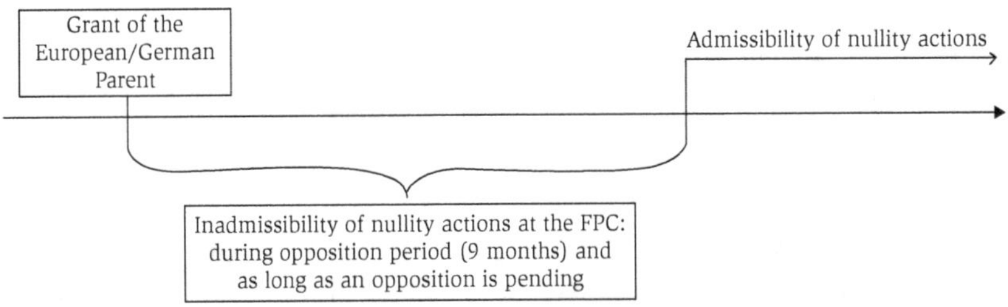

Even a "straw man," i.e., someone who acts in his own name, without interest in the proceedings, but on behalf of an anonymous party, may file such an action. This is in fact a common practice of staying anonymous.[11] Often competitors prefer to stay in the background and involve a "straw man" to take measures against disagreeable and uncomfortable patents of competing companies. In many of these cases, they prefer to take the anonymous route in order to avoid problems in their relationship with the

8. Federal Supreme Court, Decision of Jan. 1, 1963, Ia ZR 174/63, GRUR 63, 253, "Bürovorsteher."
9. Federal Supreme Court, GRUR 1996, 753, Zahnkranzfäser.
10. Federal Supreme Court, Ia ZR 64/63, GRUR 1964, 18, "Konditionierungseinrichtung."
11. Federal Patent Court, Decision of Nov. 13, 2008—10 Ni 30/07.

patentee, or they simply do not want to raise awareness of their business intentions. There are, however, limits to the straw man action, in particular if the party standing behind the straw man is contractually obligated not to challenge the patent, as may be the case in a license agreement.[12] Using a straw man is also impermissible for a party who has already lost a nullity action and is seeking to retry it on the same ground for revocation.[13] But the burden falls upon the patentee to prove an objection to a nullity proceeding on the basis of prohibited party, and this can be a difficult burden to meet.

The nullity action shall be directed against the person or legal entity registered as the patentee in the patent register (section 81(1) Patent Act). This provision applies regardless of whether or not that person or entity actually owns the patent. Only the party registered as the patentee is the right addressee of the complaint. This is also applicable if the actual owner differs from the registered one. The patentee must appear in the register at the latest by at the day of the oral hearing; otherwise, the court would dismiss the action.[14] Third parties with a legal interest in the suit may intervene on the side of either the nullity plaintiff or defendant.

[D] Timing of a Nullity Action

Nullity actions are decided in the first instance by the Federal Patent Court, usually within twenty-two to twenty-four months from the filing date of the complaint. The appeal proceedings usually last roughly an additional two years. Thus, the total length of nullity actions through two instances generally amounts to approximately four years.

[1] Chronology of First Instance (Federal Patent Court)

Complaint: The complaint contains the grounds for revoking the patent.[15] According to section 82 of the GPA, as soon as the nullity complaint is filed, the court serves the complaint on the named defendant. This should be the person or entity named as patentee in the register of the Patent Office,[16] even if the patent has been assigned to a third party and no longer belongs to the person or entity named in the register.[17]

Reply: The court invites the defendant to reply to the complaint within one month. If the patentee fails to object to the revocation in due time, a decision complying with the plaintiff's requests may be rendered without a hearing (section 82(2) Patent

12. Federal Patent Court, Decision of Mar. 30, 2004—1 Ni 28/02.
13. Federal Patent Court, Decision of Nov. 13, 2008—10 Ni 30/07.
14. Federal Supreme Court, Ia ZR 261/63, GRUR 1966, 107, "Patentrolleneintragung."
15. *See* Ch. 8, §8.05.
16. The register is available online: https://dpinfo.dpma.de/. It contains information about name/address of the patentee, name/address of the representative, if there is any, as well as the status of the patent, i.e., whether it is in force or not. It also contains some information about the history of the patent, in particular, whether nullity actions have been filed against the patent. If this is the case, the register provides the docket number by which means a files inspection can be made at the Federal Patent Court.
17. Federal Patent Court, Decision of Apr. 16, 2015, 2 Ni 8/13.

Act). In this default situation, the factual allegations of the plaintiff are regarded as proven by the court, and if the plaintiff's requests are coherent, the court will grant them.

Self-limitations: The patentee may choose to strengthen his position by narrowing the patent—i.e., by offering additional limitations to restrict the scope of the patent (so-called self-limitations). It is thus common practice to file an appropriate number of auxiliary requests in view of sustaining the patent in an amended form. Typically, the patentee submits a main request followed by one or more auxiliary requests. The auxiliary requests which are focused on a more limited scope of the granted claim(s) are made in case the court considers the main request not allowable. Such auxiliary requests may be based on features taken from the description and combined with an independent claim or, if suitable, by combining an independent claim with the features of one or more dependent claims. The limited claim must itself comply with the patentability requirements. In that respect, it is essential that the feature combination in the limited claim be sufficiently disclosed in the application as originally filed.[18]

Qualified note: After having given the parties the opportunity to present their arguments in writing, the Federal Patent Court (FPC) issues an order, called a "qualified note" highlighting aspects of particular importance, and setting forth a deadline for the parties to submit additional pleadings (section 83(1) and (2) Patent Act). According to new rules,[19] the qualified note shall already be issued within six months after service of the nullity complaint. The qualified note shall contain a preliminary opinion on patentability which may affect parallel infringement proceedings. The introduction of this six-month time limit is intended to streamline the proceedings. In addition, the qualified note on the validity of the patent shall be made available in parallel infringement proceedings prior to the issue of any decision on the infringement of the patent. This aim has not yet been achieved in all proceedings. Furthermore, the Federal Patent Court (FPC) may set a further deadline for the parties to prepare written statements in response to the note. The FPC may disregard arguments received after the expiry of that deadline. This provision is primarily intended to ensure that the notice is not delayed for reasons of procedural tactics, in particular with regard to infringement proceedings pending between the same parties before an ordinary court.

With the note, the court directs the parties to the facts that it considers of particular importance for the decision. Also, the court typically provides a preliminary opinion as to the controlling legal issues. The qualified note is of particular importance for the parties because it sets forth the panel's understanding of the state of the art being applied for an assessment of novelty and inventive step (nonobviousness). It thus enables the parties to adequately react on the position of the court and to focus their previous submissions through new facts and arguments.[20] Accordingly, the court may ask the parties to file further pertinent pleadings concerning issues of particular

18. Federal Supreme Court, GRUR 2002, 49 "Drehmomentübertragungseinrichtung"; Federal Supreme Court, GRUR 2015, 249, Schleifprodukt.
19. Bill to simplify and modernize patent law of Aug. 30, 2021 (BGBl. I S. 4074).
20. Federal Supreme Court, GRUR 2012, 1236, "Fahrzeugwechselstromgenerator."

importance, and to complete their pleadings within a deadline. Typically, the court sets a deadline of one month for additional pleadings. To this deadline, one further month is added in order that each party may respond to the pleadings of the adversary party. Submissions, such as new facts and new requests,[21] filed after these deadlines may be rejected as untimely if the delay is not sufficiently excused (section 83(1), (2) and (4) of the Patent Act). Prior to the deadline set in the qualified note, a submission of new facts can in principle not be rejected as being untimely.[22]

Hearing: The hearing takes place approximately two years after filing the complaint.[23] At the beginning of the oral hearing, the presiding judge may ask the parties if they are interested in settling the matter in an amicable way without a court decision. If unsuccessful, the court then proceeds with substantive issues of the case. Witnesses are only heard in exceptional cases. The discussion of the facts follows after the presiding judge has given an introduction regarding the decisive facts of the case and relevant questions of law. He reports on the essential content of the files. Following the presiding judge's introduction, the court gives the parties the opportunity to argue the matter (section 90(2) Patent Act). This discussion takes, in average cases, one day. In more complicated cases, this can extend to two or more days. If the matter—in the view of the court—is sufficiently discussed, normally at the end of the hearing day, the presiding judge declares the hearing closed. In contrast to the infringement courts, which do not announce an oral judgment the same day, the Federal Patent Court usually renders and announces a judgment. This judgment is announced orally in front of the parties after deliberation. The judges' deliberations (nonpublic, of course) take place at the end of the hearing, usually last no longer than an hour, and the parties await the judges' return. In exceptional cases, the parties are sent away and the decision is rendered at a later, separate session.

[2] Appeal to the Federal Supreme Court

Notice of Appeal: According to section 110 of the GPA, the notice of appeal must be filed within one month of the service of the written judgment of first instance. The one-month deadline for the notice of appeal is not extendable. The written judgment is usually provided four to six weeks after the rendering of the oral judgment. The one-month deadline starts to run on the date of the receipt of the full text of the judgment. However, in the rare instances when a written decision is not provided in a timely manner, the appeal must be filed at the latest five months after the announcement of the oral judgment (section 110(3) GPA).

Bases for Appeal: The appellant must also state the bases for the appeal. These bases may be contained in the notice of appeal or in a subsequent brief, which must be filed within a term of three months after a timely reception of the written judgment (section 112(2) GPA). However, upon request of the appellant, this term may be extended by the Chairman of the Chamber at the Federal Supreme Court in charge of

21. Federal Patent Court, Decision of Jul. 31, 2014—6 Ni 3/14.
22. Federal Patent Court, Decision of May 28, 2013—3 Ni 6/12.
23. BPatG Annual Report 2015 Business Report.

nullity appeal proceedings (presently Chamber *X*) if the opposing party consents to it. The Chairman of the Chamber may extend this deadline even without the consent of the opposing party if the appellant demonstrates considerable reasons for the extension, or if the proceedings would not be delayed by the request (section 112(2) GPA).

Before the Patent Law Modernization Act[24] came into force in 2009, the Federal Supreme Court usually appointed court experts. These experts were selected from the specific technical field in question (in many cases professors at universities). They mostly helped to provide the appropriate understanding of the terminology used in the disclosure of the originally filed documents and to illustrate the knowledge of the person skilled in the art at the priority date.

A court does not rely on court experts for assessing inventive step. The question of whether or not an inventive step is involved in a particular case was and still is regarded as a question of law for the court to decide. In other words, the court must take its own decision on inventive step. Under the present law, the Federal Supreme Court will not take evidence and appoint court experts to the extent it did in the past. Nevertheless, if the facts gathered in first instance are not sufficient to determine whether there is an inventive step, it is likely that the Federal Supreme Court will remand the case back to the first instance court (section 119 of the GPA).

According to section 118(1) GPA, the decision of the Federal Supreme Court is rendered on the basis of an oral hearing. If a party duly summoned to the proceedings does not attend the oral hearing, a decision can nevertheless proceed (section 118(4) GPA). In the oral hearing, the parties submit their requests and the Chairman of the Chamber of the Federal Supreme Court introduces the factual and legal issues. The parties are then given an opportunity to present their conclusive arguments. Finally, usually at the end of the hearing day, the Federal Supreme Court sets a date for the rendering and announcement of the decision.

Since the decision of the Federal Supreme Court is a final decision—i.e., no legal remedy is provided against a decision of the Federal Supreme Court—it takes effect upon its announcement.

§8.04 OBJECT OF NULLITY ACTIONS

A nullity action may be initiated against:

- German patents; or
- during the transitional period of Article 83 UPCA,[25] German parts of ordinary European patents. However, nullity actions against European patents with unitary effect (UPs) are inadmissible;

24. Federal Gazette BGBl. 2009 (Patent Law Modernization Act came into force on Oct. 1, 2009).
25. Chapter 4, §4.02[A][1][b]: There is no possibility for the patentee of an ordinary European patent to exclude the split competence between the national courts and the UPC imposed under Art. 83(1) UPCA. During the transitional period, the national courts will remain competent in any way.

- SPCs issued for patents covering medical or plant protection products. According to section 16a of the Patent Act, SPCs form a separate category of IP rights. However, their main purpose is to extend the term of a basic patent, which is in force when filing the application covering products that required an administrative authorization for their commercialization according to Regulations of the European Economic Community (EEC), such as the EEC Directive concerning medical products[26] or plant protection products.[27] SPCs are particularly aimed at alleviating the consequences resulting from lengthy administrative authorization proceedings during which a commercialization of the product is not possible.

It is the object of nullity actions to determine whether or not the challenged patent is to be revoked in total, revoked in part or maintained as granted. The requests of the plaintiff in the complaint are binding for the scope of the nullity action.[28] If the plaintiff's requests are limited to particular claims, the court will not render a decision on the remaining claims not covered by the request.[29]

§8.05 GROUNDS FOR REVOCATION

The grounds that may be raised to challenge a patent in nullity proceedings are limited to those listed in sections 22 and 21(1) of the GPA (for German national patents) or in Article II section 6 IntPatÜG (for German parts of European patents). This listing is exhaustive and contains in total five grounds of revocation. These grounds do not exactly match the grounds for opposition in EPO proceedings. In particular No. 3 "Usurpation" is unknown at the EPO level. Sections 22 and 21 of the Patent Act are applicable to German Patents; however, Article II section 6(1) IntPatÜG in connection with Article 138 EPC aligns the situation for EPs. Therefore, there is no reason to differentiate between German parts of European patents and national German patents.

No. 1—Lack of patentability (sections 22 and 21(1) No. 1 Patent Act): This refers to the lack of a patentable invention, which might be a lack of novelty, inventive step and/or industrial applicability. Also, statutorily barred subject matter, such as schemes, rules and methods of doing business as such, aesthetic creations as such, and computer programs as such[30] fall under this category.

No. 2—Lack of an enabling disclosure (sections 22 and 21(1) No. 2 Patent Act): This ground refers to the patentability requirement that the claimed subject matter shall be disclosed in a manner sufficiently clear and concise as to enable a person skilled in the art to carry out the invention. The relevant skilled person in the art must,

26. Council Regulation (EEC) No. 1768/92 of Jun. 18, 1992 concerning the creation of a supplementary protection certificate for medicinal products (OJ L 182, Jul. 2, 1992, 1).
27. Regulation (EC) No. 1610/96 of the European Parliament and of the Council of Jul. 23, 1996 concerning the creation of a supplementary protection certificate for plant protection products (OJ L 198, Aug. 8, 1996, 30).
28. Federal Supreme Court, I ZR 49/53, GRUR 1954, 317, "Entwicklungsgerät."
29. Federal Patent Court, BPatGE 24, 36; Federal Patent Court, BlPMZ 04, 58.
30. *See* Ch. 5, §5.01 "Patentable Subject Matter."

with the aid of his general skills, be in a position to implement the invention with the information he takes from the patent's disclosure. In general, lack of an enabling disclosure is a minor issue in most nullity proceedings, but may be of greater significance particularly for patents covering biotechnological inventions.

No. 3—Usurpation (sections 21 and 22(1) No. 3 Patent Act): If the injured party was in possession of an invention which was unlawfully taken away from him (usurpation) and then filed—without his consent—as a patent application, this is ground for revocation of the patent.[31] If the court finds that there was indeed usurpation, a revocation of the patent will result. In the alternative, an action can be filed seeking an assignment of the patent right according to section 8 of the Patent Act. An action filed on the basis of section 8 Patent Act is usually the better option for the injured party because it results in the assignment of the patent, whereas a nullity action based on ground No. 3 of section 21(1) Patent Act "Usurpation" would lead to a revocation of the patent.

No. 4—Inadmissible extensions (section 21(1) No. 4 Patent Act): A further ground for revocation exists where the subject matter of the patent extends beyond the content of the application, such as when extensions incorporated into the application during the course of the proceedings reach beyond the application as originally filed. This ground for revocation requires a comparison of the subject matter of the patent with the content of the application as filed. Where the subject matter exceeds the application as filed, there is an inadmissible extension. The subject matter of the patent is defined by the patent claims, specifically their scope of protection, which can be determined according to the general rules of claim construction.[32] The comparison requires a determination of the content of the application as originally filed from the standpoint of what a skilled person may deduce in total from the claims, descriptions and figures. If the skilled person may directly and unambiguously deduce the subject matter of the patent, i.e., its claims, from the content of the original application, then the extension would be admissible.[33]

No. 5—Extension of the scope of protection (section 22(1) Patent Act (second alternative)): The grant of the patent limits the right of the patentee to amend the claims in subsequent proceedings such as opposition, limitation or nullity proceedings. The scope of the patent, defined by the subject matter of the claims as granted, is the reference for assessing the admissibility of amendments. Inadmissible amendments limit the patentee's options with regard to claim amendment during nullity proceedings. Whereas amendments enlarging the scope of protection are not admissible, amendments which limit the scope of the patent are admissible, provided the combination of features is disclosed in the application underlying the patent as originally filed and is also comprised in the patent as granted. It is also admissible to introduce new features into a claim as long as the combination of features of the amended claim does

31. If the German part of a European patent is subject to a German nullity action, reference should be made to Art. 138(1)(e) EPC, Art. II s. 6 No. 5 IntPatÜG.
32. Federal Supreme Court, X ZR 184/98, GRUR 2001, 140, "Zeittelegramm."
33. *See* Ch. 5, §5.05 "Standards on Original Disclosure."

not extend beyond the disclosure of the patent application underlying the challenged patent as originally filed.[34]

Almost all grounds of revocation find their analogs in the provisions applicable to European opposition proceedings. The plaintiff of a nullity action may base the action on the same grounds as were argued in prior opposition proceedings, without estoppel.

§8.06 SPECIAL PROCEDURAL ASPECTS

[A] Scope of Nullity Actions

Nullity proceedings are adversarial. They are not initiated ex officio and depend on the requests of the plaintiff (section 99(1) GPA in combination with section 308 Code of Civil Procedure). Accordingly, if the plaintiff requests the invalidation of particular claims, the court would not review the validity of claims that are not covered by that request. The court's review is also limited to the asserted grounds of revocation. For instance, lack of enabling disclosure (sections 22 and 21(1) No. 2 GPA) is not contained in the court's review if it is not explicitly asserted.[35] Furthermore, the patentee is entitled to either fully object to the defendant's requests or to pursue a limited defense in view of a limited maintenance of the patent. He can request the complete or partial dismissal of the action. A partial dismissal of the request may be sought if only a limited scope of protection is reasonably defendable due to newly discovered prior art.

Even though the proceedings are adversarial in nature, the court considers the legal questions of the case and evaluates the facts on its own motion (ex officio) once the lawsuit has been initiated. According to section 87(1) of the GPA, the court investigates ex officio the facts of the case. The court is not bound by the parties' statements or their offers of proof. The court can even search for prior art on its own initiative if this is considered to be reasonable. However, in the context of an alleged public prior use, the court may request the alleging party to substantiate the alleged public prior use in detail, namely as to what was used, by whom, when and where. Due to the concept of ex officio proceedings, it is less problematic to submit newly discovered prior art during the proceedings provided that such submission is not considered abusive. However, if the court has set a deadline for submitting suitable requests or completing the pleadings, the need is even greater for submitting new prior art. Such a deadline could be set in a court order issued early in the proceedings in compliance with section 83(1) of the GPA. In such an order, the court will point to the aspects of the case that are presumably important to the decision and to which the parties are asked to adequately respond. If this order contains a deadline, the parties should do their best to sufficiently respond within the set timeframe because further attacks, including the submission of prior art, might be considered untimely and would only be admitted if sufficiently excused (*see* section 83(4) GPA).

34. *See* in detail Ch. 5, §5.05 "Standards of Original Disclosure."
35. Federal Patent Court, Decision of Jul. 9, 1980, 3 Ni 31/79.

[B] Withdrawal of Nullity Actions

The nullity proceedings can be terminated by means of a withdrawal. The plaintiff can file such a withdrawal at any time until the final termination of the nullity proceedings, even without the consent of the defendant.[36] The court would then not decide on the validity of the patent.[37] In contrast to opposition proceedings, the court cannot continue the proceedings on its own motion.

An already-issued negative preliminary opinion/qualified note of the court expressing concerns as to the validity of the patent becomes legally ineffective if the nullity action is withdrawn. No further legal effects would result from that negative preliminary opinion. It nevertheless has an unfavorable effect for the patentee because it is a public document, which could be discovered by any third party through a file inspection[38] and used in support of subsequent nullity proceedings. Even if the parties agree on it, there is no way to render the preliminary opinion confidential.

Even a first instance decision invalidating the patent would become ineffective if the withdrawal occurs prior to the rendering of the second instance decision of the Federal Supreme Court.[39] Withdrawals of nullity actions are usually caused by settlements reached during the proceedings. Of course, the first instance decision of the Federal Patent Court is publicly discoverable through a file inspection. It could challenge competitors to attack the patent with the same arguments in subsequent proceedings. Due to the withdrawal, the decision has no legal effect and does not represent a legal obstacle in enforcing the patent. However, it must be anticipated that a third party would refer to the negative decision and argue that it could successfully challenge the decision by means of a new nullity action. The strength of such argument depends on the particular situation and the extent to which the patentee can demonstrate that the first instance decision was wrong.

[C] Amendment of the Nullity Action During the Proceedings

Even though the principle of ex officio proceedings is applicable once the proceedings have been started, the subject matter of the proceedings lies basically in the hands of the parties. It is mainly determined by the allegations of the plaintiff in the complaint. The potential for later amendments to the action is determined by section 263 Code of Civil Procedure. This provision requires either that the defendant agree to the amendment or that the court find the amendment pertinent.[40] For example, if the plaintiff failed in the complaint to attack an independent claim of the granted patent, the court may include that omitted independent claim in the proceedings if the defendant agrees

36. Federal Supreme Court, GRUR 2014, 911, "Sitzgelenk."
37. Federal Supreme Court, BlPMZ 1953, 382, 386, "Konservendose"; Federal Supreme Court, Decision of Sep. 30, 2010, Xa ZR 57/08, BeckRS 2010, 28218.
38. *See* Ch. 8, §8.07 "Inspection of the Files."
39. Federal Supreme Court, I a ZR 64/63, GRUR 1964, 18, "Konditioniereinrichtung"; Federal Supreme Court, X ZR 25/86, GRUR 1993, 895, "Hartschaumplatten"; Federal Patent Court, decision from May 14, 2014, 5 Ni 50/12.
40. Federal Patent Court, decision from Sep. 9, 2015, 5 Ni 30/13 (EP).

(which he likely would not) or if the court considers it pertinent. The same applies if the plaintiff raises a new ground of revocation[41] that is not yet included in the filed nullity complaint.[42] The court is bound to the grounds of nullity as raised by the plaintiff and is not entitled to consider new grounds that were not raised.[43] An amendment to the action is difficult if it is requested after the lapse of the deadline set by the court's order pursuant to section 83(2) of GPA. This is the court order issued early in the proceedings wherein the court points to those aspects that are presumably important for the decision and to which the parties are asked to respond. If this order contains a deadline, the parties should do their best to sufficiently respond within the set timeframe. Further procedural changes requested by the parties after the lapse of the deadline might be considered untimely and would only be excusable in exceptional cases (*see* section 83(4) GPA).

Therefore, unless there are strategic reasons for limiting the attack on the patent, the plaintiff should include all of the granted claims in the nullity action and preferably base his attack on all possible grounds of nullity to avoid a possible preclusion of a later amendment of the action.

[D] Admissibility of Claim Amendments Filed During the Proceedings

The patentee may usually amend the claims of the patent during the course of validity proceedings, provided that the amendment does not exceed the scope of the original disclosure and/or the scope of protection of the patent as granted. Accordingly, the patentee may defend his patent with a main request and a set of auxiliary requests that generally represent suitable fallback positions. The court may set deadlines for filing such requests (section 83(2) Patent Act). An auxiliary request may combine features of an independent claim with features of dependent claims and/or features disclosed in the description.[44]

§8.07 INSPECTION OF THE FILES

In contrast to opposition proceedings at the EPO,[45] the files of the Federal Patent Court cannot be investigated through an online service. They can be inspected—in the form of photocopies or disks—by either party or by third parties on request (section 99(3) Patent Act). The third party need not provide any reason or justification for inspecting the files, or reveal for whom the inspection is carried out.[46]

41. *See* Ch. 8, §8.05.
42. Federal Supreme Court, Decision of Jun. 24, 1997, X ZR 13/94, Vorrichtung zum Auspressen; Federal Supreme Court, Decision of May 11, 2010, X ZR 51/06, GRUR-Prax 2010, 366, "Polymerisierbare Zementmischung."
43. Federal Patent Court, BlPMZ 2004, 58.
44. The combination of features contained in auxiliary request must be sufficiently disclosed and shall not extend beyond the disclosure of the patent application underlying the challenged patent as originally filed. *See* details in Ch. 5, §5.05.
45. *See* www.epoline.org.
46. Federal Supreme Court, X ZR 4/00, GRUR 2001, 143, "Akteneinsicht XV"; Federal Supreme Court, X ZR 84/11, Decision of Dec. 7, 2011.

Objections by the patentee to grants of inspection requests usually fail. In exceptional cases, provided that the patent owner can demonstrate a *protectable interest* (section 99(3) Patent Act), the Court may exclude parts of the file from inspection. Such protectable interests may concern trade and commercial secrets or internal company data.[47] Information that has been introduced under violation of a protective order from US-pretrial discovery proceedings may likewise be excluded from inspection.[48] Even statements concerning the scope of protection of the patent with respect to an infringing device have been excluded from inspection.[49]

However, usually the interests of the public in reviewing the files are considered more important. In particular, the patentee will not be protected against the discovery of facts, such as expert opinions,[50] or prior art contained in the file that may be problematic for the validity of the patent. The patentee is also not protected against a file inspection if the nullity action has been withdrawn after a settlement.[51]

If the request is accepted, the files are rendered available to the claimant usually by means of copies taken from files or provided electronically.

§8.08 INTERPLAY WITH PARALLEL PROCEEDINGS

[A] German Infringement Proceedings

[1] Stays of Infringement Proceedings Pending the Resolution of Validity

An important aspect of the split system is section 148 of the Code of Civil Procedure, which allows the infringement court to stay the proceedings pending resolution of the nullity challenge. The threshold questions that need to be addressed by the court before it can stay the infringement proceedings are illustrated in a separate chapter.[52]

[2] Effects of the Nullity Decisions

Once the patent has been finally revoked in part or in total—i.e., by a decision that cannot be appealed—the revocation of the patent is effective *ab initio* and has effect on everyone. In other words, it is as if the patent and application had never existed (section 21(3) GPA).

The revocation of a patent also has important implications for pending infringement proceedings. The infringement proceedings will be closed to the extent the patent was revoked. In situations where a patent has been nullified after termination of the infringement proceedings, and the proceedings have already been closed by an

47. Federal Supreme Court, X ZA 1/71, GRUR 1972, 195, "Akteneinsicht VIII."
48. Federal Patent Court, BPatGE 34, 83.
49. Federal Supreme Court, X ZR 133/05, GRUR 2007, 133, "Akteneinsicht XVII"; Federal Supreme Court, Decision of Jan. 30, 2008, X ZR 1/07, GRUR 2008, 633, "Akteneinsicht XIX."
50. Federal Patent Court, BPatGE 22, 66, 68.
51. Federal Patent Court, BPatGE 34, 9.
52. *See* Ch. 10, §10.02[D][2] "Suspension of the Proceedings."

executable final decision (favorable to the patentee), the adversary party, i.e., the former accused infringer, must begin a separate new trial if he seeks to correct an inconsistency between the nullity and infringement proceedings.[53] This action is called an action for restitution. It would be directed against the final infringement judgment and is aimed at obtaining a reopening of the infringement proceedings so that the action for infringement can be lifted. This remedy can also be applied in case of only a partial nullification of the patent, for instance, where the use of a feature additionally incorporated in the patent claim by the revocation decision was not considered in the previous infringement proceedings and is not used in the alleged infringement.[54] The filing of an action for restitution is subject to a time limit of one month from the date on which the party concerned becomes aware of the cause for restitution.[55] In addition, the action for restitution can only be filed during a time of five years after the infringement judgment became final. This even applies if the cause of restitution, such as the revocation of the patent, occurs after the five-year time period. That time limit shall provide legal peace even though it may have a detrimental effect on the accused "infringer" in such an exceptional case of late patent revocation.

Limitations of the claim imposed in nullity proceedings by the Federal Patent Court result in a retroactive legal change to the wording of the claim. An added feature must then be considered when construing the claim. Such a change should be anticipated by the plaintiff in the infringement proceedings, and if possible, the factual submissions should cover features of the accused embodiment that are also reproduced by a presumably limited scope of protection.

The relevant grounds of the decision dealing with the change to the wording of the claim are deemed to replace or stand alongside the patent description and have to be considered for the claim construction, even though these parts of the grounds have no binding effect on the infringement courts.[56] Accordingly, if a European patent is maintained in limited form, the reasons for the decision can be used, like a part of the description, to interpret the claims, but only insofar as they concern the amendment,[57] and only if the description is not also amended.

Although the grounds rejecting an action for nullity do not bind the trial judge, they may give an indication as to how the skilled person would interpret the claim.

Moreover, licenses become cancellable to the extent the license is based on a revoked patent or on revoked parts of the patent from the time of revocation of the patent. The revocation, however, has generally no impact on the validity of the license in general, and for the payment of royalties in particular, for the past.[58] That is,

53. Section 580 No. 6 Code of Civil Procedure (action for restitution).
54. Federal Supreme Court, Decision of Apr. 17, 2012, X ZR 55/09, GRUR 2012, 753 = IIC 2012, 855, "*Tintenpatrone III.*"
55. Section 586(1) and (2) ZPO.
56. Federal Supreme Court, GRUR 2007, 778, "Ziehmaschinenzugeinheit I"; Decision of Apr. 15, 2010, Xa ZB 10/09, GRUR 2010, 950 = IIC 2011, 363, "*Walzenformgebungsmaschine.*"
57. Federal Supreme Court, Decision of May 12, 1998, X ZR 115/96, GRUR 1999, 145 = IIC 1999, 805, "Stoßwellen-Lithotripter"; Decision of Apr. 17, 2007, X ZR 72/05, GRUR 2007, 778 = IIC 2008, 223, "Zugmaschinenzugeinheit."
58. Federal Supreme Court, GRUR 1957, 595, "Verwandlungstisch"; GRUR 2002, 787, "Abstreiferleiste"; GRUR, 2005, 935, "Vergleichsempfehlung II m.w.N."

royalties paid for the past must not be reimbursed even if the patent is later revoked. This case law has recently by confirmed by a decision of the ECJ.[59] It ruled that competition law does not prevent royalties being paid for technology protected by revoked patents.

[3] Inconsistent Statements

Statements made during the prosecution are basically without relevance for the interpretation of the patent claim so long as such statements are not explicitly taken from the patent specification.[60] Thus, problematic statements made by the patentee during prosecution concerning the understanding of the patent claim are irrelevant for the claim construction.[61] They may however represent an indication of how the relevant skilled person in the art would understand the patent.[62] Even statements made by the patentee during nullity proceedings are principally irrelevant for the claim construction.[63] There is however an exception to this rule,[64] namely where the patentee declares during nullity proceedings that she or he does not claim patent protection for particular embodiments. The accused infringer may refer to that statement or declaration provided that he was involved in those proceedings. He is thus allowed to argue in the parallel infringement proceedings that a narrower scope of the claim must be applied. The accused infringer can rely on these statements made by the patent owner, provided the statements were made in parallel nullity proceedings between the same parties.[65] This is taken from the general prohibition of *venire contra factum proprium* which prohibits the same party from taking inconsistent positions and acting contradictorily vis-à-vis the other party in the two proceedings. This is an exception to the rule that statements made by the applicant in grant proceedings, or by the patentee in nullity proceedings, are irrelevant for the claim construction in infringement proceedings. Because this prohibition against contradictory behavior also applies to the accused infringer, his submissions should be uniform in both proceedings as well.

[B] UPC Proceedings

[1] Unitary Patents

UPs do not and will never fall under the jurisdiction of the Federal Patent Court. Accordingly, an overlap of UPC proceedings relating to UPs and proceedings of the Federal Patent Court is unlikely.

59. ECJ C-567/14.
60. Federal Supreme Court, X ZR 43/01, GRUR 2002, 511, 513, "Kunststoffrohrteil."
61. Federal Supreme Court, X ZR 73/95, NJW-RR 1998, 184, "Weichvorrichtung II."
62. Federal Supreme Court, X ZR 57/96, GRUR 1998, 895, "Regenbecken."
63. Federal Supreme Court, X ZR 6/91, GRUR 1993, 886, "Weichvorrichtung I"; Federal Supreme Court, X ZR 73/95, NJW-RR 1998, 184, "Weichvorrichtung II."
64. *Ibid.*
65. Federal Supreme Court, X ZR 6/91 and X ZR 73/95, Weichvorrichtung I/II, respectively.

[2] Ordinary EPs

Opted-out ordinary European patents: Owners of ordinary European patents may opt out from the exclusive jurisdiction of the UPC until the end of the transitional period. The opt-out takes effect upon registration in the public register provided that all conditions for it have been fulfilled. The opt-outs for European patents only apply to the patent as a whole. It is not possible to opt out only some national parts of the European bundle patent. The European patent thus remains outside the jurisdiction of the UPCA even after the end of the transitional period.[66] A European patent for which a valid opt-out has been filed will remain beyond the jurisdiction of the UPC and may only be litigated through the appropriate national courts or authorities, on a country-by-country basis.[67] In this manner, the Federal Patent Court will have authority to adjudicate the validity of the German part of an ordinary European patent. Accordingly, it is unlikely that UPC proceedings will directly impact the proceedings of the Federal Patent Court in the case of patents that are the subject of a valid opt-out.

Non-opted-out ordinary European patents or withdrawal of the opt-out: An owner of an ordinary European patent may decline to file an opt-out. Alternatively, a patent owner that had previously filed an opt-out may decide to reverse course, and subsequently file an "opt-in."[68] In both these cases, ordinary European patents would fall within the jurisdiction of the UPC as well as of the national courts (so-called split jurisdiction). Accordingly, a conflict between UPC proceedings and proceedings of the Federal Patent Court may thus occur. Despite the misleading wording of Article 83(1) UPCA, it is common understanding that the national courts retain jurisdiction over ordinary European patents. Possible conflicts of jurisdiction are governed by the Brussels-I-Regulation (Regulation EU 1215/2012), as amended by Regulation EU 542/2014. Accordingly, the UPC is deemed to be an ordinary court like any other court of an EU Member State.[69] If a court case is pending with a court of an EU Member State, any other court invoked in a lawsuit with the same parties and having the same subject matter has to await the decision of the court with the first-filed matter.[70]

§8.09 FINANCIAL ASPECTS OF NULLITY ACTION

Court fees along with attorney fees need to be considered when budgeting a case. When filing the nullity action, the plaintiff has to advance the court fees for the first instance proceeding. At the end of the proceedings, these costs have to be paid by the

66. This can be concluded from the wording of Art. 83(3) sentence 2 UPCA: It allows opt-outs to be registered until one month before expiry of the transitional period.
67. Despite the somewhat misleading wording of Art. 83(3) UPCA, it seems that an opt-out takes away every jurisdiction from the UPC, not only the "exclusive competence." The UPC will not have a "non-exclusive competence" after an opt-out. This can be followed from the wording of Art. 32(1) and (2) UPCA. The UPC is either exclusively competent (Art. 32(1) UPCA) or has no competence at all (Art. 32(2) UPCA). By taking away the "exclusive competence," no competence remains and the parties have to litigate on a national basis.
68. Article 83(4) UPCA.
69. Article 71a(2)(a) Reg. 1215/2012 as amended by Reg. 542/2014.
70. Article 29 Reg. 1215/2012 as amended by Reg. 542/2014.

party which loses the case. If there is no fully prevailing party, then the costs are shared among the parties. A further financial aspect concerns the question of whether a security for the defendant's costs of the proceedings must be provided (*see* §8.09[B] below).

[A] Court Fees

The court fees depend on the litigation value. At the beginning of the proceedings, the plaintiff provides a preliminary estimate, which is stated in the complaint. The litigation value should correspond to the plaintiff's objective economic interests of the claims as requested in the complaint. It is often difficult to determine the litigation value. If the defendant does not object to the plaintiff's estimation, usually the court renders a decision based on the preliminary fixed litigation value. However, a litigation value that is applied in parallel infringement proceedings is usually decisive for the nullity proceedings. Due to the public nature of nullity proceedings, the value of the infringement proceedings is even increased by 25%.[71] The court fees of both instances can be taken from the charts below, which start from a rather low litigation value (EUR 0.5 million) to the maximum cap value (EUR 30 million).

[1] Court Fees: First Instance (Federal Patent Court)

Table 8.1 shows the court fees in case of first instance proceedings. They are capped if the amount in dispute exceeds EUR 30 million. These fees, which must be advanced by the plaintiff when filing a nullity action, represent a serious hurdle. Opposition proceedings are comparably inexpensive. However, they can only be filed until expiration of the opposition period. Even revocation proceedings at the UPC are less expensive (*see* above §7.07).

Table 8.1 Court Fees: First Instance (Federal Patent Court)

Litigation Value (EUR)	*Court Fees (EUR)*
500,000	17,554.50
1,000,000	26,464.50
2,000,000	44,284.50
5,000,000	97,744.50
10,000,000	186,844.50
30,000,000	543,244.50

71. Federal Supreme Court, GRUR 2011, 757, "Nichtigkeitsstreitwert."

[2] *Court Fees: Second Instance (Federal Supreme Court)*

Table 8.2 shows the court fees in case of second instance proceedings.

Table 8.2 Court Fees: Second Instance (Federal Supreme Court)

Litigation Value (EUR)	*Court Fees (EUR)*
500,000	23,406.00
1,000,000	35,286.00
2,000,000	59,046.00
5,000,000	130,326.00
10,000,000	249,126.00
30,000,000	724,326.00

[3] *Costs for Court Expert*

Due to modified rules, the Federal Supreme Court does in principle not appoint court experts. In the authors' experience, the costs of court experts range from EUR 10,000 to EUR 20,000, depending on the complexity of the case.

[B] Security for Defendant's Costs of the Proceedings

Upon request of the defendant, the plaintiff must furnish security for the costs of the proceedings, provided its general residence lies outside the European Community (section 81(6) Patent Act). Some countries—e.g., Japan, the Russian Federation, and Switzerland—have concluded bilateral agreements with Germany exempting their residents from this duty. However, residents of the USA, China, Canada and Korea are currently not exempted from the duty to furnish security of costs. These costs are determined by the court and have to be paid within a time limit set by the court. Instead of payment of the security costs, a bank warranty of an accredited German bank may be furnished as a security.

§8.10 OTHER EUROPEAN JURISDICTIONS

National patents, the national parts of European patents or, if available, utility models may be subject to review by national authorities, i.e., national patent offices or national courts, as to whether or not the requirements for patentability are satisfied. A number of national measures exist across Europe for challenging the validity of patents, either in separate revocation or cancelation proceedings to be initiated in national decision-making bodies, such as courts or patent offices. These national measures are not harmonized in Europe. There might be differences from one national system to another. These differences must be well considered when establishing a patent portfolio strategy.

In most European jurisdictions, the validity of a patent can be challenged as a counterclaim or defense in infringement proceedings in view of the revocation of the asserted patent. The judicial authority thus also takes a decision on the validity of the patent right.

Such counterclaims are not available in Germany, nor in jurisdictions such as Austria and Hungary. They operate a "split system" as described above for the German system. In contrast hereto, unified proceedings are characterized in that infringement is not considered independently of the analysis of validity. This may lead to a more consistent approach of claim construction. The plaintiff is thus prevented from putting forward a broad construction in the infringement proceedings but a narrow construction for validity in the revocation proceedings. The latter is the situation at the UPC.

CHAPTER 9

Pre-suit Considerations

§9.01 INTRODUCTION

A patent owner who discovers that his or her patent is being disregarded by competitors must first establish a suitable strategy to remedy the harm as efficiently, quickly, at low risk and at low cost as possible. The patentee's options initially depend on the territorial scope of patent protection. The simplest scenario is if the patentee only holds a single national patent, in which case the sole opportunity is to pursue infringement in that country's national courts. More typically, the patentee owns a European patent that has been validated in several countries. If he additionally owns a US or Chinese patent, or patents in relation to the same invention in other countries, and if patent infringements occur in many countries of protection, the possible avenues of enforcement expand to potentially assert patents in parallel in all these countries. However, a parallel enforcement of patent rights in many countries of protection is usually associated with high costs. To economize, it is advisable to identify preferred jurisdictions that are primarily used to implement enforcement measures. The selection depends on a case-by-case analysis. The following questions may play a role in this analysis:

- In which countries enforcement actions against the infringer(s) are most effective? From the patent owner's perspective, it could make sense to enforce the patent in a country where the infringing products are manufactured. The harm can thus be tackled at the root.
- In which countries does the injunction have the greatest effect? It might be purposeful to interrupt trade routes. The Netherlands is a small country. Nevertheless, gateways for infringing products can be found there, as important trade ports (especially Rotterdam) are located there. The strategy could be to close such gateways.
- In which countries can the greatest damages be expected? It is important to understand the interplay between the size of the country, or size of the

infringer's market, and the potential size of the award under the governing legal framework. Therefore, larger compensation can be expected in the US than in Germany.

- In which countries of protection do reliable enforcement systems exist? How fast do the enforcement systems work? Is the enforcement systems structured in a patentee-friendly manner? How predicable is the outcome of a lawsuit?
- Are positive enforcement results in one country helpful for the enforcement of the patent in other countries?
- What is the scope of transterritorial enforcement? For instance, the UPC has the jurisdiction to grant injunctions in any Member State of the UPCA.
- What risks must the patent owner consider when enforcing his patents? The patentee should assess potential counterclaim risks, as well as risks flowing from loss of the IP, including loss of existing royalty streams.
- In which court are the costs of proceedings low?
- To what extent is discovery available? The possibility of obtaining needed evidence through compulsory process depends on the procedural rules applicable in the countries of protection. There are major differences between European countries. Even though some discovery is available under the UPC and in many European countries, it is typically more restricted than in the US.

The list of questions is not exhaustive. The questions depend on the individual case. The task of the legal representative is to ask the right questions and to work out the different aspects in answer to the questions so that, as a result, a strategy tailored to the client can be worked out.

§9.02 UPC OR GERMAN COURTS

The selection of either the UPC or a German court for an infringement action depends at a threshold level on the underlying type of patent to be asserted against an accused infringer. UPs fall exclusively under the jurisdiction of the UPC.[1] They cannot be litigated in German national courts. By contrast, German national patents and German utility models are exclusively in the hands of the German national courts. The UPC has no jurisdiction over German national patents or utility models. This jurisdictional distinction depends neither on the protected technology nor on the scope of protection conferred by the patent. It is driven by the type of patent obtained. Accordingly, thinking downstream to the choice of forum is an important strategic consideration when choosing the types of patent rights to build into a patent portfolio.

Ordinary European patents provide a more complex array of enforcement options, particularly in view of the seven-year transitional provision of Article 83 UPCA.[2] During this time (which may be extended an additional seven years by the Administrative Committee), it will remain possible to enforce ordinary European

1. Article (3)(a) UPCA.
2. *See* Ch. 4, §4.02[A][1][b].

patents through national courts.[3] With respect to such traditional patents, the jurisdiction of the UPC is not exclusive during that transitional period. Rather, during the transitional period, actions based on ordinary European patents can be filed either with the UPC or with the national courts ("shared jurisdiction"). Patentees wishing to avoid having their claims subject to revocation actions at the UPC may proactively "opt out" from the UPC's jurisdiction by filing a notification as provided by Article 83(3) UPCA. Opting-out is not possible if an action has already been brought before the UPC. Rule 5(6) of the RoP clarifies that even if the action has already been concluded, an opt-out from the UPC jurisdiction would be impossible. Accordingly, once an action has been filed at the UPC under an ordinary European patent, the patent is forever precluded from an "opt-out" from the UPC's jurisdiction. The purpose of this rule is to avoid conflicting judgments of the UPC and of national courts. Strategically, patent owners should note that third parties might attempt to exploit this rule by preemptively filing actions at the UPC, to lock in jurisdiction there for the life of the patent. Thus, patent applicants may wish to proactively file an opt-out notification to block challengers' recourse to the UPC. The applicant may still withdraw its opt-out notification later.[4] However, according to Rule 5(8) RoP, a withdrawal of an opt-out (i.e., an "opt-in") is no longer possible once an action has been commenced in a national court. The withdrawal is even ineffective after the action has been concluded (Figure 9.1).

Figure 9.1 Jurisdiction in Relation to the Underlying Patent Right

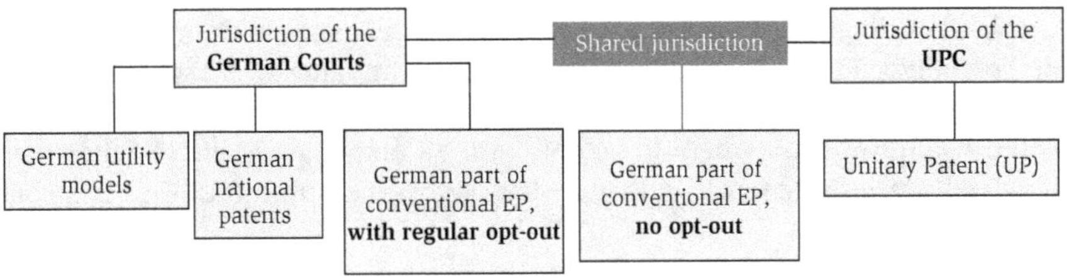

§9.03 INTERNATIONAL ASPECTS

[A] UPC

[1] Introduction

A question of jurisdiction may concern the relationship:

(1) between divisions of the UPC (internal attribution of jurisdiction);
(2) between the UPC and national courts of the Contracting Member States;

3. Article 83(1) UPCA.
4. Article 5(8) RoP.

(3) between the UPC and courts of EU States without adherence to the UPCA, such as Croatia, Poland, and Spain; and
(4) between the UPC and courts of non-EU States, such as UK and US.

[2] Subject Matter Jurisdiction of the UPC

The Brussels Ia Regulation and Lugano Convention provide a framework for establishing and exercising jurisdiction. Both frameworks govern the UPC.[5] The UPC is a court with limited jurisdiction for particular kinds of actions spelled out in Article 32(1) UPCA. The list of actions that are under the UPC's jurisdiction includes, for example, actions for actual and threatened infringement of patents; actions for declaration of noninfringement, actions for revocation of patents; and actions for monetary and injunctive relief arising from patents. The UPC's jurisdiction over these actions in relation to European patents will be exclusive upon lapse of the seven-year transitional period. In other words, the "subject matters" listed in Article 32(1) are assigned to the UPC, and the Contracting Member States will have lost that jurisdiction following the expiration of the transitional period. Outside the enumerated causes of action, the UPC has no jurisdiction, and those matters must be litigated through national courts.[6]

[3] Allocation of Jurisdiction among the UPC and National Courts

The Brussels Ia Regulation treats the UPC as a court belonging to Contracting Member States' own judicial system. The UPC thus ranks on the same level as a national court of a Contracting Member State. According to Article 71(b)(1) Brussels Ia Regulation,[7] the UPC has jurisdiction where the courts of the Contracting Member States would otherwise have jurisdiction in a matter that is governed by the UPCA. The consequences of this include:

- The UPC cannot revoke ordinary European patents regarding their national parts validated in non-Contracting Member State, such as Spain. This follows from Article 24(4) Brussels Ia Regulation, which provides that the courts of each Member State shall have exclusive jurisdiction in proceedings concerned with the registration or validity of any European patent granted for that Member State.
- Persons domiciled in a Member State may, regardless of their nationality, be sued in the courts of that Member State, pursuant to Article 4(1) Brussels Ia Regulation.
- A person domiciled in a Member State may be sued in another Member State in matters relating to tort, delict, or quasi-delict, in the courts for the place

5. Article 31 UPCA.
6. Article 32(2) UPCA.
7. Regulation (EU) No. 542/2014.

where the harmful event occurred or may occur, pursuant to Article 7(2) Brussels Ia Regulation.
- Jurisdiction over a plurality of defendants through the binding effect of "close connection" is governed by Article 8 Brussels Ia Regulation.

[4] Internal Allocation of Jurisdiction Within the UPC

There are unresolved inconsistencies among the ways that jurisdiction is allocated within the UPC. Article 33 UPCA governs the internal allocation of that jurisdiction. The allocation of cases within the UPC does not consistently follow the traditional assignment rules of the Brussels Ia Regulation. Whereas the Brussels Ia Regulation generally prohibits EU Member States from establishing agreements on jurisdiction, enforcement, and recognition of judgments, Articles 71a-d Brussels Ia Regulation deviates from this approach. Thus, if it is argued that the rules of the UPCA must comply with the Brussels Ia Regulation, a conflict may become apparent because the allocation of jurisdiction among the divisions of the UPC according to the UPCA is not fully in line with the rules of the Brussels Ia Regulation. For instance, according to Article 33(1) UPCA, the UPC's Central Division has jurisdiction over patent infringement cases against defendants that are domiciled outside the EU, such as in the US. It could be argued that the allocation contradicts Article 6(1) Brussels Ia Regulation because this provision refers to the national law according to which the court of the place of tort has jurisdiction. Likewise, the UPC's Central Division has jurisdiction over cases where the infringement occurs in a State without local division. The allocation to the UPC's central division thus deviates from the provisions of the Brussels Ia Regulation. It could be argued here that the allocation of jurisdiction under Article 33 UPCA represent an internal arrangement of the UPC for which the Brussels Ia Regulation is inapplicable. Nevertheless, concerns cannot be fully eliminated.

These exemplary inconsistencies create legal risks for plaintiffs that base their cases on a assumed jurisdiction of the UPC, which do not comply with the standards of the Brussels Ia Regulation and may thus be challenged by the defendant. Even if there are arguments in favor of the lawfulness of the rules, it is certain that defendants will take advantage of this uncertainty. They will question the jurisdiction of the central division. Such cases might trigger an appeal, with ultimate resolution by the ECJ. Plaintiffs bear the risk of delay and potential upsetting of judgments for cases in which these jurisdictional inconsistencies are challenged.

[5] Conflicts in Relation to Non-opted-out EPs Within Transitional Phase

The UPCA provides for exclusive jurisdiction in the UPC for those kinds of cases enumerated in Article 32(1) UPCA. Nonetheless, that exclusive jurisdiction is subject to the transitional period during which national courts continue to possess concurrent jurisdiction over ordinary European patents, as governed by Article 83 UPCA. An infringement or revocation action could be filed with a national court or the UPC, which could create conflicts. A patent owner may avoid the parallel (or shared) jurisdiction by duly declaring an opt-out to remove the patent from the jurisdiction of the UPC.[8]

The overlapping jurisdiction between the UPC and national courts during the transitional phase is governed by the Brussels Ia Regulation, which seeks to mitigate conflicts between these courts. In particular, Article 71c(2) Brussels Ia Regulation provides as follows:

> Articles 29 to 32 shall apply where, during the transitional period referred to in Article 83 of the UPC Agreement, proceedings are brought in the Unified Patent Court and in a court of a Member State party to the UPC Agreement.

The basic idea behind this provision of the Brussels Ia Regulation is that the court of a first-filed action will predominate in adjudication of the conflict over another court of a second-filed action in relation to the same matter. For example, consider a matter based on an ordinary European patent (without "opt-out") that is brought before the UPC. Later, another action is brought before a court of a Contracting Member State. If these proceedings involve the "same cause of action" and the "same parties," the second court shall of its own motion stay its proceedings until the jurisdiction of the court of the firs filed action is finally established. A case arises from the "same cause of action" if the same patent is asserted against the same accused product or method and same party. According to Article 71c(1) Brussels Ia Regulation, the same rules apply to the relationship between the UPC and courts of non-Contracting Member States of the EU.

The jurisdictional gaps between the UPC and the courts of non-Contracting Member States create potential for strategic maneuvers. For example, "Torpedo" actions may have a resurgence. The tactic behind a so-called Torpedo is to file a declaratory judgment case (for instance, claiming noninfringement not only of the Italian part but also of the German part of the ordinary European patent, and maybe of other national parts of that patent) in a slow-acting jurisdiction. This could preclude fast-acting courts, like German courts, from proceeding with an infringement action (on the German part of the ordinary European patent). Now, the opportunity to pursue such measure may arise by filing a declaratory action on a non-opted-out European patent before a national court of a non-Contracting Member State of the EU (such as Spain), which may block a later UPC action on the same patent. For example, if a challenger files a negative declaratory judgment action for noninfringement in Spain in relation to the Spanish, German, French and UK part of an ordinary European patent, this action would preempt a corresponding infringement action at the UPC. The UPC would have to stay the proceedings commensurate with the scope of the first-filed matter in Spain. The same applies in relation to a court belonging to the State of the Lugano Convention (such as Switzerland) and an infringement action subsequently filed with the UPC.

It will take time for case law to develop to resolve additional complexities associated with the jurisdictional interplay between the UPC and the courts of the

8. Article 82(3) UPCA.

Member States. Several aspects arising from Article 71 Brussels Ia Regulation present open issues. For example, the extent of the blocking effect of a first-petitioned court is not yet determined. For instance, it could be that the first-filed infringement action does not cover all national parts of the European patent. Those parts which are not covered by the subject matter pending with the first-filed action apparently do not represent the "same cause of action" and consequently do not block the UPC to adjudicate the case, in particular with respect to those parts of the European patent which are not coterminous with the first-filed action. A similar problem may occur if a revocation action against a traditional non-opted-out European patent has been filed with a national court. Article 24(4) of Brussels Ia Regulation provides that in this situation, this national court shall have the exclusive jurisdiction as to the national part of the European patent which has been validated in the country of that court. The blocking effect of such action is apparently limited to the national part of the European patent against which the revocation claim is made. The UPC may thus still take a decision with respect to all other UPCA States, in which the ordinary European patent has been validated. However, Article 30 of Brussels Ia Regulation might be applicable in the present context. This provision allows staying the proceedings in cases where "related actions" are pending. Any court other than the first-petitioned court may then stay its proceedings. Article 30 of Brussels Ia Regulation functions as a sort of "safety-net" for actions which do not meet the requirements of Article 29 of Brussels Ia Regulation. Matters that carry a risk of conflicting judgments, even if the judgments can be separately enforced, may represent "related actions" for the purposes of this provision.[9]

[6] Forum of Location of Assets: Long-Arm Jurisdiction

The UPC may provide a forum to pursue a claim for damages arising from acts of infringement arising outside the territory of the EU. That is, Article 71(b)(3) of Brussels Ia Regulation provides a mechanism to extend the jurisdiction of the UPC to EPC Member States which do not belong to the EU and are not Lugano convention states (e.g., UK, Turkey).

> Article 71(b) reads: "(3) where a common court has jurisdiction over a defendant under point 2 in a dispute relating to an infringement of a European patent giving rise to damage within the Union, that court may also exercise jurisdiction in relation to damage arising outside the Union from such an infringement."

The provision could be interpreted in a broad manner that the UPC may consider itself to have jurisdiction over EP patents with designations outside the EU (e.g., UK, Turkey), so long as there is also infringement within the EU and the defendant has assets within the reach of the UPC. Does this mean that UPC may take decisions, for instance, on the Turkish designation of an EP patent? The provision seems to have a narrower scope. The provision literally deals with damages arising in a third country from infringing acts taking place within a Contracting Member State. The scope of the

9. ECJ, Case C 144/86, *Gubisch Maschinenfabrik v. Palumbo*.

provision is thus limited to the assessment of damages in relation to infringing acts committed in UPCA States but having (exceptionally) damaging effects or results outside the territory of the UPC. This follows from the words "*from such an infringement.*" A broader understanding would likely conflict with Article 34 of the UPCA stipulating that "Decisions of the Court shall cover, in the case of a European Patent, the territory of those Contracting Member States for which the European Patent has effect." That said, the requirements of the long-arm jurisdiction under Article 71(b)(3) Brussels Ia Regulation are met, for example, in the following case.

The defendant is domiciled/seated in Turkey. He infringes the European patent in a UPCA state and causes damage there. In addition, it is required that:

(1) assets of the defendant are available in a UPCA state and, at least, part of the damages can be covered by these assets; and
(2) the dispute has a sufficient connection with the Member State of the UPC in which the assets are located.

Such a connection is sufficient if the plaintiff is domiciled in the Member State where the assets are located,[10] or the defendant has committed acts of infringement in the Member State where the assets are[11] or evidence is located there. Thus, the assets substitute a missing domicile, seat, or residence of the defendant. Furthermore, the "long-arm" jurisdiction is not available in respect of infringements occurring in any of the Lugano Convention states if the defendant is domiciled in a Lugano Member State. This follows from the primacy of the Lugano convention which does not acknowledge the "long-arm" jurisdiction of the UPC.

[B] German Courts

[1] International Aspect: Perspective of German Courts

According to section 143 of the GPA, there are special District Courts in Germany (twelve) with jurisdiction to hear patent infringement actions. These courts are geographically distributed throughout the German territory. These courts are namely: District Court Berlin, District Court Braunschweig, District Court Düsseldorf, District Court Erfurt, District Court Frankfort, District Court Hamburg, District Court Leipzig, District Court Magdeburg, District Court Mannheim, District Court München, District Court Nürnberg-Fürth and District Court Saarbrucken. The district courts of Düsseldorf, Mannheim and Munich adjudicate the vast majority of patent infringement cases. The selection of one of these courts depends in part upon the question of "local competence." It is permissible to file a complaint with the court where the defendant is located or has its seat (section 12 Code of Civil Procedure), but more important is the forum of *actus in tort* (section 32 Code of Civil Procedure). Accordingly, the plaintiff

10. Explanatory Memorandum of Brussels Ia Regulation (3.3).
11. *Ibid.*

can file the lawsuit within a district wherein the infringement has been committed. These are the places where the accused product has been produced, has been offered or brought onto the market. In the case of an offer, the infringing acts are not only committed where the offer has been made but also where the offer is received or can be perceived by potential interested parties.[12] This basically also applies to an offer published through a webpage that can be perceived by an internet user in Germany. The decisive factor is whether the internet offer may establish a sufficient connection to the German territory. The language of the offer does often not affect the forum determination. Thus, the webpage of interest need not be written in German to confer jurisdiction. Any widely used language, such as English, could be sufficient. It is not necessary that the internet state a price or recite the sale conditions. Rather, at least an objective visitor and potential customer should be sufficiently notified to consider the presentation on the website as a trigger to ask for more information about the product in view of an eventual purchase. Accordingly, when there has been an internet offer of the accused product, a lawsuit could be filed in any of the twelve district courts, and the choice of the court would only depend upon the plaintiff's strategic considerations. A foreign company, even without any affiliates in Germany and without having shipped any products in the past to Germany, which presents its products on its website, could unknowingly infringe a German patent, provided that the webpage is objectively addressed to the German public.[13] This is usually the case as long as German Internet users might have the impression that the webpage is addressed to them. A diligent company could avoid these consequences by means of a disclaimer posted on its website clearly indicating that the concerned products are not available for sale in Germany. However, such disclaimer would not be effective if the accused products are nevertheless shipped to the German market, even if the transaction was triggered by a test purchase prior to litigation, for instance, by a straw man tied to the patentee.[14]

Indeed, patentees may secure jurisdiction in Germany by ordering a product through a straw man, particularly in cases where there is no clear offer on the internet to sell into Germany. Even the shipment of accused products to a company situated outside the German territory might be considered to be an infringement of a German patent as soon as it is known that these products are supposed to be commercialized on the German market.[15] Accordingly, it may be sufficient to establish jurisdiction in Germany by showing that a shipment was made to a company which the accused infringer knows would subsequently sell the products on the German market.[16] The first offer or presentation of a product at a trade show in Germany may be sufficient to establish jurisdiction in Germany.[17] Even an international trade show taking place

12. Appeal Court Düsseldorf, Decision of Feb. 23, 2012, I-2 U 134/10, "Run-Flat-Vorrichtung."
13. Court of Justice of the European Union, Decision of Jan. 22, 2015, C 441/13, "Hejduk."
14. Appeal Court Düsseldorf, Decision of Jan. 28, 2010, GRUR-RR 2010, 368, I-2 U 131/08, "Testkauf patentverletzender DVDs."
15. District Court Düsseldorf, 4b O 199/06, "Elektrisches Steckergehäuse."
16. District Court Düsseldorf, InstGE 1, 154, "Rohrverzweigung"; District Court Düsseldorf, 4a O 212/08, "Schneeketten."
17. District Court Düsseldorf, 4a O 113/06, "GPRS-Mobiltelephone," Appeal Court Düsseldorf, Decision of Feb. 23, 2012, I-2 U 134/10, "Run-Flat-Vorrichtung"; Appeal Court Düsseldorf, Decision of Mar. 27, 2014, 15 U 19/14, "Sterilcontainer II."

outside Germany could potentially provide a basis for exercising jurisdiction in Germany if German visitors attend such fairs. The plaintiff must aver sufficient facts to show that the offer made by the accused infringer on such an international trade show has an impact on German territory. It would thus not be sufficient to only refer to the attendance of German visitors at such a trade show and to infer from that attendance that an offer to sell a product had thus impacted the German territory. However, it could be sufficient if the plaintiff names at least one German visitor who took along advertisement material, which was subsequently used in discussions with colleagues or superiors in Germany.[18] Accordingly, a company presenting products on an international trade show outside Germany is not completely immune from the jurisdiction of German courts.

German courts need to satisfy additional jurisdictional requirements if a foreign party is sued. German courts must address the established rules concerning international jurisdiction over any such foreign defendant, in addition to the aforementioned rules of jurisdiction from the German Civil Code. In particular, the Brussels Ia Regulation has to be taken into account. The general rule, which complies with the national rule of section 12 Code of Civil Procedure, is contained in Article 4 of the Regulation, according to which "persons domiciled in a Member State shall, whatever their nationality is, be sued in the courts of that Member State." Furthermore, almost identical to the German national provision of section 32 Code of Civil Procedure, it is possible to select the forum of the *actus in tort*. Article 7(2) of Regulation 1215/2012 provides "in matters relating to tort, delict or quasi-delict," one may also be sued "in the courts for the place where the harmful event occurred or may occur." Beyond the application of EuGVVO, in particular, with respect to US or Japanese companies, it is generally accepted that the international jurisdiction will follow from the local rules.[19] Thus, once local jurisdiction is established by satisfying the *actus in tort* requirement, for example, German courts would also look to confirm that international jurisdictional rules have been satisfied.

In light of the above considerations, choosing among Germany's courts involves far fewer jurisdictional considerations than in the US. For the vast majority of patent infringement cases, each of Germany's district courts will have jurisdiction to hear the suit. Accordingly, much of the wrangling over forum choice that is typical in the US is inapplicable in Germany.

[2] Transborder Jurisdiction

An important jurisdictional issue is whether national courts within the EU can decide on patent infringement that occurs outside the national territory. If the UPC is not chosen as the forum, this question must basically be answered in the negative. In the past, a few European courts, in particular the Netherlands[20] and Germany, were open to granting injunctions with an effect outside the national territory. Such transborder

18. Appeal Court Düsseldorf, Decision of Feb. 23, 2012, I-2 U 134/10, "Run-Flat-Vorrichtung."
19. Federal Supreme Court, GRUR 2015, 467, "Audiosignalkodierung."
20. *Expandable Grafts v. Boston Scientific* (Gerechtshof Den Haag, Apr. 23, 1998).

decisions were based on a generous interpretation of the so-called Brussels Regime, which regulates which courts have jurisdiction in legal disputes of a civil or commercial nature between individuals residing in different Member States of the EU and the European Free Trade Association. This open-minded transborder jurisdiction case law was later restricted by two decisions of ECJ.[21] Their rulings have been transposed into Regulation 1215/2012 (Brussels Ia), applicable since January 10, 2015.[22]

According to the Regulation, "... persons domiciled in a Member State shall, whatever their nationality be sued in the courts of that Member State" (Article 4(1) of Regulation 2015/2012). Accordingly, a patent infringement suit can be brought at the location where the accused infringer lives or—in the case of a company—at its corporate seat. However, this does not mean that the patentee is free to file a lawsuit at the seat of the infringer asserting the infringement of foreign patents based on infringing activities occurring outside the German territory. Such action is restricted by Article 24(4) of Regulation 1215/2012.[23] This provision stipulates that courts of a Member State have exclusive jurisdiction over cases challenging the validity of patents issuing from that Member State (including EPO patents designating that Member State). Accordingly, validity proceedings must be filed in the country where the patent has been granted or in which a European patent has been designated. The provision also interferes with infringement proceedings wherein foreign patents have been asserted. For example, if a non-German patent is asserted in a German court, as soon as the validity of the foreign patent is challenged in such proceedings either by means of a plea for invalidity or in a request to stay the infringement proceedings in reaction to a validity challenge pending with a foreign court, the German court would be unable to proceed with the infringement action based on that foreign patent. Upon the filing by the defendant of a plea of invalidity of a foreign patent, an infringement case in Germany as to that foreign patent would have even to be dismissed.[24] For instance, if a patent holder asserts infringement of both the German part and the French part of a European patent (due to infringing activities in Germany and France) in Germany, the accused infringer would have the ability to stop the proceedings with respect to the French part of the European patent. Typically, it is thus not recommended to add a foreign patent to the case. Of course, the situation is different when the UPC is chosen as the form. The UPC can make decisions with pan-territorial effect. This trans-territoriality is often a decisive factor for the choice of this forum.

21. *Primus v. Roche* (C-539/03); GAT/LUK C-4/03.
22. Regulation (EU) No. 1215/2012 of the European Parliament and of the Council of Dec. 12, 2012 on jurisdiction and the recognition and enforcement of judgments in civil and commercial matters (recast).
23. Article 24(4) states that: "... shall have exclusive jurisdiction, regardless of the domicile of the parties in proceedings concerned with the registration or validity of patents, ... irrespective of whether the issue is raised by way of an action or as a defense, the courts of the Member State in which the deposit or registration has been applied for, has taken place or is under the terms of an instrument of the Union or an international convention deemed to have taken place. Without prejudice to the jurisdiction of the European Patent Office under the Convention on the Grant of European Patents, signed at Munich on 5 October 1973, the courts of each Member State shall have exclusive jurisdiction in proceedings concerned with the registration or validity of any European patent granted for that Member State."
24. Advocate General Philippe Léger (C-539/03) and L.A. Geelhoed (C-4/03).

Regulation 1215/2012 is not literally applicable to a lawsuit filed in Germany by a US company asserting the infringement of a US patent against a company seated in Germany. The court would have to apply the general international rules applicable to civil procedures. These rules do not provide a clear answer to the question as to how the assertion of US patents is handled in front of German courts. There is a strong likelihood that German courts would draw parallels to Regulation 1215/2012. Initially, it would not be prohibited from filing a lawsuit on the basis of a US patent against an accused infringer in Germany. However, a German court would likely dismiss an action focused on that US patent as soon as a plea of its invalidity has been raised in the German proceedings.

[3] "Torpedo"

The so-called Torpedo refers to a tactic which is aimed at preempting the exercise of jurisdiction by a national court by commencing proceedings before another court in a different country which usually, though not always, lacks jurisdiction. Typically, such a "Torpedo" action is filed in a country with a notoriously slow docket. Torpedo actions were often pursued by seeking a declaratory judgment in a slow docket jurisdiction, which had the effect of preventing proceedings on the merits by the patentee before a court of its choosing. This tactic relied on Article 29 of Regulation 1215/2012 (Brussels Ia) which provides:

> 1. ... where proceedings involving the same cause of action and between the same parties are brought in the courts of different Member States, any court other than the court first seized shall of its own motion stay its proceedings until such time as the jurisdiction of the court first seized is established.
> 2. ...
> 3. Where the jurisdiction of the court first seized is established, any court other than the court first seized shall decline jurisdiction in favor of that court.

For instance, Company A sends a warning letter to Company B due to infringement of the German part of a European patent. Company B reacts and files a declaratory judgment action seeking a declaration of noninfringement of the German patent in an Italian court, just prior to any lawsuit filed by Company A in Germany. What happens if Company A later files a regular infringement lawsuit in Germany? A "negative" action seeking a declaration judgment on noninfringement filed in Italy by the accused infringer and its "positive" counterpart, i.e., an action on the merits filed by the right holder in Germany represent the *same cause* according to Article 29 of Regulation 1215/2012.[25] The German court would thus stay the proceedings, at least, until the jurisdiction of the first-petitioned court is established. Thus, the action in Germany is "torpedoed" and blocked for a considerable period of time.

For some time, Italian courts were notorious for their slow pace. Most of the torpedoes were thus fired in Italy. However, Italian courts became speedier and some

25. European Court of Justice, Decision of Dec. 6, 1994, C-406/92, BeckRS 2004, 77078; Appeal Court Düsseldorf, GRUR-RR, 2009, 401 "Italian Torpedo."

of them have curtailed the effects of the torpedo.[26] This development has removed some impact of the torpedo tactic. It needs to be evaluated case by case if it represents a useful strategy for the accused infringer. The evaluation needs to take into account that a torpedo can also be filed in other European jurisdictions than Italy. Each may have its own approach to deal with such tactical measure.

Some German courts, in particular the District Court Düsseldorf,[27] however render the application of the torpedo tactic more difficult. They allow an objection based on an abuse of rights, namely if the jurisdiction of the first-petitioned court is obviously unfounded and if the accused infringer abusively delays the proceedings of the first-filed action. This does not completely eliminate the effects of a torpedo because the objection requires that at least some time has passed to demonstrate a delay of the proceedings at the foreign court. The tactic is thus still a strategic aspect which needs to be considered before warning the accused infringer. A complete description of the various strategic options for an accused infringer to block German proceedings goes beyond this presentation.

[C] Other National Courts

The considerations outlined in §9.01 may lead to a national court being chosen as the forum. This could be challenged by the circumstances of the case. For instance, it could be that the infringer manufactures the accused product in the country in question, or he holds a large market share there. In addition, as long as the UPC has not yet developed an established practice and case law, cautious patent owners may feel more comfortable to follow the national path for patent enforcement. This is supported by the fact that the case law of national courts is well known and thus the likelihood of success of an enforcement action can be better determined. Another aspect that mitigates in favor of choosing a national court is the fact that their decisions basically have territorial effect. Thus, the patent rights can only be revoked in the respective court country. This is different at the UPC where the possibility of transnational enforcement is given. However, the UPC has the power to revoke the European patent for all UPCA Member States, which is a disadvantageous consequence for the patent owner. The latter is often overestimated. Experiences show that when a national part of a European patent is revoked in an important country, such as Germany, the commitment to pursue enforcement in other countries decreases anyway. Even though the national revocation of the patent has no binding effect on courts in other countries, nevertheless, it creates a situation that calls into question the validity of the patent decided by an impartial body. Provided the revocation is not obviously wrong, such a decision has a spill-over effect to other forums.

---

26. Court of Milan, Decision of Jan. 27, 2014, Judgment No. 1143/2014; in favor of a more generous application of the torpedo standards: Italian Supreme Court, Decision of Jun. 10, 2013 (Judgment No. 14508/2013, *The General Hospital Corporation and others v. Asclepion Laser Technologies*).
27. District Court Düsseldorf, InstGE 3, 8, "Cholesterin-Test."

§9.04 CONTACTING THE ACCUSED INFRINGER

[A] Pre-suit Investigations

Before contacting the alleged infringer, the right holder (patentee) should exhaust its investigative options. This includes the collection and analysis of information the alleged infringer produced in proceedings in other jurisdictions, including new prior art. Test purchases may be useful means to gather information on the accused product. In particular, they are useful and permissible means to prove that the accused product is sold on the German territory or in a Member State of the UPC.[28] Information and evidence produced in US discovery proceedings, for example, may be used in German infringement proceedings (subject to applicable constraints from US protective orders). Failure to perform due diligence at this investigatory stage could cause problems later (*see* "Unjustified Warning Letters" below).

Once these investigations are completed, the question arises whether and how to contact the accused infringer. Contacting the alleged infringer prior to commencing court proceedings is not legally required. Indeed, filing a lawsuit without advance warning might be advisable in some situations. But there are potential penalties involved with suing without forewarning.

An accused infringer that had not been previously and sufficiently warned by the patentee may in German proceedings, as soon as the complaint is served, admit the claims asserted, in which case the court would render a decision pursuant to this admission. This follows from section 307 of the German Code of Civil Procedure. This refers to the situation where the accused infringer immediately gives up and discontinues the accused activities. In this situation, the right holder would indeed win the case immediately, but the costs of the proceedings might be imposed on him, including the accused infringer's "statutory costs." This follows from section 93 Code of Civil Procedure which provides that "if the defendant did not induce the bringing of a suit by his conduct, the costs of the proceedings shall be paid by the plaintiff if the defendant immediately admits."[29] Thus, the right holder may—in German proceedings—avoid the imposition of these costs if he gives the accused infringer a sufficient opportunity to comply with a warning letter. The UPCA and the Rules of Procedure do not provide for such a provision. Nevertheless, Article 69(4) UPCA stipulates that "a party should bear any unnecessary costs it has caused the Court or another party." If the defendant did not give any cause for an action and behaves in such a way that the proceedings can be swiftly brought to an end, it is equitable to impose the costs on the plaintiff even if the asserted claims are well founded.

There are of course situations where a prior warning is not recommended. The prior warning might be superfluous if it is expected that the accused infringer would anyway not respect the holder's rights. A lawsuit without prior warning could also

28. Federal Supreme Court, GRUR 1999, 1017, "Kontrollnummernbeseitigung"; Appeal Court Düsseldorf, Decision of Jan. 28, 2010, I-2 U 124/08.
29. Unofficial translation.

reduce the risk of the so-called Torpedo[30] which might be fired off by the warned infringer to create a temporary obstacle for a lawsuit in a different judicial forum. These strategic considerations must be carefully weighed when approaching the accused infringer. Of course, there might be good reasons to contact the accused infringer prior to the lawsuit:

- The contact could result in a settlement without judicial proceedings. A lawsuit is not a regular element of a company's business. Lawsuits are distracting and may create unexpected effects on the financial situation of a company. As the speed of infringement proceedings does not leave much time to find acceptable design-arounds and solutions for the company's customers, the possible result of a lawsuit could have dramatic consequences for the business of a company. This situation gives leverage for settlements.
- The contact may result in discussions through which the accused infringer furnishes information with respect to the accused embodiment which was previously unknown to the right holder. The accused infringer may also provide strategically valuable information with regard to previously undisclosed prior art.

There are two usual methods used for extrajudicially approaching the accused infringer: the "warning letter" and the "inquiry letter."

[B] Warning Letter (*Abmahnung*)

A warning letter immediately puts the alleged infringer on notice that he is infringing and demands that he cease and desist. If the alleged infringer ignores the warning letter, the patentee may then file a lawsuit, without being exposed to the risk that the costs of the proceedings might be imposed on him after an immediate acknowledgement of the asserted claims by the accused infringer. One of the main reasons of a previous warning of accused infringer consists in avoiding the imposition of these costs.

[1] Content of Warning Letter

A warning letter usually contains information on the identity of the right holder and the enforceability of the asserted right. As evidence, it is sufficient to reference the patent register. A copy of the excerpt of the register and the asserted patent or utility model should be enclosed to that letter. The status of the right should also be described. Thus, if there are pending invalidity actions or opposition proceedings, they shall be mentioned in the letter as well.

Furthermore, the warning letter must contain sufficiently concrete information about the accused infringing activities. The accused infringer must be able to verify

30. *See* Ch. 9, §9.03[B][3] (above).

whether the warning letter is justified.[31] A vague allegation is not sufficient. If there are particular infringing products, these should be identified, and photos may be helpful in this regard to avoid confusion. Once the identification and description is complete the letter should contain a clear demand that the accused infringer cease and desist from the infringing activities described.

The warning letter should include a draft of an undertaking. The undertaking identifies the different claims asserted by the right holder, such as the right to prevent the use of the patent which obliges the accused infringer to cease and desist with the accused activity. It also covers the other claims resulting from the patent, namely the rendering of accounts, and states that the accused infringer has to pay damages to be calculated on the basis of the figures to be furnished by the accused infringer when rendering the accounts.

Finally, the letter should set forth a deadline for the accused infringer to return a signed copy of the undertaking. The deadline should leave sufficient time to the accused infringer to verify the allegations. Normally, three weeks are reasonable. If the deadline is too short, the warning letter does not become ineffective, but a reasonable deadline starts to run and replaces the unreasonably short deadline.[32]

There might be situations where a shorter deadline is permitted, such as in a trade show situation where a quick intervention is required. In that case, it might be sufficient if only a few days or even one day are left to the accused infringer.[33]

Finally, the warning letter needs to contain a threat that in case of noncompliance with the right holder's demand, a lawsuit might be filed.[34]

According to the recent case law of the German Constitutional Court, if the patentee intends to apply for a preliminary injunction,[35] a pretrial involvement of the opposing party is required even if an ex parte decision could be issued due to urgency. This requirement follows from the procedural equality of arms as an expression of the rule of law and the general principle of equality in civil proceedings This involvement usually takes place by means of a pretrial warning letter.

[2] Unjustified Warning Letter

Before sending out a warning letter the right holder must perform an adequate investigation to warrant a warning letter. The investigation shall reasonably allow the conclusion that the patent is indeed infringed (which requires sufficient knowledge of the accused activity or embodiment) and that the underlying patent right is valid.[36] An unjustified warning letter may trigger a claim for damages. The damages typically consist at least of the costs incurred by the lawyer involved by the warned party as a consequence of the warning letter.[37] Damages may also result from the termination of

31. Appeal Court Düsseldorf, Decision of Nov. 11, 2011, I-20 W 132/11.
32. Federal Supreme Court, I ZR 63/88, GRUR 1990, 381, 382, "Antwortpflicht des Abgemahnten."
33. Appeal Court Düsseldorf, InstGE 4, 159, "INTERPACK."
34. Federal Supreme Court, GRUR 2011, 995, "Besonderer Mechanismus."
35. Cf. Ch. 11.
36. Federal Supreme Court, GRZR 2005, 882, "Unberechtigte Schutzrechtsverwarnung."
37. Appeal Court Düsseldorf, Decision of Jan. 31, 2013, 1-2 U 54/11.

the production and/or commercialization of the accused product unless these measures were taken imprudently and too hastily.[38]

A sufficient factual investigation should thus precede the warning letter. In addition, the accused infringer shall be well informed through the warning letter about the factual circumstances, in particular about the status of the asserted patent and the scope of the assertion. The accused activities must be well specified and should not overreach the scope of protection of the asserted patent.[39] The right holder may assume the validity of the issued patent by relying on the granting decision of the patent office, unless that validity has been questioned by means of unexamined prior art submitted in pending invalidation proceedings.[40] If prior art has been identified in the post-grant phase that has not been considered by the patent office, then the patentee should diligently review and assess the relevance of such "new" prior art, and this assessment should be reflected in the warning letter. Decisions rendered by the EPO, the GPTO or German courts such as decisions of the Federal Patent Court and the UPC in relation to the asserted patent should be mentioned and disclosed.[41]

The need for due diligence is even more important in case of unexamined rights such as utility models. These rights require that the right holder has made a proper search and has sufficiently considered the resulting prior art before sending the warning letter.[42] That due diligence must sufficiently resolve doubts before sending out a formal warning letter.

[C] Inquiry Letter (*Berechtigungsanfrage*)

The soft warning, which we call the "inquiry letter," invites the accused infringer to a discussion about validity and infringement. It is an exchange of views and does not contain a demand to cease and desist or a threat to take judicial measures. The letter accordingly contains the simple demand to only indicate why the other party believes he is entitled to use the protected invention. Table 9.1 lists the differences between the warning and inquiry letter.

Table 9.1 Differences: Warning Letter Versus Inquiry Letter

Characteristics	*Warning Letter*	*Inquiry Letter*
Content	Demand to cease and desist including threat to start litigation in case of incompliance	Invitation to exchange views on validity and infringement

38. Federal Supreme Court, GRZR 2005, 882, "Unberechtigte Schutzrechtsverwarnung."
39. District Court Düsseldorf, InstGE 3, 86, "Hochdruckreiniger."
40. Federal Supreme Court, I ZR 98/02, GRUR 2006, 432, "Verwarnung aus Kennzeichenrecht II."
41. Appeal Court Düsseldorf, InstGE 9, 123, "Multifeed."
42. Federal Supreme Court, I ZR 59/50, GRUR 1951,452, "Mülltonne"; Federal Supreme Court, GSZ 1/04, Decision of Jul. 15, 2005, "Unberechtigte Schutzrechtsverwarnung."

Characteristics	*Warning Letter*	*Inquiry Letter*
Liability?	Only if warning is unjustified	No
Cause for Declaratory Judgment Action?	Yes	No

Such a letter would not trigger the effects of an unjustified warning.[43] Also, it would not create a sufficient cause for a declaratory judgment action (or action for negative declaration of noninfringement).[44] In fact, such action requires a "legitimate interest"[45] which is given in case the right holder issues a formal warning. However, it should not trigger such legitimate interest on the side of the accused infringer in case the right holder only informs the accused infringer about the concerned property right(s) and invites him to explain why he believes to be entitled to use the right(s). If such inquiry does not suggest that an action will be taken against the accused infringer, a "legitimate interest" for filing a declaratory judgment action should not yet be established. A prudent right holder could thus first send such an inquiry letter to the accused infringer and, depending upon the outcome, follow-up with a formal warning letter.

43. District Court Mannheim, Decision of Feb. 23, 2007, 7 O 276/06, BeckRS 2007, 03873 "Abgrenzung von Verwarnung und Berechtigungsanfrage."
44. *See* Ch. 10, §10.02[G] "Declaratory Judgment Action."
45. Section 256(1) German Code of Civil Procedure; Rule 61(1) RoP.

CHAPTER 10

Infringement Trial

§10.01 PROCEEDINGS AT THE UPC

[A] Structure of the UPC

The UPC comprises two judicial levels, the Court of First Instance with its central, national, and regional divisions and one centralized Court of Appeal. Comparable with the US Court of Appeals for the Federal Circuit, the Court of Appeal in Luxembourg plays an important role in harmonizing UPC case law (Figure 10.1).

Figure 10.1 Structure of the UPC

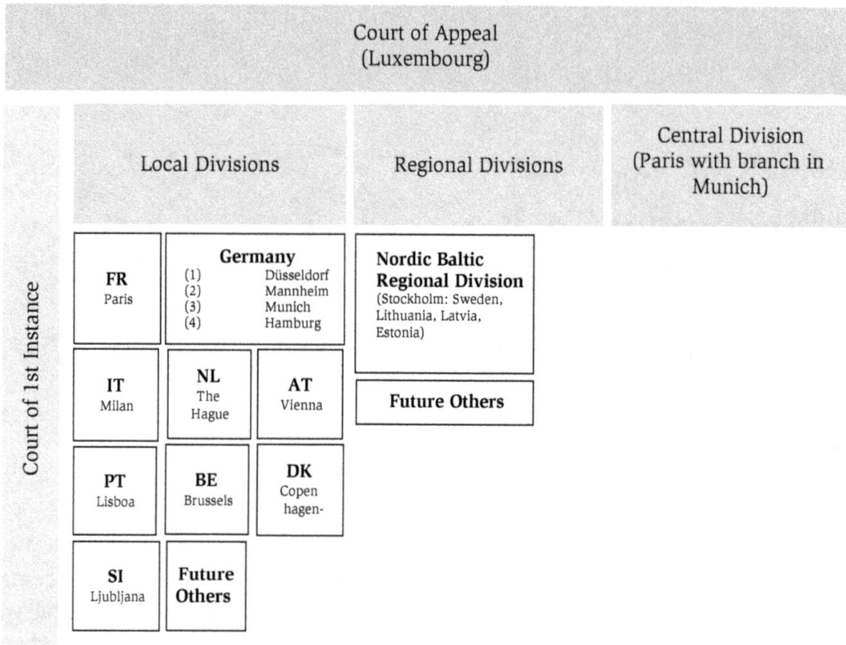

[1] Court of First Instance

The Court of First Instance compromises a central division and a plurality of local and regional divisions. Cases may be started in any of these divisions. However, the appropriate jurisdiction may depend on the nature of the case and the allocation of authority among the UPC divisions according to the UPCA and the Rules of Procedure.

[a] Local and Regional Divisions

Local divisions are set up in Contracting Member States.[1] Due to the high quantity of patent cases that have been traditionally handled by German courts, Germany has established four local divisions: They are seated in Munich, Mannheim, Düsseldorf, and Hamburg. Furthermore, France (FR), Belgium (BE), Italy (IT), the Netherlands (NL), Austria (AT), Portugal (PT), Denmark (DK) each possess their own local division. Due to the modest case load in past years, Sweden, Estonia, Latvia, and Lithuania have joined forces, and have established, by agreement signed on March 4, 2014, one common regional division, namely the Nordic-Baltic regional division located in Stockholm. Several UPCA Member States have not (yet) established a local chamber or do not (yet) belong to a regional chamber. These sates are currently

1. Article 7(3) UPCA.

Bulgaria, Luxembourg, Cyprus, Finland, Greece, Hungary, Ireland, Malta, Romania, and Slovakia. Since the decisions of the UPC may have a pan-territorial character and thus may affect the territories of these countries, there is therefore no gap in the system. These states may still join or possibly establish a chamber later. But that does not have to be the case either.

[b] Central Division

There is one Central Division with a main section in Paris and a branch in Munich. Each of the sections deal with different technical subject matter, distributed according to the International Patent Classification of the WIPO.[2] The Munich section focuses on mechanical engineering (section F) and Paris handles all other technical areas. Local and Regional Divisions of the Court of First Instance mainly decide on infringement-related issues, whereas the Central Division has mainly competency over validity-related issues. The interaction between Local, Regional and Central divisions will be explained in the following chapters.

[c] Judges

In contrast with US civil proceedings, where there is a right to jury trial in most patent cases, there are no juries at the UPC. Instead, a panel of judges renders all decisions:

- ***Judges of the Local/Regional Divisions***: In principle, the panels of local and regional divisions are composed of three legally trained judges with practical experience in patent cases. The panels of the divisions shall have a multinational composition,[3] which is guaranteed by allocating one judge from a Pool of Judges.[4] The Pool is composed of judges from Contracting States. Thus, one judge is not a national of the State hosting the local division, whereas the other two judges are nationals of that State. If a State hosting a local division has less than 50 cases per year, two judges will be allocated from the Pool to sit alongside just one national judge. The panels of regional divisions are composed of judges taken from a list of judges who are nationals of the Contracting States hosting the regional division (regional judges). A technically qualified judge will be allocated to the panel:
  - if a counterclaim for revocation has been raised;[5]
  - at the request of one of the parties; or
  - at the request of the panel.[6]

---

2. *See* http://www.wipo.int/classifications/ipc/en/.
3. Article 8(1) UPCA.
4. Article 18 UPCA: The Pool of Judges is composed of legally and technically qualified judges who are full-time or part-time judges of the Court. They will be nationals of the EU Member States.
5. Article 33(3)(a) UPCA.
6. Article 8(5) UPCA.

The local divisions in Germany extensively rely on judges of the district courts. All these judges possess experience in patent matters due to their previous professional activities. These UPC judges may continue to function as judges on the national level. This double function is allowed by Article 17(3) UPCA, which permits judges of local or regional divisions to exercise in parallel other judicial functions on national level. Having a majority of national judges in the panel of a local division will influence the development of the body of UPC law to conform to a certain extent with the national case law previously developed in the State hosting that local division. The national influence will attenuate over the time through the body of case law to be established by the UPC's Appeal Court in Luxembourg.

- *Central Division:* The panel of the Central Division is composed of one technically qualified and two legally qualified judges. The two legally qualified judges are nationals of different Contracting Member States. The technical judge is allocated from the Pool and will have qualifications and experience in the relevant field of the technology specified to that dispute (Figure 10.2).

Figure 10.2 Composition of the UPC

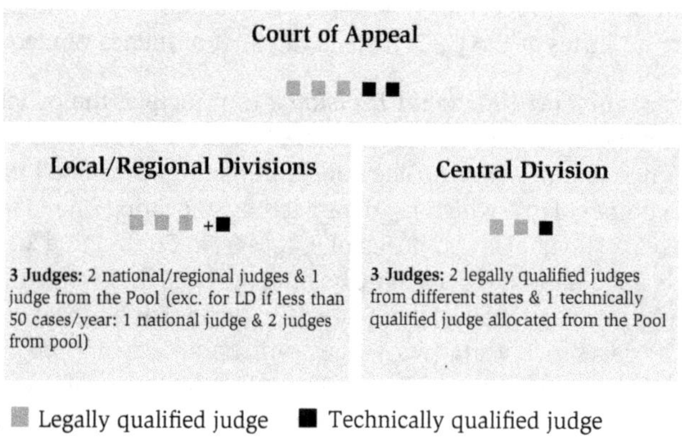

[2] *Appeal*

An appeal of a decision of the Court of First Instance may be brought before the Court of Appeal in Luxembourg by any party that has been unsuccessful, in whole or in part, in its submissions, within two months of the date of the notification of the decision.[7] An appeal can be based on both points of law and matters of fact.[8] Nevertheless, new facts and new evidence may, in principle, only be introduced where the submission of them by the party concerned could not reasonably have been expected during proceedings before the Court of First Instance. As shown in Figure 10.2, any panel of the Court of

7. Article 73(1) UPCA.
8. Article 73(3) UPCA.

Appeal will comprise five judges from different Member States, three of whom will be legally qualified and two of whom will be technically qualified. The technically qualified judges are allocated from the Pool and will have qualifications and experience in the field of the technology concerned.

Comparable with the US Court of Appeals for the Federal Circuit, the Court of Appeal in Luxembourg plays an important role in harmonizing UPC case law.

[3] European Court of Justice

The ECJ is not involved as an appellate court of the UPC's judicial system. The UPC may nevertheless refer questions of EU law to the ECJ, as national courts have traditionally done. To avoid the jurisdiction of the ECJ in substantive patent law matters, specific provisions relating to infringement laws were removed from the UP Regulation and integrated into the UPCA, which is technically not an instrument of EU law and therefore falls outside the jurisdiction of the ECJ.

[B] Course of the Proceedings

First instance proceedings are divided into three main stages: Written Procedure, Interim Procedure, and Oral Procedure (cf. Figure 10.3). First instance proceedings should normally be completed within about one year, subject to potential deadline extensions[9] (Figure 10.3).

Figure 10.3 Course of the Proceedings (with Counterclaim for Revocation)

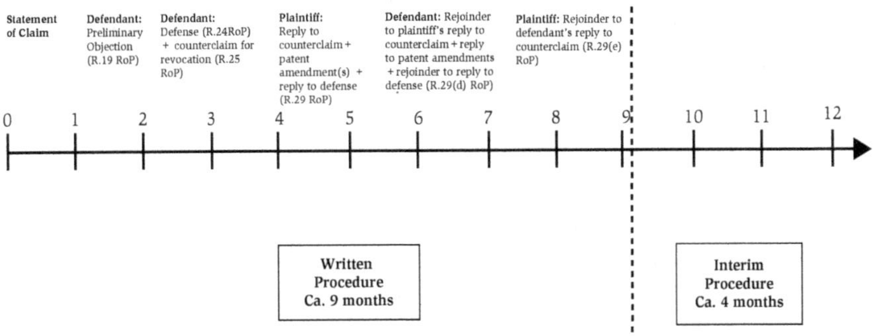

9. Preamble to the RoP: "In accordance with these principles, proceedings shall be conducted in a way which will normally allow the final oral hearing on the issues of infringement and validity at first instance to take place within one year whilst recognizing that complex actions may require more time and procedural steps and simple actions less time and fewer procedural steps."

[1] *Written Procedure*

The written procedure is initiated by electronically filling a statement of claim at the Court's registry which then serves the writ on the defendant. One of the first actions that a defendant may take when confronted by such action is to contest within one month the jurisdiction of the UPC, the jurisdiction of the division addressed in the statement of claim, or its language.[10] This can be done within one month of service of the statement of claim. This deadline is important because the failure to object renders obsolete any later jurisdictional objections, either to the UPC or to the division thereof.[11]

The written procedure follows the sequence of briefs as illustrated in Figure 10.3. This part of the proceedings usually takes up to nine months, depending on whether a counterclaim for revocation of the patent has been asserted, and the type and complexity of the action.

[2] *Interim Procedure*

The interim procedure primarily concerns the case management stage and is directed by a so-called judge-rapporteur. The presiding judge of the panel to which the action has been assigned designates himself or one legally qualified judge of his panel to take over the role of judge–rapporteur in the interim procedure.[12] This case management part of the proceedings is aimed at preparing the case for the oral hearing. It may, where appropriate, include an interim conference with the parties ("interim conference"),[13] which is typically held by telephone or video conferencing, or, on request of one party, in court.[14] During the interim procedure, the judge-rapporteur shall identify the main issues of the case, determine the relevant facts in dispute and establish a schedule for the further progress of the proceedings, including confirming the date for the oral hearing.[15] The judge-rapporteur is also empowered to issue orders regarding production of further pleadings and evidence and to decide on the value in dispute.[16] The judge-rapporteur is also responsible to explore the possibility of a settlement with the parties.[17]

It is recommended that the parties file available evidence, such as sworn witness statements and/or expert reports as soon as possible, namely as part of their pleadings in the written procedure. However, if it turns out in the course of the later proceedings that other evidence is relevant for the party's case or if the evidence is under the control of the adversary party, the concerned parties could be required to supplement their pleadings with such new evidence during the interim proceedings. The concerned

10. Preliminary Objection under Rule 19 RoP.
11. Rule 19(7) RoP.
12. Rule 18(1) RoP.
13. Rule 103(1) RoP.
14. Rule 105(1) RoP.
15. Rule 104(1) RoP.
16. Rule 103(1)(f) RoP.
17. Rule 103(1)(e) RoP.

party is thus challenged to adequately react and respond to the appropriate requests prior to the interim conference in view of bringing the evidence into the proceedings. The judge-rapporteur will consider such requests at or before the interim conference and may respond by various orders that he deems appropriate to prepare the oral hearing.

In view of properly preparing the oral hearing, the judge-rapporteur may hold preparatory meetings with witnesses and experts, which are always conducted together with the parties. These meetings are designed to identify whether a witness or expert is able to testify on issues relevant for the case. After consultation with the presiding judge, the judge-rapporteur may even set a separate hearing of witnesses and experts to take place before the panel. Such early hearing or interrogation might be meaningful, if, for instance, the hearing of a witness or expert appears to be very time-consuming and thus shall be removed from the oral hearing.[18]

Through judge-rapporteur's assessment of the case, it may be determined that a court expert would be of assistance in resolving a particular technical question. Such court expert may then be appointed as a consequence of the interim proceedings, which should be completed within three months after the end of the written proceedings.

[3] Oral Procedure

The judge-rapporteur will set the date for the final oral hearing (if one has not been already determined). The hearing will encompass infringement, as well as the validity of the patent if a counterclaim for revocation has been made. The Preamble to the Rules of Procedure points to an endeavor of the court to hold the final oral hearing within one year after filing the statement of claim. This appears to be a "soft duty" imposed on the court. The Preamble to the Rules of Procedure recognizes that "complex actions may require more time." Thus, the one-year timeline generally applies to uncomplicated normal cases.

The oral hearing enables the parties to orally present their case to the panel. If ordered during the interim procedure, witnesses and experts may also be heard at the oral hearing and questioned by the parties and the panel. Their testimony is limited to issues previously identified by judge-rapporteur or the presiding judge. Otherwise, a short oral hearing would not be possible, which basically shall be completed within one day.[19] Given that the oral hearing shall cover both infringement and validity a one-day hearing is very short. The proceedings shall be front-loaded with a great weight placed on the written and interim procedure. To enable such a short hearing, the presiding judge may also set time limits for the parties' oral submissions in advance of the oral hearing.[20] Accordingly, the written statements of the parties must be well supported in view of the risk that oral submissions cannot be sufficient to cover all relevant aspects.

18. Rule 104(g) RoP.
19. Rule 113(1) RoP.
20. *Ibid.*

Usually, a case is heard by a multinational panel of three judges, but a fourth, technical judge maybe added to the panel where a counterclaim for revocation is subject to the discussion. The presiding judge of the panel directs the hearing. At the beginning of the oral hearing, a preliminary introduction to the action is usually given by the presiding judge and questions may be put to the parties.[21] Such introduction is directed at leading the oral hearing in a certain direction. The panel typically provides its preliminary view to the parties.

The summoning and questioning of witnesses or experts depend on whether the judge-rapporteur orders such testimony. He may order a "separate hearing" of witnesses and/or experts, which takes place before the panel. Such separation appears to be reasonable where the complexity of the case presumes that the oral submissions of the parties will already fill the whole day and thus would not allow the additional testimony of witness or experts. The desire to have a short main hearing may require that the relevant issues of the case be considerably narrowed during the interim procedure. Witnesses and experts could be prepared through preparatory discussions with the judge-rapporteur and a separate hearing could be held shortly prior to the date set for the final oral hearing.

The oral hearing and any separate hearing of witnesses and/or experts are normally open to the public.[22] The Court may render them confidential, to the extent necessary to protect interests of the parties, third parties or if it is in the general interest of justice or public order.

The Rules[23] allow **oral hearings by video conference** provided that all parties agree, or the Court considers it appropriate to do so due to exceptional circumstances. Such circumstances may be established, for example, in case of travel constraints. However, no exceptional circumstances are required if the parties agree to it. Also, regardless of exceptional circumstances the Court may allow a party, representative or accompanying person to attend the oral hearing by videoconference and/or hear a party, witness, or expert through electronic means, such as video conference.[24]

[C] Important Briefs

During the course of the written procedure in an infringement case (without a counterclaim for revocation) each party is generally allowed to file two briefs. For the plaintiff this is the statement of claim and a reply to the defendant's statement of defense. The defendant may add a rejoinder to that reply. In total four briefs are thus exchanged. The timeline for these proceedings (without counterclaim of revocation) is then three months for the statement of defense. The subsequent brief (i.e., the reply to the statement of defense) is due in one month from the statement of defense. This brief is then followed by the rejoinder, which is also due within a one-month period.

21. *Ibid.*
22. Rule 115 RoP.
23. Rule 112.3(c) RoP.
24. Rule 112.3(a) and (b) RoP.

If a counterclaim for revocation is filed together with the statement of defense, then the plaintiff must respond to the revocation claim at the same time it files its reply to the statement of defense. Subsequently, in response to this, the defendant files a rejoinder to the reply as well as a reply to the defense to the revocation claim. The last brief in that sequence is then plaintiff's rejoinder to the reply to the defense against the revocation claim. The plaintiff is allowed to include an application to amend claims of the asserted patent. Such application could be the consequence of a counterclaim for revocation. The timeline for proceedings including a counterclaim of revocation is expanded, because the two briefs following the statement of defense and counterclaim are due in two months, respectively, as shown in Figure 10.3. This timeline presumes that the time limits have not been extended. Such extensions can be allowed by the court on proper request under Rule 9(3) of the Rules of Procedure (RoP).

The Rules of Procedure thus impose rigid time limits after the statement of case is filed. This approach differs from the codes of procedures of most Member States such as Germany, where the time limits are flexibly set by the courts. The proceedings at the UPC, as set out in the Preamble to the RoP, shall be swift with the goal of finalizing first instance proceedings within one year.

[1] Statement of Claim (Complaint)

[a] Content

The necessary content of a statement of claim (complaint) is codified in Rule 13 RoP. It is an important instrument of the proceedings because it sets the proceedings in motion. The plaintiff must be prepared to commit to a tight schedule. It is highly recommended for the plaintiff to dedicate sufficient time for gathering all relevant data within the pretrial phase in view of generating a thorough statement of claim because once this is filed, it is off to the races. The level of intellectual depth contained in a complaint in UPC proceedings (and likewise German proceedings) far exceeds what is expected in US proceedings. It is not a "notice pleading" standard—the statement of the claim in the UPC should strive to serve as the plaintiff's principal brief of the case. It should include the following:

- **Designation of the parties:**[25] The people entitled to assert patent infringement are listed in Article 47 UPCA. That is, in principle, the patentee, the holder of an exclusive license,[26] a nonexclusive licensee specifically authorized by the proprietor in the license agreement or by a separate authorization.
- **Details of the patent infringement[27] and reasons and arguments of law:**[28] The statement of claim must identify the patent(s) concerned, the underlying facts and the different remedies. The facts of the case must be substantiated.

25. Rule 13(1)(a)–(f) RoP.
26. Article 47(2) UPCA.
27. Rule 13(1)(l) RoP.
28. Rule 13(1)(n) RoP.

That is, the accused product or method must be described in sufficient detail. Furthermore, the technology, on which the patent is based, must be described. The asserted patent claims must be construed to be mapped to the features of the accused product or method. Finally, the different remedies sought by the plaintiff must be specified, which—in combination with the underlying facts—determine the subject matter of the case. The court is not authorized to award relief that has not been requested (*ne ultra petita*).[29] The remedies could represent:

- cease-and-desist order (injunction);[30]
- right to destruction of the accused products;[31]
- recall and remove the accused products from the distribution channels;[32]
- right of information;[33]
- claim for damages;[34]
- publication of the decision.[35]

- **Evidence relied on**: All available evidence must be specified in the statement of claim.[36] Due to the tight time schedule of proceedings at the UPC, it is highly recommended to thoroughly investigate and prepare the case prior to filing the statement of claim. It is risky to adopt a strategy that assumes that missing evidence may be identified during the course of the proceedings, particularly in view of the tight time schedule applicable for proceedings at the UPC.
- **Parallel proceedings**:[37] The statement of claim must also contain information about any prior or pending proceedings related to the patent. The latter is intended to avoid contradictory decisions and to solve potential conflicts of jurisdiction, or to assess whether the matter should be stayed.
- **Jurisdiction**:[38] The plaintiff must address the claim to the proper division of the Court, explaining why the chosen division is the correct tribunal under Article 33 UPCA.
- **Single judge option**: According to Article 8(7) UPCA, the parties may agree to have a single legally qualified judge hear the case. This refers to an exceptional situation where the case is very simple on the technical and legal side and where the defendant agrees to this. Such agreement can usually not be reached.
- **Orders to be sought during the interim procedure**:[39] During the interim conference, the judge-rapporteur is empowered to take different measures

29. Article 76(1) UPCA.
30. Articles 25 and 63 UPCA.
31. Article 64 UPCA.
32. *Ibid.*
33. Article 67 UPCA.
34. Article 68 UPCA.
35. Article 80 UPCA.
36. Article 53 UPCA; Rule 170 RoP.
37. Rule 13(1)(h) RoP.
38. Rule 13(1)(i) RoP.
39. Rule 13(1)(o) RoP.

such as ordering the production of evidence such as inspections, communication information, preserving evidence and appointing court experts. In the statement of the case, the plaintiff can specify if any such orders should be issued to fill evidentiary gaps.

- **Value of the dispute**:[40] An indication of the value of the action is necessary if the plaintiff believes that the values may exceed EUR 500,000.
- **List of documents** attached.[41]

[b] Rights and Requests

(a) ***Right to prevent the direct use of the patent***: Article 25 UPCA prohibits the direct use of a granted patent by any unauthorized third party. The provision thus enables the patent holder to act against the unlawful use of his patent. It distinguishes between product (Article 25(b) UPCA) and process claims of a patent (Article 25(c) UPCA). The same distinction can be found in section 9 of the GPA. However, the application of Article 25 UPCA is not territorially limited to Germany but covers all Contracting Member States in which the European patent is in force. Only the acts described in Article 25 UPCA are subject to prohibition. Thus, preparatory acts are typically not sufficient to fulfill the requirements of Article 25 UPCA. In the case of **product claims**, there must be a:

- ***Making***: This act refers to the manufacture of the accused product.
- ***Offer***: The prohibition on offers encompasses offers for purchase but is not so limited. Any offer for rent or a donation is sufficient.[42] The offer can be made orally or in writing. Advertisements of the accused product in sales media or on the company's webpage would suffice.
- ***Placing on the market***: A delivery of the product to a third party (such as the buyer, freight carrier or warehouse keeper) suffices for placing goods on the market, unless the "delivery" only takes place within the boundaries of the same company.
- *Use*: This act requires the use of the technical teaching, whereas the manner and purpose of use are basically irrelevant. Accordingly, the demonstration of a protected machine could represent such an unlawful use.
- ***Importing***: An importation is satisfied if the protected product enters the market in the territory where the European patent is in force provided it occurs for the purpose of offering, placing on the market or using it there.
- ***Storing***: This act refers to any possessing of the product, provided the possession is for the purpose of offering, placing on the market or using it there.

In case of **process claims** there must be either a **use** of the process or an **offering** of the process without the consent of the patentee, provided that the third party to

40. Rule 13(1)(p) RoP.
41. Rule 13(1)(q) RoP.
42. Federal Supreme Court, GRUR 2007, 221, Simvastatin.

whom the process is offered knows or should have known that using the process results in a patent infringement. The first category (i.e., the **use**) requires that the process steps as described in the patent claim be fully implemented by the accused infringer or at least by a third party whose acts are attributable to the accused infringer. The second category (i.e., the **offering**) encompasses offers of the accused infringer to use the protected process whether by himself or by a third party acting under his direction. In addition, the third party (the addressee of the offer) must know, or be grossly negligent in failing to know, that the use would infringe the patent.

In addition to the rights under Article 25(b) UPCA relating to process claims, Article 25(c) UPCA provides for a **protection of direct process products**. The protection of products directly obtained through a protected process is of importance where the patentee may not refer to a product claim or in case the protected process is implemented outside the territory of the patent. The provision however requires that the process generates a product. This requirement is satisfied if the process is only aimed at a production of an abstract result, such as a measurement result. In addition, the product must be the direct result on the process. The latter might not be satisfied if the generated product was subjected to further processing which removes the identity of the same. Products directly obtained by the protected process enjoy the same protection as those falling under a product claim.

(b) ***Right to prevent the indirect use of the patent (contributory infringement)***: Indirect use of a patent is prohibited by Article 26 UPCA. Contributory infringement consists in supplying, or offering to supply, an infringing "means relating to an essential element of the claimed invention." The term "offering" has the same meaning as the one used in Article 25 UPCA in relation to product claims. The act of "supplying" requires a physical delivery of the means in question to a third party. The offering or supplying must occur within the territory of the patent, thus, in any Contracting Member States where the European patent is in force. Furthermore, the offered and/or supplied "means" must relate to an "essential element of the invention." German case law does not set a high threshold to satisfy this requirement. It is not necessary that the means in question play a major role for the implementation of the protected teaching. Rather, it is sufficient that the means (at least) interact with one or more features of the patent claim in performing the protected teaching.[43] This provision protects the patentee in advance of a threat, without requiring an established direct infringement. However, the provision requires that the third party knows or at least should have known that the offered and/or supplied means is suitable (knowledge as to suitability) and intended to be used for putting the claimed teaching into effect (knowledge as to intended use). Positive knowledge is often difficult to prove. This is the reason why the second alternative, which only requires that the third party should have known that the means are suitable and intended to be used for putting the claimed teaching into effect, plays an important role under the doctrine of contributory infringement. The German Federal Supreme Court—with respect to the German provision (section 10 Patent Act)—typically refers to the objective circumstances and the experience of everyday

43. Federal Supreme Court, GRUR 2004, 758, Flügelradzähler.

life. Accordingly, it is sufficient to demonstrate that it is obviously expected under normal circumstances that the end user will intend to put the invention into effect. For instance, if the means in question is specifically tailored to be used in an infringing way, the subjective requirement of Article 26(1) UPCA may be satisfied. The latter is generally satisfied in case the means in question can only be used in an infringing way. In cases where the means in question may be used in an infringing and noninfringing way, additional aspects, such as the product literature or promotional data proposing or recommending an infringing use, must fill the gap.[44] This German approach is consistent with the provisions of Article 26(1) UPCA.

Nevertheless, there is a significant difference between the national situation and the UPCA. Article 26(1) UPCA refers to the "territory of the contracting Member States." The influence of the German rule, on the contrary, is limited to the German territory. This is, the acts of the contributory infringer must take place in Germany; furthermore, the means relating to an essential element of the invention must be offered or supplied for use in Germany (so-called double "domestic link"). The supply or offering of such a means in Germany does not constitute an act of contributory infringement if it occurs for the use of the claimed teaching abroad. This applies even if a national part of the (same) European patent with the same scope of protection is in force there. Other countries also have rules covering contributory patent infringement, such as Article 613-4 of the Code de la Propriété Intellectuelle (CPI) in France. Nevertheless, this does not close the gap in the scenario mentioned because a corresponding domestic link is required there as well. The double domestic link according to national rules is extended by the UPC to the "territory of the contracting Member States." Transnational activities occurring in supply chains can thus be prevented more readily.

(c) ***The remedy sought in relation to Articles 25 and 26***: Upon a finding of patent infringement, the UPC may order the defendant to cease and desist its infringing activities.[45] The best guide for the statement of claim under UPC practice is the formulation of this requested relief in German patent infringement proceedings. An example for the infringement of a product claim could be:

> It is requested in the name and on behalf of the plaintiff,
>
> i. to find the defendant liable
>   1. in order to avoid a penalty to be set by the court for each case of violation of up to an amount to be set by the court to refrain from making, offering, placing on the market, using a product or importing or storing the product for these purposes within the Contracting Member States where the patent is in force as to a product with the following features:
>
> [Description of the accused embodiment]

44. Federal Supreme Court, Mitt 2001, 21, Luftheizgerät.
45. Article 63 UPCA.

If the infringement is based on a contributory infringement, the wording of the cease-and-desist remedy must necessarily be formulated in accordance with the wording of Article 26 UPCA.

(d) ***Information rights**:* According to Article 67 UPCA, the court may order the accused infringer, and even third parties under particular conditions, to communicate information aimed at facilitating the determination of the damage claim (Article 68 UPCA). The information right may also be directed at correcting the effects of the infringement (Article 64 UPCA). Accordingly, the remedy may be directed at a communication of:

(a) the origin and distribution channels of the infringing products or processes;
(b) the quantities produced, manufactured, delivered, received or ordered, as well as the price obtained for the infringing products; and
(c) the identity of any third person involved in the production or distribution of the infringing products or in the use of the infringing process.

(e) ***The damages**:* The Court may determine a particular amount of damages in the award or leave this determination to separate proceedings.[46] If the patentee is in the position to calculate the damages on his own, he can directly request the payment of a specific amount in the statement of case. Often, this is impossible because the patentee does not yet possess the information about the infringing activities. Typically, this information is uniquely in the possession of the accused infringer. Resolving damages in separate proceedings has the advantage that the initial proceedings are not burdened by an often lengthy and controversial assessment and determination of the amount of damages. If the discussion about the amount of damages shall be excluded from the main proceedings, the plaintiff should request that the court at least indicate in the operative part of the decision that the defendant is obliged to compensate the plaintiff for all damages caused to the plaintiff by the contested acts. If infringement is found in the initial trial, then the subsequent proceeding on damages will not reopen the issue of infringement.

(f) ***Other rights**:* Besides the aforementioned rights, there are other rights which might be judicially asserted. For example, according to the UPCA, the injured party may require the destruction of the products that are the subject matter of the patent,[47] including materials and equipment that have served overwhelmingly for the manufacture of such products, provided that the enforcement is not disproportionate. The accused infringer can also be required by the plaintiff to recall the products or to remove them definitively from the distribution channels.[48] In addition, the plaintiff may assert reasonable compensation for the use of the claimed invention during the time from the publication of the patent application. Because a substantive provision is not provided for in the UPCA, the UPC must refer to Article 67 EPC in connection with

46. Rule 118(1) RoP.
47. Article 64(2)(e) UPCA.
48. Article 64(2)(c) UPCA.

Article 64 EPC, which might lead to either a reasonable compensation or full damages, depending upon in which Contracting Member States the infringement occurred.

[2] Statement of Defense

[a] Content

The defendant responds to the plaintiff's statement of claim by filing a statement of defense. This pleading is primarily aimed at showing why the action lacks merit. Like the plaintiff's statement of claim, the statement of defense should be a thorough pleading that enables the court to efficiently prepare the proceedings. The defendant must substantiate each defense and provide the different counterarguments as completely as possible. The main task consists in challenging the facts presented by the plaintiff in the statement of claim and in providing substantiated reasons why the claim lacks merit. This is important because according to Rule 17(2) RoP any statement of the plaintiff which is not sufficiently contested will be held true. A particular challenge concerns the interpretation of the claims and the determination of the scope of protection. Like the statement of claim, the defense must contain unambiguously specified offers of evidence, any orders sought in the interim procedure, an indication of the value of dispute, a list of documents, copies of the supportive documents, non-translation requests as to documents which are not written in the language of the proceedings and requests for confidentiality if appropriate.[49]

A special defense—regulated in Article 28 UPCA, which might be asserted by the defendant—is based on the right flowing from "prior use." According to German law, such prior use right is conferred upon any person who had possession of the invention and already commenced using it before the priority date.[50] If so, the defendant might be immune from liability.

Additionally, the defendant might plead the defense of exhaustion of rights. Rights conferred by a European patent can in principle not extend to acts concerning a product covered by that patent after that product has been placed by the patentee or any authorized person on the market in the EU.[51]

[b] Possible Defenses

After the statement of claim is filed and served on the defendant, the defendant must respond. This must be done within the deadlines outlined in Figure 10.3. Counterarguments can be directed against the plaintiff's presentation of facts, including the

49. Article 58 UPCA.
50. Cf. Ch. 10, §10.02[B][3][b].
51. Article 29 UPCA: "The rights conferred by a European patent shall not extend to acts concerning a product covered by that patent after that product has been placed on the market in the European Union by, or with the consent of, the patent proprietor, unless there are legitimate grounds for the patent proprietor to oppose further commercialisation of the product."

proposed claim construction. Furthermore, legal and procedural objections can be raised by the defendant at this stage:

(a) **Factual Submissions:** The defendant's defense must carefully identify those facts that are denied. Anything not expressly denied shall be deemed as admitted, unless the denial is obvious from other statements of the party. It is thus crucial to clearly point to those facts in the complaint that are denied. A simple denial (e.g., "the plaintiff's allegation is incorrect") without giving any further explanatory reasons for the denial is *not* sufficient and would be disregarded.

(b) **Legal and Procedural Defenses:** Beyond admitting or denying the facts of the complaint, and submitting the defendant's own characterization of the patent and claim construction, there are several defenses which may be available depending on the particular case. These defenses might have a legal nature, i.e., they result from the substantive law, or they may be procedural. Procedural defenses raised by the defendant are mainly directed against the venue and jurisdiction of the court, or the defendant may challenge insufficient security for the procedural costs. The main defenses resulting from the substantive law are as follows:

- **Right based on prior use:** According to Article 28 UPCA, "any person, who, if a national patent had been granted in respect of an invention, would have had, in a Contracting Member State, a right based on prior use of that invention or a right of personal possession of that invention, shall enjoy, in that Contracting Member State, the same rights in respect of a patent for the same invention." A prior user may thus invoke a right based on prior use, which must be established according to the national rules set by each Contracting Member State. Article 28 UPCA may thus not necessarily provide a remedy for all States where the European patent-in-question is in force. Rather the acquisition of such right(s) follows from the national laws of the Contracting Member State. These laws are not completely harmonized. Usually, a qualified possession of the claimed technology must be shown. This requires not only possession, in terms of availability of the claimed teaching on the side of the prior user, but also that he has knowledge of it and had already begun to commercially use the invention, or at least has made serious arrangements for doing so. In a few countries, such as France,[52] an established possession is sufficient. Also, the scope of the prior use might be different from one Contracting Member State to another. In some Contracting Member States, the use of the claimed teaching is limited to bona fide business activities and limited in scope to acts that were already committed or intended as of the priority date of the patent.[53] In particular, the defense does not provide a benefit in regard to features of the patent that

52. Article L 613-7 (Code de la Propriété Intellectuelle).
53. Federal Supreme Court, X ZR 32/99, GRUR 2002, 231, "Biegevorrichtung."

are outside of what the user effectively recognized at the priority date. Nevertheless, the defense covers not only the prior user but also subsequent trading partners,[54] such as customers who have bought a product covered by the prior use.

- **Contractual licenses**: The defendant may be entitled to rely on an existing license agreement, under which the infringement claim is barred. This requires that the agreement has actually been formalized and that the activities of the defendant are within its scope.
- **Exhaustion of patent rights**: This defense refers to a situation where the product was previously put on the EU/EEC market with the permission of the patentee or of someone who was duly authorized by the patentee. The details of the exhaustion of patent rights are described in Chapter 12.
- **Defense arising from antitrust law**: This defense may arise when a market-dominating position follows from the assertion of the patent. The details of this defense are described in the following section 3.
- **Usurpation**: The defendant may argue that he is the rightful owner and has been illegally dispossessed of the invention (usurpation).
- **Statute of limitation**: Rights resulting from the infringement of a patent may be statute-barred.
- **Forfeiture:** The defense of forfeiture refers to the exceptional situation where a right holder has knowingly tolerated, for a considerable time period, the infringing activities, such that the accused infringer may objectively presume from the circumstances that the right holder would never assert the patent-in-question. The concept of forfeiture results from the fundamental principle, according to which a right holder has a duty to proceed in good faith when asserting a claim. Nevertheless, the German Federal Supreme Court has set high thresholds establishing a defense of forfeiture:[55] first, a time aspect—the toleration of the infringing acts must have lasted for a considerable time period;[56] second, there must be particular circumstances which objectively create a reliable impression in the accused infringer that his use of the patented invention may continue into the future; and, third, he must, from such use, have thus acquired economic value.

[3] Counterclaim for Revocation

If the defendant wants to challenge in infringement proceedings the validity of the action, he must file a counterclaim for revocation in the same proceedings. The defendant of these infringement proceedings is not allowed to directly file a revocation

54. Federal Supreme Court, Decision of Jun. 12, 2012, X ZR 131/09, "Desmopressin"; Appeal Court Düsseldorf, InstGE 11, 198, "Desmopressin."
55. Federal Supreme Court, X ZR 150/98, GRUR 2001, 323, "Temperaturwächter."
56. *Ibid.*: Subject to this case was a situation where the patentee waited for more than ten years, before he started to assert his rights against the accused infringer.

action with the Central Division in such a situation,[57] even if the plaintiff is not at the same time the patentee. The Registry serves a copy of the counterclaim for revocation (which must be directed against the patent owner) on the patentee. The owner becomes a party to the revocation proceedings and will be treated as a defendant in all subsequent proceedings.[58] For instance, if the infringement proceedings have been initiated by a licensee, the licensee cannot be the addressee of the counterclaim for revocation. Rather, the patent owner becomes a party to the case after service of the counterclaim for revocation.

The counterclaim for revocation is an integral part of the statement of defense. It must be filed together with the statement of defense within three months after service of the statement of case. Because the defendant usually needs to perform prior art searches, as well as a subsequent assessment of the identified prior art, this time frame can be tight, particularly in complex cases. The three-month response period is not mandated, and the Court may grant an extension for good cause. Nevertheless, it is strongly recommended to form a team of attorneys on the defense and adequately divide the work among different legal team members. Otherwise, the workload could easily become unmanageable.

The possibility of making a counterclaim for revocation in infringement proceedings with *erga omnes* effect of the revocation is unprecedented under the German patent litigation system. In the German system, revocation (nullity) actions are filed in a separate legal proceeding, distinct from the infringement case.[59] By contrast, in the UPC system if the defendant seeks revocation of the patent, the court must adjudicate that counterclaim, even if the court dismisses the action on infringement.

The counterclaim for revocation must indicate to what extent the patent is contested. In fact, the patent can be fully contested or in relation to specific claims.[60] In addition, the counterclaim of revocation must specify the ground(s) of revocation,[61] the facts supporting the revocation and all evidence relied on.

[4] Patent Amendments (Auxiliary Requests)

In proceedings before the UPC, a counterclaim for revocation is a typical defense of the accused infringer (plaintiff). Without counterclaim for revocation, only noninfringement can be pleaded. According to Rule 30 RoP, the patentee shall indicate in his first reply to the counterclaim for revocation whether and how he wishes to amend the patent-in-suit. This is usually done by means of a main request followed by one or more auxiliary requests. The auxiliary requests are only filed as a precaution, i.e., in the alternative if the main request is not allowable. The main request usually contains a claim set with the broadest scope of protection, while the auxiliary requests form a

57. Article 33(4) UPCA: "If … an action for infringement between the same parties relating to the same patent has been brought before a local or a regional division, these actions may only be brought before the same local or regional division."
58. Rule 25(2) RoP.
59. Rule 265(2) RoP.
60. Article 65(2) UPCA.
61. Article 65 UPCA, Arts. 138, 139 EPC; cf. Ch. 7, §7.06.

cascade of claim sets limiting the scope of protection of the patent further and further. The last auxiliary request of that cascade usually contains a claim set with the smallest scope of protection. Later amendments of the patent introduced in the proceedings through such requests require the permission of the court. Thus, the patentee must define his line of defense very early. This could be problematic because in the written proceedings, neither the reporting judge nor the division's panel has expressed a preliminary opinion as to the extent to which the grounds for invalidity are considered relevant. A preliminary opinion could be issued at the earliest in the interim proceedings. Furthermore, the Rules of Procedure (Rule 30.1 (c) RoP) specify that the number of auxiliary requests should be kept "reasonable." For the patentee, the problem thus arises of having to correctly assess the relevance of the submitted attacks in advance since later amendments, i.e., as soon as a preliminary opinion of the division becomes known, could encounter delay difficulties. The patentee is therefore inclined, despite the intent of Rule 30.1(c) RoP, to file as many auxiliary requests as possible to anticipate most of the eventualities. The latter may increase the complexity of matter for the division and the parties. A possible solution to that problem would be to introduce a qualified notice issued during the interim proceeding with an opportunity for the parties to express their views and eventually add new requests or drop requests. This could be designed according to the approach applied by European opposition divisions. The UPC's procedural rules leave sufficient room for such a move, such as Rule 103.1(d) RoP, which provides that parties may file motions after the interim conference they wish to make at the oral hearing. Alternatively, the general rules of Rule 9 and Rule 334 RoP could be applied. Accordingly, a multitude of unnecessary auxiliary requests could be avoided.

[D] Language of the Proceedings

[1] Local and Regional Divisions

The local division operates in the official language (or one of the official languages) of the Member State hosting that local division. Normally the proceedings are held in the language of the seat of the court's division (language of the seat). Nevertheless, the Member States may designate one or more of the official languages of the EPO (English, German or French) in addition or instead of their official language as the language of proceedings of their division. Furthermore, there is also the possibility that the parties agree to use the language in which the patent was granted (language of the patent). With respect to regional divisions, similar rules are applicable. In principle, the proceedings are held in the language of the Member State which hosts the regional division. Alternatively, the Member States belonging to that region may agree on another official language of the region or an official language of the EPO. Again, the parties may agree to use the language of the patent. Finally, there is a further possibility to employ the language of the patent if the President of the Court of First Instance decides so, on request of one of the parties and after having heard the other parties and the members of the panel.[62]

The language of the proceedings impacts the translation requirements of written documents. The submitting party normally bears the cost of translating documents into the language of the proceedings. The translation costs can later be recovered from the losing party.[63] The Court may dispense with such translation requirements in appropriate circumstances.[64] In particular, a translation of a document written in the language of the patent should in principle be not necessary even if it deviates from the language of the proceedings

[2] Central Divisions

The language of the proceedings in the central division is the language in which the patent was granted (language of the patent). Under certain circumstances after an infringement action is brought before the Central Division, a defendant having its residence or place of business in a Contracting Member State may—on the cost of the plaintiff—require translations of relevant documents in the language of the Member State of residence or place of business.

[3] Appeal Court

The language of proceedings before the Court of Appeal shall be the language of proceedings before the Court of First Instance.[65]

[E] Jurisdiction and Venue of the UPC

[1] Introduction

Jurisdiction among the divisions of the UPC's first instance is governed by Article 33 UPCA. Where the parties do or do not agree on the venue, an action based on European patent can basically be filed at one of the two locations:

> **Location 1:** Where the actual or threatened infringement has occurred or may occur.
>
> **Location 2:** Where the defendant or, in the case of multiple defendants,[66] where one of the defendants has its residence, or principal place of business, or in the absence of residence or principal place of business, its

62. Article 49 UPCA.
63. Rule 7 RoP.
64. Article 51(1) UPCA.
65. Articles 49 and 50 UPCA.
66. An action may be brought against multiple defendants only where the defendants have a commercial relationship and where the action relates to the same alleged infringement.

place of business. Accordingly, a local division has jurisdiction if the infringement occurs in the Contracting Member State hosting that division (location 1) or if the residence or principal place of business of the defendant is located there (location 2). A regional division will have jurisdiction if the alleged infringement takes place in at least one of its Contracting States. In a situation where the actual or threatened infringement takes place in a State that neither hosts a local division nor participates in a regional cluster, the patentee may directly file his action with the Central Division. Location 1, the forum of *actus in tort*[67] will be of particular importance for patentees if the accused infringer does not have a residence or place of business in the EU, given that such a patentee could not rely on the option of location 2. The possibility to file a case at the *actus in tort* allows "shopping" among the UPC divisions. The forums of *actus in tort* are the locations where the allegedly infringing product has been produced, offered, or placed on the market.[68] In the case of an offer, the infringing act might not only be the place where the offer has been made but also in all places where the offer is received or can be perceived by potential customers. An offer published through a webpage that can be perceived by an internet user in a Contracting Member State might be sufficient. Accordingly, when there has been an internet offer of an allegedly infringing product, a case could (most likely) be filed in any division. The choice would depend upon the claimant's strategic considerations. As a result, for the majority of patent infringement cases, each division of the UPC will have jurisdiction to hear the case.

[2] Infringement Actions

Patent infringement actions, including actions for provisional and protective measures and injunctions, damages or compensation derived from provisional protection and/or prior use may be brought as indicated in the introduction before the:

- local or regional division, "where the infringement has occurred" (actual or threatened infringement); or
- where the defendant has residence or place of business;
- if the defendant has no residence or place of business within the Contracting Member States: the local/regional division where the infringement has occurred or before the central division;
- if the concerned Contracting Member State has no local/regional division: the central division.

67. Article 33(1)(a) UPCA.
68. Article 25(a) UPCA.

[a] *Jurisdiction over Actual or Threatened Infringements*

The jurisdiction of a local division may be based on **an actual or threatened infringement** that occurred in the State which hosts the local division, whereas the jurisdiction of the regional division may be based on an act of infringement that occurred within any State, which belongs to the regional group. If it is only a threatened infringement, there must be sufficient facts showing that the accused infringer will act illegally soon. A direct infringement[69] depends on whether those acts fulfill at least one of the uses as defined in Article 25 UPCA. Cases of contributory infringement are governed by Article 26 UPCA. Jurisdiction is proper in a local or regional division when the accused acts that constitute all features of a claim are performed in the State hosting the local division or within the region of the regional division. If the place of the infringer's action and the place of the end user's performance are different, then either place is likely sufficient for establishing jurisdiction. For instance, an offer posted on the internet might be initiated in a territory of a division A (i.e., seat of the accused infringer) but is visible to potential customers within the territory B. In this scenario there should be sufficient contacts for establishing jurisdiction in either division A or B, pursuant to Article 33(1)(a) UPCA. The situation becomes more difficult to determine where the acts that support infringement are carried out in different places. For instance, the steps of a method claim might be initiated in one place and completed in one or more other places. How such issues are solved need to be decided on a case-by-case assessment. General tort law may provide an appropriate legal framework, which allows the attribution of steps implemented by a third party to the accused party provided the accused party willfully embeds acts of that third party into its own activity.

[b] *Defendant' Domicile*

The jurisdiction of a division may be premised on the residence of the defendant, as well as the defendant's principal place of business or other place of business. The principal place of business is where the defendant has its registered seat and maintains its central administration. The term "place of business" opens a broader application of the provision. It may also cover temporary domiciles such as an exhibition booth at a trade show.

[c] *Multiple Defendants*

Jurisdiction over multiple defendants may be established if at least one defendant is domiciled in a Contracting Member State according to these provisions.[70] Multiple defendants may be joined in this manner only if the defendants entertain a commercial relationship with each other and the action relates to the same alleged infringement,

69. Cf. Ch. 12, §12.04.
70. Article 33(1)(b) UPCA.

such as the same accused product.[71] Therefore, it is not required that all defendants be domiciled 'n the division's area of jurisdiction. It is sufficient, for example, that one defendant (Defendant A) be domiciled in the jurisdiction of a division, while another defendant (Defendant B) is domiciled outside the area of jurisdiction of that division. For instance, defendant B is domiciled in the US. The prerequisite for an action against both defendants is that a "business relationship" exists between Defendant A and Defendant B and that the action relates to the same alleged infringing acts. The provision of Article 33(1)(b) EPC apparently deviates from the concept of Article 8(1) Brussels Ia Regulation. This provision requires that the claims are *"so closely connected that it is expedient to hear and determine them together to avoid the risk of irreconcilable judgments in separate proceedings."* Depending on which rule comes into play, the question arises whether this may lead to different results. This is especially problematic against defendants who are domiciled in non-Member States of the UPCA and for whom Article 8(1) Brussels Ia Regulation is decisive. To avoid a conflict, an interpretation of Article 33 b) UPCA in conformity with Union law and case law of ECJ[72] is therefore necessary (Article 24(1) UPCA).

[d] Defendants Without Domicile in a Contracting Member State

If a defendant has no residence or place of business within the Contracting Member States, the plaintiff may elect to proceed in either the central division or the division where the infringement occurred or is threatened. Establishing jurisdiction in the central division could conflict with the Brussels Ia Regulation. The only relevant jurisdiction under the Brussels Ia Regulation is the place of infringement, which may not coincide with the attribution of the case to the Central Division.[73] As long as this critical point remains undecided under the law of the UPC it is recommended to proceed in the division where the infringement takes place, if possible. Otherwise, the plaintiff risks having his case—with delaying effect—referred to the ECJ.

[e] Contracting Member States Without Division

If a Contracting Member State does not host a division or does not belong to a region with a regional division, the plaintiff may file the lawsuit with the central division, as provided by Article 33(1) (last sentence). Note, however, that this provision is not complaint with the jurisdictional rules set forth in Brussels Ia Regulation. As long as this critical point stays undecided by the UPC, it is recommended to proceed in a division where infringement takes place.[74] Otherwise, the plaintiff risks that his case may be—with delaying effect—referred to the ECJ.

---

71. *Ibid.*
72. CJEU C-539/03 *Roche v. Primus.*
73. Article 71(b)(2) Brussels Ia Regulation.
74. Chapter 9, §9.03[A][4].

[f] Three-Region Clause

The "three region clause" is a provision of the UPCA that deals with widespread infringing activities occurring in at least three regional divisions:[75] This is, where acts of infringement occur in the territories of at least three regional divisions, a defendant may request that the regional division where the case was originally filed should refer the case to the central division. This provision is designed to allow disputes over commercially important patents to be heard in the central division, rather than potentially before a less experienced regional division. This provision does not comply with the jurisdictional allocations of matters of the Brussels Ia Regulation. The UPC has not yet taken up the question of how to resolve such conflicts in rules.

[3] Counterclaim for Revocation

[a] Introduction

Counterclaims for revocation must be lodged together with the statement of defense in the infringement proceedings. The division hearing the infringement case may adjudicate the counterclaim for revocation in the same proceeding. In fact, when a counterclaim of revocation is lodged, the division has three options.[76] The division may:

(1) hear both the infringement action and the counterclaim for revocation (**single-track proceedings**);[77]
(2) refer the counterclaim for revocation to the central division and either suspend or further proceed with the action for infringement (**bifurcation**);[78]
(3) if agreed to by the parties, refer the entire case (i.e., infringement claim and the revocation counterclaim) to the central division (**entire case referral**).[79]

[b] Bifurcation or Single Track Proceedings

Where a patentee has brought infringement proceedings in a local or regional division under Article 33(1), the alleged infringer may lodge a counterclaim for revocation of the patent concerned. This is the case in most patent infringement proceedings. The local or regional division may then choose from several options.[80] The division may proceed in a unified manner, adjudicating both the infringement action and the counterclaim for revocation. The division may also refer the counterclaim for revocation to the central division. If the division thus takes such "bifurcation decision," it has two options:

75. Article 33(2) UPCA.
76. Article 33 UPCA.
77. Article 33(3)(a) UPCA.
78. Article 33(3)(b) UPCA.
79. Article 33(3)(c) UPCA.
80. Article 33(3) UPCA.

- **Option A**: It suspends the proceedings until a decision is reached on the validity of the patent. The division has some discretion but is obliged to suspend the infringement proceedings if there is a "high likelihood" that the patent will be revoked.[81] Rule 37(4) of the Rules of Procedure refers specifically to the question of when the local or regional division should stay the proceedings in cases where they follow the bifurcated approach and refer the revocation claim to the Central Division. The Rule states:

> Where the panel decides to proceed in accordance with Article 33(3)(b) of the Agreement, the panel may stay the infringement proceedings pending a final decision in the revocation procedure and shall stay the infringement proceedings where there is a *high likelihood* [authors' emphasis] that the relevant claims of the patent (or patents) will be held to be invalid on any ground by the final decision in the revocation procedure.

- **Option B:** The local or regional division may continue to proceed with the action for infringement.[82] If the division finds no infringement, then the case may be dismissed on the merits. If the division finds infringement, then the ruling is rendered subject to the condition that the patent may be held wholly or partially invalid pursuant to the pending counterclaim for revocation.[83] If the patent is ultimately found to be invalid, then the proceedings at the local or regional division may be resumed to account for the invalidity ruling.

Whether or not to bifurcate the proceedings, is within the discretion of the local or regional division. The relevant aspects for such a decision are still undetermined. National traditions may not provide arguments. The UPC needs to establish its own jurisprudence. The bifurcated system is advantageous to the patentee and not necessarily to the defendant. Infringement cases frequently move ahead of counterpart invalidity proceedings, thus presenting the opportunity to have infringements resolved before invalidity is tried. While the infringement court may suspend its proceedings to allow a corresponding nullity action to resolve validity first, it does so only rarely. The bifurcated approach leads to an outsourcing of the in-depth discussion on the validity of the asserted patent. In fact, it reduces the workload and thus speeds up of the proceedings. However, these are not compelling arguments in favor of the bifurcated approach.

The historical precedents of the various national court systems in Europe may not shed much light for determining how the local and regional divisions of the UPC will approach the question of bifurcation. Whereas German courts would bifurcate their proceedings by law, with nullity actions tried separately from infringement claims, that historical precedent does not necessarily inform how disputes will proceed through the divisions of the UPC, which is premised on a fundamentally different set of rules.

81. Rule 118(3)(b) RoP; Rule 37(4).
82. Article 33(3)(b) UPCA.
83. Rule 118(3) RoP.

Likewise, whereas other Contracting Member States have normally adjudicated infringement and revocation claims through single-track proceedings, it may now be appropriate to diverge from that historical precedent and adopt a new approach under the novel framework of the UPC. Now, each division must determine and decide on the most suitable option according to a case-by-case assessment and in consideration of the circumstances of the individual case, including fairness. There is a need to balance fairly the interests of the patentee (who generally seeks swift enforcement) with the interests of the accused infringer (who should not be prevented from commercial activities by an invalid patent).

There are sound arguments in favor of maintaining an action in one single track without bifurcating the case. For handling revocation claims, there is no reason to argue that the panels of the Central Division are better equipped than local or regional divisions. Local or regional divisions may be made up of four judges (with one being a technical judge), whereas the panels of the Central Division are composed of two legal and one technical judge. Apart from special cases, a single track procedure thus rather represents the normal way of handling patent litigation at the UPC. Special cases might arise, for example, if the infringing action can easily be dismissed. In such cases, where the defendant insists on proceeding with the revocation claim, that may be maintained as a stand-alone action in the central division.

[c] Stand-Alone Revocation Actions

Stand-alone actions for revocation must be brought before the central division.[84] A common scenario is that a challenger, who is commercializing or about to commercialize a patent-infringing product, files a stand-alone action for revocation. When a patent is newly granted at the EPO a competitor of the patentee may elect to challenge the patent either in opposition proceedings at the EPO or through stand-alone revocation action at the UPC, or both. At this time, that challenger may not yet have initiated activities that could be deemed an infringement. Filing a stand-alone revocation action may also be strategically motivated to preclude the patent owner from opting out of the UPC system, thus ensuring that UPC divisions be the forum for litigating disputes over the life of that patent. According to Article 83(3) UPCA, an opt-out requires that no action has yet been brought before the UPC.

If an infringement action is already pending "between the same parties"[85] before a local or regional division, the revocation claim must be brought to that division. For the purpose of procedural economy both revocation and infringement are thus decided by the same division in this scenario. Nevertheless, a revocation action which has been brought first at the Central Division does not prevent a later infringement action from being filed with an appropriate local or regional division. Article 33(5) UPCA additionally provides for a possibility to file the infringement action with the central division.[86] The latter is critical. Combining the proceedings within the central division might be

84. Article 32(1)(d) UPCA.
85. Article 33(5) UPCA.
86. *Ibid.*

appreciated for economic reasons but seems to conflict with the jurisdictional rules under Brussels Ia Regulation. This legal inconsistency will have to be solved by the UPC and eventually with the aid of the ECJ. Meanwhile, it is advisable to file the infringement claim with a competent local or regional division rather than at the central division. In that scenario, if a stand-alone revocation action is filed first with the Central Division and later an infringement action is lodged with a competent local or regional division, the infringement division may then either proceed with or stay the infringement proceedings.[87] It appears from the language of Article 33 UPCA that an accused infringer may—notwithstanding the pending revocation action with the central division—file a counterclaim for revocation in the infringement proceedings, otherwise the accused infringer would not get an opportunity to directly defend himself against an invalid patent in the infringement proceedings. Of course, allowing a revocation action and a counterclaim for revocation to proceed simultaneously in different divisions runs the risk of inconsistent results. A solution to this problem may be found, for instance, by staying the proceedings of the central division until an outcome of the infringement division is reached.[88]

[4] EPO Opposition and Parallel Infringement

EPO oppositions may proceed in parallel with infringement cases at the UPC. According to Article 33(10) UPCA, the Court shall be informed and may then stay the proceedings when a "rapid decision" of the EPO is expected.

In several European jurisdictions, opposition proceedings at the EPO and national revocation actions cannot be implemented simultaneously. For example, in Germany, commencing a national revocation action requires that no opposition proceedings against the patent be pending and that the time period for filing an opposition against the patent has passed.[89] This requirement is mainly aimed at avoiding contradictory decisions. A third party that cannot file an opposition due to the lapsed opposition period may nonetheless join pending opposition proceedings provided that an infringement lawsuit has been filed against that party.[90]

The UPCA does not prioritize opposition proceedings over revocations actions. Articles 33(8) and (10) of the UPCA permit both proceedings to continue in parallel. Article 33(8) Agreement stipulates that the claimant in revocation proceedings at the UPC is not required to file a notice of opposition with the EPO. Accordingly, the claimant can directly file a revocation action or do both.

According to Article 33(10) UPCA, the claimant is, however, required to "inform the Court of any pending revocation, limitation or opposition proceedings before the European Patent Office." Furthermore, the provision stipulates that "the Court may stay its proceedings when a rapid decision may be expected from the European Patent Office."

87. *Ibid.*
88. Rule 75(3) RoP.
89. Section 81(2) GPA.
90. Article 105 EPC.

The UPC may—but is not required to—stay proceedings in cases relating to a patent that is also the subject of opposition proceedings or limitation proceedings (including subsequent appeal proceedings) before the EPO.[91] The interplay between parallel EPO opposition proceedings and revocation proceedings at the UPC is not detailed further in the Agreement or the RoP. The establishment of standards for such stays is left to the UPC.

The UPC's decision-making authority is bounded by the determinations of the EPO. As such, a UP that has been finally revoked by the EPO (for instance, after Appeal) cannot be "revived" by the UPC. In addition, if a UP is narrowed through EPO opposition proceedings, the UPC is bound by that limited scope and is prevented from reinstating a previously applied broader scope of protection. This procedural framework must be taken into account when establishing the standards for staying proceedings at the UPC. UPC case law will have also to aim to avoid contradictory decisions among the EPO and the UPC and to reduce the duplication of work at the EPO and the UPC.

[5] Declaratory Judgment Actions

Declaratory judgment actions seeking a finding of noninfringement must be brought at the central division.[92] This action can be directly combined with an action for revocation.[93] This does not mean that a later infringement action must also be filed with the central division. Article 33(6) UPCA is premised on the concept that an infringement action can freely be brought to any appropriate infringement division. The filing of a declaratory judgment action for noninfringement may thus not be used to block the jurisdiction of particular divisions. The patent owner is not deprived of its free choice of forum for the infringement action. Nevertheless, that free choice is limited by Article 33(6) UPCA. That is, only if an infringement action is filed within a period of three month of filing the declaratory judgment action, the central division must stay the proceedings. The central division is obligated to stay the declaratory judgment action if the patent owner files an offensive infringement case within three months of the declaratory judgment action. Thus, the primacy of the patent owner's choice of forum is time limited. The three-month deadline is structured in recognition of the fact that within three months, the declaratory judgment proceedings at the central division have usually taken an advanced state. Even though the patent proprietor would not be precluded from filing an infringement action after the three-month period, the patentee would no longer benefit from a mandatory stay.

[F] Service

The RoP distinguish between service within and outside UPCA states.

91. *See also* Rule 295 RoP.
92. Article 33(4) UPCA.
93. Rule 77 RoP.

For services within UPCA states, both the EU Service Regulation and the rules set out in Chapter 2, section 1 of the RoP shall apply (Rules 270–272 RoP). The Registry serves the statement of claim or a counterclaim for revocation by electronic means if the conditions of Article 19 EU Service Regulation are met. The statement of claim shall either be served on the party directly or on a representative. The EU Service Regulation sets forth the conditions under which service of judicial documents may be effected directly on a person by electronic means. Service can either be effected using a qualified electronic registered delivery services if the defendant has consented to it. The document served electronically must use a trust service provider established by the EU or an electronic identification scheme. Service may also be effected by simple email where the addressee has consented to it and confirms receipt of the document with an acknowledgement of receipt, including the date of receipt. Service on a representative may be effected within the closed system of the Court's case management system. Where service by electronic means cannot be effected, the Registry shall serve the statement of claim on the defendant by any other method foreseen by the EU Service Regulation, and in particular by registered letter with acknowledgement of receipt or equivalent. If this is not possible, service can also be effected by any other method permitted by the law of the EU Member State where service is to be effected or authorized.

The Registry shall advise the defendant that he may refuse to accept a Statement of claim if it is not accompanied by a translation into a language that he understands or that is an official language of the place where service is to be effected.

Regarding defendants having no seat within UPCA states the service will be effected by the rules of the EU Service Regulation, by the Hague Convention or by diplomatic or consular channels from the UPCA states in which the sub-registry of the relevant division is seated or, when none of these alternatives works, the national laws on the service of the state in which the document shall be served. Where service in accordance with section 1 or 2 of Chapter 2 of the RoP cannot be implemented, the Court may permit service by an alternative method or at an alternative place, if the claimant asks to do so and gives good reasons.

[G] Enforcement

Decisions and orders of the Court are directly enforceable in any Contracting Member State under the procedure and conditions governed by the laws of the respective Contracting Member State in which the enforcement will take place.[94] No national procedures to render the decision enforceable are necessary. Prior to starting the enforcement, the claimant serves a notification to the court indicating which part of the decision he intends to enforce. An order for the enforcement of a decision is appended to the decision by the court. The Registry then serves the claimant's notification to the defendant. If a security has been ordered to ensure compensation for any damage suffered in case the underlying decision is later revoked, the enforcement can only start

94. Article 82 UPCA, Rule 354 RoP.

after the claimant has provided that security.[95] Decisions are generally immediately enforceable, but under the Court's discretion the enforcement may be made conditional upon the provision of a security.[96] The security could be provided in the form of deposit on an escrow account of a bank guarantee,[97] which must at least cover the appropriate compensation due for any injury caused by the enforcement of later revoked decision.[98] The litigation value could serve as a guideline, but is not a sufficient factor for determining the amount of the security. Of course, when enforcing pecuniary claims, the determination of the amount may easily refer to the claimed payment. This is however not possible in case of an injunction, where a cease-and-desist claim shall be subject to the enforcement. Here, the potential economic harm to the debtor must be established case-by-case.

[H] Public Access/Confidentiality

According to Article 10(1) UPCA the register shall be public. However, disclosure of pleadings and evidence collected in UPC proceedings may be restricted or prohibited. The access to such files and evidence may thus be restricted to specific people to protect trade secrets, personal data, or other confidential information of the parties to the proceedings or any third party (Article 58 UPCA). According to Article 45 UPCA, the proceedings are open to the public unless the Court decides to make them subject to secrecy, to the extent necessary to protect the interest of one of the parties or any affected third party, or the general interest of justice or public order. The Court is bound by the General Data Protection Regulation (GDPR) (Regulation (EU) 2016/679). The GDPR applies not only to administrative but also to judicial activities of the Court. A party may request that certain information of written pleadings or evidence be kept confidential. This request must be reasoned. Third parties may also lodge an application for an order that information be excluded from public access The Court shall allow the application unless legitimate reasons outweigh the interest of the applicant. During the assessment of the application (and a possible appeal) the information shall be kept confidential (Rule 262 RoP). Also, decision and orders of the Court shall be published, after redaction of personal data and confidential information.

Rule 262A deals with the protection of confidential information vis-à-vis the other party to the proceedings. A party may lodge an application for an order that certain information contained in its pleadings or the collection and use of evidence in proceedings may be restricted or prohibited or that access to such information or evidence be restricted to specific persons. The application shall be reasoned and shall contain both a redacted and unredacted version of the relevant document. In order to allow the application, it is necessary that its grounds relied upon by the applicant significantly outweigh the interest of the other party to have full access to the evidence

95. Article 82(2) UPCA.
96. Rule 352 RoP.
97. Rule 352(1) RoP.
98. Rule 354(2) RoP.

in question. In its explanatory note, the Administrative Committee states that "*restricting information from the knowledge of the other party affects its right to a fair hearing, which is, inter alia, enshrined in Art. 76(2) UPCA, Art. 47(2) of the Charter of Fundamental Rights of the European Union and Art. 6(1) of the European Convention on Human Rights. As a consequence, such restriction of information by Court order has to be limited to exceptional cases.*"

[I] Costs

[1] Losing Party Pays

The UPC system is based on a loser-pays system. Accordingly, "reasonable and proportionate legal costs and other expenses" spent by the winning party shall, as a general rule, be borne by the losing party.[99] In case of partial success or in exceptional circumstances, the UPC may order the parties to bear their own costs, or apply a different apportionment of the costs, based on equity.[100] The costs for representation (costs of the counsel and the party) are recoverable up to a ceiling set in accordance with the RoP. The ceiling to be applied to each instance of the court proceedings is tied to the value of the proceedings, to be oriented on the plaintiff's objective interest when filing the action. The latter depends on the accumulated value of the different remedies sought by the plaintiff, mainly comprising the cease-and-desist claim which represents future value through the end of the term of the patent and the damage claim, which compensates the patentee for past infringement[101] (*see* Table 10.1). These are ceilings. The ceilings do not have to be reached. Often, they are not reached because only "reasonable and proportionate legal costs and other expenses" spent by the winning party are reimbursable.

Table 10.1 Ceiling for Recoverable Costs

Value of the Proceeding (EUR)	*Ceiling for Recoverable Costs (EUR)*
Up to and including 1,000,000	Up to 112,000
Up to and including 2,000,000	Up to 200,000
Up to and including 4,000,000	Up to 400,000
Up to and including 8,000,000	Up to 600,000
Up to and including 16,000,000	Up to 800,000
Up to and including 30,000,000	Up to 1,200,000

99. Article 69(1) UPCA.
100. Article 69(2) UPCA.
101. The ceiling might be subject to reviews by the Administrative Committee and thus change over the time.

Value of the Proceeding (EUR)	Ceiling for Recoverable Costs (EUR)
Up to and including 50,000,000	Up to 1,500,000
More than 50,000,000	Up to 2,000,000

Exceptionally (for particularly complex cases), the ceiling may be raised by the UPC up to 50% if the value of the case is below EUR 1 million, up to 25% if the value ranges between EUR 1 and EUR 50 million, or up to EUR 5 million in cases the value is higher than EUR 50 million. Upon request of a party, the UPC can also lower the ceiling if the economic existence of that party is endangered.

[2] Court Fees

The UPC is self-financed, primarily through court fees, which have to be paid by the parties to the proceedings and are to be advanced by the plaintiff. Accordingly, court fees are due for both infringement and revocation actions. The statement of claim will not be deemed to have been lodged until the fee for the action has been paid.[102] If later during the proceedings the defendant launches a counterclaim for revocation of the patent, he will also be obliged to pay a court fee.[103] These fees are composed of a fixed fee and a value-based fee.[104] For actions relating to infringement, the fixed fee shall be EUR 11,000. If, in addition, the determination of damages is requested, the fixed fee for that determination shall be EUR 3,000. For actions with a value of more than EUR 500,000 a value-based fee will be added ranging from EUR 2,500 (for actions with a value between EUR 500,000 and EUR 750,000) up to EUR 325,000 (for actions with a value of more than EUR 50,000,000). For stand-alone revocation actions, a fixed court fee of EUR 20,000 will be due. The same applies to counterclaims for revocation. For provisional measures, a fixed fee of EUR 11,000 will have to be paid.

Small enterprises and microenterprises[105] may benefit from a reduction of 60% of the fixed and value-based fees.[106] However, the UPC can on its own motion order payment of the remaining 40%, if the 60% reduction is manifestly disproportionate and unreasonable with respect to the financial capacity of the applicant. The UPC can also order payment of the remainder of the regular fee plus an additional 50% if the affirmation given by the applicant is found to be wholly or partially incorrect. These security mechanisms have been introduced to avoid abuse by so-called patent trolls.

The court fees for the appeal proceedings are in principle the same as those due in first instance. This is different in German proceedings where the costs are higher, by approximately 33%. Costs for a third instance do not apply because such third instance proceedings do not exist in the UPC system. The following Table 10.2 compares the

102. Rule 15.2. RoP.
103. Rules 26 and 53 RoP.
104. Rule 370 RoP.
105. Defined in Title I of the Annex of the Recommendation of the European Commission no. 2003/361 of May 6, 2003.
106. Rule 370.8 RoP.

costs with the actual German situation. In consideration of the fact that the revocation claim brought by the defendant would only entail a maximum fee of EUR 20.000, the proceedings at the UPC are even cheaper than German proceedings.

Table 10.2 Court Fees (First Instance)

Value of the Dispute (EUR)	*Fixed Fee + Fee for Sum in Dispute (EUR)*	*Court Fees in German Proceedings (EUR)*
Up to 500,000	0 (+11,000)	11.703
Up to 750,000	2,500 (+11,000)	14.673
Up to 1,000,000	4,000 (+11,000)	17.643
Up to 1,500,000	8,000 (+11,000)	23.583
Up to 2,000,000	13,000 (+11,000)	29.523
Up to 5,000,000	32,000 (+11,000)	65.163
Up to 7,000,000	46,000 (+11,000)	88.923
Up to 10,000,000	65,000 (+11,000)	124.563
Up to 15,000,000	75,000 (+11,000)	183.963
Up to 25,000,000	125,000 (+11,000)	302.763
Up to 30,000,000	150,000 (+11,000)	362.163
Up to 50,000,000	250,000 (+11,000)	362.163
Up to 50,000,000	325,000 (+11,000)	362.163

[3] Security

At request of the defendant, the court may order the applicant to provide adequate security for legal costs and other expenses incurred by the defendant which the plaintiff may be liable to bear.[107] That is, if the court's decision is in favor of the defendant, he shall be enabled to recover costs. In German proceedings, such security must be provided by foreigners lacking a seat in the EU or at least in EEA or in countries having special arrangements with Germany. Under German procedural rules, it might be sufficient to assign the patents to a company seated in Europe to circumvent the duty to provide a security. However, it should be a company that can prove an administrative seat with operational business in Europe. A company established solely for the purpose of enforcing patents whose directors do not even live in the EU may be required to post the security.

The seat of the plaintiff is irrelevant for Article 69(4) UPCA and Rule 158 RoP. Rather, the provisions allow the UPC to exercise discretion when ordering such security. It is not the general rule to award such security. The request must be reasoned in particular taking into account the solvency of the plaintiff. For instance, pure patent assertion companies with insignificant assets other than a small patent portfolio are

107. Article 69(4) UPCA.

likely obliged to provide a sufficient security regardless of where they are seated. A strategy of assigning the patents to a Luxemburg company would thus not help.

§10.02 GERMAN PROCEEDINGS

The importance of Germany as a national jurisdiction for patent litigation is demonstrated by the number of actions filed in German courts per year. Most of the patent infringement actions filed in Europe are conducted in Germany. The existence of the UPC may shift that focus in the coming years. However, also in the future, the German system will play an important role for litigation based on patents issued by the GPTO, Germany's utility models and during the transitional period of Article 83 UPCA for German parts of ordinary European patents issued by the EPO. UPs do however not fall within the jurisdiction of the Germany's patent infringement courts and of any other national court.

[A] Overall Timeline

A key difference between patent litigation in the US and Germany is the overall timeline for a typical case. Germany has a far more streamlined process, with the main hearing on the merits taking place within about a year. Although the district court may determine that further expert proceedings are necessary, or that the proceedings should be stayed pending resolution of opposition or nullity proceedings, it is quite possible the court will take up the merits of the case, and award relief, within less than one year.

The various district courts adopt varying approaches to scheduling. For instance, the District Court Munich follows its special rules called the "Munich procedure" aimed at finishing first instance proceedings within less than twelve months.[108] Accordingly, a first oral session takes place within approximately three to six months followed by the complaint and the submission of defendant's statement of defense. In this oral session the court usually provides its first indications as to the claim construction as well as a first nonbinding view on the question of infringement of the patent-in-suit. Also in this oral session, the Court will set deadlines for further written submissions and the main hearing. Other questions, such as the question of staying the proceedings, are normally deferred until the main hearing. The time frame in-between each submission is usually about two months. The Court only grants extensions in exceptional cases for short terms not exceeding one week. In addition, the Munich Court requires compliance with certain well-defined formalities, such as the submission of a short summary limited to ten pages prior to the main hearing.

A different approach is taken by the District Courts Mannheim and Düsseldorf. At the District Court Düsseldorf, a first early session, if it takes place, does usually not result in any substantive discussion, rather it serves to set the deadlines for the different submissions to be exchanged until the main hearing, which takes place approximately twelve to fourteen months after service of the complaint. Any indications as to the

108. *See* https://www.justiz.bayern.de: Hinweise zum Münchner Verfahren in Patentstreitsachen.

claim construction or the question of infringement of the patent-in-suit will thus not be provided in that first oral session. The substantive discussion on the merits is postponed until the main hearing. At the District Court Mannheim, all is concentrated on one main hearing without any meetings of the parties and the court occurring prior to the main hearing which typically takes place eight to nine months after service of the complaint.

Figure 10.4 illustrates the typical flow of proceedings, although as noted above, the different courts commonly adopt their own variants on this basic framework.

Figure 10.4 Timeline of Patent Infringement Proceedings

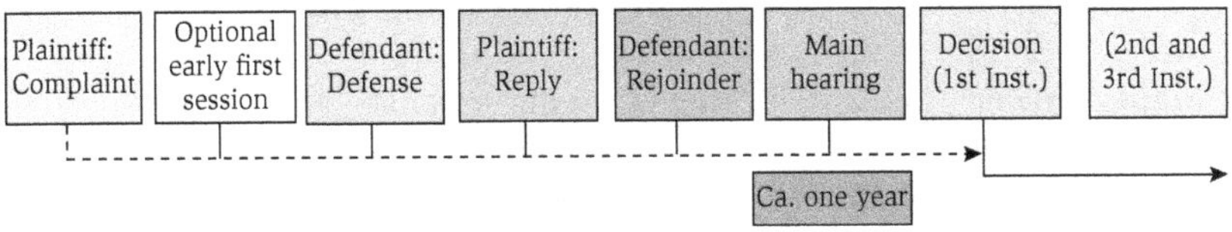

[B] Briefs of the Proceedings

[1] Introduction

Complaint: As in the US, a patent infringement case starts with a complaint (*Klageschrift*). Complaints in Germany are more detailed than in the US. Whereas complaints in the US are governed by the "notice pleading" standard, which permits patentees to file rather bare-bones complaints that merely give the defendant "notice" of the claim, Germany requires that plaintiffs set forth in their complaints a prima facie showing of entitlement to relief. As soon as the plaintiff has filed the complaint and has paid the court fee, the court will serve the complaint on the defendant(s).

Case Management Conference (CMC) or Order: After service of the complaint, the court usually sets a schedule for the case. This may be done at an in-person hearing (as is typical in the District Court Düsseldorf), or the schedule may be provided in a written order. The case management proceedings do not address the substance of the merits of the case, but may identify procedural insufficiencies in the complaint, such as inaccurately formulated requests or incomplete submissions. Normally, these insufficiencies can be corrected during the hearing or later by means of the exchanged briefs.

The court's schedule typically contains the following deadlines: a deadline which is set for the defendant's defense to the complaint brief; a deadline for the plaintiff to reply to the defendant's defense, a deadline for the defendant's final briefing and the date of the main hearing. Often the plaintiff will additionally file a brief in the days before the hearing, although this is not expressly allowed by the rules.

Defendant's Defense: Germany's analog to a US "answer" is called a "defense" (*Klageerwiderung*). This defense is typically filed two to three months after service of the complaint. And like the complaint, the defense is a much more detailed pleading than a US answer.

Plaintiffs' Reply: The plaintiff's reply (*Replik*) is usually the plaintiffs' ultimate written submission on the merits. The reply will typically contain additional arguments and refinements of position beyond what was provided in the complaint. With the defendant having set out its positions in its defense, the reply is the opportunity for the plaintiff to crystallize its case and more fully present its entitlement to relief. These briefs are styled more like "trial briefs," addressing all issues across the merits of the case. The plaintiffs' reply is typically filed—including deadline extensions—four to six months after service of the defense.

Defendants' Rejoinder: The defendants' final written submission before the main hearing is called its rejoinder (*Duplik*). Because there is no analog of "summary judgment" in Germany, these rejoinders address the overall merits of a case (unlike the more rifle-shot nature of summary judgment briefs in the US). A rejoinder is typically filed two months prior to the main hearing.

Main Hearing: The main hearing is the first instance "trial." It typically occurs twelve to thirteen months from the filing of the complaint. The main hearing is typically the court's first substantive involvement addressing the merits of the case. These main hearings are bench trials (i.e., no jury) and are remarkably fast in comparison to US-style trials. They typically last for two hours, and there are usually no live witnesses.

In this main hearing, the District Court takes up not only the ultimate issues of infringement but also the more basic issues that would tend to be resolved in the US on motions to dismiss, or for summary judgment. This main hearing is not just the court's first substantive hearing in a case, it is also frequently the last. Accordingly, threshold issues are resolved at the same time as the ultimate merits, unlike the US where a defendant would frequently have several "outs" from litigation prior to trial, such as through motions to dismiss, or *Markman* proceedings, or summary judgment.

Decision: Following the main hearing, the court determines if further proceedings will be necessary, such as by appointing an expert to resolve technical questions necessary for the claim construction and infringement,[109] or if the matter should be stayed pending opposition or nullity proceedings. In those instances, the otherwise fast-track German patent litigation may get delayed. Involving a court-appointed expert tends to add six to twelve months to the typical schedule. And a stay pending opposition or nullity actions may add a similar time, or longer, to the proceedings. The court will typically issue a formal written ruling within a few weeks after the hearing, and this normally marks the end of the first instance proceeding, from which the second instance and third instance appeals are taken. If favorable to the patentee, this decision will likely contain an injunction prohibiting the infringer from using the patented invention.

109. The task of a court expert is limited to the provision of technical knowledge for the judicial assessment of facts and to provide the technical knowledge required to understand the protected technical teaching and to enable the court to adequately interpret the patent claim(s). However, the court shall not leave the task of interpreting the patent claim to the court expert: Federal Supreme Court, Judgment of Feb. 12, 2008—X ZR 153/05—Mehrgangnabe.

Monetary Damages: If the patentee wins in the first instance, and demonstrates an entitlement to monetary damages, the amount of damages owed is subsequently determined in separate proceedings.

The following sections address in further detail each of these phases in a case.

[2] Complaint

[a] Contents

Patent infringement proceedings begin by filing a complaint. The contents of the complaint are governed by section 253 of the Code of Civil Procedure. A complaint in Germany needs to fulfill specific requirements. First, the complaint brief shall indicate the names and addresses of the parties and the selected court to which the complaint brief is addressed. In addition, the plaintiff needs to state a litigation value (which may be subject to an accounting in an ancillary proceeding, as discussed below).[110] A sample complaint is provided in Chapter 17, §17.03. Second, the plaintiff must make a precise statement of the subject matter and the grounds of the asserted rights, as well as a specific request for relief. Unlike the "notice pleading" standard of the US, Germany requires a substantiated complaint. That is, the complaint must provide enough factual basis and legal framework to justify relief in the event of a default judgment. This includes the different asserted rights, such as the asserted patent claims that are infringed, and the accused devices, complete with an explanation of why they infringe (including, where applicable, claim construction reasoning). All the above must be factually substantiated to a sufficient degree to justify relief.

[b] Rights and Requests

The complaint must specify all reliefs that the plaintiff seeks in the case. Under the rule of *ne ultra petita*, specified in section 308(1) of the Code of Civil Procedure, the court is bound by the plaintiff's requests and is not allowed to award relief beyond what is demanded in the complaint. The formulation of the requests is therefore an important task, to which due attention must be given.

[i] Injunctive Relief

Requirements: According to section 139(1) of the Patent Act, any person who uses a patented invention without authorization may be sued by the injured party to enjoin such use. The plaintiff must be an injured party. This is usually the patentee or the exclusive licensee. The claim for injunctive relief is focused on the future and accordingly it requires that the injured party demonstrates a "danger of recidivism" or that future infringements are imminent. To show a danger of recidivism, it is normally

110. Concerning the litigation value: *see* Ch. 10, §10.02[H][1] (below).

sufficient to demonstrate past infringement. The accused infringer may avert the alleged recidivism by agreeing to cease and desist of future infringing acts, so long as such agreement is coupled with penalties in case of its contempt.[111] The accused infringer may send such written undertaking to the injured party in view of avoiding a lawsuit. Usually, such undertaking is the consequence of a warning letter sent to the accused infringer during the pre-litigation phase. In case of a sufficient undertaking to cease and desist, the injured party would be barred from filing any action with respect to claims covered by the undertaking. The accused infringer may also issue such undertaking during pending litigation, in which case the plaintiff would have to declare that the lawsuit has been settled, which finishes the proceedings. The court would then only decide on the costs (section 91a of the Code of Civil Proceedings). Nevertheless, an abandonment of infringing acts or a simple declaration to refrain from using the patent in the future may not be sufficient to remove the grounds of the action.

A request aimed at preventing the accused infringer from using the invention must indicate the different acts that are forbidden to the defendant. These acts are enumerated in section 9 of the Patent Act.[112]

Proportionality Principle: It is recognized in economics and by policy that patent law requires an effective enforcement system. Patent law protects the interests of inventors. It also serves the public interest by promoting technological progress. But patent law is not resistant to considerations of equity. Enforcement is not an intransigent automatism. Rather it must be carried out with a sense of proportion and flexibility. According to the amendment of section 139(1) Patent Act by the Bill of August 30, 2021,[113] an exclusion of the right to injunctive relief (cease-and-desist claim) may be considered insofar as the claim would lead to a disproportionate hardship not justified by the exclusive right: The wording of the provision is as follows:

> The claim is excluded insofar as its assertion, due to the special circumstances of the individual case and in consideration of the requirements of good faith, would lead to a disproportionate hardship for the infringer or third parties which is not justified by the exclusive right.

A disproportionate hardship leading to a permanent exclusion of the injunctive relief (cease-and-desist claim) is found in rare situations. The wording "*insofar*" of the provision signals that the court may order—instead of a permanent—a partial exclusion of the injunctive relief. The court may, for example, grant the infringer a reasonable conversion period to develop a noninfringing alternative, or grant a period within which the infringer may still resell the infringing products on stock. The provision protects large and small companies alike. According to the legislator's view,[114] the amendment of section 139(1) Patent Act did not change the existing legal situation. It is merely a clarification that is already rooted in Union and German case

111. Federal Supreme Court, I ZR 212/93, GRUR 1996, 290, 292, "Wegfall der Wiederholungsgefahr."
112. A translation of s. 9 Patent Act is contained in Ch. 18.
113. Federal Law Gazette, BGBl. I p. 4074.
114. Gazette of the German Parliament, 19/25821.

law. The ECJ[115] understands the principle of proportionality not only as a minimum standard, but as an upper limit of protection conferred by the patent. Therefore, Union law already requires that injunctive relief be subject to proportionality. The principle of good faith (section 242 German Civil Code), to which belongs the principle of proportionality, also applies to claims for injunctive relief under patent law.[116] In addition, according to the widespread and correct view, section 275(2) of the German Civil Code also applies to patent law, according to which a debtor may refuse the enforcement of a right if it is grossly disproportionate to the creditor's interests in the performance. Thus, the Federal Supreme Court explicitly acknowledged these standards in 2016 in its "*Wärmetauscher*" judgment.[117] In the Federal Supreme Court's view a grace period, i.e., limited period of permitted use and a conversion time ("*Aufbrauchsfrist*"), can be granted on the basis of the principle of good faith "*if the immediate enforcement of the patent proprietor's claim for injunctive relief, even taking into account his interests, would represent a disproportionate hardship vis-à-vis the infringer due to special circumstances of the individual case, which would not be justified by the exclusive right and the regular consequences of its enforcement, and would therefore be contrary to good faith.*" The Federal Supreme Court made it however clear that a limitation of the injunctive relief is only applicable in special situations.

Considerations of proportionality have played only a limited role in practice so far. This was caused by a widespread view, that a consideration of proportionality would contradict the intention of the legislator due to a lack of explicit codification in the Patent Act. This view is now obsolete due to the clarification introduced in Sec. 139 Patent Act.

In view of the large number of conceivable cases, the legislator has not drawn up a list of criteria for the equity test under Sec. 139 Patent Act. This is left to the case law.[118] The granting of a limited period of permitted use and conversion time may be justified, if, for example, the economic consequences of an immediate enforcement of the injunctive relief would affect the infringer to a particularly high degree due to special circumstances (hardship); i.e., the injunctive relief would cause exceptionally great damages on the side of the infringer, for example, because extensive investments have already been made in the development and manufacture of the accused product and these consequences are completely disproportionate to the value of the infringed patent.

In supply chains, the patent owner may act not only against the manufacturer but also against the distributor. While the injunctive relief may have disproportionate consequences for the manufacturer, especially if the patented component is only a small and unsubstantial element of the accused product, it may have little effects on the distributor of the patented component. Even though it is likely that such considerations would be found to be tolerable consequences of patent enforcement, they may play a role within the overall assessment of circumstances. Also, it may be relevant that the

115. C-324/09, L'Oréal/eBay, para. 139 f.
116. Federal Supreme Court, X ZR 114/13, GRUR 2016, 1031.
117. *Ibid.*
118. Gazette of the German Parliament: 19/25821, p. 30.

infringed party itself manufactures or has manufactured corresponding products which are in direct competition with the patent-infringing product, or the infringed party is primarily interested in the monetization of its rights.[119] The latter is usually applicable to nonpracticing entities focusing on the conclusion of lucrative license agreements without tangible interests in a protection of own developments and production activities. Exaggerated license claims, which shall be enforced with the aid of an injunctive relief in an unfaithful manner, may form an argument against granting the claim for injunctive relief. However, the mere fact that the infringed party does not use the patent itself by means of own or licensed production might not per se represent a sufficient reason for limiting the right to injunctive relief.[120] Even a temporary exclusion of the injunctive relief requires a particular degree of "hardship" on the side of the patent infringer or a third party which is beyond regular effects and consequences of patent law.

Also interests of third parties can be considered according to section 139(1), sentence 3. Such interests could be affected if, for example, a drug or medical device is no longer available to patients due to the patent enforcement. But it is also true for third-party interests that regular effects of patent enforcement must be tolerated. Accordingly, it might not be sufficient for proving disproportionality to point to the normal effects of patent-protected drugs being more expensive and thus burdening the health care system.

The accused patent infringer bears the burden of presentation and proof for the disproportionality of the claim. Doubts are thus at the infringer's expense. A corresponding submission by the plaintiff for the injunctive relief is therefore only required if the patent infringer presents substantial reasons for an exceptional limitation of the claim for an injunction.

If the infringer is allowed to continue to use the invention for reasons of proportionality, it is not free of costs. The principle of proportionality regularly requires that the patentee be compensated for the use. Section 139(1), sentence 4 PatG provides for a claim for compensation regardless of fault. According to German law, compensation and damages cannot be cumulative. "Compensation" according to section 139(1), sentence 4 may thus not constitute punitive damages as known under U.S. law. According to the calculation method recognized in Germany's case law compensation necessarily reduces the damage claim. It remains to be seen how the courts will quantify this claim. It seems reasonable to calculate it according to the license analogy,[121] whereby the downsides for the right holder following from the (temporary) exclusion of the injunctive relief could be adequately priced in.

In sum, because the exclusion of injunctive relief is the exception, rather than the rule, these developments are not expected to mark a major change in the German case law.

Product Claims: If a product claim is asserted, the prayer for relief may be directed against the manufacture and commercialization of accused embodiments

119. *Ibid.*, p. 54.
120. *Ibid.*
121. Chapter 14, §14.02.

(section 9 Patent Act: "manufacturing, offering, putting on the market or using or possessing for the aforementioned purposes" the accused embodiment). The prayer for relief addresses the acts that the defendant shall be prohibited from performing. The prayer should not reach beyond the provable "risk of recidivism." If infringing acts have been committed, it is typically assumed that there is a risk that infringing acts would also occur in the future. The risk of recidivism can be proven by means of previously occurred infringing acts. If manufacturing activities can be detected on the German territory it can be assumed from these activities that the produced products will subsequently be sold. The request could thus address all acts defined in section 9 Patent Act, namely "manufacturing, offering, putting on the market or using or possessing" of the accused products. However, in case of a company which commercializes but does not manufacture the accused products in Germany, the request should not refer to acts of manufacturing; otherwise, the request would be too broad and thus partially incorrect.

A typical request in the case of an asserted product claim may have the following language:

> *It is requested in the name and on behalf of the plaintiff,*
>
> *I. to find defendant liable*
>
> *1. in order to avoid a penalty to be set by the court for each case of violation of up to € 250,000.— as an alternative confinement, or confinement of up to 6 months, in case of repeated violations a confinement of up to a total of 2 years, to refrain from manufacturing, offering, putting on the market or using or possessing for the aforementioned purposes a product comprising .... .*
>
> [Description of the accused embodiment]

In addition, the request must contain a description of the accused product or process. The request, if granted by the court, shall form a proper basis for the enforcement of the judgment. It shall specify the features of the accused product in relation to the features of the asserted claims. In case of literal infringement of the claim, lower courts usually accept the use of the features of the asserted claim(s) to describe the accused embodiment.

However, mere reproduction of the wording of the claim for the description of the accused embodiment may not be sufficient if the alleged infringement does not literally make use of features of the asserted patent claim and represents an infringement of the patent claim outside its literal wording.[122] For instance, if the infringement is based on the doctrine of equivalents[123] and thus the accused embodiment makes use of equivalent features, the request shall specify those feature(s) that are replaced and are different from the asserted claim. According to the Federal Supreme Court,[124] the courts shall ensure that the patentee's infringement allegations are identified in the

122. Federal Supreme Court, Decision of Mar. 30, 2005, X ZR 126/01, IIC 2006, 83, "Blasfolienherstellung."
123. The doctrine of equivalents is described in Ch. 12.
124. Federal Supreme Court, Decision of Mar. 30, 2005, X ZR 126/01, IIC 2006, 83, "Blasfolienherstellung."

request so specifically that a wording of the judgment in accordance with the petition can form a proper basis for a later enforcement.

In situations where the defendant is himself manufacturing the product within German territory, the request should also be directed against the manufacture of the product. If the defendant is an importing company or a reseller of the accused products without own production, the term "manufacturing" would have to be removed from the request.

Method/Process Claim: Where the request refers to a method claim, various strategies may be deployed. Section 9 No. 2 of the Patent Act distinguishes between infringing acts in relation to a method or process claims.

First, according to section 9 No. 2 of the Patent Act (first alternative), the request can be aimed at preventing the defendant "from using a method." This is the main case. The accused method must be described in the requests in the same way, and with sufficient particularity, as with product claims (*see* above).

The second alternative deals with a situation where the accused infringer, by offering the process for use within German territory, suggests to a third party that he holds or owns the patent rights. Furthermore, the third party must know, or it must be obvious from the circumstances that the use of the process is prohibited without the consent of the patent proprietor. This alternative rarely occurs in practice. It may apply to a situation where the accused infringer offers and sells a machine or device that implements the patented method.

Protection of Directly Obtained Products: Third, under the assumption that a product can be directly obtained from the method, the request may furthermore be aimed at excluding the accused infringer "*from offering, putting on the market, using or importing or stocking for such purposes the product obtained directly by a claimed process*"[125] (*see* section 9 No. 3 Patent Act). Thus, the patentee may not only prohibit the implementation and commercialization of the process, he can also foreclose offers and sales of products which have been directly obtained from the patented process. Physical products, as well as nonphysical products such as video data, may fall under the provision.[126]

The claim according to section 9 No. 3 Patent Act is particularly useful if the claimed method is not used within the German territory. That is, even for products produced outside Germany by a method that would otherwise infringe, section 9 No. 3 Patent Act nevertheless applies, as long as the accused product is subsequently commercialized on the German market.[127] Accordingly, a method claim can be infringed by a product which has been (maybe legally) produced outside Germany but later sold within Germany.[128] Protection of directly obtained products applies even if the product itself is not patentable, for example, because it is not new. However, the provision requires that the product emerges from a manufacturing process. Thus, this

125. Unofficial translation.
126. Federal Supreme Court, judgment of Aug. 21, 2012, X ZR 33/10, "MPEG-2 Videosignalcodierung."
127. Schulte, Patentgesetz, Kühnen s. 9 Rn. 81.
128. Details concerning the infringement of method and process claims can be found in Ch. 12.

cannot be a mere working or measuring method. The provision requires "immediacy" of the obtained product. This is the case if the process contributes significantly to the formation of the product and, thus, the product obtained has not lost its characteristics through further treatment. The latter can be problematic in the case of intermediate products in the chemical industry. Additional treatment steps may change the essential properties of the product and thus the (treated) product cannot anymore be considered as a product being directly obtained through the patented process.[129] If the product is new, a reversal of the burden of proof under section 139(3) Patent Act also applies. In this case, the product is deemed to have been produced by the patented process. If, however, the product in question already existed at the priority date of the patent, the reversal of the burden of proof does not apply. On the contrary, if the product is new, it is than up to the accused infringer to prove that the product was manufactured by another process which does not make use of the patent.

Contributory infringement: Contributory infringement consists in supplying or offering to supply infringing "means relating to an essential element of the claimed invention"[130] (*see* section 10(1) of the Patent Act). It protects the patentee in advance of a threat, without requiring an established direct infringement. On the contrary, it does not confer an absolute prohibition on supplying such means. It thus requires additionally that the supply occurs in view of an exploitation of the invention within German territory. This involves a certain level of knowledge on the part of the contributory infringer.[131] This contributory aspect[132] must be reflected in the prayer for relief. When formulating the prayer, care should be taken to avoid attempting to prohibit those activities that do not represent an infringement of the patent. This is of particular importance where the offered or supplied means can also be used in a noninfringing manner. The request is thus aimed at preventing the activities of the contributory infringer that would result in patent infringement. The manner of drafting these requests differs from court to court. A typical way is to seek to impose on the contributory infringer an obligation to include in future offers and sales a warning notice stipulating that a particular use of the means would fall within the scope of a patent-in-dispute. Another approach consists of attempting to impose on the contributory infringer an obligation to pursue a contractual stipulation with customers to use the means only in a noninfringing manner, and with incompliance triggering the payment of a penalty.[133] Such a request may have the following language:

> It is requested in the name and on behalf of the plaintiff,
>
> I. to find defendant liable
>
> 1. in order to avoid a penalty to be set by the court for each case of violation of up to € 250,000.00, as an alternative confinement, or confinement of up to 6 months, in case of repeated violations a confinement of up to a total of

129. DC Düsseldorf, GRUR 1989, 896 "Grasherbizid."
130. Unofficial translation.
131. Details concerning the concept of contributory infringements can be found in Ch. 12.
132. Federal Supreme Court, X ZR 79/04, GRUR 2006, 570, "extracoronales Geschiebe."
133. Federal Supreme Court, X ZR 153/03, GRUR 2006, 839, "Deckenheizung."

2 years, to refrain from offering and/or supplying within the German territory a means with the following features:

[Description of the accused means]

for a product with the following features:

[Description of the product according to the patented invention]

without

a) in case of an offer, explicitly and visibly indicating that the means ... [indication of the accused means] cannot be used without the authorization of the plaintiff as owner of the German Patent [indication of the Patent N°] ... for a product ... [indication of the product according to the patented invention];
b) in case of a delivery, imposing on customers the written obligation not to use the ... [indication of the accused means] for ... [indication of the product according to the patented invention] without the authorization of the patentee whereby each non-compliance with this obligation by the customer is subject to a penalty of the amount ... to be paid to the plaintiff.

[ii] Right to Claim Damages

According to section 139(2) Patent Act, the injured party also has the right to damages. In contrast to the right to enjoin the accused infringer from using the invention, this right requires that the infringement has been negligently or intentionally committed. However, it is generally presumed that the accused infringer acted at least negligently.[134] It is commonly accepted that anybody who participates in a commercial environment is required to sufficiently investigate and analyze opposing rights of third parties (e.g., through the publicly accessible patent registers). For that investigation, only a one-month period is given to the market participants. This is a commonly accepted standard. If the accused infringer fails to sufficiently investigate and analyze his exposure within the one-month period, he is deemed to have failed to exercise reasonable care. He thus acted negligently (section 276 of the German Civil Code). This presumption is undisputed in most cases. This means that, in contrast to the US, a marking of the product with the label "patented" is not required to ensure the patentee's right to damages and the failure to mark a patented product does not limit the period by which one can recover damages. It is rather presumed that the accused infringer knew about the patent or should have known that it exists. This is a sufficient trigger for a damage claim.

Only in exceptional instances can this presumption be refuted, for example, if the accused infringer's acts are limited to transporting or storing the accused products. Such a party would not be held liable, at least until he becomes aware of the patent rights concerned, for instance, through a warning letter.[135]

The scope of the damage claim is usually unknown when starting the proceedings. Due to the missing information, the injured party is not yet able to request a

134. Federal Supreme Court, X ZR 79/90, GRUR 1993, 460, "Wandabstreifer."
135. District Court Düsseldorf, Decision of Dec. 14, 2006, InstGE 7, 172; Federal Supreme Court, GRUR 2009, 1142, Decision of Sep. 17, 2009, "MP3-Player-Import."

specific amount of money. The Code of Civil Procedure provides an opportunity to file a declaratory action (section 256 of the Code of Civil Procedure) requesting the court to find that a damage claim exists for infringing acts committed by the defendant since the date of publication of the mention of the patent grant.[136] Such request could have the following language:

> It is requested in the name and on behalf of the plaintiff,
>
> ...
>
> ii. to find, that the defendant is obliged to compensate plaintiff for all damages invoked on plaintiff by the acts indicated under I.1, committed since ... [date of the mention of the grant plus one month[137]] and which will be invoked in future.

The assessment of the amount of damages is separate from the infringement proceedings on the merits. This assessment depends on the plaintiff's discovery of information provided by the accused infringer through a rendering of accounts, which is discussed in the following chapter.

[iii] Right to Be Informed and Rendering of Accounts

The injured party has the right to be informed about the scope of the infringing acts to assess the amount of damages. Such right is commonly accepted, and its legal basis is taken from customary law.[138] In addition, rights of information shall help to identify the origin of infringing products and distribution channels (section 140b of the GPA). It shall also give information to calculate the reasonable compensation for use of the claimed invention after the publication of the patent application (section 33 of the GPA).[139] Thus, the injured party usually files a request aimed at a so-called rendering of accounts. It specifies what the defendant will have to do. The request typically contains the following language:

> *It is requested in the name and on behalf of the plaintiff,*
>
> I. to find defendant liable
>   1. ...
>   2. to render plaintiff account as to the extent to which defendant committed the acts defined under number I.1. since ... [date of the publication of the patent application plus one month] namely by indicating:
>   a) production amount and production time;
>   b) amount of received and ordered products, names and addresses of the manufactures, supplier and other pre-possessors, including the paid price;

136. Federal Supreme Court, I ZR 189/99, GRUR 2001, 1177, "Feststellungsinteresse II."
137. The damage claims are calculated starting one month from the publication of the grant of the patent. The one-month period is considered to be sufficient for identifying the patent.
138. Federal Supreme Court, X ZR 72/94, GRUR 1997, 116, "Prospekthalter."
139. *See* Ch. 14.

c) the individual deliveries, broken down by amounts, times and prices of delivery and type names as well as names and addresses of the commercial recipients and the selling points, for which the deliveries were supposed;
d) the individual offers, broken down by amounts, times, and prices of offer as well as the names and addresses of the commercial recipients of offers;
e) the advertisement conducted, broken down by advertisement media, their number of edition, period and area of distribution;

and for time the from ... [date of the mention of the grant plus one month]

f) the overall costs and the profits made, broken down by the individual cost factors;
   - whereby the names and addresses of non-commercial recipients and addressees of offers shall not be disclosed to the plaintiff, but to a certified auditor domiciled in Germany and bound to confidentiality vis-à-vis the plaintiff, which shall be named by the defendant, provided the defendant bears the costs of the auditor and instructs and authorizes him to respond to concrete questions of plaintiff whether a particular recipient or addressee of an offer is named in the report.
   - whereby the indications as to b) and c) shall be supported by the provision of sales documents (invoices or bill of delivery) wherein confidential information which is irrelevant for the rending of account may be redacted.

If this request is granted by the court (in the first instance decision), the injured party can then enforce the corresponding operating part of the judgment to get the necessary information for a proper assessment and determination of the amount of damages and reasonable compensation. That is, during the first instance proceedings, no discussions concerning the amount of damages and the relevant basis for calculating them take place. Rather, the assessment and determination are allocated to subsequent proceedings, which are discussed in more detail in the following chapters.[140]

[iv] Other Rights

Besides the aforementioned rights, there are other rights which might be judicially asserted. For example, according to section 140(a) of the Patent Act, the injured party may require the destruction of the products that are the subject matter of the patent, including materials and equipment that have served overwhelmingly for the manufacture of such products, provided that the enforcement is not disproportionate in the individual case. The accused infringer can also be required by the plaintiff to recall the products or to remove them definitively from the distribution channels (section 140(a)(3) Patent Act). In addition, the plaintiff may assert reasonable compensation for the use of the claimed invention during the time from the publication of the patent application (section 33 Patent Act)[141] (*see* Table 10.3).

140. Details concerning the calculation of damages can be found in Ch. 14.
141. *See* Ch. 14.

Table 10.3 Typically Asserted Rights

Right to prevent the use of the patent	**Section 139(1) Patent Act:** - Requires "danger of recidivism" which can be deduced from already committed infringing acts or requires at least a danger of imminent infringements. Injunctive relief may be limited in case of **disproportionality**.
Right to claim damages	**Section 139(2) Patent Act:** - Dependent on fault: Acts must be committed intentionally or negligently (usually presumed). - Assessment/calculation of the amount of damages is separated from proceedings on the merits: Only declaratory judgment as to the existence of the claim, but no decision on the amount.
Right to be informed/rendering of accounts	**Customary law, section 140b Patent Act:** - To enable the injured party to determine amount of damage claim and to identify other infringers.
Destruction	**Section 140(a)(1) Patent Act:** - Destruction must be proportionate.
Recall of accused products and/or removal from distribution channels	**Section 140(a)(3) Patent Act:** - Recall or removal must be proportionate.
Reasonable compensation	**Section 33 Patent Act:** (in addition to damage claim) - For use of the invention during the time between publication of the application and the grant.

[c] Information about the Subject Matter of the Case

A further purpose of the complaint brief is to sufficiently inform the court about the subject matter of the case. The complaint brief should be well prepared. It should provide the facts that were gathered prior to the proceedings, followed by the requests for relief described in the previous chapters.

The factual part of the complaint brief is typically subdivided into two main subchapters. The first subchapter basically describes the subject matter of the patent-in-suit with respect to the asserted claims of the patent. The description may provide additional illustrative background information. The invention should be described in the context of the prior art cited in the patent document. This information is aimed at facilitating the understanding of the technical field and the inventive teaching for the court. The court is presumably composed of judges who do not have the level of knowledge of the skilled person to whom the patent description is addressed. Thus, for the sake of comprehensibility it is also helpful to provide illustrative material demonstrating the working of embodiments of the prior art and of the invention. Emphasis needs to be put on prior art that is decisive in understanding the claimed invention and is thus relevant to the interpretation of the asserted claims and the underlying claim construction. Because the language of the proceedings is German, German translations of these prior art documents must usually be provided. In recent years, courts have become more flexible toward English language documents. That is, depending on the seized court, not every document needs to be translated in German.

This part of the complaint brief ends with the formulation of the technical problem solved by the invention. This technical problem must have been objectively determined, without hindsight, in the light of the prior art. If the technical problem was inaccurately formulated in the patent, the complaint may clarify this. The complaint is the appropriate place to correct existing inaccuracies.[142]

After the technical problem is properly determined, the teaching of the claimed invention needs to be described. This description of the invention should be presented with an eye to the claim construction, to facilitate a favorable claim scope determination from the court. The asserted claims, in particular the independent claims, are broken down in a logical and comprehensive outline of features, which is called the feature chart. The feature chart is aimed at facilitating the court's reading and understanding of the claims. Care should be given to breaking down the elements of the claims in a manner that promotes a favorable claim construction. In many cases the feature chart, which is decisive for the infringement test, is subject to discussions between the parties later during the proceedings.

A very simple example of such a feature chart is provided below. Here the patent concerns an invention relating to a sports shoe, particularly a running shoe that features a rigid cover covering the upper on the exterior surfaces thereof, in the region of the ball of the foot and extending from the sole. The features of claim 1 could be subdivided in the following manner:

A sport shoe comprising
1) a sole;
2) an upper portion attached to the sole and
3) a rigid cover
   3a) made of resisting material;
   3b) angular in cross-section and
   3c) defining a securing band and a protective shield;
4) the securing band is affixed between said sole and said upper portion,
5) the securing band extends from said sole, upwardly over the exterior of the upper portion in the area of the ball of the shoe.

The complaint must then describe the accused technology. The feature chart is used to show, feature by feature, that the accused embodiment or method uses the

142. Significance of the formulated problem for the claim construction: *see* Ch. 12.

asserted claim. This requires each feature to be mapped onto the accused embodiment. For this feature mapping the plaintiff should refer to evidence that has been collected prior to the introduction of the proceedings. It may be—if available—the accused product itself, photos of it, literature describing the accused embodiment, advertisements or tests which have been previously carried out by the plaintiff. In the example above, it would be useful to have a photo of the shoe, which might be taken, for instance, from the advertisement collected at a trade show, in which the references of the claim features are incorporated.

This demonstration is more complicated if the claim contains features referring to characteristics of a product which need to be detected through tests or analysis, for instance, if the product claim refers to a particular composition of a chemical substance. The available product literature of the accused infringer might be sufficient for demonstrating the infringing quality of the product. Nevertheless, it may be worthwhile to carry out independent tests and analysis, especially where the publicly available information on the accused product is insufficient or cannot be relied upon because it contains errors or could be misinterpreted. If the accused product is a chemical substance, these tests and analysis can be carried out by laboratories and attached, either as a report or in the form of a private expert opinion, to the complaint brief.

Unlike in US litigation, general discovery proceedings do not take place under German law. However, there may be situations where some form of limited discovery is necessary and available. Discovery and evidence taking is discussed in detail in Chapter 13.

An outline of a complaint brief with its usual subparts can be found in Chapter 17.

[3] Defendant's Defense

After the complaint brief is filed and served on the defendant, the defendant will have to respond to the complaint. Depending on the deadlines set in the court's schedule, this will have to be done approximately two to three months after the filing of the complaint. Counterarguments can be directed against the plaintiff's presentation of facts, including the proposed claim construction. Furthermore, legal and procedural objections can be raised by the defendant at this stage.

[a] Factual Submissions

The defendant's defense must carefully identify those facts that are admitted or denied. Anything not expressly denied shall be deemed as admitted unless the denial is obvious from other statements of the party (section 138(3) Code of Civil Procedure). It is thus crucial to emphasize and clearly point to those facts in the complaint that are denied. A simple denial (e.g., "the plaintiff's allegation is incorrect") without giving any further explanatory reasons for the denial is insufficient. It would be disregarded. According to section 138(1) Code of Civil Procedure, statements made by the parties concerning factual circumstances must be "complete and truthful." This duty is independent of which party carries the burden of proof. In order to comply with this duty, the denial must be substantiated, and thus, contain a complete and truthful explanation. The duty requires that the denying party have knowledge of the factual circumstances or could reasonably obtain access to it.[143] This is usually the case if the concerned factual circumstances are within the knowledge of the denying party. Thus, the assertion of the plaintiff that a chemical substance is composed of A, B and C requires a substantiated denial. This means the accused infringer cannot offer only a bare denial that his or her product does not contain these components. He must at least state that the product is composed of different components (specifying components A, B, C (which is different to C), etc.). An unexplained bare denial would not be accepted by the court. It could lead to a shift in the burden of proof. However, an assertion of lack of knowledge is permissible, and must be considered by the court, if it concerns facts that are outside the knowledge of the denying party (section 138(4) Code of Civil Procedure).

This procedural interplay between substantiated submissions and substantiated denials serves to crystallize triable questions of fact and facilitates the court's understanding of the patent and claim construction.

[b] Legal and Procedural Defenses

Beyond admitting or denying the facts of the complaint, and submitting the defendant's own characterization of the patent, there are several defenses which may be available depending on the case. These defenses might have a legal nature; i.e., they result from the substantive law, or they may be procedural. Procedural defenses raised by the defendant are mainly directed against the venue and jurisdiction of the court, or the defendant claims a missing security for the procedural costs.[144] The main defenses resulting from the substantive law are as follows:

(a) ***Right based on prior use:*** According to section 12 of the Patent Act, a patent has no effect against a person who, at the time of filing the application,[145] possessed the inventive teaching in Germany. That is, he had already begun to use the invention, or at least has made serious arrangements for doing so. The prior user may use the invention for the needs of his own business in his own premises or the premises of others. If the defendant proves the circumstances of such prior use—provided that the use does not go beyond the indicated scope—the action is to be dismissed. The right requires that the user (the accused infringer) have had possession of the invention at the priority date of the asserted patent. Such possession is deemed to exist if the claimed teaching is objectively completed and if it is subjectively recognized that the actual implementation of the invention is possible.[146] That is, the user must

143. Federal Supreme Court, BGHZ 100, 190, 196.
144. *See* Ch. 10, §10.02[H][3].
145. That is, prior to the filing date or priority date of the application underlying the asserted patent.
146. Federal Supreme Court, Decision of Jun. 12, 2012, X ZR 131/09, "Desmopressin."

have recognized the inventive teaching as described in the asserted patent and was therefore in a position to methodically realize and repeat the inventive result.[147] The prior user need not have understood the physical or chemical reactions that are responsible for the effects according to the teaching of the patent.[148] Likewise, it is irrelevant whether he had realized the particular advantages of the inventive teaching or not.[149] Such right based on prior use is to be denied, however, if the patented subject matter was only unknowingly and coincidentally used, which would not have enabled the user to methodically realize and repeat the inventive result.[150] It would not be sufficient if the realization is merely achieved by chance in only some instances.[151] In addition, the possession of the invention must be confirmed—i.e., the user must at least have implemented bona fide arrangements to manufacture or commercialize it.[152] The right based on prior use is limited in scope to acts that were already committed or intended at the priority date of the patent.[153] It does not extend to inventive features of preferred embodiments of the asserted patent that are outside of what the user effectively recognized at the priority date. Nevertheless, it covers not only the prior user but also subsequent trade levels,[154] such as customers who have bought a product covered by the prior use.

(b) ***Contractual licenses***: The defendant may be entitled to rely on an existing license agreement, under which the infringement claim is barred. This requires that the activities of the defendant fall within the scope of a concluded agreement (section 15(2) Patent Act). Licenses granted by a previous right holder are not affected by a later assignment and can be asserted against a new owner (section 15(3) Patent Act).

(c) ***Exhaustion of patent rights***: This defense refers to a situation where the product was previously put on the EU/EEC market with the permission of the patentee or of someone who was duly authorized by the patentee. The details of the exhaustion of patent rights are described in Chapter 12.

(d) ***Defense arising from antitrust law***: This defense may arise when a market-dominating position follows from the assertion of the patent. The details of this defense are described in the following section 10.03.

147. Federal Supreme Court, I ZR 114/58, GRUR 1960, 546, "Bierhahn"; Federal Supreme Court, Ia ZR 224/63, GRUR 1964, 496, "Formsand II."
148. Appeal Court Düsseldorf, InstGE 11, 198, "Desmopressin."
149. Federal Supreme Court, Decision of Jun. 12, 2012, X ZR 131/09, "Desmopressin"; Appeal Court Düsseldorf, InstGE 11, 198, "Desmopressin."
150. Federal Supreme Court, I ZR 114/58, GRUR 60, 546, "Bierhahn"; Federal Supreme Court, Ia ZR 224/63, GRUR 64, 496, "Formsand II."
151. Federal Supreme Court, Decision of Jun. 12, 2012, X ZR 131/09, "Desmopressin."
152. Federal Supreme Court, I ZR 114/58, GRUR 60, 546, "Bierhahn"; Federal Supreme Court, Ia ZR 224/63, GRUR 64, 496, "Formsand II."
153. Federal Supreme Court, X ZR 32/99, GRUR 2002, 231, "Biegevorrichtung."
154. Federal Supreme Court, Decision of Jun. 12, 2012, X ZR 131/09, "Desmopressin; Appeal Court Düsseldorf, InstGE 11, 198, "Desmopressin."

(e) ***Usurpation***: The defendant may argue that he is the rightful owner and has been illegally dispossessed of the invention (usurpation). In such a situation, plaintiff's requests based on a patent protecting the invention would not be made in good faith and thus violate a fundamental requirement of the civil law (section 242 of the Civil Code). Such situation may also arise where the plaintiff did not acquire ownership of the asserted patent (often unknowingly) due to incorrect application of the rules governing employees' inventions. These rules are important formalities that have sometimes posed problems for plaintiffs. Under the previous Employees' Invention Act, employers frequently claimed their employees' inventions incorrectly, and therefore did not acquire ownership of the inventions, despite filing and obtaining patents. The employers' failure to comply with the complex laws on employee inventions usually came to light after patent enforcement had begun—much to the plaintiffs' surprise and annoyance undoubtedly. These rules can be exploited by a defendant, who, if he acquires the patent from the employee, can succeed with an usurpation defense.[155]

(f) ***Statute of limitation***: According to section 141 of the Patent Act, rights resulting from the infringement of a patent shall become time-barred in compliance with the provisions of Chapter 5 of Book 1 of the Civil Code. These provisions are applicable to European and German patents:

- For all rights the *standard limitation of three years* is principally applicable, which commences at the end of the year in which the right arose and in which the right holder obtained or could have obtained knowledge of the accused infringement (sections 195 and 199 of the German Civil Code).
- If the standard limitation is not applicable, the rights principally become statute-barred ten years after they arose, provided the right holder did not know the circumstances giving rise to the right, or if it cannot be proven that he at least negligently ignored these circumstances (section 199(3) No. 1 Civil Code).[156]
- However, the right to prevent the use of the patent arises continuously with each act of infringement. Therefore, a defense based on the statute of limitations does usually not lead to a dismissal of the action, rather it may reduce the time for which damages can be claimed.
- Even if the short standard limitation of three years is applicable and accordingly a damage claim (section 139(2) Patent Act) is barred for infringing acts committed prior to the three-year period, the accused infringer is still not released from any payments. In fact, he is obliged to provide restitution for the benefits he obtained without legal grounds at

155. The Employees' Inventions Act is discussed in Ch. 15.
156. For the sake of completeness, it must be noted that a thirty-year limitation may exceptionally be applicable if the moment of the infringing act and the occurrence of the injury diverge in time (s. 199(3) No. 2 Civil Code). In that case the right becomes statue barred latest thirty years from the infringing act.

the expense of the right holder or patentee. The right holder or patentee may claim to get return of unjust enrichments according to section 812 of Civil Code. That is, even if the damages claim is time-barred, a restitution claim under the provisions for the return of unjust enrichment would be applicable, calculated analogous to a reasonable license. This claim would be time-barred ten years after it arises, or, irrespective of the date on which it arises, thirty years after the date on which the act causing the injury was committed.[157]

(g) ***Forfeiture***: The defense of forfeiture arises in the exceptional situation where the right holder has knowingly tolerated, for a considerable period, the infringing activities, such that the accused infringer may objectively presume from the circumstances that the right holder would never assert the patent-in-question. The defense of forfeiture includes:
- first, a time aspect—the toleration of the infringing acts must have lasted for a considerable period;[158]
- second, there must be circumstances which objectively create an impression in the eyes of the accused infringer that his use of the patented invention is accepted and thus may continue in future; and
- third, he must, from such use, have thus acquired economic value.

The concept of forfeiture results from a fundamental principle, according to which a right holder has a duty to proceed in good faith when asserting a claim (section 242 of the Civil Code). The Federal Supreme Court sets very high thresholds for this defense.[159] The forfeiture statute term starts to run from each infringing act.[160]

[c] Requests of the Defendant

Usually, the defendant requests the dismissal of the complaint and, as a precautionary or additional request, the suspension of the proceedings.[161] Requesting the suspension of the infringement proceedings requires that opposition or nullity proceedings against the asserted patent be already pending, regardless of whether the proceedings were instituted by the defendant or a third party.

The interplay of invalidation and infringement proceedings could have an impact on the claim construction proposed by the defendant since his or her interests might be different in both proceedings. It might be more favorable for challenging validity to have a broad understanding of the asserted claims, whereas it is easier to argue noninfringement on the basis of narrow claim understanding.

157. Federal Supreme Court, X ZR 81/72, GRUR 1977, 250, "Kunststoffhohlprofil"; Federal Supreme Court, X ZR 7/80, GRUR 1982, 301, "Kunststoffhohlprofil II."
158. Federal Supreme Court, X ZR 150/98, GRUR 2001, 323, "Temperaturwächter": Subject to this case was a situation where the patentee waited more than ten years, before he started to assert his rights against the accused infringer.
159. Federal Supreme Court, X ZR 150/98, GRUR 2001, 323, "Temperaturwächter."
160. Federal Supreme Court, NJW-RR 2006, 235.
161. *See* Ch. 10, §10.02[D][2].

[4] Further Briefs until the Main Hearing

When drafting the complaint, the plaintiff cannot anticipate all the arguments of the accused infringer. Thus, it is necessary for the plaintiff to reply to the various defenses in a subsequent brief (reply brief, *Replik*), and, in particular, to any new elements raised by the defendant.

A patentee's complaint typically assumes the validity of a granted patent and usually does not contain a critical discussion as to the validity of the patent. But a discussion of validity will likely be warranted upon responding to the defendant's defense. If the defense contains a request for suspending the proceedings it must also contain a discussion of the merits of the request. This discussion, which is aimed at convincing the court to suspend the proceedings, might be built up on prosecuted prior art or previously unknown prior art documents.[162] The plaintiff will have to respond to these aspects of the defense in the third brief of the proceedings.

Thereafter, in response to the plaintiff's reply, the defendant is afforded a second opportunity to submit additional arguments and facts with relevance to plaintiff's reply. Accordingly, at least four briefs, including their exhibits, are on file on the day of the hearing. In contrast to the typical volume of materials familiar in US litigations, the records in German litigations are typically quite thin, sometimes numbering less than 100 pages.

[C] Hearing

The chambers of the District Courts are composed of three judges. One judge, usually the most experienced judge, presides over the chamber. He or she has the predominant role of directing the hearing. Due to the quantity of patent cases, the District Courts of Mannheim and Munich each have two chambers, the District Court Düsseldorf has even three chambers for trial of such cases.

Besides the setting of deadlines and the grant of time extensions, the court does not substantially involve itself during the proceedings until the day of the hearing. Of course, the court internally prepares the case by means of the submitted briefs. But until the day of the hearing, which takes place approximately one year after filing of the complaint (in some courts later), the parties do not know which claim construction will be applied. The various disputes analogous to "motions to dismiss," which a US court would have resolved on a Rule 12(b) motion (such as for lack of standing, lack of jurisdiction, and lack of controversy), are all handled at the main hearing, along with the overall merits of a case. Generally, the court does not issue any preliminary opinions on the claim construction or any other decisive aspect of the case prior to the hearing.

The hearing is introduced by the presiding judge. This introduction is the result of an internal deliberation among the judges of the chamber, which takes place after they have studied the exchanged briefs and shortly prior to the day of the hearing. One

162. Details concerning the suspension of the proceedings can be found in Ch. 10, §10.02[D][2].

of the three judges, the so-called reporting judge, is responsible for drafting an internal preliminary opinion for the purpose of the preliminary internal deliberation.

This introduction usually contains an outline of a preliminary opinion containing the main aspects that the court expects to be of particular importance for the decision. The presiding judge's introduction is aimed at concentrating the subject matter under discussion during the hearing, focusing only on the critical aspects of the case. This is one reason why the hearings tend to be of short duration. The introductory remarks of the court may also contain statements as to a particular favored claim construction. Typically, this preliminary opinion disfavors one of the parties, but that party will most probably get the first opportunity to argue his case, preferably with an emphasis on those aspects which have been highlighted in the introduction of the presiding judge. These pleadings are followed by the arguments of the other side, which might be short if no persuasive new elements or arguments have been brought up, and if the judges seem to follow the preliminary opinion. Of course, the judges pose questions during the hearing, or comment in response to statements of the counsels.

Once the parties have sufficiently exchanged their arguments—this usually takes one to two hours, longer in more complex cases—the presiding judge closes the hearing and indicates a day for the announcement of the decision. This usually takes places four to six weeks after the hearing. In contrast to the Federal Patent Court, the trial court does not deliver a decision at the end of the hearing. Because the hearing is dominated by the preliminary opinion contained in the presiding judge's introduction, it is often possible to deduce from the hearing which party will likely win the case. Accordingly, the written portion of the proceedings is very important, and well-prepared submissions represent a key element for success.

[D] Outcome of the First Instance Proceedings

The decision may take different forms. Most likely, the court either grants the requests of the complaint or either completely or partially dismisses the complaint. Due to rather high standards, the chances are moderate that the court suspends the proceedings. This may, however, happen if highly pertinent prior art is discovered which was not considered during the prosecution proceedings. Usually there is no evidence taking. The court decides based on the evidence and facts submitted by the parties. In exceptional situations, such as if the relevant facts are still in dispute or not sufficiently proven by the evidence submitted by the parties, the court will appoint an expert. It is seldom that witnesses will be heard in patent infringement proceedings. It may occur, for instance, in cases where the accused infringer asserts a right based on prior use (section 12 of the Patent Act). Accordingly, in patent infringement proceedings, the most important means of taking evidence are court experts, rather than witnesses. The most frequent forms of decision taken after the hearing are illustrated in Figure 10.5.

[1] Grant of the Action or Complete/Partial Dismissal

A decision granting the requests follows basically the same structure as the complaint. It starts with an operating part containing plaintiff's requests and a decision imposing the costs of the proceedings on the defendant. According to section 91 of the Code of Civil Procedure, the losing party bears the statutory costs of the proceedings. The operating part forms the basis for the enforcement of the judgment.

Figure 10.5 Possible First Instance Decisions

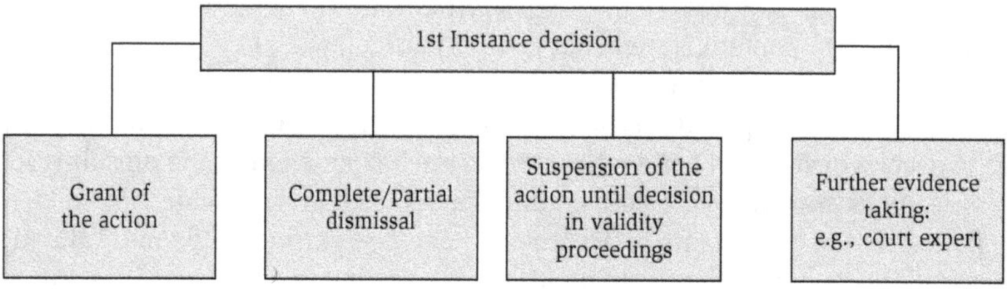

In case of partial dismissal, the court grants the requests with a reduced scope and dismisses the rest of the action. The costs are then proportionally divided (section 91 of the Code of Civil Procedure). For instance, where the plaintiff succeeds to a large extent with his claims, the court may impose one-quarter of the costs on the plaintiff and three quarters of the costs on the defendant. In case of a complete dismissal, all statutory costs of the proceedings are borne by the plaintiff.

In all these cases, the decision will contain an detailed reasoning highlighting why the court has decided in a particular way. This reasoning typically refers to the case law established through the decisions of higher courts. A particular emphasis is put on the most pertinent decisions of the Federal Supreme Court which are decisive for the subject matter of the case. Accordingly, besides other important elements, the court's claim construction is part of the decision. Samples of first court decisions translated into English can be found in the *International Review of Intellectual Property and Competition Law* published by the Max Planck Institute for Intellectual Property, Competition and Tax Law, in Munich, Germany.

[2] Suspension of the Proceedings

The District Courts may order suspension of the proceedings in anticipation of another action (section 148 Code of Civil Procedure). Requesting the suspension of the infringement proceedings requires that opposition or nullity proceedings against the asserted patent be already pending by the time of the suspension request, regardless of whether the proceedings were instituted by the defendant or a third party. The defendant thus does not need to be a party to these parallel opposition or nullity proceedings. According to section 148 Code of Civil Procedure there are two aspects that are decisive to the District Court's decision to suspend. The first aspect requires a dependency between both proceedings, namely that a decision of the infringement court depends on the decision to be expected in the parallel invalidation proceedings. Typically, such dependency could be denied if the court concludes that the asserted patent is not infringed. In that case, the court would simply dismiss the action. Nevertheless, as the indicated dependency between both proceedings has an abstract meaning, it is not a compelling requirement that the court—prior to a decision on the suspension—first concludes that there is infringement. In particular, in complex cases where such decision on the infringement cannot easily be answered and would require substantial evidence taking, it may be appropriate to first determine whether the case should be stayed.[163]

Second, the court has discretionary power to suspend the proceedings, pursuant to section 148 Code of Civil Procedure. Based on the submitted record,[164] the court makes its determination as to whether there is a predominant probability (or high likelihood) that the asserted claim will be invalidated in parallel invalidation proceedings.[165] The court's usual reasoning is roughly summarized in Figure 10.6.

Figure 10.6 Court's Reasoning as to the Question of Suspension

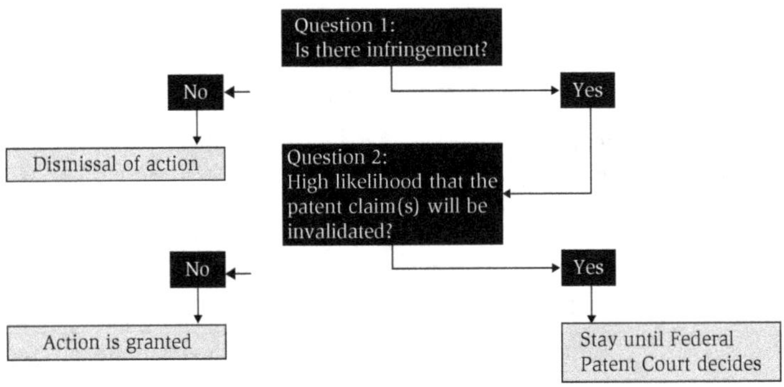

When approaching this decision, the court will weigh the interests of the parties. On the one hand, there is the depreciation in the value of the patent, as the enforcement would be delayed until a decision is taken in parallel invalidation proceedings. On the contrary, there is the interest in avoiding an infringement ruling when the patent may be invalid. Also, the behavior of the parties during the proceedings with regard to timing may be influential. An invalidation attack made very late in the proceedings lowers the chances of a suspension.[166] Since there is no evidence taking in respect to the question of suspension, the court makes a summary assessment based on the material submitted by the parties. The parties submit the briefs and the prior art documents that have been filed in the parallel invalidation proceedings. Because the district court's determination on the stay request is based on the probable outcome of the parallel invalidation proceedings, the district court's ruling is concerned only with

163. *See* Kühnen, Schulte, 9th ed., s. 139, No. 281.
164. District Court Düsseldorf, 4b O 8/09, GRUR-RR 2010, 369.
165. Federal Supreme Court, X ZR 56/85, GRUR 1987, 284, "Transportfahrzeug."
166. District Court Düsseldorf, InstGE 3, 54, "Sportschuhsohle."

the prior art that is the subject of these parallel proceedings. Table 10.4 lists the considerations favoring or disfavoring a stay of the proceedings.

Table 10.4 Considerations in the Suspension Decision

Pro	*Contra*
- Prior art which was not considered during prosecution proceedings and is novelty-anticipating.[1]	- Simple doubts on the validity of the patent, doubts referring to inventive step.[2]
- The inventive step has become so questionable in view of the prior art presented by the infringer that there is no reasonable argument in favor of validity left.[3]	- The nullity action only contains validity attacks (prior art) which were already considered by the patent office.[4]
- Patent has been invalidated in first instance by the Federal Patent Court[5] provided that this is not based on a clearly wrong decision.[6]	- The patent has been confirmed in first instance, unless new, unknown, novelty-anticipating prior art will be identified during the second instance.[7]
- The decision of the patent office is based on a clear and obviously wrong decision.[8]	- The validity attack is based on a prior public use which cannot be consistently proven by means of written documents (testimony by witnesses and affidavits are not sufficient).[9]
	- Accused infringer unnecessarily delays the parallel invalidation proceedings; that is, he does not expeditiously file a nullity complaint with the FPC or an opposition with the EPO after he became aware of the accused infringement.[10]

1. Federal Supreme Court, X ZR 56/85, GRUR 1987, 284, "Transportfahrzeug."
2. Schulte section 139, No. 273.
3. Court of Appeals Düsseldorf InstGE 7, 139, 146, GRUR-RR 2007, 259, "Thermocycler."
4. Federal Supreme Court, I ZR 93/57, GRUR 1959, 320, "Moped-Kupplung."
5. Appeal Court Munich, InstGE 3, 62, "Aussetzung bei Nichtigkeitsurteil II."
6. Court of Appeals Düsseldorf decision of May 29, 2008, Az. 2 W 47/07, GRUR 2008, 1077, "Olanzapin."
7. Federal Supreme Court, I ZR 93/57, GRUR 1959, 320, "Moped-Kupplung."
8. Schulte section 139, No. 273.
9. Appeal Court Düsseldorf, 2 U 129/78, GRUR 79, 636, "Ventilanbohrungsvorrichtung."
10. District Court Düsseldorf, InstGE 3, 54, "Sportschuhsohle."

The likelihood of a suspension is typically low if defendant's request is exclusively based on prior art documents which were already considered by the patent office during the granting or opposition proceedings. The chances for obtaining a stay are higher if the request is based on previously unknown, novelty-destroying prior art. It is commonly understood that there is a high threshold to achieve a stay of infringement proceedings. Statistical information on the success of stay requests is not available. Based on our experience of litigating many patent disputes in Germany, suspensions, or the appointment of court experts (*see* next section) generally occur in less than a quarter of the cases.

The Federal Supreme Court since recently seems[167] to have loosened the strict standards for suspending infringement proceedings toward a greater protection of the accused infringer. This trend is reflected in the following statements of the Federal Supreme Court[168] emphasizing the importance of due process rights for the accused infringer which has mounted a credible challenge to the patent's validity:

> A provisionally enforceable judgement ... to cease and desist, to provide information, to render accounts, and to destroy products in accordance with a patent is generally not justified if it can be expected with reasonable certainty that the basis underlying such a judgement will be eliminated by the revocation of the patent-in-suit. The right to due process that derives from a rule-of-law principle (Art. 20 Para. 3 of the Constitutional Law) in combination with fundamental rights, which is therefore constitutionally guaranteed (see e.g. BVerfGE 88, 118, 123), demands that the party accused of infringement be permitted to an effective legal recourse by means of a counterattack against the legal validity of this patent if the party wishes to defend itself against a challenge arising from the patent in suit. This requires not only an effective recourse to implement this attack via a nullity action, but also adequate considerations of the fact that this attack is possibly the only defense against the claims arising from the patent. Due to statutory standards, which require a valid patent for the claims resulting from Sec. 139 ff. of the Patent Act, and which offer a nullity action, lying exclusively within the jurisdiction of the Patent Court, as the only tool to undo this legal title, the attack on the patent in suit cannot be conducted as an objection in infringement proceedings or by filing a countersuit for nullity, as would be the case in other legal systems. However, the resulting effect cannot be that such an attack has no impact on the infringement proceedings. Rather, the suspension of the infringement proceedings is fundamentally appropriate if it can be expected with sufficient certainty that the patent in suit will not survive the challenge of a nullity action.[169]

If the court finds that there is a sufficient likelihood that the patent will be invalidated in the parallel proceedings, it stays its own proceedings until a decision on the validity is rendered, resuming only if the patent validity has been upheld. But if the patent is held valid, the infringement proceedings may be resumed regardless of any appeal proceedings. There have also been cases where an infringement proceeding was suspended when new prior art was identified for the first time on appeal of a first instance nullity decision.[170] Some courts apply a more defendant-friendly approach in case a patent assertion company or so-called nonpracticing company is asserting the patent. Indeed, the strategy of a nonpracticing company is typically aimed at a

167. Federal Supreme Court, X ZR 61/13, "Kurznachrichten I," Federal Supreme Court, X ZR 68/13, "Kurznachrichten II."
168. Federal Supreme Court, X ZR 61/13, "Kurznachrichten I."
169. Unofficial translation of the authors.
170. Federal Supreme Court, I ZR 93/57, GRUR 1959, 320, "Moped-Kupplung."

pecuniary result by forcing the conclusion of a licensing agreement. The stakes are not the same for an original patent holder. He might be locked in commercial competition. He may thus refer to legitimate interests in getting swifter relief than a company exclusively pursing a pecuniary interest. The following simplified situation presents the typical suspension scenario (*see* Figure 10.7).

Figure 10.7 Typical Suspension Scenario

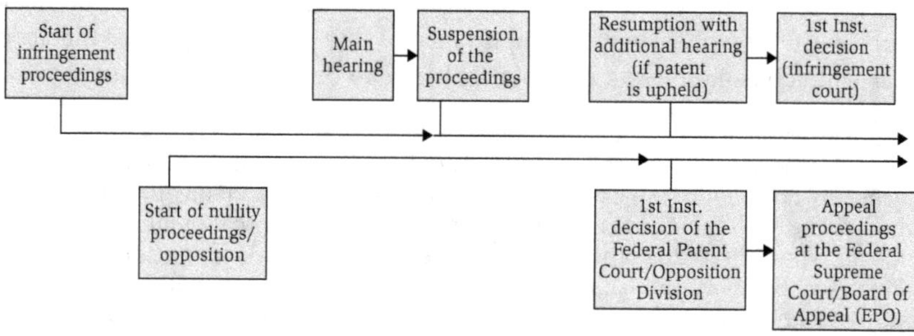

If the validity of the patent is reasonably doubtful, the patentee may consider asserting a narrower claim to better differentiate over the prior art. Of course, this new limited claim still needs to be infringed by the accused embodiment. Such a claim could be construed by features of one or several dependent claims, or the new feature combination could be based on features taken from the description. Of course, this requires a sufficient disclosure of the new combination in the patent description[171]—in particular, if features are taken from the description and then combined with an independent claim, resulting in a "new claim." Plaintiff will need to unconditionally limit the request on the new combination. This is a risky strategy. It increases the risk of a stay of the proceedings until a decision on the validity has been rendered by the EPO or the Federal Patent Court. Some courts, such as the District Court Düsseldorf, deal with such strategy generously, whereas other courts are more conservative and would rather suspend the proceedings. It is a last resort strategy to deal with problematic prior art. In fact, the assertion of a claim with a narrower scope of protection as granted through the inclusion of additional feature(s) in the granted claims could be understood as an admission that the scope of protection as granted is not valid, impairing the value of the underlying patent office's granting decision.[172] The granting decision may not serve anymore as sufficient proof for the validity of the asserted claim. In addition, the amended claim may give rise to formal challenges such as the question of whether the amended claim is sufficiently disclosed.[173] Such formal challenges are typically not heard by infringement courts in case of granted claims. These aspects should be taken into account before filing a lawsuit on the basis of a limited patent claim.

171. *See* Ch. 5, §5.05.
172. Benkard, 11th ed., Grabinski/Zülch on s. 139 PatG, marginal no. 107.
173. Federal Supreme Court, Xa ZR 70/08, "Maschinensatz."

If the court does order a suspension of the proceedings, the plaintiff may file within two weeks an immediate request for relief (section 577 of the Code of Civil procedure). The appeal court is, however, only entitled to review whether the infringement court has properly exercised its discretion. That is, the immediate request is only successful if the first instance court is found to have abused its discretion in granting the suspension.

[3] Further Evidence Taking: Appointment of a Court Expert

The court may conclude that the technical expertise of an expert is necessary. The appointment of a court expert is the most frequently used form of judicial investigation. According to the Supreme Court,[174] even an experienced court must order an expert opinion if the skilled person's understanding of the technical expressions in the patent claim is in doubt. Whether and to what an extent an expert opinion is necessary depends on the circumstances of the case.

On the contrary, fact witnesses are rather rare in patent infringement cases. Their appearance might be important, for instance, if the defendant raises the defense of prior use according to section 12 of the Patent Act.

In most cases, the court renders a decision without appointing an expert. The probability of the involvement of a court expert differs from court to court. It also depends on the subject matter of the case. Precise estimations are difficult but based on our experience litigating many patent disputes in Germany, the appointment of a court expert generally occurs in less than a quarter of the cases. In most cases, the court bases its decision on its own assessment of the technology, as understood through the material submitted by the parties.[175] The following approximation concerning three major infringement courts might additionally be taken into consideration when selecting the court.[176]

The likelihood of the court appointing an expert also depends on the technical field of the concerned subject matter, which might be differently distributed among German infringement courts. That is, certain courts have built up technical expertise over the years by nature of the cases over which they have previously presided. Because the court files are not public, the patentee must necessarily rely on the expertise of his German counsel, who must continuously acquire this knowledge through a multitude of sources, such as discussions with colleagues, articles written by colleagues, and published and unpublished decisions to which he might have access through involvement in a case. Patentees will typically want to avoid the court appointing an expert, which may significantly lengthen the proceedings, sometimes by more than one year.

174. Federal Supreme Court, Decision of Oct. 28, 2003, X ZR 76/00, GRUR 2004, 413, "Geflügelkörperhalterung."
175. Federal Supreme Court, X ZR 121/88, GRUR 1991, 436, Befestigungsvorrichtung II; Federal Supreme Court, X ZR 41/89, GRUR 1991, 744, "Trockenlegungsverfahren."
176. Magazine, JUVE Rechtsmarkt 04/10.

A judicial investigation by means of a court expert might be necessary to illuminate the knowledge of the "skilled person" in the art, and to facilitate an understanding of the patent. Likewise, an expert may be appointed if the configuration of the accused embodiment remains disputed with respect to details that cannot be readily assessed by the court.[177] Usually, university professors within the relevant technical field, selected from lists and proposed by the parties, are appointed. Unlike in the US system, these experts are not experts retained by a particular party. They are neutral experts appointed by the court. Accordingly, the parties must avoid any contact with the expert prior to and after the appointment. Parties may successfully object to proposed experts if they can establish that there is a past or actual relationship between the expert and the opposing party giving sufficient reason to believe that there is a risk of bias.

The parties should have no direct contact with the expert during the proceedings. The correspondence with the expert is conducted through the court. The expert's working guidelines are contained within the court's order. This order contains a set of questions to be answered by the expert, as well as explanatory instructions to limit the expert's inquiry to particular matters within the expert's expertise (and to avoid straying beyond that competence). The expert is tasked with explaining to the court the knowledge and experience of the skilled person in the art in question, as well as his working method and how he deals with technical problems. Whether the patent's solution was obvious is a question for the judge and not the expert.[178] Statements of the expert are therefore reviewed and placed in a legal context by the judge. For instance, if the expert defines a term used in the patent claim in compliance with the concerned specialized field, it does not release the judge from the duty to make use of the description in order to clarify the meaning of this term in the context of the patent claim.[179] The interpretation of the patent falls within the responsibility of the court.[180]

The expert prepares a written report. This may take time and is the primary reason for the prolongation of the proceedings. As soon as the written expert opinion is ready, it will be submitted to the parties, which then have an opportunity to make statements in response. Following this exchange of briefs, a further hearing will take place. The court may also order the appearance of the expert, and is in fact obliged to do this upon request of any party. These further proceedings will prolong a decision on the merits far beyond the usual one-year timeline. It may be two years from the filing of the complaint to receive a first instance decision if an expert is appointed (Figure 10.8).

177. Kühnen in Schulte s. 139, No. 292.
178. Federal Supreme Court, Decision of Nov. 25, 2003, X ZR 162/00, GRUR 2004, 411, "Diabehältnis."
179. Federal Supreme Court, Decision of Feb. 13, 2007, X ZR 74/05, GRUR 2007, 410, "Kettenradanordnung," an English translation of this decision can be found in IIC 2007, 726.
180. Federal Supreme Court, X ZR 76/04, GRUR 2006, 131, "Seitenspiegel," an English translation of this decision can be found in IIC 2007, 743.

Figure 10.8 Usual Course of Infringement Proceedings with Appointed Expert

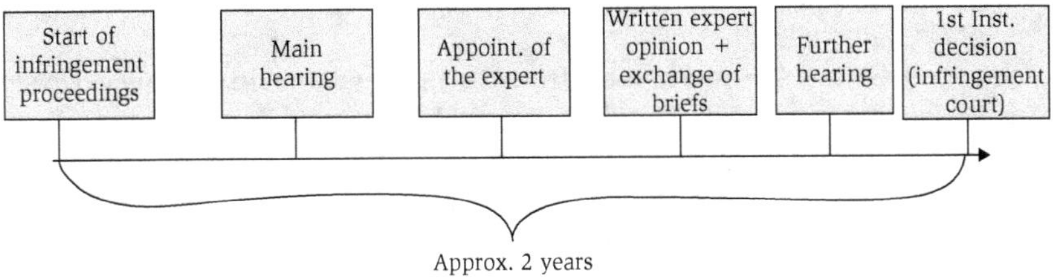

In view of the delay that appointing an expert may cause, it is incumbent on the plaintiff to attempt to streamline the issues and thoroughly digest the technology to simplify the issues for the court. Well-prepared arguments and submissions naturally help frame the issues for the court, and there is an increasing trend for parties to submit their own expert statements. These expert statements are often submitted along with the briefing papers of the parties. Whether or not to submit such a statement is a case-by-case determination and should be discussed depending on the strategic goals of the case.

[E] Relief

[1] Appeal of First Instance Decisions

An appeal may be taken against first instance decisions granting either completely or partially plaintiff's requests or dismissing the action (section 511 Code of Civil Procedure). The period for filing the appeal is one month as shown in Figure 10.9 (section 517 Code of Civil Procedure). This term begins upon service of the first instance decision.[181] It is not extendable.

Figure 10.9 Usual Course of Appeal Proceedings

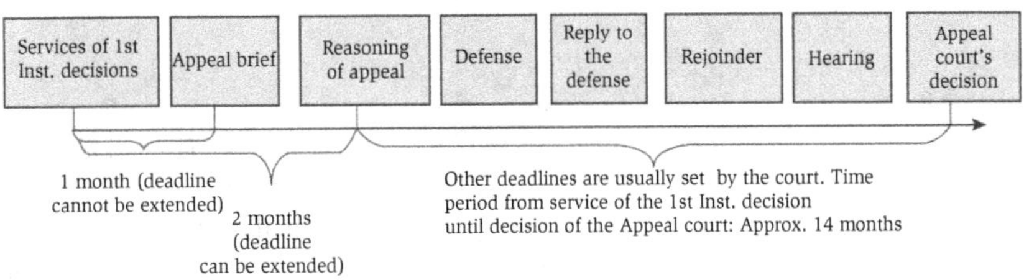

181. The term ends latest upon the expiration of five months after the pronouncement of the decision, assuming a written decision has not been served in time.

The appeal brief (notice of appeal) usually does not contain the reasons or grounds for the appeal. It is thus a very short brief indicating the first instance decision against which the appeal is directed, including a certified copy of that decision (section 519 Code of Civil Procedure).

The appellant then has two months from the service of the first instance decision to file his "reasoning of appeal." This deadline can be extended by the presiding judge upon request, provided the opposing party consents to the extension, or, without that consent, if the court determines that the proceedings will not be delayed, and the appellant presents material grounds justifying the deadline extension (section 520(2) Code of Civil Procedure).

The reasoning of appeal contains a declaration stating to what extent the first instance decision is contested and what modifications are requested. The reasoning may allege a legal mistake—that a provision of law was incorrectly applied by the first instance court—or that the submitted facts justify a different judgment (section 513 Code of Civil Procedure). When drafting the reasoning of appeal, the general rule is that parties may not submit new facts. There are exceptions, namely if there are concrete indications that the facts as established by the first instance court are incorrect or incomplete (section 529(1) No. 1 Code of Civil Procedure). In addition, according to section 529(1) No. 2 Code of Civil Procedure, the submission of new facts will be allowed if they were unknown during the first instance, or at least if their omission was excusable. According to section 531 of the Code of Civil Procedure, new attacks and defenses are only allowed if:

- they concern aspects of the case which have obviously been ignored by the first instance court, or could not be asserted in first instance due to a procedural mistake; or
- the missing submission is not caused by carelessness.

The parties are accordingly well advised not to hold back facts, evidence, possible claims or defenses that could be brought forward in the first instance proceedings. The risks are too high that such evidence may be deemed belated in the second instance.

[2] Appeal of Appellate Decisions: Federal Supreme Court

Only a few cases may be appealed to the Federal Supreme Court, which reviews cases in the third instance. The threshold to bring a case to the Federal Supreme Court is very high. An appeal to the Federal Supreme Court requires leave of the second instance appellate court. If such leave is denied, the appellant may petition directly to the Federal Supreme Court, which may then grant the appeal right directly. To be successful, special grounds of admissibility (section 543 Code of Civil Procedure) must be given, namely that:

- the case is of fundamental importance; or
- a decision of the Federal Supreme Court is necessary for the development of law or to unify the case law.

Most cases do not meet these standards. In most cases, the appeal court of second instance will not allow the appeal to the Federal Supreme Court, or the petition against the denial will be rejected by the Supreme Court. In the rare cases where the appellant manages to surmount these thresholds, the proceedings will usually be limited to violations of law (sections 546 and 547 Code of Civil Procedure).

[F] Enforcement Proceedings

[1] Provision of Security

Even though an appeal has no suspending effect, a first instance decision is not automatically enforceable. As long as the decision is not final, the prevailing party needs to provide a security for the enforcement. Thus, a first instance decision usually contains the additional sentence: "*The decision is provisionally enforceable against a security of an amount of* … ." This sentence may be more precise in that it requires that the security shall be provided by a guarantee of a bank with a seat in Germany. It must be a bank that is officially accredited to operate and provide financial services within Germany territory. It does not necessarily need to be a German bank, but it must be a financial institution with sufficient capital to answer for the amount of the guarantee.

An injunction and the claim to render account can only be enforced—prior to a final decision—by means of such security. The purpose of the security is to cover eventual damages which could arise from an unjustified enforcement of the decision, namely if an appeal is successful in the second or third instance proceedings. The amount of the security typically corresponds to the damages potentially caused on the side of the defendant through the enforcement of the decision which later turns out to be unjustified. Accordingly, it shall secure the claim for damages due to unjustified enforcement under section 945 of the German Code of Civil Procedure (ZPO) as well as attorney and court fees.[182] In principle, the amount of the security relates to the litigation value. However, the defendant is entitled to substantiate and demonstrate that he risks higher damages through the enforcement. This amount is then decisive for the provision of the security.[183] The estimation of such threatened damages is often challenging. It could become an insurmountable financial obstacle for the plaintiff. He may not afford the enforcement, when the security amount is driven up by the defendant. Of importance is primarily the question how long the distribution of the challenged embodiments is interrupted due to the enforcement.[184] In a few telecom disputes, the amount of security has even been pushed into the billions of Euros.

If the right holder intends to enforce only a part of the claim (for instance, a rendering of accounts), he should accordingly request a particular attribution of the litigation value to the different requested claims.

182. Appeal Court Düsseldorf, NJOZ 2007, 451, 454; Cepl/Voß/Lunze, ZPO, 1st ed. 2015, §709 no. 4.
183. Cepl/Voß/Lunze, *supra*, §709, no. 6 f.
184. Appeal Court Düsseldorf, NJOZ 2007, 451.

The amount of the guarantee must comply with the form set forth in section 108(1) Code of Civil Procedure. The security shall be provided by a written instrument, be irrevocable, unlimited in time, absolute, unconditional, and directly bank guaranteed. If it is too difficult or time-consuming to find a suitable bank, the enforcing party may also deposit the amount with a special office of the court, namely the deposit agency where the money is deposited in a trust account. However, this requires the availability and transfer of the full amount. A sample of such bank guaranteed can be found in Chapter 17.

[2] Motion for Temporary Suspension of Enforcement

Permanent injunctive relief primarily depends on whether there is infringement. In contrast to the US,[185] except in cases of disproportionate hardships,[186] German courts are reluctant in applying equity principles when considering whether to award permanent injunctive relief to the prevailing party. Whether the patentee or right holder uses or intends to use the patent is predominantly irrelevant to the permanent injunction analysis. This situation has not fundamentally changed even after the introduction of the amendment to section 139 PatG providing for an equity test.[187]

Thus, German infringement courts do usually not consider, during regular proceedings on the merits, whether the patent or right holder is a practicing or nonpracticing company. In contrast, US courts would apply a four-factor test (eBay), which requires a plaintiff to demonstrate that: (1) it has suffered an irreparable injury; (2) remedies available at law are inadequate to compensate for that injury; (3) considering the balance of hardships between the plaintiff and defendant, a remedy in equity is warranted; and (4) the public interest would not be disserved by a permanent injunction. The decision to grant or deny such relief is an act of equitable discretion by a US court.

In enforcement proceeding the judgment debtor, faced with enforcement of the judgment, may file a motion for a temporary suspension of the enforcement (sections 719(1) and 707 Code of Civil Procedure), which the court may grant at its discretion. In such enforcement-related proceedings the court may weigh conflicting interests of the creditor (plaintiff) and the debtor (defendant). When weighing these interests, precedence is usually given to the judgment creditor, i.e., the patentee or right holder who wants to enforce the decision against an accused infringer (judgment debtor). The duration of the patent and thus the conveyed cease-and-desist order are restricted as to time, and each delay in the enforcement would lead to a diminishing of the injunctive relief. Therefore, it is generally assumed that the judgment debtor (or accused infringer) is sufficiently protected by the security that has been posted by the creditor

---

185. *eBay v. MercExchange*, 126 S. Ct. 1837 (2006).
186. *See* above: §10.02[B][2][a][i].
187. Federal Law Gazette, BGBl. I p. 4074.

when starting the enforcement.[188] A suspension of the enforcement is only exceptionally possible,[189] but could occur if the enforced judgment is obviously wrong.[190] More frequent situations justifying a stay of the enforcement proceedings are given if the patent on which the enforced judgment is based was later nullified in parallel invalidation proceedings.[191] If the patent was only partially invalidated, it is additionally required to justify that the limited claim is clearly not infringed by the accused product(s). Also, prior art which was identified too late for being considered in the decision-making process of the instance, could be exceptionally sufficient, provided that the newly identified prior art would have justified a suspension of the proceedings on the merits.[192]

A motion to stay the enforcement proceedings may also be given if the enforcement reasonably endangers the existence of the debtor, or at least poses a threat of significant and unexpected damages. Due to the high threshold, motions for temporary suspension of injunction enforcement are rarely successful, even if the patentee is a nonpracticing company. The fact that the patentee is a nonpracticing company may however have the effect to tip the scale. In a decision rendered in 2009,[193] the Appeal Court Karlsruhe had to address the enforcement of an injunction granted by the District Court Mannheim initiated by a nonpracticing company. The Court weighed the conflicting interests of both parties and finally concluded that the interests of the nonpracticing company were of lower importance. When weighing these conflicting interests the court took into account the unsettled validity of the patent, as evidenced by the pending parallel invalidation proceedings. The court also determined that the nonpracticing company was interested in a license agreement, based on earlier negotiations where the defendant had made a reasonable offer (in the court's view) that was rejected. The significance of the damages to the defendant (85% of his annual sales) was also considered. Although this case may appear at first blush to disfavor injunction enforcement by nonpracticing companies, the conclusion of the court was rather based on a combination of a plurality of factors.

[3] Compliance with Injunctive Relief

When injunctive relief is awarded, incompliance with the court's cease-and-desist order is punishable by a fine of up to EUR 250,000, or imprisonment. The fine can be imposed several times if the violations of the judgment are repeated. The amount of the fine depends on the seriousness of the continued infringement.[194]

188. Appeal Court Karlsruhe, 6 U 38/09, GRUR-RR 2010, "Patentverwertungsgesellschaft."
189. Appeal Court Düsseldorf, I-15 U 132/14, Decision of Dec. 21, 2015; Appeal Court Düsseldorf, I-2 U 24/15, Decision of Oct. 27, 2015; Appeal Court Karlsruhe, GRUR-RR 2015, 326, Mobiltelefone; Appeal Court Düsseldorf, GRUR-RR 2010, 122, "prepaid telephone calls."
190. Appeal Court Düsseldorf, I-15 U 65/15, Decision of Jan. 13, 2016.
191. Federal Supreme Court, GRUR 2014, 1273, "Kurznachrichten."
192. Appeal Court Düsseldorf, Decision of Aug. 10, 2010, I-2 U 19/10.
193. Appeal Court Karlsruhe 6 U 38/09, GRUR-RR 2010, "Patentverwertungsgesellschaft."
194. Federal Supreme Court, I ZR 323/98, GRUR 2001, 758, "Mehrfachverstoß gegen Unterlassungsverpflichtung."

In the case of a provisionally enforceable decision, the compliance obligations only become effective if the winner has posted a security bond—that is, the decision is not automatically enforceable. As soon as the requirements of enforceability are fulfilled, the debtor needs to take reasonable measures to avoid any noncompliance with the judgment. In bigger entities this requires that employees, salespeople, sales agents—in particular people who were involved in sales activities related to the accused products—be sufficiently informed of the judgment. The remainder of infringing merchandise stock must be taken out of circulation. Sufficient protective measures must be undertaken to avoid future unintended incompliance with the injunctive relief by subsidiaries and associates.

The accused infringer might have meanwhile changed the accused embodiment. Whether the modified embodiment still falls under the judgment depends on its scope. The determination of the scope of the judgment requires a careful analysis of the judgment. In principle, the cease-and-desist order is not limited to those acts to which the decision explicitly refers, but also applies to acts that fall within the "kernel of the infringement."[195] Minor and insignificant modifications of the accused embodiment, such as changing its color, are usually not sufficient to escape the scope of the judgment.

[4] Rendering of Accounts and Lawsuit Concerning the Amount of Damages

A favorable decision requires the accused infringer to render an account on which the calculation of the amount of damages can be subsequently based. Assuming the right holder has fulfilled the requirement to enforce the decision—he has posted a bond or deposited a security—he may then demand the accused infringer to render an accounting, usually by means of a letter written by his counsel wherein he sets a deadline for provision of the report. Because the creation of the report usually takes some time, the deadline should give sufficient flexibility to fulfill the duty. Usually, three to four weeks should be allotted to the accused infringer. He must then provide a report containing all items as required by the ruling. Usually, the following information with respect to a particular timeframe must be provided:

(a) the production amount and production time;
(b) the amount of received and ordered products as well as the names and addresses of the producers, suppliers and previous possessors of the products;
(c) the individual deliveries, broken down by amounts, times and prices of delivery as well as names and addresses of the commercial purchasers;
(d) the individual offers, broken down by amounts, times, and prices of offer as well as the names and addresses of the commercial recipients of offers;

195. Federal Supreme Court, I ZR 15/92, NJW 1994, 2820.

(e) the advertisement conducted, broken down by advertisement media, their number of edition, period and area of distribution; and
(f) the overall cost and the profits made, broken down by the individual cost factors.

The report containing the rendering of accounts of the infringer should enable the right holder to decide on which calculation mode he intends to use for calculating the damages.[196] The figures should be sufficiently clear to calculate the amount of damages[197] by means of the selected calculation mode. Furthermore, the report shall give relevant information as to the distribution channels and origins of the accused products. The report shall enable the patentee to eventually identify still unknown infringers.

The patentee can reject a partial or incomplete rendering of account. If the infringer does not comply in time with his duty, the judgment creditor (plaintiff) may request the imposition of fines until a sufficient and complete report is provided.

If it turns out, or if there are reasons to believe, that the report is wrong, the creditor should additionally force the accused infringer to make a sworn declaration. The sworn declaration, made before a competent court, should state for the record that he has rendered the accounts to the best of his knowledge and as completely as he is able (section 259(2) of the Civil Code). This applies to situations where there is reason to assume that the information contained in the account has not been provided with the requisite care. A false declaration made by the accused infringer would represent a criminal offense (section 156 of the Penal Code).

Once a sufficient report is provided by the accused infringer, the patentee should be in a position to decide how to calculate the amount of damages. He would most likely select the calculation mode that appears most favorable. Accordingly, he should be in a position to derive an amount from the figures in the report and demand the accused infringer pay that amount.

The parties may also negotiate a damages amount. If however they cannot reach an agreement on an amount, it may be necessary for the right holder to file an additional lawsuit seeking a court determination of the proper damages figure (so-called *Höheverfahren*). These proceedings would only concern the correct amount and would not cover other issues such as the question of infringement or validity of the patent. This lawsuit is based on the findings of the first instance decision wherein it is ordered "that the defendant is obliged to compensate plaintiff for all damages invoked on plaintiff by the acts indicated under ... committed since ... [date of the mention of the grant plus one month] and which will be invoked in future." In these separate proceedings, the court would thus apply the principles as described in Chapter 14 and use the information submitted by the party, in particular, the result of the rendering of accounts, to determine the right amount of damages. Frequently, a separate court determination is not necessary because the parties extrajudicially reach agreements on the amount.

196. Details concerning the calculation of damages can be found in Ch. 14.
197. Federal Supreme Court, X ZR 54/81, GRUR 1982, 723, "Dampffrisierstab I."

[5] Reimbursement of Costs

It is a characteristic of German patent infringement proceedings that the losing party has to reimburse the costs of the proceedings. The costs of the proceedings are the court fees and the statutory fees of the winning party. Depending upon the litigation value, these fees can be derived precisely from tables which are predetermined by the legislature. If the plaintiff does not completely prevail, the court then accordingly apportions the costs among the parties. The allocated reimbursement claim can then be enforced against the other party through special cost fixing proceedings pursuant to which the court will issue an order containing the exact amount that has to be paid by the debtor.

[G] Declaratory Judgment Action

A declaratory judgment action is defensive in character and is aimed at preventing the patentee from asserting rights against an alleged infringer. A declaratory judgment action for a finding of no infringement would not address the validity of the underlying patent because this is an issue on which only the invalidation authorities (Federal Patent Court, Patent Offices) may render a decision. The declaratory judgment action usually comes as a response by the accused infringer to a warning letter by the right holder.

The admissibility requirements of a lawsuit on the merits, in particular as to jurisdiction and venue, are mirrored in a declaratory judgment action. However, the declaratory judgment action additionally requires a legitimate interest of the plaintiff (the accused infringer) in the declaration sought from the court (section 256 Code of Civil Procedure).[198] Such legitimate interest is usually given if a warning letter has been sent to the accused infringer. A simple inquiry letter[199] of the right holder asking the party why he believes that he is entitled to use the claimed teaching is not sufficient to create such legitimate interest in the judicial declaration.[200] Accordingly, the legal system leaves some margin to the right holder to approach the accused infringer without risking a declaratory judgment action. But the inquiry should be carefully formulated.

A declaratory judgment action does not hinder the patentee's ability to file a positive action on the merits. Accordingly, the accused infringer cannot take advantage of an earlier filing of a declaratory judgment action. Irrespective of a pending declaratory judgment action, the patentee is still free to select any court of his choice, according to the general rules. He is not bound by the choice taken by the plaintiff in the declaratory action. The legitimate interest required for a declaratory judgment action ceases to exist when a later positive action on the merits is later filed in a

198. Section 256 Code of Civil Procedure: "An action may be brought for the determination of the existence or non-existence of a legal relation ..., if the plaintiff has legitimate interest that the legal relation ... is judicially determined" (unofficial translation).
199. Form and content of an inquiry letter are described in Ch. 9, §9.04[C].
200. Appeal Court Munich, Decision of Mar. 6, 1997, 6 U 4793/96, Mitt. 1998, 117.

different court.[201] This is a consequence of the principle of subsidiarity of declaratory judgment actions when weighed against the positive action on the merits filed by the patentee.

Take for example a situation where a declaratory judgment action has first been filed with the District Court Munich, and the patentee later files an action on the merits with the District Court Düsseldorf, bringing a mirror image set of claims for infringement. It will have the effect that the case pending at the District Court Munich will have to be discontinued without a decision on the merits and the action at the District Court Düsseldorf will take its normal course. This is contrary to the jurisprudence in the US, in which the first-filed litigation will generally take precedence.

[H] Financial Aspects of Infringement Proceedings

When filing a lawsuit, the plaintiff must advance the court fees for the first instance proceedings. Even though the losing party is liable for these costs, one party, namely the plaintiff, must pay these fees in advance. Of course, the plaintiff may later, if he wins the case, claim reimbursement of the advanced court fees from the loser, along with other costs such as the fees paid to his lawyer.

If the plaintiff is a non-European company, he must additionally provide a security for the potential cost reimbursement claim of the defendant in case the complaint is dismissed. Both the security and court fees are calculated on the basis of an estimated litigation value. As soon as the litigation value is determined, the exact fee can be taken from a table.

[1] Litigation Value

The litigation value is set at the free discretion of the court, taking into account the objective economic interest of the plaintiff. However, at the beginning of the proceedings, the plaintiff gives a rough and preliminary estimation of the litigation value, and indicates this amount in the complaint.[202] If the defendant does not object to the plaintiff's estimation, usually the court renders a decision based on the preliminary fixed litigation value. In most cases, the litigation value is not in dispute between the parties. Accordingly, the preliminary estimation of the plaintiff at the beginning of the proceedings is decisive for the calculation of the overall costs of the proceedings, including the financial risk assessment. However, if the patentee negligently or intentionally indicates a lower litigation value in order to "save" court fees in consideration of an uncertain outcome of the litigation, it could have severe consequences in case it is later revealed to the court. The indication of lower litigation value could be considered to be an act to the detriment of the State which accordingly

201. Federal Supreme Court, GRUR 2006, 217, X ZR 17/03, "Detektionseinrichtung I." The legitimate interest ceases to exist as soon as the subsequently filed positive action cannot be withdrawn anymore. This is typically the case if a hearing has taken place and/or in case the plaintiff of the positive action has waived the right to withdraw his action.

202. A sample of a complaint is contained in Ch. 17, §17.03.

receives lower court fees than it would otherwise be entitled.[203] Prior to filing a lawsuit, the facts underlying the litigation value should be thoroughly discussed with counsel. They should be able to base the litigation value on reasonable argument.

The litigation value should correspond to the plaintiff's objective economic interests. It is represented by the value of the claims as requested in the complaint. In the case of a regular infringement lawsuit, this is the value of the right to prevent the use of the patent. This value depends not only on the expected lifetime of the patent but also on the market share and market position of the parties, and more precisely the turnover related to the accused embodiment. Furthermore, the amount of the expected damages has to be added to the litigation value. As a rule of thumb, the request founded on the potential injunction value usually corresponds to approximately 80% of the litigation value, whereas the other claims asserted in the complaint (such as expected damages, rendering of accounts) amount to 20% of the litigation value. This means that if the sales figures would expectedly result in a damage claim of EUR 1 million, a litigation value of EUR 5 million would typically be reasonable, assuming that the patent still has an average expected lifetime. For a soon-to-expire patent, the litigation value would be limited to objectively expected damages. The calculation of the litigation value is based on an approximation whereby the court has a considerable margin of discretion.

Typically, litigation values range in patent cases between EUR 1 and EUR 5 million. EUR 30 million is a maximum value and is a ceiling for the fees.

[2] Court Fees

As soon as the litigation value is fixed, the plaintiff may take the corresponding court fee from a cost table which can be found in the Court Fees Act.[204] Tables 10.5 and 10.6 are taken from this Act. The Act is more detailed and contains a more precise breakdown of litigation values starting from values of EUR 10–EUR 30 million, which represents the highest value and is a ceiling for the fees.

[a] Court Fees for the First Instance

Table 10.5 categorizes the values from very low, which are below average, to values which are definitely above average.

Table 10.5 Court Fees for the First Instance

Litigation Value (EUR)	*Court Fees (EUR)*
250,000 (= very low)	6,951
500,000 (= low value)	11,700

203. Appeal Court Düsseldorf, Decision of Apr. 15, 2010, I-2 W 10/10; InstGE 12, 107, "Du sollst nicht lügen!."

204. GKG Gerichtskostengesetz.

Litigation Value (EUR)	*Court Fees (EUR)*
1,000,000 (= moderate)	17,643
2,000,000 (= average)	29,523
5,000,000 (= above average)	65,163
10,000,000 (= high value)	124,563
30,000,000 (= maximum)	362,163

[b] Court Fees for the Second Instance

Average court fees for the second instance proceedings are slightly higher than for the first instance. Table 10.6 illustrates this.

Table 10.6 Court Fees for the Second Instance

Litigation Value (EUR)	*Court Fees (EUR)*
1,000,000	23,524
2,000,000	39,364
5,000,000	86,884

[c] Costs for the Third Instance

Third instance proceedings are extremely rare. The court fees are increased by about 30% relative to the second instance.

[3] Provision of a Security for Defendant's Legal Costs

[a] Principle

Upon request of the defendant, plaintiffs, depending on their origin, must provide security for the potential cost reimbursement, which is due if the defendant finally prevails, and the complaint is dismissed. The provision of security for litigation costs is an unpleasant hurdle to overcome by many plaintiffs, depending on their national origin. Companies domiciled in the EU and the EEA are not affected by that obligation. The same applies to companies with registered offices in a state that is a member of the Hague Convention on Civil Procedure (§112 (2)No. 1 ZPO). Companies, e.g., from Switzerland, Israel, Japan, Russia, and Turkey are therefore exempted from the obligation.

Companies from the US,[205] Taiwan and China are however not exempted. Since the security for litigation costs represents a considerable cost factor for the plaintiff, the

205. District Court Munich I, GRUR-RR 2005, 335; LG Düsseldorf InstGE 1, 157.

question arises whether the obligation can be circumvented by assigning the patent-in-suit, for instance, to a German company. This could be considered as an abuse of rights and thus an improper circumvention. Such an abuse of rights is discussed above all if it turns out that the company was founded solely for the purpose of enforcing the patent in Germany.

The courts have developed case law in the past years. It is recognized by German courts that section 110 of the German Code of Civil Procedure (ZPO) does not protect against the fact that a claim for reimbursement of costs cannot be realized due to the debtor's lack of assets.[206] Nevertheless, in some cases, even German companies have been ordered to provide a security for litigation costs, especially in cases where the administrative headquarter of the company could not be identified in Germany. This could be assumed, for example, if the (sole) managing director is not domiciled in the EU and manages the (German) company from the US.[207]

[b] *Amount of the Security*

The amount of the security depends upon the litigation value. The higher the litigation value is, the higher are the corresponding statutory fees and thus the higher is the amount of the security to be provided by the foreign plaintiff. Table 10.7 considers cases having only one defendant and indicates the security to be provided in compliance with the standards of the DC Düsseldorf. The indicated amount would be slightly higher in cases having more than one defendant. Pursuant to section 112(2) ZPO, the amount to be taken as a basis for determining the security corresponds to the amount that the defendant is likely to spend on court and out-of-court legal costs.[208] There is disagreement between German courts on whether the security should cover costs for all three instances. The District Court Mannheim is satisfied with the costs for first instance and for starting the appeal instance (less than all costs of the appeal), whereas the District Court Düsseldorf and the District Court Munich basically include all costs of first and appeal instance plus costs for starting the third instance. This makes a big difference and often influences the choice of the court. In compliance with section 108(1) Code of Civil Procedure, the security can be provided by means of a bond issued by a bank officially accredited to operate in Germany. Sometimes it is difficult for foreigners to find a bank, which meets these criteria. In that case, the foreign plaintiff may also deposit the money in a trust account at the deposit agency of the court.

206. Federal Supreme Court, NJW 1984, 2762; LG Düsseldorf BeckRS 2016; 08353.
207. Appeal Court Munich, BeckRS 2010, 18320; Appeal Court Düsseldorf, BeckRS 2013, 10038.
208. Cf. Celp/Voß, commentary, 2. ed., 2018, §112 Rn. 5 et seqq; District Court Munich I, GRUR-RR 2005, 335; LG Düsseldorf InstGE 1, 157.

Table 10.7 Amount of the Security

Litigation Value (EUR)	*Security (EUR)*
250,000	57,500
500,000	79,500
1,000,000	112,500
2,000,000	178,500
5,000,000	376,500
10,000,000	706,500

§10.03 FRAND

[A] Introduction

Patented inventions may encompass subject matter that is covered by technical standards. A conflict may arise if technical standards, which have been defined either individually by an enterprise or jointly by a group of firms (so-called club-standards or de facto standards) or collectively by industry-wide operating standard-setting organizations (SSO), cannot be applied without using a patented invention (so-called standard-essential patents (SEP)).[209] The telecommunication sector, for example, is heavily dependent on standards, including USB, 3G, 4G, USTM, 5G and many others. Standards make it possible for telecommunication devices, such as smartphones, to work almost anywhere in the world and run applications from a plurality of software developers. SEPs may conflict with the need for market participants or entrants to have access to standards. This situation is particularly critical in areas where standards have obtained market- or industry-wide recognition and where products that do not provide "standard compliance" may therefore be unsalable. The SEP may provide a market-dominating position within the meaning of Article 102 TFEU. Such position usually applies if the patented teaching cannot be circumvented without waiving important functions[210] or in case the technical teaching on which the SEP and the standard is based cannot be substituted by another technical design of the product.[211] The abuse of that position would be illegal under Article 102 TFEU. This is an important issue, particularly in view of waves of cases such as those relating to smartphones and tablets taking place in the German courts and elsewhere. Conflicts between the exclusionary effects of patent protection, in particular in cases where the standard has obtained market or industry-wide recognition and the need and desire to have access to

209. Federal Supreme Court, KZR 36/17, WRP 2020, 1194, no. 54, 58—FRAND Einrede; Federal Supreme Court, judgment of Jul. 13, 2004—KZR 40/02; Federal Supreme Court BGHZ 160, 67, 74—Standard-Spundfass.
210. Federal Supreme Court, WRP 2020, 1194, no. 58—FRAND Einrede; ECJ, judgment of Jul. 16, 2015—C-170/13, WRP 2015, 2783, no. 49—Huawei/ZTE; European Commission, Decision of Apr. 29, 2014—C (2014) 2892 para. 52—Motorola.
211. Federal Supreme Court, WRP 2020, 1194, no. 58—FRAND Einrede; cf. ECJ, [2004] ECR I-5039, no. 28—IMS Health; Federal Supreme Court, BGHZ 160, 67, 74—Standard-Spundfass.

standards, are inherent. A patentee of a standard-essential invention might be tempted to exploit these effects by requesting, on the basis of his exclusivity, the acceptance of unreasonable licenses.

The legal framework of the defense under antitrust law, in particular in connection with SEP, has been hotly debated. It led to a decision of the ECJ,[212] rendered in the summer of 2015, in which general principles have been determined. Meanwhile, these principles have been refined by the national courts.

[B] Situation Prior to the Decision of the ECJ

The Federal Supreme Court[213] was faced with such a conflict for the first time in 2004 when an Italian manufacturer of barrels for chemical liquids, who had been sued for damages, objected to the claim with an antitrust defense. The accused infringer argued that the patentee's refusal to grant him a license constituted an abuse of the patentee's market-dominating position by discriminating against him in comparison to other manufacturers of the patented product to whom licenses had been granted. The Federal Supreme Court concluded that in case of an industry standard (or standard-like general conditions) that forces entrants to a downstream market to adhere to the technical specifications of a patent, a market-dominating patent proprietor can be in breach of the antidiscrimination provisions when he exploits this situation to restrict access to the market by applying criteria for granting licenses that contradict the purpose of the freedom of competition. The German Federal Supreme Court thus recognized a duty to license a patent in that standardization situation, which could be raised as a defense by an accused infringer.

In a second important decision, in May 2009, which is called the *Orange Book Standard* decision,[214] the Court maintained its general position that the defendant can raise an antitrust defense in patent litigation when a market-dominating position results from the assertion of a patent (Article 102 TFEU).[215] The *Orange Book Standard* case refers to joint innovation efforts mainly made by Philips and Sony, which have been internationally accepted under the IPR declaration and licensing policies of the

212. ECJ, judgment of Jul. 16, 2015—C-170/13, WRP 2015, 2783, no. 49—Huawei/ZTE.
213. German Federal Supreme Court, Jul. 13, 2004, 36 IIC 2005, 741, Standard Tight-Head Drum.
214. Federal Supreme Court, Decision of May 6, 2009, KZR 39/06, Orange Book Standard.
215. Article 102 (previously Art. 82 TEC): Any abuse by one or more undertakings of a dominant position within the internal market or in a substantial part of it shall be prohibited as incompatible with the internal market insofar as it may affect trade between Member States. Such abuse may, in particular, consist in:
   (a) directly or indirectly imposing unfair purchase or selling prices or other unfair trading conditions;
   (b) limiting production, markets or technical development to the prejudice of consumers;
   (c) applying dissimilar conditions to equivalent transactions with other trading parties, thereby placing them at a competitive disadvantage;
   (d) making the conclusion of contracts subject to acceptance by the other parties of supplementary obligations which, by their nature or according to commercial usage, have no connection with the subject of such contracts.

European Computer Manufacturers Association (ECMA), and internationally recognized by International Organization for Standardization/International Electrotechnical Commission (ISO/IEC). The parties in that case were not competitors within the product market—rather, the patentee was essentially in the business of selling licenses offered publicly on the Internet at standard terms. The defendant, who found these terms to be commercially unacceptable, mainly sought to obtain more favorable conditions. When he continued to use the patented invention by adhering to the technical standard, the plaintiff brought an infringement action seeking injunctive relief. The defendants claimed that they were entitled to a license under Fair, Reasonable and Non-Discriminatory (FRAND) terms. This was refused by the patent owners and, according to the defendant, should therefore have barred them from asserting claims for patent infringement.

The Federal Supreme Court concluded that such defense was admissible and could be applied against a request for an injunction, provided that the defendant had behaved like a "hypothetical licensee." Accordingly, a successful defense requires that:

(1) the patentee has a market-dominating position;
(2) the hypothetical licensee:
   (a) has made an unconditional offer to license the technology under fair, reasonable and nondiscriminatory terms which could not be rejected by the proprietor without violating the prohibition of discrimination and obstructive practices;
   (b) behaves like a licensee and renders account; and
   (c) pays a reasonable royalty (or deposits the amount into a trust account) for the time he uses, or has used, the technology covered by the patent.

The Federal Supreme Court admitted that the hypothetical licensee may have difficulties determining the proper royalty rate. The hypothetical licensee may solve this problem by leaving the specification of the amount of the royalty to the patentee at his reasonably exercised discretion. It would not be binding on the defendant to the contract if such an amount is evidently inequitable. The specification is made in this case by judicial decision (*see* section 319 of the German Civil Code).

In a decision rendered on March 21, 2013, the District Court Düsseldorf[216] raised concerns as to the case law under the *Orange Book Standard*. The District Court Düsseldorf also referred to a view of the European Commission (EC) expressed in a press release dated December 12, 2012: Therein the EC indicated, "where a commitment to license SEPs on FRAND terms has been given by ... [i.e., the patentee], and where a potential licensee, ..., has shown itself to be willing to negotiate a FRAND license for the SEPs, then recourse to injunctions harms competition."

In the light of these concerns, the District Court Düsseldorf asked the CJEU to consider a set of questions concerning the understanding of how patent monopolies

216. District Court of Düsseldorf, *Huawei v. ZTE*, Mar. 21, 2013, 4b 104/12.

and standard-essential proprietary technologies can be incorporated into EU's rules on competition and antitrust. A translation of these questions can be found here:

1. Does the owner of a SEP, who has declared to a standardization body that he is willing to grant any third party a license on FRAND terms, abuse his dominant market position if he files an action for an injunction against an infringer although the infringer has declared that he is willing to negotiate concerning such a license,

   or

   is an abuse of the dominant market position only given if the infringer has made to the owner of a SEP an acceptable, unconditional offer to conclude a license agreement which the owner cannot refuse without unfairly impeding the infringer or breaching the prohibition of discrimination, and the infringer fulfils—in anticipation of the license agreement to be conclude—his contractual obligations for acts of use already committed?
2. If abuse of a dominant market position is already to be presumed as a consequence of the infringer's willingness to negotiate:

   Does Article 102 TFEU lay down particular qualitative and/or time requirements in relation to the willingness to negotiate? In particular, can such willingness to negotiate be presumed if the patent infringer has merely stated (orally) in a general way that he is prepared to enter into negotiations, or must the infringer already have entered into negotiations by, for example, submitting specific conditions upon which he is prepared to conclude a licensing agreement?
3. If the submission of an acceptable, unconditional offer to conclude a license agreement is a prerequisite for an abuse of a dominant market position:

   Does Article 102 TFEU lay down particular qualitative and/or time requirements in relation to that offer? Must the offer contain all the provisions which are normally included in licensing agreements in the field of technology in question? In particular, may the offer be made subject to the condition that the SEP is actually used and/or is shown to be valid?
4. If the fulfilment of the infringer's obligations resulting from the licence agreement to be concluded is a prerequisite for an abuse of a dominant market position:

   Does Article 102 TFEU lay down particular requirements as to those acts of fulfilment? Is the infringer particularly required to render account for acts of use committed in the past and/or to pay royalties? May the payment of the royalties fulfilled by the provision of security?
5. Do the conditions under which an abuse of a dominant position is committed by the owner of the SEP apply also other claims resulting from a patent infringement (rendering of accounts, recall of products, damages)?

On November 20, 2014, the Advocate General published his opinion[217] about the conditions of the commitment to grant licenses to third parties on FRAND terms, and it seemed that the (patentee-friendly) approach taken by German courts following the *Orange Book Standard* decision of the German Federal Supreme Court could not be maintained.

217. Opinion WATHELET, Nov. 20, 2014, Case C-170/13, *Huawei Technologies Co. Ltd v. ZTE.*

[C] Decision of the ECJ

The CJEU confirmed in its judgment of July 16, 2015, that the owner of an SEP subject to a FRAND commitment may seek an injunction against an alleged infringer that fails to negotiate toward a license in good faith without infringing Article 102 of the TFEU. The ECJ notes the need to "strike a balance between maintaining free competition … and safeguard[ing] that proprietor's intellectual-property rights and its right to effective judicial protection." In an effort to strike that balance, the ECJ describes the conditions in which the owner of an SEP subject to a FRAND commitment may pursue an injunction without the risk of violating Article 102 TFEU:

- It is not abusive for the owner of an SEP subject to a FRAND commitment to seek an injunction if he has, first, alerted the alleged infringer by designating the patent-in-question and specifying the way in which it has been infringed, and second, the alleged infringer has failed to signal his willingness to conclude a license under FRAND terms.
- Where the alleged infringer has expressed his willingness to conclude a license on FRAND terms, the SEP owner may pursue an injunction if he has, first, provided a written offer, specifying the royalty and the way in which it is to be calculated, and, second, the alleged infringer has failed to respond to the written offer in good faith.

Accordingly, Article 102 TFEU limits an SEP owner's ability to seek an injunction where the alleged infringer acts in good faith to negotiate a license after receiving a written offer. This stands under the proviso that a market-dominant position is conferred by the SEP to its owner. A patent, even an SEP, does not necessarily have such a quality.[218] That is, the existence of a market-dominant position needs to be assessed on a case-by-case basis. It is typically found if the patent bars or at least significantly impedes the market access for the accused infringer in downstream markets.[219]

Good faith of the alleged infringer is to be determined according to objective factors which may include whether the alleged infringer has promptly provided the SEP owner with a specific FRAND counteroffer, has not employed delay tactics, and has otherwise acted "in accordance with recognized commercial practices." The patentee is however not prohibited from filing an action for infringement against the infringer seeking the rendering of accounts in relation to past acts of use of that patent or an award of damages in respect of those acts of use. The FRAND defense represents a defense against the injunction, i.e., the cease-and-desist claim, the destruction claim, and recall claim. That is, while negotiating with the accused infringer, the patent owner can file an infringement action asserting claims for accounting and for a finding of liability for (past) damages.[220] Such lawsuit could later be extended by bringing claims

218. *Ibid*. Appeal Court Düsseldorf, Decision of Jan. 13, 2016, I-15 U 65/15.
219. Appeal Court Düsseldorf, Decision of Jan. 13, 2016, I-15 U 65/15.
220. *Ibid*.

for injunctive relief if the negotiations fail because of non-diligent behavior of the infringer.

Where the alleged infringer makes a counteroffer, but the parties cannot reach an agreement, he must demonstrate continued good faith from the time its counteroffer is rejected by providing the SEP owner with appropriate security (bank guarantee or deposit) for ongoing use of the patent according to recognized commercial practices.

An alleged infringer does not, however, demonstrate bad faith by merely challenging infringement or validity while negotiating the terms of a license.

Where the alleged infringer does not evidence good faith by reference to objective criteria, Article 102 TFEU does not bar the SEP owner from pursuing an injunction after it has provided notice and a written offer to license on FRAND terms. The Court also held that the owner of an SEP subject to a FRAND commitment may seek damages or a rendering of accounts without restriction.

[D] Application of the Decision of the ECJ by German Courts

[1] Introduction

The decision of the ECJ fundamentally deviates from the patentee-friendly *Orange Book Standard* decision.[221] Standard users received more flexibility under the ECJ approach (so-called *Huawei Program*). Nevertheless, German courts tend to apply the principles of the ECJ decision in a patentee-friendly manner. At present, the FRAND defense requires the following steps:

[2] Huawei Program (Steps)

Prior to applying the Huawei Program, it is necessary to determine whether the patentee possesses a market-dominating position on an individual market (here: licensing market) within the meaning of Article 102 TFEU. This requires establishing that the patent is standard-essential, and thus is indispensable for the implementation of a standard.[222] An individual licensing market is typically found if the patented teaching cannot be circumvented without foregoing important functions,[223] or the technical teaching on which the patent and the standard are based cannot be substituted by another technical design of the product.[224]

221. Federal Supreme Court, Decision of May 6, 2009, KZR 39/06, Orange Book Standard.
222. Federal Supreme Court, KZR 36/17, WRP 2020, 1194, no. 54, 58—FRAND Einrede; Federal Supreme Court, judgment of Jul. 13, 2004—KZR 40/02; Federal Supreme Court BGHZ 160, 67, 74—Standard-Spundfass.
223. Federal Supreme Court, WRP 2020, 1194, no. 58—FRAND Einrede; ECJ, judgment of Jul. 16, 2015—C-170/13, WRP 2015, 2783, no. 49—Huawei/ZTE; European Commission, Decision of 29 Apr. 2014—C (2014) 2892 para. 52—Motorola.
224. Federal Supreme Court, WRP 2020, 1194, no. 58—FRAND Einrede; cf. ECJ, [2004] ECR I-5039, no. 28—IMS Health; Federal Supreme Court, BGHZ 160, 67, 74—Standard-Spundfass.

Step I Notification: The patentee must inform the accused infringer about the infringed patent. This notification requirement shall occur prior to the filing of the complaint.

Step II Declaration of Willingness: The accused infringer swiftly[225] declares its willingness to take a license. He must clearly and unambiguously declare his willingness to conclude a license agreement with the patentee on FRAND terms. Also, he must subsequently contribute to the license negotiations in a targeted manner.[226] An infringer who remains silent for several months in response to the notice of the patentee thus regularly indicates that he is not interested in taking a license.[227] A continuing willingness to license is required, which is an indispensable prerequisite for successful licensing negotiations. An abuse of a market-dominating position of the patentee may thus only occur if such continuing willingness is not determinable (anymore).[228] As long as the infringer, for his part, makes the efforts that are required and possible and reasonable under the given circumstances to conclude a license agreement on FRAND terms, an ongoing infringement of the patent may be considered acceptable.[229] The duties of conduct of the patentee, on the one hand, and the duties of conduct of the user of the patented teaching, on the other hand, are intercorrelated and mutually dependent.

Step III FRAND Offer: The patentee must provide a specific written offer to license the SEP on FRAND conditions. The offer with which the patentee fulfills its responsibility as a market dominator to make it possible for the user of the patented teaching to conclude a license agreement on FRAND terms is the starting point of the license negotiations. In a complex situation, as is typically the case when licensing SEPs, it is regularly not obvious which contractual terms in a specific case[230] provide an appropriate balance of interests and, at the same time, do not violate the prohibition of discrimination under antitrust law. FRAND conditions may be satisfied by a range of possible appropriate solutions. The patentee is normally able to consider legitimate interests of the user once he is aware of them.[231] It is thus important for producing a fair and appropriate end result that the interests of both parties are well articulated and that factual and legal aspects are demonstrated during the negotiations which may be of significance for this result.

Step IV Reaction of the SEP User—Counter-FRAND Offer: The accused infringer must react in good faith and without delay. He must deal with

225. Five month is clearly to long: District Court Düsseldorf, 4a O 73/14.
226. Federal Supreme Court, WRP 2020, 1194, no. 83—FRAND Einrede.
227. Federal Supreme Court, WRP 2020, 1194, no. 92—FRAND Einrede.
228. Federal Supreme Court, KZR 35/17, no. 68—FRAND Einrede II.
229. *See* High Court of England and Wales [J Birss], judgment of Apr. 5, 2017, [2017] EWHC 711 [Pat] para. 562.
230. Cf. Gerechtshof Den Haag, GRUR Int. 2020, 174, 179 para. 4.34.
231. Cf. High Court of England and Wales [J. Birss], Judgment of Oct. 23, 2018, [2018] EWCA Civ 2344, GRUR Int. 2019, 357 para. 121; Appeal Court Karlsruhe, GRUR 2020, 166 para. 95; cf. on s. 19 (4) no. 4 GWB; Federal Supreme Court, BGHZ152, 84, 96—Fährhafen Puttgarden I.

the SEP owner's offer in such a way that it becomes apparent that he is pursuing the goal of reaching a mutually beneficial result as soon as possible. If the accused infringer does not accept the FRAND offer, he must make a counteroffer in reasonable time on FRAND conditions. The obligation of the alleged infringer to respond diligently by providing a FRAND counteroffer will be triggered provided the patentee previously complies with Step III.[232] However, an offer by the SEP owner that does not comply with FRAND terms (Step III) does not necessarily constitute an abuse of a market-dominating position that would remove the user's obligation to continue the negotiations.[233] If the offer (Step III) obviously does not comply with FRAND terms and appears to represent a denial to conclude an agreement on FRAND terms, the SEP user shall at least point to the facts justifying such view.[234] The court has a duty to assess and determine whether the license offer of the SEP owner complies with FRAND terms. This also requires that the SEP owner has explained in Step III "the way in which that royalty is to be calculated." He must thus indicate why he believes that the proposed royalty rate is nondiscriminatory and non-abusive under the conditions prevailing on the relevant market. The latter could be done, for instance, by submitting comparable licenses concluded in the past.[235] Unless those agreements have been concluded under the pressure of an injunction, such previously concluded license agreements based on the SEP provide a strong indication for those terms being reasonable.

Step V Rendering of Account and Provision of Security: If the patentee does not accept the counteroffer, the accused infringer must—also for the past—render account and provide security for the royalties. The latter represents a minimal requirement. It needs to be fulfilled independently upon the specific details of the offer and the counteroffer. In addition, the rendering of account and the provision of the bond has to be done swiftly[236] after the rejection of the counteroffer.

Step VI Third-Party Determination: In case of deadlock "where no agreement is reached on the details of the FRAND terms following the counter-offer by the alleged infringer"—the parties "may, by common agreement, request that the amount of the royalty be determined by an independent third party, by decision without delay." If offer and counteroffer complies with FRAND and the parties may still not agree, the determination of the royalty amount may, even must[237] be deferred to a third party.

232. Appeal Court Karlsruhe, Decision of May 31, 2016, 6 U 55/16; Appeal Court Düsseldorf, Decision of Nov. 3, 2015, 4a 4a O 144/14.
233. Federal Supreme Court, KZR 35/17, para. 76.
234. Federal Supreme Court, BGHZ 152, 84, 92—Fährhafen Puttgarden I; Federal Supreme Court, KZR 35/17, marginal no. 68.
235. District Court Düsseldorf, 4a O 73/14.
236. Within one month: Appeal Court Düsseldorf Decision, Nov. 3, 2015, Cases 4a O 93/14 and 4a O 144/14.
237. T: Kühne, Handbuch der Patentverletzung, 8th ed., 2016, pp. 537–538, E. 304.

It is crucial for both sides to deal with these requirements thoroughly, during any already-pending patent infringement proceedings and, preferably, well in advance of a potential litigation. Swift and diligent fulfillment of these requirements is particularly advantageous for the accused infringer, which may resort to this FRAND defense to avoid an injunction.

In principle, the negotiation obligations must be fulfilled before the lawsuit has been initiated, i.e., notification of infringement, notification of willingness to license, license offer, possible counteroffer, etc. However, the courts in Düsseldorf tend to be more generous in their approach for satisfying these different steps during the course of the proceedings. Accordingly, omissions may thus in principle be cured even after the proceedings have already been initiated.

[3] Details of the License Offer

The license offer must be made in writing and must contain the FRAND conditions. This offer must be detailed enough to provide an understanding, on the basis of objective criteria, why the submitted offer meets FRAND criteria. The SEP holder bears the burden of presentation and proof that he has fulfilled the standards set up in the decision of the ECJ. The mere indication of the factors for the calculation of the license fee is not sufficient. Other license agreements must be made transparent. A mere reference to further licensees or a reference to a portfolio of a third party is not sufficient. Whether the submission of license agreements alone is sufficient depends in particular on the number of license agreements concluded. If a sufficient number of license agreements and market acceptance (e.g., the market share of the products licensed at a certain fee level) are reached, no further information on the appropriateness of the license fee will normally be required. The SEP holder must also submit other decisions on infringement and the validity of the SEP rights to be licensed. If this information is not available, the SEP holder must present evidence of the appropriate license fee, for example, through comparable license agreements (if possible, in the same or comparable technical area). Also, more detailed explanations of the portfolio and its effects on the fee amount are required if the patent suit is not licensed individually.

Many details have been recently ruled upon by lower courts, in particular by the District Courts Mannheim and Düsseldorf.

[4] What Is FRAND?

FRAND terms constitute a set of principles with which SEP owners must generally agree to in return for inclusion of their technology into the relevant standard. There is no precise definition of what FRAND is. In a complex situation, as is typically the case when licensing SEPs, it is regularly not obvious which contractual terms in a specific case provide an appropriate balance of interests and, at the same time, do not violate the prohibition of discrimination under antitrust law.[238] Generally, there is agreement on that FRAND terms could be satisfied by a range of possible appropriate solutions.[239]

"*Non-discriminatory*" means that the SEP owner treats the SEP user in an equal manner in comparison to other licensees. In principle, he must offer licenses on comparable terms. An unequal treatment is sometimes possible but must be based on good and plausible reasons. Such reasons must be explained in a comprehensible manner.

"*Fair*" means that both parties should have equal access to relevant information in order to be able to negotiate on par. In the case of an established licensing practice, the SEP owner must present the existing agreements.[240]

"*Reasonable*" is a criteria which addresses the outcome of the negotiation. If the license rate cannot be taken from existing agreements, comparisons with license rates of other license programs are suggested. They are at least an indication of a reasonable license fee if there is comparability in terms of subject matter, quality, and scope.

In the field of telecommunications, there is often not only one patent-in-question, but an entire portfolio that is to be the subject of the agreement. A portfolio license can also be FRAND compliant. Worldwide portfolio licenses are also generally acceptable.[241]

Larger portfolios often require considerable efforts to clarify the infringement issue for all patents. In such a case, it is considered sufficient if a substantiated factual argument on the use of a representative selection of portfolio patents is provided. The submission of so-called claim charts "Proud-list" of approx. 10–15 may be sufficient in individual cases. It is then up to the infringer to show when certain patents of the portfolio are not used.

The question often arises as to how to deal with patents which subsequently prove to be invalid. This problem can be dealt by adjustment clauses with corresponding price corrections. For example, the license could be reduced as soon as a licensed patent hat been invalidated.

Finally, adjustment clauses may be warranted with respect to maximum license burdens. Each product can only be licensed up to a maximum limit. Some courts allow the integration of maximum limits in the contract others not.[242]

[5] FRAND in the Supply Chain

The question is still in dispute whether and under what circumstances and with what legal consequences an SEP owner having made a FRAND declaration abuses its

238. Cf. Gerechtshof Den Haag, GRUR Int. 2020, 174, 179 para. 4.34.
239. Cf. High Court of England and Wales [J. Birss], Judgment of Oct. 23, 2018, [2018] EWCA Civ 2344, GRUR Int. 2019, 357 para. 121; Appeal Court Karlsruhe, GRUR 2020, 166 para. 95; cf. on s. 19(4) no. 4 GWB; Federal Supreme Court, BGHZ152, 84, 96—Fährhafen Puttgarden I.
240. Appeal Court Düsseldorf, dec. Jan. 17, 2017—I-2 U 31/16.
241. Appeal Court Düsseldorf, Düsseldorf I-15 U 66/15.
242. Yes: Appeal Court Düsseldorf I-15 U 65/15 (license rates of 25%–30% of the profit margin are common).
Not required: District Court Mannheim, dec. Jan. 24, 2017—2 O 131/16.

market-dominating position under Article 102 TFEU if the SEP owner brings a lawsuit to enjoin the distributor of an end product in which an SEP infringing component is integrated without having first complied with a licensing demand of the supplier of that infringing component. The question is whether an SEP owner is free to decide at which stage of a supply chain it grants licenses on FRAND terms. There is disagreement about this question among the German courts. The District Court Düsseldorf referred this question including a set of other FRAND-related questions to the ECJ.[243] However, on June 1, 2021, the parties (Nokia and Daimler) settled this matter on an extrajudicial basis. Thus, the ECJ may no longer rule on the questions and accordingly legal uncertainty may not be removed from the picture. The right of each supplier to demand a FRAND license for itself exists at least in principle and unconditionally. This suggests that a demand for a FRAND license represents a permissible exercise of rights which, in the event of a refusal by the SEP holder, involves an abuse of a market-dominating position, which might be invoked both by the SEP user at the end of the supply chain and by the supplier situated earlier in the supply chain. It appears that the granting of a FRAND license to a supplier is also not to the detriment of the SEP holder in terms of remuneration for the use of the invention.

[E] Application of the Decision of the ECJ by Other European Courts: UK

A further important judgment in the context of FRAND relates to several SEPs that Unwired Planet asserted, *inter alia*, against Huawei.[244] For the first time, a UK Court made a FRAND determination and set a FRAND royalty rate. The lengthy judgment sets out the fundamental principles of FRAND and an analysis on the rates and terms of a FRAND license. The court also created a so-called FRAND injunction, namely an injunction that automatically ceases to have effect if the defendant enters into a FRAND license determined by the court. The court held that Unwired Planet did not abuse its position of dominance as an SEP holder by prematurely issuing proceedings. Obviously, the steps set out in *Huawei v. ZTE* were not so strictly applied by the court. Unwired Planet did also not abuse its dominant position by seeking an injunction, insisting on a worldwide license on a bundle of SEPs and non-SEPs.

A controversial aspect of the judgment concerns the finding that there shall be only one set of FRAND terms and rates to be set by the court. In addition, the judgment provides guidance on how parties should approach a FRAND negotiation. As long as the SEP owner and user negotiate in a FRAND manner, the offers themselves do not have necessarily to be FRAND. The declaration itself creates a legally enforceable contract. In addition, the judgment says that non-FRAND license terms are not automatically anticompetitive. When determining a FRAND royalty rate, a "benchmark rate" should be set on which the value of the SEP portfolio can then be adjusted. Unwired Planet and Huawei both put forward methods for calculating the total number of SEPs relevant to various European Telecommunications Standards Institute (ETSI)

243. DC Court Düsseldorf 4c O 17/19 Decision of Nov. 26, 2020.
244. *Unwired Planet v. Huawei* [2017] EWHC 711 (Pat).

standards, as well as the shares held by Unwired Planet and Ericsson, which was then used by the court to reach a conclusion. However, many conclusions as to the total number of relevant SEPs in the concerned patent pool and valuation remain vague.

§10.04 OTHER EUROPEAN JURISDICTIONS

In addition to the UPC, national court systems, such as the German system are playing an important role for solving patent infringement issues. During the transitional phase (of seven years) provided for in Article 83 UPCA, patent enforcement based on national parts of conventional European patents can be pursued through national courts. National patents, for which the UPC does not have jurisdiction, must be enforced through national courts anyway. Because the territorial scope of the UPC does not cover the entire European area, in certain countries, such as in Spain, in Switzerland and the UK, national enforcement of patents remains basically the only way of judicially acting against infringers. Thus, a patent owner possesses a broad range of enforcement possibilities. The scope for decision-making leaves margin for the development of a balanced international strategy. The most important European jurisdictions are outlined below. This outline is aimed at providing a rough insight into the main characteristics of these systems to get a first impression of whether they should be further assessed for a broader pan-European patent enforcement campaign.

[A] France

[1] Saisie Contrefaçon

French patent infringement proceedings are usually initiated by a seizure, a so-called ***saisie contrefaçon***. It is a tool dominantly used in France to obtain proof of infringement. This procedure is ordered by a judge, on request of the owner of a valid right (patent, utility certificate or SPC). Also, it is necessary to provide the judge with the beginning of proof of infringement. The law provides that the owner of the right may, on request, be authorized, by order, to get a report drawn up by a bailiff to prove the infringement. Once the judge has issued the seizure order, the operation is carried out by the bailiff without any prior notification to the alleged infringer, other than the presentation of the order prior to the implementation of the seizure. The bailiff may be assisted by an expert who, in practice, is the patent attorney of the right holder. The seizure may be carried out at the place of production of the alleged infringing product where the bailiff proceeds, in accordance with the order, with a description of the allegedly infringing product or process accompanied by a description and photographs if necessary, and with, if necessary, the seizure of a certain number of samples of these same products. The bailiff is usually assisted by the patent attorney of the right holder, as well as by a police commissioner and any other admitted person if necessary (photographer, etc.). The bailiff draws up a report in which all the material evidence is included (photographs, photocopies, notices of the infringing products or processes, etc.).

[2] *Proceedings on the Merits (No Bifurcation)*

A **complaint** for infringement must be filed before the competent Court of First Instance within thirty days following the seizure of the infringing goods, against at least one of the presumed infringers. The complaint shall specify the plaintiff's arguments, establishing, for example, the essential characteristics of the patented invention and the similarities observed with the counterfeit product, as demonstrated by the seizure report. The complaint must contain an exact and complete list of the allegedly infringing claims that are being asserted, and in addition, it must state the grounds for the action as well as the requests for cessation of the infringement and compensation for damages suffered. The action for infringement of a patent, utility certificate or SPC must be brought before the **Tribunal de Grande Instance de Paris**, which has **exclusive jurisdiction** in this matter. If the action is based on a patent application that has not yet been granted, the court shall stay the proceedings pending the grant of the patent and the end of any opposition proceedings. Once the defendant has been summoned, a period (ca. 6–12 months) is granted to him to present his arguments in writing (**defense brief**). In the defense brief, he may, on the one hand, contest the facts of which he is accused, the infringement, and on the other hand, contest, by means of a **counterclaim for invalidity**, the validity of the patent right (patent, utility certificate or SPC) due to lack of novelty or inventive step, insufficient description of the invention, or any other ground for invalidity provided for by the law. The plaintiff can then present his arguments, demonstrating, for example, that the invention remains patentable despite the arguments developed by the opposing party. Further exchanges of pleadings may take place between the parties. Although it is possible to introduce new arguments during these exchanges, it is naturally preferable to maintain the same strategy throughout the proceedings. The final pleadings usually take the form of summary pleadings, which allow the judges to have all the arguments of each party in a single document.

[3] *Experts*

The court is not required to appoint an **expert**. However, in some cases, the parties may prefer to request the court to appoint a technical expert. This may be necessary where the allegedly infringing products require a certain amount of analysis and comparison tests. If the court decides to appoint an expert, it submits several questions to him. The expert organizes meetings with the parties concerned, during which they can present their arguments.

[4] *Hearing*

After a certain number of exchanges (generally 2 to 4 briefs) the court usually closes the case and sets a deadline for filing of final briefs, as well as a date for the **hearing.** The hearing usually takes place one to two years after filing the complaint brief, unless an expert is appointed, which lengthens the proceedings of about one or two further years.

The pleading of each representative during the hearing lasts from 1 to 3 hours. The plaintiff intervenes first, the defendant gets the opportunity to respond to the plaintiff's arguments. Depending on the complexity of the case a hearing represents a day, or two days event. The **court's decision** comes a few months after the hearing. An **appeal** takes place before the Appeal Court Paris. Appeal proceedings generally have the same speed as 1st instance proceedings. Decisions rendered by the Appeal Court Paris maybe subject to appeal to the Supreme Court which only rules on points of law.

[5] Costs

First, **court fees** are not due to commence proceedings before French courts. The filing of an appeal is subject to a little fee of EUR 225. Accordingly, the costs of own representatives are the **main cost driver**. Also, under Article 700 of the Code de Procédure Civile (CPC), the prevailing party can request that the losing party pay the costs incurred during the proceedings. The winning party usually submits a report proving the total amount of costs incurred, covering fees of legal representatives, patent attorneys, experts, and bailiffs. The award, which can be substantial, is granted under the court's discretion. It usually represents approximately one-third of the actual costs.

[B] Italy

[1] Courts

Infringement actions in Italy are subject to the exclusive jurisdiction of **specialized divisions** comprising judges skilled in patent matters. The divisions are spread throughout the Italian territory. There are presently 22 courts having such divisions. However, only 11 of them have jurisdiction on cases involving foreign defendants. The **most active divisions** are **in Milan, Turin, Venice, Bologna, and Rome**. Like in France, the proceedings are pursued without bifurcation, i.e., dealing with both, infringement, and validity of the patent. Lawsuits on the merits in relation to patent infringements and patent validity are pending once the plaintiff has served the complaint on the defendant, who is then entitled to respond by a **statement of defense** with counterclaims and exceptions, including, the invalidity of the asserted patent. Of course, the challenge of the validity of the patent is the most common defense of the accused infringer against the patentee. A **first hearing** may take place within 90 days if the defendant is based in Italy, whereas the term is extended to 150 days for foreign defendants. After that first hearing, the parties are allowed to exchange three briefs and submit documents as evidence and/or provide other evidence to support their respective claims and assertions. In almost all patent matters, **Italian courts appoint a technical expert** skilled in the specific field of the patent, who evaluates the validity of the patent and the interference of the attacked product with the existing scope of protection of the enforced patent. Following the appointment of the expert, a technical debate between takes place often accompanied by their own technical experts. After conclusion of that technical debate, the court expert issues a report. The report is not binding for the court, but often anticipates the result of the proceedings. The parties have the option to discuss the report before the judge, who will then invite plaintiff and defendant to exchange their final statements. A final hearing to discuss the case takes place only upon request of a party.

In each stage of the proceedings the patentee may submit **amendments of claims** provided they stay within the scope of the content of the application as originally filed:[245] The law states: "*In proceedings concerning nullity, the owner of the patent has the right to submit to the Court, at any stage or instance of the proceedings, amended claims that remains within the limits of the content of the patent application as originally filed and that does not extend the protection conferred by the patent granted.*"[246]

Depending on the complexity of the matter, a first instance decision can be expected within **two or three years** from the first hearing. The proceeding may take longer if the patentee amends the claims during the proceedings under Article 79(3) of the Industrial Property Code (IPC). Because of this considerable time span, in many cases quicker preliminary injunction proceedings are initiated.

[2] Discovery or Inspection

Limited **discovery or inspection**, comparable to the French *Saisie Contrefaçon* can be obtained by the patentee. He must provide reasonable indications to support its claims and, in substantiating those claims, specify evidence that is under the control of the opposing party. Under the same conditions, in case of infringing activities on a commercial scale, the patentee can also obtain the disclosure of banking, financial or commercial documents under the control of the opposing party, subject to the protection of confidential information.[247] He may also be entitled to obtain information on the origin of the infringing products or services, distribution channels and the identity of any third party involved in the infringing activities. Such inspection proceedings are often used in Italy to collect evidence about suspected patent infringement, especially if the infringement cannot reasonably be proven through other tools. The inspection is followed by the main proceedings which need to be introduced within a deadline imposed by the court or, in its absence, within 20 working days or 31 calendar days (if the latter is a longer period) from the decision ordering the inspection.

[3] Costs

The **costs of patent litigation** in Italy are low. The court fees for filing a patent lawsuit on the merits or patent validity proceedings amount to EUR 1,000, while the filing fees of preliminary injunctions proceedings are about EUR 500. Of course, the fees for the

245. Details: Decision No. 21402 of Aug. 14, 2019, of the Italian Supreme Court.
246. Article 79 Italien IPC.
247. Article 121 Italien IPC.

representatives must be added. The winning party can usually recover at least a part of the incurred costs, in average a sum in-between EUR 25,000 to EUR 50,000 may be granted for cases on the merits, and EUR 10,000 to EUR 15,000 for preliminary injunction proceedings.

[C] The Netherlands

[1] Discovery

A main entry point for patent cases in the Netherlands is the **District Court of The Hague**. This court has exclusive jurisdiction to hear patent infringement and invalidity cases. Pretrial measures, such as seizure measures do not fall within the exclusive jurisdiction of the court of The Hague. The patentee may request a district court to grant permission, often on **ex parte** basis to **seize evidence** that is in the possession or under the control of the accused infringer. A successful request requires to demonstrate at least a legitimate fear of infringement. Following the permission granted by the court on a successful request, a bailiff may be instructed to inspect the premises of the infringer, often with the help of technical experts. To protect confidential information of the accused infringer, the data collected by the bailiff during this operation will not directly be handed over to the patentee. The patentee will have to request in *inter partes* proceedings to get disclosure of the seized documents.

[2] Proceedings on the Merits

Patent infringement proceedings are initiated with a complaint brief, describing the background technology and protected teaching of the invoked patent, the infringing activities, and the relief that is requested. After service of the **complaint**, the defendant can file a **statement of defense** usually accompanied by a **counterclaim of revocation** against the patent-in-suit. The plaintiff then gets an opportunity to respond to the counterclaim for revocation. He is allowed to file auxiliary requests (**amendments** to the granted claims).

The court either schedules a **hearing** after the plaintiff has had the opportunity to respond to the counterclaim for revocation, or it allows the parties to continue the exchange of briefs, after which the court summons to a hearing (three to five hours and in complex cases longer).

[3] Experts

Even though Dutch courts may appoint **court experts,** or they may be appointed on request of the parties, this rarely happens. Instead, the parties refer to their own, i.e., individually selected technical experts, who may support their arguments by written expert statements and through testimony in the hearing.

[4] Costs

Court fees are insignificant. They can be neglected for a cost estimate. The main cost factors of Dutch patent proceedings relate to the involvement of legal representatives, patent attorneys, experts, and translations. The amount also depends on the complexity of the case, the technology involved, and the number of patents invoked. Generally, these costs roughly range between EUR 50,000 to EUR 250,000. Furthermore, the losing party is, in principle, ordered to pay the costs of the prevailing party based on indicative fees depending on the complexity of the matter. For preliminary relief proceedings, the indicative fees range from EUR 10,000 to EUR 120,000. The indicative fees for proceedings on the merits in first instance range from EUR 30,000 to EUR 250,000.

[D] United Kingdom

[1] Territorial Scope

The **territorial scope** of the UPC does not reach the UK. The Unitary Patent will also have no effect there. Due to UK's withdrawal from the EU, these instruments do not have effect there. Nevertheless, the UK will continue to play an important role in patent enforcement through **UK national patents**, prosecuted via the UK Intellectual Property Office (the UK IPO), and UK parts of **traditional European patents** prosecuted via the EPO that designate the UK.

[2] Courts and Proceedings

Although certain courts in Scotland and Northern Ireland also have jurisdiction over UK patents, patent actions are usually initiated in either the **Patents Court** or the **Intellectual Property Enterprise Court**. They represent first instance courts and are part of the High Court of England and Wales. Both courts have jurisdiction over infringement and validity. A defendant to an infringement action may, and usually will, challenge validity by way of counterclaim, but it may also initiate revocation proceedings at any time. A common defense in UK's infringement proceedings is thus a counterclaim aimed at revoking the patent-in-suit. The procedures in both courts do not profoundly differ. However, the Intellectual Property Enterprise Court is supposed to deal with smaller disputes of small and medium-sized enterprises with a cap on costs. Also, it can only award financial relief of up to GBP 500,000.

Patent actions at the Patent Court are initiated by a service of a claim form and the statement of case. At a CMC, the schedule until the hearing and the date for the hearing will be set, usually about a year after the action has been started. The parties are accompanied by one or rarely more than two expert witnesses. They will provide expert reports submitted in line with the set schedule set at the CMC. In addition, the court orders on whether and to which extent disclosure of documents relating to the matters in issue is necessary. Expert reports and parties' statements are exchanged according to the dates fixed at the CMC, timely before the hearing, whereby the other side shall have an opportunity for cross-examination. "Skeleton arguments" setting out the respective parties' arguments are then exchanged shortly before the hearing.

The hearing can take up to several days. The patentee usually introduces the case followed by the examination and cross-examination of its experts and witnesses of fact. Subsequently, the defendant gets the opportunity to explain its view of the case. The experts and witnesses of fact of the defendant are also subject to examination and cross-examination. A patentee should make **amendments to its patent** before the hearing so that the court can determine the permissibility of the amendments and whether these suffice to meet the validity attack. The court typically does not allow such amendments to be made after the hearing. Usually, several weeks after the hearing, a written judgment is delivered by the court. In case the patentee is successful, the court usually orders an injunction and decides whether to stay the proceedings pending the outcome of the appeal. It also orders a rendering of account directed to providing the patentee with sufficient information to make an informed election between. If a patent is held to be invalid, the court (partially/completely) revokes it, which will be suspended pending the outcome of any appeal. Appeals from the Patents Court and, in patent matters, the Intellectual Property Enterprise Court are in the hands of the English Court of Appeal.

Proceedings at the Intellectual Property Enterprise Court differ from that of the Patent Court: The initial briefs in these proceedings are usually more detailed. But, unless otherwise ordered at the CMC, the proceedings are less burdened because no disclosure, no oral testimony a cross-examination takes place at the hearing, which is shorter, usually not longer than one or two days.

[3] Costs

In each court, the winning party may recover an important part of its legal costs. The loser may be exposed to the other side costs in the order of several hundred thousand pounds, and sometimes even more, in addition to having to meet its own costs. In the Intellectual Property Enterprise Court, costs recovery is capped at EUR 50,000 for the liability phase and EUR 25,000 for the damages phase.

CHAPTER 11
Summary Proceedings and Provisional Measures

The UPC as well as German courts can grant provisional measures, such as preliminary injunctive relief. For example, provisional measures may be sought when infringing goods are detected for the first time at a trade show exhibited by a company that resides outside Europe, with need for judicial intervention prior to the end of the tradeshow. In such situations, the UPCA and the related Rules of Procedure[1] provide for a mechanism to protect the legal position of the patentee.

§11.01 UPC

[A] Aim of Summary Proceedings

In exceptional cases, the patent holder should not be forced to wait for a full trial on the merits. Requiring a full trial on the merits would not sufficiently protect the right holder's legal interests. Summary proceedings allow the court to order tailored measures for that purpose. The different provisional measures are indicated in Article 62(1) and (3). After weighing the parties' interests, including the degree of urgency, the risk of harm and the possibility of making a wrong decision, the court may:

- grant injunctions,[2] mandating cessation of the infringing activity. The injunction will be enforced to cease the activity by ordering a penalty in case of violation of the order;[3]
- make any continuation of an infringing activity depend upon guarantees securing a possible compensation claim of the patentee;[4]

1. Article 62 UPCA; Rules 205–213 RoP.
2. Article 62(1) UPCA.
3. Article 82(4) UPCA.
4. Article 62(1) UPCA.

- order the seizure or surrender of products suspected of infringing a patent;[5] this measure is aimed at preventing the accused products from entering the channels of commerce;
- order the seizure of property of the alleged infringer, including blocking bank accounts and other assets of the accused infringer, to secure payment for later damage awards.[6] If requested, the applicant must describe circumstances from which it can be determined with a sufficient probability that a subsequent claim for damages would be endangered.

These provisions from Article 62 UPCA are not an exhaustive list. Thus, other measures which are better suited to a particular case may be applied by the court.

[B] Timing and Urgency

According to Rule 206(1) RoP, an application for provisional measures can be lodged at any time prior to or after the commencement of the main proceedings. A common approach is to file the application either prior to the main proceedings or simultaneously with its commencement. Summary proceedings can provide swift relief in urgent matters which may not be available in main proceedings on the merits. The requirement of "urgency" is critical, and failure to seek provisional relief within a reasonable time period may lead to a denial of the request.[7] "Urgency" is an undefined legal concept which is not defined in the UPCA or the RoP. The court must give meaning to that concept within the framework of its discretionary authority. It must be clear that main proceedings with a later decision would not sufficiently protect the right holder. The request must therefore be urgent. This requires that the validity of the patent be sufficiently supported and that after weighing the interests of the parties in consideration of all circumstances it becomes clear that plaintiff's interests in a swift reaction of the court prevail. The plaintiff is therefore advised to proceed swiftly in initiating the preliminary injunction proceedings.[8] He should not give the impression that he is reluctant to pursue his rights. The concept of urgency is not tied to statutory time limits. Rather, it depends on the circumstances of the individual case, which may result in a shorter or longer period of time. As soon as the plaintiff has gained positive knowledge of the circumstances of the patent infringement, he should pursue his claims expeditiously and without negligence. This knowledge is present if all facts giving rise to an infringement of the patent and the infringer are reliably known to him. Thus, if the patent owner has tangible indications of infringing acts, he may not close his eyes, but must swiftly act. Any inactivity may be understood that he is not in a hurry to pursue his legal interests, which is harmful for the issuance of a preliminary injunction. From the moment of gaining knowledge, the plaintiff must thus immediately decide whether he wants to act against the infringement and then, without delay,

5. Article 62(3) UPCA.
6. *Ibid.*
7. Rule 209(2)(b) RoP.
8. Rule 211(4) RoP.

do everything necessary to clarify and prepare the facts of the case in such a way that he can initiate the proceedings. Carefully investigating of the facts and evidence and procuring of suitable means of establishing credibility for the preparation of a quality application are understood as necessary prerequisites. However, in accordance with the urgent nature of the preliminary injunction proceedings, he must apply all possible and reasonable efforts to get hold of the targeted product as quickly as possible and, as soon as he has the target in his hands, investigate it (or have it investigated). A "new" urgency could start to run if the situation changes fundamentally, for example, if it turns out that the infringement has become more intense or has a different, more far-reaching quality and nature than initially known.

The UPC has not yet established case law on the concept of urgency. However, the ECJ—in a recent decision[9]—has clarified the question of whether patents that have not yet been reviewed by a court, such as through EPO opposition proceedings or national nullity proceedings, can also be the subject of preliminary injunction proceedings. The ECJ answered in the affirmative and ruled: "*Article 9(1) of Directive 2004/48/EC of the European Parliament and of the Council of 29 April 2004 on the enforcement of intellectual property rights must be interpreted as precluding national case-law under which applications for interim relief for patent infringement must, in principle, be dismissed where the validity of the patent in question has not been confirmed, at the very least, by a decision given at first instance in opposition or invalidity proceedings.*" The ECJ thus ruled that according to the Enforcement Directive, a completed validity proceeding is not a *conditio sine qua non* for injunction proceedings. It is expected that the UPC will comply with this requirement.

[C] Stages of the Proceedings

Summary proceedings under the UPCA are divided into two main stages.[10] The first stage consists of a written part initiated by a written application for provisional measures. The second stage consists of oral proceedings. Oral proceedings are not mandatory if the case is sufficiently urgent. This is similar to German preliminary injunction proceedings.

A characteristic of such summary proceedings is that the court does not need to be fully convinced about the presented facts as required in main proceedings. Of course, a mere possibility that an alleged fact is correct or true does not provide a sufficient amount of proof for ordering a provisional measure. Rather a "sufficient degree of certainty"[11] must be given that facts presented are correct.

Depending on the degree of "urgency," such summary proceedings may follow different tracks:

9. C-44/21.
10. Rule 205 RoP.
11. Article 62(4) UPCA, Rule 211(1) RoP.

(1) The court informs the defendant about the application and directs the defendant within a set time limit to lodge a written objection to the application.[12] The time limit set by the court must weigh the explained urgency with the defendant's interests to be fairly heard. On the contrary, this allowance for filing objections would likely not be reasonable if it endangers the purpose of the requested measure.

(2) The court summons—as soon as possible—to a hearing:
   - either both parties (i.e., plaintiff and defendant are summoned to a hearing); or
   - only the plaintiff may be summoned in cases of sufficient urgency such that any delay would cause irreparable harm or there is a risk that evidence being destroyed.[13] Such ex parte approach could harm the defendant. Accordingly, the court must in principle order a sufficient security, from the applicant.[14] This could be a bank guarantee to cover the potential harm caused to the defendant by an erroneous decision.

   The court provides a written decision as soon as possible after the hearing.

(3) In exceptional cases, the court may issue a decision without any hearing. In fact, the plaintiff can request an ex parte decision without any hearing if the case is extremely urgent.[15] These are only extreme situations where the loss of time would make it impossible to enforce the right.

[D] Content of a Successful Application

The application must indicate the provisional measure(s) to be ordered by the Court. The application should be drafted like a statement of claim.[16] In addition, the application must contain facts justifying why the requested measures are necessary. That is, in addition to the description of the patent infringement, the applicant must demonstrate reasons for immediate action by the Court. The applicant must show why he would not be sufficiently protected by the tools available through normal proceedings on the merits. A provisional measure requires "urgency." There must be a reason why waiting for a decision on the merits would be insufficient to protect the plaintiff's interests. Under the UPCA, the requirement of urgency is not bound by a fixed time limit for filing the request for provisional relief. Rather, it is left to the Court to decide on a case-by-case assessment. The time by which the applicant needs to file the application certainly plays a role in that decision. The more the applicant waits, the harder it is to establish urgency. This is explicitly required in Rule 211(4) RoP which mandates that court consider any unreasonable delay by the applicant in seeking provisional measures.[17]

12. Rule 209(1) RoP.
13. Rule 212(1) RoP.
14. Rule 212(2) RoP.
15. Rule 209(3) RoP.
16. Rule 13 RoP.
17. Chapter 11, §11.01[B].

Winning provisional relief requires sufficiently substantiating the underlying facts of infringement, including presenting the evidence from which a sufficient degree of certainty can be drawn on which to base the requested remedy. A sufficient degree of certainty must be given as to the ownership and validity of the patent. In addition, it must be demonstrated that the infringing activities fall within the scope of protection of the patent. According to Rule 8.5(c) RoP, patent ownership can be demonstrated by means of an excerpt of the patent register. It is still unsettled as to how the Court could ascertain a sufficient degree of certainty as to the validity of the patent. The validity may be more forcefully established if the patent has successfully survived opposition or revocation proceedings. Completed validity proceedings are not a *conditio sine qua non* for injunction proceedings.[18] However, the Court will likely ask the defendant to file an objection or at least summon both parties to a hearing if the underlying patent has not yet been upheld in opposition or revocation proceedings.

The applicant must also substantiate the potential harm caused by the infringing activities. Submitting relevant business data, which can be supported by affidavit, may satisfy the evidentiary burden. The Court's discretion depends on weighing up the interests of the parties, including the potential harm for either of the parties resulting from the granting or the refusal of the injunction.[19] Furthermore, the application shall contain a concise description of the merits of the main proceedings.

Any attempt to seek provisional relief on an ex parte basis requires the plaintiff to justify such exceptional measure. An ex parte order substantially restricts the defendant's procedural right to be heard. Typically, the plaintiff will have to demonstrate an irreparable harm to justify ex parte relief. For instance, trade show cases where the alleged infringer will have departed the jurisdiction following the exhibition, or if there is a risk that assets will be moved outside the jurisdiction of the court, could justify such ex parte proceedings.

[E] Protective Letter

Potential targets of actions for provisional relief may file "protective letters" with the Registry of the court. A protective letter is a written defense against a potentially later-filed application for provisional measures. It is a way for potential defendants to preemptively lodge an exculpatory pleading with the Court in anticipation of a patent holder's request for provisional relief. The protective letter remains confidential as long as an application for provisional measures is not filed. In this manner, the lodging of a protective letter does not attract the attention of the patent holder. In Germany, the use of protective letters is a well-accepted and recognized tool used by parties concerned with potential accusations of infringement.

For instance, a company may plan to introduce a new product on the European market and knows that there is a patent that could be asserted against such activity. The company may thus file a protective letter in anticipation of an application for

18. C-44/21; Ch. 11, §11.01 [B].
19. Rule 211(2) RoP.

provisional measures. The protective letter shall contain all arguments and facts challenging the right holder's attempt to block the new product from the market. It may contain noninfringement arguments, it may challenge the patent's validity and it may assert that there is no urgency in the matter. Statements of facts presented in the protective letter should be supported by available written evidence, such as sworn witness statements, expert opinions or data stored on video or audio carriers.

If an application for provisional measures is lodged with a division, the Registry of the court verifies whether a protective letter has been filed by the defendant concerning the asserted patent. The Court must take note of a protective letter when taking a decision in summary proceedings. Unless the arguments presented in the protective letter are without merit, the protective brief could at least prompt the court to disregard an ex parte order and, instead, set a date for a hearing or invite the defendant to prepare an objection.

A protective letter must be accompanied by a small fee of EUR 200.[20] The letter will stay in the register for six months,[21] a timeframe which could be extended on request.

[F] Withdrawal of the Application

The applicant might be interested in an "ex parte" decision by the Court. If the court is not willing to grant ex parte relief, often the applicant would prefer to withdraw the application to avoid the target learning about this unsuccessful attempt. The RoP provide for such a mechanism.[22] That is, the applicant can request the opportunity to withdraw an unsuccessful ex parte application and to have the application maintained confidential. The defendant would thus not be informed about the application.

[G] Revocation of the Order

In the context of the UPCA, a provisional measure becomes challengeable if, within a time period not exceeding thirty-one calendar days or twenty working days—whichever is the longer period—specified in the court order, the applicant does not initiate proceedings on the merits. After that time period, the defendant may request the revocation of the provisional measures. The threat of such revocation may force the applicant to initiate the main proceedings on the merits. In addition, where the provisional relief is revoked because the indicated time period has ended, compensation may be claimed for damages caused by the enforcement of the order.[23] A similar mechanism is applicable under French law.[24] In France, it is not necessary that the action be a civil action on the merits. It can also be a penal action, as through a complaint filed with the public prosecutor (L615-3 CPI [5]). The starting point of the

20. Rule 207(4) RoP; Table of Court Fees, Jul. 8, 2022.
21. Rule 207 (9) RoP.
22. Rule 209(4) RoP.
23. Rule 213(2) RoP.
24. L615-3 CPI, (5) in combination with R615-1 CPI.

time limit is the date "specified" in the order, which might not be the date of the notification of the order. The situation becomes problematic if the date of the order is not mentioned in the order, in which case it might be arguable—as proposed in a decision of the Appeal Court Paris[25]—to defer the starting point of the time limit to the date of notification of the order, or, in the absence of a notification, to the date on which the party concerned obtained actual knowledge of the order. The date of notification and the date mentioned on the order are usually different. Typically, the time period begins to run at a point in time when plaintiff is not yet aware of the order, which may be cause to stretch the start of the time period to the date of notification, regardless of the date mentioned on the order.

[H] Financial Aspects

In contrast to litigation in Germany where court fees based on litigation value are due in preliminary injunction cases, the litigation value of the underlying matter is irrelevant for determining the court fees for provisional measures requested at the UPC. The court fee is fixed: EUR 11,000. Nevertheless, it is necessary to determine the litigation value for the assessment of the recoverable costs. However, the litigation value for provisional measures is typically lower than the value of the action on the merits in the same matter. Also, German courts usually apply a significantly lower litigation value for preliminary injunction cases. With respect to the recoverable costs, reference can be made to Chapter 10, §10.07.

§11.02 GERMANY

[A] Framework

Proceedings similar to those available under the UPCA can be initiated in German courts. Such expedited proceedings also allow for swift injunctive relief. A claim for destruction may also be secured through an order to surrender the accused goods to a bailiff who stores them until a decision on the merits is taken on the destruction claim. In addition, the proceedings may yield discovery into the nature of distribution channels of the accused products, and to eventually determine the identities of previously unknown infringers (section 140b(7) Patent Act).[26] However, in most instances, preliminary injunction proceedings are used in German courts for obtaining quick injunctive relief.

A request for a preliminary injunction is usually filed prior to the introduction of a regular lawsuit. A preliminary injunction may be granted in an *inter partes* proceeding. In very urgent cases, the grant of injunctions in ex parte proceedings is possible.

25. Appeal Court Paris, 2nd Ch., Mar. 26, 2015, RG:14/12790.
26. An unofficial translation of s. 140b Patent Act can be found in Ch. 18, §18.03.

German courts are generally reluctant to grant preliminary injunctions,[27] but some German courts apply more generous preliminary injunction rules than others. The differences are substantial among the courts in Germany because preliminary injunctions are not appealable to the Federal Supreme Court (section 542(2) Code of Civil Procedure). In view of the absence of the harmonizing effect of the Federal Supreme Court, it is thus crucial to appreciate the differences among local practices in selecting the most appropriate court for preliminary injunction proceedings.

[B] Proper Court

A request for preliminary relief must be filed with an appropriate court having jurisdiction over the matter. The selection of the court follows the same standards that are applicable to regular lawsuits (*see* Chapter 10). Accordingly, patentees have considerable leeway in selecting a favorable forum within Germany, to maximize the chances of obtaining preliminary relief. In the case of a Germany-wide commercialization, which can be demonstrated sufficiently by, for example, a single offer made through a webpage, all twelve district courts have jurisdiction.

[C] Basis for a Preliminary Injunction

A request for injunctive relief must provide a sufficient basis to justify entitlement to this extraordinary remedy. In that respect, in addition to satisfying the requirements for a complaint in regular proceedings, the applicant must additionally substantiate the urgency needed to justify preliminary relief.

In the US, courts apply a four-factor test to govern the award of preliminary injunctive relief. That is, US courts consider: (1) the likelihood of the patentee's success on the merits; (2) whether the patentee will suffer irreparable harm if the injunction is denied; (3) the balance of hardships between the parties; and (4) the public interest.[28]

In Germany, comparable aspects are considered when deciding on a request for a preliminary injunction; however, the courts apply a different methodology. The requirements essentially rely on two main criteria: first, the claim on which the preliminary injunction shall be based (*Verfügungsanspruch*), and second, a well-founded reason to grant this claim in preliminary injunction proceedings (*Verfügungsgrund*). Both the foundation of the claim as well as the well-founded reason for extraordinary remedy must be sufficiently substantiated and supported by prima facie evidence. Regular evidence taking proceedings will not take place, and the court has to decide within a tight time framework.[29]

---

27. District Court Düsseldorf, 4 O 286/79, GRUR 1980, 989, "Sulfaveridin."
28. For example, *Abbott Laboratories v. Andrx Pharmaceuticals, Inc.*, 473 F.3d 1196, 1200–1201 (Fed. Cir. 2007).
29. District Court Düsseldorf, 4 O 286/79, GRUR 1980, 989, "Sulfaveridin."

[1] Claim on Which the Injunction Is Based (**Verfügungsanspruch**)

[a] Validity of the Asserted Patent

The injunction is typically aimed at preventing the use of the patent according to section 139(1) Patent Act. Thus, the patentee must proffer sufficient evidence to carry a prima facie basis for entitlement to a finding that the asserted patent is infringed. This shall include a demonstration that the asserted patent is in force and that he is entitled to assert rights resulting from it. He could provide an excerpt from the register of the Patent Office, which is available online (https://dpinfo.dpma.de/). However, a statement in the register that the "patent is in force" does not legally presume the validity of the patent. The same applies to other entries in the register such as the named owner. That entry does not itself suffice in establishing entitlement to proceed with a preliminary injunction claim.[30]

In a decision of April 28, 2022, the ECJ ruled[31] on a question referred to by the DC München:[32] "Is it compatible with Article 9(1) of Directive 2004/48 if German higher regional courts, which have jurisdiction at last instance in proceedings for interim relief, refuse, in principle, to grant interim measures for patent infringement if the validity of the patent in dispute has not been confirmed in opposition or invalidity proceedings at first instance?" The vagueness of the term "in principle" used by the DC Munich in the referral question led to some discussion. It can either be broadly construed as a general rule allowing exceptions or be narrowly understood as an almost necessary condition. The narrow understanding does not correspond to the German approach: According to the case law of the Appeal Courts Düsseldorf, Karlsruhe, and Munich,[33] the grant of a preliminary injunction in patent matters depends on whether the question of patent infringement and validity of the patent can be forecasted so clearly in favor of the plaintiff that an erroneous decision is not seriously to be expected. Besides the infringing quality of the accused product, there must be a sufficient certainty that the patent is valid. This assumption of validity is commonly affirmed if the asserted patent survived (at least one instance in) invalidation proceedings, such as an EPO opposition or nullity proceedings at the Federal Patent Court. The ECJ might have understood that this is a mandatory requirement under the German case law. However, there are other cases where a sufficient certainty of validity could be assumed, such as:

- the defendant or any other renowned competitor was involved with observations in the granting procedure of the underlying patent application;[34]

30. Federal Supreme Court, Decision of May 2, 2013, X ZR 69/11, "Fräsverfahren."
31. C-44/21.
32. 21 O 16782/20.
33. Appeal Court Munich, GRUR 2020, 385—Elektrische Anschlussklemme.
34. Appeal Court Düsseldorf, InstGE 12, 114, 121—Harnkatheterset; Decision of 07.11.2013—I-2 U 94/12 = BeckRS 2014, 04902; GRUR-RR 2013, 236, 239 f.—Flupirtin-Maleat; Decision of Dec 10, 2015—I-2 U 35/15 = BeckRS 2016, 06208; Decision of Dec. 14, 2017—I-2 U 18/17 = BeckRS 2017, 142305 Rn. 14.

- the patent is generally respected as a valid right by renowned competitors (such as renowned licensees);
- the objections raised against the validity of the patent are obviously groundless;
- in exceptional circumstances, it may appear reasonable to grant quick relief. Such circumstances may be given, for example, in the area of generic medicines.[35]

A preliminary opinion of the opposition division or a qualified indication of the Federal Patent Court could provide sufficient certainty of the validity.[36] Admittedly, these opinions are not binding and do not anticipate the later decision. Nevertheless, a clearly expressed and carefully reasoned preliminary opinion may possibly allow the assumption that the opinion will be reflected in the later decision. The decisive factor is therefore whether the preliminary opinion takes an unambiguous and well-founded position, or whether it neutrally addresses only possible considerations and points for discussion.

According to the German case law, the term "in principle" thus describes a general rule, which allows the issuance of an interim injunction in individual cases even without the requirement for the patent to have survived invalidation proceedings. The ECJ affirmed that approach: *"Article 9(1) of Directive 2004/48/EC of the European Parliament and of the Council of 29 April 2004 on the enforcement of intellectual property rights must be interpreted as precluding national case-law under which applications for interim relief for patent infringement must, in principle, be dismissed where the validity of the patent in question has not been confirmed, at the very least, by a decision given at first instance in opposition or invalidity proceedings."* The ECJ thus ruled that according to the Enforcement Directive, validity proceedings are not a *conditio sine qua non* for granting a preliminary injunction. This does however not mean that the ECJ lowered the degree of certainty for preliminary injunction proceedings. Rather, it seems that the ECJ's decision did not substantially change the prior situation.

[b] Licensee

The patentee's licensee may also bring the request for preliminary relief, insofar as the licensee's status can be substantiated. Specifically, the licensee needs to submit a copy of the license agreement including an affidavit demonstrating that the agreement is still valid (and not terminated). If the applicant is not an exclusive licensee, but a simple licensee, he needs to submit an authorization (in addition to the copy of the agreement and affidavit) granted by the patentee, permitting him to file the suit.

---

35. Appeal Court Düsseldorf, InstGE 12, 114, Harnkatheterset; Appeal Court Düsseldorf, GRUR-RR 2013, 236, 240—Flupirtin-Maleat; Decision of 07.11.2013—I-2 U 94/12 = BeckRS 2014, 4902—Desogestrel; Decision of Feb. 19, 2016—I-2 U 54/15 = BeckRS 2016, 6344 Rn. 13; Decision of 14.12.2017—I-2 U 18/17 = BeckRS 2017, 142305 Rn. 15.
36. Appeal Court Düsseldorf, Decision of 21.07.2108—I-2 U 19/17; 29.01.2021—I-2 W 26/20 = GRUR-RS 2021, 1830.

[c] *Infringement of the Asserted Patent*

Second, the patentee needs to demonstrate that the patent is infringed. Similar to a complaint filed in regular proceedings,[37] the request must describe the prior art to which the patent-in-suit specifically refers and explain the invention and propose a claim construction. An appropriate claim chart, mapping feature by feature of the claim to the accused embodiment, is usually contained in the request as well.

It is necessary to provide an evidentiary basis for all factual statements made in the request, although in a request for preliminary relief a prima facie basis is sufficient (section 294 of Code of Civil Procedure). Regular evidence taking will not occur in preliminary injunction proceedings. The kinds of evidence typically relied on by a patentee in establishing this prima facie basis include:

- samples of the accused product, provided a submission is feasible;
- copies of documents, such as promotional documents, manuals describing the application of the accused product;
- photos of the accused embodiment;
- affidavits, sworn witness statements; and
- private expert opinions.

[2] *Particular Reasons for a Preliminary Injunction* (Verfügungsgrund)

[a] *Urgency*

Beyond establishing a likelihood of success on the merits, the patentee (or licensee as the case may be) also needs to substantiate the urgency of the case. He must file the request quickly after he becomes aware of the patent infringement. This does not mean that the patentee has a duty to monitor the market to identify suspect products. A defense alleging that the right holder could have identified the accused products earlier would, as a matter of principle, not be successful.[38] The right holder must at least become aware of tangible indications that the patent is infringed. As soon as he has such knowledge, a swift handling of the matter is recommended. That is, if the right holder learns of suspect products by which infringement cannot be readily determined, he should swiftly analyze them, carry out necessary tests, and attempt additional investigations as needed in order to confirm whether the patent is infringed or not. Unnecessary and inexcusable delay with such investigations may endanger the success of the request.[39] The time period conferred to the right holder depends on the complexity of that investigation. The right holder shall have sufficient time for determining the infringing quality of the suspect product. A longer time period is granted to the right holder if complex and sophisticated tests are necessary to clarify the

37. Chapter 8 deals with regular infringement proceedings.
38. Appeal Court Cologne, GRUR-RR 2014, 127.
39. Appeal Court Düsseldorf, Decision of Jul. 5, 2012, I—2 U 12/21.

technical particularities of the suspect product.[40] As soon as the right holder has sufficient knowledge of the infringing quality of the accused product, he needs to file the request.[41] He should not wait longer than one month.[42] Even though this is not a fixed deadline, the right holder needs to pursue the proceedings without delay.

Attempting negotiations with the accused infringer may be to the detriment of the patent owner, due to the prolonged time before filing.[43] The right holder should take into account that the accused infringer may tactically use ongoing negotiations to "burn the clock" and make it more difficult for the right holder to obtain a preliminary injunction.

Some important courts[44] have an established practice of not granting preliminary injunction requests unless the validity of the patent was previously confirmed by a first instance decision in invalidation proceedings, either through the EPO opposition or nullity proceedings. A request based on a recently granted patent which did not undergo invalidation proceedings might thus be considered too weak for successful enforcement in a preliminary injunction proceeding because a reasonable prior search could not yet have been implemented by the accused infringer. As long as the court is not thoroughly convinced that the patent will survive invalidation proceedings, the request will likely not be successful.[45] If there are already-pending invalidity proceedings, the right holder may be allowed to wait for the final outcome of those invalidation proceedings to file for preliminary relief.[46]

Thus, in order to make a patent suitable for preliminary injunction proceedings, it is typically necessary to have a positive decision rendered through opposition proceeding, or by the Federal Patent Court. This rule is premised on the fact that granted patents statistically withstand an *inter partes* validity challenge in only one out of three cases, notwithstanding the examination undergone during the granting proceedings. This finding can be explained by the fact that the grant of a patent is preceded by a merely one-sided exchange between patent office and the applicant. Conversely, it follows from a positive decision on the validity of the patent that, as soon as it is available, the validity of the patent must be assumed to be sufficiently established for preliminary injunction proceedings. Notwithstanding the requirement to proceed with urgency, the patent owner may await a decision in invalidation proceedings to seek preliminary relief.[47]

---

40. Appeal Court Hamburg, 3 U 83/87, GRUR 1987, 899, "Verbandsmaterial."
41. Appeal Court Hamburg, MDR 2011, 557.
42. Appeal Court Munich, WPR 2008, 972; Decision of Jun. 28, 2012, 29-U-539/12.
43. Appeal Court Munich, InstGE 3, 301, "Fälschungsverdacht II."
44. Appeal Court Düsseldorf, InstGE 12, 114, "Harnkatheterset"; Appeal Court Karlsruhe, Decision of Sep. 23, 2015, 6 U 52/15.
45. District Court Mannheim, InstGE 11, 159, VA-LCD, Fernseher II; Appeal Court Düsseldorf, InstGE 12, 114, "Harnkatheterset"; District Court Munich I, Decision of Nov. 16, 2015, 21 O 20498/15 seems to apply a more patentee-friendly approach.
46. District Court Düsseldorf, Decision of Apr. 22, 2014, Case 4c O 3/14, BeckRS 2014, 19176.
47. Appeal Court Düsseldorf, InstGE 9, 140, 146—Olanzapin; InstGE 12, 114—Harnkatheterset; Decision of Dec. 18, 2014—I-2 U 60/14 = BeckRS 2015, 01829; Decision of Dec. 10, 2015—I-2 U 35/15 = BeckRS 2016, 06028; Decision of 31.08.2017—I-2 U 6/17 = BeckRS 2017, 125978; Appeal Court Karlsruhe, GRUR-RR 2015, 509—Ausrüstungssatz; Appeal Court München, GRUR 2020, 385—Elektrische Anschlussklemme.

[b] Other Interests Weighed

Preliminary injunctions are awarded for the provisional protection of the right holder. This consequently leads to a lower degree of judicial analysis of the critical subject matter of the case. On the contrary, preventing a competitor from commercializing particular products by means of an injunction may critically impact, and endanger, his business. The law requires weighing these conflicting interests to find an equitable solution. Favorable and unfavorable arguments taken from the case law are set forth in Table 11.1.

Table 11.1 Pros and Cons for Granting a Preliminary Injunction

Pros	*Cons*
- Teaching of the patent is simple and understandable and infringement can easily be assessed.[1] - Patent is literally infringed.[2] - Patentee has already successfully asserted the patent in court proceedings against other infringers and the validity of the patent has not been sufficiently questioned.[3] - The validity of the patent is sufficiently established. This is in principle the case if the patent successfully survived opposition proceedings at the EPO or first instance nullity proceedings with the Federal Patent Court in Munich.[4] - The accused infringer or other competitors was already involved in granting proceedings and was able to make objections. - Competitors have acknowledged the validity of the patent, for instance, through license agreements. - Credible concerns against the validity of the patent could not be brought up. This can even exceptionally be the case if the patent has been revoked in first instance nullity proceedings with the Federal Patent Court provided that this decision is evidentially wrong and that significant interests of the right holder are at stake.[5]	- Delay by the patentee in asserting rights.[6] - If the validity of the patentee is doubtful to a degree which would justify a suspension of regular lawsuit.[7] In particular, in case of pending parallel nullity or opposition proceedings containing critical fresh prior art; at the District Court Mannheim and Düsseldorf, the request will—in principle—not be granted.[8] - The accused infringer could credibly demonstrate that the patent will be invalidated in parallel opposition proceedings.[9] - Technical subject matter is complex and complicated. - Infringement is questionable; infringement is based on the doctrine of equivalents.[10] - High risks of significant economic disadvantages for the accused infringer's market position in case of interruption of activities due to an injunction. - Patentee does not practice the inventive technology (unless he shows that he has particular interests in the injunction such as to protect his licensee's interests).[11] - Private prior use could be credibly demonstrated.[12]

Pros	*Cons*
- Expiration of the patent is close. The accused infringer should not benefit from the normal length of regular proceedings which would typically not allow the grant of an injunction until the expiration of the patent. - Risk of significant economic disadvantages for the patentee's market position in case of ongoing activities of the accused infringer. - Accused infringer is a foreign company and exhibits infringing products at a trade show.	- Preliminary injunction shall not be granted if the patent has been revoked in first instance opposition or nullity proceedings except for the very exceptional case that the appealed decision nullifying the patent is evidently wrong and that the patentee would suffer serious disadvantages if the injunction is not granted.[13] - Patentee is exploiting the patent exclusively through licenses.

1. Appeal Court Karlsruhe, decision of Jul. 26, 1989, Mitt. 1990, 120.
2. Appeal Court Frankfurt, 6 U 83/81, GRUR 1981, 905, "Schleifwerkzeug."
3. District Court Düsseldorf, decision of May 26, 1994, Mitt 1995, 190.
4. Appeal Court Düsseldorf, InstGE 12, 114, "Harnkatheterset"; Appeal Court Karlsruhe, decision of September 23, 2015, 6 U 52/15.
5. Appeal Court Düsseldorf, decision of May 29, 2008, Az. 2 W 47/07, "Olanzapine."
6. Appeal Court Frankfurt, 6 W 58/84, GRUR 1984, 693, "Messe-Abmahnung."
7. Appeal Court Düsseldorf, Mitt 1996, 87, "Captopril."
8. District Court Mannheim, InstGE 11, 159, VA-LCD Fernseher II; Appeal Court Düsseldorf, InstGE 12, 114, "Harnkatheterset"; the District Court Munich I, decision of Nov. 16, 2015, 21 O 20498/15 seems to apply a more patentee-friendly approach.
9. Appeal Court Frankfurt, 6 U 83/81, GRUR 1981, 905, "Schleifwerkzeug."
10. *Ibid.*
11. District Court Düsseldorf, 4 O 187/99, GRUR 2000, 692, "NMR—Kontrastmittel."
12. District Court Mannheim, InstGE 6, 194, "Etikettieraggregat."
13. Appeal Court Düsseldorf, decision of May 29, 2008, Az. 2 W 47/07, "Olanzapin."

[D] Particular Situation: Trade Shows

Preliminary injunctions are particularly useful in trade show situations. Germany hosts a large number of high-profile trade shows in a wide variety of industries. For many companies, trade shows are their most important sales points and critical to their business. Right holders are therefore understandably interested in disabling the alleged infringer's ability to display infringing products at trade shows. Furthermore, as soon as the trade show is over and the accused infringer has left German territory, the application of judicial measures are, due to lengthy international service proceedings and the necessary involvement of foreign authorities, more difficult, more expensive and less effective. The particular situation is taken into account when weighing the conflicting interests as illustrated in the previous sections. Since trade shows usually take place over the span of a few days, there is consequently a compressed time period to investigate and file a preliminary injunction, if appropriate. Accordingly, the retention of counsel sufficiently prior to any German trade show where infringing products are likely to be shown is imperative. In some instances, the measures can be accompanied by customs action proceedings.[48]

[E] Normal Course of Preliminary Injunction Proceedings

The process starts with the right holder's investigation and the preparation of a writ requesting the grant of a preliminary injunction. As previously mentioned, counsel should be retained at the earliest possible stage. While normal evidentiary proceedings do not take place, facts must be consistently and coherently demonstrated based on prima facie evidence. The early involvement of appropriate counsel is crucial to identify and fill remaining gaps in the storyline and to efficiently gather any missing information, documents and, in particular, to prepare sufficient affidavits. The result of the investigation will be incorporated in the writ. Due to the compressed timeframe for the court to assess the matter, the quality of the written submission decisively contributes to the success of the request. Decisions on preliminary injunctions may be appealed to the Appeal Court, but a further appeal to the Federal Supreme Court is not permitted (section 542(2) Code of Civil Procedure). Accordingly, because Federal Supreme Court review does not apply, a diverse body of procedural rules has developed within the twelve jurisdictions.

Historically German courts have often granted ex parte preliminary injunctions. However, in two decisions of September 30, 2018, the German Federal Constitutional Court (1 BvR 1783/17 and 1 BvR 2421/17) ruled that preliminary injunctions granted without previously sending a warning letter to the accused infringer and without hearing him may violate the principle of procedural equality and the right to be heard of the accused infringer. These rights are guaranteed by Germany's Constitution (Articles 3(1) and 20(3) of the Constitution). It is required that the patentee send a warning letter to the alleged infringer before applying for a preliminary injunction to give him a reasonable time to respond. Any response must then be disclosed to the court. If the patentee has not sufficiently allowed the defendant to respond to the allegations, an oral hearing must take place. The court must also provide to the accused infringer any communication it had with or received from the patentee, such as minutes of telephone calls. Nevertheless, issuing a preliminary injunction without an oral hearing is still possible in cases of extreme urgency according to section 937(2) of the German Code of Civil Procedure. Such extreme urgency could be given in the situations of trade shows.

[1] Ex Parte Proceedings

The right holder may try to obtain the preliminary injunction in ex parte proceedings (section 937(2) Code of Civil Procedure). Nevertheless, ex parte preliminary

48. Cf. Ch. 16.

injunctions, without having an oral hearing or notifying the accused infringer, are the exception. Given that an ex parte proceeding interferes with a fundamental right, namely the right to be heard, a successful applicant must demonstrate why a few days' delay to summon the accused infringer for a hearing would cause irreparable harm.

Such situations might occur where foreign companies present infringing products at trade shows. *Inter partes* proceedings would not sufficiently protect the interest of the right holder. There is not enough time until the end of the trade show for *inter partes* proceedings and the measure would be pointless if the parties are summonsed for a hearing that takes place after the end of the trade show.

In such an exceptional case, it is likely that an injunction can be obtained in less than twenty-four hours. The speed of the proceedings significantly depends on the interaction between the right holder and the court. An efficient handling of the case and counsel's knowledge of the particularities of the selected court is critical.

Although ex parte proceedings are, in theory, the exception, some German courts nevertheless have followed a flexible approach and have granted ex parte injunctions even outside the context of trade shows.[49] Accordingly, any company that is about to bring an important product to market should evaluate the risk of an ex parte injunction and take adequate preparatory measures. Indeed, a cautious company, under the right circumstances, might consider the preparation and filing of a protective brief that can be filed in anticipation of an eventual request for a preliminary injunction.[50]

That more flexible approach of these German courts must be seen in the context of two recent decisions of the German Federal Constitutional Court (1 BvR 1783/17 and 1 BvR 2421/17). These decisions require, before filing an application for a request for a preliminary injunction, that a warning letter is sent to the alleged infringer. Even though issuing a preliminary injunction without oral hearing is still possible in cases of extreme urgency according to section 937(2) of the German Code of Civil Procedure, there will likely be less ex parte preliminary injunctions in the future.

An ex parte injunction is granted in the form of a court order. The applicant's task is to serve the order on the accused infringer. This is a necessary and therefore important element of the enforcement. Service is only effective if done within one month from the notification of the order (section 929 Code of Civil Procedure). Thus, if a month has expired since the date on which the right holder was notified of the grant of the order and it has not been properly served on the infringer, it becomes unenforceable. If the injunction is confirmed—i.e., after an objection of the accused infringer, or by the Appeal court—this decision must be served on the accused infringer as well, even though the court serves the decision on its own.[51]

The right holder certainly can, and in certain strategic situations should, withhold the granted order from the accused infringer, for instance, while waiting for a positive reaction from the accused infringer to a warning letter, or otherwise to see how

49. District Court Munich I, Decision of Nov. 16, 2015, 21 O 20498/15.
50. *See* Ch. 11, §11.02[F][1] "Protective Brief" (below).
51. Appeal Court Düsseldorf, Decision of Apr. 21, 2015, I-20 U 181/14; Appeal Court Munich, MDR 2013, 422.

negotiations with the infringer progress. If negotiations appear to be unsuccessful, the right holder may then serve the order, so long as it is within the specified term.

In the trade show situation, the right holder is presumably interested in quickly implementing the service proceedings, usually as soon as a certified and enforceable copy of the order is available. Typically, counsel does not wait until the court provides notice of the order by mail. Rather, the attorney personally obtains the order at the courthouse and brings it to the local bailiff who serves the order at the trade show at the accused infringer's booth.[52] The injunction then becomes effective vis-à-vis the accused infringer.[53]

The accused infringer then needs to stop the commercialization of the accused embodiment. Otherwise, the infringer risks harsh fines, imposed through enforcement proceedings. Counsel may additionally include in the request further duties that must be fulfilled by the accused infringer, such as providing the accused embodiments to the bailiff who will keep them in custody.[54]

If the court is unwilling to grant the injunction, which might be ascertainable from the first reaction of the court to the request (phone call, indications by the court in writing, etc.), the applicant can withdraw the request. If the request is directed on an ex parte injunction, the presiding judge may inform the applicant by phone that the court intends not to grant the injunction without a hearing. A right holder who is only interested in ex parte proceedings may choose at this point to withdraw the request, in which case the opposing party would not be informed about the intentions of the right holder, the application or the withdrawal. The normal course of ex parte preliminary injunction proceedings is illustrated in Figure 11.1.

Figure 11.1 Normal Course of Ex Parte Preliminary Injunction Proceedings

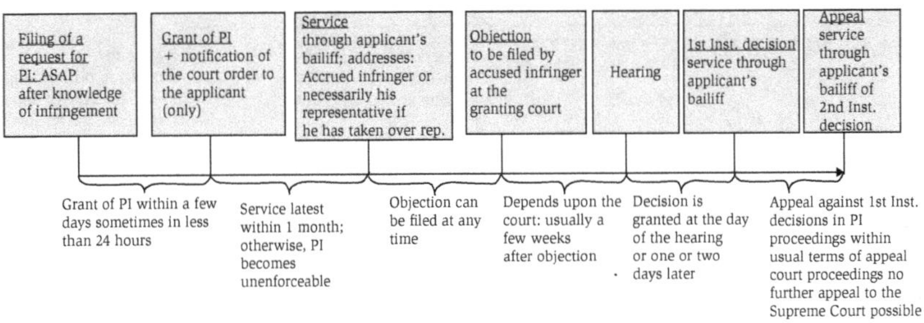

52. The service can be effectuated at any place of business of the accused infringer, the momentary booth of the accused infringer on the trade show is sufficient (Zöllner, s. 178 ZPO, No. 15).
53. The addressee of the service is the accused infringer, but if a representative (legal counsel) has officially taken over the representation, the order has necessarily to be served to the representative.
54. District Court Düsseldorf, Decision of May 11, 2004, 4a O 195/04.

[2] Inter Partes *Proceedings*

In case of *inter partes* proceedings, the parties are summoned for a hearing. An *inter partes* hearing is mandatory for any right holder who desires that the injunction also be enforceable outside German territory. Enforcement abroad requires that the German court order be first recognized by the foreign authorities, which require that the accused infringer be heard by the court prior to the grant of the injunction. Article 34 of the Council Regulation 44/2001,[55] applicable for any EC Member State, provides that a judgment shall not be recognized, "where it was given in default of appearance, if the defendant was not served with the document which instituted the proceedings or with an equivalent document in sufficient time and in such a way as to enable him to arrange for his defense." This requirement would not be fulfilled in case of an ex parte order.

The hearing takes place generally a few weeks after the right holder's request has been filed. The accused infringer gets an opportunity to raise the usual defenses directed against validity. In addition, the accused infringer may show that there are no reasons for an injunction, such as by demonstrating that the requirement of urgency is not met. Usually, this is done in a defense brief filed prior to the hearing. The normal course of ex parte preliminary injunction proceedings is illustrated in Figure 11.2.

Figure 11.2 Normal Course of Inter Partes Preliminary Injunction Proceedings

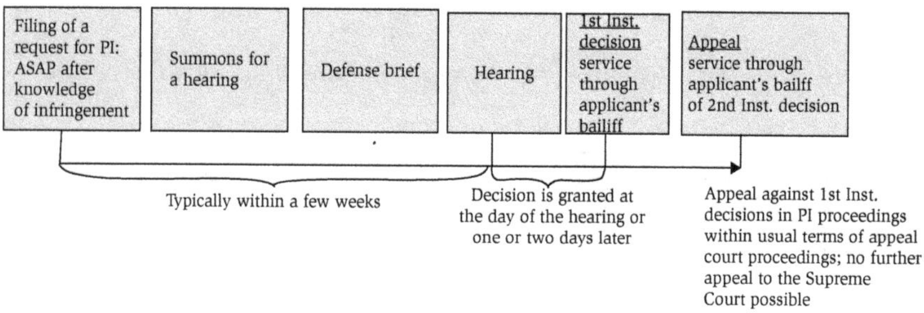

[F] Possible Reactions of the Accused Infringer

[1] Protective Brief

A cautious party seeking to avoid a preliminary injunction may file a so-called protective brief with courts in which a preliminary injunction request is likely to be filed. This is appropriate where a party that believes it will be accused of infringement and has sufficient knowledge to name both the right holder and the particular product that will likely be the subject of judicial action. As sample request for a protective brief is provided in Chapter 17, §17.06.

55. Council Regulation (EC) No. 44/2001 of Dec. 22, 2000, on jurisdiction and the recognition and enforcement of judgments in civil and commercial matters.

For instance, the presumably accused infringer may intend to introduce a new product on the German market and knows that there is a patent that could be asserted against it. The urgent need for a protective order could occur in other scenarios besides a new product launch. Even products that have been available for sale for some time could potentially be subject to a preliminary injunction. The urgency could arise on the day of the grant of the patent, i.e., the day when the patent becomes enforceable, or if a decision (in opposition or invalidation proceedings) confirming the validity of the patent is rendered.

The protective brief is thus filed under the presumption that the right holder will file a request for a preliminary injunction. The protective brief contains all arguments that could be raised against the claim of the injunction (in particular all noninfringement arguments) and its reasons, namely that there is no urgency, and/or that the patent is invalid. Unless these arguments are obviously without merit, the protective brief would at least cause the court to withhold issuing an ex parte decision. Instead, the court would set a date for a hearing.

The "protective brief" must be filed centrally via a mailbox of a central register located in Frankfurt am Main, called "Zentrales Schutzschriftenregister" (§945a Code of Civil Procedure). It is therefore not necessary to send the same brief to all courts that may potentially be seized by the patent holder. Assuming the patent owner files a preliminary injunction with one of the competent courts, the judge first checks the central register to determine whether a protective brief has been deposited. The protective briefs are deleted six months after entry in the register.

[2] Acceptance and Final Warning Notice

If the accused infringer does not have sufficient grounds to oppose the preliminary injunction, for instance, if the infringement of the patent is clear and validity is uncontested, he could simply acknowledge the preliminary injunction. If a warning letter was not previously sent to him, that acknowledgement could be accompanied by a request to impose all costs on the applicant (right holder). This follows from section 93 of the Code of Civil Procedure.

A preliminary injunction has a preliminary character and principally covers only a right to refrain from using the patent. Typically, so-called final warning notices are used to settle the matter also with respect to the other claims (damage claim, rendering of account, etc.). It contains a draft of an undertaking.

If the accused infringer accepts the undertaking the situation is settled between the parties and no regular proceedings are necessary anymore. Without such final settlement through a "final warning notice," either party (section 926 Code of Civil Procedure) may request in addition to the remedies available in preliminary injunction proceedings (*see* Figures 11.1 and 11.2)[56] the implementation of regular proceedings on the merits to affirm or lift the preliminary injunction measures.

56. The accused infringer may file an objection against a preliminary injunction order rendered in ex parte proceedings (s. 924(1) Code of Civil Procedure). The preliminary injunction will then be either confirmed or lifted after a hearing in a court decision which can be appealed (*see* Figure

§11.03 OTHER EUROPEAN JURISDICTIONS

Germany is not the only place where preliminary injunctions are available. Other European countries provide for such measures, such as Italy, where a party may request a preliminary relief either before or during proceedings on the merits. As with Germany, it is necessary in Italy to show by prima facie evidence that the asserted right is infringed and valid. When considering the validity of the patent an important factor for the Italian courts is whether the Italian patent being enforced has also been granted in other countries which conduct a full examination procedure. In addition, a risk of serious and irreparable damage must be demonstrated. Usually, a delay of even six months between knowledge of the infringement and bringing the request may still be acceptable. Such a long waiting period would typically be fatal to a request for provisional relief in German courts. Preliminary injunction proceedings might be a very powerful tool in patent enforcement campaigns. Also, the jurisdictions of UK, France[57] and the Netherlands are known to provide for swift, flexible and cost-efficient preliminary relief measures.

11.1). In *inter partes* proceedings, the preliminary injunction is rendered after a hearing in a decision which can be directly appealed (Figure 11.2).

57. L615-3 CPI.

CHAPTER 12

Claim Construction and Infringement

§12.01 APPLICABLE LAW

German patents granted by the GPTO and utility models stand outside the jurisdiction of the UPC. They may only be litigated in German courts. Accordingly the rules for enforcing German patents and utility models remain unchanged by the UPCA. The same applies to national rights of other UPCA Member States, such as French national patents or utility models. These national rights do not fall into the jurisdiction of the UPC.

During the seven-year transitional phase,[1] ordinary European patents may either be litigated in national courts or at the UPC ("Shared Jurisdiction"[2]), whereas for European patents with unitary effect, the UPC has exclusive jurisdiction. The overall aim of harmonization of the patent law through the UPC would not succeed if the case law of individual Member States has "binding character." Rather, the jurisprudence of the UPC will have to be developed itself, likely synthesizing its approach using appropriate guidance from the various authorities of the Member States. The established case law traditions of the national member countries thus only serve as a source of inspiration or guideline without binding character.

In contrast to common law systems, civil law systems do not recognize precedents or court decisions as a source of law. Most of the Participating Member States of the UPCA are based on civil law systems. However, the Republic of Ireland, has a common law system and other Participating Member States, such as Denmark and Malta apply a mixture of both systems. This may result in differences in the way patent infringement and revocation (nullity) proceedings are handled on a national level. Even though the UPC rules incorporate some elements taken from European common law systems, the civil law concepts of the Europe's mainland predominantly influence

1. Article 83 UPCA.
2. Chapter 4, §4.02[A][1][b].

the legal framework of the UPC. The UPC does not recognize precedents as a source of law. In that respect it follows the concept of civil law systems.

Based on Article 69 EPC and the related Protocol on the "Interpretation of Article 69 EPC,"[3] the UPC must take a fresh look at the principles applicable to the interpretation of European patents (with or without unitary effect) whereby there is no obligation to follow the case law of individual Participating Member States of the UPCA. To harmonize the law of the UPC, national courts are challenged to apply the same approach to European patents.

There are good justifications that Article 83 UPCA only opens a choice of forum, and not a choice of law.[4] For a transitional period Article 83(1) UPCA establishes a parallel jurisdiction of the UPC. According to Article 83(3) UPCA, the patentee—subject to conditions—may through an opt-out declaration "carve out" the jurisdiction of the UPC, with the effect that only the single track of national proceedings remains possible. These rules do however not concern the application of the substantive law to opted-out European patents. This is supported by the wording of the provision, which specifically refers to the court's jurisdiction and not to the application of substantive law. Thus, the opt-out declaration does not affect the applicability of the substantive law of the UPCA. Accordingly, the laws applicable to an ordinary European patent are the same regardless of whether an opt-out has been declared or not. In other words, the opt-out does not change the substantive law related to the claim construction of ordinary European patents. Consequently, national courts are required to implement the new European harmonization process as to European patents that are litigated through those national courts. The contrary view[5] which advocates that, in case of a declared opt-out, the European patent shall be exclusively subject to national laws carving out the substantive UPCA law would have unreasonable results: it would allow the applicant through his opt-out and later opt-in to unilaterally change the substantive foundation of the patent. This does not comply with the principles of private international laws.

It can thus be anticipated that the described perception concerning European patents will also have a harmonizing influence on the case law generated by German courts in the context of German patents and utility models. There is no compelling reason that different standards will be developed for these different types of IP rights.

Nevertheless, German case law will play an influential role in the development of the jurisprudence of the UPC, even if it is not binding legally. Germany is the country with most of the court decisions related to the scope of protection of patents.

§12.02 CLAIM CONSTRUCTION PROCEDURE

There is no "Markman" hearing in the UPC and German courts. Because there is no jury in patent infringement trials, the concerns addressed by the US Supreme Court's

3. Protocol on the Interpretation of Art. 69 EPC of Oct. 5, 1973 as revised by the Act revising the EPC of Nov. 29, 2000.
4. Tilmann, The Transitional Period of the UPCA, Mitt 2/2014.
5. Preparatory Committee: Cf. Note of the Preparatory Committee of Jan. 29, 2014.

Markman ruling,[6] such as asking a lay jury to interpret the scope of legal documents, are inapplicable. It is the role of the court to interpret patent claims, and this duty is carried out in the context of the court's other decision-making tasks. Thus, in contrast to the US system, which commonly provides for a dedicated claim construction hearing, with specialized briefing (and a vast body of case law focused solely on claim construction), the UPC and German system simply includes claim construction as part of the overall proceedings.

The infringement proceedings start with the filing of a complaint. Beyond merely setting out the claims of the plaintiff to put the defendant on notice of the basis of the lawsuit (as is typical under the US-style notice pleading rules), a complaint in UPC and German proceedings commonly serves as an opening claim construction brief. The plaintiff provides a description of the patent and its claims in a way that provides a prima facie basis for the court to find infringement by the defendant's accused embodiments or actions. After the court serves this complaint on the defendant and announces the schedule and deadlines of the case, the defendant files its defense, which will typically provide a contrary view of claim construction, to support its noninfringement position.

§12.03 CLAIM CONSTRUCTION

[A] Legal Framework of the Claim Construction

The claim language, of course, is the basis for determining the scope of protection. This is codified in Article 69 of the EPC, which provides as follows:

> (1) The extent of the protection conferred by a European patent, or a European patent application shall be determined by the claims. Nevertheless, the description and drawings shall be used to interpret the claims.

The description and drawings are accordingly used only to facilitate the interpretation of the claims. Subject matter that is not specifically claimed may not be asserted even though it is disclosed in the description or drawings.[7] A Protocol[8] on the Interpretation of Article 69 EPC, which is an integral part of the EPC, further describes the often-difficult task of interpreting the claim language in view of the teachings of the specification as follows:[9]

> **Article 1**
>
> **General principles**
>
> Article 69 should not be interpreted as meaning that the extent of the protection conferred by a European patent is to be understood as that defined by the strict,

6. *Markman v. Westview Instruments*, 517 U.S. 370 (1996).
7. Federal Supreme Court, X ZR 20/86, GRUR 1987, 626, "Rundfunkübertragungssystem."
8. Protocol on the Interpretation of Art. 69 EPC of Oct. 5, 1973 as revised by the Act revising the EPC of Nov. 29, 2000.
9. The Protocol is applicable not only on European Patents but also on German Patents: Federal Supreme Court, Mitt. 2002, 216, 218, "Schneidmesser."

literal meaning of the wording used in the claims, the description and drawings being employed only for the purpose of resolving an ambiguity found in the claims. Nor should it be taken to mean that the claims serve only as a guideline and that the actual protection conferred may extend to what, from a consideration of the description and drawings by a person skilled in the art, the patent proprietor has contemplated. On the contrary, it is to be interpreted as defining a position between these extremes which combines a fair protection for the patent proprietor with a reasonable degree of legal certainty for third parties.

Article 2:

Equivalents

For the purpose of determining the extent of protection conferred by a European patent, due account shall be taken of any element which is equivalent to an element specified in the claims.

This Protocol thus frames the same challenges faced by US courts in cases such as the *Philips v. AWH* opinion from the US Court of Appeals for the Federal Circuit.[10] The Protocol recognizes that there is a tension between interpreting the claims solely on the basis of claim language versus relying on the teachings of the patent description and drawings to help interpret the claims. In fact, there is an inevitable conflict between the interests of the patent applicant in an appropriate degree of protection and the public interest in clarity, legal certainty and maximizing competition.

The Protocol acknowledges that there is no bright line in terms of how to interpret claims in light of the specification. It seems to be clear from Article 1 of the Protocol that the skilled person shall not be tied to the literal meaning of the words used in the claims when defining the scope of protection. However, it is left open how far a court may move away from that literal meaning of the claim language. Article 2 provides that equivalents must be taken into account, but no specific guidance is given as to what constitutes an equivalent. The ultimate aim of the interpretation consists in finding a balance between a "fair protection" for the patentee, on the one hand, and a "reasonable degree of legal certainty" for third parties, on the other hand. In other words, the patentee must be compensated for the disclosure of his invention, but third parties must be reasonably informed about the scope of protection through the patent claims.

The legal framework resulting from the EPC also applies in national jurisdictions and is considered by national courts. Nevertheless, even within the same legal framework, a complete consistency between the different national courts was never achieved absent a centralized court of last resort. Nonetheless, the development over the years showed that national courts were willing to learn from each other, seeking to move toward, rather than away from, each other's approaches.

A description of the differences between the national approaches is difficult because those differences are often marginal. Often the approaches appear conceptually different but do not differentiate in their results. For that reason, the following

10. *Phillips v. AWH Corp.*, 415 F.3d 1303 (Fed. Cir. 2005 (en banc)).

sections primarily focus on the German situation, whereby major differences from prominent jurisdictions such as France will be highlighted in the text.

The UPC applies Article 69 EPC and its Protocol when it comes to construing the claim.[11] At the time of the publication of this manual the UPC has not yet issued decisions related to these provisions. It is thus still undefined how the UPC fills out the margins given by Article 1 and 2 of the Protocol. The body of national case law has no binding effect on the UPC. The UPC will take national case law into account as it develops its own case law, and accordingly the following illustrations only provide suggestions of how claim construction could be implemented under the UPC. The fact that infringement and validity of the patent are typically decided in unified proceedings at the UPC in contrast to the German split system, might have a balancing effect on the claim construction. Indeed, an attempt by the patentee to pursue a broad claim construction in infringement proceedings, while simultaneously attempting to assert a narrow interpretation of the claims for defeating validity challenges, should fail in the context of unified proceedings at the UPC.

Harmonization of law at the UPC will be driven by a centralized second instance of the UPC, namely its Court of Appeal in Luxembourg. Of course, this will be a gradual process of harmonization by the Appeal Court in Luxembourg as the various issues in claim construction are appealed and a sufficient body of law develops at the appellate level.[12]

[B] Significance of the Claims

According to Article 69(1) EPC and the corresponding national provisions, such as section 14 of the GPA or the French provision of Article L.613-2 CPI, the terms of the claims govern the scope of protection. Descriptions and drawings have an auxiliary function for the claim construction. They are the main sources of interpreting the content of the claims.

[1] Semantic Content

The claims of the patent are construed in view of the overall teachings of the patent, to arrive at the "semantic content" of the claims.[13] That is, when determining the scope of protection, the skilled person is not tied to the strict literal meaning of the claim language, as imposed by Article 1 of the Protocol. Rather, terms of the claim are interpreted to sufficiently cover the technical teaching as disclosed in the description. Terms are given the broadest possible technical understanding under the disclosed teaching. For the determination of the scope of protection, claim terms are construed in

11. Article 24(1)(c) UPCA refers directly to the EPC.
12. In order to guarantee a coherent jurisprudence within the UPC Court of Appeal, the Court of Appeal may refer the case to the full court, which means all chambers of the Court of Appeal, Art. 21(2) UPCA Statute.
13. Federal Supreme Court, X ZR 74/05, IIC 2007, 726 (in English), "Kettenradanordnung"; Federal Supreme Court, X ZR 82/03, GRUR 2004, 845, "Drehzahlermittlung."

the context of the solution to a defined problem the patent specification objectively discloses.[14] This exercise is done in the same manner independent upon the legal context in which the claim construction is needed, i.e., be it for the assessment of patent infringement, of patentability or the assessment of any other potential ground for revocation.[15] The skilled person needs to read the specification in a reasonable way to identify the understanding of the terms in the context of the claimed teaching in a manner that harmonizes the language of the claims and the technical description of the invention.[16] In particular, the patent claim should be read in a way to cover the preferred embodiments illustrated in the description in the context of the claimed teaching, insofar as the claim language accommodates that reading.[17] In making the determination of the semantic content of a claim, the meanings of the claim terms are to be analyzed step by step, in order to assess the overall meaning of the claimed teaching as a unit.[18] It is thus necessary to determine the semantic content of the claim in its entirety as well as the contribution of the individual features to the overall performance of the claimed teaching.[19] In principle, the latter determination requires a previous identification of the objective problem to be solved by the claimed teaching. That is, the problem to be solved by the claimed teaching shall comply with the interpretation result.[20]

German courts often apply a "function-oriented interpretation" of patent claims: Thereby, terms of the claim are construed in the context of the solution that the patent application objectively discloses.[21] In other words, the skilled person needs to read the specification in a reasonable way to identify the particular function(s) of the terms. The understanding of a term is thus primarily influenced by the function it fulfills within the claimed teaching. The function-oriented interpretation may find its limits where terms used in the claim have a clear spatial or physical defined configuration. The unambiguousness of such terms may not be circumvented by means of a function-oriented interpretation. For instance, a "nail," which is explicitly required in the claim, could likely not be generalized, through a function-oriented interpretation, to the mere function of a "fixing means," which would involve screws even if a merely functional approach allows it. Or a chemical compound specified in the patent claim such as "pemetrexed disodium" may not be converted into "pemetrexed dipotassium" by such "function-oriented interpretation."[22]

14. Federal Supreme Court, Decision of Nov. 7, 2000, X ZR145/98, GRUR 2001, 232, "Brieflocher."
15. Federal Supreme Court, Decision of Jun. 2, 2015, X ZR 103/13, GRUR 2015, 972, "Kreuzgestänge."
16. Federal Supreme Court, X ZR 16/09, Decision of May 10, 2011, "Okklusionsvorrichtung."
17. *Ibid.*
18. Federal Supreme Court, X ZR 82/03, GRUR 2004, 845, "Drehzahlermittlung."
19. Federal Supreme Court, X ZR 117/11, Decision of Jul. 17, 2012 BGHZ 194, 107 = GRUR 2012, 1124 Rn. 27, "Polymerschaum"; Federal Supreme Court; X ZR 29/15, Decision of Jun. 14, 2016, GRUR 2016, 921, "Pemetrexed."
20. Federal Supreme Court, X ZR 29/15, Decision of Jun. 14, 2016, GRUR 2016, 921, "Pemetrexed."
21. Federal Supreme Court, X ZR145/98, Decision of Nov. 7, 2000, GRUR 2001, 232, "Brieflocher."
22. Federal Supreme Court, X ZR 29/15, Decision of Jun. 14, 2016, GRUR 2016, 921, "Pemetrexed."

[2] *Main Sources for the Claim Construction*

Descriptions and drawings are used to construe and clarify the patent claims and the terms used in the patent specification (Article 69(1) EPC). As noted above, the descriptions and drawings serve as a source for interpreting the claim language, but they do not themselves constitute the scope of protection of the patent. That is, the description and drawing cannot extend the scope of protection conferred by the claims, beyond what the claim terms themselves may permit. Thus, no protection can be provided for subject matter that is not included in the patent claims, even though it is explicitly contained in the description and drawings.[23] Thus, like in the US, it is essential to identify a "hook" in the claim language to justify interpreting that claim language in light of the teachings of the patent specification.

[a] *Definitions in the Description*

German courts often state that the patent specification forms its "own dictionary"[24] (similar to the rule in the US that a patentee may be his or her own lexicographer). The definition for a term found in the description shall govern the claim construction, even if this definition differs substantially from the usual technical meaning of the term. That is, if terms differ from the general (technical) language then ultimately the terms as defined in the description are authoritative. Terms of the patent claim may thus have a broader or narrower meaning than definitions taken from the common technical literature or belonging to a common use in the relevant technical field.[25] Nevertheless, this does not mean that recourse to the habitual language use of technical terms is excluded. The patent description does not have to provide a definition for all terms, and it is usually assumed that the patent is written in the typical and common language of the concerned technical field. However, interpreting the patent requires determining whether a different understanding is applicable.[26] For instance, if the person skilled in the art concludes, in the light of the description and drawings, that a possible interpretation of the claim needs to be excluded from its scope of protection, then that claim can be restricted to a narrower teaching even where the literal understanding of the claim term could suggest a broader construction. This rule comes from the landmark Federal Supreme Court *Spannschraube* (Tension Screw)[27] decision. In that decision, the German Supreme Court refers to an exceptional case, which was decided differently than other national courts, such as the French and Swiss courts. This is an example of diverging decisions among national courts. Nevertheless, French courts, i.e., like the German Federal Supreme Court in *Spannschraube*, also have a history of excluding those embodiments from the scope of protection which would run against

23. Federal Supreme Court, X ZR 9/89, GRUR 1992, 305, "Heliumeinspeisung"; Federal Supreme Court, Decision of May 10, 2011, X ZR 16/09 "Okklusionsvorrichtung."
24. Federal Supreme Court, X ZR 85/96, IIC 1999, 932 (in English), "Spannschraube."
25. *Ibid.*
26. Federal Supreme Court, X ZR 74/05, GRUR 2007, 410, "Kettenradanordnung."
27. Federal Supreme Court, X ZR 85/96, IIC 1999, 932 (in English), "Spannschraube."

the purpose of the inventive teaching as defined in the description. In such cases, a restrictive interpretation of the claim is suggested. This was made clear in the decision *Filmop v. Dit et al.* decided by the Paris Court of Appeal.[28] The fact that decisions rendered by courts of different states diverge from time to time does not mean that these courts apply fundamentally different concepts. In most cases, the diverging effect is because those courts are not controlled by the same last instance.

[b] Examples and Preferred Embodiments

Preferred embodiments and examples disclosed in the description shall not—as a general rule—limit the scope of protection of a claim describing the invention in more generic terms.[29] This rule of claim construction is similar to the approach taken in the US. Preferred embodiments are supposed to explain the claimed invention in an exemplary manner.[30] Likewise, numbered references pointing to the drawings that have been left in the patent claim shall not restrict the scope of protection either.[31] Nonetheless, claim interpretation shall consider the preferred embodiments. A claim construction that excludes all described preferred embodiments from the scope of protection of the claim usually cannot prevail.[32] Drawings only serve to explain the principle of the claimed teaching and thus do not disclose particular dimensions.[33] However, drawings are an equally relevant part of the patent specification and may also serve as an independent basis of disclosure.[34]

[c] Dependent Claims

An independent claim determines the protected teaching in the most general form within the same claim hierarchy. By definition, dependent claims that refer back to the main claim contain more specific embodiments of the invention, but do not extend beyond the scope of protection of the independent claim. Such dependent claims usually protect preferred embodiments, whereas the main claim aims at protecting a more generic form of the invention, which includes the more specific preferred embodiment. Consequently, a more generic definition of the invention in the independent claim must consequently be interpreted in a way that it also covers the more specific embodiments or the embodiments of its dependent claims. This hierarchy is an important aspect of the claim construction.[35]

---

28. Paris Court of Appeal, Oct. 2, 2013, *Filmop v. Dit et al.*; RG 11/23300.
29. Federal Supreme Court, X ZR 255/01, IIC 2005, 971(in English) "Bodenseitige Vereinzelungseinrichtung."
30. Federal Supreme Court, Decision of Feb. 12, 2008, X ZR 153/05, Mitt 08, 271, "Mehrgangnabe."
31. Federal Supreme Court, X ZR 17/02, GRUR 2006, 316, "Koksofentür."
32. Federal Supreme Court, X ZR 35/11, GRUR 2015, 159, "Zugriffsrechte."
33. Federal Supreme Court, X ZB 10/11, GRUR 2012, 1242, "Steckverbindung."
34. Federal Supreme Court, X ZR 112/13, GRUR 2016, 50, "Teilreflektierende Folie."
35. Federal Supreme Court, Decision of Feb. 12, 2008, X ZR 153/05, Mitt 08, 271, "Mehrgangnabe."

[d] *Indications of Purpose*

Indications of purposes, effects and functions mentioned in the patent claim usually do not restrict the scope of protection.[36] They illustrate, for instance, a possible field of application or an intended use of the claimed embodiment. If the particular effects and functions sought by the protected teaching are sufficiently achieved by the other physical features of the claim, such indications of purpose could be neglected when determining the scope of protection. Nevertheless, where the indication of purpose makes demands on a particular spatial or physical attribute which is not yet reflected by the other features of the claim but required to produce the effect or function sought be the protected teaching, the indication of purpose may have a limitative character. In such a situation, they are thus treated like other features of the claim.[37]

[e] *Numerical Indications*

A numerical indication (such as "an angle of less than 90°" or a parameter range between "5 to 20 Newton") in a patent claim may also be subject to interpretation. As a general rule, numerical limitations give more concrete boundaries than descriptive terms,[38] and so accused products falling outside the numerical limitations do generally not infringe.[39] Nonetheless, depending on the context of the patent, some variation may be tolerated.[40] It may depend on how the skilled person in the art understands the meaning of the terms within the general context of the patented invention, taking into account the explanations in the description and the drawings. Numerical indications may differ within various contexts, so an accused embodiment that deviates slightly from a claimed numerical indication does not necessarily avoid infringement.[41] Typically, the departure from a range or numerical value is acceptable if it stays within technical tolerances. For legal certainty reasons, the doctrine of equivalence generally does not help if the departure is more significant, even if the effects and advantages of the claimed teaching are still achieved by the accused embodiment. This is because numerical indications are deemed concretely selected by the patent applicant, and, in only exceptional cases the skilled person would consider a solution outside the claimed range representing a still sufficient implementation of the teaching, for instance, if the specification of the patent provides evidence that the observation of the range is not critical for the teaching.

---

36. Federal Supreme Court, X ZR 121/88, GRUR 1991, 436, "Befestigungsvorrichtung II."
37. Federal Supreme Court, X ZR 105/04, GRUR 2006, 923, "Luftabschneider für Milchsammelanlage."
38. Federal Supreme Court X ZR 33/88, GRUR 1989, 903, "Batteriekastenschnur."
39. Federal Supreme Court, X ZR 43/01, GRUR 2002, 511, "Kunststoffrohrteil"; Federal Supreme Court, X ZR 73/01, GRUR 2002, 527, "Custodiol II"; Federal Supreme Court, X ZR 135/01, GRUR 2002, 519, "Schneidmesser II"; Federal Supreme Court, X ZR 12/00, GRUR 2002, 523, "Custodiol I."
40. *Ibid.*
41. Federal Supreme Court, X ZR 135/01, GRUR 2002, 519, "Schneidmesser II."

[f] *Reference to the Prior Art*

Prior art discussed in the body of the patent specification represents a source for interpretation and understanding of the claim.[42] For instance, if the patent describes the claimed invention in reference to embodiments of the prior art, then such qualification may be relevant for the proper understanding of the patent claims and, thus, represents a source of interpretation. The extent to which prior art documents mentioned in the description may be used for the claim construction is decided on a case-by-case basis. If prior art documents are not mentioned in the patent specification, then they are likely to be irrelevant for claim construction.[43] This is true even if this prior art was available at the date of the application or the priority date.[44] Nonetheless, such prior art may possibly help to identify and demonstrate the general expertise of the person skilled in the art. In jurisdictions like Germany where validity and infringement are resolved in separate proceedings before different panels, it is less likely that prior art that was not before the examiner will have any effect on claim construction. Such prior art may become more relevant to claim construction in jurisdictions like the UPC, where validity and claim construction are considered together, because such proceedings will entail a more holistic view of how a person of skill would interpret the claims.

[3] *Evidence Outside of the Patent Document*

[a] *General Expertise of the Skilled Person*

The subject matter of the invention and the scope of protection have to be identified through the eyes of the person skilled in the art.[45] This fictitious person is tasked with giving the content of the patent a meaningful and consistent understanding.[46] He has the average skills of someone who is typically in charge of research and development in the technical field of the teaching of the patent. Although fictitious, he demonstrates the general expertise available in the concerned technical field, including the experiences and abilities of his professional peers,[47] at the time of the patent application, more precisely its priority date. The skilled person is not necessarily an expert with exceptional skills. For instance, he does not have an overview of all prior art. Rather, he is deemed to have a solid education with enough experience to properly perform his tasks within the technical field addressed by the patent. When determining the content of the patent disclosure, the court can refer to self-evident technical information which the skilled person reads in-between the lines when studying the patent. If the patent

42. Federal Supreme Court, X ZR 56/96, Mitt 1999, 365, "Sammelförderer."
43. Federal Supreme Court, X ZR 45/85, GRUR 1987, 280, "Befestigungsvorrichtung."
44. Federal Supreme Court, X ZR 124/88, GRUR 1991, 811, "Falzmaschine."
45. Federal Supreme Court, X ZR 255/01, IIC 2005, 971 (in English), "Bodenseitige Vereinzelungseinrichtung."
46. Appeal Court Düsseldorf, Mitt. 98, 179.
47. Federal Supreme Court, X ZR 255/01, GRUR 2004, 1023 and IIC 2005, 971 (in English) "Bodenseitige Vereinzelungseinrichtung."

addresses several technical fields, the general expertise of all the fields involved must be considered.

[b] *Inadmissibility of Prosecution File Estoppel*

A fundamental distinction between claim construction approaches in Germany and the US concerns the role of the prosecution history. In the US, the prosecution history forms one of the core bodies of intrinsic evidence for construing patent claims, both in terms of ascertaining the ordinary meaning of claim terms, as well as for determining if there has been a surrender of patent scope (i.e., prosecution history estoppel).

By contrast, in many European jurisdictions, such as in Germany the prosecution history is basically not taken into account.[48] Thus, courts of UK, Italy, Germany and the Netherlands more or less discourage use of the prosecution file for the claim construction. The concept behind this approach is based on the view that the interpretation of the inventive teaching should not change according to whether or not the person skilled in the art has access to the files. The claim construction process rests on an analysis of the patent claims, taken in view of the patent description and the drawings. These are the only interpretation sources explicitly listed in Article 69 EPC and the identical national provisions such as section 14 of the GPA.[49] The patentee's or the examiner's statements in grant proceedings may however represent a strong indication of how the relevant skilled person in the art would understand the technical reaching.[50]

There are exceptions to the general rule that the prosecution file is excluded from consideration when evaluating claim scope. Even though statements made by the applicant or the examiner during the grant procedure cannot be readily used as the sole basis for claim construction, it is permissible to use such statements as an indication of how the person skilled in the art understands the subject matter of the patent. A reference to the prosecution file may be of particular interest when the assessment comes to the doctrine of equivalence. In a landmark decision of the German Supreme Court,[51] the question was raised whether a limitation of a claim in the grant procedure may exclude an infringement based on the doctrine of equivalence and whether the prosecution files are a proper source of evidence for answering that question. The court agreed that referring to the prosecution history might be necessary to determine whether the patent proprietor was forced to limit the claim in the granting procedure for material grounds, especially to delimit the claimed invention from prior art that restricted the patentability of a claim set. Understandably, a patent owner who amends the asserted claim during prosecution to exclude subject matter from the scope of its patent, should not be allowed to resort to the doctrine of equivalents to reclaim protection for this same subject matter which was previously surrendered to avoid prior art. This is, inventiveness or novelty reasons for the amendment tend, in

48. Federal Supreme Court, X ZR 43/01, GRUR 2002, 511, 513, "Kunststoffrohrteil."
49. *Ibid.*
50. Federal Supreme Court, X ZR 57/96, GRUR 1998, 895, "Regenbecken."
51. Federal Supreme Court, X ZR 29/15, Decision of Jun. 14, 2016, "Pemetrexed" (No. 28, 56, 64 etc).

principle, to limit the reach of the doctrine of equivalence. According to the German Supreme Court this should count even if the amendment would not have been necessary from an objective legal standpoint.[52] On the contrary, a different, more flexible approach favoring an infringement by the doctrine of equivalence might be reasonably applied if the limitation or amendment made during prosecution was aimed at overcoming formal patentability issues, such as amendments made for clarity reasons or for avoiding an inadmissible broadening of the scope of protection.[53]

The question of the use of the prosecution history in claim construction is not harmonized amongst the European courts. However, it is unclear how much, if any, difference there is in the outcome. The French courts[54] are more inclined to refer to the prosecution file on issues of claim interpretation than the German courts. The UK courts also allow, at least on an exceptional basis, a reference to the contents of the prosecution file when considering a question of interpretation or infringement, along substantially the same lines as the German courts.[55] Ignoring the prosecution file when defining the scope of protection of a patent claim is not convincing, especially when the doctrine of equivalence is in question. For instance, the question of whether the integration of an amendment into the claim during the granting procedure was caused due to substantive or formal reason can, in the vast majority of cases, only be answered by referring to the prosecution file. Therefore, in the opinion of the authors, it is not appropriate to answer this question solely by comparing the original application with the granted version of the patent.

[c] Effects of Invalidation Proceedings on the Claim Construction

In split systems like Germany, when infringement and validity are tried separately, questions of patent validity still maintain an impact over infringement proceedings, particularly in claim construction. When co-pending proceedings, such as through the Federal Patent Court or in opposition proceedings, impose new limitations on the claims through a final decision, these limitations result in a retroactive and binding legal change to the wording of the claim. Only the newly limited claims may then be asserted against an infringer. The relevant grounds of the decision dealing with the change to the wording of the claim are deemed to replace or stand alongside the patent description in the consideration of the claim construction.[56] Other elements of the nullity or opposition ruling do not have binding effect on the infringement courts.[57] It does not bind the trial judge but may be regarded as persuasive as to how a skilled person would interpret the claim.

52. *Ibid.*
53. *Ibid.*
54. Cour d'Appel, no. 08/00882, *Hewlett Packard GmbH v. Agilent Technologies Deutschland GmbH*, Jan. 27, 2010; TGI Paris, 3rd Chamber, "Institut Pasteur v Siemens Healthcare Diagnostic," May 28, 2010; Court of Appeal Paris, "Pemetrexed," *Eli Lilly v. Zenitva*, Nov. 9, 2021, RG 19/06927.
55. UK Supreme Court Judgment, *Actavis v. Eli Lilly* [2017] UKSC 48.
56. Federal Supreme Court, X ZR 63/75, GRUR 1979, 308, 309, "Auspuffkanal für Schaltgase."
57. Federal Supreme Court, X ZR 72/05, GRUR 2007, 778, "Ziehmaschinenzugeinrichtung."

Statements made by the patentee at the Federal Patent Court in nullity proceedings or in opposition proceedings are in principle not binding for the claim construction. However, an exception may apply in the situation where the patentee declares, during nullity or opposition proceedings, that he does not claim patent protection for particular embodiments and this declaration causes the maintenance of the patent with a specific scope.[58] A third party may refer to that statement or declaration provided that the third party was involved in the invalidation proceedings. In such a scenario, the third party may assert that, according to the declaration, a narrower understanding of claim must be applied. Other parties which were not involved in these proceedings cannot rely on such a declaration. Thus, statements of the patentee/proprietor can be used in German infringement proceedings if those statements have been made in parallel nullity or opposition proceedings between the same parties.[59] This is an exception to the rule that declarations made by the applicant in granting proceedings, or by the patentee in invalidation proceedings, are basically irrelevant to the claim construction. Nevertheless, such declarations, like statements made in the prosecution history, could potentially be useful to demonstrate how a person skilled in the art would understand the patent.[60]

§12.04 IDENTICAL AND EQUIVALENT INFRINGEMENT

[A] Identical Infringement

Once a claim has been interpreted, it remains to be determined if there has been infringement. An identical infringement is found if all features are reproduced in a literal or semantic manner by the accused embodiment. So-called sub-combinations, i.e., where the accused use does not reproduce all features of the claim, are not protected. The German case law is unclear whether an exception to this rule can be made where the omitted feature is not substantial or decisive for the protected teaching.[61] However, it seems likely that even in those cases the principle of legal certainty prevails. That is, competitors should be in a position to identify the scope of protection with sufficient reliability, which might not be guaranteed in case of such partial infringements.

Account must thus be taken of all features, irrespective of whether they are contained in the preamble or the body of the claim. Nevertheless, German case law does allow that certain features do not limit the scope of protection, including indications of purpose contained in the claim describing, for example, a particular use of the teaching. These features only have a limiting effect if they are necessary for the qualification of the teaching, i.e., the teaching is not already fully implemented by its other substantive features.

58. Federal Supreme Court, X ZR 6/91, GRUR 1993, 886, "Weichvorrichtung I"; Federal Supreme Court, X ZR 73/95, 1997 Mitt. 364, "Weichvorrichtung II."
59. *Ibid.*
60. Federal Supreme Court; X ZR 29/15, Decision of Jun. 14, 2016, "Pemetrexed."
61. Federal Supreme Court, X ZR 55/89, GRUR 1991, 444, "Autowaschvorrichtung."

When determining whether there is infringement, it is irrelevant whether individual features of the claim were known.[62] Likewise, in the case of dependent claims, they include all features of the claim to which reference is made.

In case of an identical use, there is no room for a "defense of the free state of the art" in German patent infringement proceedings. Thus, the accused infringer cannot argue that the challenged use or the accused embodiment was known or obvious in consideration of the state of the art. The German infringement court is bound by the decision of the patent office granting the asserted patent.[63] However, this argument plays an important role as soon as it comes to the question of whether the asserted patent claim is valid, as evaluated in separate nullity proceedings. Indeed, if the challenged use or the accused embodiment was known or obvious in consideration of the state of the art, the asserted patent claim may be found invalid in view of that prior art.

This is an aspect of the German bifurcated legal situation. It would not apply to UPC proceedings where the defendant in the infringement action may counterclaim for revocation before the same division of the UPC and thus simultaneously challenge the validity of the asserted patent.

The concept of identical infringement ("contrefaçon littérale") is not viewed so narrowly in France. Decisions are known from French courts which distinguish between essential and nonessential means. "Essential means" are features of the claim without which the claim cannot be considered novel and inventive; and which are indispensable for the fulfillment/solution of the technical problem underlying the claimed invention. In contrast hereto, nonessential features do not limit the scope of protection. So-called secondary differences[64] between the accused embodiment and claimed teaching do not exclude infringement. Nonessential means are thus features that are not decisive for the claimed teaching's novelty and inventiveness. These features are not indispensable to perform the function sought by the claimed invention. Accordingly, prior to considering the doctrine of equivalence, a French Court would first assess whether a difference between patent claim and accused embodiment relates to nonessential means.

[B] Doctrine of Equivalents

[1] Introduction

If one or several features of the claim are not reproduced identically, there may still be infringement under the doctrine of equivalents, as provided for in the EPC (*see* Figure 12.1), namely in the Protocol on the Interpretation of Article 69 EPC as provided in Article 2:

62. Federal Supreme Court, X ZR 102/91, GRUR 1994, 357, "Muffelofen."
63. Federal Supreme Court, X ZR 22/97, GRUR 99, 914, "Kontaktfederblock."
64. TJ Paris, 3rd Ch., "Pemetrexed," *Eli Lilly v. Fresenius*, Sep. 1, 2020, RG 17/1042.

Equivalents

For the purpose of determining the extent of protection conferred by a European patent, due account shall be taken of any element which is equivalent to an element specified in the claims.

[2] Germany

For assessing the question of an equivalent infringement, the following questions have been established by the German Federal Supreme Court.[65] In order to find infringement of the patent on the basis of the doctrine on equivalents, questions (1), (2) and (3) must each be answered in the affirmative, and the accused infringer's *Formstein* defense (4) must fail.

(1) *Same Effect (Gleichwirkung)*: Does the accused embodiment solve the problem—underlying the claimed invention—with a feature which, although modified, has objectively the same effect? That is, to prove infringement by equivalents, the modified feature must achieve the same effect as the explicitly claimed feature, both in a feature-by-feature comparison[66] and as viewed in the context of the overall invention.[67]

Figure 12.1 Doctrine of Equivalents

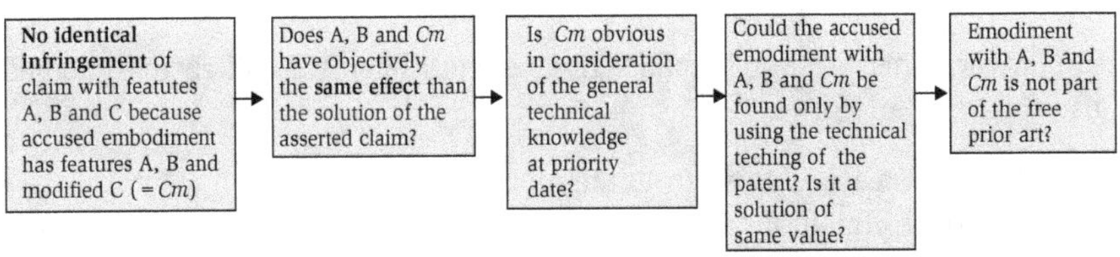

(2) *Obviousness of the Modified Feature (Auffindbarkeit)*: Would the general technical knowledge in the field have taught a skilled person to practice the invention with the allegedly equivalent modification? The modified feature must be obvious for the skilled person after reading the patent specification. When determining if an accused technology is equivalent to the claimed invention, courts thus look to whether the feature that is not literally present in the claim is an obvious variant of what is claimed.[68] Infringement by equivalents is unavailable if the modified feature is inventive over the feature

65. Federal Supreme Court, X ZR 135/01, GRUR 2002, 519, "Schneidmesser II"; Federal Supreme Court, X ZR 81/13, "Kochgefäß."
66. Federal Supreme Court, X ZR 1/05, GRUR 2007, 959, "Pumpeinrichtung" and Federal Supreme Court, X ZR 128/98, GRUR 2000, 1005, "Bratgeschirr."
67. Federal Supreme Court, X ZR 128/98, GRUR 2000, 1005, "Bratgeschirr."
68. Federal Supreme Court, X ZR 16/93, GRUR 1994, 597, "Zerlegvorrichtung für Baumstämme."

that is recited in the claim.[69] Infringement under the doctrine of equivalents is only available if the use of the modified feature would have been obvious in view of the literally claimed feature. The Federal Supreme Court did not yet finally rule on how to deal with alternatives which were unknown at the priority date. If such previously unknown alternative would be identifiable by the skilled person with the general technical knowledge available at the priority date, the question could be easily answered in the affirmative. However, the issue becomes critical where the alternative means was not identifiable by the skilled person with knowledge available at the priority date but is obvious from the general technical progress. For instance, the patent-in-suit concerns a method of reducing emissions from diesel engines using dissolved cerium, whereas the attacked embodiment used stabilized cerium nanoparticles instead. However, on the priority date of the patent-in-suit, the nanotechnology was still in its infancy, and such cerium nanoparticles were therefore not yet available to the skilled person. Nevertheless, the Appeal Court Düsseldorf ruled for patent infringement in that case.[70]

(3) *Same Value (Gleichwertigkeit)*: Is the modified feature so closely oriented toward and tied to the essence of the expressly claimed teaching that the accused embodiment has equal value as compared to the solution provided by the invention recited in the claims? The skilled person needs to identify the modified solution as an obvious variant and must additionally consider it to be of the same value in comparison to the claimed teaching.[71]

In practice, this question is challenging, and infringement is likely to be denied on this basis, particularly if:

- the patent teaches away from the modification;[72]
- numerical limitations of the claims are not met, unless it is exceptionally possible to deduce from the patent description that the effect(s) of the claim can also be achieved with deviating values;[73] or
- the patent encourages particular materials to be used, and the accused embodiment does not make use of one of those.

More generally, the German case law refers to the notion of a "concrete selection" taken by the applicant or patentee. This means, if it appears from the patent claim, that the applicant or patentee wanted to make a "concrete selection" for a particular variant, leaving the impression that he wanted to say "for whatever reason I do it my way,"[74] he has disqualified the scope of protection for other variants. Under the notion of a "concrete selection," two groups of cases must be distinguished: (1) the first group

69. *Ibid.*
70. Appeal Court Düsseldorf, Judgment, Jul. 7, 2016, I-2 U 5/14.
71. Federal Supreme Court, X ZR 135/01, GRUR 2002, 519, "Schneidmesser II"; Federal Supreme Court, X ZR 132/18, GRUR 2021, 574—Kranarm.
72. Federal Supreme Court, X ZR 55/89, GRUR 91, 443, 447, "Autowaschvorrichtung."
73. Federal Supreme Court, X ZR 135/01, GRUR 2002, 519, "Schneidmesser II."
74. Federal Supreme Court, Decision of May 10, 2011, X ZR 16/09, "Okklusionsvorrichtung."

relates to the situation where the alternative means used in an accused embodiment is disclosed in the asserted description, but is not explicitly claimed; or (2) the alternative means used in the accused embodiment is not mentioned in the specification:

(a) Examples for the first group: The patent description explicitly describes a plurality of specific embodiments suitable to achieve the effects of the invention, whereas only one of these embodiments has been included in the patent claim. This case would fall under the notion of a "concrete selection" made by the applicant or patentee. Therefore, an accused infringer, who uses an embodiment which is described in the description but not explicitly claimed, would not qualify as an infringer under the doctrine of equivalence.[75] The question of whether such "concrete selection" was made by the applicant or patentee must be responded from the perspective of the public audience faced by the patent. The notion of a "concrete selection" does not require a particular motivation on the part of the patentee. As it is explained by the Federal Supreme Court, such "concrete selection" can be made "for whatever reason."[76] The inclusion of the particular variant in the patent claims can thus even be unnecessary in the light of the patent's validity. Accordingly, if there is such "concrete selection" among different means or variants disclosed in the patent description, the third question ("same value") must usually be denied and the use of means or variants, which are not claimed (but disclosed in the description), would not fall within the scope of protection. An exception to this rule might be given if the equivalent means used by the accused embodiment is disclosed in the patent description but in a different context than in the context of the replaced claim feature.[77]

(b) With respect to the second case where the replaced means used by the accused embodiment is not disclosed in the patent description, the case law seems, at present, not yet settled. Even though not providing a complete picture, reference can be made to a set of guidelines determined by Federal Supreme Court. First, the Court clarified[78] that the patent description does not necessarily have to contain statements which would lead the skilled person to the equivalent means. Furthermore, the Court provided further guidelines in a case where the patent description generally referred to the use of a group of embodiments, such as a category of agents, but only one specific embodiment, i.e., one specific agent of that category was explicitly described and claimed by the patent. The Court indicated that such situation does not mean that the applicant or patentee made a "concrete selection" excluding from the scope of protection all other undisclosed embodiments of that group or category.[79] The Court also indicated that the situation might be different and

75. *Ibid.*; Federal Supreme Court, Decision of Sep. 13, 2011, X ZR 69/10, "Diglycidverbindung."
76. Federal Supreme Court, Decision of May 10, 2011, X ZR 16/09, "Okklusionsvorrichtung."
77. Appeal Court Düsseldorf, Decision of Nov. 7, 2013, I-2 U 29/12, "WC—Sitzgelenk."
78. Federal Supreme Court, X ZR 36/13, GRUR 2014, 852, "Begrenzungsanschlag."
79. Federal Supreme Court, X ZR 29/15, "Pemetrexed."

mitigate against patent infringement if the claimed embodiment(s) of the group is/are linked to specific characteristics, which are necessary to achieve the effect(s) of the invention. Likewise, it would lean against a finding of infringement under the doctrine of equivalents if it becomes apparent from a comparison of the different claim versions submitted during the granting proceedings that the claims were narrowed down to particular embodiments in the granted patent in order to distinguish from the prior art, not just for formal reasons such as to better satisfy the requirement of clarity of the claim or to conform to written support. If the narrowing was to comply with such formalities, resort to the doctrine of equivalence would still be allowed.[80] Even though the prosecution file shall principally not be used as the (sole) basis for claim construction, at least in the context of the doctrine of equivalence, a limited reference might be acceptable. That is if the prosecution file shows that the patent proprietor has limited the claim in the granting procedure for "material" grounds, namely in order to distinguish the claimed invention from the prior art and to eliminate doubts about patentability, a barrier to an infringement based on the doctrine of equivalence might have been set. The right holder shall not recapture protection for subject matter through the doctrine of equivalents which was previously surrendered by an amendment of the claim. On the contrary, the door might be left open for an infringement by the doctrine of equivalents if the limitation was aimed at overcoming formal grounds, such as clarity reasons or to avoid an inadmissible broadening of the scope of protection.[81]

In another decision, called "V-shaped guiding arrangement" of August 2016,[82] the Federal Supreme Court again dealt with the requirements of the selection decision. In that matter, "V-shaped guiding arrangement" was claimed in the asserted patent, whereas the attacked embodiment provided for a "U-shaped guiding arrangement." The court clarified that embodiments, similar to "foreseeable equivalents" as known under the American patent law, are not necessarily excluded from the scope of protection even if the patentee has recognized (or could have recognized) that the equivalent means were conceivable for being integrated in the claim, but nevertheless did not work toward a wording of the claim in which the equivalent means would have been encompassed by the literal sense of the patent claim. Even if a precise specification of a feature in the patent claim might have effects on the determination of the type and scope of possible equivalent means, such a specification does not in itself justify an exclusion of all or certain equivalent means from the scope of protection of the patent claim. This decision also shows that the previously prevailing narrow application of the doctrine of equivalence should no longer apply.

80. *Ibid.*
81. *Ibid.*
82. Federal Supreme Court, Decision of Aug. 23, 2016, X ZR 76/14, "V-förmige Führungsanordnung."

The scope of the doctrine of equivalence is thus still in flux in the case law. The case law is most unsettled when the patent description does not contain particular hints to the modified and replaced feature used by the accused embodiment. With two decisions rendered in 2016,[83] the Federal Supreme Court seems to direct the rather restrictive case law of the past toward a more patentee-friendly handling of the doctrine of equivalence.

(4) *Formstein Defense:* Does the allegedly equivalent solution belong to the prior art?

If questions (1), (2) and (3) are answered affirmatively, the accused infringer may rely on a counter-defense called the *Formstein Defense,*[84] named after a landmark decision of the Federal Supreme Court rendered in 1986. That is, the accused infringer can defend himself by stating that the accused embodiment is either identical to the prior art or could have not been patented at the priority date of the asserted patent due to lack of inventive step. This defense has been exclusively developed for the doctrine of equivalents. It is inapplicable if the infringement is based on an identical infringement.[85] The reasoning behind this defense, which finds its counterpart in the US in the *Wilson* case,[86] is derived from competition law, according to which the prior art should be free and available to the public. Under the German split system, the infringement courts are bound by the grant decision of the patent office. Accordingly, since infringement courts do not have jurisdiction to decide validity, the *Formstein defense* is not permitted in cases of identical infringement. This defense might not possess the same importance in a court system which jointly deals with infringement and revocation under the same procedural umbrella.

[3] Other Jurisdictions

[a] UK

The UK does not belong to the UPC system. Nevertheless, despite Brexit, the UK stays an EPC Member State. Ordinary European patents can still be validated in the UK. UK courts will therefore continue to rule on ordinary European patents, i.e., the corresponding national part validated in the UK. The view on UK may have been pushed into the background by Brexit. Nevertheless, the case law of the UK courts on European patents will also have to be considered in the future in the context of patent law harmonization under the EPC.

83. Federal Supreme Court, Decision of Jun. 14, 2016, X ZR 29/15, "Pemetrexed"; Federal Supreme Court, Decision of Aug. 23, 2016, X ZR 76/14, "V-förmige Führungsanordnung."
84. Federal Supreme Court, X ZR 28/85, GRUR 1987, 279, IIC 1987, 795 (in English), "Formstein."
85. Federal Supreme Court, X ZR 22/97, GRUR 1999, 914, "Kontaktfederblock."
86. *See Wilson Sporting Goods Co. v. David Geoffrey & Assocs.*, 904 F.2d 677, 14 U.S.P.Q. 2d 1942 (Fed. Cir.).

In *Eli Lilly v. Actavis*,[87] the UK Supreme Court reassessed the doctrine of equivalence under English law. The so-called protocol questions,[88] which more or less corresponded to the "Schneidmesser" questions, had been replaced by a *purposive construction* by the Amgen decision.[89] Now the protocol questions shall be applicable in a modified form for the assessment of a patent infringement. The Supreme Court formulates the questions as follows:

(1) "Notwithstanding that it is not within the literal meaning of the relevant claim(s) of the patent, does the variant achieve substantially the same result in substantially the same way as the invention, i.e. the inventive concept revealed by the patent?"
(2) "Would it be obvious to the person skilled in the art, reading the patent at the priority date, but knowing that the variant achieves substantially the same result as the invention, that it does so in substantially the same way as the invention?"
(3) "Would such a reader of the patent have concluded that the patentee nonetheless intended that strict compliance with the literal meaning of the relevant claim(s) of the patent was an essential requirement of the invention?"

The first protocol question seems to correspond essentially to the first "Schneidmesser" question. The UK Supreme Court states that the variant must first achieve substantially the same result in substantially the same manner, i.e., the inventive performance disclosed in the patent must be achieved. This is an objective test which apparently does not diverge from the first "Schneidmesser" question.

The second protocol question of the UK Supreme Court seems to be different from the German approach (second "Schneidmesser" question). In principle, both approaches refer to the priority date. According to the UK Supreme Court, the person skilled, on being told what the variant does, must be able to see that its effect is achieved in essentially the same way as supposed by the claimed teaching. This approach seems to be broader than the German approach. It may allow including variants in the scope of protection which became known or developed after the priority day. This has not yet been ruled out by the highest court in Germany but was accepted in one decision of the Appeal Court Düsseldorf.[90] In the German view, however, the second "Schneidmesser" question may only be affirmed if the skilled person is able to identify the variant without applying inventiveness. The UK Court doubts that this is correct. An inventor of a variant may obtain a patent for it, which does not necessarily mean that the variant may not fall within the scope of protection of the earlier patent. Nevertheless, legal certainty might require that new and inventive solutions are excluded from the scope of protection. Also, the search for new and inventive solutions circumventing a patent is an important engine of innovation and progress. Accordingly, the UK's approach might be too far-reaching.

87. UK Supreme Court Judgment, *Actavis v. Eli Lilly* [2017] UKSC 48.
88. *Improver v. Remington* [1990] FSR 181, 189 = GRUR Im 1993, 245 (246 f.).
89. *Kirin Amgen Inc. v. Hoechst Marion Russel Ltd.* = GRUR Im 2005, 343.
90. Appeal Court Düsseldorf, Decision of Jul. 7, 2016, I-2 U 5/14, BeckRS 2016, 21120, "Partikel-Auffangvorrichtung."

The third protocol question of the UK Supreme Court seems to differ from the third "Schneidmesser" question of the Federal Supreme Court. The Supreme Court asks whether the reader of the patent can assume that the patentee intended a strict observance of the literal meaning of the claims. This seems to correspond to the concept of selection decisions under the German jurisprudence, which is why the approaches probably do not differ.

[b] France

When it comes to claim construction, French courts apparently follow a conceptually different approach than the UK and Germany. Nevertheless, often it is difficult to predict whether there will be major differences in the outcome of particular cases. The claim construction is purpose-oriented and thus, French courts aim at giving the claim its full meaning.

However, the French case law differentiates between three types of infringement:

(1) literal infringement ("contrefaçon littérale");
(2) infringement by reproduction of the essential means; and
(3) infringement based on the doctrine of equivalents.

Literal infringement ("contrefaçon littérale") is found if the contested embodiment reproduces the claimed means both in their form or structure and function. A second form of infringement may be given,[91] even if there are differences between the claimed and the contested embodiment. This requires that these differences only relate to details and do not concern essential means of the asserted claim. This raises the question of what is meant under "essential means" and what are nonessential means. A lack of corresponding "non-essential means" may still allow for patent infringement. Generally, a feature of the claim is essential if the claimed product or method would not work without that feature.[92] On the contrary, if it does not contribute to the performance sought by the technical teaching, it could be disregarded as nonessential. This determination must be checked against the public interests of an audience which relies on the wording of claims. "Essential" features are those features of the claim without which the claimed teaching cannot be considered novel and inventive; and which are necessary for solving the technical problem underlying the claimed invention.

Also, the French doctrine of equivalents seems to deviate from the German and UK approaches. First, French courts are more inclined to look into the prosecution file to solve issues of interpretation or scope than German or UK courts.[93] The deviation can be explained by the fact that revocation and infringement are procedurally embedded in the same proceedings in contrast to the German split situation. If it comes

91. Cour de Cassation, Decision of Jan. 3, 1985.
92. *Ibid.*
93. Cour de Cassation, Decision of Nov. 23, 2010, Case No. 1194 F-D.

to doctrine of equivalents, French courts may rule that a patent is deemed to be infringed[94] where a variant:

(1) is used to perform the same function as the claimed means; and
(2) reaches an identical or similar result to that of the claimed means; and
(3) the function of the claimed means is new.[95]

The "function" indicated in prong (1) refers to the primary technical effect produced by the claimed means,[96] whereas the "result" of prong (2) refers to the technical advantages provided by the concerned means.[97] That result must be of the same nature and efficiency.[98] Prongs (1) and (2) of the test are more or less reflected in Germany's question 1 (Q1—Germany: "Same effect"). On the contrary, in contrast to Germany, no importance is given in France to the question of whether the variant would have been obvious to the skilled person (Q2—Germany: "Obviousness of the Modified Feature). Accordingly, the variant may be inventive under French law. Also new variants which were unknown at the priority date are eligible for infringement under the doctrine of equivalence.[99]

Prong (3) of the French test also differs from the analysis in Germany. It requires a reviewing of whether the function of the concerned claimed means was known or not known at the priority date. Consequently, the French case law does not recognize infringement by equivalence if the function of the claimed means is not new. Thus, it would not be sufficient if the claimed means only differ from the prior art by structure.[100] The claimed means must also differ from the prior art by the function. For example, a claim encompasses features A, B, C, D whereby the accused embodiment reproduces A, B, C, but D in a different form (D*). D* must perform the same function as the claimed means (1); and also reach an identical or similar result (2). Prong (3) thus raises the question whether the means performing the same function as feature D was already known in combination with A, B, and C. If this can be affirmed, no infringement under the doctrine of equivalence is allowed. Prong (3) thus answers the question whether patent protection would have been possible for the modified means. The latter is generally excluded if modified means are known fulfilling the same function.

§12.05 INFRINGING ACTS

The central provisions governing the consequences of infringing acts are contained in Articles 25 (*direct acts of use*) and 26 (*indirect acts of use; contributory infringement*) of

94. *Ibid.*
95. Cour de Cassation, *Newmat v. Normalu*, Feb. 6, 2019, 1721585.
96. Cour de Cassation, Com., 16 20.644, Jun. 27, 2018.
97. Paris Court of Appeal, Decision of May 17, 2016, Case No. 14/10335.
98. TGI Paris, Decision of Apr. 3, 2014; PIBD 2014, No. 1010-III-597; TGI Paris, Decision of Nov. 22, RG No. 10/10117.
99. TGI Paris, Sep. 29, 2004, RG No. 00/14083.
100. Cour de Cassation, Decision of Apr. 16, 2013, PIBD 2013, No. 972-III-735.

the UPCA. These provisions are applicable to European patents with or without unitary effect. National courts apply the UPCA provisions if they adjudicate ordinary European patents, even if an opt-out was declared as to the ordinary European patent at issue.[101] Thus, national courts are required to adapt their case law to the new provisions of the UPCA, at least in cases involving ordinary European patents. National courts thus get a chance to take a fresh look at long-established jurisprudence.

The question whether the provisions of Articles 25–28 UPCA or the corresponding national provisions must be applied by the national courts in relation to ordinary European patents is still undecided and in dispute among commentators. However, there is no doubt that sections 9 and 10 of the GPA with an almost identical wording are applicable to German national patents.[102]

Although the German case law established under the GPA and the case law of other European courts result from similar provisions, this body of law is not authoritative for the interpretation of the corresponding provisions of the UPCA. These provisions belong to an international treaty. Their interpretation primarily follows the interpretation framework of the Vienna Convention of the law of treaties. According to Article 31 of the Vienna Convention, "a treaty shall be interpreted in good faith in accordance with ordinary meaning to be given to the terms of the treaty in their context and in the light of its object and purpose." Article 32 of the Vienna Convention adds supplementary means of interpretation, namely "the preparatory work of the treaty and the circumstances of its conclusion" may be used in order to confirm the meaning resulting from the application of Article 31. The Vienna Convention only provides a basic set of interpretative rules. It does not exclude consideration of other sources of authority, in particular the case law of the Member States. This is particularly germane to those provisions of the UPCA which correspond to identical national provisions under which extensive case law has been established over decades. For this reason, it is incumbent upon the UPC to take into consideration the decisions and opinions of courts and industrial property offices in the Members States of the UPCA.

Accordingly, the interpretation of the UPCA starts from an independent legal framework. The German case law established under similar substantive provisions only serves as a nonbinding guideline for the interpretation of Articles 25 and 26 UPCA. The same applies to the jurisprudence of other states adhering to the UPCA. The UPC will have to establish its own case law. During the coming years the case law of the UPC will be in development. Until the UPC's Appeal Court has developed its own body of governing law, the question of how the UPCA and RoP are to be interpreted lays in the hands of the UPC's divisions and their judges. These judges might be inclined to adopt legal standards with which they are already familiar.

101. Cf. Ch. 12, §12.01.
102. For German Utility Models, equivalent provisions can be found in s. 11 of the German Utility Model Act.

[A] Direct Infringement

If a feature of the asserted claim is neither met literally nor by equivalents in the accused embodiment, then there is no infringement (*see* previous sections). The infringement test starts from a comparison of the claimed invention and the accused embodiment. The patent is infringed if the accused embodiment practices all features of the patent claim. Differences in efficiency, in particular in case of improved or inferior realizations, suggest not excluding patent infringement, as long as all features of the claim are met. That is, an apparatus claim might be infringed as long as the embodiment is objectively suitable to achieve the claimed properties and the effects as described in the description of the patent. It should be sufficient if the infringing properties are the result of normal use made by the user, for instance, if a particular wheel circumference of a tire (as claimed) is later achieved by the normal use of the tire. At least this is how German courts have considered it in the past.[103] It seems to be irrelevant if the producer or supplier of the infringing devices explicitly proposes in the instruction manual another (presumably noninfringing) use of the apparatus, as long as the use of the teaching of the patent is possible. Accordingly, infringement may be found even if the user of the product does not necessarily use it in an infringing way. On the contrary, if the user of the accused embodiment needs to apply particular measures in view of achieving the claimed properties and the effects as described in the description of the patent, the seller or producer of such embodiment might not be an infringer, as the user's activities do not fall within his responsibility.

The accused infringer may escape liability if he disables a particular functionality of the accused product that is recited in the patent. For example, the accused infringer sells a device with a multitude of software-based functionalities, but one functionality (allegedly infringing) is disabled. The question whether there is still infringement could be answered depending on the "objective user" of the accused product and how easily the user could enable the disabled functionality. For instance, a device, which does not make use of all features of the patented teaching when it is delivered, may still represent a direct infringement of the patent if it is self-evident and certain that the purchaser; i.e., the "objective user" will manipulate it and realize the patented teaching. This could be the case if the accused infringer guides and controls that last act of manipulation committed by the "objective user." He then deliberately adopts the manipulation of the "objective user" with his delivery, which justifies treating him as if he had delivered an infringing device.[104] One decision of the German Federal Supreme Court[105] stated:

> The patent is infringed provided the features of the patent claim are reproduced and the accused embodiment is objectively suitable to achieve the patented properties and effects. It does not preclude infringement if the device is usually applied in a different manner and if normally the user does not make use of [the

103. Appeal Court Düsseldorf, Decision of Jul. 29, 2010, 2 U 139/09, BeckRS 2010, 21759.
104. Appeal Court Düsseldorf, Decision of Feb. 19, 2015, I-15 U 39/14.
105. Federal Supreme Court, X ZR 14/02, GRUR 2006, 399, "Rangierkatze"; District Court Düsseldorf, Decision of Jan. 23, 2007, 4a O 34/06, BeckRS 2009, 12319.

> infringing functionality]. Patent infringement is also given if the manufacturer explicitly recommends another use of the devices as long as the use of the patented teaching is possible.[106]

In this manner, German law is more accommodating to the patentee than US law in establishing a case of direct infringement. The law in the US would, by contrast, require proof of induced infringement in this circumstance, which entails a level of scienter absent from German law.

[1] Products

Introduction: The central provision governing a direct infringement of a product claim is Article 25(a) UPCA, which prescribes that a person not having the consent of the patentee is prohibited:

> from making, offering, placing on the market or using a product which is the subject matter of the patent, or importing or storing the product for such purposes.

Section 9(1) No. 1 of the GPA has an identical text. At least one of the indicated activities must be demonstrated and proven for the grant of an injunction against the infringement of a product claim. Usually, it is sufficient to demonstrate one case of offering for sale the accused product.

Territoriality: The coverage of a patent infringement lawsuit at the UPC goes well beyond national borders. An offer in any UPCA country may be sufficient provided that the asserted European patent is in force in that UPCA country. In case of a European bundle patent these are those UPCA countries where the patent has been validated and is still in force, whereas for a unitary European patent, an infringing act occurring in any UPCA countries would be sufficient to establish the UPC's jurisdiction.

This is typically different in German national proceedings. A German patent or the German counterpart of a European bundle patent, which is subject to a lawsuit in front of a German court, entitles the patent proprietor to prohibit acts that led to an infringement within the boundaries of the German territory. A main reason for the limited reach of German courts resides in high thresholds for allowing "trans-border litigation," namely, litigation where national courts decide on patent infringement occurring in foreign states.[107]

Offer: An "offer" is generally broadly construed to cover any holding out of the prospect of making available the product, pursuant to Article 25(a) UPCA as well as section 9(1) No. 1 of the GPA. A legally binding offer is not mandatory. Rather, any act that promotes sales is sufficient (as opposed to the law in the US, which is more restrictive in requiring a formal offer). Also, it is not required that the offer leads to any result or that the offered product be delivered.[108] However, the offer must occur during

106. Unofficial translation.
107. Cf. Ch. 9, §9.03[B][2].
108. Federal Supreme Court, GRUR 2003, 1031, "Kupplung für optische Geräte."

the lifetime of the patent.[109] A promotional brochure showing the product might thus be sufficient to establish an infringing offer. An infringing offer may be originated outside the territory of the court's jurisdiction as long as the offer is received inside the territory of the court's jurisdiction and accessible to potential customers there. At least a domestic connection must be substantiated.

Offer through a webpage: An offer posted through a webpage on the Internet that could be perceived and understood by a potential customer situated in the concerned jurisdiction is generally sufficient regardless of the server's location, which could be thus located outside that territory, for instance, in the US or Asia. It is well established under German case law that an English webpage is sufficient to constitute a potentially infringing "offer" under section 9 of the GPA. Thus, a foreign company, even without any affiliates in Europe and without having previously shipped any products onto the European Market, which presents its products on its website, could unknowingly infringe a European or German patent, provided that the webpage is objectively addressed to the European public. A diligent company could avoid these consequences by means of a disclaimer posted on the website clearly indicating that the concerned products are not available in Europe.[110] The disclaimer might however not be helpful as soon as the accused products are shipped into the court's jurisdiction, an event which could potentially be triggered by a test purchase[111] initiated by a straw man associated with the patentee. Such test purchases are commonly accepted to justify the jurisdiction of German courts.[112]

Offer at trade shows: Even the first offer or advertisement of a product at a trade show taking place within the territory covered by the court's jurisdiction might likely meet the requirements of Article 25(a) UPC or section 9 of the GPA.[113] However, the trade show must have the quality of a sales exhibition for the purpose of trading goods. If the exhibition is simply for information purposes, without trading of goods, the demonstration of a product would not be considered to be an infringing act.[114]

Offer abroad: A supplier that is based abroad and delivers patent-infringing products to a customer, who is also based abroad, may be liable for patent infringement in Germany if he had knowledge of "concrete indications" that the goods would further be delivered by the customer to Germany. In such a situation, even the sale of the product outside of Germany could constitute a patent infringement in Germany.[115]

109. Federal Supreme Court, GRUR 2007, 221, "Simvastatin": The entry of a generic drug in an announcement list represents an offer, even if it explicitly indicates that the generic is only available after the expiration of the patent. Nevertheless, a generic company can initiate the regulatory process in view of getting an approval for the generic drug prior to the expiration of the patent: Appeal Court Düsseldorf, Decision of Sep. 20, 2012, I-2 U 44/12.
110. Federal Supreme Court, GRUR 2006, 513, "Arzneimittelwerbung im Internet."
111. Appeal Court Düsseldorf, Decision of Jan. 28, 2010, 2 U 131/00, NJOZ 2010, 1781, "Testkauf patentverletzender DVDs."
112. *Ibid.*
113. Appeal Court Düsseldorf, Decision of Mar. 27, 2014, Az. I-15 U 29/14, "Sterilcontainer."
114. *Ibid.*
115. Federal Supreme Court, Decision of May 16, 2017, X ZR 120/15, GRUR 2017, 785, "Abdichtsystem."

Transit: Goods entering the EU are declared in transit if they are not intended to be put on the market in the country where the goods enter the borders. Either these goods are shipped to another EU Member State (so-called internal transit) or to a country outside of the EU (external transit). The Federal Supreme Court[116] recently repeated its case law that the placing of goods in transit proceedings at a German boarder does not infringe rights in Germany under section 9 GPA.[117] Infringement of a German patent may only be found if the goods are subject to trading transactions taking place on the German territory or if the goods are imported for that purpose. This view is in line with the case law of the ECJ[118] on "suspensive proceedings" under the Community Customs Code.[119] Accordingly, goods in transit do not infringe upon the exclusive rights resulting from a patent, unless the proprietor can demonstrate at least a concrete risk that the goods are intended to be put on the market in the country in question. That is, it must be shown that the suspected products may possibly not reach their destination and could thus enter into circulation on the market which is covered by the court's jurisdiction.[120] A mere risk is not sufficient.[121] Rather there must be reliable indications to justify such suspicion. Those indications may include, *inter alia*, the fact that the destination of the goods is not declared, the lack of reliable information as to the identity or address of the manufacturer or consignor of the goods, or a lack of cooperation with the customs authorities. Although the ECJ puts the thresholds for the interception of goods in transit on the basis of the customs regulation relatively low, such indications might, as such, not be sufficient to establish infringement before the national courts.

The aforementioned "transit" case law is not decisive for the UPCA and the UP Regulation. If the transit goods are not destined for a UPCA country, the transit should, in principle, not constitute an infringement under Article 25 UPCA. If goods are declared in transit because they are not intended to be put on the market in the EU entry state, but shipped to another EU Member State (so-called internal transit), the situation is the following: In case of a European patent with unitary effect, even if the entry State and the destination State are both States in which the UPC has jurisdiction over that patent, the transit, as such, might not yet represent an infringing act under Article 25 UPCA. However, the fact that the goods shall be transported into a country, where the patent has unitary effect, with the apparent intention that it shall be brought there into circulation would likely represent a sufficient "threat" that the goods will be placed "on the market" in the sense of Article 25 UPCA. This could justify a claim for cease and desist. This does also apply in case of an ordinary European patent as long as the patent is in force and valid in the State of destination, where the goods shall be later brought into circulation. This would equally represent a sufficient "threat" that the goods will

116. Federal Supreme Court, Decision of Jun. 25, 2014, X ZR 72/13.
117. Federal Supreme Court, I ZR 246/02, GRUR 2007, 876, "Diesel II."
118. European Court of Justice, Decision of Nov. 9, 2006; Case C-281/05, *Montex Holdings Ltd v. Diesel SpA*; decisions of Dec. 1, 2011, Cases C-446/09, *Philips* and C-495/09, *Nokia*.
119. *See* Ch. 14.
120. District Court Hamburg, Decision of Apr. 30, 2009, 315 O 72/08, BeckRS 2009, 29649; *see also* Decision of the European Court of Justice, C-281/05, GRUR 2007, 146 *Montex/Diesel*.
121. Federal Supreme Court, Decision of Apr. 25, 2012, I ZR 235/10 "Clinique happy."

be deemed placed "on the market" in the sense of Article 25 UPCA and justify a claim for cease and desist. As recently ruled by the Federal Supreme Court[122] the transit of goods—even though not representing an infringement of rights in the country of entry—could constitute an infringement of a patent which is in force in the country of destination. It needs to be decided case by case whether this is the case.

Making: This act of "making" refers to all steps of the manufacturing process up to the completion of the product.[123] Accordingly, the act of "making" might not be satisfied if the accused activities are limited to preparatory acts unless the accused infringer controls the process from the beginning to the final step (extended workbench).[124]

Putting on the market: The act of "putting on the market" broadly extends to all acts where the power of disposal of the product is passed to a third party, without the necessity that its ownership is assigned. Thus, the delivery to the carrier or shipper is normally sufficient.

[2] Processes

Introduction: Process claims relate to a physical activity, such as a method, process or use.[125] The central provisions governing infringing acts of a process claim are contained in Article 25 b) UPCA and in section 9(1) No. 2 of the GPA. Both provisions prescribe that a person not having the consent of the patentee shall be prohibited (*see* Table 12.1).

Table 12.1 Comparison of UPCA and GPA (Infringement of Process Claims)

Article 25 b) UPCA	*Section 9(1) No. 2 GPA*
... from using a process which is the subject-matter of the patent or, where the third party knows, or should have known, that the use of the process is prohibited without the consent of the patent proprietor, offering the process for use within the territory of the Contracting Member States in which that patent has effect.	... from using a process which is the subject-matter of the patent or, where he knows or it is obvious from the circumstances that the use of the process is prohibited without the consent of the patentee, from offering the process for use within the territory to which this Law applies.[1]

1. Unofficial translation.

The provisions cover two case scenarios. The first scenario refers to the situation where the accused infringer uses himself the protected process ("using a process"),

122. *Ibid.*
123. Federal Supreme Court, GRUR 1951, 452, "Mülltonne."
124. Federal Supreme Court, GRUR 1990, 997, "Ethofumesat."
125. Enlarged Board, G 2/88.

whereas the second scenario concerns an offer made by the accused infringer to a third party to perform the claimed process ("offering a process").

Process claims encompass all kinds of methods, namely methods of working, manufacturing methods and use methods. The main difference between both provisions relates to their territorial application. Article 25 b) UPCA is applicable to ordinary European patents and European patents with unitary effect. The latter type of patent has effect in all Contracting Member States. Accordingly, the use of a process claim in any of these States would, in principle, fall under Article 25 b) UPCA. As to ordinary European patents, an infringement is basically governed by Article 25 b) UPCA in those Contracting Member States where the patent has been validated and thus has effect. The ordinary European patent might have been validated also in other EPC Member States, which do not belong to the group of Contracting Member States of the UPCA. Due to the missing applicability of Article 25 b) UPCA in those States, the provisions of national law prevail.

A method is used if the essential steps of the claimed method are performed by the accused infringer. Thus, preparatory acts alone are usually not sufficient. Nevertheless, it has been decided by the Appeal Court Düsseldorf that the infringer does not need to have necessarily implemented all the steps of the protected method in order to be liable for direct infringement. He would still infringe the patent if, for example, the final steps of the method are implemented by a third party, and these acts of the third party can nonetheless be imputed to him.[126] Because of the proximity to the concept of contributory patent infringement, these are exceptional cases. The concept of contributory patent infringement is reserved for cases in which the infringer does not realize all features of the claim. Direct patent infringement shall therefore only be assumed if the acts of the third party completing the infringement can be clearly allocated or imputed to the infringer. If such allocation of responsibility is not possible, only patent infringement under the umbrella of the concept of contributory patent infringement can be considered.

As a consequence of territoriality, the use of the claimed method outside the territory addressed by Article 25 b) UPCA or section 9(1) No. 2 GPA does not represent an infringement. However, an infringement might be found even if only a part of the method is implemented by the accused party within the territory, as long as the remaining method steps that are accomplished outside that territory are attributable to the accused party. The same approach can be mirrored to the inverse situation, namely if one part of the method steps is implemented outside the relevant territory by a third party and the remaining acts are accomplished by the accused infringer inside the relevant territory. In both scenarios the acts that were committed outside the territory addressed by Article 25 b) UPCA or section 9(1) No. 2 GPA may be imputed to the accused infringer in order for infringement to be found.[127]

In client-server systems, where the server, database and user are situated in different countries, the approach described here for method claims may likely also be

126. Appeal Court Düsseldorf, Dec. 10, 2009, I-2 U 51/08, GRUR-RR 2010, 122, "Prepaid-Telefonkarte."

127. *Ibid.*

applicable to system claims. This would have the effect that all components of the system need not necessarily be located within the territory addressed by Article 25 b) UPCA or section 9(1) No. 2 GPA. These cases must dogmatically be distinguished from the concept of contributory patent infringement. As long as acts of infringement cannot be concentrated on one person by means of an attribution of facts, patent infringement can only be considered under the doctrine of contributory infringement.

The second scenario ("offering a process") requires not only that the accused infringer makes an offer but also that he knows or—at least—that he should have known that the use of the process is prohibited.[128] The principle of territoriality is explicitly reflected in that the offer must be oriented to a use of the process in territory addressed by Article 25 b) UPCA or section 9(1) No. 2 GPA. If the product is offered for a use which shall take place outside the territory belonging to the court's jurisdiction, then there would be no patent infringement.

Product directly obtained by the process: Furthermore, the patentee may exclude any third party—according to Article 25(c) or section 9(3) GPA:

> from offering, placing on the market, using or importing or storing for such purposes the product obtained directly by a process which is the subject-matter of the patent.

This means in case of a process claim, similar rights as are known in the US are conferred to the patentee. If the process is a manufacturing process, the patentee can also prohibit the commercialization of products directly generated by that method even though his patent does not contain any product claim. The product generated by the method must not necessarily possess a physical or corporal nature. The product could also represent a sequence of electronic signals, as long as the signals are reproducible by a reader, at least under the law of the German Supreme Court.[129] However, the legal protection is limited to a "direct" generation of the product through the process. This should be the case if the accused product was directly obtained by the patented process and was not subsequently subject to other manufacturing measures of the product generated by the process. In fact, the question of what is meant by a direct process product causes difficulties in cases where the product has been modified by further measures. Such a claim might fail as soon as the process product loses its characteristic properties due to a further treatment. For example, protection does not extend to a final product obtained by chemical conversion from intermediate products obtained after completion of the patented process steps. In this case, the essential properties of the process product are changed by the additional steps.[130]

Moreover, for the application of Article 25(c) UPCA or section 9(3) GPA, it is irrelevant where the method has been implemented and where the product has been generated by the process. It would be sufficient for infringement if the method was

128. Section 9(1) No. 2 GPA reads "obvious from the circumstances."
129. Federal Supreme Court, Decision of Aug. 21, 2012, X ZR 33/10 "MPEG-2-Videosignal-codierung."
130. District Court Düsseldorf GRUR 1989, 896 "Grass herbicide."

implemented in the US and the product obtained by the method was later imported onto markets where the UPC or a German court has jurisdiction.

Shift of burden of proof: The position of the patentee asserting a process claim is strengthened by a shift of burden of proof as shown in Table 12.2.

Table 12.2 Comparison of Article 55 UPCA with §139(3) GPA

Article 55 UPCA	*Section 139(3) GPA*
(1) ... if the subject matter of a patent is a process for obtaining a new product, the identical product when produced without the consent of the patent proprietor shall, in the absence of proof to the contrary, be deemed to have been obtained by the patented process. (2) The principle set out in paragraph 1 shall also apply where there is a substantial likelihood that the identical product was made by the patented process and the patent proprietor has been unable, despite reasonable efforts, to determine the process actually used for such identical product. (3) In the adduction of proof to the contrary, the legitimate interests of the defendant in protecting its manufacturing and trade secrets shall be taken into account.	... if the subject matter of a patent is a process for obtaining a new product, the identical product when produced by any other party shall, in the absence of proof to the contrary, be deemed to have been obtained by the patented process. In the adduction of proof to the contrary, the legitimate interests of the defendant in protecting his manufacturing and business secrets shall be taken into account. [1]

1. Unofficial translation.

Both provisions, Article 55 UPCA and section 139(3) GPA, provide a shift of the burden of proof in the case of process claims. Both provisions require that the patentee must first prove that the product obtained by the patented process is "new." This suggests a showing of at least one aspect that differentiates the obtained product over prior art products at the priority date of the patent-in-question. If the patentee can do so, he only needs to show that the product obtained by the accused infringer's process is identical to that product. In principle, it is generally sufficient if the products are the same or equivalent with respect to their properties.[131]

Sections 1 and 3 of Article 55 UPCA are identical with section 139(3) GPA. However, Article 55 UPCA contains an additional section 2 which is unknown under the German law and further strengthens the position of the patentee. It reduces the scope of proof in that a "substantial likelihood that the identical product was made by the patented process" is sufficient. Thus section 2—in contrast to section 1—does not require a "new" product obtained by the patented process. However, the shift of the

131. Federal Supreme Court, Decision of Jun. 25, 1976—X ZR 4/75, Alkylendiamine II.

burden of proof according to section 2 additionally requires that proprietor "has been unable, despite reasonable efforts, to determine the process actually used for such identical product."

[3] Product-by-Process Claims

A product-by-process claim defines a product in terms of the method used in its manufacture. This type of claim typically provides a way for protecting products, like chemical compounds, that are difficult to describe by chemical makeup or structure but can only be described by the way they are made. The patentability of such claims requires that the product can only be described in terms of how it can be made and, thus, cannot be described in terms of its composition, structure or other physical properties. The determination of the scope of protection conferred by such claims creates particular problems. According to a decision of the Federal Supreme Court,[132] the scope of protection shall not be limited to the manufacturing methods or processes recited in the claims. This is because the claims set forth the manufacturing method merely as an example of how the product is obtained (typical claim language: "is obtainable"). Thus, products, which meet the particular properties conferred by the process, but are in fact obtained by another process, would thus also be covered by the claim. Nevertheless, the particular effects that the processes recited in the claims produce upon the final product shall be taken into account for the determination of the scope of protection.[133]

Product-by-process claims are important for the enforcement of utility models. Utility models generally do not cover processes. A way to circumvent this restriction is through the use of product-by-process claims, which are centered on a product. This approach allows for indirect protection for a process through the utility model framework.

[B] Contributory Infringement

[1] Legal Framework

Contributory patent infringement facilitates, for example, the enforcement of multistep process claims, and system claims composed of a plurality of components. Such claims may be collaboratively fulfilled by different entities. For instance, the accused party only offers an element for an embodiment which is supposed to be assembled by a third party into a patent-protected embodiment. The patentee may act against someone who causes a danger for a direct patent infringement. He does not have to wait until the patent infringement finally occurs. The concept of contributory patent infringement

132. Federal Supreme Court, X ZB 13/90, GRUR 1993, 651, "Tetraploide Kamille."
133. Federal Supreme Court, X ZR 188/01, GRUR 2005, 749, "Aufzeichnungsträger."

thus only requires a danger of direct infringement. Typical cases of contributory patent infringement are:[134]

- offer and/or delivery of an apparatus with which a patent-protected process can be carried out;
- offer and/or delivery of a component which can be combined with other components to form a protected system or a multipart apparatus;
- offer and/or delivery of an apparatus with which a patented product can be manufactured.

In applying the law, the boundaries between contributory and direct patent infringement must be defined. Drawing the line is not always easy because there are forms of direct infringement which could be confused with the concept of contributory infringement. For instance, according to German case law, direct infringement is also given in case of a negligent inducement or negligent assistance of a direct patent infringement committed together with someone else.[135] The demarcation between direct and contributory infringement is important because the legal consequences of both types of infringement are different. A claim for compensation according to section 33 Patent Act which may result from a published patent application is excluded in case of contributory infringement. Also, the claim for recall and destruction (Sec. 140a Patent Act) is not applicable in case of contributory patent infringement. The concept of contributory patent infringement is provided in Article 26 UPCA and in section 10 GPA. The provisions and its counterpart in the UPCA read as shown in Table 12.3.

Table 12.3 Comparison: Article 26 UPCA Versus Section 10 GPA

Article 26 UPCA	*Section 10 GPA*
(1) A patent shall confer on its proprietor the right to prevent any third party not having the proprietor's consent from supplying or offering to supply, within the territory of the Contracting Member States in which that patent has effect, any person other than a party entitled to exploit the patented invention, with means, relating to an essential element of that invention, for putting it into effect therein, when the third party knows, or should have known, that those means are suitable and intended for putting that invention into effect.	(1) A patent shall have the further effect that a third party not having the consent of the proprietor shall be prohibited from supplying or offering to supply, within the territory to which this Law applies, any person, other than a party entitled to exploit the patented invention, with means relating to an essential element of that invention for putting it into effect therein, when the third party knows or it is obvious from the circumstances that such means are suitable and intended for putting the invention into effect.

134. Federal Supreme Court, Decision of Jul. 27, 2007, X ZR 113/04, "Rohrschweißverfahren."
135. Supreme Court, GRUR 2009, 1142—Mp3-Player-Import.

Article 26 UPCA	*Section 10 GPA*
(2) Paragraph 1 shall not apply when the means are staple commercial products, except where the third party induces the person supplied to perform any of the acts prohibited by Article 25. (3) Persons performing the acts referred to in Article 27(a)–(e) shall not be considered to be parties entitled to exploit the invention within the meaning of paragraph 1.	(2) Paragraph 1 shall not apply when the means are staple commercial products, except where the third party induces the person supplied to perform any of the acts prohibited by the second sentence of section 9. (3) Persons performing the acts referred to in section 11.1–3, shall not be considered persons entitled to exploit the invention within the meaning of paragraph 1.[1]

1. Unofficial translation.

Neither section 10(1) GPA nor Article 26 UPCA requires that the contributory infringement finally leads to a direct infringement. A threat of direct infringement is thus sufficient.

[2] Prerequisites

The framework for assessing contributory infringement has requirements having both an objective and subjective character. The subjective requirements are to be examined with regard to the offeror/supplier and the offeree/consignee as mentioned in Table 12.4.

Table 12.4 Overview: Contributory Infringement

Objective Conditions	*Subjects Requirements*	
	Offeror/Supplier	**Offeree/Acquirer**
[1] offering or supplying a means in Germany; [2] means referring to an essential element of the invention; [3] suitability of the means for direct use of the protected teaching; [4] unauthorized Offeree or Acquirer; [5] lack of consent of the patent proprietor;	[6] knowledge of the objective suitability of the means for direct use and knowledge of the intended use in Germany or obviousness	[7] intended use: Intention to use the offered/supplied means in Germany in a way that infringes the patent.

[a] General Outline

The concept of contributory infringement provides the patentee an avenue for relief without having to prove all the elements of direct infringement. The scope of protection for contributory infringement is limited, recognizing that the supplied or offered means do not themselves suffice to establish a claim for direct infringement. Thus, the offer and supply of the means are basically not illegal. Also, the rule against contributory infringement does not provide an absolute prohibition against supplying or offering such means.

The rule against contributory infringement is limited to situations where the offered or supplied means relate "to an essential element of the invention." Additional substantive conditions must also be satisfied in order to penalize the offeror or supplier of the means.[136]

The offered or supplied means must be suitable for putting the claimed teaching into effect and must additionally be intended for that purpose. The contributory infringer must know that the supplied means is suitable for an infringing use and intended for that use by the offeree/acquirer, who himself must have the intention to use it in an infringing way. Although proving such knowledge or intention is typically difficult, the patentee can establish its case by demonstrating that—in consideration of the circumstances—the supplied means are suitable and intended for an infringing use. According to section 10(1) GPA, the knowledge and intention must be "obvious from the circumstances." In contrast to German law, Article 26 UPCA uses a different terminology. It reads, "the third party should have known that those means are suitable and intended for putting the invention into effect." The terminology "should have known" commonly refers to the concept of negligence corresponding to a disregard of care objectively required in business life. As the case law of the UPC develops, it should become clear whether the German provision and Article 26 UPCA will be applied harmoniously. The UPC will likely base the existence of "should-have-known" on the availability of objective facts taken from the circumstances, consistent with the German provision.

The more it is clear that the supplied means could be used for an infringement, the less problematic it is for the patentee to prove the existence of that knowledge on the side of the contributory infringer and the offeree/acquirer. Of course, if the supplied means can only be used in an infringing way and there are no noninfringing uses, that knowledge can be assumed.[137] The assessment is more complex if the concerned means can be used in an infringing and a noninfringing manner. The situation becomes even more complicated if the delivered means must first proactively be manipulated or adapted to render it suitable for a patent infringement. In such a situation, concrete evidence showing that the acquirer is indeed using the supplied means in an infringing manner must be established.[138] Typically, recommendations or instructions contained

136. Federal Supreme Court, May 4, 2004, X ZR 48/03, GRUR 2004, 758, "Flügelradzähler."
137. Federal Supreme Court, X ZR 173/02, GRUR 2007, 679, "Haubenstretchautomat."
138. *Ibid.*

in manuals, or the product literature of the accused contributory infringer represent useful sources for such evidence.

[b] *Offer and Delivery of a Means in Germany*

The meaning of the terms "offer" and "supply" as stated above, likewise apply under section 9 of the GPA.[139] Both terms are broadly construed. A legally binding offer is not mandatory (as opposed to the law in the US, which is more restrictive in requiring a formal offer). Also, it is not required that the offer lead to any result or that the offered product be delivered.[140] "Supply" means any physical transfer of the means.[141]

Infringement may be satisfied if the acquirer supplied by the contributory infringer does not himself intend to complete the direct patent infringement, but supplies the means to a third party, who intends to use it in a patent-infringing manner.[142] That is, infringement may be established as long as there is any entity in the supply chain that finally possesses the intention to use the acquired means in an infringing manner, regardless if the contributory infringer himself does not supply the goods to that entity directly.[143]

Section 10 of the GPA, which proscribes the supply and offers to supply of a means, does not limit the production and possession of such means. The same applies to Article 26 UPCA. Accordingly, both provisions do not confer any rights to prohibit the manufacture of the means, even though it may be known from circumstances that the means is offered and delivered in an infringing manner.

According to recent case law, it is not necessary for the means to be a physical object. A limitation to physical objects is not justified. The means could be nonphysical, such as a software.[144] In principle, the means must be suitable for use in a directly infringing manner at the time of the offer or delivery.[145]

[c] *Quality of the "Means"*

To be actionable under the concept of contributory infringement, a "means" must have a particular quality. That is, it must "*relate to an essential element of the invention.*" The case law interprets this provision broadly. Generally, this requirement can be satisfied if the means is capable of interacting with an element which contributes to the realization of the protected invention.[146] In other words, the offered or supplied means must be capable of interacting functionally with one or more features of the patent

139. Cf. §12.05.
140. Federal Supreme Court, GRUR 2003, 1031, "Kupplung für optische Geräte."
141. Cf. §12.05.
142. Appeal Court Karlsruhe, GRUR 2014, 59—MP2 devices.
143. *Ibid.*
144. District Court Munich Decision dated 05.12.2019—7 O 5336/18; Appeal Court Düsseldorf, InstGE 1, 26, 32—Cam. Carpet.
145. Supreme Court, GRUR 2013, 713, Fräsverfahren.
146. Federal Supreme Court, X ZR 48/03, 04.05.2004—Flügelradzähler; Federal Supreme Court GRUR 2007, 769—Pipettensystem.

claim to implement the protected invention. A means is essential whenever it is an integral part of the claim, i.e., the means realizes one or part of the claim features, whereby it does not matter that they belong to the preamble of the characterizing part of the claim. It is therefore not necessary that the means is individualized with regard to the effects of the invention.[147] It is thus not necessary that the interaction relates to the "core" of the invention. But it should at least represent a "(little) cog in the wheel"[148] to be considered as a "means relating to an essential element of the invention." This is, for instance, the case if the use of the means is causal for realizing a step of the method set forth in the patent claim.[149]

Example: The patent protects a decoding method, while the alleged infringer offers a CD with encoded data. There is an essential connection between the encoded data and the protected decoding method: The data must be encoded in a certain way in order to be decoded by the decoding method. However, the encoded data are only processed by the method. Even though the encoded data represent an essential object for the video signal obtained through the decoding method, the encoded data themselves are subject of the method, but do not contribute to the implementation of the claimed method. The connection between encoded data and decoding is thus not sufficient for a contributory infringement according to §10 Patent Act.[150]

Likewise, a means that is subordinated to the technical teaching of the invention could be insufficient for a contributory infringement. For instance, means that only create preconditions for implementing the protected method may not suffice to fulfill the requirement of the provision.[151] This is the view of the German Federal Supreme Court.[152]

[d] Objective Suitability for Direct Use

In order to be the target of a contributory infringement claim, the offered or supplied means must be objectively suitable for directly infringing the patent. The availability of noninfringing uses does not necessarily disqualify a claim for contributory infringement. However, the possibility of noninfringing uses may influence the legal consequences following from the contributory infringement.

A patent owner can establish a case for contributory infringement by relying on the acts of third parties in order to substantiate that the accused means is suitable for use in the implementation of a patented process. Accordingly, a claim for contributory infringement can succeed if evidence of actions of third parties is relied on to satisfy claim steps that are not met by the accused means itself.[153]

147. BGH GRUR 2007, 769—Pipet system.
148. Federal Supreme Court, Decision of Feb. 3, 2015, GRUR 2015, 467, "Audiosignalkodierung."
149. *Ibid.*
150. Federal Supreme Court, decision dated 21.08.2012, X ZR 33/10 "MPEG-2-Videosignalcodierung."
151. Federal Supreme Court, Feb. 3, 2015, GRUR 2015, 467, "Audiosignalkodierung."
152. Federal Supreme Court, May 4, 2004, X ZR 48/03, GRUR 2004, 758, "Flügelradzähler"; Federal Supreme Court, Decision of Feb. 3, 2015, GRUR 2015, 467, "Audiosignalkodierung."
153. Federal Supreme Court, GRUR 2007, 773—Pipe welding process.

Example: A patented process is divided into three steps. The first step requires that data be encoded. The second step requires that data be transmitted, and the third step relates to the decoding of the received encoded data. Someone who offers or supplies a device (a decoder) with which the encoded data may be decoded can be a contributory infringer, even though the acquirer of the decoder only decodes the data (process step (3)). He thus does not carry out the first two process steps. The indirect infringer makes use of the circumstance that the first two steps are necessarily carried out by third parties which may thus be imputed to him.[154]

[e] Unauthorized Offeree/Acquirer and Lack of Consent

The doctrine of patent exhaustion may exonerate a supplier of a means if a downstream acquirer of the means might be shielded by the exhaustion doctrine. The doctrine of exhaustion is relevant in practice when, for example, a means is offered or supplied which is to be used for repairing or maintaining an apparatus for which exhaustion has previously occurred, for example, because it was acquired from the patent proprietor. Exhaustion of patent rights depends primarily on whether the protected product was placed onto the European market by the patentee or by a person who is authorized by the patentee (such as a licensee). According to European rules, patent rights are exhausted if the authorized goods are placed on the market anywhere within the EU or the EEA.[155] Accordingly, the authorized goods may be used within the scope of an objectively intended use. Maintenance and repair of the product are possible, without the consent of the patentee, if the utility of the product is impaired or negated in whole or in part, or damaged. In principle, this also includes the replacement of a part of which the replacement is expected during the normal service life of the protected product. The patentee's authorization is not needed to replace those parts which tend to be regularly renewed, provided that the technical effects of the invention do not appear precisely in the replaced part. On the contrary, an illegal remake of the product may be found, for instance, if the service life of the product is artificially lengthened. A means which is used for such remake could be actionable. The same applies if the means is a spare part which is partly responsible for the advantages of the invention, or the invention influences the function or lifetime of the part to be replaced. This would go beyond the boundaries of an objectively intended use and would not be covered by the concept of exhaustion.[156]

[f] Knowledge of the Contributory Infringer

At the time of the offer or delivery, the contributory infringer must have knowledge of the suitability of the means and of the intended use of the offeree/acquirer. At least, this must be obvious in consideration of the overall circumstances. Because the

154. Federal Supreme Court, X ZR 69/13, Decision of Feb. 3, 2015.
155. Cf. §12.07.
156. Federal Supreme Court, May 4, 2004, X ZR 48/03, GRUR 2004, 758, "Flügelradzähler."

subjective intentions of the offeree/acquirer are usually difficult to establish and prove, section 10 GPA allows this prong to be substantiated if it is shown that the offeree's/acquirer's intention to use the means in accordance with the patent is obvious from the circumstances.[157] In this respect, experience from everyday life may be considered.[158]

[g] Intention of Use by the Offeree/Acquirer

The patentee may be able to prove contributory infringement against the seller of a means by showing that the offeree/acquirer would normally use the means for performing the claims of the patent. However, this offer of proof can be negated if the offeree/acquirer is bound to an undertaking to refrain under penalty from using the patent-in-suit.

In order to establish that the offeree/acquirer intends to use the means in an infringing manner, it is not necessary to establish contemporaneous evidence of this intent.[159] Often the offeree is not even identifiable. Accordingly, to fulfill the subjective condition, it is sufficient that, from an objective point of view, there is a sufficiently certain expectation from the viewpoint of the contributory infringer that the acquirer would use the means in a patent-infringing manner.[160] The subjective determination of the acquirer to use an offered or supplied means in a directly patent-infringing way may be obvious under the circumstances, such as if the means can be only used in a patent-infringing manner.[161] If the means can be used both in an infringing and noninfringing manner and the contributory infringer points to both possibilities in his product documentation and/or advertising material, the acquirer's intention to act in a patent-infringing manner might be assumed.[162] If, on the contrary, the instructions only teach a noninfringing use, concrete factual indications that at least a patent-infringing use of the means is possible must be shown to substantiate the intent of the acquirer to use the means in an infringing manner. To establish the intent of the acquirer to use the means in an infringing manner, a variety of sources of evidence might be relied upon, such as the intent of the supplier, the customary nature of a specific use, the orientation of the supplied company, or tacit indications of the supplier.

[h] Staple Commercial Products

According to the second subsection of the provisions, even means that are staple commercial products (nails, screws, etc.) might be suitable for contributory infringement.

157. Federal Supreme Court, GRUR 2006, 839—Ceiling heating.
158. Federal Supreme Court, GRUR 1958, 179, 182—Resin.
159. Federal Supreme Court, GRUR 2007, 679—Haubenstretchautomat.
160. Federal Supreme Court, GRUR 2006, 839—Ceiling heating.
161. Federal Supreme Court, GRUR 2005, 848—Antriebsscheibenaufzug; BGH, GRUR 2007, 679—Haubenstretchautomat.
162. Federal Supreme Court, GRUR 2007, 679—Haubenstretchautomat.

However, for these types of products, the requirements for a contributory infringement are tightened. The supply of staple commercial products would only represent a contributory infringement if the supplier deliberately induces the purchaser to commit a direct infringement. In addition, it is required that completed act of patent infringement is committed by the induced purchasers. These higher thresholds protect the supplier of objects that are generally traded. It cannot be expected that suppliers of staple commercial products monitor the intentions of their purchasers.

[i] International Context/Double-Territorial-Link

In transborder cases, the assessment of contributory infringement requires an analysis of where the "offering for sale" or the "supplying" of the means took place and whether the disputed acts fall within the scope of the provision. In that respect, a major difference exists between the German provision of section 10 GPA and Article 26 UPCA. Under section 10 GPA, the concerned contributory acts, namely "offering for sale" or "supplying," must occur on the German territory. This is one side of the so-called double-territorial-link requirement. Acts occurring outside the German territory thus remain outside section 10 GPA. The German provision is explicitly confined to acts occurring on "the territory to which this Law [German Patent Act] applies." Because the GPA only applies to the German territory, it would not be actionable under German law if the act-in-dispute occurs in a country where the corresponding European patent is also valid and in force with the same claims.

Furthermore, the other side of the so-called double-territorial-link requirement under section 10 GPA requires that the offering or supplying of the means must be performed with the intention that the invention be put into effect within German territory.[163]

The UPCA is advantageous to the patentee by expanding the scope of the territorial boundaries for satisfying the requirement of the "double-territorial-link." Article 26(1) UPCA refers to the territory of the Contracting Member States in which the patent is in force. The patent proprietor may thus prohibit acts performed "within the territory of the Contracting Member States in which that patent has effect." Also, the "double-territorial-link" requirement must necessarily be given in only one national territory. It is sufficient if the "offering for sale" or the "supplying" takes place in any Contracting Member States in which that patent has effect.

By contrast, if the assessment of contributory infringement is based on section 10 GPA, the "double-territorial-link" must be demonstrated within the German territory. Thus, both the supply of the means and the act of putting the invention into use must occur in Germany under section 10 GPA. For example, if an invention is protected by a bundle patent, which is in force in Germany and France, a competitor supplying a means in France—even if the means is intended by the acquirer to be used in an infringing manner in Germany—could, in principle, not be sued under section 10 GPA. The double-territorial-link under section 10 GPA would require that either the "offering

163. Federal Supreme Court, GRUR 2005, 845, "Abgasreinigungsvorrichtung."

for sale" or the "supplying" takes place in Germany. The limitation falls away under Article 26(1) UPCA because it is sufficient if the acts occur in "the territory of the Contracting Member States in which that patent has effect."

Despite the limited territorial application of section 10 GPA, nonetheless German courts have applied this provision broadly in transborder cases. The Federal Supreme Court[164] has ruled that a contributory patent infringement can even be committed under section 10 GPA by exporting means that relate to an essential element of a claimed invention, if such means contribute to the manufacture of an infringing product that is intended to be commercialized on the German market.[165] That ruling arose from a case in which the accused infringer manufactured wheelwork mechanisms for radio clocks. He supplied these wheelwork mechanisms from Germany to a company located in the UK, which used them to manufacture radio alarm clocks (according to the claimed invention). The foreign company subsequently imported the radio alarm clocks onto the German market. The accused company, namely the company that only manufactured the wheelwork mechanism, did not make a direct use of the patented teaching. It supplied only a component of the device, according to the claimed invention, to the foreign manufacturer. Section 10(1) Patent Act requires a "supply within the German territory," and this was critical in the *Funkuhr II* case as the supplied means was first exported to a company located in a foreign country. Nevertheless, the Federal Supreme Court ruled that it is sufficient for contributory infringement if the contributor knows or should know in consideration of the circumstances that the final product will ultimately find its way back into German territory.

Since the subjective conditions, such knowledge and negligent ignorance, on the side of the accused infringer, are in most cases not readily verifiable, German courts refer to objective criteria (objective indications) in such cases. It is recognized in German case law that a supplier located abroad who supplies a customer also located abroad with patent-infringing products can be held accountable for an act of infringement in Germany. This applies as soon as concrete evidence shows that the customer will offer the delivered goods or put them on the market in Germany.[166] The merely abstract possibility that the customer could sell the delivered goods in Germany or offer them there is thus not sufficient for a liability.[167] The fact that the customer has business relations in Germany or that he has already delivered or offered similar products in Germany would not yet establish a sufficient basis for the subjective side of a contributory infringement. Concrete indications of a further delivery to Germany are necessary to trigger the foreigner's liability. This burden of proof may be established, for example, if the supplier has become aware of a delivery onto the German Market that has actually taken place or is imminent. Depending on the circumstances of the individual case, sufficiently concrete indications may already exist on the basis of other circumstances—for example, because the delivered quantity is so large that it can

164. Federal Supreme Court, Decision of Jan. 30, 2007, X ZR 53/04, "Funkuhr II."
165. *Ibid.*
166. Federal Supreme Court, X ZR 47/19, Jun. 8, 2021—Ultraschallwandler; Federal Supreme Court, Feb. 26, 2002—X ZR 36/01, GRUR 2002, 599—Funkuhr I.
167. *Ibid.*

hardly be distributed only on markets free of patent rights, or because the purchasing behavior correlates conspicuously with a perceptible and potentially infringing activity of the customer on the German market. If such concrete indications manifest, the supplier may no longer rely on the fact that his customer will refrain from patent-infringing activities. Rather, he has reason to ask the customer about deliveries and offers to the domestic market and to point out the possibility of a patent infringement therein as a precaution. If there is no plausible answer to such an inquiry, the supplier must seriously reckon with the possibility that he is participating—even without positive knowledge—in a third-party patent infringement.[168]

[3] Legal Consequences

[a] Absence of Noninfringing Uses

Contributory patent infringement usually does not result in an unconditional prohibition of offering and delivering the means. Offer and supply of a means is not as such illegal. However, an unconditional prohibition could be conferred to the patentee if the offered or supplied means can only be used in a patent-infringing manner, i.e., if an alternative use outside the patent does not exist. The patentee carries the burden to show the absence of noninfringing alternatives in order to win an unconditional prohibition on offering and supplying the means.[169]

[b] Where Noninfringing Uses Exist

If noninfringing uses of the means exist, then less drastic legal consequences are applicable. On the one hand, the commercial use of a means outside the scope of the patent must remain unimpaired. On the other hand, a patent-infringing use by the offeree/acquirer shall be avoided with sufficient certainty.[170] Suitable measures to achieve that goal include warning notices attached to the offers and which are aimed at dissuading the offeree/acquirer from using the patented teaching without the consent of the owner of the patent. Contractual cease-and-desist agreements concluded between the supplier and the acquirer of the means may also be considered. This could be tied to the payment of a contractual penalty to the patentee in the event of a violation of the cease-and-desist agreement.[171] It depends on the individual case and circumstances to identify appropriate measures which sufficiently protect the patentee, and which do not unfairly overburden the contributory infringer in this business activities. The greater the risks are for patented use, the more drastic the imposed measure can be.

168. Federal Supreme Court, X ZR 47/19, Jun. 8, 2021—Ultraschallwandler.
169. Federal Supreme Court, GRUR 2013, 713—Fräsverfahren.
170. Federal Supreme Court, GRUR 2004, 758—Flügelradzähler; BGH, GRUR 2006, 839—Deckenheizung.
171. Federal Supreme Court, GRUR 2007, 679—Haubenstretchautomat.

[4] *Application of Article 26 UPCA by National Courts*

Also, in the future, national courts may be concerned with the question of infringement of traditional European patents (bundle patents). According to Article 83(1) UPCA, this applies even if no opt-out has been declared for that patent. On the contrary, the UPC has exclusive jurisdiction over enforcement of European patents with unitary effect. Thus, if it comes to the question of contributory infringement of a bundle patent, a national court may take the position that the entry into force of the UPCA did not change the legal situation and thus simply applies the provisions known from national law. For instance, the German courts would continue to apply section 10 GPA in conjunction with Article 64(1) EPC. Consequently, these courts would require that the "double-territorial-link" must be established for the German territory.

The question of which legal provision is applicable has not yet been decided by the courts. There are sound reasons to conclude that Article 26 UPCA represents the decisive rule for bundle patents. In fact, the bundle patent is subject to the UPCA, per Article 3c UPCA. The application of Article 26 UPCA to bundle patents does not necessarily conflict with Article 64 EPC. Accordingly, a bundle patent shall confer on its proprietor, "in each Contracting State in respect of which it is granted, the same rights as would be conferred by a national patent granted in that state." At a first glance, this provision suggests the application of those provisions applicable to German national patents, i.e., section 10 GPA. However, Article 149(a) EPC explicitly provides that nothing in the EPC shall be construed "as limiting the right of some or all of the Contracting States to conclude special agreements on any matters concerning European patent applications or European patents which under this Convention are subject to and governed by national law." The UPCA Contacting Member States were thus allowed to agree on provisions that also relate to national patent law. This has been done through the UPCA. The applicable law thus extents the scope of contributory infringement of European patents. It is not contradictory if the patent proprietor is entitled to more than a national patent would provide. Article 64 EPC does not prohibit that rights reaching beyond "the rights as would be conferred by a national patent granted in that state" be added to the set of rights on which the patent proprietor may base his claims. Accordingly, contributory infringement may be premised on actions across a bigger territory based on Article 26 UPCA. This has the positive effect that "offering for sale" or "supplying" the means and its intended use are not required to occur within the boundaries of the same country, as it is required under the national rule Article 64(1) EPC, section 10 GPA. It is thus sufficient if the double-territorial-link is satisfied within the group of States where the UP, or European patent, has effect. Thus, in the context of contributory infringement, the UPCA can provide a patent owner broader protections than would otherwise be available from a bundle of separate national patents.

According to the contrary view, during the transitional period national courts shall simply apply national law rather than the UPCA. This view refers to a risk of inconsistent application of the UPCA in the individual Contracting States. The supporters of this view assert that it was not the intention of the Contracting States to pose such risk. Also, reference is made to Recital 5 of the UPCA which mentions that the

Contracting States were guided by the desire to strengthen legal certainty through the establishment of a single patent court. However, this objective, as mentioned in the recital, does not depend on the law which the national courts have to enforce. This view is thus not convincing.[172]

[5] Inducement

A person who actively and intentionally induces or aids a third party to willfully commit an infringement of a patent is also liable. This liability relies on the general rules of active and intentional inducement or aid (*see* sections 26 and 27 German Criminal Code in conjunction with section 830 of the German Civil Code), which could be applicable in parallel to section 10 GPA or Article 26 UPC. However, it would require that both the inducer and the induced party act willfully. Negligence is not sufficient.[173] In addition, the liability for inducement also requires that a direct infringement has effectively been committed by the third party.[174] For instance, a person who instructs a third party on how to use a staple commercial product or any other component to exercise the patented invention may be liable as an active inducer. In contrast hereto, several infringers who jointly and consciously act together in view of a patent infringement (such as distributor, producer or importer) are individually liable as direct infringers (*Nebentäter*). They must not necessarily act with intent. Negligence would be sufficient.

§12.06 LIMITATIONS OF THE EFFECTS OF A PATENT

[A] Privileged Acts

Categories of uses exempt from infringement are defined by Article 27 UPCA. The limitations provided by that provision shall balance out, on the one hand, the right holder's interests in an uncommitted commercial exploitation of the right conferred by the patent, and, on the contrary, the interest of the public in getting access to the patented teaching. In other words, there are particular uses of the claimed teaching which are privileged such as the **private and noncommercial use** made by a third party.[175] This use of a patented technology for that purpose would not represent an infringement of the patent.

172. *Note*: This question is undecided and presently in dispute: Cf. Michael Nieder, GRUR 2015, 1178 ff. and Horst Vissel, GRUR 2015, 619; Gesetzentwurf der Bundesregierung "Entwurf eines Gesetzes zur Anpassung patentrechtlicher Vorschriften auf Grund der europäischen Patentreform," Explanations.
173. Busse, Patentgesetz, s. 11, No. 30.
174. *Ibid.*
175. Article 27(a) UPCA.

[1] Experimental Privileges

Experimental privileges[176] play an important role in practice: Article 27(b) UPCA requires that the experimental use relates "to the subject matter" of the patented teaching. Thus, not any experimental use falls under Article 27(b) UPCA. It is required that the experimental use be aimed at obtaining (more) data on the patented teaching, such as any research which is interested in data obtainable through exploring the effects of a patented substance and/or new possibilities of application of a substance or process (Research on the Subject Matter):[177]

(a) **Research on the Subject Matter:** Acts are exempt from patent liability if the research is **directed to** the patented subject matter *as such*. The latter can directly be taken from the provision exempting (only) acts done "for experimental purposes relating to the subject matter of the patented invention." Accordingly, a privileged experiment is a planned measure for obtaining information about the subject matter of the patented invention.[178] The requirements of a research exemption are fulfilled if an experiment is directed to resolving questions and/or obtaining further information about the subject matter of the patented invention. Accordingly, experiments relating to the constitution of a patented substance are not critical. This includes the investigation of its composition, reproducibility, technical usability, and technical effects. Also allowed are experiments testing the functionality of the patented invention or in view of verifying data contained in the patent description. Thus, the patented subject matter could be used for finding new, previously unknown applications of the teaching. Experiments in view of further developing or optimizing the claimed teaching including experiments aimed at identifying non-infringing alternatives seem to be exempted under the Supreme Court's case law.[179] This seems to be the prevailing view of the commentators. Even though older decisions of lower courts (rendered prior to the landmark decisions *Klinische Versuche I and II* apply a narrower view,[180] it is to be expected that the standards outlined in this paragraph will be applied by the courts in future cases. Also, experiments for obtaining information about properties and effects of a patented substance within known (pharmaceutical) indications is allowed. On the contrary, activities done for the only purpose of generating revenues or clarifying commercial factors of the protected teaching, such as market needs, price acceptability and marketing options, would not fall in the scope of the exemption.

(b) **Objectives of the research**: Nevertheless, as long as the experiments are conducted to gain knowledge about the patented invention, (secondary)

176. Article 27(b) UPCA.
177. Federal Supreme Court, NJW 1997, 3092 ff., Klinische Versuche II.
178. BGH, GRUR 1996, 109, Klinische Versuche I.
179. Benkard; Patentgesetz, s. 11 Rn. 7 with further references.
180. DC Düsseldorf GRUR Int. 86, 807; DC Berlin GRUR 85, 375.

aim(s) or objectives of the experiment/research are not harmful for the application of the exemption. That is, the experiments must not necessarily be motivated by scientific research interests. They can also be driven by commercial interests.[181] The research exemption may, thus, even apply in cases in which the experimental acts are primarily directed to realizing commercial purposes and in which further technical and/or scientific knowledge is acquired and obtained as a side effect only.[182] Thus, it does not matter where the research is carried out; the researcher could be a private company, industrial entity or a public entity, such as a university.[183]

(c) **Scale:** The provision does not contain limits as to the extent and quantity of the experiment. The case law, in particular under the decision *Clinical Trials II*,[184] is however intended to avoid abuses of the research exemption. Experiments performed on a large-scale reaching beyond the actual experimental purpose of gaining information about the claimed teaching may not be considered permissible acts under section 11 No. 2 GPA. For instance, patent-protected products, such as a patented substance of formulation should only be produced in a quantity and used to an extent which is necessary to achieve the purpose of the envisaged research. Accordingly, stockpiling of patent-protected products which are not necessary for conducting experiments may be actionable. For instance, patent-protected products could have been produced for the experiment—which is in principle is allowed because otherwise the experiment could not be conducted—but it turns out that the products were generated in a quantity far in excess of what was needed for the experiment. Even if the purpose of the stockpiling is directed to a future marketing after the expiry of patent protection, a patentee could argue that the previous production was partly unjustified, particularly as to the surplus quantity generated. On the contrary, it could be argued that a stockpiling of the surplus is only infringing if it is purposeful under section 9 GPA, which might not be established because the stocked products are not supposed to be used in an infringing manner but rather are supposed to be sold after the expiration of the patent. However, this special situation belongs to a grey area without settled case law. The main reason for the missing case law is likely because the stockpiling is typically not visible to the outside world. That is, the patentee would have not sufficient factual information to make a claim against the possessor of the stockpiled products. Furthermore, the ruling in *Clinical Trials II*[185] also indicates that abuses are actionable when the underlying actions are aimed at disturbing the patent holders commercialization efforts as a means for obtaining a competitive advantage. In practice, however, such cases are difficult to prove.

181. BGH Mitt. 1997, 253, Klinische Versuche II.
182. Cf. Kühnen, Handbuch der Patenverletzung, 10th ed. 2018; p. 721, s. 33 IV.
183. BGH, GRUR 1996, 109, Klinische Versuche I; Kraßer, s. 787; Busse, Patentgesetz, 7. Auflage, s. 11 Rn. 13.
184. BGH Mitt. 1997, 253, Klinische Versuche II.
185. *Ibid.*

(d) **Research Tools:** Research tools themselves will not be exempt from infringement, particularly if the tools are not aimed at the patented subject matter itself. For example, protected laboratory equipment might be used for an experiment. However, as long as the research tool is only an aid for conducting the experiment, its use would not be exempted by section 11 No. 2 GPA. As long as the experiment is not aimed at gaining knowledge about the patented aid, the research exemption would not apply.

(e) **Outsourcing:** A prevailing view in the literature[186] is that, in principle, outsourcing of research to contractors, such as specialized laboratories, might be exempted as long as the work remains focused on the subject matter of the patent. Therefore, it is advisable to specifically define the purpose and limits of the contractual work in agreements with such contractors.[187] The research exemption is purpose-driven and may thus only extend to contractors knowing that their work is performed in the context of privileged research. The more it is possible to show that both, i.e., the outsourcing entity and the contractor, pursue valuable interests in gaining information on the envisaged activities, the stronger the case for an exemption is. The underlying (written) contract between both entities may thus present evidence/arguments in favor of the exemption. It is recommended to involve an IP lawyer in drafting such contract in order to maximize the chances of sustaining a claim to an exemption from infringement.

(f) **Supply:** Producing and supplying patented means or substances for use in research may be outside the research exemption.[188] The wording of section 11 No. 2 GPA suggests that acts done for experimental purposes are privileged as long as they are carried out for performing the experiment. Nevertheless, production, offer and sale of patented means/substances by a supplier are not *as such* acts done for experimental purposes even if the acquirer (researcher) exclusively uses the patented means/substances for a privileged research. However, there are serious voices in the literature and lower courts[189] saying, that—under certain limited conditions—the activities by the supplier of patented means/substances should also be sheltered by the research exemption. In fact, it would be unfair if the privileged acts must necessarily be concentrated on one person or entity. For instance, it could be that that party interested in privileged research is for economical or other reasons not in the position to prepare/produce the necessary test substance/means. Such party should also be enabled to benefit from the privilege. Thus various authorities including the Appeal Court Düsseldorf[190] suggests construing the contractual relationship between supplier and the researching entity in a particular way to guarantee that the supplied means or substances be used only for purposes

186. Cf. Kühnen, Handbuch der Patenverletzung, 10th ed. 2018, p. 721, with further references; Benkard; Patentgesetz, s. 11 Rn. 8 with further references.
187. Appeal Court Düsseldorf, GRUR-RR 2014, 100.
188. Cf. Kühnen, Handbuch der Patenverletzung, 10th ed. 2018; p. 721, with further references.
189. *Ibid.*; Appeal Court Düsseldorf, GRUR-RR 2014, 100.
190. Appeal Court Düsseldorf, GRUR-RR 2014, 100.

that fall within the exemption. The contract might explicitly point to the contemplated experiments and provide a provision according to which the supplied means/substances must be exclusively used as objects of the experiment. Aided by contract language limiting the use of the supplied means/substances to privileged experiments only, the supplier can strengthen its case that the production and distribution of the means/substances should be privileged. Nevertheless, it is likely not permitted to advertise and offer patent-protected test substances to an indefinite group of customers by merely indicating in the advertisement or offer "for experimental purposes."[191] In one case, the District Court Düsseldorf applied a narrower view[192] ruling that suppliers of test substances are only privileged if they are "co-participants of the research," requiring that the supplier have an individualized interest in (also) gaining further knowledge regarding the patent-protected substance. In sum, it is likely in the light of the literature and the indicated Appeal Court decision that German courts would apply the broader view as outlined above. Because the underlying contract between both supplier and research may provide evidence/arguments concerning application of the exemption, it is recommended to involve an IP lawyer when it comes to the drafting of such contract.

[2] Other Privileges

Certain acts required for obtaining a drug approval are not necessarily covered by Article 27(b) UPCA because these acts would not "relate to" the protected teaching as such. However, acts in connection with drug approvals could be exempted according to Article 27(d) UPCA (so-called Bolar exemption). Accordingly, acts, pursuant to Article 13(6) of Directive 2001/82/EC or Article 10(6) of Directive 2001/83/EC, in respect of any patent covering the product within the meaning of either of those Directives are exempted. This includes not only experiments but also studies, trials and their practical requirements necessary for obtaining the approval of human and veterinary medical products for the marketing of them within the EU or in a Member State of the EU or abroad. In contrast to Article 27(b) UPCA, this exemption is not limited to research on the subject matter of a protected product or process.

It has to be noted that the parallel German provision seems to be broader. The German provision is not limited to acts in connection with generic medical products. It also covers trial activities with patented drugs for the purpose of obtaining regulatory approval of a drug, generic or otherwise. So far there are no decisions as to whether and to what extent differences exist between the German provision and the UPCA.

---

191. Cf. Chrocziel, Die Benutzung patentierter Erfindungen zu Versuchs- und Forschungszwecken, MIP-Schriftenreihe Bd. 67, Koln, 1986, 195; Straus, GRUR 1993, 308, 311; Chrocziel/Hufnagel, Versuchsprivileg und Unterstützungshandlungen: Abgrenzungsfragen im, "Bermuda-Dreieck" der Doppelparagraphen 9, 10, 11 Nr. 2/2b GPA, Festschrift Mes, 2009, pp. 59 et seq.
192. DC Düsseldorf, Decision date Jul. 16, 2012, 4a O 282/10.

There are sound reasons to conclude that Article 27 UPCA needs to be applied not only to European patents with unitary effect but also to the traditional bundle patent. The same discussion can be applied in respect to Article 26 UPCA as to the question of contributory infringement.[193] In fact, the bundle patent is subject to the UPCA as provided in Article 3c UPCA. As the UPCA Contacting Member States did agree on new provisions through the UPCA, there are sound reasons that Article 27 UPCA represents the decisive rule when it comes to question of whether particular acts are privileged (*see* Table 12.5).

Table 12.5 Overview: Experimental Use/Bolar

	Admissible	*Inadmissible*
Article 27(b)	- Testing whether the substance is eligible to cure/relieve other illnesses.[1] - Testing options for developments or alternatives to the patented substance. - Testing in case of uncertainties of effects or/and tolerability of a substance even if it is done in view of obtaining an authorization for a pharmaceutical composition.[2]	Tests which are not aimed at gaining knowledge about the patented invention or are without relevance for the teaching of the patented invention.
Article 27(d)	- All uses of the patented teaching aimed at enabling/preparing studies/trials in view to the application, such as own manufacture and importation of the patented ingredient, but there must be a direct relationship between study/tests and use of the patent.	- Use of patented research tools, except the tools are exclusively used for the research needed for the drug approval.[3]

1. Federal Supreme Court, X ZR 99/92.
2. Federal Supreme Court, X ZR 68/94.
3. Disputed.

Other Privileges: Article 27 UPCA provides for other exemptions. They relate to special situations, such as the plant research privilege,[194] or those related to the extemporaneous preparation of medicines,[195] use on board of vessels,[196] in the construction or operation of aircraft or land vehicles, etc. However, these exemptions play only a limited role in the patent literature and case law.

193. Cf. above §12.05[B].
194. Article 27(c) UPCA.
195. Article 27(e) UPCA.
196. Article 27(f) UPCA.

[B] Right Based on Prior Use

A special defense against the assertion of patent rights is set forth in Article 28 UPCA. The provision explicitly refers to the national laws, and the parallel German national provision can be found in section 12 GPA. According to German law, such prior use right is conferred to a person who had possession of the invention as of the priority date already commenced using it. The use must be performed in good faith and for business purposes. Bona fide preparations for such use prior to the filing date or priority date might be sufficient.

Such user has the right to continue to use the invention or to use the invention as planned during the preparations. The right of the prior use may only be transferred in combination with the company holding the right of prior use. No right based on prior use arises from the mere knowledge or documentation of the invention. A prior user may thus invoke a right based on prior use acquired in a Contracting Member State. It must be established according to the national rules of and for each Contracting Member State.

Article 28 UPCA does not necessarily provide a remedy for all States where the European patent-in-question is in force. Rather the acquisition of such right(s) follows from the national laws of the Contracting Member State. These laws are not completely harmonized. Usually, a qualified possession of the claimed technology must be shown. This requires not only possession, in terms of availability of the claimed teaching on the side of the prior user, but also that he has knowledge of it and had already begun to commercially use the invention, or at least has made serious arrangements for doing so. In a few countries, such as France,[197] an established possession is sufficient. Also, the scope of the prior use might be different from one Contracting Member State to another. In some Contracting Member States, the use of the claimed teaching is limited to the needs of the user's own business and limited in scope to acts that were already committed or intended at the priority date of the patent.[198] In particular, the user might not be able to exploit benefits of the patent-in-question that are outside of what the user effectively recognized as of the priority date. Nevertheless, the benefits of this protection cover not only the prior user but also downstream users,[199] such as customers who have bought a product covered by the prior use.

§12.07 EXHAUSTION

[A] Putting onto the EU/EEA Market

Exhaustion of patent rights depends primarily on whether the protected product was placed onto the European market by the patentee or by a person who is authorized by

197. Article L 613-7 (Code de la Propriété Intellectuelle).
198. Federal Supreme Court, X ZR 32/99, GRUR 2002, 231, "Biegevorrichtung."
199. Federal Supreme Court, Decision of Jun. 12, 2012, X ZR 131/09, "Desmopressin"; Appeal Court Düsseldorf, InstGE 11, 198, "Desmopressin."

the patentee (such as a licensee). According to European rules, patent rights are exhausted if this occurs anywhere within the EU or the EEA.[200]

Article 6 of the UP Regulation contains an exhaustion provision for European patents with unitary effect. It corresponds to the parallel provision of Article 29 UPCA, which covers ordinary European patents and those with unitary effect. The exhaustion provisions establish a Union-wide exhaustion resulting in a limitation of the rights inherent to a patent.

In the event that the patented object is put into circulation by the patent holder or by a third party with his consent in the EU or the EEA, the consequence of exhaustion follows also from Article 34 of the TFEU[201] (formerly Article 28 EC Treaty). According to this provision, all quantitative restrictions on imports and all measures having equivalent effect are prohibited between Member States of EU. The right holder acquires, in return for his inventive activity, the exclusive right to manufacture and put into circulation commercial products, hence the right to exploit the invention either himself or by means of granting licenses to third parties. But if the product, according to the invention, is put into circulation by the holder himself, or with his consent, he loses this right. The right holder must accept the consequences of this choice as far as concerns trade within the Common Market. Indeed, if the product was first sold outside Europe, there may be an exhaustion of the patent rights in the particular market (e.g., Canada, China, etc.). Exhaustion of patent rights in a country outside the EU/EEA does not have any effect on European patent rights, so long as the patentee did not intend via agreement for ultimate delivery into the EU/EEA. The burden of proof for the existence of such an agreement would be on the defendant.[202]

[B] Assertion of a Patent with Device Claim

As soon as the concerned product is deliberately put onto the EU/EEA market by the patentee, the patent product claims are exhausted as to that product.[203] Thus, the exhaustion has a Europe-wide effect, which is also a consequence of the EU/EEA public law aimed at avoiding trade barriers. Thus, the buyer of the product is entitled not only to use but also to sell the product. A device or product claim cannot be asserted against a third party buying the product. The patentee has received the benefits of his invention through the sale of the product. He has used up the patent rights with respect to the specific item covered by the patent and can no longer control its subsequent use in commerce.

200. Federal Supreme Court, Decision of Dec. 14, 1999, X ZR 61/98, GRUR 2000, 299, "Karate."
201. Article 34 TFEU reads "Quantitative restrictions on imports and all measures having equivalent effect shall be prohibited between Member States."
202. Federal Supreme Court, Dec. 14, 1999, X ZR 61/98, GRUR 2000, 299 "Karate."
203. Federal Supreme Court, X ZR 72/94, GRUR 1997, 116, "Prospekthalter" and Federal Supreme Court, X ZR 137/99, GRUR 2001, 223, "Bodenwaschanlage."

[C] Assertion of a Patent with a Method Claim

According to the German Supreme Court,[204] the situation is different with respect to method claims. A method or process can be used, but literally, it cannot be put on the market. Products produced through the protected method can be put on the market. They might be subject to exhaustion. However, if an apparatus, which is necessary for the implementation of a method/procedure, is put onto the market with the agreement of the patentee, the concept of exhaustion is not directly applicable. Method patents can implicitly or explicitly be licensed and the patentee is free to determine the scope of the use of the apparatus in the agreement with the buyer.[205] In case of method patents, the extent to which the buyer of the apparatus is entitled to implement the method must be determined by the contractual relationship between the patentee and the buyer. As there is no exhaustion of rights, the contractual liberty is not limited by antitrust law, and the parties are free to shape this relationship. If there is no written agreement, it would be necessary to establish the intention of the parties. In order to identify the implicit expression of intention, they usually refer to the interests of the parties at the specific moment of agreement and the related specific factual circumstances. Typically, the implicit arrangement between right holder and the buyer of the apparatus contains the consent that the protected method can be used with the apparatus in a more or less unrestricted manner.[206]

[D] Assertion of a Patent Containing Apparatus and Method Claims

According to a general opinion in the German case law,[207] the sale of an apparatus that is protected by a method claim and by an apparatus claim of the same patent leads to the exhaustion of the patent rights also with respect to the method claim (as opposed to patents having only method claims). Accordingly, the third party could use the method without the permission of the patentee. In this situation, the patentee is considered to have obtained the benefits from the invention through his apparatus claim. This is not the case if only the method claim is used, but not the apparatus claim.

The existing case law deals mainly with situations where the apparatus claim is composed of features analogous to the method claims (i.e., the method claim describes the only use of the apparatus). This case law does not, however, give a clear answer as to cases where the method claim and the apparatus claim are focused on technically different aspects or teachings. There are good reasons to believe that the method claim is not exhausted in such a situation.

---

204. Federal Supreme Court, X ZR 137/99, GRUR 2001, 2003, "Bodenwaschanlage"; cf. Commentary: Benkard/Scharen, s. 9 GPA, No. 16 ff.
205. For instance, District Court Düsseldorf, 4 O 175/98.
206. Federal Supreme Court, X ZR 113/04, Decision of Feb. 27, 2007, "Rohrschweißverfahren" and Decision of Sep. 24, 1979, KZR 14/78, "Fullplastverfahren."
207. Federal Supreme Court, X ZB 21/94, GRUR 1998, 130, "Handhabungsgerät"; District Court Düsseldorf, Mitt. 1999, 179, "Levitationsmaschine."

[E] Limits to the Exhaustion of Rights (Maintenance, Refurbishment and Rebuilding)

There are limits to the exhaustion doctrine.[208] It is recognized that the buyer of a patented apparatus is entitled to a normal use of the patent exhausted apparatus. This is, he may resell the apparatus without further permission of the patentee. A normal use also includes the repairing and maintenance of the apparatus occurring during normal lifetime of the product.[209] On the contrary, a "rebuilding" of the apparatus may represent patent infringement. Such illicit rebuilding may be established where spare parts for patent exhausted products are reassembled to create a (new) device.[210] The concept of exhaustion does not extend to such a newly manufactured device even though only spare parts of patent exhausted products are used.

There are cases where it is difficult to determine whether there has been an authorized repairing versus an illicit rebuilding of the apparatus. To assess whether the exchange of a part of a patent exhausted apparatus represents an infringement, the Federal Supreme Court balances the patentee's interests in the economical exploitation of the invention against the interests of the buyer in an unhindered use of the acquired apparatus.[211] A criterion for the distinction between illicit and authorized activities is the period of normal deterioration to be expected during the lifetime of the concerned product. The accused activities shall not artificially prolong the lifetime of the product.[212] According to the Federal Supreme Court, the decisive question is to what extent the replaced spare part interferes with the technical effects of the claimed invention.[213] For instance, an illicit rebuilding of a patent-protected apparatus may be established if the advantage(s) of the claimed invention is/are contained in the replacement spare part or, at least, it is partly responsible for the advantages sought be the claimed invention.

In a recent decision, the Federal Supreme Court Germany applied a two steps analysis:[214] In a first step, it should be assessed whether the replacement of the spare part forms part of the normal use of the product. If no, the rebuilding is not allowed. If this question is answered in the affirmative, then it must be determined in a second step whether the technical effects of the invention are realized in the replacement means. If that is not the case, then the patent is not infringed. Accordingly, for an infringement it is necessary that the replacement means are more than a mere object to the invention. This is, they need to take part in realizing the invention.

208. Federal Supreme Court, X ZR 48/03, GRUR 2004, 758 and IIC 2005, 963 (in English) "Flügelradzähler."
209. Federal Supreme Court, GRUR 2006, 837, "Laufkranz."
210. Federal Supreme Court, GRUR 1973, 518, "Spielautomat II."
211. Federal Supreme Court, GRUR 2004, 758, "Flügelradzähler."
212. Federal Supreme Court, GRUR 1959, 232, "Förderrinne."
213. *Ibid.*; Federal Supreme Court, GRUR 2006, 837, "Laufkranz"; Federal Supreme Court, GRUR 2007, 769, "Pipettensystem."
214. Federal Supreme Court, GRUR 2018, 170, "Trommeleinheit."

CHAPTER 13
Discovery and Evidence Taking

§13.01 INTRODUCTION

Although in general, US-style pretrial discovery proceedings are unknown in patent infringement proceedings at the UPC or in German courts, some discovery is available. The comparatively limited form of discovery in Europe usually challenges patentees, prior to commencing a court action, to privately investigate and gather the relevant facts and evidence from openly available sources, sometimes by means of private investigators or through reverse engineering of the accused embodiment. However, discovery may be obtained through judicial measures if independent fact-finding is not successful. That is, the UPC and in German courts do provide avenues of discovery that may allow the patentee to have access to evidence that is otherwise inaccessible. Judicial measures can be applied *prior* to the filing of a lawsuit, as well as during main proceedings.[1] Most of the time, it is recommended to initiate discovery measures, preferably through swift interim measures, prior to filing the main proceedings. This is true for both the UPC and German courts. Such interim measures minimize the risk that the evidence might be altered; in addition, obtaining evidence before the main proceedings may allow the right holder to structure the litigation more properly and to increase the chances of success. These advantages can usually not be achieved if discovery measures are combined with main proceedings. Discovery proceedings may help in situations in which the patent infringement is still uncertain, and in which compulsory process may resolve the questions underlying infringement Importantly, these questions can be resolved prior to filing the main enforcement action. Therefore, in most cases a stepwise approach is recommended, with the discovery procedure carried out before filing the main proceedings.

1. Appeal Court of Düsseldorf, Decision of Nov. 8, 2012, 2 U 108/10, "Fluidflusssimulation II."

The remainder of this chapter will explain the types of discovery available at the UPC and in German patent litigation, their rationale, historical development, and procedural mechanics.

In many cases, the facts relevant to the infringement proceedings are openly accessible to the patentee. For instance, the contested product may be freely available on the market and can be dismantled, reverse engineered and then analyzed. In many cases, extrajudicial investigations carried out by the patentee on his own initiative are sufficient and thus no discovery procedure is necessary. The patentee may use various means at his disposal to conduct this investigation and analysis. For example, he could hire a private investigator or a private expert. The private investigator could help to identify further factual material concerning the contested embodiment. A private expert might be retained to carry out testing, or analyze the properties of the accused product, such as the composition of a chemical substance.

Information on the contested method and documents that were discovered through proceedings before courts of other jurisdictions could also be used as evidence. US discovery may form an important source of evidence, unless applicable protective orders limit such use.[2] If the accused embodiments are not available on the territory covered by the court's jurisdiction, a diligent counsel needs to include in his assessment the possibility of applying legal tools available in foreign countries. With respect to the US, an important tool is a request under 28 U.S.C. section 1782 which allows the conduct of discovery (testimony or document production) through a US federal district court for use in a foreign court such as the UPC or a German court. Section 1782 requests may be initiated either by a letter rogatory issued by the court or directly by the party to the proceedings, i.e., without any letter rogatory, addressed to the US district court. Furthermore, customs actions may also be used to gather information relevant for later patent infringement proceedings. If infringing products are detected and detained by customs, the right holder is usually informed about the origin of the product and their distribution channels, and he may take samples of the shipment to analyze, test and prove the infringing quality of the products.[3]

§13.02 BURDEN OF PROOF

The burden of proof to substantiate factual matters "shall be on the party relying on those facts" as provided in Article 54 UPCA, and likewise in German proceedings. The plaintiff in infringement proceedings thus typically bears the burden of proof *inter alia,* to establish the existence and the infringement of the patent. Consequently, he needs also to provide the facts from which the existence and the infringement of the patent can be deduced. On the contrary, the defendant needs to provide the facts on which his

2. It needs to be taken into account that a German court is not bound by a protective order issued by a US court. The protective order is addressed to the parties of the US proceedings, for which reason it is likely that a German court would disregard US protective orders, in case a party introduces material from US proceedings into German proceedings and thus violates that order.
3. *See* Ch. 16, "Customs Actions."

defenses are based. For instance, he needs to show the factual circumstances from which a right of a prior use according of Article 28 UPCA can be taken.

There are important exceptions of the basic rule of burden of proof. If the subject matter of a patent is a process for obtaining a new product, the identical product when produced without the consent of the patent proprietor shall, in the absence of proof to the contrary, be deemed to have been obtained by the patented process. This reversal of burden of proof is provided by Article 55(1) UPCA. This provision is meant to accommodate difficulties of the patentee who has no or insufficient evidence about facts occurring in the sphere of the accused infringer. In fact, the patentee may have information on the product itself but no insight into the production process from which the product results.

This provision corresponds to section 139(3) of the GPA. According to both provisions, the owner of the process patent may rely on the reversal of burden of proof if the product to be produced is a new product. "New" means the product must be distinguishable at least with respect to one particularity from products known at the priority date.[4] The reversal of proof would thus not apply if products with the same particularities were already known at the priority date. In addition, the reversal of burden of proof requires that the protected process generates "identical" products. According to the German case law, this does not require a complete identity between the product generated by the protected process and the accused product. Typical production related differences are usually not critical.

Article 55(2) UPCA, which does not find an explicit analogous provision in the German law, further eases the requirements of the reversal of proof. Accordingly, only a substantial likelihood is sufficient to prove that the identical product was made by the patented process and the patent proprietor has been unable, despite reasonable efforts, to determine the process actually used for such identical product. In contrast to Article 55(1) UPCA, this provision does not even require that the concerned product is a "new product."

The concept of burden of proof goes hand in hand with a duty of presentation. The claimant must sufficiently provide facts in support of the allegation that are the basis of the desired legal consequences.[5] This duty arises from an obligation under procedural law to provide facts and circumstances fully, completely, and truthfully. German courts have developed a system of mutual obligations to substantiate facts corresponding to the information the parties may reasonably provide. The obligation to substantiate facts may depend on the other parties' pleading. For instance, it would not be permissible to deny a detailed submission without providing explicit facts to the contrary. Finally, if a party does not explicitly dispute certain facts, those facts can be deemed acknowledged.

4. Appeal Court Munich, Decision of Dec. 23, 2010, 6 U 4719/08.
5. *See* below §13.04[A][1] "General Principles."

§13.03 DISCOVERY BEFORE OR AFTER FILING A COMPLAINT

[A] At the UPC

[1] Basic Considerations

Similar to a *saisie contrefaçon* available under French law, preservation proceedings can be initiated prior to any action. It allows the claimant to obtain an order permitting a bailiff to seize evidence of infringing goods. Under special conditions, it is even possible to enter premises for that purpose. Nevertheless, the UPCA sets burdensome requirements for such seizure measures. For that reason, they might be used less frequently than in France, where almost all patent infringement actions are preceded by a *saisie contrefaçon*. According to Rule 192 RoP, besides other formal indications, the application for preservation proceedings shall contain the following:

- A clear indication of the measures requested and the exact location of the evidence to be preserved:[6] Unspecified searches for information or evidence, so-called fishing expeditions, may thus be excluded by the UPC. The evidence must be particularized as to location and—at least to some extent—identifiable. Of course, if the measure shall take place in areas that are unknown to the plaintiff, such as the premises of the accused infringer, it should be sufficient to refer to the location of the concerned premises where the evidence is presumingly expected to be found. Some of the measures to which the applicant may refer are described in Rule 196 RoP. They range from preparing detailed descriptions, with or without the taking of samples, to the disclosure of digital media and data plus any passwords necessary to access them, to the physical seizure of allegedly infringing goods, even materials and implements used in the production and/or distribution of these goods and any related document. From the ratio of these provisions, it can be deduced that the court may compel the defendant to actively support the investigation and to render the concerned evidence accessible, such as the provision of necessary passwords or giving access to those parts of the premises where the object of the investigation is located.
- Reasons why the proposed measures are needed:[7] As a consequence of the principle of proportionality,[8] there must be a justification for the relief sought. Notably, there is no urgency requirement. Likewise, there is no urgency requirement in Directive 2004/48/EC.
- Facts and evidence in support of the application: Accordingly, "reasonable available evidence"[9] must be provided showing that the patent has been infringed or is about to be.[10] The provisions of the UPCA and Rules of

6. Rule 192(2)(c) RoP.
7. *Ibid.*
8. Article 42 UPCA.
9. Article 60(1) UPCA.
10. *Ibid.*, Rule 192(2)(d) RoP.

Procedure (RoP) do not provide a guideline on how clear the infringement of the patent must already be established in that request. It is thus left to the court to assess whether the requirement of Article 60(1) UPC "reasonably available evidence" is satisfied. On the one hand, a request based on mere allegations will likely be rejected by the UPC. On the other hand, applying too tight standards of showing the infringement would undermine the rationale of the provision, which is aimed at filling evidentiary gaps. Under German law, a "sufficient probability" of infringement must be at least shown to be successful with such requests. In addition, there should not be serious doubts as to the validity of the patent. Such approach is guided by the principle of proportionality which must also be ensured by the UPC.[11]

- If the order is sought prior to the commencement of main proceedings, a concise description of the action which will be started and the facts and evidence which will be relied on, must be provided.[12]
- If the order is requested as an ex parte measure, it is also required to provide a justification for not hearing the defendant in adversarial proceedings. Such reasons are usually where any delay is likely to cause irreparable harm to the applicant or where there is a demonstrable risk of evidence being destroyed or otherwise ceasing to be available.[13]

For ex parte applications, there is another issue to be considered. The UPCA provides for a "protective letter" system. According to Rule 207 RoP, potential defendants may have the opportunity to file a letter with the UPC to challenge a possible application, such as the missing validity of the underlying patent or any other grounds, justifying the rejection of the application. Under Rule 209.2(d), the court "shall in particular consider summoning parties to an oral hearing if a relevant protective letter has been filed by the defendant." While a protective brief does not guarantee that a seizure order will not be made on an ex parte basis, it lessens its chances. Rule 194(6) RoP provides that the court must inform the applicant about the protective letter who may than withdraw the application before the defendant is notified of the application.

[2] Procedural Implementation

[a] Introduction

The application shall be filed with the division where the applicant has already started infringement proceedings on the merits, or, when the application is filed prior to the filing of a lawsuit, at the division where the filing of such proceedings is intended.[14] The

11. Article 42 UPCA.
12. Rule 192(2)(e) RoP.
13. Rule 197(1) RoP.
14. Rule 192(1) RoP.

UPCA gives discretionary authority to the appropriate division as to how to proceed with the application. The division may:[15]

- inform the defendant about the application and invite him to object to it;
- summon to an early[16] oral hearing, of either both parties or only the applicant without the defendant;
- take an ex parte decision.

The applicant may not wish that the defendant be informed about the attempt to get an ex parte measure. The RoP is indulgent with the applicant in such a situation and requires the court to inform the applicant prior to informing the defendant. The applicant may then withdraw the application and request that the court shall order that the application and its contents remain confidential.[17] This mechanism renders an application less risky. It provides an opportunity to test whether an ex parte application would be granted without any involvement of the defendant.

[b] Execution of the Measure

A predominant concern during the execution of the measure to preserve evidence relates to the protection of trade secrets, personal data or other confidential information of the defendant or any third party. The rules guaranteeing a sufficient protection of the defendant or a third party must be defined by the court in the order. An important limitation is that the measures to preserve evidence may only be used in the proceedings on the merits of the case.[18] Furthermore, the RoP limits the group of people who are allowed to be present when the measures to preserve evidence are being carried out. The court's order shall specify who shall carry out the measures.[19] This person shall be a professional person or an expert, who guarantees expertise, independence and impartiality. Where appropriate and allowed under applicable national law, the person may be a bailiff, or an expert assisted by a bailiff. In no circumstances may an employee or director of the applicant be present at the execution of the measures. The person prepares and presents a written report. In addition, the applicant may be represented by a person when the measures to preserve evidence are being carried out. This is principally a legal representative, to be named in the order.[20] Nothing restricts the court from additionally imposing on the legal representative the duty to keep the results of the measure confidential vis-à-vis the applicant. They must wait until the court lifts the secrecy obligation. Under German law, the secrecy obligation under which attorneys may receive confidential information is considered to be sufficient for

15. Rule 194(1) RoP.
16. Rule 195(1) RoP: "the oral hearing shall be set as soon as possible after the date of receipt of the application."
17. Rule 194(5) RoP.
18. Rule 196(2) RoP.
19. Rule 196(4) and (5) RoP.
20. Rule 196(3)(a) RoP.

protecting the accused infringer's secrecy rights.[21] Attorneys-at-law and patent attorneys are considered "independent judicial bodies"[22] and could thus be named in the order.

[c] Necessity to File a Lawsuit on the Merits

The court shall ensure that the measures to preserve evidence are revoked or otherwise cease to have effect, at the defendant's request, without prejudice to the damages which may be claimed, if the applicant does not bring, within a period not exceeding thirty-one calendar days or twenty working days, whichever is the longer, an action leading to a decision on the merits of the case before the court. This deadline starts to run from a date specified in the court's order,[23] which might be reasonably not earlier than the date on which the written report on the measures to preserve to be prepared by the independent expert or bailiff in accordance with Rule 196(4) RoP is prepared and available.

Where the measures to preserve evidence are revoked, or where they lapse due to any act or omission by the applicant, or where it is subsequently found that there has been no infringement or threat of infringement of the patent, the court may order the applicant, at the defendant's request, to provide the defendant with appropriate compensation for any damage suffered as a result of those measures.[24] This provision puts pressure on the applicant, and requires careful consideration of whether to bring the evidence preservation action in the first place, and then whether to proceed on the merits. The downside risk of having to pay compensation for an unfruitful seizure helps to discourage the use of these proceedings in unsupported cases.

[B] German Proceedings

In Germany, inspection proceedings are codified in section 140c PatG, which transposes the Directive on the Enforcement of Intellectual Property Rights (2004/48/EC, Enforcement Directive) into German law. These proceedings offer a possibility of obtaining evidence under judicial supervision. Nevertheless, due to higher thresholds inspection proceedings in Germany are less common than with France's "saisie contrefaçon" measures.

21. Federal Supreme Court, Nov. 16, 2009, X ZB 37/08, IIC 2010, 724 (in English), "Lichtbogenschnürung."
22. In German: "Organ der Rechtspflege" (s. 1 BRAO).
23. Rule 198(1) RoP.
24. *Ibid.*

[1] Basic Requirements

[a] *"Sufficient Probability" of Patent Infringement*

The first section of section 140c of the GPA provides:

> (1) Any person who, with sufficient probability, uses a patented invention in contravention of §§9 to 13 may be required by the right holder or another authorised person to present a document or to tolerate the inspection of an object that is within his power of disposal or of a method that is the subject matter of the patent if such is necessary to establish such party's claims. If there is a sufficient probability of an infringement to a commercial extent, the claim also extends to the submission of banking, financial or trading documents. If the alleged infringer claims that such information is confidential, the court shall adopt the necessary measures to ensure the protection required in the individual case.[25]

Accordingly, if the patentee is in a position to show a "sufficient probability" that his patent is infringed, he may seek production of documents and the inspection of the object in dispute, as set forth below. A sufficient probability is less than a "considerable degree"[26] of probability as defined by the case law under section 809 of the German Civil Code which represented the only legal basis for discovery claims prior to the introduction of section 140c Patent Act. The Appeal Court Frankfurt opined that as a "practical indication" a sufficient probability exists if the patent infringement is more probable than improbable, i.e., from a degree of probability of more than 50%.[27] Facts which may establish a sufficient probability of patent infringement are, for example, the nature of products sold by the presumed infringer in foreign countries (where there might not be patent coverage), as well as statements made by the presumed infringer in advertisement, which indicate a certain nature of the product, or industrial standards by which the accused party is likely complying.[28]

The existence of a sufficient probability is a substantive requirement that needs to be demonstrated in the request. The demonstration shall allow an assessment to be made on the basis of objectively determinable facts.[29] A minimum of facts must be provided by the patentee, otherwise the discovery claim would fail. For instance, if the distributed product originated from the protected process can also be manufactured in a way other than by the protected process and public statements about the manufacturing process are simply not available, the patentee may likely not prevail. Requests that are based on mere allegations, the proverbial "shot in the dark," will be dismissed.[30] However, the requirement of sufficient probability of infringement is fulfilled where concrete indications pointing to an infringement could be deduced from

25. Unofficial translation.
26. Federal Supreme Court, GRUR 1985, 512—Druckbalken.
27. Appeal Court Frankfurt, Decision of Nov. 27, 2019, 6 W 100/19, Juris marginal no. 3.
28. Commentary: Busse/Keukenschrijver, PatG, 9th ed. 2020, s. 140c marginal no. 8; Kühnen, Handbuch der Patentverletzung, 13. ed. 2021 marginal no. B.28-31.
29. Appeal Court Frankfort, Decision dated Nov. 27, 2019, 6 W 100/19, Juris no. 3.
30. Kühnen, Handbuch der Patentverletzung, ed. 2021; Rn. B.26; Busse/Keukenschrijver, PatG, 9. ed. 2020, §140c Rn. 8.

a thorough examination of the defendant's commercial catalogues and advertising.[31] Even in technically complex cases, difficulties as to whether there is in fact an infringing activity shall in principle, not minimize the success of a request. For instance, a request may even be successful if it is foreseeable that the question of infringement will later require the involvement of a technical expert in the subsequent main proceedings. However, a request for inspection will be unsuccessful if it can be clearly shown without the help of an expert that the contested product or method falls outside the scope of protection of the asserted patent.[32] The different German courts apply slightly different standards as to the existence of a "sufficient probability," for which reason the selection of the right court is an important element for the success of the request.

Finally, the object or the document to be inspected must be in the possession or custody of the accused infringer. At least, he must be entitled to a claim of surrender in case the item to be inspected is in the possession of a third party.[33]

[b] Necessity and Principle of Proportionality

The request must comply with the principle of proportionality. First of all, the patentee must show that he is unable to obtain the evidence in any other suitable way. For example, the District Court Braunschweig[34] rejected a claim for inspection because the patentee did not exhaust own reasonable possibilities for clarifying the facts. The claim would thus be denied if there are other appropriate and accessible means to obtain the desired evidence. The plaintiff must demonstrate in detail that he tried all available avenues and each attempt failed.

Section 140c of the Patent Act states that the claim seeking judicially enforced discovery "is excluded if its enforcement is disproportionate in the individual case."[35] Generally, the interests of the patentee predominate, but there might nevertheless be situations where the desired discovery intervention would be considered disproportionate to the infringing activity. The proportionality may however exceptionally be denied in a case where there are serious doubts as to the validity of the patent or its infringement. Different courts and chambers weigh such interests differently, but German counsel should be able to reasonably predict, on a case-by-case basis, the extent to which judicial discovery intervention is likely.

[2] Procedural Implementation of the Request

[a] General Outline

The discovery claim may be pursued through main action proceedings. Often it is desirable to pursue a discovery claim through preliminary injunction proceedings

31. Appeal Court of Karlsruhe, Decision of Oct. 16, 2012, W 6 72/12.
32. Appeal Court of Düsseldorf, InstGE 11, 298, "Weißmacher."
33. District Court of Nürnberg/Fürth, InstGE 5, 153, "Betriebsspionage."
34. DC Braunschweig, decision dated Aug. 5, 2016—9 O 2539/15.
35. Unofficial translation.

(section 140c(3) Patent Act). Accordingly, at an early stage, before the infringement suit is filed, the right holder, usually the patentee or its licensee, may file for a preliminary injunction enabling the inspection of a device or a machine. Such a court order could be rendered ex parte, with a view to surprising the accused infringer and avoiding any manipulation of the evidence by the accused infringer.

It should be noted that the scope of any order, ex parte or otherwise, would be limited to an object or document specified by the right holder in his request.[36] It is not a general search right and even in its broadest conception does not approach the scope of discovery proceedings known in the US.

If the discovery claim is enforced through preliminary injunction proceedings, it is questionable whether the applicant must file the request as soon as possible to satisfy a requirement of urgency. This requirement is normally applicable to preliminary injunction proceedings.[37] Some courts are of the opinion that a delay could be detrimental to the request;[38] other courts, such as the Appeal Court of Düsseldorf, do not apply a time requirement.[39]

Another instrument of obtaining discovery in the course or outside of patent infringement proceedings results from section 485 Code of Civil Procedure. This instrument is called "independent evidentiary proceedings." Its admissibility follows its own rules and does not depend on the requirements of a substantive discovery claim, such as the claim resulting from section 140c Patent Act. The request based on section 485 Code of Civil Procedure is permissible if there is a "concern that the evidence might be lost, or that it will become difficult to use it."[40] In addition, such request may be filed prior to the main proceedings and may involve an expert who prepares a written report to substantiate the "state or the value of an object"[41] and other related aspects with an object to be discovered. This instrument may thus represent a helpful option in case the requirements of the substantive discovery claim are not fulfilled or difficult to prove. The measures of section 485 Code of Civil Procedure may also be combined with a preliminary injunction based on section 140c Patent Act.

[b] Protection of the Defendant's Secrecy Interests

Secrecy interests of the accused infringer will have to be sufficiently protected. This is not dependent upon which legal form of discovery is applied. Section 140c(3) of the Patent Act considers valid secrecy interests and states: "*The court shall take necessary measures to ensure the protection of confidential information. This shall apply in particular in cases in which the injunction is imposed without prior hearing of the*

36. Federal Supreme Court, I ZR 187/01, GRUR 2004, 420, "Kontrollbesuch."
37. *See* Ch. 11, §11.02[C][2][a] "Urgency."
38. Appeal Court of Cologne, OLG-Report 2009, 258; Appeal Court of Karlsruhe, Decision of May 18, 2010, 6 W 28/10; Appeal Court of Nürnberg, Decision of Aug. 17, 2015, "3 W 1412/15."
39. Appeal Court of Düsseldorf, InstGE 12, 108; Appeal Court of Frankfort/Main, Decision of Jun. 10, 2010, 15 U 192/09.
40. Section 485(1) Code of Civil Procedure (CCP).
41. Section 485(2) CCP.

opposing party."[42] The text does not further specify how this should be implemented and leaves it to the courts to decide on a case-by-case basis. It has already been outlined by the Federal Supreme Court in the landmark *Faxkarte* decision that the secrecy conflict should be solved flexibly by including in the inspection order a provision that takes into account both the right holder's interest in the inspection and the defendant's interest in secrecy. If discovery measures of section 485 Code of Civil Procedure are combined with a summary measure based on section 140c Patent Act involving the preparation of an expert opinion, secrecy interests may be protected through the application of the following steps:[43]

- First, the court appoints an independent expert (the right holder proposes a suitable person in the request).
- The expert carries out the investigation (e.g., the inspection of a machine that is located on the premises of the defendant). If the accused infringer refuses the investigation (for instance, he refuses access to the location), police powers could be applied. The accused infringer is not required to actively support the inspection. His duty is mainly confined to positively tolerating the inspection.[44] Nevertheless, in case of a software-related infringement, the accused infringer might be obliged to provide passwords necessary to execute the inspection.[45]
- To efficiently protect the interests of the accused infringer, only the right holder's legal representatives, namely his attorney-at-law and/or patent attorney (and not the right holder himself), shall be allowed to attend the inspection. In addition, the right holder's representatives will be bound by court order not to disclose to their client (the right holder) the information they obtain during the inspection. This is an unusual situation for the right holder's legal representatives, who are not allowed to tell their client the results of the investigation. They must wait until the court lifts the secrecy obligation. The secrecy obligation under which attorneys may receive confidential information is considered to be sufficient for protecting the accused infringer's secrecy rights.[46] Attorneys-at-law and patent attorneys are considered "independent judicial bodies"[47] who are required to not violate a court order of secrecy, all the more since such violation would represent a criminal offense:[48]
- The expert then establishes an expert report.
- The expert submits the report to the court.

42. Unofficial translation.
43. District Court of Düsseldorf, InstGE 8, 103, Etikettiermaschine.
44. Federal Supreme Court, WuM 2007, 209.
45. *Ibid.*
46. Federal Supreme Court, Nov. 16, 2009, X ZB 37/08, IIC 2010, 724 (in English), "Lichtbogenschnürung."
47. In German: *Organ der Rechtspflege* (s. 1 BRAO).
48. Federal Supreme Court, Nov. 16, 2009, X ZB 37/08, IIC 2010, 724 (in English), "Lichtbogenschnürung."

- The court forwards the report to the representatives of both sides.[49] The report is not yet forwarded to the claimant (or right holder). The accused infringer (defendant) can then make statements regarding his secrecy interests.

The court then decides whether and to what extent the findings of the expert are to be disclosed to the right holder and to what extent the secrecy obligation of the right holder's representative may be lifted. This includes weighing of the reciprocal interests.[50] The interests of the right holder typically prevail if a patent infringement can be deduced from the report. If the report indeed contains confidential information that should not be disclosed to the right holder, then there are different means that could be applied. For instance, the confidential parts of the report could be redacted[51] before forwarding the document to the right holder. That is, in a first step, the accused infringer may be asked to redact those parts of the expert report which he claims contain protectable "secret information." Accordingly, the disclosure of the redacted report to the right holder poses no problem.[52] Which items in dispute that have been redacted, i.e., the allegedly secret information, are to be disclosed against the will of the accused infringer depends then on a court decision weighing the secrecy interests of the accused infringer and the patentee's interests. As indicated, the interests of the right holder typically prevail if the court is able to conclude that the report sufficiently supports the allegation of patent infringement.[53] If the court concludes that no prevailing secrecy interests of the accused infringer are concerned, the right holder's representative will be fully released from his secrecy obligation. This mechanism could also be combined with other available means for protecting the secrecy of confidential information, such as exclusion of the public from the hearing or from the pronouncement of the decision. This mechanism used by German courts to protect secrecy interests may well serve as a guideline for the proceedings at the UPC.

[c] Scope and Aim of the Request

While the discovery request may target a concrete object for inspection, such as a machine on the defendant's premises, the accused infringer is not required to actively assist the inspection. His duty is merely confined to render the inspection possible. In the above example, he would have to enable access for the court-appointed inspector, including access to his property if that is where the machine is located. In the software context, he may have to provide passwords when necessary for executing a software. Often, a simple inspection of the object is not sufficient and a dismantling of the object—even when such dismantling amounts to destruction—is necessary to determine if it is infringing. The extent to which a destructive modification of the object is permitted requires weighing of interests and might depend on whether and to what

49. *Ibid.*
50. Appeal Court of Düsseldorf, InstGE 10, 198, "zeitversetztes Fernsehen."
51. District Court of Düsseldorf, InstGE 6, 189, "Walzen- Formgebungsmaschine."
52. Appeal Court of Düsseldorf, Aug. 20, 2012, I_2 W 13/12.
53. Appeal Court of Düsseldorf, InstGE 10, 198, "zeitversetztes Fernsehen."

extent the patentee/right holder pays for the cost of the modified or destroyed object. In some circumstances, the inspection could also include the seizure of samples.[54]

The discovery request could also cover the production of documents or the disclosure of the source code.[55] This includes documents that relate to the contested device or apparatus with which the contested method is carried out, such as user manuals, operating guidelines or engineering drawings. In case of infringements being committed on a broader scale, the claim may even be extended to the submission of banking, financial or trading documents (section 140c(1) Patent Act). All this discovery would not have the characteristic of a US-style discovery. The request is limited to documents and objects that are sufficiently specified by the patentee/right holder. He may not simply ask for "all documents related to" or all "relevant documents" as might be sought in US discovery proceedings. Rather, the right holder is required to sufficiently specify the focus of the discovery in the request. To some extent, his disadvantageous situation is taken into account, namely that his insight into the accused infringer's business is limited, but this does not release him from a basic duty to sufficiently specify the focus of the discovery.[56]

[3] Discovery after Filing the Complaint

[a] Section 140c Patent Act

The demand for discovery according to section 140c Patent Act is considered a substantive and judicially enforceable claim of the patentee. It is typically a claim which is asserted and enforced in preparation for a lawsuit on the merits. Nevertheless, the claim may also be asserted as part of the main infringement proceedings[57] (the right to prevent the accused infringer from using the patent, rendering of accounts, etc.). The parallel assertion of the discovery claim, together with the other patent infringement-related claims, by means of the same lawsuit on the merits, may prompt the court to rule on the different claims at different times. Indeed, if the court determines, after a hearing, that the submitted evidence is not completely sufficient to prove the infringement, a partial judgment (section 301 Code of Civil Procedure) could be rendered concerning only the discovery claims, and a decision on the other asserted claims could come after the ordered discovery has been implemented.[58]

[b] Procedural Means

German procedural law provides additional mechanisms to allow patentees to gather evidence for proving infringement. However, in contrast to section 140c Patent Act,

54. Federal Supreme Court, GRUR 2013, 316, "Rohrmuffe."
55. Federal Supreme Court, GRUR 2013, 509, I ZR 90/09, "UniBasic IDOS."
56. Federal Supreme Court, I ZR 187/01, GRUR 2004, 420, "Kontrollbesuch."
57. District Court of Düsseldorf, Decision of Aug. 10, 2010, 4b O 54/09 (not published); Appeal Court of Düsseldorf, Decision of Nov. 8, 2012, 2 U 108/10, "Fluidflusssimulation II."
58. District Court of Düsseldorf, Decision of Aug. 10, 2010, 4b O 54/09 (not published).

these procedural means do not represent not substantively and judicially enforceable claims. They depend on the court's discretion.

According to sections 142 and 144 Code of Civil Procedure, a court may order the disclosure of documents and the production of the contested device and product, provided that disclosure is proportionate and appropriate. The likely use of the protected subject matter may also be taken into account when rendering an order for disclosure. These provisions are as follows:

> **§142 Code of Civil Procedure:**
>
> The court can order that a party to the proceedings or a third party discloses a deed or other documents which are in its possession and which a party to the proceedings has referred to. To do so, the court may set a deadline and order that the disclosed documents are to remain, for a predetermined period, in the possession of the court. … .[59]
>
> **§144 Code of Civil Procedure:**
>
> The court may order the inspection or an expert opinion. For that purpose, the court may order, from a party to the proceedings or a third party, the production of an object which is in its possession and may set a deadline therefor. Is may also order the acquiescence of it provided a home is not involved. … .[60]

Accordingly, sections 142 and 144 Code of Civil Procedure may help if it turns out during the proceedings that submitted evidence is not yet sufficient. A disclosure and inspection order requires that such disclosure be suitable and necessary to clarify the facts of the case, and that the request be proportionate and appropriate. When a court weighs the factors before rendering a disclosure order, the court will consider the nature of the rights of the party. A disclosure order may be made where there is a likelihood of patent infringement. Similar to section 140a Patent Act, an order based on sections 142 and 144 Code of Civil Procedure requires that the right holder show at least a sufficient probability that the patent is infringed.[61] Unless this minimum requirement is met, the court is under no duty to issue an order based on sections 142 and 144 Code of Civil Procedure.[62] Where the documents requested contain commercially sensitive or confidential information, they may be protected by redaction and/or the different legal means available under the German procedural law. In its decision of August 1, 2006, the Federal Supreme Court[63] advised:

> German law must be construed in such a way that it complies with the requirements of the TRIPS Agreement (Federal Supreme Court, GRUR 2002, 1046, "Faxkarte" …). Like the substantive provision of §809 Civil Code, the provision of §142 new Code of Civil Procedure is a means of overcoming a plaintiff's inability to produce evidence, as may particularly occur in the field of the especially vulnerable technical property rights. In the field of industrial property, a provision

59. Unofficial translation.
60. Unofficial translation.
61. Federal Supreme Court, GRUR 2013, 316, "Rohrmuffe."
62. *Ibid.*
63. Federal Supreme Court, Aug. 1, 2006, X ZR 114/03, IIC 2007, 97 (in English) "Restschadstoffentfernung."

> like that of §142 new Code of Civil Procedure also has the function of executing the measures that are required for the production of evidence pursuant to Article 6 Enforcement Directive, 2004/48/EC, to be implemented into national law by 26 April 2006, and which are known in French law in the form of the "saisie contrefaçon" or in the laws of the United Kingdom in the form of the search order ("Anton Piller Order").[64]

This decision demonstrates the effort of the Federal Supreme Court in recent years to effectively reach the international standards codified in the Agreement on TRIPS and in the Enforcement Directive. This effort must be understood in light of the limited discovery that characterizes the history of German civil court procedures. The more flexible approach, which finds its basis in a case law starting with the *Faxkarte* decision in 2002 and the introduction of more discovery friendly provisions in the following years, is still evolving.

[C] French *saisie contrefaçon*

[1] Introduction

French law provides for a so-called *saisie contrefaçon. Saisie contrefaçon* procedures are widely used in France for obtaining evidence of the existence and extent of patent infringement. It is a means of obtaining proof of infringement of IP rights, in particular patents. The central provision is Article L615-5 CPI. It reads:

> Infringement may be proven by any means.
>
> Any person being entitled to bring an action for infringement shall be entitled to have carried out, in any place and by any bailiff, assisted by experts appointed by the plaintiff, by virtue of an order issued on request by the competent civil court, either a detailed description, with or without taking samples, or the actual seizure of the allegedly infringing products or processes, as well as any document relating thereto.
>
> The court may order, for the same evidentiary purposes, the actual seizure of the materials and instruments used to manufacture or distribute the allegedly infringing products or to implement the allegedly infringing processes.
>
> It may make the execution of the measures it orders subject to the provision by the plaintiff of guarantees intended to ensure the possible indemnification of the defendant if the infringement action is subsequently judged unfounded or the seizure annulled.
>
> If the plaintiff fails to take civil or criminal action on the merits of the case within a time limit set by regulation, the entire seizure, including the description, shall be cancelled at the request of the seized party, without the latter having to state the reasons for his request and without prejudice to any damages that may be claimed.

[2] Requirements

Seizure orders may be obtained through ex parte proceedings on the basis of a presumption of infringement. Obtaining seizure orders are not a priori subordinated by

64. Unofficial translation.

law to the production of prima facie evidence. Until the transposition of the Enforcement Directive[65] on October 29, 2007, it was thus established case law that a request for seizure could not be denied if the forms and justifications provided by law were submitted in the request.[66] This approach required less of a showing than is required by the Enforcement Directive. Its Article 7(1) requires that the seizing party shall submit at least "reasonably accessible evidence to support its allegations." Following the transposition of Directive of April 29, 2004, 2004/48/EC in 2007 French judges have raised the question of whether evidence must be provided in support of a request for an order. A decision of the Appeal Court Paris of January 28, 2014[67] ruled that mere allegations which are not supported by a minimum of documents are insufficient for a successful request. This ruling seemed to bring French law closer to the more restrictive German and Nordic concepts. The parliamentary work on the 2007 law however confirms the French legislator's desire to maintain the previous law by allowing the national law to be more favorable to the rights holder.[68] In two decisions dated May 26, 2017,[69] the Appeal Court Paris ruled that a seizure order may be granted "*without requiring proof or even the beginning of proof of the infringement that the measure requested is precisely intended to bring about.*" A slightly different approach emerged in a decision of the Appeal Court Paris denying a request for a seizure order, considering that the means invoked in support of the request were inaccurate[70] Even if the current French case law is not entirely consistent, it can be assumed that the District Court Paris is more generous in granting seizure requests than German courts.

[3] Implementation

Other complications may arise if the bailiff carrying out the seizure is assisted by experts appointed by the applicant. In fact, when the seizure of counterfeit goods concerns complex objects, it is suggested that the bailiff be assisted by a person who may technically support him. In earlier times that expert was often an employee of the plaintiff.[71] The link between such expert and the seizing party poses an obvious problem of partiality and generates a risk of industrial espionage. Accordingly, the Supreme Court[72] prohibited the involvement of the seizing party's employee. However, the party's patent attorney, as ruled in a decision of March 8, 2005,[73] may participate in the seizure operation, even if he is the usual counsel of the seizing party. He may thus contribute his notes to the seizure report. In a recent decision, rendered

65. Apr. 29, 2004, 2004/48/EC.
66. Cass. com., Jun. 29, 1999, no. 97-12.699: JurisData no. 1999-002744; D. 1999, p. 207, prec. no. 54.
67. Appeal Court Paris, 3rd Ch, Jan. 28, 2014, No. 13/08128.
68. P. Gosselin Report to the National Assembly no. 178, October 2007, p. 93.
69. Appeal Court Paris, Ch. 2, May 26, 2017, no. 15/10201 and 15/10204.
70. Appeal Court Paris, Sep. 11, 2018, No. 18/01099: PIBD 2018, No. 1104, III, p. 682.
71. Appeal Court Paris, Apr. 18, 1984: RTD com. 1985, p. 11, commented by. A. Chavanne and J. Azéma.
72. Cass. Com., Apr. 28, 2004, JCP G 2004, II, 10171.
73. Cass. Com, Mar. 8, 2005, no. 03-15.871, Sté Miniplus c/Sté Capitole Carton.

by the Appeal Court Paris on March 27, 2018,[74] the problem of partiality became apparent again. The court ruled that the experts appointed by the seizing company were not impartial, since they had previously worked for the requesting client in relation to one of the suspected infringing objects. The court therefore ordered the cancelation of the seizure report and prohibited any use or communication concerning the seizure report and the seized items. The bailiff conducting the seizure may thus usually be assisted by the patent attorney of the seizing party. He is bound by a code of ethics to ensure impartiality and the nondisclosure of sensitive and confidential data to a competing party.

§13.04 MEANS OF EVIDENCE

[A] At the UPC

[1] General Principles

In case of proceedings pending with the UPC, a plurality of evidence gathering tools are available. These rules combine the predominantly written procedure of civil law litigation, as it is applicable in Germany as well as an "Anglo-Saxon" type of procedure wherein evidence may be adduced during an oral hearing. Without suggesting any order of preference, Article 53 UPC contains an indicative and non-exhaustive list of admissible "means of evidence," namely written documents, expert reports, physical objects, electronic files and even audio and video recordings. The UPCA provides for a very broad understanding of what may constitute a means of evidence. A written document could constitute a legal instrument such as a concluded agreement or circumstantial evidence such as an object documented by a photo. Physical objects can be brought into the courtroom or might be viewed in situ during a local inspection. However, no classification of their evidentiary value is made in Article 53 UPCA. In paragraphs 2 and 3, the admissible means of obtaining evidence are listed:

- hearing the parties;
- requests for information;
- the production of documents;
- hearing witnesses;
- opinions by private or court-appointed experts;
- inspections; and
- experiments and affidavits.

These means of evidence are further elaborated in Part 2 of the RoP. However, neither the UPCA nor the RoP ranks these means of evidence. For instance, the current French law prioritizes documentary evidence over witness testimony. According to the German procedural law, statements of the parties to the proceedings are basically not

74. Mar. 27, 2018, rendered by the Appeal Court Paris in *JC BRAMFORD EXCAVATORS Limited v. SA MANITOU BF.*

considered as formal "means of evidence." Even opinions of private experts are assimilated to parties' statements under German law.[75] This does, however, not mean that such statements are irrelevant to the outcome of the proceedings. They play a role in the court's decision-making process under German law in evaluating evidence based on "discretion and conviction."[76] In fact, the reliability of the means of evidence depends on many factors, such as the degree of impartiality. This is typically not the same for opinions of independent experts appointed by the court and statements of the parties to the proceedings biased by their own interests. A rigid ranking of the means of evidence is not suggested by the UPCA. Rather it is left to the court to rank their values on a case-by-case assessment. Also, it is left to the court to determine the degree of certainty to find a fact proven or not. Under Article 76(3) UPCA, a free assessment of evidence is established. Complete certainty is not needed to establish a fact, although, depending on the context, a predominant or high probability might not be sufficient to prove a fact. Rather, the court must sufficiently be convinced, and its conviction must be documented in its decision.[77] A lesser evidentiary standard is applied under German procedural law when it comes to the assessment of damages, where the court may apply extensive discretion.[78]

A basic principle on evidence is set forth in Article 54 UPCA. It stipulates that the "burden of proof of facts shall be on the party relying on those facts." A fact or statement does, however, not need to be supported by evidence if it is not contested. In such case, it shall be held to be true.[79] Similar principles are applicable in German proceedings and many European jurisdictions. The plaintiff usually bears the burden of proof. This burden of proof is accompanied by a duty of presentation, which means that the plaintiff must sufficiently provide facts in support of the allegation from which the legal consequences can be drawn.

A party making a statement of fact that is contested or likely to be contested by the other party shall indicate the means of evidence to prove it.[80] This obligation is further detailed in Rule 13 RoP which imposes on the plaintiff that all relevant facts, evidence, legal arguments and claims for relief must be put forward in the statement of claim. This complies with the duty of the plaintiff who "shall set out their full case as early as possible" in the proceedings, according to the Preamble to the RoP. This follows from the burden of proof which is on the party relying on those facts. However, if it turns out that the means of evidence is available only to one party, and that

75. Federal Supreme Court, NJW 09, 2894.
76. Section 286 of the German Code of Procedure:

> (1) The court is to decide, at its discretion and conviction, and taking account of the entire content of the hearings and the results obtained by evidence being taken, if any, whether an allegation as to fact is to be deemed true or untrue. The judgment is to set out the reasons informing the conviction of the judges.
> (2) The court shall be bound to statutory rules of evidence only in the cases designated in the present Code. [Unofficial Translation]

77. Federal Supreme Court, BGHZ, 53, 245.
78. Section 287 German Code of Procedure.
79. Rule 171(2) RoP.
80. Article 171(2) RoP.

evidence is not available to the party bearing the burden of proof, then the UPCA goes one step further and puts that first party under duty to produce available evidence of such a fact.[81] Under Rule 191 RoP, information must be communicated that is under the control of the other party.

Nevertheless, a patentee is well advised to perform reasonable work before filing a complaint. Similar to German proceedings, the plaintiff is challenged to assemble all documents and evidence, accessible and obtainable to him, prior to the start of the proceedings. He has every motivation to do so because once his complaint is on record, the procedural deadlines are tight. If the UPC does indeed work under these time constraints as set out in the RoP, a plaintiff should not speculate as to whether the evidence in support of his position might be identified during the course of the proceedings.

Nothing in the UPCA or RoP prohibits a party from simply denying alleged facts. Article 48(6) UPCA imposes on representatives of the parties the obligation not to misrepresent facts knowingly or with good reasons to have known. This duty may reflect on the represented party who shall comply with the general rule to act in good faith. However, when the plaintiff has fulfilled his duty and sufficiently substantiated his claim by means of facts in the complaint, it is reasonable that the defendant be required to present facts and to give reasons why he believes that a particular factual assertion made by the plaintiff is incorrect or incomplete. This is a common approach in German court proceedings, and it is likewise applicable under the UPC. Rule 172(2) of the RoP requires allegations to be specified. This mechanism renders a bare denial inadmissible. Many issues can be solved by such a mechanism without taking of evidence. Often the factual assertion concerns the attacked product or method which is the specialization of the defendant. The defendant is then closer to the relevant information. In such a situation, it is reasonable to impose on the defendant a duty to respond in a substantiated manner to the allegations of the plaintiff. Of course, there is an exception: facts that are not subject to the party's own activities or personal perception and may not be easily uncovered can be denied without giving reasons. In German Proceedings, this can be taken from section 138(4) of the Code of Civil Procedure.[82]

The evidence available to a party regarding a statement of fact that is contested or likely to be contested by the other party must be produced by the party making that statement of fact.[83] The court may at any time during the proceedings order a party making a statement of fact to produce evidence that lies in the control of that party. If the party fails to produce the evidence, the court shall take such failure into account when deciding on the issue in question.[84]

81. Article 191 RoP.
82. Federal Supreme Court, BGHZ 100, 190, 196: "*A party may declare its lack of knowledge only where this concerns facts that were neither actions taken by the party itself, nor within its ken.*"
83. Rule 172(1) RoP.
84. Rule 172(2) RoP.

[2] Witnesses

A party seeking to offer evidence through a witness shall lodge a sworn statement or a written summary of the evidence to be given.[85] The party may choose between sworn statement and an application for interrogating the witness. For the latter case, at least, a summary of the expected testimony must be given. The approach of the UPCA is different from German procedural law where sworn witness statements are in principle insufficient for the purpose of lawsuits on the merits; rather, they are used in preliminary injunction proceedings to render allegations credible.[86] It only constitutes prima facie evidence. Both a sworn statement and a written summary of the testimony anticipate that the party's representative must contact the witness in order to elicit such a statement or summary. In German proceedings, it is in principle permissible for lawyers to contact potential witnesses as long as the contact is not aimed at manipulating the witness. Such contact is necessary to identify the witness' knowledge of a particular fact in support of the party's allegation.

If the form of a sworn statement—in contrast to a simple summary—is used, which represents an official means of evidence,[87] the witness must indicate therein that he is aware of his obligation to tell the truth and of his liability under applicable national law in the event of any breach of this obligation.[88] In addition, the statement shall disclose any current or past relationship between the witness and the party offering the evidence, and any actual or potential conflict of interest that may affect the impartiality of the witness.[89] The inclusion of such statements serves to sensitize the witness of potential conflicts of interest and to avoid potential manipulations of the witness. The witness also needs to appreciate that in case the court orders him to be heard in the oral hearing, he will be asked by the court to confirm the evidence given therein.[90]

A party seeking to offer oral witness testimony must make an application during the interim procedure[91] for the hearing of a witness in persona, setting out the reasons why the witness should be heard in person and the facts which the party expects the witness to confirm.[92] Such application may be appropriate in particular if a sworn statement could not be acquired from the witness. Indeed, a witness cannot be compelled to produce a sworn statement. The court may also order that a witness be heard in person on its own motion, or where a sworn witness statement is challenged by the other party.[93]

---

85. Rule 175(1) RoP.
86. Section 294 Code of Civil Procedure: "Anyone who is to demonstrate an allegation as to fact to the satisfaction of the court may use all evidence and may also be permitted to make a statutory declaration in lieu of an oath."
87. Rule 170(2)(h) RoP.
88. Rule 175(2) RoP.
89. Rule 178(3) RoP.
90. Rule 177(1) RoP.
91. Rules 13(1)(m), 112(2)(b).
92. Rule 176 RoP.
93. Rule 177(1) RoP.

When conducting the evidentiary hearings, the RoP confer on the presiding judge and the judges of the panel a leading role. They start the questioning of the witness, followed by the parties. The presiding judge may prohibit any question which is not designed to adduce admissible evidence.[94] The court may allow a witness to give evidence through electronic means, such as video conferencing. In German proceedings, such tools principally depend on whether the parties agree to it. Patent litigation has often an international dynamic requiring the testimony of foreigners living outside the court's territory. Such a flexible approach of using technical means for the interrogation may be an important cost-saving measure.

Unless a privilege to refuse to give evidence is applicable,[95] witnesses who have been duly summoned shall obey the summons and attend the oral hearing, and in case they fail to do so, may be sanctioned by a penalty.[96] If the witness breaches this duty, the court may impose sanctions.

[3] Private Experts

Parties may put forward their own expert evidence by submitting a written expert report commissioned by that party. In contrast to German national law, such private expert opinions possess a higher evidentiary value. The expert must sign the report and indicate that he is aware of his duty to tell the truth. The rules for witnesses apply *mutatis mutandis* to experts of the parties. Accordingly, either a summary of the evidence to be given by the private expert shall be provided by the party in advance or the private expert prepares a written statement (sworn statement). It represents an official means of evidence.[97] In case the expert shall be heard in the oral hearing, the court's order will impose on him the duty to assist the court impartially on matters relevant to his area of expertise. The latter shall override any duty to the party retaining him. Accordingly, he must be independent and objective, and shall not act as an advocate for any party to the proceedings.

[4] Court-Appointed Experts

Where the court must resolve a specific technical or other question in relation to the action, it may appoint a court expert on its own motion, after hearing the parties. The parties may make suggestions regarding the identity of the court expert, his technical or other relevant background and the questions to be put to him. He can be selected from a list of experts maintained by the Registry of the court. The court expert shall be responsible to the court and shall possess the expertise, independence and impartiality required for being appointed as court expert. The parties shall be entitled to be heard on the expertise, independence, and impartiality of the court expert. Once the written report of the court expert has been presented to the court, the court shall invite the

94. Rule 177(5) RoP.
95. Rule 179(3) RoP.
96. Rule 179(1)(2) RoP.
97. Rule 170(2)(h) RoP.

parties to comment on it either in writing or during the oral hearing. A main difference with a private expert is that the court-appointed expert's activities are carried out under the supervision of the court. Also, the parties are prohibited from directly communicating with the court-appointed expert.

[5] Judicial Cooperation

Rule 173 RoP refers to Regulation (EU) No. 2020/1783 for evidence to be taken within the EU and to the Hague Convention of March 18, 1970, for evidence to be taken outside the EU. Articles 5 to 22 of Regulation (EU) No. 2020/1783 contain the provisions for the transmission and execution of requests. Article 19 regulates the direct taking of evidence by the requesting court in another EU Member State. Article 20 provides for taking of evidence by videoconferencing or other distance communications technology.

[B] German Proceedings

[1] Court-Appointed Experts

Court experts may be appointed to clarify technical aspects of the case. Their function consists of providing the court with technical knowledge and expertise. They may be appointed, for instance, if the interpretation of a complex patent is problematic or if properties of the accused embodiment are in dispute and require a more complex technical examination. The court may appoint an expert if such an examination is required, or even if the court simply wants to be educated in an area of technical knowledge it does not already possess.

The expert may provide his understanding of technical terms used in the patent. His involvement may also be important to determine the scope of the relevant prior art and the common general knowledge at the priority date, in order to assess how the skilled person would understand the disclosures in the patent.[98] However, the court is not permitted to simply adopt the view of the expert, or to leave the construction of the patent claims entirely to an expert.[99]

In general, German courts are reluctant to appoint experts, and in the vast majority of cases, the court renders a decision without appointing an expert. The probability of the involvement of a court-appointed expert differs from court to court[100] and depends on the subject matter of the case. Based on the authors' experience, the appointment of a court expert occurs in less than one-quarter of all cases. The Federal Supreme Court[101] holds that courts with significant experience in patent matters may issue a decision on technical questions without the appointment of court experts, since usually the parties' submissions within the scope of the duties of presentation (*see*

98. Federal Supreme Court, X ZR 176/99, GRUR 2001, 770, "Kabeldurchführung."
99. Federal Supreme Court, X ZR 76/04, GRUR 2006, 131, "Seitenspiegel."
100. *See* Ch. 10, §10.02[D][3].
101. Federal Supreme Court, X ZR 126/01, GRUR 2005, 569, 571, "Blasfolienherstellung."

above) suffice to make clear the technical aspects of the case and provide a sufficient basis for a decision.

If the court does order the appointment of an expert, the parties are usually asked to provide names of experts within the technical field concerned (such as professors). Parties should avoid identifying experts with whom they already have relationships. An expert that worked for or still keeps a scientific or business relationship with either party might be disqualified.[102] To avoid any disqualification of the expert, the parties should not directly contact him prior and during the proceedings. The rules for court-appointed experts under German law are comparable to those applicable under the UPCA and the RoP. The main difference between both bodies of laws relates to private expert opinions. Under German law, they only represent qualified party submission, whereas private expert opinions enjoy—at least formally—a higher evidentiary value in UPC proceedings.

[2] Witnesses

Fact witnesses are rare in German patent infringement proceedings. Compared to the US, many grounds of dispute that would necessitate witnesses do not exist in German and UPC proceedings. There is basically no defense of inequitable conduct. Facts outside the patent document are mainly irrelevant for the construction of the claim and, if they are relevant, they usually do not require testimony from a fact witness. Prosecution file estoppel is inapplicable.[103] All critical issues concerning damages are raised in separate proceedings.[104] These areas for potential disputes are thus taken away from the main infringement proceedings. Accordingly, there are only a few areas where a witness could be of use for evidence taking in German infringement proceedings. One exception might be the situation where the defendant asserts a right based on prior use (Article 28 UPCA, section 12 Patent Act), for example, if he claims that he independently invented the subject matter of the asserted patent.

§13.05 ATTORNEY-CLIENT PRIVILEGE

In UPC and German court proceedings, it is unlikely that a court would order a party to disclose correspondence with its attorneys. In US court proceedings, the situation regarding a possible disclosure of correspondence of a party with its German or European attorneys is more complex. Unlike under US law, general discovery proceedings are not conducted in UPC and German court proceedings. Basically, no party is obliged to give the other side access to any document or other communication, such as emails, memos or letters. This is mainly the reason why "attorney-client privilege" has a different meaning in Europe than in US litigation. The plaintiff has a limited right to request disclosure of documents from the defendant, which generally would not

102. Federal Supreme Court, X ZR 126/01, GRUR 2008, 191, "Sachverständigenablehnung II."
103. *See* Ch. 12, §12.03[B][3][b] "Inadmissibility of Prosecution File Estoppel."
104. *See* Ch. 10, §10.02[F][4] "Rendering of Accounts and Lawsuit Concerning the Amount of Damages."

include attorney-client communications. To the extent such communications could potentially be relevant to the dispute, there are nonetheless mechanisms to shield these documents from production. That is, German attorneys-at-law and patent attorneys have a special right to refuse to give evidence, which sufficiently protects them from disclosing documents relating to their clients (section 383(1) No. 6 Code of Civil Procedure: 6. "Persons to whom facts are entrusted by virtue of their office, profession or status, the nature of which mandates their confidentiality, or the confidentiality of which is mandated by law, where their testimony would concern facts to which the confidentiality obligation refers"). Indeed, German attorneys-at-law are bound by a professional secrecy obligation for both general advice and litigation (section 43a (2) Federal Attorney Regulation (BRAO)). The scope of the right complies with the UPCA, conferring on the representatives of the parties the rights and immunities necessary for the independent exercise of their duties, including the privilege from disclosure in proceedings before the court in respect of communications between a representative and the party or any other person, unless such privilege is expressly waived by the party concerned.[105] This duty relates to everything that has become known to the lawyer in connection with his professional relationship to a client. The duty thus covers any document or material that has become known to him in his professional relationship with the client, irrespective of its specific type or content.

For professional representatives at the EPO (European patent attorneys), the attorney-client privilege is explicitly enshrined in Rule 153 EPC:

(1) Where advice is sought from a professional representative in his capacity as such, all communications between the professional representative and his client or any other person, relating to that purpose and falling under Article 2 of the Regulation on discipline for professional representatives, are permanently privileged from disclosure in proceedings before the EPO, unless such privilege is expressly waived by the client.
(2) Such privilege from disclosure shall apply, in particular, to any communication or document relating to:
  (a) the assessment of the patentability of an invention;
  (b) the preparation or prosecution of a European patent application;
  (c) any opinion relating to the validity, scope of protection or infringement of a European patent or a European patent application.

It is questionable whether communication with in-house counsel is protected as well. An in-house counsel may act in his capacity as his employer's legal advisor. Being admitted to the bar, he observes a general duty of confidentiality[106] a breach of which represents a criminal offense under section 203 Criminal Law. Such in-house counsel admitted as an attorney-at-law needs to have a lawyers' office separate from the offices of his employer. To best ensure the privilege, it is thus required that communications

105. Article 47(5) UPCA, Rule 287 RoP.
106. Section 2 BRAO ("Bundesrechtsanwaltsordnung": Regulations Concerning the Legal Profession).

between in-house counsel and employees, officers or directors of the company be separately stored and kept in the counsel's single custody. Accordingly, communications containing legal advice, rather than business advice, are likely privileged even if they are made with in-house attorneys, although this is less certain than in the US. However, not every in-house lawyer in Germany is admitted to the bar. There are thus two requirements which need to be fulfilled to secure the data from production: First, that the in-house be admitted to practice as an attorney-at-law in Germany and, second, that the information be obtained in the course of providing legal advice and cannot be attributed to management, controlling, accounting or similar services. Rule 287 RoP applicable to proceedings at the UPCA explicitly extends the privilege to communications between a client and a lawyer or patent attorney employed. However, he must be instructed by his employer to act in such professional capacity. This provision implies that the in-house counsel must separate these activities from other activities done on behalf of his employer. Similar to German standards, he will be well advised that communications falling under professional privilege are separately stored and kept in the counsel's single custody.

CHAPTER 14

Damages

§14.01 GENERAL REMARKS

The patentee, or its exclusive licensee,[1] can obtain an award of monetary damages following a successful infringement ruling. The patentee may claim an amount to compensate for his injury. Often the parties will resolve the amount of damages out of court. If no agreement can be reached, the patentee may file a separate lawsuit seeking a court determination of the damages. These proceedings, which are ancillary to the main infringement trial, are confined to the measuring of the amount.[2] Like the infringement trial, there is no jury.

§14.02 STANDARDS FOR DETERMINING DAMAGES UNDER THE UPCA

[A] Introduction

According to Article 32(f) UPCA, the UPC has authority to award damages (as well as compensation derived from the provisional protection conferred by a published European patent application). The scope of this authority is provided in Article 68 UPCA, which empowers the UPC to order an infringer who has infringed a UP, European bundle patent or a SPC to pay the injured party damages. Article 68 UPCA contains the basis for the rules of awarding damages. This provision complies with Article 13 of the Enforcement Directive.[3] Article 24(1) UPCA permits the UPC, if necessary, to apply national law to fill gaps in the EU laws, EPC, UPCA and other treaty

1. Article 47 UPC; the nonexclusive licensee is in principle not entitled to claim damages. He is not harmed by an unauthorized use of the patent as he would have anyway to accept other licensees of the patent besides him.
2. Under German law, such proceedings are called "Höheverfahren." Also at the UPC, these are "Separate Proceedings," cf. Rules 125 et seq. RoP.
3. Article 13 of the Enforcement Directive:

laws. In determining the correct approach, the UPC may refer to general principles common to the laws of the UPCA States. Also, the UPC applies national law for determining compensation derived from the provisional protection conferred by a published European patent application.

[B] Liability for Fault

According to section 139(2) GPA, "*any person who performs the act intentionally or negligently shall be obliged to compensate the injured party for the damage caused.*" German law does not differentiate between degrees of fault, whereas Article 68 UPCA forms two groups of infringers. To the first group belong infringers who have "*knowingly infringed.*" This is someone who acts intentionally. An infringer of the first group is someone who has had "*reasonable grounds to know*" about the infringement. The infringers of the first group shall be ordered to pay damages in accordance with sections (1)-(3), whereas infringers who did not knowingly infringe or did not have reasonable grounds to know about the infringement, belong to the second group. They may only be ordered the recovery of profits or the payment of compensation in accordance with section (4).[4] The basis for this provision is Article 13(2) Enforcement Directive, an optional provision which has not been implemented in all EU Member States, including Germany. Article 4(4) of the Translation Regulation (TR—1260/2012) gives hints of what kinds of infringers may fall into the second group. The provision, which applies to European patents with unitary effect, states that the UPC shall assess and take into consideration when assessing a damage claim, particularly "*where the alleged infringer is a small- or medium-sized enterprise (SME), natural person, a non-profit making organization, a university or a public research organization, whether the alleged infringer acted without knowing or without reasonable grounds for knowing that he was infringing a UP before having been provided with the translation referred to in Article 4(1) TR.*" The lack of willful intent on the part of such infringer could thus be

---

1. Member States shall ensure that the competent judicial authorities, on application of the injured party, order the infringer who knowingly, or with reasonable grounds to know, engaged in an infringing activity, to pay the rightholder damages appropriate to the actual prejudice suffered by him as a result of the infringement. When the judicial authorities set the damages:
   (a) they shall take into account all appropriate aspects, such as the negative economic consequences, including lost profits, which the injured party has suffered, any unfair profits made by the infringer and, in appropriate cases, elements other than economic factors, such as the moral prejudice caused to the rightholder by the infringement; or
   (b) as an alternative to (a), they may, in appropriate cases, set the damages as a lump sum on the basis of elements such as at least the amount of royalties or fees which would have been due if the infringer had requested authorisation to use the intellectual property right in question.
2. Where the infringer did not knowingly, or with reasonable grounds to know, engage in infringing activity, Member States may lay down that the judicial authorities may order the recovery of profits or the payment of damages, which may be pre-established.

4. This corresponds to Art. 13(1) and (2) of the Enforcement Directive.

deduced from the fact that the patent was not available in the language of the infringer. Even though this still remains to be decided by the UPC, this provision likely represents a catchall element that allows at least the general determination that such "low profile" infringers of the second group are the exception, rather than the norm.

For infringers of the first group, Article 68(1) UPCA requires either intent (first alternative) or existence of facts from which one would arrive at the relevant knowledge (second alternative). The first alternative, namely "intent," is difficult to prove. Therefore, most of the damage cases will be decided on the second alternative. It is expected that courts will not set the scale of the fault according to Article 68(1) to be very high, which should cover simple negligence, not just gross negligence. In German case law, for example, the fault is linked to the question of whether the infringer has sufficiently fulfilled his obligation to check the registers for upcoming conflicting patents. If he did not comply with this obligation within a sufficient period of time—in Germany one month from the publication of the event—to review the legal situation when entering with a product or service on the market, he shall be held liable. In practice, this standard removes from the infringement discussion the issue of whether the infringer acted willfully or with negligence, because it is thus usually the case. The UPC will develop its own jurisprudence on this issue.

[C] Calculation Methods

Article 68(2) UPCA is premised on three main principles for establishing the proper framework for determining damages, namely:

(1) the injured party shall, to the extent possible, be placed in the position it would have been in if no infringement had taken place;
(2) the infringer shall not benefit from the infringement;
(3) damages shall not be punitive.

Unlike under US law, there are no punitive damages under the UPCA. The same is true in Germany. At the same time the infringer shall not benefit from the infringement. This concept is also a known principle under German law. In fact, an infringer shall not be brought in a position which is better than the one of an authorized user, such as a normal licensee. As provided in Article 68(3)(b) UPCA, this position represents a minimum which shall not be undercut. Also, the first principle refers to a known concept under German law, as can be taken from section 249 German Civil Code, indicating that the infringer must restore the position that would exist if the circumstance obliging him to pay damages had not occurred. The indicated principles are thus well known and accepted concepts under the German patent law.

In addition, Article 68(3) UPCA sets out the basic details on which damages shall be calculated. Article 68(3) UPCA corresponds literally to Article 13(1)(a) of the Enforcement Directive. It provides that all appropriate aspects must be taken into account, such as:

(1) the negative economic consequences, including lost profits, which the injured party has suffered;
(2) any unfair profits made by the infringer; and
(3) in appropriate cases, noneconomic factors, such as the moral prejudice caused to the injured party by the infringement.

The court must thus refer to: (1) the effects of the infringement on side of the injured party, which are typically reflected in the so-called lost profits; (2) and on the side of the accused infringer, who might have made profits, so-called unfair profits of the infringer, thanks to the use of the accused patent; (3) other noneconomic factors, such as a moral prejudice. The latter factor is obviously a factor increasing the typical damage amount. Article 68(3) UPCA does not resolve the relationship between the three aspects. It is however suggested that, if it turns out that the identified lost profits are higher than the profits made by the infringer or vice versa, the higher amount counts for the damage award. This is similar to the German case law which leaves it to the injured party to select between three calculation methods, namely to measure the damages by either the "lost profits" or "unfair profits of the infringer" or "reasonable royalties by analogy." Often the method of "lost profits" is not chosen by the injured party because it requires that the injured party discloses its own financial situation.

Article 68(3) UPCA proposes as an "alternative" a further calculation method namely to award a lump sum payment on the basis of elements such as at least the amount of the royalties or fees which would have been due if the infringer had requested authorization to use the patent-in-question. This seems to comply with the method for measuring damages under German law referring to a reasonable royalty.

[D] Statute of Limitation

Article 72 UPCA provides that "without prejudice to Article 24(2) and (3), actions relating to all forms of financial compensation may not be brought more than five years after the date on which the applicant became aware, or had reasonable grounds to become aware, of the last fact justifying the action." The UPCA thus sets a time limit of five years for filing an action aimed at damages (or compensation derived from the provisional protection conferred by a published European patent application). With respect to European bundle patents, which could be asserted at the UPC or a national court, national law may provide for more flexible statutory limitations, as it might be the case under German law (*see* the following sections). However, such national rules should not be applied at the UPC, unless equity and fairness require doing so. For example, a claim that was already time-barred under the applicable national law shall not be enforceable under the UPC later on. In such a situation, the lapse that already occurred under national law shall remain applicable. In any other situation, the UPC shall apply the five-year period, so that the court will not have to make reference to a bundle of different national rules. Despite the wording of Article 72 UPCA, the limitation should not be treated ex officio, but remain subject to a defense raised by the defendant.

Another important aspect is: According to Rule 12 RoP, the claimant has to lodge an application for the determination of damages no later than one year from service of the final decision on the merits (including any final decision on appeal) on both infringement and validity.

§14.03 LESSONS FROM THE GERMAN CASE LAW

[A] Introduction

Unlike under US law, there are no punitive damages under the UPCA and the German law for patent infringement. Nonetheless, it is recognized that infringement damages must be sufficiently high to provide a deterrent effect.[5] Such a demand would comply with the requirement that the infringer shall not benefit from the infringement (Article 68(2) UPCA). The infringer shall not be better positioned than an authorized user. That is, it should not be advantageous for the alleged infringer to contest a patent that is valid and infringed. Someone who has previously asked for permission and pays licenses to the patent holder is acting properly. Thus, the legal system must favor such legal conduct and accordingly discourage a potential infringer. Thus, the deterrent effect should be sufficiently serious to discourage would-be infringers from including patent infringement in their business model (i.e., the so-called rule of "efficient infringement" must be discouraged by law).

German case law has established three methods for measuring the actual damages:[6]

(1) reasonable royalty;
(2) patentee's lost profits; or
(3) infringer's profits.

This damages framework arises from the following statutory sections and also comports with Article 68(2) UPCA. Section 139(2) of the Patent Act provides as follows.

Any person who commits these acts intentionally or negligently shall be liable for compensation to the injured party for the damage suffered therefrom. For the assessment of the compensation account can be taken of the profits, which the infringer has made due to the infringement. The assessment of the damages can also be based on the amount which would have been due as a reasonable compensation if the infringer had requested authorization for the use.[7]

The "reasonable royalty" calculation method and the "patentee's lost profits" are explicitly mentioned in section 139(2) of the Patent Act, whereas the "the infringer's lost profits" can be claimed according to general civil rules (sections 249 and 252 of the Civil Code).

5. BGBl. I S. 1191.
6. Federal Supreme Court, X ZR 60/06, GRUR 2008, 94, "Zerkleinerungsvorrichtung."
7. Unofficial translation.

It is up to the injured party to select the appropriate methodology, depending on the figures provided by the accused infringer. Even though the provisions of section 139(2) Patent Act seem to leave this open, it is impermissible to "mix and match" these various damages calculation methods.[8] The injured party can only select one of the three methods for calculating the damages. The following is an overview of the various damage methodologies recognized by German courts, and a summary of how they play out in practice.

[B] Reasonable Royalty

The award of a "reasonable royalty" provides a baseline measure of damages in those cases where the lost profits of the infringer or patentee do not justify a higher award. The royalty calculation is premised on the principle that an unauthorized user should not be better positioned than an authorized licensee.[9] The reasonable royalty is thus the price on which reasonable parties would have agreed if they had known the extent of the use of the patent when concluding a hypothetical agreement.[10] For this reason, this calculation method is also commonly called a "license analogy." The following is a framework for arriving at the appropriate royalty base and royalty rate.

*[1] Royalty Base (*Bezugsgröße*)*

The royalty base for calculating royalty damages typically refers to the net revenues[11] achieved by the infringer with the sales of the product or assembly. The royalty-based calculation method relies on an abstract assessment of the infringing sales without investigating whether or to what extent the revenues are caused using the infringed patent or whether the accused product or assembly could have been sold at the same price even without using the accused features.[12]

Where the defendant sells an assembly that is composed of many different components or features, but the inventive aspects of the patent-in-suit are directed to only one or several components, parts or features of the assembly, the assessment additionally involves the question as to whether the royalty rate is to be applied against the revenue from the whole product or assembly or only of parts of it. This typically depends on what objective parties would have hypothetically considered as an appropriate reference in a license agreement. According to the case law of the Federal Supreme Court,[13] it has first to be determined which part(s) of the product or assembly is/are characterized by the invention. These are the parts of the assembly which considerably improve the device with respect to the asserted advantages of the

8. This results from the reasons of the legislator accompanying the Act when implementing s. 139(2) Patent Act: BR-DR 64/07, 76.
9. Federal Supreme Court, X ZR 36/80, GRUR 1982, 286, "Fersenabstützvorrichtung."
10. Federal Supreme Court, X ZR 54/93, GRUR 1995, 578, 581, "Steuereinrichtung II."
11. These are the revenues excluding sales tax: Federal Supreme Court, I ZR 169/07, GRUR 2010, 239, "BTK."
12. Federal Supreme Court, I ZR 169/07, GRUR 2010, 239, "BTK."
13. Federal Supreme Court, X ZR 54/93, GRUR 1995, 578, 581, "Steuereinrichtung II."

invention of the patent-in-suit. If such parts can be identified within the concerned assembly, the next question is whether such parts represent marketable units and can individually be bought on the market.[14] If this is the case, it is typically suggested to apply the royalty against the value of the marketable unit in which the invention resides and not of the entire assembly. The assessment thus leads to the smallest marketable unit of the entire assembly. This is similar to the "smallest salable patent practicing unit" (SSPPU) concept in US patent law. For instance, if the invention concerns a part of the assembly (for instance, passenger car rearview mirror), which can be bought as part of or together with the whole assembly (in this example the car), it can be assumed that the parties would have agreed on a royalty which is applied against the smallest salable part, here the car's rearview mirror. Of particular importance for that assessment are industry customs. In cases where the smaller part is not separately marketable, or the technical improvement is applicable to the entire assembly, then the royalty rate may be applied to the entire assembly. In addition, a strong interrelationship between the royalty rate and royalty base needs to be taken into account. That is, if it is not possible to refer to a small marketable unit and if consequently the entire assembly must be used as the royalty base, the applicable royalty rate will have to be reduced, thus providing a balancing effect.

For determining the base, all sales which are triggered by an offer made in Germany by the accused infringer are accounted for. This even includes sales to customers situated outside Germany. The base excludes accessory charges such as operational costs like sales taxes, freight costs, cash discounts and so on. Typically, the figures for determining the base will be obtained through the accounting ordered upon the successful conclusion of an infringement trial. In case of an infringed process claim, it is commonly accepted to calculate the royalties on the net sales price of the sold products that were produced with the patented process.[15]

The territorial scope for assessing damages depends on the court in which they are sought. Before a national court, this is basically limited to the national boundaries, whereas an action before the UPC can be extended to all UPCA States as long as patent protection exists there.

[2] Royalty Rate

[a] General

The amount of the royalty is based on a hypothetical negotiation, namely what would have been due as a reasonable compensation if the infringer had requested authorization for the use on the basis of a nonexclusive license agreement.[16] All relevant facts need to be taken into account to achieve as appropriate a rate as possible. The assessment should start by determining the usual royalties in the concerned market. If

14. Federal Supreme Court, X ZR 8/90, GRUR 1992, 599, "Teleskopzylinder"; Appeal Court Düsseldorf, Decision of Jul. 17, 2009, 2 U 38/08, BeckRS 2010, 21821, "Kappaggregat."
15. Appeal Court Düsseldorf, InstGE 4, 165, "Spulkopf."
16. Appeal Court Karlsruhe, GRUR-RR 2014, 55, "Schadensberechnung."

there are preexisting license agreements, those shall first and foremost be used as a benchmark for calculating the royalty rate. If such preexisting license agreements can be used for determining the royalty fee, it is widely accepted to considerably increase the fee in order to compensate any benefits to the infringer who was not required during the time of the infringing use to satisfy any duties of a licensee, such as keeping records to establish the royalty reports necessary under standard license agreements. In particular, the infringer compared to a licensee does not bear the risk of paying royalty fees for an invalid patent.[17]

If such agreements are not available, the court will look to customary industry practice. In the pharmaceutical sector, we have seen royalty rates up to 10%. Within the chemical sector generally we have seen rates up to 8%. These are the known peak rates, and values can of course vary. The situation is more modest in the sectors of mechanical engineering, where royalties of 3%–5% are usual. In the telecommunication area, these values might be even significantly lower. Customary rates form a rough starting point for the determination of the rate.

[b] Specific Factors

Other factors that may influence the royalty rate include the following considerations, which point to the value of the patented invention:

- Technological and economic importance of the invention:[18] The most critical fact is based on the characterization of the technical improvement itself, as provided by the patented invention. Of importance are the advantages offered by the invention in view of the state of the prior art. In particular, the rate would be higher in a case where it is particularly difficult if not impossible to circumvent the patented invention and if reasonable and feasible alternatives to the invention do not exist.
- Interaction between the royalty base and the amount of the rate: If an invention concerns an assembly that is composed of different parts, the base will be assessed either on the value of the entire device or on the part that most directly embodies the invention (*see* above). If a bigger base is identified, that will tend to lead to a lower royalty rate.
- Volume of sales: Mass-produced products usually justify lower rates, due to lower profits gained per item, whereas high value products sold in smaller quantities may confer higher rates. A further indicator which is taken into account is the infringer's profit attributable to the infringing product.

17. Royalties paid prior to the revocation of the patent are not reimbursable. The argument behind this concept is that the licensee had an advantage over its competitors due to the factual existence of the patent until its revocation. *See also* District Court Mannheim, InstGE 12, 160, "Orange Book License"; District Court Munich I, NJOZ 2011, 1318, "Gülleausbreitungseinrichtung": The District Court Munich found an increase of 66% reasonable.
18. Federal Supreme Court, X ZR 19/92, GRUR 1993, 897, "Mogul Anlage."

- An elevating factor for the rate is premised on the consideration that the infringer did not bear the typical risks of a normal licensee. The normal licensee bears the risk of paying a license for an invalid patent.[19]
- A factor that tends to favor a lower rate may be that the product or part of the assembly against which the royalty is assessed embodies other inventions unrelated to the patented invention. And another factor that may reduce the royalty rate is if it can be shown that the revenue from the sales of infringing products are attributable to the marketing efforts or business connections of the accused infringer, more than the technical benefit of the patented technology.[20]

Back damages are typically augmented by prejudgment interest. It is understood that the infringer shall not benefit from the fact that the payment for damages is claimed and paid a long time after the use of the patent started. By analogy, a licensee is under the duty to continuously pay royalties after the conclusion of the agreement. Typically, the licensee is obliged to report and pay royalties for the use of the licensed patent at the beginning of each year for the past calendar year, with this amount typically due on February 1st for the past calendar year. A licensee in default would have to pay this default interest starting from that date for the past calendar year. It is accepted case law that the infringer must pay this default interest for the respective time of the infringing use just like a licensee in default.[21] Accordingly, he would have to pay interest for each past calendar year starting from February 1st up to the present, compounded. Due to the fact that the use of the patent by the infringer might have started many years back, that element of the damages could amount to a large sum of money. The interest rate is significant, presently set (since July 29, 2014)[22] at nine percentage points above the basic rate of interest. Pursuant to section 247(2) of the German Civil Code, the Deutsche Bundesbank announces the current basic rate of interest in the Federal Law Gazette.[23]

[C] Lost Profits of the Right Holder

Another measure of damages is based on the actual losses that the patentee (or licensee) incurred because of the infringement. The patentee has the burden to prove the extent of its lost profits. In practice, this means that the patentee will have to open its books for the infringer, which may be undesirable from a competitive perspective. Moreover, the burden is on the patentee to show that it did indeed lose profits due to

19. Appeal Court Karlsruhe, GRUR-RR 2014, 55, "Schadensberechnung"; District Court Düsseldorf, InstGE 1999, 83, GRUR 2000, 690, "Reaktanzschleife."
20. Appeal Court Düsseldorf, InstGE 4, 165, "Spulkopf II."
21. Appeal Court Karlsruhe, GRUR-RR 2014, 55, "Schadensberechnung"; Federal Supreme Court, GRUR 2010, 239, "BTK."
22. Section 288(2) of the German Civil Code: The amount was set prior to Jul. 29, 2014, at 8% over the basic rate of interest, prior to Jan. 1, 2002, at 5% over the basic rate of interest, and prior to May 1, 2000, at 3.5% over the basic rate of interest.
23. Previously and currently applicable basic rates of interest can be found on the website of the Deutsche Bundesbank: https://www.bundesbank.de.

the infringing acts—this is akin to the concept of "but for" infringement under US law. The assessment thus requires that the injured party (patentee or exclusive licensee) demonstrate and prove that he uses the patent, and that there is at least a probability that he would have realized the lost profits.[24] For instance, he can show that particular business dealings were not possible due to the infringing activity.[25] This is a concrete, but challenging, way for demonstrating lost profits, and requires showing that the injured party would have indeed satisfied the needs of the market. It also is possible to show and prove the amount of lost profits hypothetically, by demonstrating that through the normal course of business a certain level of profits would have been made but for the infringement. The injured party must sufficiently substantiate this assumption based on facts to enable the court to estimate the amount. According to section 287 of the Code of Civil Procedure, the Court may then decide on this at its discretion by taking into consideration all the circumstances. Nevertheless, it is difficult to show in a normal market situation that the right holder would have made the sales but for the infringement. This calculation methodology tends to be used most successfully in well-defined markets.

[D] Profits Made by the Infringer

The third method for calculating damages is based on the profits made by the infringer. Section 139(2) of the GPA explicitly states that "when assessing the compensation, consideration may also be given to the profit which the infringer has obtained by infringing the right." Most lawsuits seeking a court determination of damages are based on this framework. The court will apply some discretion in determining the amount (section 287 of the Code of Civil Procedure) considering the factual circumstances as a whole.[26] The calculation method does not consider whether the harmed right holder was in the position to make the profits on his own. Thus, it is not necessary that the right holder possesses its own operation enabling the production of products falling under the asserted patent. Unlike a compensation for actual damages suffered by the right holder, this method rather compensates for the unlawful acts committed by the infringer and the hypothetical possibility that this harmed right holder could have made the infringer profits.[27]

The following factors are relevant for the calculation method based on the infringer's profits.

[1] Infringer's Revenue

The calculation method first requires the determination of the revenues realized with the product infringing the patent. This information is typically provided by the infringer

24. Federal Supreme Court, I ZR 132/60, GRUR 1962, 509, "Dia-Rähmchen II."
25. Federal Supreme Court, VIII ZR 392/03, NJW 2006, 843, "Abstrakte Berechnung entgangenen Gewinns."
26. Appeal Court Düsseldorf, InstGE 5, 251, BeckRS 2005, 10332, "Lifter"; District Court Düsseldorf, Decision of Jun. 30, 2009, 4a O 146/08, "Rolladen II."
27. Federal Supreme Court, I ZR 132/60, GRUR 1962, 509, "Dia-Rähmchen II."

through a "rendering of accounts" proceeding.[28] Even if the patent covers only a part of an assembly, unit or composition, the revenues realized through the marketing of the whole product shall usually be taken into account.[29]

[2] Deductible Costs

When assessing the infringer's profits, disputes often arise over what costs may, and may not, be deducted from the revenues to ascertain to the relevant amount of profits made. Generally, variable costs are deductible, whereas fixed or overhead costs are not. According to a decision of the Supreme Court,[30] overhead costs do basically not represent deductible costs because these costs would have accrued anyway, even without the infringing activity. Overhead costs refer to those expenses associated with running the company that cannot be directly linked to creating or producing a product or service. The allegation that overhead costs have been spent and are equally necessary for the production and distribution of the infringing product is usually not sufficient to render these costs deductible. In rare exceptions, if overhead costs are directly linked to the infringing device/product, they are deductible. This direct attribution must be demonstrated and proven by the accused infringer.[31] The same applies to the variable costs that are necessary for the production of the accused product and are usually deductible costs. Typical variable costs are the material costs which by necessity must be spent to produce the infringing device.

By way of examples, the following are costs that are typically deductible:

- The actual material costs necessary for the production and assembling of the infringing product.[32]
- Costs for transportation of the infringing product, including packaging and freight costs.
- Costs for employees being specially recruited and used for the manufacturing of the infringing device.[33] Thus, costs for employees, in particular their salaries are usually not deductible, even if the employee was involved in the production of the infringing products.[34] The accused infringer has to prove that he would have saved the costs for particular employees without the infringing activity. This might be possible if he is able to show that he has specially recruited the employee for the production of the infringing device.[35]

28. *See* Ch. 10, §10.02[F][4].
29. Appeal Court Düsseldorf, InstGE 7, 194, "Schwerlastregal."
30. Federal Supreme Court, I ZR 246/98, BGHZ 145, 366, "Gemeinkostenanteil": This decision is based on a design patent infringement. It is commonly accepted that the guidelines given by the Federal Supreme Court in that decision are also applicable to patent infringements: Appeal Court Düsseldorf, decision from Jun. 3, 2015; I-15 U 34/14.
31. Appeal Court Düsseldorf, InstGE 5, 251, BeckRS 2005, 10332, "Lifter."
32. Federal Supreme Court, I ZR 6/04, GRUR 2007, 431, "Steckverbindergehäuse."
33. *Ibid.*
34. District Court Düsseldorf, Decision of Jun. 30, 2009, 4a O 146/08, "Rolladen II"; this is however in dispute: Appeal Court Köln, GRUR-RR 2013, 398, "Bigfoot II."
35. Appeal Court Düsseldorf, InstGE 5, 251, BeckRS 2005, 10332, "Lifter"; District Court Düsseldorf, Decision of Jun. 30, 2009, 4a O 146/08, "Rolladen II."

- Costs for the acquisition of a machine that is exclusively used for the production of the infringing device. These costs are prorated according to the time of infringement and durability of the machine.[36]
- Costs for the energy used in connection with the manufacturing of the infringing product.[37]
- Lease of the production facility and stockroom used exclusively for the infringing embodiment.

Following are examples of expenses that are typically not deductible from the revenues when determining the infringer's profits:

- costs of the management, salary of administrators, salary of employees also dealing with other products;[38]
- lease of the production facility and stockroom not exclusively connected with the infringing activity;[39]
- general marketing costs;[40]
- research and development costs;[41]
- costs for products that can no longer be sold because of an injunction;[42]
- costs in relation to liability claims of customers.[43]

*[3] Share Factor (***Anteilsfaktor***)*

The damage claim is focused on the profits that are specifically caused by the infringing activity.[44] That is, the accused infringer must only surrender the part of the profits that can be effectively attributed to the use of the invention.[45] Accordingly, it is important to identify the different factors that might have contributed to the profits. These factors need to be weighted and prorated. The "share factor" is the portion of the infringer's profits attributable to the patented invention, and thus subject to the damages claim.

In case of a device or an apparatus, the profits are tied to the purchase decision of the customer. This decision is usually triggered by factors beyond, or in addition to, the inventive aspects of the infringed patent. Many factors could potentially influence the purchase decision. For instance, the accused product makes use of a plurality of other IP rights. These rights likely contribute to the achieved sales volume to some

36. Federal Supreme Court, I ZR 6/04, GRUR 2007, 431, "Steckverbindergehäuse"; District Court Düsseldorf, Decision of Jun. 30, 2009, 4a O 146/08, "Rolladen II."
37. Federal Supreme Court, I ZR 6/04, GRUR 2007, 431, "Steckverbindergehäuse."
38. *Ibid.*
39. *Ibid.*; the Appeal Court Köln seems to apply a more flexible approach to employees which do not exclusively deal with the production of the patent-infringing products: Appeal Court Köln, GRUR-RR 2013, 398, "Bigfoot II."
40. Federal Supreme Court, I ZR 6/04, GRUR 2007, 431, "Steckverbindergehäuse."
41. *Ibid.*
42. *Ibid.*
43. *Ibid.*
44. *Ibid.*
45. Federal Supreme Court, I ZR 322/02, GRUR 2006, 419, "Noblesse"; Federal Supreme Court, I ZR 107/90, GRUR 1993, 55, "Tchibo/Rolex II"; Appeal Court Düsseldorf, InstGE 5, 251, BeckRS 2005, 10332, "Lifter."

degree, or the accused product disposes of unique features which are unrelated to the inventive teaching but influential for the buyer's decision. Advertisement and sales efforts made by the infringer are typically disregarded.[46] However, a strong trademark, trade name or a predominant good will may positively influence the infringer's profits and thus influence the share factor, driving it down. The patentee shall not benefit from these attributes of the alleged infringer's product because they are not tied to the infringing activity.[47]

The determination of a share factor is particularly necessary if the inventive aspects of the infringed patent are only realized in particular parts or elements within an assembly. Another important aspect of this assessment is the question of whether there are alternative solutions available and the extent to which the accused infringer was in a position to design around the patent. The particular advantages resulting from the use of the patented invention, and to what extent these advantages influence the decision to buy, shall be taken into account.[48]

Usually courts determine a share factor within a range of 20%–60% of the established profits. Thus, the resulting compensation to be paid by the infringer will amount to 20%–60% of the actual profits that have been determined from the net revenue minus deducible costs as explained in the previous section. The court may exercise some discretion to determine the exact percentage, taking into account the circumstances (section 287 German Code of Civil Proceedings). The totality (100%) of the profits may be considered in only one exceptional situation: if the misappropriated invention opens a new area of application. In other words, a situation where noninfringing alternative solutions are not available and, consequently, the technical solution provided by the infringed patent represents the only factor that could trigger the customer's purchase decision. For example, such a situation might arise if the infringed patent concerns a drug with a particular active agent against a particular disease for which no alternative solutions are available. Where the effect provided by the patented active agent cannot be obtained from any other drug it is assumed that the purchaser buys the infringing medicament for no other reason than curing the disease. In such a situation it could be justified to award the totality of the established profits without any reduction through a share factor.[49]

[E] Period for Which Damages Are to Be Paid

A question often arises as to the time period over which damages must be paid.

46. Appeal Court Düsseldorf, decision from Jun. 3, 2015; I-15 U 34/14.
47. Federal Supreme Court, I ZR 322/02, GRUR 2006, 419, "Noblesse"; Federal Supreme Court, I ZR 107/90, GRUR 1993, 55, "Tchibo/Rolex II"; Appeal Court Düsseldorf, InstGE 5, 251, BeckRS 2005, 10332, "Lifter."
48. Appeal Court Düsseldorf, decision from Jun. 3, 2015; I-15 U 34/14; Federal Supreme Court, GRUR 2012 1226, "Flaschenträger."
49. District Court Düsseldorf, Decision of Jun. 30, 2009, 4a O 146/08, "Rolladen II."

[1] General

The damages calculation time period generally runs from the commencement of the infringing activities until the end of the damages period as described below in section 14.03[E]. However, there is a requirement of fault on the part of the infringer. Unlike under US law, German law presumes that anyone who participates in a commercial environment is required to sufficiently investigate and analyze opposing rights of third parties through publicly available means (e.g., patent registers). Thus, under German law, the infringer usually cannot escape liability by arguing that he did not know about the existence of the asserted patent or utility model. Accordingly, he must exercise reasonable care.[50] It is generally presumed that the infringer acted at least with negligence.[51] Furthermore, the award of damages does not require that the patentee mark the patented article as "patented,"[52] and failure to mark does not limit the damage claim. This is an advantage for patentees who do not exercise the invention, such as nonpracticing companies and holding companies. It is presumed that the accused infringer knew about the patent or should have known about its existence.[53] Effective notice of the granted patent (and hence the availability of damages) is calculated starting one month from the publication of the grant of the patent or the publication of the registration of the utility model, unless the infringer was given earlier actual knowledge of the right (for instance, by means of a special notice or communication from the right holder shortly after the publication). This one-month-from-publication period is considered to be sufficient for identifying and analyzing the granted right.[54] Ignorance of the right would be typically excusable only during that one-month period. Accordingly, it is recommended that potential defendant companies establish patent monitoring programs.[55]

[2] Published Patent Applications

Damages claims result from the infringement of a granted patent or a registered utility model. Damages claims cannot be based on patent applications. Nevertheless, a patent application may confer provisional protection from the date of its publication. According to Article 67 EPC,[56] it is left to the Contracting States of the EPC to prescribe the content of this provisional protection. It could be less than what is conferred by a granted patent but shall not be less than that which the laws of the State concerned attach to the compulsory publication of unexamined national patent applications. These are minimum conditions, and hence there might be differences from country to country (*see* Table 14.1 for key European countries). The German law provides this

50. This is a consequence of s. 276(2) of the German Civil Code: "A person acts negligently if he fails to exercise reasonable care."
51. Federal Supreme Court, X ZR 79/90, GRUR 1993, 430, "Wandabstreifer."
52. Chapter 10, §10.02[B][2][b][ii] "Right to Claim Damages."
53. Federal Supreme Court, X ZR 79/90, GRUR 1993, 430, "Wandabstreifer."
54. Federal Supreme Court, X ZR 28/85, GRUR 1986, 803, "Formstein."
55. Chapter 6, §6.02.
56. The text of Art. 67 can be found in Ch. 18, §18.01.

minimum protection by means of Article II, section 1 IntPatÜG for European patent applications corresponding to section 33 of the Patent Act applicable to national applications:

> **§33**
> (1) As from publication ... the applicant may assert from any person who has used the subject matter of the application, although he knew or should have known that the invention used by him was the subject matter of the application, a claim for compensation appropriate to the circumstances. Further claims are excluded.
> (2) The claim for compensation cannot be asserted if the subject matter of the application is obviously unpatentable.[57]

[a] Requirements

Use of the subject matter: Pursuant to section 33 of the GPA, the patent applicant may demand compensation appropriate to the circumstance for the "use of the subject matter" of the patent application. The scope of protection of the claims contained in the application as published is key, provided the claims are supported by the application as originally filed. The demand for compensation is thus triggered by the use of these claims. The scope of protection is determined according to the general rules applicable to granted patents.[58] A later limitation, such as by adding an additional feature to the claim as published,[59] has a retroactive effect. However, compensation is only due if the use still falls within the scope of the claim(s) as later narrowed.[60] Compensation that was paid earlier due to a broader claim contained in the published application, which was then narrowed to a scope that no longer covers the use, would have to be reimbursed.[61] Furthermore, any use of other (unclaimed) subject matter of the application which goes beyond the subject matter as claimed is not compensable.[62] Of course, such unclaimed and inventive subject matter could be detached from the application and explicitly claimed in a divisional application[63] from which publication a liability according to section 33 Patent Act might exist.

Contributory use: As there is not yet a granted patent, the use of the invention described in the patent application is not deemed to be unlawful, and thus the applicant cannot prohibit that use. It is not sufficient if someone only contributes to a use of the subject matter or induces a third party[64] to use it. Someone who only furnishes means for such use would not be liable, but of course the user is liable.[65]

57. This is an unofficial translation.
58. Chapter 12, Claim Construction and Infringement.
59. Please note that the claim may be modified after publication of the application. Such modifications may occur even after grant in opposition proceedings or later in national invalidation proceedings.
60. Federal Supreme Court, X ZR 22/73, GRUR 1977, 598, "Autoskooter-Halle."
61. Schäfers in Benkhard, Patentgesetz, 10th ed., s. 33, No. 4.
62. Kühnen in Schulte, Patentgesetz, 8th ed., s. 33, No. 6.
63. *See* Ch. 4, §4.02[D] "Divisional Application."
64. Federal Supreme Court, X ZR 79/04, GRUR 2006, 570, "extracoronales Geschiebe."
65. This is the opinion of the Federal Supreme Court (previous footnote) but still in dispute: *see* Schäfers in Benkhard, Patentgesetz, 10th ed., s. 33, No. 4.

Level of knowledge of the user: The compensation claim requires that the person who has used the subject matter knew or should have known that the use falls within the subject matter of the invention claimed in the application. As with damages claims, usually a one-month-from-publication period is considered to represent a sufficient time window for the user to identify the published application[66] and to acquire that level of knowledge. If he is not doing this investigation, it is presumed that he acted at least with negligence and consequently he would be liable.

Translation of claims: Finally, section 33 Patent Act necessarily requires, if the application is not in German, that a translation of the claims must be made available to the public by the GPTO or communicated to the user of the claimed invention.[67] An applicant who filed a European patent application in English or French could not assert any provisional rights during the time from publication until grant of the patent without such published or notified translation of the claims. Typically, a translation is filed if the claimed invention in the application is already used by third parties or if there is a likelihood of such use. In any event a German version of the claims has to be submitted after grant of the patent (Rule 71(3) EPC).

[b] "Compensation Appropriate to the Circumstance"

According to the Federal Supreme Court, the amount of compensation attributable to published patent applications is limited to a "reasonable royalty"[68] calculated in compliance with the method as previously described in connection with damage claims (section 14.02). The calculation methods "own lost profits" or "the infringer's profits" are specific to the infringement of granted patents and are not applicable to section 33 of the GPA, which only covers the time period up until the grant of the patent. After the grant of the patent, the other damages claim methodologies can be asserted.

Table 14.1 Provisional Protection

	Germany	*France*	*Italy*	*UK*
Provisional right arises when?	When translation of the claims (in German) is made available to the public GPTO or communicated to the user	When translation of the claims (in French) is made available to the public through the French Patent Office (INPI) or communicated to the user	When translation of the claims (in Italian) is made available to the public through the Italian Patent Office (UIBM) or communicated to the user	When translation of the claims (in English) is made available to the public through UK's Patent Office (IPO) or communicated to the user

66. Federal Supreme Court, X ZR 22/73, GRUR 1977, 598, "Autoskooter-Halle."
67. Article II, s. 1(2) of IntPatÜG.
68. Federal Supreme Court, X ZR 26/87, GRUR 1989, 41, "Offenend-Spinnmaschine."

	Germany	*France*	*Italy*	*UK*
Content of the right	Reasonable compensation only in case of direct use	Damages	Damages	Damages
Enforceability	Reasonable compensation can judicially be asserted against user, but court may stay the proceedings until grant	Seizure of products possible; court would stay the proceedings until grant	Seizure of products possible	Seizure of products possible; court proceedings possible after grant

[F] Statute of Limitation

According to section 141 of the Patent Act, damage claims shall become time-barred by statute in compliance with the provisions of Chapter 5 of Book 1 of the Civil Code.[69] Damages claims thus become time-barred ten years after they arise, provided the right holder did not know the circumstances giving rise to the damages, or at least if it cannot be proven that he negligently ignored these circumstances (section 199(3) No. 1 Civil Code).[70] In contrast, a limitation period of only three years is applicable where the right holder obtained or could have obtained knowledge of the accused infringement. This period commences at the end of the year in which the right arose (sections 195 and 199 of the German Civil Code). Accordingly, the relevant period for which damages have to be paid depends on the right holder's knowledge. If he was not aware of the infringing activity, he could claim damages for ten years. In the case of established knowledge, a shorter time limit is applicable.

Nevertheless, for the time-barred period, the right holder could claim restitution for all the benefits the accused infringer has obtained without legal grounds at the right holder's expense (claim to return of unjust enrichment according to section 812 of Civil Code). This claim would be time-barred ten years after it arises, or, irrespective of the date on which it arises, thirty years after the date on which the act causing the injury was committed. Accordingly, if the damages claim is already time-barred, at least a

69. *See also* Ch. 10, §10.02[B][3][b] "Legal and Procedural Defenses," point (f): "Statute of Limitation."
70. For the sake of completeness, it has to be noted that a thirty-year limitation may exceptionally be applicable if the moment of the infringing act and the occurrence of the damage, i.e., the moment when the right arose, diverge in time (s. 199(3) No. 2 Civil Code). In that particular case, the right becomes statue barred at the latest thirty years from the infringing act. This limitation is usually irrelevant as the moment of the infringing act and occurrence of the damage do not diverge.

restitution claim under the provisions for the return of unjust enrichment would be applicable, calculated by analogy to a reasonable license.[71]

The right holder can avoid having his claims becoming time-barred by means of triggering a suspension of the limitation period. The period of time for which the limitation period is suspended is not included in the calculation of the limitation period. For instance, the limitation period is suspended during the time of pending negotiations up to a refusal to continue these negotiations. The right holder may also trigger a suspension by means of filing a lawsuit against the infringer or by means of other similar proceedings (*see* section 204(1) of the German Civil Code).

71. Federal Supreme Court, X ZR 81/72, GRUR 1977, 250, "Kunststoffhohlprofil"; Federal Supreme Court, X ZR 7/80, GRUR 1982, 301, "Kunststoffhohlprofil II."

CHAPTER 15
Inventorship and Ownership

The legal concepts of inventorship and ownership of patents or patent applications are complex and multilayered. The concept of inventorship relates to the inventor or inventors who have contributed the ingenuity necessary for the invention. The inventor or inventors are those who have identified the inventive technical teaching in a reproducible and demonstrable manner. From that intellectual performance or inventive act of human beings may follow patent rights. A legal entity thus cannot be an inventor. Also, artificial intelligence (AI) *as such* may not be the sole origin of an invention.[1] From the inventive act emerges a legal position. This legal position includes the right to the patent which originally belongs to the inventor(s).[2] It contains the entitlement to file a patent application, to obtain a patent and to exclude third parties from using the technical teaching as protected by a subsequently granted patent. The owner of a patent is thus the person who enjoys the rights and benefits from a patent. Even though ownership originates from inventorship, the inventor and owner of the patent are not necessarily the same person.

As further specified in Article 60(1) EPC, if an inventor is an employee, the right to a European patent is determined in accordance with the laws of the state in which the employee is predominantly employed or, if such state cannot be determined, the state in which the employer has the place of business to which the employee is attached. Of particular note is Germany's Act on Employees' Inventions (hereinafter "ArbEG"), which governs the extent to which employees' inventions are assigned to their employers. The employment of workers in Germany and the acquisition of German entities thus require knowledge about the unique provisions of the ArbEG. Questions of whether employee inventions are, indeed, assigned to the employer can be quite challenging, and may be problematic when patents on these inventions are asserted in court. The following is an overview of the rules for inventorship, ownership

1. Melullis, in Benkard, Commentary of the EPC, 3rd ed., 2019, Art. 60, nos 14, 15.
2. Article 60(1) EPC.

and assignments, and in particular the requirements of the ArbEG for securing ownership of inventions developed by the employees.

§15.01 APPLICABLE LAW

The law applicable to a particular matter or relationship is a primary question for any legal assessment. The determination of the applicable law follows from the rules of private international law. These rules are spread over many different legal texts contained in national law, international conventions, such as the EPC, and different Regulations of the EU. Of importance are three Regulations, called "Recast-Brussels,"[3] "Rome I"[4] and "Rome II,"[5] establishing common rules to govern the applicable jurisdiction, the choice of law in disputes of contractual and noncontractual nature (so-called Brussels Regime). It is a complex task to work out which law will be applied in a given matter. The identification of the applicable law needs to be assessed case by case. The present chapter only aims at pointing to the most important aspects in relation to patents as an asset of property.

The EPC contains rules on the applicable law. The general rule is that, unless the EPC provides otherwise, the substantive aspects of property of a European patent or a European patent application are basically left to the national laws (*lex loci protectionis*). For European patent applications, this is explicitly provided for in Article 74 EPC.[6] For granted European patents, the principle of national protection follows from Articles 2(2) and 64(1) EPC. In each of the Contracting States for which it is granted, a European patent has the effect of and is subject to the same conditions as a national patent granted by that State, unless otherwise provided in the EPC. The referral is additionally overlaid by the special provisions of the UPCA and the UP Regulation.[7]

For UPs, the special rule of Article 7 of the UP Regulation is of importance. The provision provides that a UP as an "object of property" shall be treated in its entirety and in all Contracting Member States as a national patent of the Contracting Member State in which that patent has unitary effect and in which, according to the register, the applicant had its residence, principal place of business or a place of business on the filing date of the application. In case of joint applicants, this counts for the joint applicant indicated first in the European Patent Register. The first named joint applicant's residence or place of business is thus decisive for the applicable law. Accordingly, the order in which joint applicants, who are located in different States, are listed in the register may determine the applicable choice of law. If none of the applicants has its place of business in a participating Member State, German law

3. Recast-Brussels; EU 1215/2012 on jurisdiction and enforcement.
4. Rome I Regulation (Regulation (EC) No. 593/2008) of the European Parliament and of the Council of Jun. 17, 2008 on the law applicable to contractual obligations.
5. The Rome II Regulation (EC) No. 864/2007 regarding the conflict of laws on the law applicable to noncontractual obligations.
6. "Unless this Convention provides otherwise, the European patent application as an object of property shall, in each designated Contracting State and with effect for such State, be subject to the law applicable in that State to national patent applications."
7. Cf. Ch. 12, §12.01.

always applies.[8] This is because for nonresidents Article 7(3) of the UP Regulation refers to the State where the EPO has its headquarters. This is Munich. Thanks to the latter provision, German law plays an important role.

§15.02 INVENTORSHIP

An invention arises from the mental acts of a human being. Consequently, if German law is applicable, an inventor cannot be a legal entity. There is currently an ongoing debate about how AI can be linked to the aspect of inventorship. The Legal Board of Appeal of the EPO has ruled in its decision J 8/20 that under the EPC an inventor designated in a patent application must be a human being. This is also the view of the Federal Patent Court.[9] It is therefore recommended to designate a human being as an inventor. AI is a tool used by human beings. Even if the human contribution to the invention becomes a background feature, this contribution, as small as it may be, is nevertheless decisive for the question of inventorship. The discussion about the question of whether an AI system shall thus be named as inventor is, at least for the time being, far-fetched.

When the invention is developed jointly by several people, they are coinventors. Inventorship under German law starts from the principle that each inventor must have made at least an independent and creative contribution to the inventive teaching. This contribution does not necessarily need to be inventive on its own.[10] This is analogous to the requirement under US law that a person must "contribute to the conception" of an invention in order to be deemed a coinventor. As in both Germany and the US, the employee's contribution in relation to an achievement of a group of people must be more than insignificant in order to be inventive.[11] The simple provision of tools to the inventor, as would be usually found in an employer/employee situation, is insufficient to establish a coinventorship. It would also be insufficient if the contributor purely follows the instructions of the inventor.[12] The employee must enhance the intellectual underpinnings in order to qualify as an inventor.

The process of determining who is or is not an inventor on a patent may be difficult. For the reasons discussed below in the context of the ArbEG, there may be financial stakes for being included as an inventor on a patent, particularly for those inventions that become commercially successful for the company. Thus, the individual motivations for German employees to assert that they are inventors may be different than for US-based inventors, and the challenge for legal departments is to resolve these inventorship claims in a manner consistent with the ArbEG.

8. Article 7(3) UP Regulation.
9. Federal patent Court, Nov. 11, 2021, 11 W (pat) 5/21.
10. Federal Supreme Court, X ZR 142/01, GRUR 2004, 50, "Verkranzungsverfahren."
11. Federal Supreme Court, X ZR 130/93, "Gummielastische Masse."
12. Federal Supreme Court, X ZR 142/01, GRUR 2004, 50, "Verkranzungsverfahren."

§15.03 RIGHT TO THE INVENTION

The property rights arising from the invention follow from the inventorship determination. Article 60(1) EPC, section 6 of the Patent Act provides as follows:

> The right to a ... patent shall belong to the inventor or his successor in title.

Inventorship confers "the right to the patent, the right to the grant of a patent and the rights deriving from a patent."[13] As long as it is not an employee's invention for which the special rules of the Employee Invention Act are applicable (*see below*), the right to the invention can freely be assigned from the inventor to any third party. For instance, persons not considered "employees" by the ArbEG (*see below*), such as CEOs,[14] are basically free to transfer their rights to their inventions unless their contract with the company provides otherwise. For instance, a CEO, who is involved in the research and development of the company, makes an invention. He could be obliged to offer the invention to the company, even if this is not explicitly stipulated in his contract, provided that the invention falls into the business of the company and is largely achieved with the company's resources.[15] It results from contract interpretation but not from the ArbEG. That contract interpretation could also imply that the duty to assign the rights to the invention shall be adequately compensated.[16] The obligation to assign the invention could implicitly be contained in any contractual relationship between parties, such as between principal and service providers.[17] It would not be sufficient to confine the analysis to literal wording of a contract.

The inventor who assigns his rights to the invention remains an inventor. The status of inventorship is a personal right which is not transferable. But the assignment of the rights to the invention triggers a transfer of the property rights connected to the invention, namely "the right to the patent, the right to the grant of a patent and the rights deriving from a patent"[18] to the assignee. The assignee can be a natural person or a legal entity.

The assignment of a patent or patent application can even be based on an implied agreement.[19] But this exceptional situation must be deduced from a special relationship between assignor and assignee, and the party that seeks to assert rights from an implied agreement must prove the existence of such a special relationship. Thus, even though a written assignment agreement is not legally mandatory, it is highly recommended.

Note that in the case of pending European patent applications, a written and signed agreement is mandatory to transfer ownership. This is based on Article 72 of the EPC, which supersedes the more flexible German law.[20] That is, an assignment of a

---

13. Unofficial translation of s. 15(1) Patent Act.
14. Appeal Court Düsseldorf, 2 U 11/98, GRUR 2000, 49, "Geschäftsführer-Erfindung."
15. Appeal Court Frankfurt, 6 U 69/16, Decision of Apr. 13, 2017.
16. BGH GRUR 2007, 52, Rollenantriebseinheit II.
17. Federal Supreme Court, X ZR 42/67, Decision of Apr. 28, 1970; Appeal Court Düsseldorf, Mitt. 2014, 337, 341 "Rapssaatenschälung."
18. Section 15(1) Patent Act.
19. Federal Supreme Court, X ZR 42/67, Decision of Apr. 28, 1970.
20. Federal Supreme Court, X ZR 98/90, GRUR 92, 692, "Magazinbildwerfer."

European patent application shall be made in writing and shall require the signature of the parties to the contract. According to the case law[21] that strict formality exclusively relates to the assignment of the formal position resulting from the patent application.[22] Article 72 EPC does not apply to the right to the European patent (Article 60 EPC), for which the laws of the respective designated countries apply. Thus, the assignment of the German part of a European patent would not require a formal written assignment agreement, although it would nonetheless be highly advised.

§15.04 CO-OWNERSHIP

[A] Under German Law

[1] Legal Framework

Where the invention is developed jointly by several people, they are deemed co-owners of the invention (section 6 of the Patent Act):

> If two or more persons have jointly made an invention, the right to a patent shall belong to them jointly.[23]

As noted above, to be a joint inventor it is necessary that each inventor has at least made an *independent and creative contribution* to the inventive teaching. The legal relationship between co-owners (including organization and administration of their co-ownership) may be governed by an agreement concluded by all of them. To avoid disputes about organization and administration of the co-owned invention, in particular, about the individual shares of the co-owners in the invention, the conclusion of a written agreement is recommended. Thus, as soon as a group of researchers intend to undertake a joint research and development project, they would agree on a written agreement, a so-called R&D Agreement, which sufficiently addresses these matters. The co-owners may also establish a civil law partnership (§§705 et seq. of the German Civil Code, in the following "GbR").[24] It is an association uniting individuals or entities in view of achieving a joint purpose, which could be, for instance, the joint exploitation of the co-owned invention.[25] The formation of a GbR requires the conclusion of a partnership agreement. A written partnership agreement is recommended but the written form is not compulsory. As soon as one establishes a GbR, that

---

21. District Düsseldorf, 4a O 406/06; Decision of Nov. 14, 2006.
22. There are three categories of rights which basically follow from an invention: The **first category** is called the ***right to the patent*** (*see* Art. 60 EPC) and encompasses the sum of proprietary rights resulting from the invention. These rights emerge from the invention itself and do not require a patent application. The **second category** is the ***right to the grant of the patent***. This is the formal position which arises from the patent application vis-à-vis the patent office. Finally, there is the **third category** which is called ***rights out of the patent*** and relates to the effects of the patent such as the rights resulting from non-authorized use (ss. 9 and 10 Patent Act). The formalities of Art. 72 EPC only apply to rights of the second category.
23. Unofficial translation.
24. Federal Supreme Court, GRUR 1979, 540, 542.
25. Benkard, Patentgesetz, Commentary, 11 ed., §6, Rn. 59.

triggers application of a set of provisions contained in the German Civil Code (§§705 et seq.), which govern details about the treatment of the company's assets and possible dissolution. The involved parties need to consider that the legal consequences for a co-owner in a situation where there is an agreement between them may significantly differ from the legal situation without any written explicit or tacit agreement. In order to avoid undesirable legal consequences, it is therefore advisable to prevent these by formalizing an agreement.

In the absence of any agreement between the co-owners and provided that German law is applicable, the provisions of the German Civil Code dealing with the "community of co-owners" (section 741 of the Civil Code)[26] apply.[27] Such co-owners will have a share in the invention that corresponds to their creative contribution.[28] The determination of that share requires an evaluation of the performance of each contributor.[29] "In case of doubt it is to be assumed that the co-owners are entitled to equal shares" (section 742 of the Civil Code).[30] Each co-owner is also entitled without the consent of the other co-owners to individually transfer his share in the community to a third party.[31] The law does not contain a provision for a right of first refusal ("Vorkaufsrecht") that could be exercised by the other co-owners in case one co-owner is about to sell his share. Thus, a co-owner may exert pressure on the other co-owners through the threat of selling his share to any third party, for instance, an unpleasant competitor.[32] The question as to the extent to which such a co-owner is bound by the principle of good faith and can therefore be prevented from such (possibly damaging) sale by the other co-owners has not yet been decided by the courts.[33]

In principle, each co-owner is allowed to individually assert patent claims[34] against infringers through court proceedings without the other co-owners necessarily joining these proceedings. This follows from an application by analogy of section 1011 of the Civil Code according to the case law.[35] The co-owner is thus also litigating on behalf the other co-owners of the community. This follows from the external relationship of the community, which must not necessarily comply with the internal arrangements of the co-owners. Also, co-owners can principally use the invention for their own purposes to the extent that joint use by other co-owners is not impaired (section 743(2) Civil Code).[36]

26. A translation of the German Civil Code can be found on the webpage of the German Ministry of Justice: www.gesetze-im-internet.de/englisch_bgb/.
27. Federal Supreme Court, X ZR 152/03, GRUR 2005, 663, "Gummielastische Masse II"; Appeal Court Düsseldorf, I-2 U 5/11, GRUR-RR 2012, 319, "Einstiegshilfe für Kanalöffnungen."
28. Federal Supreme Court, X ZR 152/03, GRUR 2005, 663, "Gummielastische Masse II."
29. Federal Supreme Court, X ZR 54/67, GRUR 1971, 210, "Wildverbissverhinderung."
30. Federal Supreme Court, X ZR 63/77, GRUR 1979, 540, "Biedermeiermanschette."
31. Federal Supreme Court, X ZR 223/98, GRUR 2001, 226, 227, "Rollenantriebseinheit."
32. Busse/Keukenschrijver, Commentary, 9th ed., §6 PatG, no. 44.
33. For further details *see* Krasser/Ann, §19, no. 97.
34. The assertion may include the right to prevent the use of the patent, to claim damages and to be informed about the extent of use.
35. Federal Supreme Court, I ZR 168/97, GRUR 2000, 1028, "Ballermann," Appeal Court Düsseldorf, I-2 U 39/09.
36. Federal Supreme Court, X ZR 152/03, GRUR 2005, 663, "Gummielastische Masse II."

[2] Compensation Between Co-owners

Unless it is not regulated otherwise in an agreement, a co-owner is basically not required to compensate the other co-owners for his individual use of the invention unless that use considerably exceeds his share in the invention and if such financial compensation in-between the co-owners is demanded for equity reasons.[37] When evaluating the question of whether a co-owner is entitled to a monetary compensation, the circumstances of the individual case must be comprehensively assessed.[38] Typically, financial balancing between owners is unnecessary, especially if their individual scopes of exploitation are equal and well balanced. The situation becomes complicated if there is an imbalance among the individuals' scope of exploitation or if one co-owner is not exploiting the invention at all, but the others do. Of importance for the evaluation are the reasons for which the co-owner refrains from exploiting the invention, leading to that imbalance.[39] If certain co-owners are limited in their ability to exploit the invention, for example, due to their field of activity or the resources available to them, it is suggested as a rule that such co-owners should be compensated by co-owners who make considerable use of the invention through their own production or distribution activities. In such cases, a co-owner who does not possess sufficient experiences or resources, such as an individual inventor who typically exploits the rights to which he is entitled by granting licenses, need not, in principle, elaborate on the reasons for which he has refrained from exploiting the patent.

The license analogy is generally well suited to provide an appropriate balance of interests. It is generally to be regarded as an appropriate calculation method unless special circumstances exist which make the calculation on this basis appear unsuitable in the specific case.[40]

[3] Administration of Co-owned Inventions

Unless the co-owners have agreed to do it otherwise, the administration of the co-owned invention is organized jointly by the community (section 744(1) of the Civil Code). Administrative acts would cover the filing of patents or utility models and the granting of licenses. It is usually sufficient if the co-owners agree on proper administrative acts by a simple majority (section 745(1) of the Civil Code). The vote need not be unanimous. But in the case of only two co-owners, a simple majority would require that both co-owners agree on whether or not a particular administrative act shall be performed. Accordingly, one co-owner could in principle block the other co-owner and in exceptional situation even hinder patent exploitation, as through licensing or

37. *Ibid.*
38. Federal Supreme Court, judgment of Mar. 22, 2005—X ZR 152/03, BGHZ 162, 342, 348, Gummielastische Masse II; Federal Supreme Court, judgment of May 16,2017, Az. X ZR 85/14.
39. *See* Ann in Ann/Kraßer, Patentrecht, 7th ed., §19 marginal no. 85; Federal Supreme Court, judgment of May 16, 2017, Az. X ZR 85/14.
40. Federal Supreme Court, judgment of Dec. 21, 2005—X ZR 165/04, GRUR 2006, 401, 404—Zylinderrohr.

enforcement against infringers[41] as a result of the internal relationship between the co-owners. A way to overcome such a conflict is to compel consent from the denying co-owner through a court action. This action would, however, only be successful if the denial is considered abusive or clearly unreasonable (section 745(2) Civil Code). Nevertheless, necessary acts of administration (section 744(2) Civil Code) aimed at safeguarding the right to the invention can individually be carried out by each co-owner even without the consent of the other co-owners.

A co-owner may—at any time—request the dissolution of the community (§749(1) Bürgerliches Gesetzbuch (BGB): Civil Code).[42] An economically weak co-owner thus has considerable leverage over his co-ownership. The dissolution is then implemented by sale and division of the generated proceeds; in the absence of special agreements, the sale is means of mortgage sale (§753(1) BGB). This can lead to unsatisfactory solutions in individual cases.

In practice, these provisions may create problems between the co-owners. It is thus recommended that co-owners have a written agreement in place to avoid disputes about the administration of the co-owned invention. As soon as a group of researchers intends to undertake a joint research and development project, they should discuss these issues and agree to them in writing.

[B] Other National Laws: France and UK

If the co-owners do not agree on how to organize the co-ownership, French law provides for a default provision: it gives a co-owner individual discretion to organize the exploitation of the patent in parallel with the other co-owner(s). This discretion is balanced out by financial compensation.[43] Accordingly, each co-owner may independently exploit the invention but must pay a fair indemnity to the other nonexploiting owners. Each co-owner is entitled to start a patent infringement action if he notifies the other co-owners. The co-owner can even grant a nonexclusive license against a fair indemnity to the other co-owners. Also, the assignment of the co-ownership is possible, provided the (selling) co-owner previously offers it to the other co-owners.[44]

Under UK law, unless agreed otherwise, each applicant (co-owner) has an equal undivided share in it.[45] Each co-owner is entitled to use the patented teaching for his own benefits without the consent of the other co-owner(s). On the contrary, a sole co-owner may not, without the consent of the other co-owner(s), grant a license under the patent. Therefore, if one co-owner wishes to use the rights by licensing, an agreement between the two co-owners needs to be reached.

The relationship between co-owners is handled differently in the laws of the various European States. To avoid legal uncertainty related to the application of these laws, it is thus highly recommended to establish an agreement between the parties at

41. Busse, s. 6 No. 38, Federal Supreme Court, BGHZ 146, 341 (NJW 01, 1056).
42. Federal Supreme Court, X ZR 152/03, GRUR 2005, 663, "Gummielastische Masse II."
43. Article L. 613-29 (CPI).
44. Article L. 613-29, (e) (CPI).
45. UK Patent Act 1977, s. 36.

an early stage when the coinventions have not been made. In practice, such agreements are important to advance the special interests of the parties.

§15.05 LEGAL TITLE TO THE INVENTION

[A] Legal Fiction in Favor of the Applicant

In the proceedings before the patent offices, the applicant is deemed to be entitled to exercise the rights to the patent (Article 60(3) EPC or section 7(1) GPA): "the applicant ... shall be deemed to be entitled to request the grant of the patent."[46] This legal fiction is aimed at avoiding a delay of the examination. Accordingly, an investigation about who is the right inventor or owner of the rights does not take place at the patent office. What counts is the name of the person or entity indicated in the documents filed and mentioned in the register.

If someone contends that he has been wrongly omitted from the right to the invention, it is left to the challenger to file a court action seeking an assignment of the application (section 8 Patent Act, Article 60 EPC, Article II section 5 IntPatÜG). By means of this action, for which the civil courts have jurisdiction, an examination of rights to the invention takes place. If a final decision determines that someone other than the applicant is entitled to the grant of the patent, the applicant can be replaced in the course of the granting proceedings by the previously omitted person, and if the patent is already granted, the rights can be assigned to him.

The EPO will stay granting proceedings if a third-party institutes proceedings against the applicant to establish that the third party is entitled to the grant of the European patent, instead of the original applicant.[47] Such inventorship challenges are typically filed in national courts of the EPC States. Their jurisdiction may follow from the applicable (national) employment law,[48] or the applicant's seat or the claimant's seat,[49] and by default, the courts of Germany having jurisdiction.[50] The patent will not be granted during the time of the stay. This stay of the granting proceedings can, of course, significantly delay the enforcement of the patent rights against infringers.[51] In exceptional cases, the EPO can order that the granting proceedings be resumed regardless of the pending national entitlement proceedings.[52] In order to determine whether the granting proceedings are to be resumed, all aspects relevant in balancing the interests of the parties have to be taken into account. Relevant factors include, for example, if there are facts or evidence showing that the third party is not actively

46. Unofficial translation.
47. *See* Rule 14(1) EPC.
48. Article 4, Protocol on Jurisdiction and the Recognition of Decisions in respect of the Right to the Grant of a European Patent (Protocol on Recognition).
49. Article 3, Protocol on Jurisdiction and the Recognition of Decisions in respect of the Right to the Grant of a European Patent (Protocol on Recognition).
50. Article 2, Protocol on Jurisdiction and the Recognition of Decisions in respect of the Right to the Grant of a European Patent (Protocol on Recognition).
51. EPO-J 0002/14 (Stay of proceedings) of Jun. 15, 2015.
52. EPO-J 15/13 of May 9, 2014.

seeking a decision by the national court. Also, the length of the proceedings before the national court or national authority is to be taken into consideration in a decision on whether to resume the granting proceedings.[53]

[B] Legal Effects of the Register

[1] German Proceedings

Entries in the patent register do not establish a legal presumption of their correctness. The acquisition of a patent is not dependent on any entry in a national patent register.[54] The true legal ownership of the patent may thus differ from what appears in the register. This divergence between the entries in the register and the actual legal situation occurs if the patent has been assigned by means of an agreement and so long as the new owner is not yet registered. Thus, if the entitlement of the registered owner is challenged by the defendant, the plaintiff must demonstrate that he is the entitled owner. Under German law, there is no legal presumption that the entry in the register of the ownership of a granted patent is true. However, it seems to be reasonable even under German law to attribute to an entry in the register at least some circumstantial evidence that the registered party is in fact legally entitled to assert the rights resulting from the patent. This assumption is however refutable. If the defendant refers to factual inconsistencies, it is the right holder's duty to provide evidence for his entitlement. In patent infringement proceedings, the entitlement of the registered owner could thus be challenged. He would be forced to prove that he is the owner of the patent and entitled to the damages for the claimed period. The problem becomes apparent if the patent has been assigned from the original applicant to a new entity and later to other entities. In such a situation it may thus be necessary to submit into the proceedings copies of the different assignment contract(s) showing an unbroken chain from the original applicant to the entity named in the patent register. This may be a complicated and difficult task, in particular, in cases where a long chain of assignments has occurred. The problem becomes acute if the originals of the agreements are no longer traceable and other evidence, such as evidence by witnesses, is unavailable or only available abroad. In addition, it has to be taken into account that often the assignments have been construed under foreign law, which burdens the assessment with considerations of foreign law. It is thus essential to assess the assignment situation prior to filing the patent infringement lawsuit.

If the legitimate owner is not mentioned in the register, it is necessary under German law that the registered party explicitly authorize the new and legitimate owner to take action. Therefore, an assignment agreement should contain provisions dealing with the period until the new owner is finally named in the register after a requested change of the register (section 30(3) Patent Act). Without any explicit authorization the

53. For instance, EPO-J 6/10 of Nov. 13, 2012.
54. Article 7(4) Regulation on the Unitary Patent.

new owner would be considered an entitled party in the infringement proceedings until the patent office actually changes the registration.

[2] UPC Proceedings

It is still undecided how an objection against the entitlement by the accused infringer should be treated in UPC proceedings. Rule 8(5)(c) RoP stipulates that for the purposes of the proceedings under the RoP, "there shall be a rebuttable presumption that the person shown in each national patent register and the European Patent Register kept by the European Patent Office is the person entitled to be registered as proprietor or applicant as the case may be." Thus, the entry in the register does provide some evidence that the registered entity is in fact legally entitled to assert the rights resulting from the patent. However, this presumption is refutable. Accordingly, a defendant who points to concrete factual inconsistencies which makes it at least sufficiently doubtful may challenge the registered owner to provide evidence for his claimed entitlement. The situation is clearer with respect to European patents with unitary effect. Rule 8(4) RoP provides for a non-rebuttable presumption. The registered person shall be treated "as such" for the purpose of the proceedings at the UPC. As long as he appears in the register, he is the only person who can commence or continue UPC actions or against whom UPC actions can be commenced or continued.

§15.06 EMPLOYEE INVENTIONS

[A] National Laws

Article 60(1) EPC provides in its second sentence that if the inventor is an employee, the right to a European patent shall be determined in accordance with the law of the State in which the employee is mainly employed and if that State cannot be determined, the law of the State in which the employer has the place of business to which the employee is attached. This applies to ordinary European patents as well as to patents with unitary effect. The rule must be brought into the context of Article 7 of the UP Regulation. The UP Regulation constitutes a special agreement under Article 142 EPC[55] which must be interpreted in way that the binding provisions of the EPC are not affected. Accordingly, the question of the applicable law must be determined case-by-case. It depends on the legal situation between employee and the employer. This may lead to the involvement of national law.

[1] France

For instance, if French law is applicable, the provisions contained in Article L 611-7 Code de la Propriété Intellectuelle (CPI) must be taken into account:

55. Article 1(2) UP Regulation.

If the inventor is an employee, the property right, in the absence of a contractual provision, which is more favorable to the employee, shall be defined in accordance with the following provisions:

1. Inventions made by the employee in the performance of either an employment contract involving an inventive mission corresponding to his actual functions, or studies and research explicitly entrusted to him, belong to the employer. The employer shall inform the employee who has made such an invention when it is the subject of an application for an industrial property title and when it is granted, where applicable, about that title. The conditions under which the employee, who is the author of an invention belonging to the employer, receives additional remuneration are determined by collective agreements, company agreements and individual employment contracts.

   If the employer is not subject to a collective agreement, any dispute relating to additional remuneration shall be submitted to the conciliation commission set up by Article L. 615-21 or to the Tribunal de Grande Instance.
2. All other inventions belong to the employee. However, where an invention is made by an employee either in the course of the performance of his duties, or in the field of the company's activities, or through knowledge or use of techniques or means specific to the company, or of data procured by the company, the employer shall have the right, under conditions and within periods fixed by decree of the Council of State, to be granted ownership or enjoyment of all or part of the rights attached to the patent protecting his employee's invention.

   The employee must obtain a fair price which, in the absence of agreement between the parties, is fixed by the conciliation commission set up by Article L. 615-21 or by the Tribunal de Grande Instance: they shall take into consideration all elements which may be provided to them, in particular by the employer and the employee, in order to calculate the fair price both in terms of the initial contributions of both parties and the industrial and commercial utility of the invention.
3. An employee who is the author of an invention shall inform his employer, who shall acknowledge receipt of the invention in accordance with the procedures and time limits laid down by regulation.

   The employee and the employer must provide each other with all relevant information on the invention in question. They shall refrain from any disclosure likely to compromise in whole or in part the exercise of the rights conferred by this act.

   Any agreement between the employee and his employer concerning an employee's invention must, under penalty of nullity, be evidenced in writing.
4. The conditions for the application of this article shall be determined by decree of the Council of State.
5. The provisions of this article shall also apply to civil servants, public authorities and all other legal persons governed by public law, in accordance with procedures laid down by decree in the Council of State.[56]

[2] UK

If UK law is applicable, the rules for determining ownership of employees' inventions are set out in sections 39–43 of the Patents Act 1977. Section 39 reads:

56. Unofficial Translation.

(1) Notwithstanding anything in any rule of law, an invention made by an employee shall, as between him and his employer, be taken to belong to his employer for the purposes of this Act and all other purposes if—
  (a) it was made in the course of the normal duties of the employee or in the course of duties falling outside his normal duties, but specifically assigned to him, and the circumstances in either case were such that an invention might reasonably be expected to result from the carrying out of his duties; or
  (b) the invention was made in the course of the duties of the employee and, at the time of making the invention, because of the nature of his duties and the particular responsibilities arising from the nature of his duties he had a special obligation to further the interests of the employer's undertaking.

(2) Any other invention made by an employee shall, as between him and his employer, be taken for those purposes to belong to the employee.

The employer is not obliged to file a patent or to protect the employee's invention. According to section 40, on an exceptional basis, the employee may receive an additional compensation, in particular for patent-protected inventions being of outstanding benefit to the employer.

The differences between the national laws are thus quite significant.

[B] Germany: ArbEG

Where German law is applicable, the law on employee inventions is applicable. The statute governing the assignment of employee inventions to an employer is the Act on Employees' Invention (ArbEG). Most of the provisions of the ArbEG are mandatory on employers. For instance, the employer cannot simply require (as is common in the US) that all inventions be assigned to the company. Rather, section 22 of the ArbEG states that "*the provisions of the Act cannot be modified by contract to the detriment of the employee.*"[57] For international entities acting within the German market, including through affiliates, it is crucial to correctly apply these rules.

The law is based on the concept that inventions made by employees initially belong to them. Under the ArbEG, special mandatory proceedings have to be applied in order for the invention to become the property of the employer. The employer and employee may not agree in advance upon an automatic transfer of rights as to inventions or technical improvements made by the employee during the employment. Such clause would be invalid according to section 22 ArbEG.

An unofficial translation of the most important provisions of the ArbEG can be found in Chapter 18.

[1] Scope of Application of the ArbEG

[a] Material Scope of Application

The ArbEG covers technical inventions and mere "technical improvements." Technical inventions could be subject to a patent or a utility model, whereas technical

57. Unofficial translation.

improvements are not eligible for protection under an industrial property right (sections 3 and 20 ArbEG).[58]

The ArbEG does not apply to other achievements of employees made during the employment relationship. This means that artistic creations and designs do not fall under the binding rules of the Act and accordingly the parties are usually free to agree on these rights in advance.

[b] Personal Scope of Application

The ArbEG defines "employee" as a person employed by the employer according to the German Labor Act.[59] This is a person who provides contractually owed labor tasks within an organization, in which he is under the direction of the contract partner (employer) with respect to content, way, time and location of implementing these tasks.[60] This applies to normal employees, and also to some executive employees.[61] The Act does not apply to the employer and to people holding positions in the company that are similar to the position of an employer (such as high officers[62]). Moreover, commercial agents and independent freelancers do not benefit from the provisions of the Act. Thus, in agreements concluded with such persons it is possible to agree in advance that inventions made in the course of the contractual relationship have to be assigned to the company. Without such an agreement a separate assignment would be necessary and additional compensation would be owed.

[c] Territorial Application

The application of the ArbEG depends upon whether German law is applicable to the employment relationship. If the employment relationship falls under German law, the ArbEG would be applicable.[63]

A question often arises as to whether it is possible to evade the ArbEG by means of the choice of law agreed in the employment contract. Indeed, according to Article 8 of Regulation EC 593/2008 (Rome II),[64] an employment contract is primarily governed by the law chosen by the parties. Article 8 of Regulation EC No. 593/2008 requires that

58. Technical improvements, which are in practice of lower importance, are only eligible for compensation if they confer to the employer an advantage that is similar to a patent or utility model. This requires that the technical improvement be a useful achievement from the status quo with a commercial advantage, and not something obvious to the person skilled in the art or detectable without difficulty by any competitor: District Court Munich Decision of Jan. 17, 2007, 21 O 1788/05, BeckRS 2008, 18310, "Keramikschneidwerkzeug."
59. Federal Supreme Court, X ZR 58/88, GRUR 1990, 193, "Autokindersitz."
60. Federal Constitutional Court, Decision of Feb. 18, 2000, 1 BvR 491, 562/93, NZA 2000, 653.
61. In German *Leitende Angestellte*: Appeal Court Hamburg, 3 U 89/58, GRUR 1960, 488, "Geruchs-beseitigungsverfahren."
62. CEO of German Limited (GmbH): Federal Supreme Court, X ZR 165/04, GRUR 2006, 401, "Zylinderrohr."
63. Federal Supreme Court, Decision of Nov. 27, 1975, X ZB 24/73, GRUR 1976, 385, "Rosenmutation"; cf. Art. 60(1) EPC.
64. Regulation (EC) No. 593/2008 of the European Parliament and of the Council of Jun. 17, 2008 on the law applicable to contractual obligations (Rome I).

"such a choice of law may not, however, have the result of depriving the employee of the protection afforded to him by provisions that cannot be derogated from by agreement under the law that, in the absence of choice, would have been applicable pursuant to paragraphs 2, 3 and 4 of this Article." In the absence of a choice of law provision, the contract would generally be governed by the law of the country in which the employee habitually carries out his work in performance of the contract. This is called the "usual place of employment." It stays the usual place of employment even if the employee is temporarily employed in another country (Article 8(2) Regulation EC 593/2008).

Thus, the restrictive rules of the ArbEG are usually applicable irrespective of whether or not the parties have agreed on a choice of law when the employee's usual place of employment is in Germany. Of course, special considerations of each case must be taken into account in making this determination. For exceptions to the general rule, particular attention should be paid to situations in which the employer or the employee does not reside in Germany or where the main tasks under the agreement shall be fulfilled partly within and partly outside the German territory.

[2] Service Inventions and Free Inventions

The ArbEG is applicable to all inventions irrespective of where and in which technological area and why the invention has been made by the employee during the employment. But the Act distinguishes between two types of inventions, namely "service inventions" and "free inventions" (section 4 ArbEG).

Section 4(2) ArbEG subdivides service inventions into two subcategories:

(1) they either result from the assigned duties under the employment contract; or
(2) they are "decisively based upon experiences or activities" of the company.

Service inventions according to the first category are connected to duties actually assigned to the employee. This is mainly the case if the employee is instructed to perform research and development activities. The second category does not necessarily require the assignment of such duties. It rather suffices for that category that the employee performs the activity in relation to the employer's experiences or activities. The latter can be any technological information, knowledge, know-how, practice, etc., of the employer. An enhanced causal connection between the inventive act and the "experiences or activities" of the employer's company must be given. In the words of the law, the invention must "decisively" be based on such "experiences or activities."

The main characteristic of both categories of service inventions is that they are essentially based on the employer's own initiative or resources.[65]

By contrast, "free inventions" make up all other inventions made by the employee, which do not meet at least one of the two criteria of being "service inventions." That is, they do not result from duties under the employment contract, or they are not decisively based on the company's know-how or developments. For

65. Federal Supreme Court, X ZR 155/03, GRUR 2006, 756, "Haftetikett."

example, an employee who is employed for improving software applications for an aircraft invents a novel sports shoe. That invention would not fall within the category of a "service invention," provided that it is neither a result of the accomplishment of regular contractual duties nor decisively based on know-how or experiences of the company.

In making the assessment between service inventions and free inventions, it does not matter when, for what reason, and where the inventor developed and completed the invention. It is not necessary that a service invention be developed at the usual working place of the employee. It is also irrelevant that third parties contributed to the invention.[66] All employee inventions made during the period of employment are governed by the ArbEG. It is irrelevant, for application of the Act, that the invention was made during working hours or while staying at home in the evening. Even inventions made during holidays are either service or free inventions (*see* Table 15.1).

Table 15.1 Distinction Between Service and Free Inventions

Inventions Made During the Period of Employment	
Service inventions =	**Free inventions** =
- Either result from obligatory duties of the employee (section 4(2)(i) ArbEG) **or** - are decisively based on know-how or developments of the employer (section 4(2)(ii) ArbEG).	- All other inventions which are not service inventions.
Employer is **entitled to acquire** a service invention.	Free inventions are **basically at the free disposal of the employee,** but there is a duty to offer to the employer a nonexclusive license under reasonable conditions if it falls within the range of the employer's actual or planned activities.

[3] Duty to Report

Service Inventions. Whenever an employee has made an invention, he must fulfill particular obligations vis-à-vis his employer. A central obligation of the ArbEG is the duty to report all service inventions. This means that as soon as the employee has accomplished any service invention—including a creative improvement of a previously completed invention—he must prepare a report about that invention (section 5 ArbEG). The aim of that report is to sufficiently inform the employer about the invention so that the employer can make a decision on whether to claim ownership or to release the invention.

66. Federal Supreme Court, X ZR 165/04, GRUR 2006, 401, "Zylinderrohr."

The report need not necessarily be a signed document. The report can be submitted by fax or email so long as the report is sent in text form to the right addressee (employer or particular authorized people) and mentions the reporting party. Bigger companies usually contractually require employees to use forms with predetermined fields and questions. The use of such forms is commonly accepted[67] and is recommended for an accelerated treatment and to avoid oversights that could occur if the invention is only reported by email.[68]

A duly established report of a service invention needs to contain (section 5(2) ArbEG) the following:

- A detailed description of the technical problem (including disadvantages, drawbacks and unmet needs in the state of the art) and its solution. It should provide a clear and complete understanding of the invention including modes of application. The employee must also add any existing notes to the extent they are relevant to the understanding of the inventive solution. Preferably, he should refer to drawings and photos.
- The employee shall describe how he arrived at the invention.
- He must mention the instructions, directions and technical aid received from the employer or supervisors.
- He must also mention the extent to which internal know-how and the developments of the company were important for solving the problem.
- The report shall also indicate possible collaborators (they do not necessarily need to be coinventors) as well as coinventors, including the nature of their involvement and the scope of their contribution. However, coinventors are entitled to submit a joint report, and this is generally recommended to avoid contradictory descriptions.
- The employee should indicate—in the situation of coinventors—the contribution he considers having personally provided to the service invention (section 5(2) ArbEG).

A report which does not comply with these requirements is deemed to be valid if the employer does not declare within two months that—and to which extent—the report needs to be supplemented.[69]

Free Inventions. If the employee believes the invention is free, he nevertheless has to sufficiently inform the employer about this invention (section 18 ArbEG). The duty then shifts to the employer to object to this categorization of the invention. If the employer does not object to the categorization made by the employee within three months of the employee's notification, the invention can no longer be claimed as a service invention. Section 19 ArbEG sets forth the circumstances under which the employee needs to offer a nonexclusive license under reasonable conditions to his

67. Federal Supreme Court, X ZR 26/03, GRUR 2006, 141, 142, "Ladungsträgergenerator."
68. Reports by email are admissible since Oct. 1, 2009, Federal Gazette, BGBl. I S. 2521. Invention reports submitted by fax, telecopy and email were not admitted prior to that date: Federal Supreme Court, X ZR 26/03, GRUR 2006, 141, 142, "Ladungsträgergenerator."
69. Section 5(3) ArbEG.

employer for any such free inventions, specifically, if the otherwise free invention falls within the range of the employer's actual or planned activities.

[4] Acquisition of the Ownership of Service Inventions

The German system is based on the concept that the rights to an invention made by an employee initially belong to the employee and not the employer. Accordingly, an acquisition process must take place in order for the employer to become the owner of the invention. The acquisition process starts with the reception of the report. As soon as the employer has received a report in appropriate form, a four-month period commences during which the employer may claim ownership over the service invention by means of a declaration (section 6(1) ArbEG). This four-month period may be extended in certain circumstances, such as if the report is incomplete (section 5(3) ArbEG).

An important change in the law took place in 2009 regarding the mechanics of assigning inventions to the employer. Prior to 2009, a serious pitfall arose if the employer failed to act on the employee's report of an invention. Under the previous ArbEG, the employer's claim had to be made "in a written statement, addressed to the employee, as soon as possible, and not later than four months from the receipt of a proper report"[70] (previous section 6(2) ArbEG). The written statement had to be signed, for instance, emails were not sufficient, and the period started to run as soon as the invention was duly reported, or, in the absence of such a report, at the latest at the filing date of the patent application, which was usually filed in the name of the employer. The courts consider the filing of the application by the employer as the trigger for the four-month deadline, even without any report about the services invention having previously been made by the employee.[71] The trigger of the deadline is not affected if that report of the employee is submitted at a later stage.[72] However, the employee's own (illicit) patent filing without a proper report, for instance, by means of a verbal message to the employer may not represent a sufficient trigger for that deadline.[73]

Inadvertently, some employers failed to present adequate written statements to the employee-inventor. Often this was simply caused by lack of knowledge of the law or by a more or less disorganized handling of these issues by the employers. In such situations, the right to the invention stayed with the employee.

In many cases, such defects in the transfer of ownership went undetected for years. Many of those defects are still undetected. These oversights have caused and will continue to cause problems for companies trying to enforce or assign patents which suffer from improper compliance with the prior provisions of the ArbEG. This is particularly critical for employers, if the employee meanwhile left the company and is

70. Unofficial translation.
71. Federal Supreme Court, X ZR 155/03, GRUR 2006, 756, "Haftetikett"; Federal Supreme Court, X ZR 64/15, "Lichtschutzfolie."
72. Federal Supreme Court, X ZR 64/15, "Lichtschutzfolie."
73. Federal Supreme Court, GRUR 2011, 733, "Initialidee."

consequently less inclined to help his ex-employer. In a worst-case scenario, he even could assign his rights to competitors. The old legal situation continues to apply for inventions reported prior to October 1, 2009.[74] Patents from that time might have such a defect. Thus, it can be expected that for the next ten years courts will still have to deal with the old legal regime and complications arising thereunder.

The ArbEG was amended on October 1, 2009, to facilitate transfer of service inventions to employers. Now, after expiration of the four-month term following receipt of an invention report, an employer who stays passive automatically acquires rights to the service invention. This so-called automatism provision is provided in section 6(2) ArbEG,[75] which provides that the employer's "declaration is deemed to be executed, if the employer does not, within a four-month term starting from the receipt of a duly made report release the invention by means of a declaration executed in text form vis-à-vis the employee." Accordingly, the absence of an explicit claim no longer hinders the employer from acquiring the rights to the invention, because it is now presumed that the employer had made a claim to the service invention. This provision is not retroactive, and so the "automatism" provisions of the 2009 law do not cure any prior defects in earlier patents.

Also under the present law, the employer may explicitly claim a service invention by executing a declaration to the employee (section 6(1) ArbEG). An explicit claiming of the service invention, instead of automatically acquiring the ownership by the indicated fiction of law (section 6(2) ArbEG), might be best if the employer does not want to wait until the end of the four-month term, for instance, in order to fulfill obligations toward business partners. An explicit declaration may also be useful to create a legal certainty between the parties and in granting proceedings at the patent offices. With either an explicit claim (section 6(1) ArbEG) or an automatic claim (section 6(2) ArbEG), all rights to the service invention pass to the employer. The employer becomes owner of the service invention and will be free to dispose of it, grant licenses or assign it to third parties (*see* Table 15.2).

Table 15.2 Employer's Options with Respect to Service Inventions

Release communicated in text form to the employee: - Employee stays owner of the invention and is entitled to apply for an industrial property right.	**Explicit claiming** by means of a declaration to the employee before the end of the four-month term (section 6(1) ArbEG): - Employer becomes owner of the invention upon receipt of the declaration.	**No reaction** by employer within a time period of four months starting from receipt of duly made report (section 6(2) ArbEG): - Employer becomes owner of the invention according to a fiction of law.

74. Section 43(3) ArbEG, Federal Supreme Court, X ZR 64/15, "Lichtschutzfolie."
75. Federal Gazette, BGBl. I S. 2521.

[5] *Obligations of Employer after Acquisition of the Service Invention*

If the employer elects to acquire the service invention, the employee is entitled to compensation. The employer is the debtor of this claim, which stays with the employer even if the service invention is later assigned to a third party.[76] The compensation claim can be assigned by the employee and is inheritable.[77]

National Filing (Section 13 ArbEG): If the employer acquires the service invention, he is solely entitled, but also obliged to file a national patent application as early as possible after the acquisition.[78] This could be a German patent application, or a European patent application, or an application under the PCT, provided Germany is among the designated countries, or, in case this appears to be more appropriate, a German Utility Model (section 13(1) ArbEG: "domestic application"). The employer must keep the inventor informed about the progress of the prosecution of the patent. If the employer fails to file the application on time, the employee may start the application or registration proceedings on his own initiative in the name of the employer (section 13(3) ArbEG).

International Filing (Section 14 ArbEG): The employer must inform the employee about those countries for which he does not intend to file a foreign application. He must so inform the employee sufficiently prior to the end of the term, until which priority rights can be claimed under international treaties.[79] The employee should have enough time to decide and to permit him to file applications in these States. However, the employee would have to bear the costs of these foreign applications filed in his own name. The employer may keep a nonexclusive right to use the invention in such States (section 14(3) ArbEG).

If the employer intends to abandon a patent application or granted patent in particular countries, the employee may take over the application or the patent but will then have to handle the prosecution in his own name. The employer may retain a nonexclusive right of use as long as the employee does not show that this represents an undue burden on the employee.

The failure of the employer to sufficiently comply with the indicated duties aimed at the protection of service inventions may trigger damage claims which could be asserted by the employee against him.

Keeping the service invention as a trade secret: In case of legitimate interests, the employer could also decide to keep the invention as a trade secret (section 17 ArbEG). However, this decision requires that the employer acknowledge that he would not question the patentability of the subject matter of the invention. If such an acknowledgement is made, this would result in compensation having to be paid to the employee in the same manner as with a patented invention. If the employer intends to keep the service invention secret but believes that the employee's asserted invention is

76. Federal Supreme Court, Jun. 2, 1987, X ZR 97/86, GRUR 1987, 900, 901, "Entwässerungsanlage."
77. District Court Düsseldorf, Decision of Sep. 17, 1991, "Reißverschluss."
78. A filing without delay is aimed at ensuring early priority rights.
79. In particular: Paris Convention.

not patentable, the employer may ask for an opinion of the Arbitration Board for employees' inventions at the German Patent Office. If the Arbitration Board concludes that the invention is not patentable, and the employee does not object to that opinion, the employer is entitled to keep the invention as a company secret with possibly very little or even no compensation for the employee (*see* Table 15.3).

Table 15.3 Protection of Service Inventions

Domestic Protection	*Trade Secret (in Case of Legitimate Interests):*
- Entitlement and duty to file for national protection right (PCT/EP with designation DE, DE Patent, Utility Model). - Duty to inform the employee about status of prosecution. - Duty to assign related rights in case of intent to abandon an application/registration or granted right (but employer may reserve for himself right to use against reasonable compensation).	- Duty to acknowledge eligibility for protection or refer to Arbitration Board (section 17 ArbEG).
Foreign Protection - Entitlement for protection abroad (outside Germany). - Duty to inform the employee about states in which no protection is sought, to release the service invention for these states and to enable the employee to acquire and get protection in these states (but the employer may reserve for himself nonexclusive right to use against reasonable compensation). - Duty to assign related rights in case of intent to abandon an application/registration or granted right (but the employer may reserve for himself right to use against reasonable compensation).	

[6] Employee's Compensation

As soon as the employer has made a claim of a service invention, the employee is entitled to compensation (section 9(1) ArbEG). The employer is obliged to compensate the employee even if the invention is later assigned to a third party.[80] The compensation claim can be assigned by the employee and is inheritable.[81] The amount of compensation should economically compensate the employee for the assignment of the rights to the employer.[82]

80. Federal Supreme Court, X ZR 97/86, GRUR 1987, 900, 901, "Entwässerungsanlage."
81. District Court Düsseldorf, 4 O 13/91, Mitt. 2000, 363, 368, "Reißverschluss."
82. Federal Constitutional Court, 1 BvR 587–588, NJW 1998, 3704.

[a] Individual Agreements on the Compensation

The provisions of the ArbEG are mandatory and the parties cannot, in most instances, contract around them. For example, it is impermissible for the parties to agree in advance on conditions that are objectively disadvantageous to the employee. A stipulation in an employment agreement which confers upon the employee a kind of all-inclusive flat rate for inventions made during the employment is, as a general rule, impermissible.[83] Nevertheless, the parties may reach agreements, in particular compensation agreements, concerning service inventions as soon as they have been reported to the employer (section 22 ArbEG): "Agreements shall, however, be permissible concerning service inventions after they have been reported and concerning free inventions and proposals for technical improvement (Section 20(1)) after their notification."[84]

Nevertheless, the content of the individual agreements may be challenged in the following two events:

(i) significant inequity which can be asserted by both parties until six months after the termination of the employment agreement (section 23(1) ArbEG);[85]
(ii) both parties may claim from the other party an adaptation of the compensation in case of substantial changes being essential for the assessment (section 12(6) ArbEG).

Even though the parties may waive the claim of adaptation of the compensation according to section 12(6) ArbEG, such agreements should be carefully reviewed with an eye to later disputes. The agreement should clarify and describe the factors of the assessment that resulted in that particular compensation.

The compensation is an important aspect of motivating employees. Typically, the compensation is paid as a lump sum,[86] but it can also be an ongoing payment. The agreement on a lump sum payment may have the advantage of removing uncertainties due to future changes with respect to the scope of use of the invention and, more importantly, it eliminates administrative efforts on the side of the employer. A lump sum payment could be combined with a waiver of the claim of adaptation of the compensation according to section 12(6) ArbEG but would require an additional payment to avoid an inequity according to section 23(1) ArbEG.[87]

Lump sum payments are usually used within incentive programs in view of motivating employees for better performances. To some extent, by means of an agreed lump sum the employer may additionally get a release from formal duties, such as the duty to protect the service invention or to release the invention for foreign countries.

83. Busse, Patentgesetz s. 22 ArbEG No. 5.
84. Unofficial translation.
85. Section 23(1) ArbEG reads: "Agreements concerning service inventions, free inventions, or proposals for technical improvement (section 20(1)) permitted by this Act, shall be invalid and void to the extent that they are significantly inequitable."
86. Federal Supreme Court, Nov. 20, 1962, I ZR 40/61, GRUR 1963, 315, 317, "Pauschalabfindung."
87. Arbitration Board 2/05.

[b] Calculation Methods

The amount of the compensation is governed by a directive issued by the Federal Minister of Labor,[88] which provides three methods for calculating the compensation paid to an employee for an invention, namely:

(1) license analogy (Directive No. 6-11);
(2) benefits to the employer (Directive No. 12); and
(3) estimation of the invention's value (Directive No. 13).

All three methods decisively depend on the benefits that the employer receives from the service invention.[89] Thus, the compensation requires that the invention have an economical effect with determinable advantages for the employer.[90] A share of these benefits is allotted to the employee.[91] However, benefits relating to third parties, such as benefits of licensees or the assignee of the service invention, are irrelevant for the assessment.[92]

[i] Contribution Factor (Directive No. 30)

When assessing the amount of compensation, a so-called contribution factor must be determined. The purpose of the contribution factor is to determine how much the employee as an individual contributed to the invention. For example, a scientist, whose duties of employment are mainly characterized by research and development, receives less compensation than someone who is not principally employed to perform research and development. The "contribution factor" is based on three elements: the extent of the respective contributions of the employer and employee in defining the problem that resulted in the invention, their respective contribution in finding the inventive solution and the position and duties of the employee within the company. Accordingly, if the calculation is based on the "license analogy" method departing from a market oriented or reasonable royalty rate, the determined contribution factor would influence the royalty rate to be paid to the employee as compensation. In the case of an employee focused primarily on solving needs predetermined by the employer, the employee's compensation might be a low fraction of that reasonable royalty. The average contribution factor ranges between 10%-20%.

---

88. Directive dated Jul. 20, 1959, modified by Directive of Sep. 1, 1983 (Federal Labor Gazette, No. 169, BArbBl. 11/1983, 27).
89. Federal Supreme Court, X ZR 137/07, GRUR 2010, 223, 225, "Türrinnenverstärkung."
90. *Ibid.*
91. *Ibid.*
92. Arbitration Board, Decision 58/07.

[ii] License Analogy

The "license analogy" is commonly applied by the courts[93] if the invention can be allocated to products manufactured by the employer. A number of factors are usually taken into account for a proper calculation of the employee's compensation. Comparable factors are also used for determining damages:[94]

- *Reference Base* (Directive No. 8): A reference base needs to be identified as the relevant basis for applying a reasonable royalty. For instance, if the product (as protected by the patent) is composed of a plurality of components, German courts usually refer to those components of that product which are decisively influenced by the invention. The reference base for a patent that claims a car is not necessarily the value of the whole car. It rather depends on the influence of the invention on the car and which part or parts of the car are decisively characterized by the invention. On the contrary, if the decisive character of the invention influences the whole product (this could be the case with respect to pharmaceutical substances, where the inventive aspect is tied to an active agent), it is reasonable to refer to its whole value. If the invention influences only parts of the product, it is acceptable to take only a percentage of its value. To determine the reference value, German courts weigh the problem solved by the patented invention and its relevance for the product concerned.
- *Net Sales Revenues*: These revenues do not contain costs for packaging, discounts, value added taxes (VAT) and agents' commissions.
- *Reasonable royalty rate*: For determining this rate, reference can be made to license agreements that have already been concluded by the employer with third parties. In absence of such license agreement(s), industry practices must be considered.
- *Scaling:* If the product is manufactured and sold in very high numbers, employers like to apply a sliding scale, which has a reducing effect on the compensation starting from a certain quantity. This must, however, be common practice in the relevant industry sector[95] or require that high numbers of sold products can be attributed to efforts and achievements of the employer. The success of a product is not necessarily triggered by the patent of which the product makes use. Also, other factors, such as the branding, advertisement, reputation of the company, might be decisive for the decision of the purchaser. Accordingly, the royalty rate is progressively reduced depending on the volume of revenue attributed to the product. For instance, in one case the Appeal Court Düsseldorf[96] applied a scaling starting from a revenue in excess of EUR 13 million, i.e., for the revenue below EUR 13 million, the full royalty, from EUR 13 million to EUR 25 million only three-fourths of the royalty rate, from EUR 25 million to EUR 50 million only half of the royalty rate, above EUR

93. Federal Supreme Court, X ZR 137/07, GRUR 2010, 223, 225, "Türrinnenverstärkung."
94. *See* Ch. 14.
95. Federal Supreme Court, X ZR 71/86, GRUR 1994, 271, Vinylchlorid.
96. InstGE 4, 165, 181.

50 million only one-quarter of the royalty rate had to be paid. This is only an example. The case law gives examples where a scaling was applicable starting from even significantly lower revenue (EUR 1.5 million).

- *Plurality of Patents*: A further aspect which has decreasing effect on the royalty rate is the question as to whether other patents are used by the concerned product. If multiple patents apply to a particular product, German courts consequently decrease the royalty of the different individual inventions.

[iii] Benefit to the Employer and the Invention's Value

Another rarely used method for the calculation of the employee's compensation is based on the benefit to the employer relating to the internal cost savings that the employer can achieve as a result of the invention. This method is most useful in cases where the invention consists of technical improvements that can only be realized within the company and therefore the license analogy method would not furnish a meaningful value.

The third (also rarely used) method is based on a free estimation of the value of the invention. This calculation method may be used where the value of the patent cannot be measured by a real royalty income (*see* Table 15.4).

Table 15.4 Three Calculation Methods

License Analogy:	*Benefit to the Employer:*	*Estimation of the Invention's Value:*
Appropriate method if the invention can be allocated to the manufacture and sale of products. This is the most used calculation method.	Appropriate method for innovations and improvements which can only be realized within the company and have no direct effect on the sales of the company.	Useful in cases of cross-licensing where the value of the concerned patent can often not be measured by a royalty income.

[c] *Example (License Analogy Method)*

The compensation needs to be assessed on a case-by-case basis. However, the following simple formula can help with calculating the compensation on the basis of the commonly used license analogy method:

$$C = E \times A$$

C = Compensation of the employee: If there is more than one employee-inventor, C has to be shared according to their respective contributions.
E = Value of the invention: E refers to the quotient of the reference base (*see* above) and the reasonable royalty. If the reference base refers to the value of the whole product, the revenues of the net sales price have to be multiplied by reasonable royalty which price usually is paid for the invention on the market (revenue x reasonable

royalty). The right royalty rate depends on many factors (*see* above). If the product is sold in high numbers, the employer may apply a sliding scale to the royalty rate, with decreasing effect.

A = Contribution factor: The contribution factor depends on the circumstances surrounding the tasks that led to the invention, how the problem was solved and the employee's role and position in the company. This factor is inherently open to dispute. Average factors range between 10% and 20%. To determine the contribution factor, reference is made to the following point scale:

a + b + c	3, 4	5, 6, 7	8, 9	10, 11	13 14	15 16	17, 18	19, 20	[p]
A	2, 4	7, 13	15	21,25	32, 29	55, 63	72, 81	90, 100	[%]

The following sub-factors of A (a + b + c) are used to assess the quantity of points (p). Each quantity of points corresponds to a percentage (such as 6p = 10%):

(a) **Contribution of the employee** (1–6 points): The employer sets the problem, but also gives the employee specific instructions as to the method he needs to employ to solve the problem (low number of points, e.g., 1p). The invention lies outside or is positioned far from the employee's usual area of responsibilities and he solved the problem independently (high number of points, e.g., 6p).

(b) **Contribution of the company** (1–6 points): To what extent does the employee rely on company resources to solve the problem? The less the company contributes, the higher the number of points.

(c) **Position of the employee within the company** (1–8 points): The more the employee is involved in research and development, the lower the number of points.

Example:

- Inventor discovered the problem to be solved on his own: However, he knew of shortcomings in the company which led him to the problem:

$$a = 2$$

- Inventor found solution using a combination of individual knowledge and company resources:

$$b = 2$$

- Inventor holds a university degree and is a research assistant in the company:

$$c = 4$$

Result: a + b + c = 8 = Contribution Factor 15%. In total this would lead to compensation of 15% of the reasonable royalty rate.

[7] *Resolution of Disputes*

A special system is provided by law to resolve disputes in the context of employees' inventions. The German Patent Office provides for an Arbitration Board (section 29 ArbEG), consisting of a legal member, who serves as chairman, and two technical members. The technical members are examiners from the German Patent Office selected according to the subject matter of the particular dispute (section 30 ArbEG).

The main objective of the proceedings at the Arbitration Board is to find an amicable solution between the employer and employee. After introduction of the proceedings on petition of either the employee or the employer (section 31 ArbEG), the Board makes a proposal, which becomes final if the parties do not object to the proposal within one month after its notification (section 34(3) ArbEG). If one party objects, the proposal is null and void and the parties can then introduce court proceedings (section 37 ArbEG).

Even after termination of an employment agreement, the parties may still involve the Arbitration Board to solve existing disputes, and they can also directly file an action at a court of appropriate jurisdiction.

[8] *Special Conditions for Inventions Made at Universities*

Special conditions concerning inventions made by professors, lecturers and scientific assistants (in the following: "scientific staff"), in their capacity as such, at universities are stipulated in section 42 of the German ArbEG. Section 42 ArbEG states:

> The following special provisions apply for inventions made by persons employed by a university:
> (1) The inventor shall have the right to publish work pertaining to an invention made in the course of the performance of his or her contracted teaching and research activities (hereinafter "employee's invention") provided that he or she has informed his or her employer of his or her intention to do so in advance, the usual notice period being two months. § 24 para. 2 is, therefore, not applicable.
> (2) In the event that the inventor chooses to exercise his or her academic freedom not to publish anything in relation to the employee's invention, he or she shall not be obliged to report the invention to his or her employer. Should the inventor wish to publish anything in relation to the invention at a later date, then he or she shall undertake to report the invention to his or her employer without delay.
> (3) In the event that the university chooses to claim the employee's invention, the inventor shall retain an inalienable right to utilize the employees' invention in the course of his or her contract teaching and research activities.
> (4) Should the employer choose to exploit the employee's invention, then the inventor(s) shall be remunerated at a rate of 30 per cent of all revenues generated through the exploitation of the invention.
> (5) § 40 No. 1 is, therefore, not applicable.

Notwithstanding the right according to subsection (2) of section 42, inventions made by the scientific staff must be reported. The university may then claim the invention, as explained in the previous sections. That is, the scientific staff has a duty to report all service inventions as soon as they are created. Rights to a service invention thus first belong to the inventor (staff). However, the employer (university) is entitled to acquire the service inventions. Once the university receives the report, it may during a time period of four months explicitly claim the ownership of the invention or, if the four-month period has passed, it automatically obtains the ownership. The university is then basically free to dispose of the right, grant licenses or assign the rights to third parties. However, this acquisition by the university is comes with obligations. The university must remunerate the inventor(s) and protect the invention by applications as early as possible after the acquisition. One way in which the situation with universities differs from the general rules concerns the amount of remuneration. According to section 42(4) ArbEG the inventor gets 30% of all revenues. This is definitely more than the usual remuneration of an employee. In addition, the scientific staff may—according to section 42(2) ArbEG—refer to a "negative publication" right. In fact, a professor or any member of the scientific staff may (legally) conceal the inventions made under a particular research project. There is also a "positive publication right" of section 42(1) ArbEG subject to special conditions such as a prior notice. Another difference over the general rules is that according to section 42(3) ArbEG the university-based inventor keeps a right to use the invention in the course of his contractual teaching and research activities.

Section 42(1) ArbEG makes it sometimes difficult for a university to enter into research and development projects with third parties. Section 22 of the ArbEG states that "the provisions of the Act cannot be modified by contract to the detriment of the employee." For instance, the employer and employee may agree upon an automatic transfer of rights in advance as to inventions or technical improvements made by the employee during the employment. However, such clause would be invalid according to section 22 ArbEG. The same likely applies to rights of an inventor who benefits from section 42 ArbEG. It seems to be not an option to introduce in the contract between the university and its scientific staff, a stipulation according to which the staff waives "in advance" their rights of section 42 ArbEG. A university, when concluding a research and development agreement with a third party, must thus thoroughly consider section 42 ArbEG. The inventions under the R&D project will be generated by its scientific staff. In such situations it might be recommended either to directly involve the scientific staff in the agreement or consider possible disclaimers in the R&D agreement to avoid possible conflicts with inventors covered by section 42 ArbEG.

CHAPTER 16

Customs Actions

§16.01 INTRODUCTION

Customs actions are an important strategic tool for combating IP infringement in cross-border trade. Although originally limited to combating product piracy, customs actions are applicable against goods that infringe patents and utility patents, irrespective of piracy. Besides blocking the importation of suspect goods, customs actions can be a useful tool for acquiring information about the suspect good itself and its source, destination and distribution channels.

There are limited parallels between customs actions in Europe and proceedings before the US ITC. Both sets of actions provide for seizures of infringing goods crossing the borders. However, the US ITC will not seize such goods until conducting its own hearing and determination into the validity and infringement of the patents. By contrast, the EU and national proceedings discussed herein provide a temporary wall against suspect imports, and it is left to the national courts to decide whether this wall shall be lifted or not, i.e., insofar as the importer contests the detention. Furthermore, to establish standing at the ITC, the right holder must show that an industry in the US relating to articles protected by the patent exists or is in the process of being established. Such "domestic industry" requirement is inapplicable under the European or national customs actions rules.

In the EU, customs authorities carry out the detention of suspect products without an in-depth assessment and analysis of validity and infringement of the IP right. The customs authorities instead mainly rely on the submissions of the right holder. As soon as the authorities detect suspect goods (and usually after an initial consultation with the contact person named in the application), they order detention of the goods. The right holder even receives an opportunity to inspect the detained goods. Prior to court proceedings, customs actions are essentially formalities initiated by the filing of an application form. This application procedure is efficiently channeled through centralized offices in EU countries, such as the Zentralstelle Gewerblicher Rechtsschutz (ZGR) in Munich.

The right holder is able to stop the proceedings at any stage. The right holder can decide whether a further detention is necessary or an immediate release of the goods is preferred, and is thus in a position to minimize any further interference in the customs clearance. An importer that stays silent during the proceedings could be penalized, because silence may lead to the destruction of the products. If the importer does not explicitly object to the destruction of the seized goods, it is presumed that the importer has consented to the destruction. The number of cases where such presumed agreement leads to destruction of the products is significant. Most of these cases, however, concern clear counterfeits where the importer knows that an objection would obviously be without merit. If the owner of the seized goods objects to the detention, the right holder must initiate court proceedings. Then the case moves to the regular patent infringement courts.

§16.02 LEGAL FRAMEWORK

Customs actions can be based on both EU Community and German law. European law provides for such actions pursuant to Regulation (EU) No. 608/2013,[1] while the German law allows for seizures through section 142(a) of the GPA. The frameworks mainly differ in their territorial scope. National procedures are confined to the national borders, whereas customs actions based on EU rules refer to the protection of the borders of the EU.

[A] EU Rules

European customs enforcement law aims to provide uniform measures throughout the EU, as applied by national customs authorities. The primary EU rules are contained in Regulation (EU) No. 608/2013 of the European Parliament and of the Council of June 12, 2013 concerning customs enforcement of IP (hereinafter referred to as "the Regulation").[2] The Regulation is completed by the Commission Regulation (EC) No. 1352/2013 of December 4, 2013, which sets forth provisions for the implementation of the Regulation (hereinafter referred to as "the Implementing Regulation").[3] The Regulation is confined to procedural aspects and does not contain rules relating to the question of whether IP rights are infringing. This question needs to be answered by means of national law.

The Regulation is primarily applicable to goods which are leaving or entering the single market, i.e., from countries outside the EU into the territory of the custom-free market (so-called customs territory of the EU, Article 1 of the Regulation). Its

1. Regulation (EU) No. 608/2013 of the European Parliament and of the Council of Jun. 12, 2013 concerning customs enforcement of intellectual property rights and repealing Council Regulation (EC) No. 1383/2003(OJ L 181, Jun. 29, 2013, p. 15.).
2. The full text of the Regulation is available in English at http://eur-lex.europa.eu/.
3. The full text of the Implementing Regulation is available in English at http://eur-lex.europa.eu/.

application is questionable as to goods which are shipped from third-party countries into the EU and ultimately destined for another third-party country outside Europe. In the decision *Philips v. Nokia*,[4] the ECJ ruled that such goods in transit which are prima facie not intended for the EU market, in principle, cannot be seized by the right holder unless there is convincing evidence and a substantial likelihood that the goods will be rerouted for sale on the EU market.

The Regulation covers a wider range of IP rights, including trademarks, designs, copyright, geographical indications, SPCs for medicinal products and plants, Community and national plant variety rights, topography of semiconductor products and tradenames.[5] It also covers utility models and national patents, including the national parts of conventional European patents. Furthermore, customs actions may also be based on European patents with unitary effect. Customs actions may only cover those European countries where an enforceable right is available. For instance, customs actions based on a conventional European patent that designates certain EU Member States are limited to those EU States where the European patent is valid and in force. European patents with unitary effect will be enforceable in those EU Member States participating in the enhanced cooperation (Article 2 of Regulation 1257/2012). A Community Design, even more broadly, would be enforceable in all EU Member States. Thus, an IP portfolio may cover the EU territory in different ways. In some territorial areas of the EU, the protection may be strong and consist of multilayer rights, whereas in other perhaps less commercially active parts of Europe, the protection may be weaker. European patents with unitary effect will add a further protection layer to the right holder's toolbox.

[B] National Rules

Besides the pan-EU provisions, national law in any of the EU Member States may provide for additional protection. German law provides for additional protection under section 142a of the Patent Act. Customs actions according to German national law are particularly useful in areas that are not covered by the Regulation (section 142a(1) of the GPA). The German national rules "complete" the Regulation in the following areas:

- **Movements of goods between EU countries:** The EU Regulation covers measures applicable at the external borders of the single market. These are mainly the customs at the border delimiting the territory of the EU. The Regulation does not address transit of infringing goods across internal borders within Europe, such as between Germany and France. For instance, infringing goods that have been produced in France or Spain and are later imported into German territory cannot be blocked based on the EU Regulation. Because these are goods that are already within the single market, the proper recourse is to national laws.

4. *See* ECJ, Dec. 1, 2011, C-446/09 and C-495/09.
5. Article 2 Regulation.

- **Illegal parallel imports of original goods (i.e., "grey market" goods):** The EU Regulation is limited in that it explicitly excludes coverage of original goods that have been produced with the consent of the right holder.[6] European patent rights are not necessarily exhausted even if original goods are concerned. This is particularly applicable to goods that the right holder or an authorized person has put into a market outside the EU. Nevertheless, even if their reimportation into the European Market represents an infringement of patent rights, these goods cannot be seized pursuant to the Regulation. The new Regulation also does not apply to "goods manufactured by a person duly authorized by a right holder to manufacture a certain quantity of goods, in excess of the quantities agreed between that person and the right holder,"[7] i.e., unauthorized overruns. However, measures according to section 142a of the GPA may help in such situations. It is commonly accepted case law[8] that illegal parallel imports (grey market products) or unauthorized overruns may be combatted pursuant to national law, such as section 142a of the GPA. For instance, the right holder may use German law to block a party who bought a patented good in a developing country at a low price from importing that product into Germany. It also is a very efficient tool to hinder the commercial activity of vendors using the internet to sell original goods bought in low-price countries for resale in European high-price countries.

As set forth above, there are important areas that are left to national customs laws. If the right holder can rely upon a multitude of rights—for instance, on a portfolio composed of community designs, European patents and German utility models—he will typically use both the European and the national tracks.

§16.03 APPLICATION PROCEEDINGS

Regardless of whether the application is based on the Regulation or on section 142a of the GPA, it is principally the right holder that may apply for a customs action.[9] This is the person who is named in the register. As an exception, the right holder can also be the licensee, insofar as the licensee is formally authorized by the right holder to initiate customs proceedings.[10] Proof of ownership can be provided by means of an excerpt from the register. The application must be filed with the customs authorities of appropriate jurisdiction. In Germany, the customs authority is the Zentralstelle Gewerblicher Rechtsschutz (Bundesfinanzdirektion Südost).

The Regulation provides for two different tracks: one is applicable to the Community rights with a community-wide effect[11] (Article 4 of the Regulation), and

6. Article 1(5) Regulation.
7. *Ibid.*
8. Federal Financial Court, VII R 89/98, GRUR Int. 2000, 780, Jockey.
9. Article 3(1)(a) Regulation.
10. Article 3(2)(a) and (3) Regulation.
11. Community trademark, Community design, a Community plant variety, or a designation of origin or geographical indication or a geographical designation protected by the Community.

the other is applicable to national rights, particularly European patents, national patents, utility models, SPCs and national trademarks (Figure 16.1).

Figure 16.1 Application Proceedings

[A] Content of the Application

The application is made through standard forms,[12] which are available on the customs authority's website. In Germany, the required data can be entered directly into an online form available on the ZGR website.[13] Later, if the application is granted, the ZGR forwards the data to the border authorities. That is, it is made available through the customs intranet, which is used by border personnel to detect suspected shipments. Accordingly, the success of the measure significantly depends upon the data and illustrations given by the right holder when completing the form.

In addition to proof that the right holder is authorized to assert the patent rights,[14] the application should contain the following information:

- The name and address of a legal or technical person, usually the lawyer handling the filing procedure.[15] This person must be vested with a power of attorney. This is also the first contact person in the event that customs detect suspect goods.
- An accurate and detailed technical description of the goods—i.e., sufficient information to enable customs to distinguish authentic/original products from suspect goods. The right holder should add a list of those companies authorized to sell the original goods.
- Available information on potential infringers and infringing goods. This information should be constantly updated.
- Information (if available) regarding the particularities of the packaging; schedule of arrival or departure; means of transportation; identity of the importers, exporters and holders of suspect goods; and details of the distribution channels used by potential infringers, including information concerning upcoming trade shows. Accordingly, a list of companies that potentially import suspect products into the European market, as well as those companies potentially receiving such products, should be added and constantly updated.

---

12. *See* Annex I of the Implementing Regulation; a different form must be used if the right holder bases the application on the national regime, namely s. 142a of the GPA.
13. *See* www.ipr.zoll.de.
14. Article 6(3)(a)(c) Regulation.
15. Article 6(3)(k) Regulation.

The effectiveness of an application for action by customs depends on the accuracy and thoroughness of the information that customs authorities receive regarding the goods and the potential infringer. The more information that is available to the customs, the greater the chance that infringing items will be detected.

[B] Security

The relative ease of seizing good in Germany is counterbalanced by the potential payment of damages if it later turns out that the seizure was unjustified. The right holder must provide a guarantee. In the case of customs actions based on the Regulation, it is sufficient to provide an assumption of liability for the case where the detained goods in question are subsequently found not to infringe the asserted IP rights if the holder of the goods or declarant has suffered damage in that regard. The assumption of liability, which is contained as an undertaking in the application form (*see* Annex I of the Implementing Regulation), shall cover eventual damages resulting from an unjustified detention of goods. There is no rating of creditworthiness or other similar checks; the signed undertaking is sufficient.

The situation is different in the case of customs actions based on German national rules. Here, a security bond is necessary. According to section 108(1) of the Code of Civil Procedure, this security bond shall be a written, irrevocable, unlimited in time, absolute, unconditional and directly liable bank guarantee to cover eventual damages resulting from an unjustified detention. For the time being, the ZGR requires a bond of EUR 10,000 from a bank that is officially accredited to operate and provide financial services within German territory. If it is too difficult to find a suitable bank, the right holder may also deposit the amount into a trust account with any deposit agency of a German Court.

§16.04 GRANT OF THE APPLICATION

The application is processed ex parte. When the ZGR receives the application, it checks whether the requirements are met, specifically whether the application contains sufficient information to enable the detection of the goods in question, and whether a sufficient guarantee is provided. Following the filing of the application, the ZGR may informally contact the right holder if any information is missing. The ZGR does not, however, assess the validity of the rights. It is satisfied with an excerpt from the register showing that the rights are in force. The ZGR also does not check whether the applicant's statements are correct. Rather, the customs authorities rely on the written factual allegations and explanations of the right holder. Once the application is granted, the ZGR feeds the information contained in the application into the customs intranet, which is then available at the customs offices.

§16.05 ONGOING UPDATES TO CUSTOMS

The order of the ZGR granting the application specifies a time period during which the customs authorities take action.[16] This period shall not exceed one year, but on expiration, the ZGR can extend the period by request of the right holder.

During the time period of the validity of the customs order, the facts on the ground may change. For instance, the right holder may become aware of new potential infringers or may obtain better information on the means of transportation and the commercial channels used for shipping the suspect goods. As new or more accurate information becomes available, the customs application should be updated. This can be done easily through the ZGR website.

According to Article 15 of the Regulation, the right holder is obliged to inform customs if the IP right covered by the application ceases to have effect if the right holder ceases for other reasons to be entitled to submit an application, or if any other modifications render the application on file inaccurate.

§16.06 DETENTION PROCEDURE

A simplified picture of the detention procedure is provided in Figure 16.2. Detention is carried out by the customs authorities basically without in-depth analysis of the validity and infringement of the patent. But once goods are seized, proceedings then shift to the regular courts where the patent rights are analyzed (Figure 16.2).

Figure 16.2 Detention Procedure

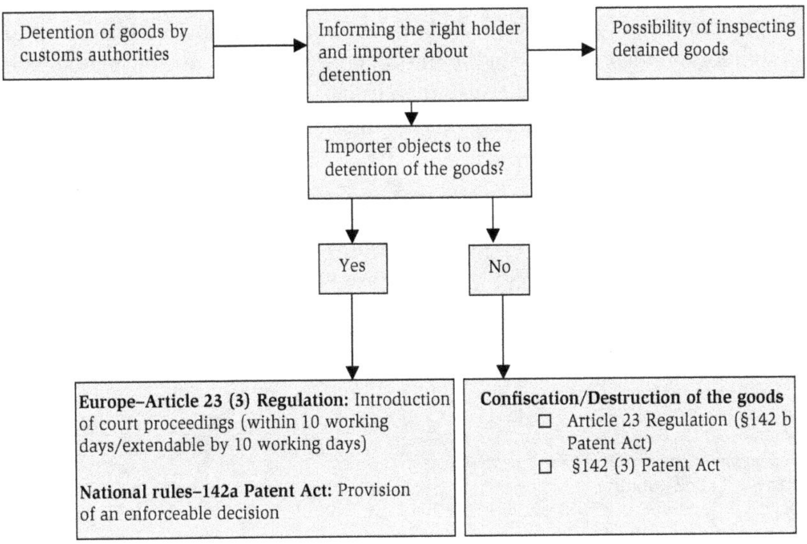

16. Article 11(1) Regulation.

[A] Customs' Detection and Assessment of Goods

If the customs authorities detect goods that they suspect are infringing, according to the information found on the customs intranet, then they will detain these goods.[17] According to Article 2(7) of the Regulation, such goods are basically goods "with regard to which there are reasonable indications that they are prima facie subject of an act of infringement." Accordingly, the determination of the infringement of a right depends on a review of the factual information and documents provided by the right holder to the customs. The infringement must be more than a mere assumption.[18] Prior to detaining the goods, customs may ask the right holder to provide them with any other relevant information with respect to the goods. This possibility allows the customs authorities to broaden the basis for their review of the situation. Nevertheless, the Regulation stays silent as to what extent it is customs' duty to investigate the legal justification of the detention. The Regulation only states that "where the customs authorities identify" suspect goods, they shall suspend the release of the goods or detain them. This sets an even lower threshold for a legal review on the side of customs than was applicable in the previous Regulation of 2003,[19] which required that customs gained satisfaction "that goods ... are suspected of infringing an intellectual property right." In practice, however, the customs authorities do not have experts on IP law, and they primarily rely on the right holders' allegations.

A detention based on the national provisions even requires that "the infringement is obvious" (section 142a(1) of the Patent Act). Even though the German framework seems to require a higher certainty as to whether the detained products indeed infringe the concerned patent, in practice, the customs authorities rely on the right holder's allegations. There has been some criticism of this practice in the literature[20] and by courts[21] because there is a risk for abuse. The trend may be thus toward greater review by customs authorities, but ultimately the likelihood of any substantial legal review, now or in the future, in the customs clearance process is low because customs officers do not have any particular IP-related expertise.

Important German customs entry points where most suspect products are detected are as follows:

- German airports, in particular the airport of Frankfurt;
- German maritime harbors, in particular Bremen and Hamburg;
- mail (close to 67% of all suspect products are detected through mail clearance);
- customs clearance at the special customs offices for trade shows.

17. Article 17(1) Regulation.
18. Rogge/Grabinski, PatG, 10th ed., s. 142a Rule 20; Cordes, GRUR 2007, 483 (485); Hermsen, Mitt. 2006, 261 (262).
19. EC No. 1383/2003.
20. *See* AIPPI, Question Q. 208, Answer of the German Group.
21. District Court Düsseldorf InstGE 9, 130, 137.

Other important entry points are harbors in France (Le Havre), Belgium (Antwerp) and the Netherlands, in particular the harbor of Rotterdam. These harbors are used for transit and have a high volume of important container traffic.

[B] Notification of Detention

As soon as the customs authorities have detected suspect goods, they act with regard to the detained goods. The customs authorities provide the following information to the right holder:

- actual or estimated quantity, and the actual or presumed nature of the detained goods, including available images thereof, as appropriate;
- the names and addresses of the declarant or the holder of the goods; and
- the origin, provenance and destination of the suspect goods (Article 17(4) of the Regulation, section 142a(2) of the Patent Act).

The right holder has an opportunity to inspect the detained goods.[22] In limited circumstances, the customs authorities may also send samples to the right holder to analyze the infringement; however, this is primarily limited to "counterfeit and pirated goods" which, according to the legal definition provided in Article 2(5) and (6) of the Regulation, do not include items only protected by patents or utility models. Accordingly, the right holder must typically visit the customs office detaining the goods in order to inspect the detained goods.

The importer (usually the declarant) of the goods also will be informed about the detention. It may happen that innocent products are detained by customs. In such a situation, the right holder should clear the situation as soon as possible and take the necessary steps such that the detained goods are quickly released to minimize any further interference in the customs clearance and to avoid possible liabilities.

[C] Measures after Notification of the Parties

[1] EU Rules

[a] Destruction

This procedure may result in the destruction of the detained products. It requires the following steps:

- The right holder confirms within ten working days from the notification of detention in writing,[23] that, in its opinion, the suspect goods infringe the IP right. The right holder must confirm its agreement to the destruction of the

22. Article 19(1) Regulation.
23. Article 23(1) Regulation: Within three working days in case of perishable goods. The ten-day period may be extended by a further ten working days where circumstances warrant.

goods. This obligation to confirm the infringement and authorize the goods' destruction shall merit careful consideration by the right holder, in view of the potential liabilities arising from an improper seizure.

- Where the owner, declarant or holder of the goods has neither confirmed its agreement to the destruction of the goods nor notified its opposition thereto to the customs authorities within those deadlines, the customs authorities may deem the owner, declarant or holder of the goods to have confirmed its agreement to the destruction of those goods.[24] Accordingly, this agreement is presumed if the owner, declarant or holder of the goods has not explicitly objected to the destruction within the indicated ten-day period.[25]

Once the right holder informs the authorities that the detained goods infringe the patent, and provides an explicit or presumed agreement, the goods will be destroyed. In the case of clear counterfeits, the holder of the goods will commonly not object, and this leads to destruction of the goods without any further legal review.

[b] Regular Proceedings

Destruction proceedings are unavailable if the goods' owner, holder or declarant objects to the destruction in a timely manner. In that event, the right holder must initiate court proceedings within ten working days[26] from the receipt of the notification of detention. This deadline can be extended further by ten working days in appropriate cases, upon the duly justified request by the right holder. The Regulation, in particular Article 23, does not provide for a definition of the term "proceedings, to determine whether an intellectual property right has been infringed," but it is commonly understood that it is sufficient to file a regular lawsuit[27] with one of the competent patent infringement courts.[28] The requirement also is fulfilled by means of a request for a preliminary injunction, which may constitute a precautionary measure according to Article 24(2)(b) of the Regulation, and would have the additional effect of defeating a subsequent request of the importer to release the detained products (*see* following section 16.06[C][1][c]). Accordingly, the right holder has ten, at most twenty, working days to prepare and file a complaint brief or to request a preliminary injunction with a German infringement court or a division of the UPC. The customs authorities do not provide a forum for adjudicating whether the patent is valid and infringed (as is the case with the US ITC). Rather, the customs authorities form a temporary barrier against suspect imports, and it is principally left to the courts to decide whether this barrier shall stay or be removed. Figure 16.3 illustrates the main procedural steps after the detention of suspect goods.

---

24. Article 23(1)(c) Regulation.
25. *See also* s. 142b(4) Patent Act.
26. In the case of perishable goods, the period shall be three working days, which is not extendable.
27. This can also be a request for a preliminary injunction.
28. Rundschreiben der Bundesfinanzdirektion Südost, Aug. 20, 2008.

Figure 16.3 Procedure after Detention

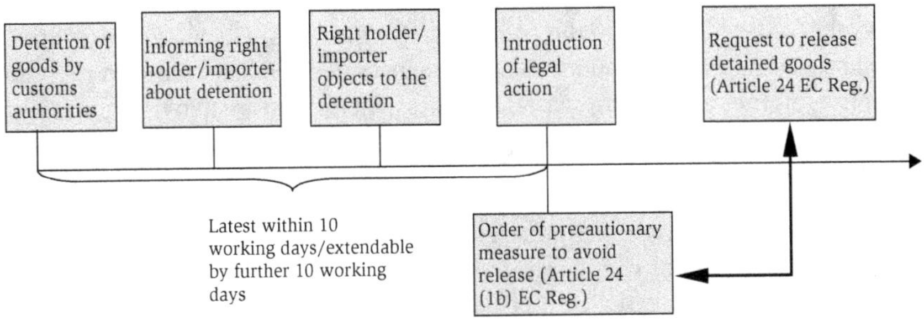

[c] *Possibility of Release*

If the right holder has initiated court proceedings and thus fulfilled the requirements of Article 23 of the Regulation, and absent action on the part of the declarant, owner, importer, holder or consignee, the goods will remain with the customs authorities. But the Regulation provides for relief to obtain an early release of the detained goods. This procedure is described in Article 24 of the Regulation. The early release can be requested by the owner, declarant or holder of the goods. The customs authorities then typically release the detained goods on provision of a guarantee, which shall be sufficient to protect the interests of the right holder. The amount of the guarantee shall basically be equal to the amount the importer of the goods would have to pay as damages for the infringement of the detained goods. The right holder's indications will be taken into account when determining the amount of the guarantee. However, if no agreement between right holder and importer can be reached on a reasonable amount, the customs authorities will determine it.

However, according to Article 24(2)(b) of the Regulation, the customs authorities will not release the detained products if the "authority empowered for this purpose has authorized precautionary measures." That is, customs will not release the detained goods even on the provision of a sufficient guarantee by the importer if the right holder can provide an executable court decision ordering the impounding of the detained goods. Accordingly, the maintenance of the detention requires not only that court proceedings have been initiated by the right holder but also that a court reviews the situation and renders an executable decision. Without this decision ordering precautionary measures, the goods would be released against the guarantee. In view of the speed of the early release proceedings according to Article 24 of the Regulation, it seems to be necessary that the right holder requests precautionary measures through preliminary injunction proceedings.

Often the right holder is satisfied with the release because the short interruption in importation is enough to at least hinder exhibition at a trade show, and in the meantime, the right holder can inspect the suspect good and obtain relevant information on parties and distribution channels.

[d] Proceedings for Small Consignments

A specific procedure for small consignments of counterfeit and pirated goods has been introduced in order to minimize the administrative burden and costs.[29] It simplifies the standard proceedings and responds to the growing amount of infringing goods ordered through the internet and sent by postal services. The procedure allows for such goods to be destroyed without the explicit agreement of the applicant in each case. It only applies if the following are true:

- The suspect goods are counterfeit or pirated goods.[30]
- The goods are not perishable goods.
- The goods are covered by a decision granting an application.
- The right holder has specifically requested the use of the procedure. The form contains a box, which needs to be checked.
- The goods are transported in small consignments.[31]

Requesting the procedure entails an undertaking from the applicant to bear the costs related to the destruction of goods under this procedure, where requested by the customs authorities.

[e] Ex Officio Proceedings

According to Article 18 of the Regulation, the customs authorities can also act without any underlying request of the right holder. If the customs authorities detain goods suspected of infringing an IP right that are not covered by a valid application, they will try to locate the person or entity entitled to submit the application, which will then have four working days to file it.

[2] German Rules (Section 142a of the GPA)

The procedure based on the German national rules is comparable to European rules but not completely the same. Even under German law the absence of an objection and appropriate subsequent action may lead to the destruction of the detained products. Where no opposition to the detention is made by the importer, at the latest within two weeks of service of the notification of the detention, the customs authorities shall order confiscation of the detained products, which consequently results in the destruction of the detained products (section 142a(3) of the Patent Act).

If the importer objects to the detention, the customs authorities must inform the right holder, which must then indicate to the customs authorities whether it still seeks

29. Article 26 of Regulation (EU) No. 608/2013.
30. In particular infringements concerning signs which are identical to trademarks or cannot be distinguished in its essential aspects from them (Art. 2(5)) and goods which infringe copyrights, related rights or designs (Art. 2).
31. These are postal or express courier consignments, which contain three units or less or have a gross weight of less than 2 kilograms.

the maintenance of the detention. If the right holder withdraws its request, the customs authorities will release the detained products.

If the right holder intends to proceed, it must submit an executable court decision ordering the impounding of the detained goods. This is different from the European customs action proceedings, where it is sufficient to simply prove that regular proceedings on the merits have been initiated. The detention triggered by a German customs action requires not only that court proceedings have been initiated but also that a court review the situation and render an executable court decision. As this decision must be provided within a short timeframe, namely within two weeks, the right holder must initiate preliminary injunction proceedings to achieve this goal. Where the right holder can show that a court decision has been requested, but has not yet been received, the seizure shall be maintained for a further two weeks at most.

Where the detention proves to have been unjustified from the beginning (for instance, where it is later found that there is no infringement of the asserted patent, or if the patent is invalidated), and the right holder did not timely withdraw the request to maintain the detention, the right holder shall be required to compensate the damages that the detention has caused to the person entitled to dispose of the goods.[32] The amount of damages may consist of the difference between the price the owner of the goods would have received when selling them earlier and the value of the goods after the detention. Because the detained products are released by customs in case of an unjustified detention, the calculation of damages is consequently linked to the temporary unavailability of the detained products. The claimant has the burden of proving the cause and amount of the damages. This is difficult to do in practice, and liabilities are usually kept within reasonable limits.

§16.07 COSTS OF THE PROCEEDINGS

Except for the costs related to the storage, handling and destruction of detained goods, there are no fees to be paid to the customs authorities for the application procedure. The preparation of the application will involve some legal costs, as will the maintenance of the detention measures, depending on the number of seizures performed and the extent of follow-up court proceedings.

32. Article 28 of the Regulation.

CHAPTER 17
Samples

This chapter contains samples of the most frequently encountered documents used in German patent infringement proceedings. They represent schematic outlines, meant to illustrate the matters described in detail in the previous chapters. The samples only server as a basic guidance to draft writs for matters falling in the scope of EU Patent Package. For such writs, attention must be drawn to relevant provisions of the UPCA and the Rules of Procedure, which are not identical with the German Law. Both procedures have in common that the court takes decisions on the basis of the parties' requests. Courts may not award more than has been requested.[1] The parties and not the court are the "masters of the proceedings."

The following samples are for illustrative purposes only. When drafting motions and pleadings, it is strongly recommended to consult a legal expert of the patent field. In particular, it is strongly advisable to investigate recommendations published by the courts, including the practical guidance and templates published by the UPC, when drafting legal texts.

§17.01 WARNING LETTER

Explanations concerning the content of the warning letter can be found in Chapter 9, §9.04[A].

1. Article 76(1) UPCA.

[A] Body of the Warning Letter

Registered Mail[2]

Management

Company X

Address

Date

Ref.

Due to infringement of EP ...

Dear Sirs,

This is to inform you that the patent attorneys and lawyers of our firm are representing the well-known Company Y.[3] *We have been instructed by our client to inform you about the following:*

Our client is the owner of the EP ... concerning a sports shoe (in the following: "the Patent"). The mention of the grant of the Patent has been published on October 20, 2016, and its application has been published on October 15, 2015. A copy of the Patent is enclosed as

—Enclosure 1—

The Patent is in force in the countries ... .[4] *A nullity action filed against the asserted Patent has recently been dismissed by the Federal Patent Court. The decision is final and confirms the validity of the patent as granted and is enclosed as*

—Enclosure 2—

An excerpt of the register of the ... is enclosed as

—Enclosure 3—

Our client has taken note that on the present trade show ISPO Winter 2022 in Munich your company is exhibiting sports shoes having the features of at least claim 1 of the Patent. Our client became also aware that you are manufacturing the accused products in Germany.

---

2. The warning letter shall be addressed to the party who will be the prospective defendant. The letter is typically sent by registered mail to obtain a certificate of receipt to prove that the accused infringer received the warning letter.
3. It is advisable to add to the warning letter a power of attorney.
4. It is advisable to mention that no opposition or invalidation proceedings are pending. It is advisable to disclose all decisions of the EPO, UPC and national courts addressing the validity of the patent.

These sports shoes, which infringe our client's Patent, are named: "... ." (hereinafter "the Model)"[5] *A brochure of your company in which these sports shoes are shown and advertised is enclosed as*

—Enclosure 4—

Brochures according to Enclosure 4 are distributed by employees of your company on the ongoing tradeshow. By producing and distributing the Model you are infringing our client's Patent.

The claimed teaching of the Patent of our client concerns a sports shoe, particularly a running shoe which is provided with a rigid cover which covers the upper portion on the exterior surfaces thereof in the front region of the shoe. The main claim 1 reads:

A sports shoe comprising

1) *a sole;*
2) *an upper portion attached to the sole; and*
3) *a rigid cover:*
    - *made of resisting material;*
    - *angular in cross-section; and*
    - *defining a securing band and a protective shield.*
4) *the securing band is affixed between said sole and said upper portion;*
5) *the securing band extends from said sole, upwardly over the exterior of the upper portion in the area of the ball of the shoe.*

Further explanations of the patented subject matter can be taken from the description of the asserted patent (see Enclosure 1).[6]

A comparison of the features of main claim 1 with your Model exhibited by you on the ongoing ISPO Winter 2022 reveals that the accused sports shoes make use of all features of this claim of the patent and, thus, infringe our client's rights.[7]

Our client is thus entitled (Article 25 UPCA) to ask you to refrain from the indicated activities in the Federal Republic of Germany, France [list of countries where the patent is valid and for which a cease and deists claim is made]. Furthermore, you are obligated to render full and true account about the indicated infringing activities in order to enable our client to calculate and determine the damages resulting therefrom. Additionally, for the time after the publication of the patent application until the mention of the grant, our

5. The accused product should be concretely designated, such that the accused infringer understands to which products the accusations are addressed. This requires that the warning letter exactly identifies which products/infringing activities are concerned.
6. A warning letter requires a sufficient description of the subject matter and scope of protection. Nevertheless, reference can be made to the specification of the patent in case of simpler technologies. This applies to the example.
7. The accused technology should be well described in the warning letter, whereby the indicated claim chart can be used to show, feature by feature, that the accused embodiment uses the claimed invention. For this feature mapping, it is advisable to use available evidence (photos, advertisements, etc.).

client claims a reasonable compensation according §33(1) German Patent Act for activities in Germany.[8] *The duty to recall the accused shoes from customers and the duty to destroy them follows from Article 64 (2) UPCA.*[9]

Finally, according to law our client is also entitled to claim the reimbursement of the legal costs caused by the intervention of our firm which became necessary due to your unlawful conduct.

*In order to avoid otherwise inevitable commencement of legal actions against your company, we have to request you to sign and return the enclosed undertaking (**Enclosure 5**)*[10] *not later than*

Date[11]

at the latest.

According to law, only a binding and sufficiently penalized declaration of cease and desist as requested is considered as appropriate to avoid a lawsuit for infringement. A power of attorney is enclosed in the present letter.

Very truly yours,

Patent- und Rechtsanwälte

(signature)	*(signature)*
Rechtsanwalt	*Patentanwalt*

Enclosures:

German Patent EP. ... (Enclosure 1)

Decision of the Federal Patent Court (Enclosure 2)

Excerpt of the registers (Enclosure 3)

Brochure (Enclosure 4)

Undertaking (Enclosure 5)

Power of Attorney (Enclosure 6)

8. *See* Ch. 14, §14.03[E][1][b]; the claim can be given also for other jurisdiction; for instance, in France, the provisional protection under Art. 67 confers damages, cf. Art. L. 614-9, L. 613-3 to L. 613-7, L. 615-4, and L. 615-5 CPI; the Netherlands: Art. 72(1), (2) PA.
9. The provisions can be found in Ch. 18, §18.03.
10. This undertaking can be found in the following section.
11. In patent infringement cases, a time frame of two to three weeks is usually given to the accused infringer.

[B] Undertaking of Cease and Desist

UNDERTAKING

Company X hereby undertakes toward Company Y

I. *in order to avoid the payment of a contractual penalty to Company Y for each case of noncompliance of EUR 25,000.00, to refrain from manufacturing, offering, placing on the market or using, or importing or storing for those purposes a product with the following features:*

A sports shoe comprising

1) *a sole;*
2) *an upper portion attached to the sole; and*
3) *a rigid cover:*
   - *made of resisting material;*
   - *angular in cross-section; and*
   - *defining a securing band and a protective shield.*
4) *the securing band is affixed between said sole and said upper portion;*
5) *the securing band extends from said sole, upwardly over the exterior of the upper portion in the area of the ball of the shoe.*

In particular, a sports shoe (insert precise description and designation of the sports shoe) as shown in the following photographs (insert photographs of the shoe).

II. *to render account of the extent of the acts covered by section I and committed since November 15, 2015 [one month after publication of the patent application] by establishing a list indicating:*
1) *the production quantities and times;*
2) *the individual supplies; broken down according to delivery quantities, delivery times, delivery prices and type designations, and the names and addresses of commercial buyers;*
3) *the individual offers for sale, broken down according to quantities offered for sale, times of the sales, prices of goods offered for sale and type designations, and the names and addresses of commercial recipients of offers for sale;*
4) *the advertisement carried out, broken down according to advertising media, their circulation, the dissemination period, and the dissemination territory;*
5) *production costs broken down according to individual cost factors, and profits made, whereby this information is only to be provided for infringing activities carried out in the period since November 20, 2016 [1 month after publication of the grant of the patent];*

III. *to pay to Company Y*
1) *a reasonable compensation for all acts covered by section I and committed since November 15, 2015, until November 20, 2016;*

2) *all damages arisen and arising in the future by the acts covered by section I and committed since November 20, 2016.*

IV. *Company X shall recall delivered sports shoes according to section I from customers who are still in possession of these sports shoes, whereby these customers shall be informed by Company X about the infringing quality of these sports shoes, and Company X shall seriously demand the back transfer of these sports shoes. Company X shall take a binding undertaking toward these customers to reimburse eventual payments and to bear eventual packaging and transport costs for the back transfer.*

V. *Company X shall—at its own cost—destroy or surrender to a bailiff, to be named by Company Y, all sports shoes according to section I, which are in its direct or indirect possession, for the purpose of destruction;*

VI. *to reimburse the costs attributable to the intervention of the patent attorneys and lawyers of the law firm .... .*[12]

Date, Place	*Signature*

§17.02 INQUIRY LETTER[13]

Registered Mail

Management

Company X

Address

Ref.

Dear Sirs,

This is to inform you that the patent attorneys and lawyers of our firm are representing the well-known Company Y. We have been instructed by our client to inform you about the following.

Our client is the owner of the EP ... concerning a sports shoe. The mention of the grant of the patent has been published on October 20, 2016, and its application has been published on October 15, 2015 (in the following: the "Patent"). A copy of the Patent is enclosed as

—Enclosure 1—

The patent is in force in Germany, France, Italy, and the Netherlands. A nullity action filed against the Patent has recently been dismissed by the Federal Patent Court. The

12. The costs are tied to the litigation value and to an act identifying corresponding statutory fees.
13. *See* Ch. 9, §9.04[C].

decision is final and confirms the validity of the patent as granted. This decision is enclosed as

—Enclosure 2—

Excerpt of the registers of the … are enclosed as

—Enclosure 3—

The teaching of the patented invention concerns a sports shoe, particularly a running shoe which is provided with a protection cover which covers the upper portion of the exterior surfaces thereof in the front region of the shoe. Main claim 1 reads:

A sports shoe comprising:

1) *a sole;*
2) *an upper portion attached to the sole; and*
3) *a rigid cover:*
   - *made of resisting material;*
   - *angular in cross-section; and*
   - *defining a securing band and a protective shield.*
4) *the securing band is affixed between said sole and said upper portion,*
5) *the securing band extends from said sole, upwardly over the exterior of the upper portion in the area of the ball of the shoe.*

Our client has taken note that on the ISPO Winter 2022 trade show in Munich your company is exhibiting sports shoes with such protection cover.

It appears that these sports shoes infringe our client's patent. The relevant sports shoes are named: "…" A brochure of your company in which these sports shoes are shown and advertised is enclosed as

—Enclosure 4—

Brochures according to Enclosure 4 are distributed by employees of your company on the ongoing tradeshow.

A comparison of the features of main claim 1 with your Model "…" exhibited by you on the ongoing ISPO Winter 2022 appears according to our opinion that the accused sports shoes make use of all features of at least claim 1 of the Patent and, thus, infringe our client's rights.

The commercialization of the sports shoe with the designation "…" constitutes in our view an unlawful use of our client's patent rights, and accordingly we demand that within … business days you indicate why you believe that you are entitled to continue selling your Model "…," in view of our client's patent rights.

A power of attorney is enclosed in the present letter.

Very truly yours,

Patent- und Rechtsanwälte

(signature)	*(signature)*
Rechtsanwalt	*Patentanwalt*

Enclosures: *EP ... (Enclosure 1)*

Decision of the Federal Patent Court ... (Enclosure 2)

Excerpts of the registers of (Enclosure 3)

Brochure (Enclosure 4)

Power of Attorney (Enclosure 5)

§17.03 COMPLAINT BRIEF (INFRINGEMENT ACTION)

Explanations concerning the complaint in infringement proceedings can be found in Chapter 10. The following sample is drafted in the lines of Article 63(1) UPCA. Please consult the practical guidance and templates published by the UPC when drafting legal texts.

...

[Address of the Court]

Munich, date

Our Reference:

Complaint

Of

Company Y., *[address], represented by its CEO ...*

Litigation counsel: *Attorneys-at-law of the law firm ...*

In cooperation with: *Patent attorneys of the law firm*[14] *...*

—plaintiff—

versus

Company X, [address] *legally represented by its chief executive director, at the same place,*

—defendant—

14. The patent attorneys and litigation attorneys need not necessarily be from the same firm.

due to patent infringement.

Litigation value: EUR 1,000,000 (preliminary estimated).

In the name and by authorization of plaintiff, we file suit against defendant and request,

I.1. *to establish that defendant has infringed within the scope of Germany, France, and the Netherlands the patent ...*[15] *by selling a product with the following features:*

1) *a sole;*
2) *an upper portion attached to the sole; and*
3) *a rigid cover:*
   - *made of resisting material;*
   - *angular in cross-section; and*
   - *defining a securing band and a protective shield.*
4) *the securing band is affixed between said sole and said upper portion,*
5) *the securing band extends from said sole, upwardly over the exterior of the upper portion in the area of the ball of the shoe in particular a sports shoe (insert precise description and designation of the sports shoe) as shown in the following photographs (insert photographs of the shoe).*

I.2. *in order to avoid a penalty to be set by the court for each case of violation of up to ..., to refrain in Germany, France, and the Netherlands (list of countries for which an injunction is sought) from making, offering, placing on the market or using, or importing or storing for the aforementioned purposes sports shoes according to [I.1] within the scope of Germany, France and the Netherlands.*

I.3. *to disclose information to the plaintiff about the extent to which defendant committed the acts designated in I.1 since November 20, 2016 [publication of the grant of the European patent], specifying:*

a) *the names and addresses of the producers, suppliers and other previous holders of the goods, as well as the commercial customers and the wholesalers and retailers for whom they were intended;*
b) *the quantities produced, manufactured, delivered, received or ordered, as well as the price obtained for the infringing products;*
   - *whereby the names and addresses of noncommercial recipients of offers shall not be disclosed to the plaintiff, but to a certified auditor domiciled in Germany and bound to confidentiality vis-à-vis the plaintiff, which shall be named by the defendant, provided the defendant bears the costs of the auditor and instructs and authorizes him to respond to concrete questions of plaintiff whether a particular recipient of an offer is named in the report.*

II. *to find that the defendant is obliged to:*

15. It is assumed that the asserted European patent is in force and valid in Germany, France and the Netherlands.

a) pay a reasonable compensation for all acts covered by section I.1. and committed since November 15, 2015, until November 20, 2016;
b) compensate Plaintiff for all damages invoked on plaintiff by the acts indicated under I.1, committed since November 20, 2016, and which will be invoked in future;

III. to have defendants bear the costs of the proceedings;
IV. ...

REASONING

A. Introduction

Plaintiff is the proprietor of the EP (in the following "Patent-in-suit") on which the present complaint is based. The Patent-in-suit is filed as

—Enclosures K 1—

The grant of a Patent-in-suit was published on October 20, 2016. The corresponding patent application has been published on October 15, 2015. The Patent-in-suit is in force in Germany, France, and the Netherlands.

Evidence: *Excerpts of the patent registers, enclosed as:*

—Enclosure K 2—

A nullity suit was filed on ... against the German Part of the EP (Patent-in-suit), but was finally dismissed by the Federal Patent Court on. ... This decision is enclosed as

—Enclosure K 3—

This decision has not been appealed and is thus final. With the present complaint, plaintiff asserts patent rights as to a shoe.

B. The Parties

The plaintiff is a renowned sports equipment manufacturer. It is an innovative enterprise, which invests on an annual basis several Millions of Euros in its Research & Development (R&D). The achievements of plaintiff's R&D are protected by IP rights, such as patents. Among these patents is the presently asserted patent. The features of the claimed invention are reproduced in plaintiff's shoe models such as ... of which photos are enclosed as

—Enclosures K 4—[16]

The defendant operates in the same field. The parties are in direct competition. The defendant commercializes a sports shoe which is referenced as ... (hereinafter "accused

16. It is not necessary for asserting claims from that patent that the right holder uses the invention. This information contained in the complaint is aimed at giving more background information and to illustrate the significance of the case to the court.

sports shoe") The accused sports shoe is illustrated on the second page of a flyer, provided as

—Enclosures K 5—

C. Patent-in-suit

i. Subject matter of the patent

The invention relates to a sports shoe. It relates, in particular, to a running shoe which is provided with a protective cover. It covers the upper on the exterior surfaces thereof in the region of the ball and extends from the sole.

Not only the sole but also the upper portion on the exterior surfaces of the sports shoe in the vicinity of the ball are subject to heavy stresses. In the case of running shoes, the stress is particularly high. Therefore, the prior art proposes, as illustrated in the German Patent Application DE … provided as

—Enclosure K 6—

to provide protecting supports which cover the critical areas. The document of Enclosure K 6 is cited in the description and is the closest prior art according to the decision of the Federal Patent Court (see page …, enclosure K 3). If these supports are subsequently fitted, for example, by means of a lace, perfect fitting can usually not be obtained. If, however, the supports are formed on the sole and drawn up over the edge thereof a certain distance over the upper portion, the problem arises that, on the one hand, only soles with folds formed thereon can be used and, on the other hand, the fixing of the folds composed, for instance, of rubber on to the upper portion by gluing is not sufficiently durable.

ii. Objective/Solution

The objective of the patent is to provide an improved sports shoe in view of the problem shown in the prior art. The invention overcomes this problem by providing a protecting cover of angular cross-section and permanent shape, one band of which serves for holding the cover in position and engages the underside of the shoe, preferably inserted between the upper portion and the sole. At the same time, the holding band of the shoe cover is preferably located between the margin of the upper portion and the sole composed of one or several layers. It is preferably in the form of a thin tongue tapering toward its end. The advantage offered by the invention is that the normal components of the shoe, irrespectively of whether it is the upper portion or the sole, can be worked into the shape, and that no supplementary or securing means are required for fitting the protecting cover. This is realized by sports shoes with the following features, namely:

A sports shoe comprising:

1) *a sole;*
2) *an upper portion attached to the sole; and*

3) *a rigid cover:*
   - *made of resisting material;*
   - *is angular in cross-section; and*
   - *defining a securing band and a protective shield;*
4) *the securing band is affixed between said sole and said upper portion;*
5) *the securing band extends from said sole, upwardly over the exterior of the upper portion in the area of the ball of the shoe.*

This feature chart is separately provided on a sheet as

—Enclosure K 7—

C. Infringement of the patent-in-suit

Defendant commercializes the infringing shoe via its website www.yyy.com. The accused sports shoe violates claim 1 of the patent-in-suit. The accused shoe is illustrated in a photo used in defendant's advertising, provided here as:

—Enclosure K 8—

The photo contains the references of features 1)–5) of the asserted claim 1: It is a sports shoe with a sole (Feature 1) with an upper portion attached to the sole (Feature 2) and a protective (Feature 3) which is

- *made of resisting material;*
- *is angular in cross-section; and*
- *define a holding arm and a cover arm.*

Furthermore, the holding band is secured between said sole and said upper portion (Feature 4) and the cover arm extends from said sole, upwardly over the exterior of the upper portion in the area of the ball of the shoe (Feature 5).

Accordingly, at least claim 1 of the patent-in-suit is infringed.

D. Legal assessment

The jurisdiction of the … follows from … . Defendant is marketing the infringing products in Germany, France, and the Netherlands.

The claims asserted in the present action are justified in view of the above stated facts. The defendant is obliged to cease and desist an illegal use of the subject matter of the patent-in-suit.

Furthermore, defendant must pay damages to the plaintiff according … . As a company which is specialized in this particular field, defendant could have recognized the patent infringement through ordinary diligence.

Since the plaintiff is not able to quantify damages caused by the infringing act of the defendant, because the extent of the infringing acts are not yet known, there is a legitimate interest of the plaintiff in the Court's determination of the liability for damages.[17]

In order to enable the plaintiff to quantify the damages, the defendant is obliged to render account. Plaintiff needs the required account to determine the amount of damages and the defendant is not unreasonably demanded with the provision of the required information.[18]

(signature)

Rechtsanwalt

Enclosures K1–K 8

§17.04 SETTLEMENT AGREEMENT

Sample 4 is based on a typical scenario: The patentee won the first instance trial. Accordingly, the patentee was able to enforce the decision. Even though the patentee still needs to provide security for the enforcement, it is a critical situation for the accused infringer. An appeal may not have suspending effect and thus the uninterrupted marketing of the contested products is endangered by the immediate enforcement of the first instance decision. Against this background, the accused infringer (defendant) might be interested (now more than at the beginning and during the first instance proceedings) in finding a solution and would try to settle the case with the patentee. This is the situation which led to the present settlement agreement:

Settlement Agreement

Between Company (right holder)

[Address] … duly represented by …

—in the following referred to as the Licensor—

and Company Licensee

[Address] … duly represented by …

—in the following referred to as Licensee—

Preamble

Licensor is the owner of the German counterpart of the European patent … relating to a sports shoe (hereinafter "the Patent").

17. The binding confirmation of a committed patent infringement by way of a declaratory judgment is essential. It forms the basis for subsequent adjudications of the court. It shall be binding in future proceedings establishing the amount of damages.
18. The sample does not include the destruction claim. Also, it does also not include a claim to recall the infringing products or to remove them definitively from the distribution channels.

Licensee has sold sports shoes. These sports shoes have been held in an infringement proceeding to infringe the patent of Licensor. The decision of first instance rendered by the ... on ... [Docket number] has granted all requests of the complaint (hereinafter "the Decision"). In order to terminate the litigation between the parties enter into the following settlement agreement.

§1 Royalty for the past

(1) Licensee shall provide for the time until the execution of the present Agreement a written, complete and itemized listing comprising all offers, sales and deliveries of products as defined in section I of the Decision. This list shall contain individual deliveries, classified according to delivery amounts, times, prices.
(2) Licensee promises to pay a royalty of ... € per pair to Licensor for the sale of the sports shoes covered by the Decision, in particular those with the product name. ...
(3) The submission of the list according to §1 (1) as well as the payment of the resulting amounts shall be made within three weeks after the execution of this contract.

§2 License for the future

(1) Licensor grants to Licensee a nonexclusive license to produce and sell products that make use of the Patent (hereinafter "Licensed Products").
(2) Licensee pays a royalty of € ... per pair for sales of the Licensed Products after the execution of the present contract.
(3) The parties agree that the sports shoes produced by Licensee with product number ... do not fall under the patent in litigation.

§3 Termination of litigation

(1) Licensee will withdraw the appeal filed with the Court ... within two weeks after the execution of this agreement.
(2) Further, Licensee promises to pay all court fees, attorney fees and patent attorney fees in accordance with the statutory rules. The payment of these costs shall be made within two weeks after receipt of the respective invoice.

§4 Royalties and payment

(1) With respect to future sales Licensee shall report quarterly on the first day of the month with respect to the sales of the Licensed Product starting three months after execution of this agreement. The payment of the royalties is due with the report.
(2) If Licensee delays the report and/or the royalty payment more than two weeks, Licensor has the right to terminate this agreement for cause.

§5 *Bookkeeping and review*

(1) *Licensee promises to keep a separate list on the deliveries of Licensed Products showing the precise number of the articles produced by Licensee under this agreement, the customers and the delivery dates, as well as other significant facts.*
(2) *Licensor will have the right to have an independent auditor, who is subject to confidentiality, review Licensee's bookkeeping and its compliance with Licensee's general bookkeeping. Patentee will bear the costs of reviewing the books.*
(3) *If errors are discovered Licensee will bear the auditing costs. In addition, the royalties shall be doubled for the review period, if the deviation is more than 5 percent under the owed amount.*

§6 *No guarantees*

(1) *Licensor does not guarantee the validity, technical utility, or commercial exploitability of the patented invention.*
(2) *Licensor is not liable for the dependency of the patent on patents of third parties.*
(3) *Licensee holds Licensor harmless of any possible claims for product liability as far as these are based on the production of Licensee under the patent.*
(4) *If the patent should be declared invalid, then this contract shall end on the date of the final decision in the invalidation proceedings. Paid royalties shall not be refunded.*

§7 *Assignment and sublicenses*

This agreement cannot be assigned to third parties, and Licensee does not have the right to grant sublicenses.

§8 *Obligation to defend and proceed against infringers*

(1) *Licensor is not obligated to defend the Patent against attacks by third parties.*
(2) *In the case of infringement of the Patent, Licensor shall decide on bringing infringement action taking into account commercial aspects.*

§9 *Duration of the contract*

This contract is for the remaining duration of the Patent. The contract can be terminated by Licensee with a termination notice of six months to the first of January and the first of July of each year.

§10 *Mutual release*

With the performance of this agreement all mutual claims deriving from this litigation are settled.

§11 Jurisdiction and Applicable Law

German Law shall be applicable to the present Agreement. For all controversies under this agreement the District Court Düsseldorf shall have jurisdiction.

Place, Date Signatures

§17.05 REQUEST FOR A PRELIMINARY INJUNCTION[19]

Please consult the practical guidance and templates published by the UPC when drafting such texts.

...

(Address of the Court)

Munich,..., date

Our ref.:

Request to grant a preliminary injunction

of

the Company Y ... duly represented by the Executive Directors,

—plaintiff—

Authorized representatives: Attorneys-at-law and patent attorneys of the law firm ...

versus

the Company X ... duly represented by its legal representatives.

—defendant—

on grounds of alleged patent infringement.

Litigation value: Preliminarily estimated. ...

In the name and on behalf of plaintiff, we request—on a provisional basis—to order defendant, due to particular urgency without prior hearing of defendant,[20]

I.1. subject to a penalty to be set by the court for each case of violation of up to ..., to refrain from making, offering, placing on the market, or using a product which is the subject matter of the patent, or importing or storing the product for those purposes within the scope of Germany, France, and the Netherlands[21] *having the following features ...*

1) a sole;

19. Explanations concerning a request for preliminary injunction can be found in Ch. 11.
20. Rule 209.2 RoP.
21. The example is based on European patent validated and in force in Germany, France and the Netherlands.

2) an upper portion attached to the sole; and
3) a rigid cover:
- *made of resisting material;*
- *angular in cross-section; and*
- *defining a securing band and a protective shield.*

4) the securing band is affixed between said sole and said upper portion;
5) the securing band extends from said sole, upwardly over the exterior of the upper portion in the area of the ball of the shoe.

II. to place in custody of a sequestrator to be appointed by the Court all sports shoes according to section I, being in defendant's possession, to prevent their entry into; or movement, within the channels of commerce.[22]

III. to have defendant bear the costs of the proceedings.

Reasoned statement:

a. The parties

The plaintiff is a renowned sport equipment manufacture. It is an innovative enterprise, which invests several Millions of Euros in its Research & Development (R&D).[23] *Main achievements of Plaintiff's R&D are protected by IP rights, such as patents, including the patent at issue. The features of the claimed invention are reproduced in plaintiff's shoe models such as … of which photos are enclosed as*

—Enclosure AST 1—

The defendant operates in the same field. The parties are in direct competition. At the ongoing tradeshow ISPO 2022, which takes place from February 6 to 11, 2022, plaintiff became aware that defendant exhibits and commercializes a sports shoe which is referenced as. … (hereinafter "accused sports shoe") The accused sports shoe is illustrated on the second page of a flyer, provided as

—Enclosure AST 2—

which is distributed by employees of the defendant on the ongoing tradeshow. The flyer is also available at the defendant's booth which is in Hall B, and the booth can be found in position B134. [**Note:** Under the present case law of the German Federal Constitutional Court (cf. decisions of September 30, 2018 (1 BvR 1783/17 and 1 BvR 2421/17), even in tradeshow situations, it might be necessary to previously warn the accused infringer, then on very short notice (*see* Chapter 11, section 11.02[E])).

22. Article 62(3) UPCA: Seizure and blocking of accounts of the defendant is not only requested here but also possible to ensure payment of damages or compensation or for payment of court costs.
23. The right holder does not need to be using the invention in order to assert the patent against the defendant. This section in the request serves to give more background information to illustrate the significance of the case to the court.

B. Patent

i. Background

The plaintiff is owner of the EP ..., provided as

—Enclosure AST 2—

concerning a sports shoe. The application date for the patent was. ... The patent application was published on ... . The mention of the grant of the patent occurred on ... . The Patent (in the following: Patent) is in force and valid in Germany, France, and the Netherlands, which can be taken from excerpts of the patent registers, provided as

—Enclosure AST 3—

An EPO opposition was filed on ... against the Patent but was finally dismissed by the Boards of Appeal on. ... This decision is enclosed as

—Enclosure AST 4—

This decision has not been appealed and is thus final.

ii. Subject matter of the Patent

The invention of the Patent relates to a sports shoe. It relates, in particular, to a running shoe which is provided with a protective cover. It covers the upper portion on the exterior surfaces thereof in the region of the ball and extends from the sole.

The sole and upper portion on the exterior surfaces of the sports shoe, in the vicinity of the ball of the foot, are subject to heavy stresses. In the case of running shoes the stress is particularly high. Therefore, the prior art proposes, as illustrated in the German Patent Application DE ... provided as

—Enclosure AST 5—

to provide protecting supports which cover the critical areas. If these supports are subsequently fitted, for example, by means of a lace, perfect fitting can usually not be ensured. If, however, the supports are formed on the sole and drawn up over the edge thereof a certain distance over the upper, the problem arises that, on the one hand, only soles with folds formed thereon can be used and, on the other hand, the fixing of the folds composed, for instance, of rubber on to the upper by gluing is not sufficiently durable.

iii. Objective/Solution

The objective of the patent is to provide an improved sports shoe in view of the problem shown in the prior art. The invention overcomes this problem by providing a protecting cover of angular cross-section and permanent shape, one band of which serves for holding the cover in position and engages the underside of the shoe, preferably inserted between the upper portion and the sole. At the same time, the holding band of the shoe cover is preferably located between the margin of the upper portion and the sole composed of one or several layers. It is preferably in the form of a thin tongue tapering toward its end. The advantage offered by the invention is that the normal components of the shoe, irrespectively of whether it is the upper portion or the sole, can be worked into the shape, and that no supplementary or securing means are required for fitting the protecting cover. This is realized by sports shoes with the following features, namely

A sports shoe comprising

1) *a sole;*
2) *an upper portion attached to the sole; and*
3) *a rigid cover:*
   - *made of resisting material;*
   - *is angular in cross-section; and*
   - *defining a securing band and a protective shield.*
4) *the securing band is affixed between said sole and said upper portion;*
5) *the securing band extends from said sole, upwardly over the exterior of the upper portion in the area of the ball of the shoe.*

This feature chart is separately provided on a sheet as

—Enclosure AST 6—

C. Infringement of the patent-in-suit

The plaintiff became aware that the defendant is exhibiting at the present trade show ISPO 2022 a running shoe, namely the type … which makes use of claim 1 of the patent-in-suit. The accused shoe is illustrated on a photo which has been taken from the flyer of Enclosure AST 2, but separately provided as

—Enclosure AST 7—

The photo contains the references of features 1)–5) of the asserted claim 1: It is a sports shoe with a plastic sole (Feature 1) and an upper portion which is attached to the sole (Feature 2) and a rigid cap (Feature 3) which is:

- *made of resisting material;*
- *is angular in cross-section; and*
- *defines a holding arm and a cover arm.*

Furthermore, the holding arm is secured between said sole and said upper portion (Feature 4) and the cover arm extends from said sole, upwardly over the exterior of the upper portion in the area of the ball of the shoe (Feature 5).

D. Reason for the preliminary injunction/urgency

The plaintiff became aware of the accused shoe on. … The present matter is particularly urgent because the patent-in-suit concerns an invention of particular importance to the plaintiff. Its sports shoes … use the patented features and are one of its most successful products, also thanks to significant promotional investments. As already indicated, plaintiff invests Millions of Euros in its Research & Development (R&D) and main achievements of Plaintiff's R&D are protected by IP rights, including the patent at issue.

The plaintiff also exhibits these products at the present tradeshow. It is indicated that the ongoing accused commercial activities of defendant with the accused shoe will negatively influence the sales of plaintiff and considerably harm plaintiff's business. Most companies conduct their annual European business through the ISPO tradeshow. Since the defendant is an Asian company, it will no longer be reachable after the end of the tradeshow. Therefore, there is a considerable interest that the activities of the defendant are stopped still during the ongoing trade fair. The grant of the application without hearing the defendant is thus justified.

On … the plaintiff informed the defendant of the patent-in-suit with reference to the accused products. Nevertheless, the defendant indicated that it did not intend to stop the commercialization.

The validity of the patent-in-suit is sufficiently secured and confirmed by the final decision of the Boards of Appeal according to Annex AST 4.

The factual details described in the present request for a preliminary injunction are contained in an affidavit of the CEO of the plaintiff, who has knowledge of the circumstances. This affidavit is provided as

—Enclosure AST 8—

e. Legal assessment

The jurisdiction of the … follows from … and from that the present case concerns a patent matter. Defendant is marketing the attacked products in Germany, France, and the Netherlands. The accused sports shoe is offered for sale at the present tradeshow and meanwhile advertised on defendant's website www.yyy.com and can thus be bought by any potential customer within any of the indicated jurisdictions.

The claims raised with the present action follow from the above made submission. The defendant is obliged to cease and desist due to an illegal use of the subject matter of the patent-in-suit.

Furthermore, the claim to place in custody of a sequestrator all sports shoes follows from Article 62(3) UPCA.

It is respectfully requested that the chamber indicate, if possible, by phone, whether any further evidence is necessary to substantiate the claim.

(signature)

Rechtsanwalt

(Signature of the Counsel)

Enclosures AST 1–AST 8

§17.06 PROTECTIVE BRIEF

In order to avoid an ex parte preliminary injunction, a prudent company that has reason to believe it will be accused of infringement should preemptively file a protective brief. Details concerning protective briefs are contained in Chapter 11, sections 1.5 and 2.6.1. The following sample presents an outline of the body of a protective brief. The following sample follows the German standards.

District Court. ...

(Address)

Munich, ... date

Our ref.:

Protective brief

In presumed preliminary injunction proceedings of

Company Y ... represented by the Executive Directors,

—presumed plaintiff—

versus

Company X ... represented by its legal representatives;

—presumed defendant[24]—

Authorized representatives: Attorneys-at-law and patent attorneys of the law firm ...

on grounds of alleged patent infringement.

We hereby declare to be authorized representatives in presumed proceedings against the presumed defendant in case that the presumed plaintiff should file a request for a preliminary injunction on grounds of the following facts of the case.

We request,

i. *that a presumed request for order of a preliminary injunction be dismissed, or in the alternative that a decision about a presumed request for a preliminary injunction shall not be made without conducting previously an oral hearing;*
ii. *that in case of a dismissal of the request for injunction or its withdrawal the costs for the injunction proceedings including the costs for the deposit of the protective letter be imposed upon the plaintiff.*

In case the plaintiff should file a request for an order of preliminary injunction, we consent to providing the present protective letter to the plaintiff.

24. It is recommendable to include all possible accused infringers: US mother company; all affiliates provided they are commercially active on the German market.

We agree to the determination of a date for an oral hearing on the terms of a shortened period of summons, to make the present protective letter accessible to the presumed plaintiff in case they should request a preliminary injunction.

Reasoned statement:

A. The parties

The presumed plaintiff supplies systems for the treatment of biological material. Also, the defendants operate in this field. The parties are in direct competition with each other. The presumed defendant plans the introduction of a new product on the market (hereinafter "presumingly accused product")

This protective letter is primarily based on lack of validity and lack of infringement of the Patent. The presumed defendant reserves to extend the counterstatement in presumed preliminary injunction proceedings.

B. The patent-in-suit[25]

1. Background

The presumed plaintiff is owner of the European patent … (in the following: the Patent), provided as

—Enclosure AG 1—

concerning a method for isolating a portion of a layer of a biological material.

It is possible that a new product, i.e., the presumingly attacked product of the defendant, is challenged by the presumed plaintiff.

2. Subject matter of the patent-in-suit

(…)

3. Objective/Solution

The objective of the patent is to provide (…)

C. Apparent lack of validity of the patent-in-suit

Initially, the Court's attention should be directed on the fact that the presumed plaintiff would proceed based on an invalid patent. (…)[26]

Conclusion: *All features of claim 1 are anticipated. A request for order of a preliminary injunction based on claim 1 is not justified due to lack of validity.*

25. This part of the protective brief is similar to the complaint and request for a preliminary injunction (*see* above).
26. This section contains all reasons why the possible defendant believes that the patent-in-suit is not valid.

D. Lacking infringement of the patent-in-suit

The order of a preliminary injunction on the basis of the patent cannot be considered under any aspect. The presumed defendant reserves to provide further facts for noninfringement. Nevertheless, as

—Enclosure AG ...—

a chart is provided, which contains an overview showing that none of the independent and dependent claims are realized.[27]

v. Missing cause for a preliminary injunction

The present case is also not urgent.[28] *...*

The factual details described in the present protective brief are contained in an affidavit of the CEO of the defendant, who has knowledge of the circumstances. This affidavit is provided as

—Enclosure AG ...—

It is respectfully requested that the chamber indicate, if possible, by phone, whether any evidence is missing. The defendant will see to it that it is provided as soon as possible.

Signature of the Counsel

—Enclosures AG 1–AG ...—

§17.07 BANK GUARANTEE

This sample is in line with German standards. Such a guarantee is needed to render a first instance decision enforceable. The UPCA does not prescribe a particular type of security. This is subject to the discretion of the UPC. Of course, a security must provide sufficient protection for damages caused by the enforcement. A bank guarantee must thus be directly enforceable, irrevocable, unlimited, and unconditional, as it is required in German proceedings.

BANK GUARANTEE (REF. NO.)

Issuing Bank: [a bank, which is officially accredited and entitled to operate in Germany]

Amount: Euro € ...

Issue Date: ...

Beneficiary: [Complete Address]

---

27. It is advisable to include a noninfringement argument. Without a noninfringement argument, there is a risk that the Court gets the impression that the accused infringer's activities are done in full awareness of the infringement.
28. This section of the protective brief shall contain all facts and arguments that may present obstacles to the grant of a preliminary injunction, such as missing "urgency."

Applicant: [Complete Address]

Ladies/Gentlemen:

in the lawsuit at the District Court Düsseldorf with the court docket n°... between ... (hereinafter "Plaintiff"), and ... (hereinafter "Defendant"), the District Court Düsseldorf requested the Plaintiff by Court Decision of ... to provide a security. This security can be provided by a written, irrevocable, unlimited in time, absolute, unconditional, and directly liable bank guarantee in view of the provisional enforcement of item ... of the aforementioned Decision

By order of the Plaintiff and for the account of Plaintiff in respect of eventual costs caused to the Defendant through the provisional enforcement of item ... of the aforementioned Decision provided that the provisional enforcement turns out to be unjustified in case the Defendant finally prevails, we hereby establish our irrevocable, unlimited in time, absolute, unconditional, and directly liable Bank Guarantee ("Bank Guarantee") to the amount of

[...€][29]

and waive the defense of rescission and setoff, including the plea of exhausted remedies according to §§770, 771 of the Civil Code.

The guarantee expires under §158 paragraph 2 of the Civil Code if the guarantee is handed back to us by the defendant or with his consent by a third party.

Authorized Signatures(s)

29. Normally 110% of the litigation value.

CHAPTER 18

Legal Texts

This chapter contains English translations of most of the legal provisions referred to throughout this handbook. The quoted articles and rules of the EPC (sections 18.1 and 18.2) and the Council Regulation (EC) concerning custom actions (section 18.06) are official texts. The excerpts from the German Patent Act, Utility Model Act and Act on Employees' Inventions are unofficial translations, and in some instances represent the only available English translations. The complete text of the EPC can be found on the website of the EPO (www.epo.org). The excerpts of the UPCA and RoP and the UP Regulations are official texts. Complete texts can be found on the website of the Preparatory Committee https://www.unified-patent-court.org/. The legal texts include the following:

(1) Excerpt of the EPC.
(2) Chapter V of the Rules to the EPC—Biotechnological inventions.
(3) Excerpts of the German Patent Act.
(4) Excerpts of the Utility Model Act.
(5) Excerpts of the Act on Employees' Inventions.
(6) Council Regulation (EC) concerning custom actions.
(7) Excerpts of the UPCA.
(8) UP Regulations.

EPC

§18.01 EXCERPTS OF THE EPC[1]

Article 52—Patentable inventions

(1) European patents shall be granted for any inventions which are susceptible of industrial application, which are new and which involve an inventive step.
(2) The following in particular shall not be regarded as inventions within the meaning of paragraph 1:
   (a) discoveries, scientific theories and mathematical methods;
   (b) aesthetic creations;
   (c) schemes, rules and methods for performing mental acts, playing games or doing business, and programs for computers;
   (d) presentations of information.
(3) The provisions of paragraph 2 shall exclude patentability of the subject matter or activities referred to in that provision only to the extent to which a European patent application or European patent relates to such subject matter or activities as such.
(4) Methods for treatment of the human or animal body by surgery or therapy and diagnostic methods practised on the human or animal body shall not be regarded as inventions which are susceptible of industrial application within the meaning of paragraph 1. This provision shall not apply to products, in particular substances or compositions, for use in any of these methods.

Article 53—Exceptions to patentability

European patents shall not be granted in respect of:

(a) inventions the publication or exploitation of which would be contrary to "order public" or morality, provided that the exploitation shall not be deemed to be so contrary merely because it is prohibited by law or regulation in some or all of the Contracting States;
(b) plant or animal varieties or essentially biological processes for the production of plants or animals; this provision does not apply to microbiological processes or the products thereof.

Article 54—Novelty

(1) An invention shall be considered to be new if it does not form part of the state of the art.
(2) The state of the art shall be held to comprise everything made available to the public by means of a written or oral description, by use, or in any other way, before the date of filing of the European patent application.
(3) Additionally, the content of European patent applications as filed, of which the dates of filing are prior to the date referred to in paragraph 2 and which

1. *See* website of the EPO: www.epo.com.

were published under Article 93 on or after that date, shall be considered as comprised in the state of the art.

(4) Paragraph 3 shall be applied only in so far as a Contracting State designated in respect of the later application, was also designated in respect of the earlier application as published.

(5) The provisions of paragraphs 1 to 4 shall not exclude the patentability of any substance or composition, comprised in the state of the art, for use in a method referred to in Article 52, paragraph 4, provided that its use for any method referred to in that paragraph is not comprised in the state of the art.

Article 55—Non-prejudicial disclosures

(1) For the application of Article 54 a disclosure of the invention shall not be taken into consideration if it occurred no earlier than six months preceding the filing of the European patent application and if it was due to, or in consequence of:

(a) 31 an evident abuse in relation to the applicant or his legal predecessor, or

(b) the fact that the applicant or his legal predecessor has displayed the invention at an official, or officially recognized, international exhibition falling within the terms of the Convention on international exhibitions signed at Paris on November 22, 1928 and last revised on November 30, 1972.

(2) In the case of paragraph 1(b), paragraph 1 shall apply only if the applicant states, when filing the European patent application, that the invention has been so displayed and files a supporting certificate within the period and under the conditions laid down in the Implementing Regulations.

Article 56—Inventive step

An invention shall be considered as involving an inventive step if, having regard to the state of the art, it is not obvious to a person skilled in the art. If the state of the art also includes documents within the meaning of Article 54, paragraph 3, these documents are not to be considered in deciding whether there has been an inventive step.

Article 57—Industrial application

An invention shall be considered as susceptible of industrial application if it can be made or used in any kind of industry, including agriculture.

Article 58—Entitlement to file a European patent application

A European patent application may be filed by any natural or legal person, or anybody equivalent to a legal person by virtue of the law governing it.

Article 59—Multiple applicants

A European patent application may also be filed either by joint applicants or by two or more applicants designating different Contracting States.

Article 60—Right to a European patent

(1) The right to a European patent shall belong to the inventor or his successor in title. If the inventor is an employee, the right to a European patent shall be determined in accordance with the law of the State in which the employee is mainly employed; if the State in which the employee is mainly employed cannot be determined, the law to be applied shall be that of the State in which the employer has the place of business to which the employee is attached.
(2) If two or more persons have made an invention independently of each other, the right to a European patent therefore shall belong to the person whose European patent application has the earliest date of filing, provided that this first application has been published.
(3) In proceedings before the European Patent Office, the applicant shall be deemed to be entitled to exercise the right to a European patent.

Article 61—European patent applications filed by non-entitled persons

(1) If by a final decision it is adjudged that a person other than the applicant is entitled to the grant of the European patent, that person may, in accordance with the Implementing Regulations:
 (a) prosecute the European patent application as his own application in place of the applicant;
 (b) file a new European patent application in respect of the same invention; or
 (c) request that the European patent application be refused.
(2) Article 76, paragraph 1, shall apply mutatis mutandis to a new European patent application filed under paragraph 1(b).

Article 62—Right of the inventor to be mentioned

The inventor shall have the right, vis-à-vis the applicant for or proprietor of a European patent, to be mentioned as such before the European Patent Office.

Article 63—Term of the European patent

(1) The term of the European patent shall be 20 years as from the date of filing of the application.
(2) Nothing in the preceding paragraph shall limit the right of a Contracting State to extend the term of a European patent, or to grant corresponding protection which follows immediately on expiry of the term of the patent, under the same conditions as those applying to national patents:
 (a) in order to take account of a state of war or similar emergency conditions affecting that State;
 (b) if the subject matter of the European patent is a product or a process of manufacturing a product or a use of a product which has to undergo an administrative authorization procedure required by law before it can be put on the market in that State.

(3) Paragraph 2 shall apply mutatis mutandis to European patents granted jointly for a group of Contracting States in accordance with Article 142.

(4) A Contracting State which makes provision for extension of the term or corresponding protection under paragraph 2(b) may, in accordance with an agreement concluded with the Organization, entrust to the European Patent Office tasks associated with implementation of the relevant provisions.

Article 64—Rights conferred by a European patent

A European patent shall, subject to the provisions of paragraph 2, confer on its proprietor from the date of publication of the mention of its grant, in each Contracting State in respect of which it is granted, the same rights as would be conferred by a national patent granted in that State.

If the subject matter of the European patent is a process, the protection conferred by the patent shall extend to the products directly obtained by such process.

Any infringement of a European patent shall be dealt with by national law

Article 65—Translation of the European patent

(1) Any Contracting State may prescribe that if the text, in which the European Patent Office intends to grant a European patent or maintain a European patent as amended for that State, is not drawn up in one of its official languages, the applicant for or proprietor of the patent shall supply to its central industrial property office a translation of this text in one of its official languages at his option or, where that State has prescribed the use of one specific official language, in that language. The period for supplying the translation shall end three months after the date on which the mention of the grant of the European patent or of the maintenance of the European patent as amended is published in the European Patent Bulletin, unless the State concerned prescribes a longer period.

(2) Any Contracting State which has adopted provisions pursuant to paragraph 1 may prescribe that the applicant for or proprietor of the patent must pay all or part of the costs of publication of such translation within a period laid down by that State.

(3) Any Contracting State may prescribe that in the event of failure to observe the provisions adopted in accordance with paragraphs 1 and 2, the European patent shall be deemed to be void *ab initio* in that State.

Article 67—Rights conferred by a European patent application after publication

(1) A European patent application shall, from the date of its publication under Article 93, provisionally confer upon the applicant such protection as is conferred by Article 64, in the Contracting States designated in the application as published.

(2) Any Contracting State may prescribe that a European patent application shall not confer such protection as is conferred by Article 64. However, the protection attached to the publication of the European patent application may

not be less than that which the laws of the State concerned attach to the compulsory publication of unexamined national patent applications. In any event, every State shall ensure at least that, from the date of publication of a European patent application, the applicant can claim compensation reasonable in the circumstances from any person who has used the invention in the said State in circumstances where that person would be liable under national law for infringement of a national patent.

(3) Any Contracting State which does not have as an official language the language of the proceedings, may prescribe that provisional protection in accordance with paragraphs 1 and 2 above shall not be effective until such time as a translation of the claims in one of its official languages at the option of the applicant or, where that State has prescribed the use of one specific official language, in that language:
   (a) has been made available to the public in the manner prescribed by national law, or
   (b) has been communicated to the person using the invention in the said State.

(4) The European patent application shall be deemed never to have had the effects set out in paragraphs 1 and 2 above when it has been withdrawn, deemed to be withdrawn or finally refused. The same shall apply in respect of the effects of the European patent application in a Contracting State the designation of which is withdrawn or deemed to be withdrawn.

Article 68—Effect of revocation or limitation of the European patent

The European patent application and the resulting patent shall be deemed not to have had, as from the outset, the effects specified in Articles 64 and 67, to the extent that the patent has been revoked in opposition proceedings.

Article 69[2]—Extent of protection

The extent of the protection conferred by a European patent or a European patent application shall be determined by the terms of the claims. Nevertheless, the description and drawings shall be used to interpret the claims.

For the period up to grant of the European patent, the extent of the protection conferred by the European patent application shall be determined by the latest filed claims contained in the publication under Article 93. However, the European patent as granted or as amended in opposition proceedings shall determine retroactively the

---

2. Protocol on the Interpretation of Art. 69 EPC of Oct. 5, 1973 as revised by the Act revising the EPC of Nov. 29, 2000:

   Article 1—General principles

   Article 69 should not be interpreted as meaning that the extent of the protection conferred by a European patent is to be understood as that defined by the strict, literal meaning of the wording used in the claims, the description and drawings being employed only for the purpose of resolving an ambiguity found in the claims. Nor

protection conferred by the European patent application, in so far as such protection is not thereby extended.

Article 70—Authentic text of a European patent application or European patent

(1) The text of a European patent application or a European patent in the language of the proceedings shall be the authentic text in any proceedings before the European Patent Office and in any Contracting State.

(2) However, in the case referred to in Article 14, paragraph 2, the original text shall, in proceedings before the European Patent Office, constitute the basis for determining whether the subject matter of the application or patent extends beyond the content of the application as filed.

(3) Any Contracting State may provide that a translation, as provided for in this Convention, in an official language of that State, shall in that State be regarded as authentic, except for revocation proceedings, in the event of the application or patent in the language of the translation conferring protection which is narrower than that conferred by it in the language of the proceedings.

(4) Any Contracting State which adopts a provision under paragraph 3:

(a) must allow the applicant for or proprietor of the patent to file a corrected translation of the European patent application or European patent. Such corrected translation shall not have any legal effect until any conditions established by the Contracting State under Article 65, paragraph 2, and Article 67, paragraph 3, have been complied with mutatis mutandis;

(b) may prescribe that any person who, in that State, in good faith is using or has made effective and serious preparations for using an invention the use of which would not constitute infringement of the application or patent in the original translation may, after the corrected translation takes effect, continue such use in the course of his business or for the needs thereof without payment.

Article 71—Transfer and constitution of rights

A European patent application may be transferred or give rise to rights for one or more of the designated Contracting States.

EPC

---

should it be taken to mean that the claims serve only as a guideline and that the actual protection conferred may extend to what, from a consideration of the description and drawings by a person skilled in the art, the patent proprietor has contemplated. On the contrary, it is to be interpreted as defining a position between these extremes which combines a fair protection for the patent proprietor with a reasonable degree of legal certainty for third parties.

Article 2—Equivalents

For the purpose of determining the extent of protection conferred by a European patent, due account shall be taken of any element which is equivalent to an element specified in the claims.

Article 72—Assignment

An assignment of a European patent application shall be made in writing and shall require the signature of the parties to the contract.

Article 73—Contractual licensing

A European patent application may be licensed in whole or in part for the whole or part of the territories of the designated Contracting States.

Article 74—Law applicable

Unless otherwise specified in this Convention, the European patent application as an object of property shall, in each designated Contracting State and with effect for such State, be subject to the law applicable in that State to national patent applications.

Article 75—Filing of a European patent application

(1) A European patent application may be filed:
  (a) with the European Patent Office, or
  (b) if the law of a Contracting State so permits, and subject to Article 76, paragraph 1, with the central industrial property office or other competent authority of that State. Any application filed in this way shall have the same effect as if it had been filed on the same date with the European Patent Office.

(2) Paragraph 1 shall not preclude the application of legislative or regulatory provisions which, in any Contracting State:
  (a) govern inventions which, owing to the nature of their subject-matter, may not be communicated abroad without the prior authorisation of the competent authorities of that State, or
  (b) prescribe that any application is to be filed initially with a national authority, or make direct filing with another authority subject to prior authorisation

Article 76—European divisional applications

(1) A European divisional application shall be filed directly with the European Patent Office in accordance with the Implementing Regulations.[3] It may be filed only in respect of subject matter which does not extend beyond the content of the earlier application as filed; in so far as this requirement is

3. Rule 36 EPC: European divisional applications: (1) The applicant may file a divisional application relating to any pending earlier European patent application, provided that: (a) the divisional application is filed before the expiry of a time limit of twenty-four months from the Examining Division's first communication under Art. 94, para. 3, and Rule 71, paras. 1 and 2, or Rule 71, para. 3, in respect of the earliest application for which a communication has been issued, or (b) the divisional application is filed before the expiry of a time limit of twenty-four months from any communication in which the Examining Division has objected that the earlier application does not meet the requirements of Art. 82, provided it was raising that specific objection for the first time. (...)

complied with, the divisional application shall be deemed to have been filed on the date of filing of the earlier application and shall enjoy any right of priority.

(2) All the Contracting States designated in the earlier application at the time of filing of a European divisional application shall be deemed to be designated in the divisional application.

(...)

Article 82—Unity of invention

The European patent application shall relate to one invention only or to a group of inventions so linked as to form a single general inventive concept.

Article 83—Disclosure of the invention

The European patent application shall disclose the invention in a manner sufficiently clear and complete for it to be carried out by a person skilled in the art.

Article 84—Claims

The claims shall define the matter for which protection is sought. They shall be clear and concise and be supported by the description.

(...)

Article 87—Priority right

(1) Any person who has duly filed, in or for
 (a) any State party to the Paris Convention for the Protection of Industrial Property or
 (b) any Member of the World Trade Organization,

(2) an application for a patent, a utility model or a utility certificate, or his successor in title, shall enjoy, for the purpose of filing a European patent application in respect of the same invention, a right of priority during a period of twelve months from the date of filing of the first application.

(3) Every filing that is equivalent to a regular national filing under the national law of the State where it was made or under bilateral or multi-lateral agreements, including this Convention, shall be recognized as giving rise to a right of priority.

(4) A regular national filing shall mean any filing that is sufficient to establish the date on which the application was filed, whatever the outcome of the application may be.

(5) A subsequent application in respect of the same subject matter as a previous first application and filed in or for the same State shall be considered as the first application for the purposes of determining priority, provided that, at the date of filing the subsequent application, the previous application has been withdrawn, abandoned or refused, without being open to public inspection and without leaving any rights outstanding, and has not served as a basis for

claiming a right of priority. The previous application may not thereafter serve as a basis for claiming a right of priority.

(6) If the first filing has been made with an industrial property authority which is not subject to the Paris Convention for the Protection of Industrial Property or the Agreement Establishing the World Trade Organization, paragraphs 1 to 4 shall apply if that authority, according to a communication issued by the President of the European Patent Office, recognizes that a first filing made with the European Patent Office gives rise to a right of priority under conditions and with effects equivalent to those laid down in the Paris Convention.

Article 88—Claiming priority

(1) An applicant desiring to take advantage of the priority of a previous application shall file a declaration of priority and any other document required, in accordance with the Implementing Regulations.

(2) Multiple priorities may be claimed in respect of a European patent application, notwithstanding the fact that they originated in different countries. Where appropriate, multiple priorities may be claimed for any one claim. Where multiple priorities are claimed, time limits which run from the date of priority shall run from the earliest date of priority.

(3) If one or more priorities are claimed in respect of a European patent application, the right of priority shall cover only those elements of the European patent application which are included in the application or applications whose priority is claimed.

(4) If certain elements of the invention for which priority is claimed do not appear among the claims formulated in the previous application, priority may nonetheless be granted, provided that the documents of the previous application as a whole specifically disclose such elements.

(…)

Article 90—Examination on filing and examination as to formal requirements

(1) The European Patent Office shall examine, in accordance with the Implementing Regulations, whether the application satisfies the requirements for the accordance of a date of filing.

(2) If a date of filing cannot be accorded following the examination under paragraph 1, the application shall not be dealt with as a European patent application.

(3) If the European patent application has been accorded a date of filing, the European Patent Office shall examine, in accordance with the Implementing Regulations, whether the requirements in Articles 14, 78 and 81, and, where applicable, Article 88, paragraph 1, and Article 133, paragraph 2, as well as any other requirement laid down in the Implementing Regulations, have been satisfied.

(4) Where the European Patent Office in carrying out the examination under paragraphs 1 or 3 notes that there are deficiencies which may be corrected, it shall give the applicant an opportunity to correct them.

(5) If any deficiency noted in the examination under paragraph 3 is not corrected, the European patent application shall be refused unless a different legal consequence is provided for by this Convention. Where the deficiency concerns the right of priority, this right shall be lost for the application.

Article 92—Drawing up of the European search report

The European Patent Office shall, in accordance with the Implementing Regulations, draw up and publish a European search report in respect of the European patent application on the basis of the claims, with due regard to the description and any drawings.

Article 93—Publication of the European patent application

(1) The European Patent Office shall publish the European patent application as soon as possible
   (a) after the expiry of a period of eighteen months from the date of filing or, if priority has been claimed, from the date of priority, or
   (b) at the request of the applicant, before the expiry of that period.

(2) The European patent application shall be published at the same time as the specification of the European patent when the decision to grant the patent becomes effective before the expiry of the period referred to in paragraph 1(a).

Article 94—Examination of the European patent application

- The European Patent Office shall, in accordance with the Implementing Regulations, examine on request whether the European patent application and the invention to which it relates meet the requirements of this Convention. The request shall not be deemed to be filed until the examination fee has been paid.
- If no request for examination has been made in due time, the application shall be deemed to be withdrawn.
- If the examination reveals that the application or the invention to which it relates does not meet the requirements of this Convention, the Examining Division shall invite the applicant, as often as necessary, to file his observations and, subject to Article 123, paragraph 1, to amend the application.
- If the applicant fails to reply in due time to any communication from the Examining Division, the application shall be deemed to be withdrawn.

(...)

Article 97—Grant or refusal

- If the Examining Division is of the opinion that the European patent application and the invention to which it relates meet the requirements of this

Convention, it shall decide to grant a European patent, provided that the conditions laid down in the Implementing Regulations are fulfilled.

- If the Examining Division is of the opinion that the European patent application or the invention to which it relates does not meet the requirements of this Convention, it shall refuse the application unless this Convention provides for a different legal consequence.
- The decision to grant a European patent shall take effect on the date on which the mention of the grant is published in the European Patent Bulletin.

(...)

Article 99—Opposition

Within nine months of the publication of the mention of the grant of the European patent in the European Patent Bulletin, any person may give notice to the European Patent Office of opposition to that patent, in accordance with the Implementing Regulations. Notice of opposition shall not be deemed to have been filed until the opposition fee has been paid.

The opposition shall apply to the European patent in all the Contracting States in which that patent has effect.

Opponents shall be parties to the opposition proceedings as well as the proprietor of the patent.

Where a person provides evidence that in a Contracting State, following a final decision, he has been entered in the patent register of such State instead of the previous proprietor, such person shall, at his request, replace the previous proprietor in respect of such State. Notwithstanding Article 118, the previous proprietor and the person making the request shall not be regarded as joint proprietors unless both so request.

Article 100—Grounds for opposition

Opposition may only be filed on the grounds that:

- the subject matter of the European patent is not patentable under Articles 52 to 57;
- the European patent does not disclose the invention in a manner sufficiently clear and complete for it to be carried out by a person skilled in the art;
- the subject matter of the European patent extends beyond the content of the application as filed, or, if the patent was granted on a divisional application or on a new application filed under Article 61, beyond the content of the earlier application as filed.

(...)

Article 105—Intervention of the assumed infringer

Any third party may, in accordance with the Implementing Regulations, intervene in opposition proceedings after the opposition period has expired, if the third party proves that proceedings for infringement of the same patent have been instituted against him, or following a request of the proprietor of the patent to cease alleged infringement, the third party has instituted proceedings for a ruling that he is not infringing the patent.

An admissible intervention shall be treated as an opposition.

Article 105a—Request for limitation or revocation

- At the request of the proprietor, the European patent may be revoked or be limited by an amendment of the claims. The request shall be filed with the European Patent Office in accordance with the Implementing Regulations. It shall not be deemed to have been filed until the limitation or revocation fee has been paid.
- The request may not be filed while opposition proceedings in respect of the European patent are pending.

Article 105b—Limitation or revocation of the European patent

The European Patent Office shall examine whether the requirements laid down in the Implementing Regulations for limiting or revoking the European patent have been met.

If the European Patent Office considers that the request for limitation or revocation of the European patent meets these requirements, it shall decide to limit or revoke the European patent in accordance with the Implementing Regulations. Otherwise, it shall reject the request.

The decision to limit or revoke the European patent shall apply to the European patent in all the Contracting States in respect of which it has been granted. It shall take effect on the date on which the mention of the decision is published in the European Patent Bulletin.

(...)

Article 115—Observations by third parties

Following the publication of the European patent application, any person may present observations concerning the patentability of the invention in respect of which the application has been filed. Such observations must be filed in writing and must include a statement of the grounds on which they are based. That person shall not be a party to the proceedings before the European Patent Office.

The observations referred to in paragraph 1 shall be communicated to the applicant for or proprietor of the patent who may comment on them.

(...)

Article 123—Amendments

The conditions under which a European patent application or a European patent may be amended in proceedings before the European Patent Office are laid down in the Implementing Regulations. In any case, an applicant shall be allowed at least one opportunity of amending the description, claims and drawings of his own volition.

A European patent application or a European patent may not be amended in such a way that it contains subject matter which extends beyond the content of the application as filed.

The claims of the European patent may not be amended during opposition proceedings in such a way as to extend the protection conferred.

§18.02 CHAPTER V: BIOTECHNOLOGICAL INVENTIONS[4]

Rule 26—General and definitions

For European patent applications and patents concerning biotechnological inventions, the relevant provisions of the Convention shall be applied and interpreted in accordance with the provisions of this Chapter. Directive 98/44/EC of 6 July 199819 on the legal protection of biotechnological inventions shall be used as a supplementary means of interpretation.

- "Biotechnological inventions" are inventions which concern a product consisting of or containing biological material or a process by means of which biological material is produced, processed or used.
- "Biological material" means any material containing genetic information and capable of reproducing itself or being reproduced in a biological system.
- "Plant variety" means any plant grouping within a single botanical taxon of the lowest known rank, which grouping, irrespective of whether the conditions for the grant of a plant variety right are fully met, can be:
- defined by the expression of the characteristics that results from a given genotype or combination of genotypes,
- distinguished from any other plant grouping by the expression of at least one of the said characteristics, and
- considered as a unit with regard to its suitability for being propagated unchanged.

A process for the production of plants or animals is essentially biological if it consists entirely of natural phenomena such as crossing or selection.

- "Microbiological process" means any process involving or performed upon or resulting in microbiological material.

Rule 27—Patentable biotechnological inventions

Biotechnological inventions shall also be patentable if they concern:

(a) biological material which is isolated from its natural environment or produced by means of a technical process even if it previously occurred in nature;
(b) plants or animals if the technical feasibility of the invention is not confined to a particular plant or animal variety;
(c) a microbiological or other technical process, or a product obtained by means of such a process other than a plant or animal variety.

4. This chapter is part of the Implementing Regulations to the EPC. The full text can be found on the website of the EPO: www.epo.org.

Rule 28—Exceptions to patentability

Under Article 53(a), European patents shall not be granted in respect of biotechnological inventions which, in particular, concern the following:

(a) processes for cloning human beings;
(b) processes for modifying the germ line genetic identity of human beings;
(c) uses of human embryos for industrial or commercial purposes;
(d) processes for modifying the genetic identity of animals which are likely to cause them suffering without any substantial medical benefit to man or animal, and also animals resulting from such processes.

Rule 29—The human body and its elements

(1) The human body, at the various stages of its formation and development, and the simple discovery of one of its elements, including the sequence or partial sequence of a gene, cannot constitute patentable inventions.
(2) An element isolated from the human body or otherwise produced by means of a technical process, including the sequence or partial sequence of a gene, may constitute a patentable invention, even if the structure of that element is identical to that of a natural element.
(3) The industrial application of a sequence or a partial sequence of a gene must be disclosed in the patent application.

§18.03 GERMAN PATENT ACT[5]

§1 Patentable Inventions

(1) Patents shall be granted for inventions in all technical areas that are new, involve an inventive step and are susceptible of industrial application.

(2) Patents shall also be granted on inventions within the meaning of subsection (1) if they concern a product consisting of or containing biological material, or if they concern a process by which biological material is produced or modified, or in which it is used. Biological material isolated from its natural environment or produced by means of a technical process may also constitute an object of an invention, even if it was already present in nature.

(3) The following shall not be regarded as inventions within the meaning of subsection (1):

1. discoveries, scientific theories and mathematical methods;
2. aesthetic creations;
3. schemes, rules and methods for performing mental acts, playing games or doing business and programs for computers;
4. presentations of information.

(4) The provisions of subsection (3) shall exclude patentability only to the extent to which protection is sought for the above-mentioned subject matter or activities as such.

§1a Human Body and its Elements

(1) The human body, at the various stages of its formation and development, including germ cells, and the simple discovery of one of its elements, including the sequence or partial sequence of a gene, cannot constitute patentable inventions.

(2) An element isolated from the human body or otherwise produced by means of a technical process, including the sequence or partial sequence of a gene, may constitute a patentable invention, even if the structure of that element is identical to that of a natural element.

(3) The industrial application of a sequence or a partial sequence of a gene must be disclosed in the patent application stating the function performed by the sequence or partial sequence.

(4) If the object of the invention concerns a sequence or partial sequence of a gene, the structure of which is identical to the structure of a natural sequence or partial sequence of a human gene, its use for which the industrial application is specifically described under subsection (3) must be included in the patent claim.

5. Amended Version: Aug. 10, 2021.

§2 Ordre Public and Morality

(1) Patents shall not be granted in respect of inventions the publication or exploitation of which would be contrary to ordre public or morality, provided that the exploitation shall not be deemed to be so contrary merely because it is prohibited by law or regulation.
(2) Patents shall not be granted in respect of:
   1. processes for cloning human beings;
   2. processes for modifying the genetic identity of the germline of human beings;
   3. use of human embryos for industrial or commercial purposes;
   4. processes for modifying the genetic identity of animals which are likely to cause them suffering without any substantial medical benefit to man or animal, and also animals resulting from such processes.

In the application of subsections 1 to 3, the relevant provisions of the Embryo Protection Act shall take precedence.

§2a Plant and Animal Varieties, Production of Plants and Animals, Microbiological Processes, Definitions

(1) Patents shall not be granted in respect of
   1. plant and animal varieties or essentially biological processes for the production of plants and animals.
   2. methods for the treatment of the human or animal body by surgery or therapy and diagnostic methods practised on the human or animal body. This shall not apply to products, in particular to substances or compositions, for use in one of these methods.
(2) Patents can be granted in respect of inventions which concern
   1. plants or animals, if the technical feasibility of the invention is not confined to a particular plant or animal variety;
   2. a microbiological or other technical process or a product obtained by means of such a process, where this is not a plant or animal variety....

§3 Novelty

(1) An invention shall be deemed to be new if it does not form part of the state of the art. The state of the art shall be held to comprise all knowledge made available to the public before the date governing the filing or priority date of the application by means of a written or oral description, by use or in any other way.
(2) The content of the following patent applications having an earlier filing or priority date which were made available to the public on or after the date governing the filing or priority date of the later application shall also be deemed to be comprised in the state of the art:

1. national applications as filed with the German Patent and Trade Mark Office;
2. European applications as filed with the competent authority if the application seeks protection in the Federal Republic of Germany and the designation fee has been paid in respect of the Federal Republic of Germany pursuant to Article 79 paragraph 2 of the European Patent Convention, and if, in the case of a Euro-PCT application (Article 153 paragraph 2 of the European Patent Convention), the requirements laid down in Article 153 paragraph 5 of the European Patent Convention are fulfilled;
3. international applications under the Patent Cooperation Treaty as filed with the receiving Office, provided the German Patent and Trade Mark Office is the designated Office in respect of the application.

If the earlier filing or priority date of an application is based on the claim to the priority of an earlier application, the first sentence shall apply only to the extent that the version of the application in question does not extend beyond the version of the earlier application. Patent applications pursuant to the first sentence, no. 1, in respect of which an order has been made in accordance with section 50 (1) or (4) shall be deemed to have been made available to the public after the expiry of a period of eighteen months following their filing.

(3) Subsections (1) and (2) shall not exclude the patentability of any substance or composition, comprised in the state of the art, for use in a method referred to in section 2a (1) no. 2, provided that its use for any such method is not comprised in the state of the art.

(4) Subsections (1) and (2) shall also not exclude the patentability of any substance or composition referred to in subsection (3) for any specific use in a method referred to in section 2a (1) no. 2, provided that such use is not comprised in the state of the art.

(5) For the application of subsections (1) and (2), a disclosure of the invention shall not be taken into consideration if it occurred no earlier than six months before the filing of the application and if it was due to, or in consequence of

1. an evident abuse in relation to the applicant or his legal predecessor, or
2. the fact that the applicant or his legal predecessor has displayed the invention at an official, or officially recognized, international exhibition falling within the terms of the Convention on international exhibitions signed at Paris on 22 November 1928.

The first sentence, no. 2, shall apply only if the applicant states, when filing the application, that the invention has been so displayed and files a certificate to that effect within four months of the filing. Exhibitions referred to in the first sentence, no. 2, shall be notified by the Federal Minister of Justice in the Federal Gazette (Bundesanzeiger).

§4 Inventive Step

An invention shall be considered to involve an inventive step if, having regard to the state of the art, it is not obvious to a person skilled in the art. If the state of the art also includes documents within the meaning of Section 3(2), these documents shall not be considered in deciding whether there has been an inventive step.

§5 Industrial Application

An invention shall be considered susceptible of industrial application if it can be made or used in any kind of industry, including agriculture.

§6 Right to the Invention

The right to a patent shall belong to the inventor or his successor in title. If two or more persons have jointly made an invention, the right to a patent shall belong to them jointly. If two or more persons have made an invention independently of each other, the right shall belong to the person who is the first to file an application with the Patent Office.

§7 Legal Fictions in favor of the Applicant and Applications by Non-entitled Persons

(1) To avoid the substantive examination of the patent application being delayed due to the need to determine the identity of the inventor, the applicant shall be deemed in the proceedings before the Patent Office to be entitled to request grant of a patent.

(2) If a patent is revoked by reason of opposition based on usurpation (Section 21(1).3) or if opposition results in the withdrawal of the patent, the opponent may himself file an application in respect of the invention, within one month after the official notification thereof, and claim the priority of the earlier patent.

§8 Assignment of the Patent in case of Deprivation

An entitled person whose invention has been applied for by a person not so entitled or the person infringed by the usurpation may require the patent applicant to surrender to him the right to the grant of a patent. If the application has already resulted in a patent, he may require the patentee to assign the patent to him. Such right may only be asserted by an action at law within two years after publication of the grant of the patent (Section 58(1)), subject to the fourth and fifth sentences. If the injured person has filed opposition on the grounds of usurpation (Section 21(1).3), he may bring an action within one year of the final conclusion of the opposition proceedings. The third and fourth sentences shall not apply if the patentee had not acted in good faith in obtaining the patent

§9 Prohibition of Direct use of the Patented Invention

A patent has the effect that the patentee alone is authorized to use the patented invention within the limits of valid law. A person not having the consent of the patentee shall be prohibited:

1. from manufacturing, offering, putting on the market or using a product which is the subject matter of the patent or importing or stocking the product for such purposes;
2. from using a method which is the subject matter of the patent or, if he knows or it is obvious from the circumstances that the use of the process is prohibited without the consent of the patentee, from offering the process for use within the territory to which this Act applies;
3. from offering, putting on the market, using or importing or stocking for such purposes the product obtained directly by a process which is the subject matter of the patent.

§9a Rights conferred by Biological Patents

(1) If the subject matter of the patent is biological material which has certain properties as a result of an invention, the provisions of Section 9 shall be applicable to every biological material which is obtained from this biological material by generative or vegetative reproduction in the same or a deviant form and which has the same properties.

(2) If the subject matter of the patent is a process which makes it possible to obtain biological material, which has certain properties as a result of an invention, the provisions of Section 9 shall be applicable to the biological material obtained directly by this process and every other biological material having the same properties which is obtained by generative or vegetative reproduction in the same or a deviant form from the material directly obtained.

(3) If the subject matter of the patent is a product which consists of or contains a genetic information as a result of an invention, the provisions of Section 9 shall be applicable to every material which includes this product and in which this genetic information is contained and performs its function. Section 1a, subsection 1 shall remain unaffected.

§9b Exhaustion in the case of Biological Material

If the patentee or with his approval a third party puts on the market biological material which has certain properties as a result of the invention within the territory of a Member State of the EU or another Contracting State to the Agreement on the European Economic Area, and if further biological material is obtained from this biological material by generative or vegetative reproduction, the provisions of Section 9 shall not be applicable if putting on the market was for the purpose of reproduction of the biological material. This shall not apply if the material obtained in this way is subsequently used for further generative or vegetative reproduction.

§9c Farmer's Privilege

(1) If reproductive plant material is put on the market by the patentee or with his approval by a third party to an agriculturist for the purpose of agricultural cultivation, the agriculturist may contrary to Sections 9, 9a and second sentence of 9b use his crop for generative or vegetative reproduction by himself in his own farm. Article 14 of Council Regulation (EC) No. 2100/94 as amended and the implementing regulations shall apply mutatis mutandis to the conditions and the extent of this authorization. Claims resulting for the patentee shall be asserted according to the implementing regulations enacted on the basis of Article 14, subsection 3 of Council Regulation (EC) No. 2100/94.

(2) If working animals or reproductive animal material are put on the market by the patentee or with his approval by a third party to an agriculturist, the agriculturist may contrary to Sections 9, 9a and second sentence of 9b use the working animals or reproductive animal material for agricultural purposes. This authorization shall also extend to the provision of the agricultural working animals or other reproductive animal material for the continuation of his agricultural occupation, but not to the sale with the objective of or within the framework of reproduction as source of income.

(3) Section 9a, subsections 1 to 3 shall not apply to biological material which was obtained in the field of agriculture accidentally or was technically non-avoidable. An action shall therefore not lie against an agriculturist if he has not cultivated seeds or plants subject to this patent protection law.

§10 Prohibition of Indirect use of the Patented Invention

(1) A patent shall have the further effect that a person not having the consent of the patentee shall be prohibited from supplying or offering to supply within the territory to which this Act applies a person, other than a person entitled to exploit the patented invention with means relating to an essential element of such invention for exploiting the invention, where such person knows or it is obvious from the circumstances that such means are suitable and intended for exploiting the invention.

(2) Subsection (1) shall not apply when the means are staple commercial products, except where such person induces the person supplied to commit acts prohibited by the second sentence of Section 9.

(3) Persons performing the acts referred to in Section 11.1 to 3 shall not be considered persons entitled to exploit the invention within the meaning of subsection (1).

§11 Limitation of Effects of Patents

The effects of a patent shall not extend to:

1. acts done privately and for non-commercial purposes;
2. acts done for experimental purposes relating to the subject matter of the patented invention;
   2a. the use of biological material for the purpose of cultivation, discovery and development of a new plant variety;
   2b. studies and tests and practical requirements resulting therefrom which are necessary for obtaining an authorization according to the current medicinal product law regulations for putting on the market in the EU or for obtaining an authorization according to the current medicinal product law regulations in Member States of the EU or non-member States.
3. the extemporaneous preparation for individual cases in a pharmacy of a medicine in accordance with a medical prescription or acts concerning the medicine so prepared;
4. the use of the patented invention on board vessels of another State party to the Paris Convention for the Protection of Industrial Property, in the body of the vessel, in the machinery, tackle, gear and other accessories, where such vessels temporarily or accidentally enter the waters to which the territory of this Act extends on condition that such use serves exclusively the needs of the vessel;
5. the use of the patented invention in the construction or operation of aircraft or land vehicles of another State party to the Paris Convention for the Protection of Industrial Property or of accessories for such aircraft or land vehicles, where these temporarily or accidentally enter the territory to which this Act applies;
6. the acts specified in Article 27 of the Convention on International Civil Aviation of December 7, 1944, where such acts concern the aircraft of another State to which the provisions of that Article are applicable.

§12 Right based on Prior Use

(1) A patent has no effect against a person who, at the time of the filing of the application, had already begun to use the invention within the national borders, or had made the necessary arrangements for doing this. Such person shall be entitled to use the invention for the needs of his own business in his own plant or the plant of others. This right can only be inherited or transferred together with the business. If the applicant or his predecessor in title has, before applying for a patent, disclosed the invention to other persons and reserved his rights in the event of a patent being granted, a person learning of the invention as a result of such disclosure cannot, under the provisions under the first sentence, invoke measures which he has taken within six months after the disclosure.

(2) If the patentee is entitled to a right of priority, the date of the prior application shall be substituted for the date of the application referred to in subsection

(1). However, this provision shall not apply to nationals of a foreign country which does not guarantee reciprocity in this respect, where they claim the priority of a foreign application.

§13 Right to Use in the Public Interest

(1) A patent shall have no effect where the Federal Government orders that the invention be exploited in the interest of public welfare. Nor shall the effect of a patent extend to any exploitation of the invention which is ordered in the interests of the security of the Federal Republic by the appropriate supreme federal authority or, on the latter's instructions, by a subordinate agency.
(2) Appeals against orders under subsection (1) shall be heard by the Federal Administrative Court where such orders have been made by the Federal Government or the appropriate supreme federal authority.
(3) In the cases mentioned in subsection (1), the patentee shall have a claim against the Federal Republic for reasonable compensation. In the event of dispute as to its amount, legal action may be brought before the ordinary civil courts. Any order by the Federal Government under the first sentence of subsection (1) shall be communicated to the person recorded as patentee in the Register (Section 30(1)) before the invention is exploited. If the supreme federal authority by which an order or an instruction under the second sentence of subsection (1) is issued learns that an entitlement to compensation has arisen under the first sentence, it shall give notice thereof to the person recorded in the Register as patentee.

§14 Scope of Protection

The extent of the protection conferred by a patent or a patent application shall be determined by the terms of the claims. Nevertheless, the description and drawings shall be used to interpret the claims.

§15 License, Assignment

(1) The right to a patent, the right to the grant of a patent and the rights deriving from a patent shall pass to the heirs. They may be assigned to others with or without restrictions.
(2) The rights under subsection (1) may be licensed in whole or in part, exclusively or non-exclusively, for the whole or part of the territory to which this Act applies. Where a licensee contravenes a restriction of his license covered by the first sentence, the right conferred by the patent may be invoked against him.
(3) The assignment of rights or the granting of a license shall not affect licenses previously granted to other persons.

§16 Term of the Patent

(1) The duration of a patent is 20 years, beginning on the day following the filing of the application in respect of the invention. If the purpose of an invention is the improvement or further development of another invention for which the applicant has already secured patent protection, he may apply, within 18 months from the date of filing of the application or, insofar as an earlier date is claimed as relevant for the application, from that date, for a patent of addition, which shall expire at the same time as the patent for the earlier invention.

(2) If the main patent lapses due to revocation, declaration of nullity, forfeiture or abandonment, the patent of addition shall become an independent patent; its duration shall be determined by the date of commencement of the main patent. Where there are several patents of addition, only the first shall become independent; the others shall be deemed patents of addition to that patent.

§16a Supplementary Protection Certificate

(1) Pursuant to Regulations of the EU concerning the creation of supplementary protection certificates, which shall be notified in the Federal Law Gazette, supplementary protection may be requested in respect of a patent that shall follow on immediately from the expiry of the term of the patent under Section 16. Annual fees shall be paid for supplementary protection in accordance with the schedule of fees.

(2) Unless otherwise provided by the law of the European Communities, the provisions of the Patent Act concerning entitlement of the applicant (§§6 to 8), effects of the patent and exceptions thereto (§§9 to 12), order to exploit the patent and compulsory license (Sections 13, 24), extent of protection (Section 14), licenses and their registration (Sections 15, 30), lapse of the patent (Section 20), nullity (Section 22), preparedness to grant licenses (Section 23), domestic representative (Section 25), revocation (Section 64, first alternative, section 2 and 3, sentences 1–3), the Patent Court and proceedings before the Patent Court (Sections 65 to 99), further treatment (Section123a); proceedings before the Federal Court of Justice (Sections 100 to 122a), reinstatement (Section 123), obligation of truth (Section 124), electronic document (Section 125a), official language, service of documents and legal aid (Sections 126 to 128), infringement (Sections 139 to 141a, 142a and 142b), joining of actions and advertising of patent (Sections 145 and 146) shall apply mutatis mutandis to supplementary protection.

(3) Licenses and declarations under Section 23 of the Patent Act that are effective for a patent shall also apply to supplementary protection.

(…)

§21 Grounds for Revocation

(1) A patent shall be revoked (§61) if it transpires that
1. the subject matter of the patent is not patentable under §§1 to 5,
2. the patent does not disclose the invention in a manner sufficiently clear and complete in order to be carried out by a person skilled in the art,
3. the essential elements of the patent have been taken from the descriptions, drawings, models, appliances or equipment of another person, or from a method used by another person, without his consent (unlawful deprivation),
4. the subject matter of the patent extends beyond the content of the application as originally filed with the competent authorities; the same shall apply if the patent was granted on a divisional application or on a new application filed in accordance with §7(2) and the subject matter of the patent extends beyond the content of the earlier application as originally filed with the competent authorities.

(2) If the grounds for revocation affect the patent in part only, the patent shall be maintained in the form of a corresponding limitation. The limitation may be implemented in the form of an amendment to the claims, the descriptions or the drawings.

(3) In the event of revocation, the effects of the patent and of the application shall be deemed not to have existed "ab initio." This provision shall apply mutatis mutandis to limited maintenance. (...)

(...)

§24 Compulsory License

(1) The non-exclusive authorization for the industrial use of an invention is granted by the Federal Patent Court in individual cases in compliance with the following provisions (compulsory license), if
1. the applicant for a license has unsuccessfully endeavored during a reasonable time frame to obtain from the patentee an authorization to use the invention under reasonable and commercially usual conditions; and
2. the public interest demands the grant of a compulsory license.

(2) If the applicant for a license is unable to exploit an invention for which he holds protection under a patent of later date without infringing a patent of earlier date, he shall be entitled to request the grant of a compulsory license with respect to the owner of the patent of earlier date if
1. the conditions of item 1 of subsection (1) are fulfilled and
2. if his own invention comprises, in comparison with that under the patent of earlier date, an important technical advance of considerable commercial significance.

The patentee can require the applicant for a license to grant him a counter license under reasonable conditions for the exploitation of the patented invention of later date.

(3) Subsection 2 applies mutatis mutandis if a plant breeder cannot maintain or exploit a plant variety right without infringing a patent of earlier date.
(4) A compulsory license under subsection (1) may be granted for a patented invention in the field of semi-conductor technology only if such grant is necessary to remove an anti-competitive practice on the part of the patentee that has been established in judicial or administrative proceedings.
(5) If the patentee does not use the patented invention, or does not use it predominantly in Germany, compulsory licenses under subsection (1) may be granted to ensure an adequate supply of the patented product to the domestic market. Importing shall be deemed to constitute use of the patent in Germany in such case.
(6) The grant of a compulsory license in a patent shall be permissible only after the grant of the patent. It may be granted subject to restrictions and made dependent upon conditions. The scope and duration of use shall be restricted to the purpose for which they have been permitted. The patentee shall be entitled to remuneration from the holder of a compulsory license that shall be commensurate with the circumstances and shall take into consideration the commercial value of the compulsory license. In the event of a significant change, with respect to the repeated remuneration that will become due in future, in the circumstances on which the determination of the amount of the remuneration was based, each party shall be entitled to require a corresponding adjustment. If the circumstances on which the grant of a compulsory license was based no longer apply and if it is unlikely that they will reoccur, the patentee may require the withdrawal of the compulsory license.
(7) A compulsory license in a patent may only be transferred together with the enterprise involved in the exploitation of the invention. A compulsory license in an invention that is the subject matter of a patent of earlier date may only be transferred together with the patent of later date.

(...)

§30 Register of the Patent Office

(1) The Patent Office shall maintain a Register in which shall be recorded the titles of patent applications, the files of which may be inspected by any person, and of granted patents, supplementary certificates of protection (Section 16a) and the names and addresses of applicants or of patentees and appointed representatives or persons authorized to accept service, if any (Section 25), it being sufficient to record one such representative or person authorized to accept service. The commencement, expiration, lapsing, order for limitation, revocation, declaration of nullity or supplementary certificates of protection (Section 16a), as well as the filing of opposition and of a nullity action shall also be recorded therein.

(2) The President of the Patent Office may determine that further particulars be entered in the Register.

(3) The Patent Office shall record in the Register any change in the identity of the person, of the name or of the address of the applicants or the patentees and of their representatives and persons authorized to accept service, if proof thereof is furnished to it. As long as the change has not been recorded, the former applicant, patentee or representative shall remain subject to the rights and obligations as provided in this Act. If a person newly entered in the Register as applicant or as proprietor of the patent takes over opposition proceedings before the Patent Office, opposition or appeal proceedings before the Federal Patent Court or appeal proceedings before the Federal Court of Justice, the consent of other parties to the proceedings shall not be required for this purpose.

(...)

§33 Reasonable Compensation

(1) As from publication of the notification pursuant to Section 32(5), the applicant may require from any person who has used the subject matter of the application although he knew or should have known that the invention used by him was the subject matter of the application, compensation appropriate to the circumstances. Further claims are excluded.

(2) The claim to compensation cannot be asserted if the subject matter of the application is obviously unpatentable.

(3) The provisions of Book 1, Division 5 of the German Civil Code (Bürgerliches Gesetzbuch) shall apply mutatis mutandis to limitation, with the proviso that the limitation shall become effective at the earliest one year after the grant of the patent. Where the person obliged obtains something as a consequence of the infringement at the expense of the person entitled, section 852 of the German Civil Code shall apply mutatis mutandis.

(...)

§59—Opposition

(1) Within three months of publication of the grant of the patent any person may give notice of opposition to the patent, in the case of usurpation only the aggrieved party. Notice of opposition shall be given in a written reasoned statement. It may only be based on the claim that one of the grounds for revocation set out in section 21 exists. The facts justifying the opposition shall be detailed. The particulars shall, in so far as they have not already been included in the notice of opposition, be submitted in writing within the opposition period.

(2) Where a notice of opposition has been given to a patent, any third party who can prove that an action has been brought against him on account of an infringement of the patent may intervene in the opposition proceedings as an

opponent after the expiry of the opposition period if he gives notice of intervention within three months of the date on which the action claiming the infringement was filed. The same shall apply to any third party who can prove that, following a demand by the proprietor of the patent that the third party refrain from the alleged infringement of the patent, he instituted proceedings for a ruling that he is not infringing the patent. The notice of intervention shall be declared in writing and reasoned within the time limit referred to in the first sentence. Subsection (1), third to fifth sentences, shall apply mutatis mutandis.

(3) A hearing shall be held in the opposition proceedings upon request of a party or if the Patent Division deems this to be expedient. When issuing the summons, the Patent Division shall draw attention to the points which in its opinion need to be discussed for the purposes of the decision to be taken. The hearing, including delivery of the decision, shall be public. Section 169, second sentence, as well as sections 171b to 175 of the Courts Constitution Act (Gerichtsverfassungsgesetz) shall apply mutatis mutandis, with the proviso that the public may also be excluded from the hearing at the request of one of the parties if there is concern that the interests of the applicant meriting protection are at risk.

(4) The chair of the Patent Division shall ensure that order is maintained during the hearing and shall thus exercise his domestic authority.

(5) In other respects, section 43 (3), second sentence, and sections 46 and 47 shall apply mutatis mutandis in the opposition proceedings.

§81 Nullity and Compulsory License Proceedings

(1) Proceedings for a declaration of nullity of a patent or a supplementary certificate of protection or for the grant or withdrawal of a compulsory license or for the adaptation of a compensation set by a judgment for a compulsory license shall be instituted by bringing legal action. The action shall be directed against the person recorded in the register as patentee or against the holder of the compulsory license. An action against a supplementary certificate of protection may be consolidated with an action against the basic patent and may also be based on the fact that one of the grounds for nullity exists in respect of the basic patent (§22).

(2) An action for a declaration of nullity of a patent shall not be brought as long as opposition may still be filed or opposition proceedings are pending. An action for a declaration of nullity of a supplementary certificate of protection shall not be brought as long as applications pursuant to Section 49a(4) can be made or proceedings for a decision regarding these applications are pending.

(3) In the case of an unlawful deprivation, only the injured party shall be entitled to bring an action.

(4) An action shall be filed with the Patent Court in written form. Copies of the complaint brief and of all written statements shall be attached for the

opposing party. The action and all written statements are served ex officio on the opposing party.

(5) The complaint brief shall designate the plaintiff, the defendant and the matter at issue and shall contain a specific motion. The facts and documentary evidence relied on shall be stated. If the complaint brief does not fully comply with these requirements, the presiding judge shall invite the plaintiff to file the necessary additional materials within a specified period. The court file number of a patent dispute concerning the patent in suit and its litigation value shall be indicated.

(6) If the plaintiff's general residence lies outside the EU or the member states of the Treaty on the European Economic Area, he shall furnish to the defendant, upon request, security for the costs of the proceedings. §110 (2) N° 1 to 3 of the Code of Civil Procedure shall apply mutatis mutandis. The Patent Court determines, at its equitable discretion, the amount of the security and shall fix a time limit within which that amount shall be furnished. If the time limit is not observed, the action shall be deemed to have been withdrawn.

§82 Notice of Action and Objection

(1) The Patent Court shall without delay serve notice of the action on the defendant and invite him to reply thereto within one month.

(2) If the defendant fails to reply in due time, a decision complying with the plaintiff's request may be rendered forthwith without a hearing and every factual allegation of the plaintiff assumed to be proved.

(3) If the defendant files an objection in good time, the patent court shall notify the plaintiff of the objection. The defendant may provide grounds for the objection within two months after service of the action. The chairman may, on application, extend the time limit by up to one month if the respondent shows substantial grounds for doing so. The grounds shall be made credible. Section 81(5), third sentence, shall apply mutatis mutandis insofar as the relevant information is not already known from the complaint brief.

(4) The chairman shall set the earliest possible date for the oral hearing. With the parties' consent, an oral hearing can be waived. Paragraph 2 shall remain unaffected.

§83 Timely Information by the Court

(1) In proceedings for a declaration that the patent or supplementary certificate is null and void, the patent court shall inform the parties as soon as possible about the aspects that it expects to be of particular importance for the decision or that are conducive to the concentration of the hearing on the questions that are of essence for the decision. This notice shall be given within six months after service of the complaint. If a patent case is pending, the notice shall also be sent to the other court ex officio. The patent court may set a time limit for the parties to submit a final written statement in preparation for the notice

under the first sentence. If the patent court does not set a time limit, the reference may not be made before the expiry of the time limit under section 82(3), second and third sentences. Comments of the parties received after the expiry of the time limit need not be considered by the patent court in the notice. There shall be no need for a notice according to sentence 1 if the aspects to be discussed appear obvious in the light of the parties' submissions. §139 of the Code of Civil Procedure shall also apply.

(2) The patent court can set the parties a deadline within which they can comment on the indication pursuant to Paragraph 1 by means of pertinent petitions or additions to their submissions and otherwise submit a final comment. This deadline can be prolonged if the party concerned submits material reasons for such. Such reasons shall be substantiated.

(3) The powers pursuant to Paragraphs 1 and 2 can also be exercised by the presiding judge or a member of the court to be designated by the presiding judge.

(4) The patent court can reject a party's contestation or defense pleadings or an amendment of the action or a defense by the defendant on the basis of an amended version of the patent if such are not submitted until after expiry of the deadline set pursuant to Paragraph 2, and can decide the case without further investigations if

1. a postponement of an in-person hearing already set would be needed to take account of the new submission, and
2. the party concerned has failed to provide a sufficient excuse for the delay, and
3. the party concerned has been informed about the consequences of failing to comply with the deadline.

The exculpation shall be substantiated.

Infringement

§139 Right to Prevent the Use of the Patented Invention, Damages, Burden of Proof

(1) Any person who uses an invention contrary to Sections 9 to 13 may, if there is a risk of a recurrent infringement, be sued by the injured party to enjoin such use. This claim also applies in the event of the threat of a first infringement. The claim is excluded insofar as its assertion, due to the special circumstances of the individual case and in consideration of the requirements of good faith, would lead to a disproportionate hardship for the infringer or third parties which is not justified by the exclusive right. In this case, the infringed party shall be granted an appropriate compensation in money. The claim for damages in accordance with paragraph 2 shall remain unaffected.

(2) Any person who commits these acts intentionally or negligently shall be liable for compensation to the injured party for the damage suffered therefrom. For the assessment of the compensation account can be taken of the profits which

the infringer has made due to the infringement. The assessment of the damages can also be based on the amount which would have been due as a reasonable compensation if the infringer had requested authorization for the use.

(3) If the subject matter of a patent is a process for obtaining a new product, the same product when produced by any other party shall, in the absence of proof to the contrary, be deemed to have been obtained by the patented process. In the adduction of proof to the contrary, the legitimate interests of the defendant in protecting his manufacturing and business secrets shall be taken into account.

§140 Suspension in case of Reasonable Compensation

If, prior to the grant of a patent, rights based on an application, the files of which may be inspected by any person (Section 31(1), the second half of the second sentence and (2)), are claimed in court proceedings, and if the decision on the litigation depends on whether an action exists under Section 33(1), the Court may order that the proceedings be deferred until the decision is made on the grant of the patent. If a request for examination pursuant to Section 44 has not been filed, the Court may, at the request of the opposing party, set a time limit for filing the request for examination to the party claiming rights on the basis of the application. If the request for examination is not filed within that time limit, the rights deriving from the application involved in the litigation may not be claimed.

§140a Destruction and Recall

(1) Any person who uses a patented invention in contravention of Sections 9 to 13 may be required by the injured party to destroy the product that is the subject matter of the patent and that is in the possession of the infringer or is his property. The first sentence shall also apply in the case of a product that has been directly manufactured by means of a process that is the subject matter of the patent.

(2) The provisions of subsection 1 shall apply mutatis mutandis to materials and equipment that have served overwhelmingly for the manufacture of such products.

(3) Any person who uses a patented invention in contravention of Sections 9 to 13 can be required by the injured party to recall the products that are the subject matter of the patent or to remove them definitively from the distribution channels. The first sentence shall also apply in the case of a product that has been directly manufactured by means of a process that is the subject matter of the patent.

(4) The claims pursuant to subsections 1 to 3 are excluded if their enforcement is disproportionate in the individual case. The examination of proportionality shall also take account of the legitimate interests of third parties.

§140b Information about Distribution Channel and Origin of Goods

(1) Any person who uses a patented invention in contravention of Sections 9 to 13 may be required by the injured party to give information as to the origin and distribution channels of the products used, without delay.

(2) In cases where the infringement is obvious or in cases in which the injured party has filed an action against the infringer, the claim, notwithstanding subsection 1, also applies against a person who to a commercial extent
1. had infringing products in his possession,
2. made use of infringing services,
3. provided services that were used for infringing activities, or
4. according to information from a person specified in Numbers 1, 2 or 3, participated in the manufacture, production or distribution of such products or the provision of such services,

unless the person would be entitled to refuse to testify in the proceedings against the infringer pursuant to Sections 383 to 385 of the Code of Civil Procedure. If the claim pursuant to the first sentence is asserted before the courts, the court can upon application suspend the litigation pending against the infringer until settlement of the litigation conducted on the claim to information. The party obliged to provide information can require the injured party to refund the expenditure necessary for the provision of the information.

(3) The person required to give information shall give particulars of
1. the names and addresses of the manufacturers, the suppliers and other prior owners of the products, or of the users of the services, and the trade customers and points of sale for which they were intended, and
2. the quantity of the products that have been manufactured, dispatched, received or ordered and the prices paid for the goods or services in question.

(4) The claims pursuant to subsections 1 and 2 shall be excluded if their enforcement is disproportionate in the individual case.

(5) If the party obliged to give information provides the information incorrectly or incompletely with intent or gross negligence, he shall be required to compensate the injured party for the resulting loss.

(6) Any person who has given true information without being required to do so pursuant to subsection 1 or subsection 2, shall only be liable to third parties if he knew that he was not required to give the information.

(7) In cases where infringement is obvious, the obligation to provide information may be imposed by injunction in compliance with Sections 935 to 945 of the Code of Civil Procedure.

(8) Such information may only be used in criminal proceedings or in proceedings under the Act on Minor Offences against the person required to give information or against a dependent person under Section 52(1) of the Code of Criminal Procedure, in respect of an act committed before the information was given, with the consent of the person required to give the information.

(9) If the information can only be given using traffic data (Section 3 No. 30 of the Telecommunications Act), the provision of the information shall be subject to a court order concerning the admissibility of the use of traffic data, application for which shall be filed by the injured party. For the issue of this order, the regional court in whose district the party obliged to provide information has his place of residence, his registered office or a business establishment shall have exclusive jurisdiction, without regard to the value in dispute. The decision shall be rendered by the civil chamber. The proceedings shall be subject mutatis mutandis to the provisions of the Act concerning Proceedings in Family Cases and in Matters of Voluntary Jurisdiction. The costs for the court order shall be borne by the injured party. An appeal can be filed against the decision of the regional court. The appeal shall be filed within a period of two weeks. The provisions concerning the protection of personal data shall for the rest remain unaffected.

(10) Subsection 2 in conjunction with subsection 9 limits the basic right to privacy of telecommunications (Article 10 of the Basic Act).

§140c Inspection of Infringing Object and Presentation of Documents

(1) Any person who with sufficient probability uses a patented invention in contravention of Sections 9 to 13 may be required by the right holder or another authorized person to present a document or to tolerate the inspection of an object that is within his power of disposal or of a method that is the subject matter of the patent, if such is necessary to establish such party's claims. If there is a sufficient probability of an infringement to a commercial extent, the claim also extends to the submission of banking, financial or trading documents. If the alleged infringer claims that such information is confidential, the court shall adopt the necessary measures to ensure the protection required in the individual case.

(2) The claim pursuant to subsection 1 is excluded if its enforcement is disproportionate in the individual case.

(3) The obligation to present a document or tolerate the inspection of an object can be imposed by an injunction pursuant to Sections 935 to 945 of the Code of Civil Procedure. The court shall take the necessary measures to ensure the protection of confidential information. This shall apply in particular in cases in which the injunction is imposed without prior hearing of the opposing party.

(4) Section 811 of the Civil Code and Section 140b subsection 8 shall apply mutatis mutandis.

(5) If there was no infringement or threat of an infringement, the alleged infringer can claim compensation for the loss incurred by him as a result of the application from the party who has applied for the presentation or inspection pursuant to subsection 1.

§140d Presentation of Banking, Financial or Trading Documents

(1) In the case of an infringement committed to a commercial extent, in the cases covered by Section 139(2), the injured party can also require the infringer to present banking, financial or trading documents or to provide suitable access to the corresponding documents that are in the infringer's power of disposal and that are necessary for the enforcement of the claim for damages if the satisfaction of the claim for damages is in doubt without such presentation. If the alleged infringer claims that such information is confidential, the court shall adopt the necessary measures to ensure the protection required in the individual case.

(2) The claim pursuant to subsection 1 is excluded if its enforcement is disproportionate in the individual case.

(3) The obligation to present the documents specified in subsection 1 can be imposed by an injunction in compliance with Sections 935 to 945 of the Code of Civil Procedure if the claim to damages is obvious. The court shall take the necessary measures to ensure the protection of confidential information. This shall apply in particular in cases in which the injunction is imposed without prior hearing of the opposing party.

(4) Section 811 of the Civil Code and Section 140b(8) shall apply mutatis mutandis.

§140e Publication of the Judgement

Where an action has been brought under this Act, the successful party may be entitled in the judgment to make the judgment public at the expense of the unsuccessful party if the successful party demonstrates a legitimate interest. The nature and extent of the publication shall be laid down in the judgment. The entitlement shall lapse if it is not used within three months of the judgment becoming final. The pronouncement in accordance with the first sentence shall not be provisionally enforceable.

§141 Limitation

Rights based on the infringement of a patent shall become statute-barred in compliance with the provisions of the 5th Chapter of the 1st book of the Civil Code. If the infringer has obtained anything through the infringement at the expense of the claimant, section 852 of the Civil Code shall apply mutatis mutandis.

§142 Penalties

(1) Any person who, without the necessary consent of the patentee or the holder of the supplementary certificate of protection (Sections 16a and 49a)

1. makes or offers, puts on the market, uses or imports or stocks for these purposes a product which is the subject matter of a patent or a supplementary certificate of protection (Section 9, second sentence, item 1) or
2. uses or offers for use within the territory to which this Act applies a process which is the subject matter of a patent or a supplementary certificate of

protection (Section 9, second sentence, item 2), shall be liable to imprisonment not exceeding three years or a fine.

The first sentence, item 1, shall also apply if there is a product which has been directly produced by a process which is the subject matter of a patent or a supplementary certificate of protection (Section 9, second sentence, item 3).

(2) Where the offender acts by way of trade, he shall be liable to imprisonment of up to five years or a fine.

(3) The attempt to commit such an offense shall be punishable.

(4) Offenses under subsection (1) shall only be prosecuted on complaint unless the prosecuting authorities deem that ex officio prosecution is justified in view of the particular public interest.

(5) Objects implicated in an offense may be confiscated. Article 74a of the Penal Code shall apply. Where the claims referred to in Section 140a are upheld in proceedings under the provisions of the Code of Criminal Procedure with regard to compensation of the injured party (Sections 403 to 406c), the provisions on confiscation shall not be of application.

(6) If a penalty is pronounced, the Court shall, at the request of the injured party and if the latter can show a justified interest, order publication of the judgment. The nature of the publication shall be laid down in the judgment.

(7) Insofar as injunctive relief is excluded under section 139(1), third sentence, the infringer shall not be punished under subsections (1), (2) or (3).

(8) The criminal proceedings shall be suspended under section 262(2) of the Code of Criminal Procedure if opposition proceedings or nullity proceedings against the patent in dispute are pending.

§142a Customs Action

(1) A product that infringes a patent protected under this Act shall be subject, at the request of the holder of the rights and against his security, to seizure by the customs authorities, on import or export, in those cases where the infringement is obvious and provided that Council Regulation (EC) N° 608/2013 dated June 12, 2013 concerning customs action against goods suspected of infringing certain intellectual property rights and the measures to be taken against goods found to have infringed such rights, is not applicable. This provision shall apply in trade with other Member States of the EU and Members of the Agreement on the EEC only insofar as controls are carried out by the customs authorities.

(2) Where the customs authorities order a seizure, they shall advise the person entitled to dispose and also the petitioner thereof without delay. The origin, quantity and place of storage of the product, together with the name and address of the person entitled to dispose, shall be communicated to the petitioner; the secrecy of correspondence and of mail (Section 10 of the Constitution) shall be restricted to that extent. The applicant shall be given

the opportunity to inspect the product where such inspection does not constitute a breach of commercial or trade secrecy.

(3) Where no opposition to the seizure is made, at the latest within two weeks of service of the notification under the first sentence of subsection (2), the customs authorities shall order confiscation of the seized product.

(4) If the person entitled to dispose opposes the seizure, the customs authorities shall inform the applicant thereof without delay. The applicant shall be required to declare to the customs authorities, without delay, whether he maintains the request under subsection (1) in respect of the seized goods.

1. If the applicant withdraws his request, the customs authorities shall lift the seizure without delay.
2. If the applicant maintains his request and submits an executable court decision ordering the impounding of the seized copies or the limitation of the right to dispose, the customs authorities shall take the necessary measures.

Where neither of the cases according to items 1 and 2 is applicable, the customs authorities shall lift the seizure after expiration of two weeks after service of the notification to the applicant under the first sentence; where the applicant can show that a court decision according to item 2 has been requested, but has not yet been received, the seizure shall be maintained for a further two weeks at most.

(5) Where the seizure proves to have been unjustified from the beginning and if the applicant has maintained the request under subsection (1) in respect of the seized product or has not made a declaration without delay (second sentence of subsection (4)), he shall be required to compensate the damages that the seizure has caused to the person entitled to dispose.

(6) The petition under subsection (1) is to be submitted to the Regional Finance Office and shall be effective for two years unless a shorter period of validity has been requested; the request may be repeated. The cost of official acts related to the request shall be charged to the petitioner in accordance with Section 178 of the Fiscal Code.

(7) Seizure and confiscation may be opposed by the legal remedies allowed by the fixed penalty procedure under the Act on Minor Offenses in respect of seizure and confiscation. The petitioner shall be heard in the review proceedings. An immediate appeal against the decision of the Local Court shall be admissible; it shall be heard by the Provincial High Court.

§142b Simplified destruction

For the procedure according to Council Regulation (EC) N° 608/2013, the provisions of §142a (5) and (6) shall apply mutatis mutandis, with the proviso that the Council Regulation does not contain provisions which contradicts this.

Part X Procedure in Patent Litigation

§143 Patent Litigation

(1) For all actions whereby a claim arising out of one of the legal relationships regulated in this Act is asserted (patent litigation), the civil chambers of the regional courts shall have exclusive jurisdiction without regard to the value in dispute.
(2) The Governments of the Federal States shall have power to allot by statutory order patent litigation for the areas of several regional courts to one such court. The Governments of the Federal States may transfer those powers to the provincial administrations of justice. The Federal States may further by way of agreement assign tasks for which courts of one Federal State are responsible completely or partly to the competent court of another Federal State.
(3) Of the costs arising from the collaboration of a patent attorney in the case, fees according to Section 13 of the Federal Regulations on Fees for Attorneys-at-Law shall be refunded, as shall the necessary expenses of the patent attorney.

§144 Abatement of Costs

(1) If, in a patent case, a party satisfies the court that the awarding of the costs of the case against him according to the full value in dispute would considerably endanger his financial position, the Court may, at his request, order that party's liability to pay court costs to be adjusted in accordance with a portion of the value in dispute that shall be appropriate to his financial position. As a result of the order, the favored party shall likewise be required to pay the fees of his attorney-at-law only in accordance with that portion of the value in dispute. To the extent that the costs of the case are awarded against him or to the extent to which he assumes such costs, he shall be required to refund the court fees paid by the opposing party and the fees of the latter's attorney-at-law only in accordance with that portion of the value in dispute. To the extent that the extrajudicial costs are ordered to be paid by the opposing party or are assumed by that party, the attorney-at-law of the favored party may recover his fees from the opposing party in accordance with the value in dispute applying to the latter.
(2) The request under subsection (1) may be declared before and recorded at the registrar's office of the court. It shall be presented before the substance of the case is heard. Thereafter, it shall only be admissible if the presumed or fixed value in dispute is subsequently increased by the court. Before the decision on the request is given, the opposing party shall be heard.

§145 Concentration of Action

Any person who has brought an action pursuant to Section 139 may bring a further action against the defendant on account of the same or a similar act on the basis of another patent only if, through no fault of his own, he was not in a position to assert that patent also in the earlier suit.

(...)

§18.04 INTPATÜBKG

Art. I

(...)

Art. II

European patent law

§ 1 Compensation claim from European patent applications

(1) The applicant of a published European patent application seeking protection for the Federal Republic of Germany may claim from the person who has used the subject-matter of the application, although he knew or should have known that the invention used by him was the subject-matter of the European patent application, compensation which is reasonable under the circumstances. Section 141 of the Patent Act shall apply mutatis mutandis. Further claims under Article 67, paragraph 1, of the European Patent Convention are excluded.

(2) If the European patent application has not been published in German, the applicant shall be entitled to compensation under paragraph 1, first sentence, only from the date on which a German translation of the patent claims filed by him has been published by the German Patent and Trade Mark Office or the applicant has communicated such translation to the user of the invention.

(3) The preceding paragraphs shall apply mutatis mutandis in the case of an international patent application published under Article 21 of the Patent Cooperation Treaty for which the European Patent Office has acted as designated Office. Article 153, paragraph 4, of the European Patent Convention shall remain unaffected.

§ 2 Publication of translations of the claims of European patent applications

At the request of the applicant, the German Patent and Trade Mark Office shall publish the translation filed under §1(2).

(...).

§ 3 Transmission of information

(...)

§ 4 Filing of European patent applications at the GPTO

(...)

§ 5 Claim against the non-entitled patent applicant

(1) The person entitled under Article 60, paragraph 1, of the European Patent Convention, whose invention is applied for by a non-entitled person, may

request the patent proprietor to assign to him the right to the grant of the European patent. If the patent application has already led to the European patent, he may request the patent proprietor to assign the patent.

(2) The claim under the second sentence of paragraph 1 may be asserted in court within a preclusive period of two years from the date on which the European Patent Bulletin mentions the grant of the European patent, but later only if the patent proprietor was aware that he had no right to the European patent when the patent was granted or acquired.

§ 6 Revocation

(1) The European patent granted with effect in the Federal Republic of Germany shall be declared invalid upon request if the German courts continue to have jurisdiction in accordance with the Agreement of 19 February 2013 on a Unified Patent Court (Federal Law Gazette 2021 II p. 850, 851) and it is found that

1. the subject-matter of the European patent is not patentable under Articles 52 to 57 of the European Patent Convention,
2. the European patent does not disclose the invention sufficiently clearly and completely for a person skilled in the art to carry it out,
3. the subject-matter of the European patent goes beyond the content of the European patent application as originally filed with the authority competent for the filing of the application or, if the patent is based on a European divisional application or a new European patent application filed under Article 61 of the European Patent Convention, beyond the content of the earlier application as originally filed with the authority competent for the filing of the application,
4. the scope of protection of the European patent has been extended,
5. the proprietor of the European patent is not entitled under Article 60, paragraph 1, of the European Patent Convention.

Insofar as the European patent has been declared invalid, the effects of the European patent and the application shall be deemed not to have taken effect from the beginning.

(1) If the grounds for invalidity concern only a part of the European patent, the patent is limited by corresponding amendment of the claims and declared partially invalid.

(2) The patent proprietor is entitled to defend the European patent in the proceedings for a declaration of invalidity of the patent by limiting the extent of the claims. The proceedings shall be based on the limited version.

(3) In the case of paragraph 1, first sentence, No. 5, only the person entitled under Article 60, paragraph 1, of the European Patent Convention shall be entitled to file the request.

IntPatUbkG

§ 6a Supplementary protection certificates

The German Patent and Trademark Office shall grant supplementary protection certificates under Sec. 49a of the Patent Law also for the European patent granted with effect in the Federal Republic of Germany.

§ 7 Annual fees

(...)

§ 8 Prohibition of double protection

(1) To the extent that the subject matter of a patent granted in proceedings under the Patent Act is an invention for which a European patent with the same priority has been granted to the same inventor or his successor in title with effect in the Federal Republic of Germany, which patent is not subject to the exclusive jurisdiction of the Unified Patent Court by virtue of the use of the exception provided for in Article 83, paragraph 3, of the Agreement on a Unified Patent Court, the patent shall, to the extent that it protects the same invention as the European patent, cease to have effect from the time when
   (1) the period for filing an opposition to the European patent has expired without an opposition having been filed,
   (2) the opposition proceedings with maintenance of the European patent have been concluded with final effect,
   (3) the invocation of the exception under Article 83, paragraph 3, of the Agreement on a Unified Patent Court has become effective in respect of the European patent if this date is later than the date referred to in points 1 or 2, or
   (4) the patent is granted, if this date is later than the date referred to in points 1–3.

(2) The occurrence of the legal consequence under paragraph 1 is final.

(omitted)

§ 9 (...)

§ 10 Jurisdiction of courts (...)

§ 11 Central authority for letters rogatory (...)

§ 12 Withdrawal of the place of business of a professional representative (...)

§ 13 Requests for technical expert opinions (...)

§ 14 Inadmissible application to the European Patent Office (...)

§ 15 European patent with unitary effect

(1) Sections 1 to 4 and 11 to 14 shall also apply, subject to more specific provisions, to the European patent with unitary effect referred to in Article 2(c) of Regulation (EU) No 1257/2012 of the European Parliament and of the Council of 17 December 2012 on the implementation of enhanced cooperation in the area of the creation of unitary patent protection (OJ L 361, 31.12.2012, p. 1; L 307, 28.10.2014, p. 83). §5, 6a and 10 shall apply mutatis mutandis to European patents with unitary effect, subject to more specific provisions.

(2) If the unitary effect of a European patent is entered in the Register for Unitary Patent Protection pursuant to Article 2(e) of Regulation (EU) No. 1257/2012, the European patent shall be deemed not to have taken effect for the Federal Republic of Germany as a national patent on the date of publication by the European Patent Office of the mention of the grant of the European patent in the European Patent Bulletin.

(3) If the request of the proprietor of a European patent for unitary effect is rejected, the renewal fees for the European patent granted with effect in the Federal Republic of Germany shall become due on the date of service of the decision of the European Patent Office or, in the case of an action under Article 32, paragraph 1(i), of the Agreement on a Unified Patent Court, on the date of service of the decision of the Unified Patent Court on the rejection, which decision shall become final, unless a later due date results under Sec. 3, paragraph 2, first sentence, of the Patent Costs Act.

§ 16 Compulsory license to a European patent with unitary effect (...)

§ 17 Surrender of the European patent with unitary effect (...)

§ 18 Double protection and double claim defense (...)

(1) An action for infringement or threatened infringement of a patent granted in proceedings under the Patent Act shall be dismissed as inadmissible,
   1. insofar as the subject-matter of the patent is an invention for which a European patent or a European patent with unitary effect with the same priority has been granted to the same inventor or his legal successor with effect in the Federal Republic of Germany, and
   2. if proceedings are pending before the Unified Patent Court against the same party for infringement or threatened infringement of the European patent or the European patent with unitary effect under n° 1 by the same embodiment or if the Unified Patent Court has given a final decision on such a request, and
   3. provided that the defendant raises this objection at the first hearing after the objection has arisen, prior to the commencement of the hearing on the merits of the case.

(2) If the defendant raises a plea under subsection (1), the court may order that the hearing be stayed until the proceedings before the Unified Patent Court have been terminated.

(3) Paragraphs 1 and 2 shall apply mutatis mutandis to supplementary protection certificates.
(4) Paragraphs 1 and 2 shall not apply to provisional or protective measures.

§ 19 Application of the Code of Civil Procedure for the enforcement of decisions and orders of the Unified Patent Court

(1) Judgments and orders of the Unified Patent Court under Article 82 of the Agreement on a Unified Patent Court which the Unified Patent Court has ordered to be enforced shall be enforced domestically without the need for an enforcement clause. The provisions relating to the enforcement of domestic judgments shall apply mutatis mutandis, unless otherwise provided in paragraphs 3 and 4.
(2) Enforcement may commence only if the occurrence of the prerequisites necessary for enforcement is evidenced by documents drawn up in the German language or translated into the German language. The translation shall be prepared by a person authorized to do so in a Member State of the European Union. The costs of the translation shall be borne by the judgment creditor.
(3) The trial court of first instance within the meaning of section 767(1), section 887(1), section 888(1) first sentence and section 890(1) of the Code of Civil Procedure shall be replaced, irrespective of the amount in dispute, by the regional court in whose district the debtor is domiciled or, if he is not domiciled in Germany, in whose district enforcement is to take place or has taken place. The domicile of companies or legal entities shall be deemed equivalent to domicile. If the Länder have assigned jurisdiction for patent litigation to certain regional courts under Section 143(2) of the Patent Act, this assignment shall apply mutatis mutandis to the determination of the regional court having jurisdiction under the first sentence.
(4) If the action under section 767 of the Code of Civil Procedure in conjunction with subsection (1) sentence 2 is directed against enforcement under a court settlement, section 767 subsection (2) of the Code of Civil Procedure shall not apply.

§ 20 (...)

Art III-X (...)

§18.05 UTILITY MODEL ACT

§1 Admissible Subject Matter

(1) Utility model protection shall be afforded to inventions that are new, involve an inventive step and are susceptible of industrial application.

(2) The following, in particular, shall not be regarded as the subject matter of a utility model within the meaning of subsection (1):

1. discoveries, scientific theories and mathematical methods;
2. aesthetic creations;
3. schemes, rules and methods for performing mental acts, playing games or doing business, and programs for computers;
4. presentations of information.
5. biotechnological inventions (Section 1(2) Patent Act).

(3) Subsection (2) shall oppose utility model protection only to the extent to which protection is sought for the above-mentioned subject matter or activities as such.

§2 Excluded Subject Matter

Utility model protection shall not be granted in respect of:

1. inventions the publication or exploitation of which would be contrary to public policy or morality, provided that the exploitation shall not be deemed to be so contrary merely because it is prohibited by law or regulation.
2. plant or animal varieties;
3. processes.

§3 Novelty and Industrial Application

(1) The subject matter of a utility model shall be considered to be new if it does not form part of the state of the art. The state of the art comprises any knowledge made available to the public by means of a written description or by use within the territory to which this Act applies before the date relevant for the priority of the application. Description or use within the six months preceding the date relevant for the priority of the application shall not be taken into consideration if it is based on the conception of the applicant or his predecessor in title.

(2) The subject matter of a utility model shall be considered susceptible of industrial application if it can be made or used in any kind of industry, including agriculture.

§4 Application; Amendments, Divisional Applications

(1) Applications in respect of inventions for which utility model protection is sought shall be filed in writing with the Patent Office. A separate application shall be filed for each invention.

(2) The application may also be filed with a patent information center if this center was by announcement of the Federal Ministry of Justice in the Federal Law Gazette determined to receive utility model applications. An application which may contain a state secret (Section 93 Penal Code) may not be filed with a patent information center.

(3) Applications shall contain:
1. the name of the applicant;
2. a request for registration of the utility model, which must designate clearly and concisely the subject matter of the utility model;
3. one or more claims in which shall be specified what is to be protected by the utility model;
4. a description of the subject matter of the utility model;
5. the drawings to which the claims or the description refer.

(4) The Federal Ministry for Justice shall have power to issue by statutory order regulations concerning other requirements for the application. It may delegate such power by statutory order to the GPTO.

(5) Up to the time of the decision to register the utility model, alterations in the contents of the application shall be permissible insofar as they do not broaden the scope of the subject matter of the application. No rights may be derived from alterations which broaden the scope of the subject matter of the application.

(6) An applicant may at any time divide his application. The division shall be made by a statement in writing. The date of the original application and any priority that has been claimed shall continue to apply to each part of a divided application. For the period up to division the same fees which were payable for the original application shall be paid for the separated application.

(...)

§5 Branching Off

(1) Where an applicant has already sought, at an earlier date, a patent with effect in the Federal Republic of Germany for the same invention, he may file together with the utility model application a declaration claiming the date of filing relevant for the patent application. Any priority right claimed in respect of the patent application shall also apply to the utility model application. The priority right under the first sentence may be exercised up to the expiration of two months from the end of the month in which processing of the patent application or any opposition procedure is terminated, at the latest, however, by the end of the tenth year from the date of filing of the patent application.

(2) Where an applicant has filed a declaration under the first sentence of subsection (1), the Patent Office shall request him to communicate the serial number and the date of filing and to file a copy of the patent application, within two months of service of the request. Where the particulars are not provided in due time, the priority right under the first sentence of subsection (1) shall be forfeited.

§6 Priority

(1) Within a period of 12 months from the date of application for an earlier patent or utility model application filed with the Patent Office, the applicant shall enjoy a right of priority for the application for a utility model for the same invention, unless a domestic or foreign priority has already been claimed for the earlier application. Section 40(2) to (4) and (5), first sentence and (6) of the Patent Act shall apply mutatis mutandis, with the proviso in the case of Section 40(5), first sentence, that the earlier patent application shall not be deemed to have been withdrawn.

(2) The provisions of the Patent Act on foreign priority (Section 41) shall be applicable mutatis mutandis.

(...)

§7 Search

(1) The Patent Office shall upon request search for the prior art which is to be considered in assessing the registrability of the subject matter of the utility model application or the utility model.

(2) A request may be filed by the applicant or the registered proprietor or by any other party. Requests shall be filed in writing. Section 28 shall be applicable mutatis mutandis. Section 28 shall apply mutatis mutandis.

(3) (...)

§8 Registration

(1) Where an application complies with the requirements of Sections 4, 4a, 4b the Patent Office shall order registration in the Utility Model Register. No examination of the subject matter of the application as to novelty, inventive step or industrial applicability shall be carried out. Section 49(2) of the Patent Act shall apply mutatis mutandis.

(2) The registration shall contain the name and address of the applicant and of any duly appointed representative or person authorized to accept service (Section 28), together with the date of filing of the application.

(3) Summary lists of registrations shall be published in the Patent Gazette at regular intervals.

(4) The Patent Office shall record in the Register any change in the identity of the proprietor of the utility model or of his representative or the person authorized to accept service if proof thereof is furnished to it. Until such time as the change has been recorded, the former proprietor and his former representative or the person authorized to accept service shall continue to have the rights and obligations as provided under this Act.

(5) Anyone may inspect the Register and the files of registered utility models, including the files of cancellation proceedings. In addition, the Patent Office

shall permit any person so requesting to inspect the files if and to the extent that a legitimate interest has been satisfactorily proved.

(...)

§11 Effect of the Registration

(1) Registration of a utility model shall have the effect that the proprietor alone is authorized to use the subject matter of the utility model. Any person not having his consent shall be prohibited from making, offering, putting on the market or using a product which is the subject matter of the utility model, or importing or stocking the product for these purposes.

(2) Registration shall have the further effect that any person not having the consent of the proprietor shall be prohibited from supplying or offering to supply within the territory to which this Act applies persons, other than those entitled to exploit the subject matter of the utility model, with means relating to an essential element of the subject matter of the utility model, for using it within the territory to which this Act applies, when such person knows, or it is obvious in the circumstances, that the means are suitable and intended for using the subject matter of the utility model. The first sentence shall not apply when the means are staple commercial products, except when such person induces those supplied to commit acts prohibited by the second sentence of subsection (1). Persons performing the acts referred to in items 1 and 2 of Section 12 shall not be considered to be persons entitled to exploit the subject matter of the utility model within the meaning of the first sentence.

§12 Limitation of Effects

The effects of the utility model shall not extend to

1. acts done privately for non-commercial purposes;
2. acts done for experimental purposes relating to the subject matter of the utility model;
3. acts of the kind specified in items 4 to 6 of Section 11 of the Patent Act.

§12a Scope of Protection

The scope of protection of the subject matter of the utility model shall be determined by the terms of the claims. When interpreting the claims, reference shall be made, however, to the description and the drawings.

§13 Inassertability

(1) Registration shall not afford utility model protection where a claim for cancellation of the utility model (Sections 15(1) and (3)), assertable by any person, exists against the person registered as the proprietor.

(2) If the essential elements of the registration have been taken from the descriptions, drawings, models, appliances or equipment of another person

without that person's consent, protection under this Act may not be invoked against the injured party.

(3) The provisions of the Patent Act concerning the right to protection (Section 6), the right to the grant of protection (Section 7(1)), the right to assignment (Section 8), the right deriving from prior use (Section 12) and the official order of exploitation (Section 13) shall be applicable mutatis mutandis.

§14 Utility Model and Subsequently Filed Patent

If a subsequently filed patent infringes a right under Section 11, the right deriving from such patent may not be exercised without the consent of the proprietor of the utility model.

§15 Cancellation of the Utility Model

(1) Any person may assert a claim against the person registered as proprietor for cancellation of the utility model
   1. if the subject matter of the utility model is not registrable within the terms of Sections 1 to 3;
   2. if the subject matter of the utility model is already protected on the basis of an earlier patent or utility model application; or
   3. if the subject matter of the utility model extends beyond the content of the application as filed.

(2) In the case of Section 13(2), only the injured party may assert a claim for cancellation.

(3) Where the grounds for cancellation relate to a part only of the utility model, only that part shall be cancelled. The limitation may be effected in the form of an amendment to the claims.

§16 Cancellation Request

A request for cancellation of a utility model under Section 15 shall be filed with the Patent Office in writing. The request shall state the grounds on which it is based. The provisions of Sections 81(6) and 125 of the Patent Act shall apply mutatis mutandis.

§17 Cancellation Proceedings

(1) The Patent Office shall notify the proprietor of the utility model of the request and shall invite him to reply thereto within one month. If he fails to file a contesting reply in due time, cancellation shall be effected.

(2) In the contrary case, the Patent Office shall notify the person making the request of such reply and shall take all measures necessary for the investigation of the matter. It may order the examination of witnesses and experts. The provisions of the Code of Civil Procedure (Sections 373 to 401 as well as 402 to 414) shall apply mutatis mutandis to any such examination. A sworn minute-taker shall be called in for the proceedings relating to the taking of evidence.

(3) The decision on a request shall be taken on the basis of a hearing. The decision shall be pronounced at the session at which the hearing is closed or at a session to be fixed forthwith. The decision shall contain the grounds therefore, shall be in writing and shall be communicated ex officio to the parties. Section 47(2) of the Patent Act shall apply mutatis mutandis. Service of the decision is admissible instead of pronouncement.

(4) The Patent Office shall determine in what proportion the costs of the proceedings shall be borne by the parties. Section 62(2) and the second and third sentences of Section 84(2) of the Patent Act shall apply mutatis mutandis.

§18 Appeal

(1) Appeals against decisions of the Utility Model Section and the Utility Model Divisions shall be made to the Patent Court.

(2) In other respects, the provisions of the Patent Act governing proceedings on appeal shall be applicable mutatis mutandis. If an appeal is filed from a decision given in cancellation proceedings, Section 84(2) of the Patent Act shall apply mutatis mutandis in respect of the decision on the costs of the proceedings.

(3) Appeals against decisions of the Utility Model Section and against decisions of the Utility Model Divisions shall be heard by a Chamber of Appeal of the Patent Court. Appeals against rejection of an application for registration of a utility model shall be heard by a Chamber of Appeal composed of two legal members and one technical member, and appeals against decisions of the Utility Model Divisions regarding cancellation requests by a Chamber of Appeal composed of one legal member and two technical members. For appeals against decisions about requests for legal aid sentence 2 shall apply mutatis mutandis. The presiding judge must be a legal member. Section 21g(1) and (2) of the Judiciary Act shall apply with regard to the allocation of business within the Chamber of Appeal. In the case of proceedings relating to appeals against decisions of the Utility Model Section, Section 69(1) of the Patent Act shall apply and, in the case of proceedings relating to appeals against decisions of the Utility Model Divisions, Section 69(2) of the Patent Act shall apply, mutatis mutandis.

(4) An appeal on a point of law against a decision of the Chamber of Appeal of the Patent Court in respect of an appeal under subsection (1) shall be filed with the Federal Court of Justice if the Chamber of Appeal, in its decision, has given leave to appeal on that point of law. Sections 100(2) and (3) and 101 to 109 of the Patent Act shall apply.

§19 Suspension of the Infringement Proceedings

If litigation is pending during cancellation proceedings and the decision on that litigation depends on the existence of utility model protection, the court may order that the hearing be postponed until the cancellation proceedings have been settled. It shall order such postponement if it considers the utility model registration to be invalid. If the cancellation request is refused, the court shall be bound by that decision only if it was taken in respect of the same parties.

§20 Compulsory License

The provisions of the Patent Act concerning the grant or withdrawal of compulsory licenses or with respect to the adaptation of the remuneration for a compulsory license stipulated by decision (Section 24) and the procedure for the grant of compulsory licenses (Sections 81 to 99 and 110 to 122a) shall apply mutatis mutandis in the case of registered utility models.

§21 Referral to the Patent Act

(1) The provisions of the Patent Act concerning the giving of opinions (Section 29(1) and (2)), reinstatement (Section 123), further processing of the application (Section 123a), obligation to observe the truth in proceedings (Section 124), electronic conduct of proceedings (Section 125a), official language (Section 126), service of documents (Section 127) and legal assistance from the courts (Section 128) and the reimbursement of witnesses and the remuneration of experts (128a) and relief for extensive judicial proceedings (128b shall also apply to utility model proceedings.

(2) The provisions of the Patent Act granting legal aid (Sections 129 to 138) shall apply mutatis mutandis in utility model proceedings and Section 135(3) shall apply with the proviso that the representative assigned under Section 133 shall have the right to appeal.

§22 Assignment and License

(1) The right to a utility model, the right to registration of a utility model and the right derived from such registration shall pass to the heirs. Such rights may be assigned to other parties, with or without restriction.

(2) The rights under subsection (1) may be licensed in whole or in part, exclusively or non-exclusively, for the whole or part of the territory to which this Act applies. Where a licensee contravenes a restriction of his license under the first sentence, the right afforded by the registration may be invoked against him.

(3) The transfer of rights or the grant of a license shall not affect licenses previously granted to third parties.

§23 Term, Maintenance and Cancellation

(1) Utility model protection shall start on the day of application and end ten years after the expiry of the month in which the application was filed.

(2) The term of protection may be renewed for the fourth until the sixth, seventh and eighth as well as the ninth and tenth year by payment of a renewal fee, calculated from the day of application. Such renewal shall be recorded in the Register.

(3) A utility model shall lapse if

1. the registered proprietor abandons it by a written declaration made to the Patent Office or
2. the renewal fee is not paid in time (Section 7(1), Section 13(3) or Section 14(2) and (5) Patent Cost Act).

§24 Right to Prohibit Use, Damages

(1) Any person who uses a utility model contrary to the provisions of Sections 11 to 14 may, if there is a risk of a recurrent infringement, be sued by the injured party to enjoin such use. This claim also applies in the event of the threat of a first infringement.

(2) Any person who undertakes such action intentionally or negligently shall be liable for compensation to the injured party for the damage suffered therefrom. For the assessment of the compensation account can be taken of the profits which the infringer has obtained through the infringement. The assessment of the damages can also be based on the amount which would have been due as a reasonable compensation if the infringer had requested authorization for the use.

§24a Destruction Claim

(1) Any person who uses a utility model in contravention of Sections 11 to 14 may be required by the injured party to destroy the product that is the subject matter of the utility model and that is in the possession of the infringer or is his property. The first sentence shall also apply to materials and equipment in possession of the infringing party that have served overwhelmingly for the manufacture of such products.

(2) Any person who uses a utility model in contravention of Sections 11 to 14 can be required by the injured party to recall the products that are the subject matter of the utility model or to remove them definitively from the distribution channels.

(3) The claims pursuant to subsections 1 and 2 are excluded if their enforcement is disproportionate in the individual case. The examination of proportionality shall also take account of the legitimate interests of third parties.

§24b Information about Distribution Channel and Origin of Goods

(1) Any person who uses a utility model contrary to the provisions of Sections 11 to 14 may be required by the injured party to give information as to the origin and distribution channels of the product used, without delay.

(2) In those cases where infringement is obvious or in cases in which the injured party has filed an action against the infringer, the claim, notwithstanding subsection 1, also applies against a person who to a commercial extent
1. had infringing products in his possession,
2. made use of infringing services,
3. provided services that were used for infringing activities, or
4. according to information from a person specified in Numbers 1, 2 or 3, participated in the manufacture, production or distribution of such products or the provision of such services,

unless the person would be entitled to refuse to testify in the proceedings against the infringer pursuant to Sections 383 to 385 of the Code of Civil Procedure. If the claim pursuant to the first sentence is asserted before the courts, the court can upon application suspend the litigation pending against the infringer until settlement of the litigation conducted on the claim to information. The party obliged to provide information can require the injured party to refund the expenditure necessary for the provision of the information.

(3) The person required to give information shall give particulars of
1. the names and addresses of the manufacturers, the suppliers and other prior owners of the products, or of the users of the services, and the trade customers and points of sale for which they were intended, and
2. the quantity of the products that have been manufactured, dispatched, received or ordered and about the prices paid for the goods or services in question.

(4) The claims pursuant to subsections 1 and 2 shall be excluded if their enforcement is disproportionate in the individual case.

(5) If the party obliged to give information provides the information incorrectly or incompletely with intent or gross negligence, he shall be required to compensate the injured party for the resulting loss.

(6) Any person who has given true information without being required to do so pursuant to subsection 1 or subsection 2, shall only be liable to third parties if he knew that he was not required to give the information.

(7) In cases where infringement is obvious, the obligation to provide information may be imposed by injunction in compliance with Sections 935 to 945 of the Code of Civil Procedure.

(8) Such information may only be used in criminal proceedings or in proceedings under the Act on Minor Offences against the person required to give information or against a dependent person under Section 52(1) of the Code of Criminal Procedure, in respect of an act committed before the information was given, with the consent of the person required to give the information.

(9) If the information can only be given using traffic data (Section 3 No. 30 of the Telecommunications Act), the provision of the information shall be subject to a court order concerning the admissibility of the use of traffic data, application for which shall be filed by the injured party. For the issue of this order, the regional court in whose district the party obliged to provide information has

his place of residence, his registered office or a business establishment shall have exclusive jurisdiction, without regard to the value in dispute. The decision shall be rendered by the civil chamber. The proceedings shall be subject mutatis mutandis to the provisions concerning the Act concerning Proceedings in Family Cases and in Matters of Voluntary Jurisdiction. The costs for the court order shall be borne by the injured party. An appeal can be filed against the decision of the regional court. The appeal shall be filed within a period of two weeks. The provisions concerning the protection of personal data shall for the rest remain unaffected.

(10) Subsection 2 in conjunction with subsection 9 limits the basic right to privacy of telecommunications (Article 10 of the Basic Act).

§24c Limitation

(1) Any person who with sufficient probability uses a utility model in contravention of Sections 11 to 14 may be required by the right-holder or another authorized person to present a document or to tolerate the inspection of an object that is within his power of disposal, if such is necessary to establish such party's claims. If there is a sufficient probability of an infringement to a commercial extent, the claim also extends to the submission of banking, financial or trading documents. If the alleged infringer claims that such information is confidential, the court shall adopt the necessary measures to ensure the protection required in the individual case.

(2) The claim pursuant to subsection 1 is excluded if its enforcement is disproportionate in the individual case.

(3) The obligation to present a document or tolerate the inspection of an object can be imposed by an injunction pursuant to Sections 935 to 945 of the Code of Civil Procedure. The court shall take the necessary measures to ensure the protection of confidential information. This shall apply in particular in cases in which the injunction is imposed without prior hearing of the opposing party.

(4) Section 811 of the Civil Code and Section 140b subsection 8 shall apply mutatis mutandis.

(5) If there was no infringement or threat of an infringement, the alleged infringer can claim compensation for the loss incurred by him as a result of the application from the party who has applied for the presentation or inspection pursuant to subsection 1.

(…)

§25 Penalties

(1) Any person who, without the necessary consent of the proprietor of the utility model

1. makes, offers, puts on the market, uses or imports or stocks for these purposes a product which is the subject matter of a utility model (Section 11(1), second sentence) or
2. exercises the right deriving from a patent contrary to Section 14 shall be liable to imprisonment of up to three years or a fine.

(2) Where the offender acts by way of trade, he shall be liable to imprisonment of up to five years or a fine.

(3) The attempt to commit such an offense shall be punishable.

(4) Offenses under subsection (1) shall only be prosecuted on complaint, unless the prosecuting authorities deem that ex officio prosecution is justified in view of the particular public interest.

(5) Objects implicated in an offense may be confiscated. Article 74a of the Penal Code shall apply. Where the claims referred to in Section 24a are upheld in proceedings under the provisions of the Code of Criminal Procedure with regard to compensation of the injured party (Sections 403 to 406c), the provisions on confiscation shall not be of application.

(6) If a penalty is pronounced, the Court shall, at the request of the injured party and if the latter can show a justified interest, order publication of the judgment. The nature of the publication shall be laid down in the judgment.

§25a Customs Action

(1) A product that infringes a utility model protected under this Act shall be subject, at the request of the holder of the rights and against his security, to seizure by the customs authorities, on import or export, in those cases where the infringement is obvious and provided that the Council Regulation 608/2013 ... is not applicable. This provision shall apply in trade with other Member States of the EU and the EEC only insofar as controls are carried out by the customs authorities.

(2) Where the customs authorities order a seizure, they shall inform the person entitled to dispose and also the applicant thereof without delay. The applicant shall be informed about the origin, quantity and place of storage of the product, together with the name and address of the person entitled to dispose; the secrecy of correspondence and of mail (Section 10 of the Constitution) shall be restricted to that extent. The applicant shall be given the opportunity to inspect the product where such inspection does not constitute a breach of commercial or trade secrecy.

(3) Where no opposition to the seizure is made, at the latest within two weeks of service of the notification under the first sentence of subsection (2), the customs authorities shall order confiscation of the seized product.

(4) If the person entitled to dispose opposes seizure, the customs authorities shall inform the applicant thereof without delay. The applicant shall be required to declare to the customs authorities, without delay, whether he maintains the request under subsection (1) in respect of the seized copies.

1. If the applicant withdraws his request, the customs authorities shall lift the seizure without delay.
2. If the applicant maintains his request and produces an executable court decision ordering the custody of the seized copies or the limitation of the right to dispose, the customs authorities shall take the necessary measures.

   Where neither of the cases referred to in items 1 and 2 is applicable, the customs authorities shall lift the seizure on the expiry of two weeks after service of the notification to the petitioner under the first sentence; where the petitioner can show that a court decision according to item 2 has been requested but has not yet been received, the seizure shall be maintained for a further two weeks at most.

(5) Where the seizure proves to be unjustified from the beginning and if the applicant has maintained the request under subsection (1) in respect of the seized product or has not made a declaration without delay (second sentence of subsection (4)), he shall be required to compensate the damages that seizure has occasioned to the person entitled to dispose.

(6) An application under subsection (1) is to be submitted to the General Customs Office and shall be effective for one years unless a shorter period of validity has been requested; the request may be repeated. The cost of official acts related to the request shall be charged to the applicant in accordance with Section 178 of the Fiscal Code.

(7) Seizure and confiscation may be opposed by the legal remedies allowed by the fixed penalty procedure under the Act on Minor Offenses in respect of seizure and confiscation. The petitioner shall be heard in the review proceedings. An immediate appeal can be filed against the decision of the Local Court; it shall be decided by the Higher Court.

§25b

For the procedure according to Council Regulation (EC) N° 608/2013, the provisions of §25a (5) and (6) shall apply mutatis mutandis, with the proviso that the Council Regulation does not contain provisions which contradicts this.

§26 Apportion of Litigation Value

(1) If a party to civil litigation in which an action is brought to assert a claim arising from one of the legal relationships regulated under this Act satisfies the court that the award of the costs of the case against him according to the full value in dispute would considerably endanger his financial position, the court may, at his request, order that party's liability to pay court costs to be adjusted in accordance with a portion of the value in dispute that shall be appropriate to his financial position. As a result of the order, the favored party shall likewise be required to pay the fees of his attorney-at-law only in accordance with that portion of the value in dispute. To the extent that the costs of the case are awarded against him or to the extent to which he assumes such costs, he shall be required to refund the court fees paid by the opposing

party and the fees of the latter's attorney-at-law only in accordance with that portion of the value in dispute. To the extent that the extrajudicial costs are ordered to be paid by the opposing party or are assumed by that party, the attorney-at-law of the favored party may recover his fees from the opposing party in accordance with the value in dispute applying to the latter.

(2) A request under subsection (1) may be declared before and recorded at the registrar's office of the court. It shall be presented before the substance of the case is heard. Thereafter, it shall be admissible only if the presumed or fixed value in dispute is subsequently increased by the court. Before the decision is given on the request, the opposing party shall be heard.

§27 Utility Model Dispute

(1) For all actions whereby a claim arising out of one of the legal relationships regulated in this Act is asserted (utility model litigation), the civil chambers of the regional courts shall have exclusive jurisdiction without regard to the value in dispute.

(2) The Governments of the Federal States shall have power to allot by statutory order utility model litigation for the areas of several regional courts to one such court insofar as this is procedurally expedient. The Governments of the Federal States may transfer those powers to the provincial administrations of justice. The Federal States may further by way of agreement assign tasks, for which courts of one Federal State are responsible, completely or partly to the competent court of another Federal State.

(3) Of the costs arising from the collaboration of a patent attorney in the case, fees according to Section 13 of the Federal Regulations on Fees for Attorneys-at-Act shall be refunded, as shall the necessary expenses of the patent attorney.

(...)

§18.06 ACT ON EMPLOYEES' INVENTIONS

§1 Scope of Application

This Act applies to inventions and to proposals of technical improvement made by employees in private employment, by employees in public service, by civil servants, and by members of the army.

§2 Inventions

Inventions within the meaning of the Act are only those which may be the subject of a patent or of a utility model.

§3 Proposals for Technical Improvement

Technical improvement proposals within the meaning of this Act are proposals for other technical innovations that may not be the subject of a patent or of protection as a utility model.

§4 Service Inventions and Free Inventions

(1) Employee inventions within the meaning of this Act may be either bound or free.

(2) Bound inventions (service inventions) are those made during the employment relationship which:
   1. either resulted from the employee's duties in the private or public entity,
   2. or are decisively based on the experience or activities of the private or public entity.

(3) Other inventions of an employee are free inventions. They are however subject to the limitations contained in §§18 and 19.

(4) Subsections (1) to (3) apply mutatis mutandis to inventions made by civil servants and members of the army.

§5 Duty to Report

(1) An employee making a service invention is obliged to report the invention to his employer immediately in a separate notice in text form indicating that said notice represents the report of an invention. Where several employees have contributed to making the invention, a joint notice can be made. The employer shall inform the employee without delay and in text form of the date the report was received.

(2) In the report, the employee shall describe the technical problem, its solution and how the service invention was achieved. Existing notes shall be attached provided they are necessary for an understanding of the invention. The report shall indicate the service instructions and directions received by the employee, use made of the expertise and activities of the enterprise, the employee's collaborators and the nature and extent of their contribution, and

the report should indicate the contribution which the reporting employee considers to have made personally.

(3) A report which does not meet the requirements of subsection (2) shall be deemed to be in order unless the employer states within a two months period that and to what extent the report needs to be supplemented. To the extent necessary, he must assist the employee in supplementing the report.

§6 Claim of a Service Invention

(1) An employer may claim a service invention by means of a declaration executed vis-à-vis the employee.
(2) The declaration is deemed to be executed if the employer does not, within a four months term starting from the receipt of a duly made report (sentences 1 and 3 of Section 5(2)), release the invention by means of a declaration executed in text form vis-à-vis the employee.

§7 Effect of the Claim

(1) With the claim all rights in the service invention shall pass to the employer.
(2) Dispositions made by an employee as to a service invention prior to the employer declaring a claim shall have no effect on his employer insofar as the employer's rights are concerned.

§8 Free Inventions

A service invention becomes free if the employer releases it by a statement in text form. The employee may dispose of a service invention that has become free without the restrictions stipulated in Sections 18 and 19.

§9 Compensation

(1) The employee shall have a right to reasonable compensation against his employer as soon as the employer has made a claim to a service invention.
(2) For assessing the compensation, account shall in particular be taken of the commercial applicability of the service invention, the duties and position of the employee in the entity, and the entity's contribution to the invention.

§11 Compensation Directives

After hearing the leading organizations of employers and employees (in accordance with Section 12 of the Act on Collective Labor Agreements), the Federal Minister of Labor shall issue guidelines for assessing the compensation.

§12 Assessment and Determination of the Compensation

(1) The nature and amount of the compensation shall be determined by agreement between the employer and the employee within a reasonable time after the claim to a service invention has been made.
(2) If several employees have contributed to a service invention, the compensation shall be determined separately for each of them. The employer must inform the employees of the total amount of compensation awarded and of the share assigned to each inventor.
(3) Where no compensation agreement is concluded within a reasonable time after a claim to a service invention was made, the employer shall fix the amount of compensation, giving his reasons in text form to the employee, and shall pay in accordance with his settlement. The compensation shall be determined at the latest three months from the grant of the property right.
(4) An employee who disagrees with the settlement may object to it in text form within two months. If he does not object, the settlement becomes binding for both parties.
(5) If several employees have contributed to the service invention, the settlement shall not bind any of them if one of them objects on the ground that his contribution to the service invention has been incorrectly determined. In this case, the employer may make a new compensation settlement for all parties.
(6) The employer and the employee may require the other to agree to a different compensation arrangement if a substantial change has occurred in the circumstances essential to the assessment or determination of the compensation. A refund of compensation payments already received may not be requested. Subsections (1) to (5) are not applicable.

§13 Domestic Application

(1) An employer is obliged and solely entitled to apply for the grant of domestic property rights for a reported service invention. Where the invention is capable of patent protection, he shall apply for a patent unless, on an assessment of the industrial applicability of the service invention, protection as a utility model seems to be more appropriate. The application shall be filed without delay.
(2) The employer's obligation to file such an application lapses:
   1. if the service invention has become free (Section 8);
   2. if the employee agrees that no application is to be filed;
   3. if the conditions stipulated in Section 17 are fulfilled.
(3) If, after making a claim to a service invention, an employer does not comply with his duty to apply for an industrial property right and also fails to do so within a further reasonable time period set by the employee, the employee may apply for an industrial property right for the service invention in the employer's name and at the employer's expense.

(4) If a service invention has become free, only the employee is entitled to apply for an industrial property protection therefore. Should his employer already have applied for industrial property protection for the service invention, his rights resulting from such application shall pass to the employee.

§14 Protection Abroad

(1) After making a claim to a service invention, an employer is also entitled to apply for industrial property protection abroad.

(2) For foreign countries in which the employer does not intend to obtain industrial property rights, he shall release the service invention to the employee and shall, upon request, enable the employee to acquire these rights. The release must be executed in sufficient time in order that the employee can take advantage of the priority dates under international treaties in the field of industrial property.

(3) When releasing a service invention under subsection (2), the employer may reserve for himself a non-exclusive right to use the service invention in the foreign countries concerned, based on a reasonable compensation, and may require the employee, also in return for reasonable compensation, to respect the employer's obligations arising from contracts existing at the time of the invention's release when exploiting the released service invention.

(...)

§16 Surrender of application and rights

(1) If an employer, before fully meeting the demand of the employee for reasonable compensation, intends to stop prosecuting an application for a service invention, or to surrender a grant or registration issued, he shall inform his employee accordingly and, at the employee's request and expense, must assign the rights to him and forward to him any documents necessary to maintain the rights.

(2) An employer shall be entitled to surrender a grant issued if his employee does not request assignment thereof within three months from receipt of the communication made to the employee.

(3) When making the communication as provided in subsection (1), the employer is entitled to reserve for himself, against payment of reasonable compensation, a non-exclusive right to use the service invention.

§17 Trade Secrets

(1) If legitimate interests of the entity require that a reported service invention should not be disclosed, the employer may refrain from applying for industrial property protection, provided that he acknowledges vis-à-vis the employee that the service invention is capable of protection.

(2) If an employer does not acknowledge that a service invention is capable of protection, he may refrain from applying for an industrial property protection if he involves the Arbitration Board (Section 29) in view of seeking an agreement on the service invention's eligibility for protection.

(3) When determining the compensation for an invention under subsection (1), due account must also be taken of the economic drawbacks that result for the employee in connection with the fact that industrial property protection will not be obtained for the service invention.

2. *Free Inventions*

§18 Duty to Notify

(1) An employee who has made a free invention during the term of an employment contract shall inform the employer in text form thereof without delay. He shall give the employer all the details as to the invention and, if necessary, concerning its accomplishment which the employer may need to assess whether it is indeed a free invention.

(2) If the employer does not contest that the invention is a free invention by means of a declaration in text form made to the employee within three months of the notification, the invention can no longer be claimed as a service invention (Section 6).

(3) There is no obligation to notify the employer of a free invention if the invention is obviously not capable of being used in the employer's enterprise.

§19 Duty to Offer

(1) Prior to exploiting otherwise a free invention during the employment, an employee must offer to the employer at least a non-exclusive right to use the invention on reasonable conditions if the invention falls within the range of the actual or planned activities of the employer's enterprise at the time the offer is made. Such offer may be submitted together with the notification required according to Section 18.

(2) If the employer does not accept the offer within three months, the prerogative lapses.

(3) If the employer declares within the time period provided by subsection (2) that he intends to acquire the rights offered to him, but claims that the terms offered to him are not reasonable, the court shall determine the terms on action by the employer or employee.

(4) The employer or the employee may request a new determination of the terms if the circumstances essential to the terms agreed or fixed have substantially changed.

§20 Proposals of Technical Improvement

(1) For proposals of technical improvement which afford the employer an advantaged position similar to that obtained from an industrial property right, an employee shall be entitled to reasonable compensation from his employer as soon as the latter exploits the technical improvement. Sections 9 and 12 shall apply mutatis mutandis.
(2) In all other cases, technical improvement proposals shall be regulated by collective or company agreements.

§22 Mandatory Applicability

The provisions of this Act cannot be modified by contract to the detriment of the employee. Agreements shall, however, be permissible concerning service inventions after they have been reported and concerning free inventions and proposals for technical improvement (Section 20(1)) after their notification.

§23 Inequitable Agreements

(1) Agreements concerning service inventions, free inventions, or proposals for technical improvement (Section 20(1)) permitted by this Act, shall be invalid and void to the extent that they are significantly inequitable. This provision applies also to compensation settlements (Section 12(4)).
(2) The employer and employee may invoke the inequity of an agreement or compensation settlement only if they do so, by means of a statement in text form addressed to the other party, within six months following termination of the employment contract.

(...)

§26 Termination of Employment

The rights and duties arising from this Act are not affected by the termination of the employment relationship.

(...)

§18.07 COUNCIL REGULATION (EC) NO. 608/2013 OF THE EUROPEAN PARLIAMENT AND OF THE COUNCIL OF 12 JUNE 2013 CONCERNING CUSTOMS ENFORCEMENT OF INTELLECTUAL PROPERTY RIGHTS AND REPEALING COUNCIL REGULATION (EC) NO. 1383/2003

...

Whereas:

(1) The Council requested, in its Resolution of 25 September 2008 on a comprehensive European anti-counterfeiting and anti-piracy plan, that Council Regulation (EC) No 1383/2003 of 22 July 2003 concerning customs action against goods suspected of infringing certain intellectual property rights and the measures to be taken against goods found to have infringed such rights, be reviewed.

(2) The marketing of goods infringing intellectual property rights does considerable damage to right-holders, users or groups of producers, and to law-abiding manufacturers and traders. Such marketing could also be deceiving consumers, and could in some cases be endangering their health and safety. Such goods should, in so far as is possible, be kept off the Union market and measures should be adopted to deal with such unlawful marketing without impeding legitimate trade.

(3) The review of Regulation (EC) No 1383/2003 showed that, in the light of economic, commercial and legal developments, certain improvements to the legal framework are necessary to strengthen the enforcement of intellectual property rights by customs authorities, as well as to ensure appropriate legal certainty.

(4) The customs authorities should be competent to enforce intellectual property rights with regard to goods, which, in accordance with Union customs legislation, are liable to customs supervision or customs control, and to carry out adequate controls on such goods with a view to preventing operations in breach of intellectual property rights laws. Enforcing intellectual property rights at the border, wherever the goods are, or should have been, under customs supervision or customs control is an efficient way to quickly and effectively provide legal protection to the right-holder as well as the users and groups of producers. Where the release of goods is suspended or goods are detained by customs authorities at the border, only one legal proceeding should be required, whereas several separate proceedings should be required for the same level of enforcement for goods found on the market, which have been disaggregated and delivered to retailers. An exception should be made for goods released for free circulation under the end-use regime, as such goods remain under customs supervision, even though they have been released for free circulation. This Regulation should not apply to goods carried by passengers in their

personal luggage provided that those goods are for their own personal use and there are no indications that commercial traffic is involved.

(5) Regulation (EC) No 1383/2003 does not cover certain intellectual property rights and certain infringements are excluded from its scope. In order to strengthen the enforcement of intellectual property rights, customs intervention should be extended to other types of infringements not covered by Regulation (EC) No 1383/2003. This Regulation should therefore, in addition to the rights already covered by Regulation (EC) No 1383/2003, also include trade names in so far as they are protected as exclusive property rights under national law, topographies of semiconductor products and utility models and devices which are primarily designed, produced or adapted for the purpose of enabling or facilitating the circumvention of technological measures.

(6) Infringements resulting from so-called illegal parallel trade and overruns are excluded from the scope of Regulation (EC) No 1383/2003. Goods subject to illegal parallel trade, namely goods that have been manufactured with the consent of the right-holder but placed on the market for the first time in the European Economic Area without his consent, and overruns, namely goods that are manufactured by a person duly authorised by a right-holder to manufacture a certain quantity of goods, in excess of the quantities agreed between that person and the right-holder, are manufactured as genuine goods and it is therefore not appropriate that customs authorities focus their efforts on such goods. Illegal parallel trade and overruns should therefore also be excluded from the scope of this Regulation.

(7) Member States should, in cooperation with the Commission, provide appropriate training for customs officials, in order to ensure the correct implementation of this Regulation.

(8) This Regulation, when fully implemented, will further contribute to an internal market which ensures right-holders a more effective protection, fuels creativity and innovation and provides consumers with reliable and high-quality products, which should in turn strengthen cross-border transactions between consumers, businesses and traders.

(9) Member States face increasingly limited resources in the field of customs. Therefore, the promotion of risk management technologies and strategies to maximise resources available to customs authorities should be supported.

(10) This Regulation solely contains procedural rules for customs authorities. Accordingly, this Regulation does not set out any criteria for ascertaining the existence of an infringement of an intellectual property right.

(11) Under the "Declaration on the TRIPS Agreement and Public Health" adopted by the Doha WTO Ministerial Conference on 14 November 2001, the Agreement on Trade-Related Aspects of Intellectual Property Rights (TRIPS Agreement) can and should be interpreted and implemented in a manner supportive of WTO Members' right to protect public health and, in

particular, to promote access to medicines for all. Consequently, in line with the Union's international commitments and its development cooperation policy, with regard to medicines, the passage of which across the customs territory of the Union, with or without transhipment, warehousing, breaking bulk, or changes in the mode or means of transport, is only a portion of a complete journey beginning and terminating beyond the territory of the Union, customs authorities should, when assessing a risk of infringement of intellectual property rights, take account of any substantial likelihood of diversion of such medicines onto the market of the Union.

(12) This Regulation should not affect the provisions on the competence of courts, in particular, those of Regulation (EU) No 1215/2012 of the European Parliament and of the Council of 12 December 2012 on jurisdiction and the recognition and enforcement of judgments in civil and commercial matters.

(13) Persons, users, bodies or groups of producers, who are in a position to initiate legal proceedings in their own name with respect to a possible infringement of an intellectual property right, should be entitled to submit an application.

(14) In order to ensure that intellectual property rights are enforced throughout the Union, it is appropriate to allow persons or entities seeking enforcement of Union-wide rights to apply to the customs authorities of a single Member State. Such applicants should be able to request that those authorities decide that action be taken to enforce the intellectual property right both in their own Member State and in any other Member State.

(15) In order to ensure the swift enforcement of intellectual property rights, it should be provided that, where the customs authorities suspect, on the basis of reasonable indications, that goods under their supervision infringe intellectual property rights, they may suspend the release of or detain the goods whether at their own initiative or upon application, in order to enable a person or entity entitled to submit an application to initiate proceedings for determining whether an intellectual property right has been infringed.

(16) Regulation (EC) No 1383/2003 allowed Member States to provide for a procedure allowing the destruction of certain goods without there being any obligation to initiate proceedings to establish whether an intellectual property right has been infringed. As recognised in the European Parliament Resolution of 18 December 2008 on the impact of counterfeiting on international trade, such procedure has proved very successful in the Member States where it has been available. Therefore, the procedure should be made compulsory with regard to all infringements of intellectual property rights and should be applied, where the declarant or the holder of the goods agrees to destruction. Furthermore, the procedure should provide that customs authorities may deem that the declarant or the holder of the goods has agreed to the destruction of the goods where he has not explicitly opposed destruction within the prescribed period.

(17) In order to reduce the administrative burden and costs to a minimum, a specific procedure should be introduced for small consignments of counterfeit and pirated goods, which should allow for such goods to be destroyed without the explicit agreement of the applicant in each case. However, a general request made by the applicant in the application should be required in order for that procedure to be applied. Furthermore, customs authorities should have the possibility to require that the applicant covers the costs incurred by the application of that procedure.

(18) For further legal certainty, it is appropriate to modify the timelines for suspending the release of or detaining goods suspected of infringing an intellectual property right and the conditions in which information about detained goods is to be passed on to persons and entities concerned by customs authorities, as provided for in Regulation (EC) No 1383/2003.

(19) Taking into account the provisional and preventive character of the measures adopted by the customs authorities when applying this Regulation and the conflicting interests of the parties affected by the measures, some aspects of the procedures should be adapted to ensure the smooth application of this Regulation, whilst respecting the rights of the concerned parties. Thus, with respect to the various notifications envisaged by this Regulation, the customs authorities should notify the relevant person, on the basis of the documents concerning the customs treatment or of the situation in which the goods are placed. Furthermore, since the procedure for destruction of goods implies that both the declarant or the holder of the goods and the holder of the decision should communicate their possible objections to destruction in parallel, it should be ensured that the holder of the decision is given the possibility to react to a potential objection to destruction by the declarant or the holder of the goods. It should therefore be ensured that the declarant or the holder of the goods is notified of the suspension of the release of the goods or their detention before, or on the same day as, the holder of the decision.

(20) Customs authorities and the Commission are encouraged to cooperate with the European Observatory on Infringements of Intellectual Property Rights in the framework of their respective competences.

(21) With a view to eliminating international trade in goods infringing intellectual property rights, the TRIPS Agreement provides that WTO Members are to promote the exchange of information between customs authorities on such trade. Accordingly, it should be possible for the Commission and the customs authorities of the Member States to share information on suspected breaches of intellectual property rights with the relevant authorities of third countries, including on goods which are in transit through the territory of the Union and originate in or are destined for those third countries.

(22) In the interest of efficiency, the provisions of Council Regulation (EC) No 515/97 of 13 March 1997 on mutual assistance between the administrative authorities of the Member States and cooperation between the latter and

the Commission to ensure the correct application of the law on customs or agricultural matters, should apply.

(23) The liability of the customs authorities should be governed by the legislation of the Member States, though the granting by the customs authorities of an application should not entitle the holder of the decision to compensation in the event that goods suspected of infringing an intellectual property right are not detected by the customs authorities and are released or no action is taken to detain them.

(24) Given that customs authorities take action upon application, it is appropriate to provide that the holder of the decision should reimburse all the costs incurred by the customs authorities in taking action to enforce his intellectual property rights. Nevertheless, this should not preclude the holder of the decision from seeking compensation from the infringer or other persons that might be considered liable under the legislation of the Member State where the goods were found. Such persons might include intermediaries, where applicable. Costs and damages incurred by persons other than customs authorities as a result of a customs action, where the release of goods is suspended or the goods are detained on the basis of a claim of a third party based on intellectual property, should be governed by the specific legislation applicable in each particular case.

(25) This Regulation introduces the possibility for customs authorities to allow goods which are to be destroyed to be moved, under customs supervision, between different places within the customs territory of the Union. Customs authorities may furthermore decide to release such goods for free circulation with a view to further recycling or disposal outside commercial channels including for awareness-raising, training and educational purposes.

(26) Customs enforcement of intellectual property rights entails the exchange of data on decisions relating to applications. Such processing of data covers also personal data and should be carried out in accordance with Union law, as set out in Directive 95/46/EC of the European Parliament and of the Council of 24 October 1995 on the protection of individuals with regard to the processing of personal data and on the free movement of such data and Regulation (EC) No 45/2001 of the European Parliament and of the Council of 18 December 2000 on the protection of individuals with regard to the processing of personal data by Community institutions and bodies and on the free movement of such data.

(27) The exchange of information relating to decisions on applications and to customs actions should be made via a central electronic database. The entity which will control and manage that database and the entities in charge of ensuring the security of the processing of the data contained in the database should be defined. Introducing any type of possible interoperability or exchange should first and foremost comply with the purpose limitation principle, namely that data should be used for the purpose for

which the database has been established, and no further exchange or interconnection should be allowed other than for that purpose.

(28) In order to ensure that the definition of small consignments can be adapted if it proves to be impractical, taking into account the need to ensure the effective operation of the procedure, or where necessary to avoid any circumvention of this procedure as regards the composition of consignments, the power to adopt acts in accordance with Article 290 of the Treaty on the Functioning of the European Union should be delegated to the Commission in respect of amending the non-essential elements of the definition of small consignments, namely the specific quantities set out in that definition. It is of particular importance that the Commission carry out appropriate consultations during its preparatory work, including at expert level. The Commission, when preparing and drawing up delegated acts, should ensure a simultaneous, timely and appropriate transmission of relevant documents to the European Parliament and to the Council.

(29) In order to ensure uniform conditions for the implementation of the provisions concerning defining the elements of the practical arrangements for the exchange of data with third countries and the provisions concerning the forms for the application and for requesting the extension of the period during which customs authorities are to take action, implementing powers should be conferred on the Commission, namely to define those elements of the practical arrangements and to establish standard forms. Those powers should be exercised in accordance with Regulation (EU) No 182/2011 of the European Parliament and of the Council of 16 February 2011 laying down the rules and general principles concerning mechanisms for control by Member States of the Commission's exercise of implementing powers. For establishing the standard forms, although the subject of the provisions of this Regulation to be implemented falls within the scope of the common commercial policy, given the nature and impacts of those implementing acts, the advisory procedure should be used for their adoption, because all details of what information to include in the forms follows directly from the text of this Regulation. Those implementing acts will therefore only establish the format and structure of the form and will have no further implications for the common commercial policy of the Union.

(30) Regulation (EC) No 1383/2003 should be repealed.

(31) The European Data Protection Supervisor was consulted in accordance with Article 28(2) of Regulation (EC) No 45/2001 and delivered an opinion on 12 October 2011,

HAVE ADOPTED THIS REGULATION:

Chapter I Subject Matter, Scope and Definitions

Article 1 Subject matter and scope

1. This Regulation sets out the conditions and procedures for action by the customs authorities where goods suspected of infringing an intellectual property right are, or should have been, subject to customs supervision or customs control within the customs territory of the Union in accordance with Council Regulation (EEC) No 2913/92 of 12 October 1992 establishing the Community Customs Code, particularly goods in the following situations:
   (a) when declared for release for free circulation, export or re-export;
   (b) when entering or leaving the customs territory of the Union;
   (c) when placed under a suspensive procedure or in a free zone or free warehouse.
2. In respect of the goods subject to customs supervision or customs control, and without prejudice to Articles 17 and 18, the customs authorities shall carry out adequate customs controls and shall take proportionate identification measures as provided for in Article 13(1) and Article 72 of Regulation (EEC) No 2913/92 in accordance with risk analysis criteria with a view to preventing acts in breach of intellectual property laws applicable in the territory of the Union and in order to cooperate with third countries on the enforcement of intellectual property rights.
3. This Regulation shall not apply to goods that have been released for free circulation under the end-use regime.
4. This Regulation shall not apply to goods of a non-commercial nature contained in travellers' personal luggage.
5. This Regulation shall not apply to goods that have been manufactured with the consent of the right-holder or to goods manufactured, by a person duly authorised by a right-holder to manufacture a certain quantity of goods, in excess of the quantities agreed between that person and the right-holder.
6. This Regulation shall not affect national or Union law on intellectual property or the laws of the Member States in relation to criminal procedures.

Article 2 Definitions

For the purposes of this Regulation:

(1) "intellectual property right" means:
   (a) a trade mark;
   (b) a design;
   (c) a copyright or any related right as provided for by national or Union law;

(d) a geographical indication;
(e) a patent as provided for by national or Union law;
(f) a supplementary protection certificate for medicinal products as provided for in Regulation (EC) No 469/2009 of the European Parliament and of the Council of 6 May 2009 concerning the supplementary protection certificate for medicinal products;
(g) a supplementary protection certificate for plant protection products as provided for in Regulation (EC) No 1610/96 of the European Parliament and of the Council of 23 July 1996 concerning the creation of a supplementary protection certificate for plant protection products;
(h) a Community plant variety right as provided for in Council Regulation (EC) No 2100/94 of 27 July 1994 on Community plant variety rights;
(i) a plant variety right as provided for by national law;
(j) a topography of semiconductor product as provided for by national or Union law;
(k) a utility model in so far as it is protected as an intellectual property right by national or Union law;
(l) a trade name in so far as it is protected as an exclusive intellectual property right by national or Union law;

(2) "trade mark" means:
(a) a Community trade mark as provided for in Council Regulation (EC) No 207/2009 of 26 February 2009 on the Community trade mark;
(b) a trade mark registered in a Member State, or, in the case of Belgium, Luxembourg or the Netherlands, at the Benelux Office for Intellectual Property;
(c) a trade mark registered under international arrangements which has effect in a Member State or in the Union;

(3) "design" means:
(a) a Community design as provided for in Council Regulation (EC) No 6/2002 of 12 December 2001 on Community designs;
(b) a design registered in a Member State, or, in the case of Belgium, Luxembourg or the Netherlands, at the Benelux Office for Intellectual Property;
(c) a design registered under international arrangements which has effect in a Member State or in the Union;

(4) "geographical indication" means:
(a) a geographical indication or designation of origin protected for agricultural products and foodstuff as provided for in Regulation (EU) No 1151/2012 of the European Parliament and of the Council of 21 November 2012 on quality schemes for agricultural products and foodstuffs;
(b) a designation of origin or geographical indication for wine as provided for in Council Regulation (EC) No 1234/2007 of 22 October 2007 establishing a common organisation of agricultural markets and on

specific provisions for certain agricultural products (Single CMO Regulation);

(c) a geographical designation for aromatised drinks based on wine products as provided for in Council Regulation (EEC) No 1601/91 of 10 June 1991 laying down general rules on the definition, description and presentation of aromatized wines, aromatized wine-based drinks and aromatized wine-product cocktails;

(d) a geographical indication of spirit drinks as provided for in Regulation (EC) No 110/2008 of the European Parliament and of the Council of 15 January 2008 on the definition, description, presentation, labelling and the protection of geographical indications of spirit drinks;

(e) a geographical indication for products not falling under points (a) to (d) in so far as it is established as an exclusive intellectual property right by national or Union law;

(f) a geographical indication as provided for in Agreements between the Union and third countries and as such listed in those Agreements;

(5) "counterfeit goods" means:

(a) goods which are the subject of an act infringing a trade mark in the Member State where they are found and bear without authorisation a sign which is identical to the trade mark validly registered in respect of the same type of goods, or which cannot be distinguished in its essential aspects from such a trade mark;

(b) goods which are the subject of an act infringing a geographical indication in the Member State where they are found and, bear or are described by, a name or term protected in respect of that geographical indication;

(c) any packaging, label, sticker, brochure, operating instructions, warranty document or other similar item, even if presented separately, which is the subject of an act infringing a trade mark or a geographical indication, which includes a sign, name or term which is identical to a validly registered trade mark or protected geographical indication, or which cannot be distinguished in its essential aspects from such a trade mark or geographical indication, and which can be used for the same type of goods as that for which the trade mark or geographical indication has been registered;

(6) "pirated goods" means goods which are the subject of an act infringing a copyright or related right or a design in the Member State where the goods are found and which are, or contain copies, made without the consent of the holder of a copyright or related right or a design, or of a person authorised by that holder in the country of production;

(7) "goods suspected of infringing an intellectual property right" means goods with regard to which there are reasonable indications that, in the Member State where those goods are found, they are prima facie:

(a) goods which are the subject of an act infringing an intellectual property right in that Member State;

(b) devices, products or components which are primarily designed, produced or adapted for the purpose of enabling or facilitating the circumvention of any technology, device or component that, in the normal course of its operation, prevents or restricts acts in respect of works which are not authorised by the holder of any copyright or any right related to copyright and which relate to an act infringing those rights in that Member State;

(c) any mould or matrix which is specifically designed or adapted for the manufacture of goods infringing an intellectual property right, if such moulds or matrices relate to an act infringing an intellectual property right in that Member State;

(8) "right-holder" means the holder of an intellectual property right;

(9) "application" means a request made to the competent customs department for customs authorities to take action with respect to goods suspected of infringing an intellectual property right;

(10) "national application" means an application requesting the customs authorities of a Member State to take action in that Member State;

(11) "Union application" means an application submitted in one Member State and requesting the customs authorities of that Member State and of one or more other Member States to take action in their respective Member States;

(12) "applicant" means the person or entity in whose name an application is submitted;

(13) "holder of the decision" means the holder of a decision granting an application;

(14) "holder of the goods" means the person who is the owner of the goods suspected of infringing an intellectual property right or who has a similar right of disposal, or physical control, over such goods;

(15) "declarant" means the declarant as defined in point (18) of Article 4 of Regulation (EEC) No 2913/92;

(16) "destruction" means the physical destruction, recycling or disposal of goods outside commercial channels, in such a way as to preclude damage to the holder of the decision;

(17) "customs territory of the Union" means the customs territory of the Community as defined in Article 3 of Regulation (EEC) No 2913/92;

(18) "release of the goods" means the release of the goods as defined in point (20) of Article 4 of Regulation (EEC) No 2913/92;

(19) "small consignment" means a postal or express courier consignment, which:

(a) contains three units or less;

or

(b) has a gross weight of less than two kilograms.

For the purpose of point (a), "units" means goods as classified under the Combined Nomenclature in accordance with Annex I to Council Regulation (EEC) No 2658/87 of 23 July 1987 on the tariff and statistical nomenclature and on the Common Customs Tariff if unpackaged, or the package of such goods intended for retail sale to the ultimate consumer.

For the purpose of this definition, separate goods falling in the same Combined Nomenclature code shall be considered as different units and goods presented as sets classified in one Combined Nomenclature code shall be considered as one unit;

(20) "perishable goods" means goods considered by customs authorities to deteriorate by being kept for up to 20 days from the date of their suspension of release or detention;

(21) "exclusive licence" means a licence (whether general or limited) authorising the licensee to the exclusion of all other persons, including the person granting the licence, to use an intellectual property right in the manner authorised by the licence.

Chapter II Applications

SECTION 1 Submission of applications

Article 3 Entitlement to submit an application

The following persons and entities shall, to the extent they are entitled to initiate proceedings, in order to determine whether an intellectual property right has been infringed, in the Member State or Member States where the customs authorities are requested to take action, be entitled to submit:

(1) a national or a Union application:
  (a) right-holders;
  (b) intellectual property collective rights management bodies as referred to in point (c) of Article 4(1) of Directive 2004/48/EC of the European Parliament and of the Council of 29 April 2004 on the enforcement of intellectual property rights;
  (c) professional defence bodies as referred to in point (d) of Article 4(1) of Directive 2004/48/EC;
  (d) groups within the meaning of point (2) of Article 3, and Article 49(1) of Regulation (EU) No 1151/2012, groups of producers within the meaning of Article 118e of Regulation (EC) No 1234/2007 or similar groups of producers provided for in Union law governing geographical indications representing producers of products with a geographical indication or representatives of such groups, in particular Regulations (EEC) No 1601/91 and (EC) No 110/2008 and operators entitled to use a geographical indication as well as inspection bodies or authorities competent for such a geographical indication;

(2) a national application:
  (a) persons or entities authorised to use intellectual property rights, which have been authorised formally by the right-holder to initiate proceedings in order to determine whether the intellectual property right has been infringed;
  (b) groups of producers provided for in the legislation of the Member States governing geographical indications representing producers of products with geographical indications or representatives of such groups and operators entitled to use a geographical indication, as well as inspection bodies or authorities competent for such a geographical indication;

(3) a Union application: holders of exclusive licenses covering the entire territory of two or more Member States, where those licence holders have been authorised formally in those Member States by the right-holder to initiate proceedings in order to determine whether the intellectual property right has been infringed.

Article 4 Intellectual property rights covered by Union applications

A Union application may be submitted only with respect to intellectual property rights based on Union law producing effects throughout the Union.

Article 5 Submission of applications

1. Each Member State shall designate the customs department competent to receive and process applications ("competent customs department"). The Member State shall inform the Commission accordingly and the Commission shall make public a list of competent customs departments designated by the Member States.
2. Applications shall be submitted to the competent customs department. The applications shall be completed using the form referred to in Article 6 and shall contain the information required therein.
3. Where an application is submitted after notification by the customs authorities of the suspension of the release or detention of the goods in accordance with Article 18(3), that application shall comply with the following:
   (a) it is submitted to the competent customs department within four working days of the notification of the suspension of the release or detention of the goods;
   (b) it is a national application;
   (c) it contains the information referred to in Article 6(3). The applicant may, however, omit the information referred to in point (g), (h) or (i) of that paragraph.
4. Except in the circumstances referred to in point (3) of Article 3, only one national application and one Union application may be submitted per Member State for the same intellectual property right protected in that Member State. In the circumstances referred to in point (3) of Article 3, more than one Union application shall be allowed.

5. Where a Union application is granted for a Member State already covered by another Union application granted to the same applicant and for the same intellectual property right, the customs authorities of that Member State shall take action on the basis of the Union application first granted. They shall inform the competent customs department of the Member State where any subsequent Union application was granted, which shall, amend or revoke the decision granting that subsequent Union application.
6. Where computerised systems are available for the purpose of receiving and processing applications, applications as well as attachments shall be submitted using electronic data-processing techniques. Member States and the Commission shall develop, maintain and employ such systems in accordance with the multi-annual strategic plan referred to in Article 8(2) of Decision No 70/2008/EC of the European Parliament and of the Council of 15 January 2008 on a paperless customs environment for customs and trade.

Article 6 Application form

1. The Commission shall establish an application form by means of implementing acts. Those implementing acts shall be adopted in accordance with the advisory procedure referred to in Article 34(2).
2. The application form shall specify the information that has to be provided to the data subject pursuant to Regulation (EC) No 45/2001 and national laws implementing Directive 95/46/EC.
3. The Commission shall ensure that the following information is required of the applicant in the application form:
   (a) details concerning the applicant;
   (b) the status, within the meaning of Article 3, of the applicant;
   (c) documents providing evidence to satisfy the competent customs department that the applicant is entitled to submit the application;
   (d) where the applicant submits the application by means of a representative, details of the person representing him and evidence of that person's powers to act as representative, in accordance with the legislation of the Member State in which the application is submitted;
   (e) the intellectual property right or rights to be enforced;
   (f) in the case of a Union application, the Member States in which customs action is requested;
   (g) specific and technical data on the authentic goods, including markings such as bar-coding and images where appropriate;
   (h) the information needed to enable the customs authorities to readily identify the goods in question;
   (i) information relevant to the customs authorities' analysis and assessment of the risk of infringement of the intellectual property right or the intellectual property rights concerned, such as the authorised distributors;

(j) whether information provided in accordance with point (g), (h) or (i) of this paragraph is to be marked for restricted handling in accordance with Article 31(5);
(k) the details of any representative designated by the applicant to take charge of legal and technical matters;
(l) an undertaking by the applicant to notify the competent customs department of any of the situations laid down in Article 15;
(m) an undertaking by the applicant to forward and update any information relevant to the customs authorities' analysis and assessment of the risk of infringement of the intellectual property right(s) concerned;
(n) an undertaking by the applicant to assume liability under the conditions laid down in Article 28;
(o) an undertaking by the applicant to bear the costs referred to in Article 29 under the conditions laid down in that Article;
(p) an agreement by the applicant that the data provided by him may be processed by the Commission and by the Member States;
(q) whether the applicant requests the use of the procedure referred to in Article 26 and, where requested by the customs authorities, agrees to cover the costs related to destruction of goods under that procedure.

SECTION 2 Decisions on applications

Article 7 Processing of incomplete applications

1. Where, on receipt of an application, the competent customs department considers that the application does not contain all the information required by Article 6(3), the competent customs department shall request the applicant to supply the missing information within 10 working days of notification of the request.

   In such cases, the time-limit referred to in Article 9(1) shall be suspended until the relevant information is received.
2. Where the applicant does not provide the missing information within the period referred to in the first subparagraph of paragraph 1, the competent customs department shall reject the application.

Article 8 Fees

The applicant shall not be charged a fee to cover the administrative costs resulting from the processing of the application.

Article 9 Notification of decisions granting or rejecting applications

1. The competent customs department shall notify the applicant of its decision granting or rejecting the application within 30 working days of the receipt of the application. In the event of rejection, the competent customs department

shall provide reasons for its decision and include information on the appeal procedure.

2. If the applicant has been notified of the suspension of the release or the detention of the goods by the customs authorities before the submission of an application, the competent customs department shall notify the applicant of its decision granting or rejecting the application within two working days of the receipt of the application.

Article 10 Decisions concerning applications

1. A decision granting a national application and any decision revoking or amending it shall take effect in the Member State in which the national application was submitted from the day following the date of adoption.

   A decision extending the period during which customs authorities are to take action shall take effect in the Member State in which the national application was submitted on the day following the date of expiry of the period to be extended.
2. A decision granting a Union application and any decision revoking or amending it shall take effect as follows:
   (a) in the Member State in which the application was submitted, on the day following the date of adoption;
   (b) in all other Member States where action by the customs authorities is requested, on the day following the date on which the customs authorities are notified in accordance with Article 14(2), provided that the holder of the decision has fulfilled his obligations under Article 29(3) with regard to translation costs.

   A decision extending the period during which customs authorities are to take action shall take effect in the Member State in which the Union application was submitted and in all other Member States where action by the customs authorities is requested the day following the date of expiry of the period to be extended.

Article 11 Period during which the customs authorities are to take action

1. When granting an application, the competent customs department shall specify the period during which the customs authorities are to take action.

   That period shall begin on the day the decision granting the application takes effect, pursuant to Article 10, and shall not exceed one year from the day following the date of adoption.
2. Where an application submitted after notification by the customs authorities of the suspension of the release or detention of the goods in accordance with Article 18(3) does not contain the information referred to in point (g), (h) or (i) of Article 6(3), it shall be granted only for the suspension of the release or detention of those goods, unless that information is provided within 10

working days after the notification of the suspension of the release or detention of the goods.

3. Where an intellectual property right ceases to have effect or where the applicant ceases for other reasons to be entitled to submit an application, no action shall be taken by the customs authorities. The decision granting the application shall be revoked or amended accordingly by the competent customs department that granted the decision.

Article 12 Extension of the period during which the customs authorities are to take action

1. On expiry of the period during which the customs authorities are to take action, and subject to the prior discharge by the holder of the decision of any debt owed to the customs authorities under this Regulation, the competent customs department which adopted the initial decision may, at the request of the holder of the decision, extend that period.
2. Where the request for extension of the period during which the customs authorities are to take action is received by the competent customs department less than 30 working days before the expiry of the period to be extended, it may refuse that request.
3. The competent customs department shall notify its decision on the extension to the holder of the decision within 30 working days of the receipt of the request referred to in paragraph 1. The competent customs department shall specify the period during which the customs authorities are to take action.
4. The extended period during which the customs authorities are to take action shall run from the day following the date of expiry of the previous period and shall not exceed one year.
5. Where an intellectual property right ceases to have effect or where the applicant ceases for other reasons to be entitled to submit an application, no action shall be taken by the customs authorities. The decision granting the extension shall be revoked or amended accordingly by the competent customs department that granted the decision.
6. The holder of the decision shall not be charged a fee to cover the administrative costs resulting from the processing of the request for extension.
7. The Commission shall establish an extension request form by means of implementing acts. Those implementing acts shall be adopted in accordance with the advisory procedure referred to in Article 34(2).

Article 13 Amending the decision with regard to intellectual property rights.

The competent customs department that adopted the decision granting the application may, at the request of the holder of that decision, modify the list of intellectual property rights in that decision.

Where a new intellectual property right is added, the request shall contain the information referred to in points (c), (e), (g), (h) and (i) of Article 6(3).

In the case of a decision granting a Union application, any modification consisting of the addition of intellectual property rights shall be limited to intellectual property rights covered by Article 4.

Article 14 Notification obligations of the competent customs department

1. The competent customs department to which a national application has been submitted shall forward the following decisions to the customs offices of its Member State, immediately after their adoption:
   (a) decisions granting the application;
   (b) decisions revoking decisions granting the application;
   (c) decisions amending decisions granting the application;
   (d) decisions extending the period during which the customs authorities are to take action.
2. The competent customs department to which a Union application has been submitted shall forward the following decisions to the competent customs department of the Member State or Member States indicated in the Union application, immediately after their adoption:
   (a) decisions granting the application;
   (b) decisions revoking decisions granting the application;
   (c) decisions amending decisions granting the application;
   (d) decisions extending the period during which the customs authorities are to take action.

   The competent customs department of the Member State or Member States indicated in the Union application shall immediately after receiving those decisions forward them to their customs offices.
3. The competent customs department of the Member State or Member States indicated in the Union application may request the competent customs department that adopted the decision granting the application to provide them with additional information deemed necessary for the implementation of that decision.
4. The competent customs department shall forward its decision suspending the actions of the customs authorities under point (b) of Article 16(1) and Article 16(2) to the customs offices of its Member State, immediately after its adoption.

Article 15 Notification obligations of the holder of the decision

The holder of the decision shall immediately notify the competent customs department that granted the application of any of the following:

(a) an intellectual property right covered by the application ceases to have effect;
(b) the holder of the decision ceases for other reasons to be entitled to submit the application;
(c) modifications to the information referred to in Article 6(3).

Article 16 Failure of the holder of the decision to fulfil his obligations

1. Where the holder of the decision uses the information provided by the customs authorities for purposes other than those provided for in Article 21, the competent customs department of the Member State where the information was provided or misused may:
   (a) revoke any decision adopted by it granting a national application to that holder of the decision, and refuse to extend the period during which the customs authorities are to take action;
   (b) suspend in their territory, during the period during which the customs authorities are to take action, any decision granting a Union application to that holder of the decision.
2. The competent customs department may decide to suspend the actions of the customs authorities until the expiry of the period during which those authorities are to take action, where the holder of the decision:
   (a) does not fulfil the notification obligations set out in Article 15;
   (b) does not fulfil the obligation on returning samples set out in Article 19(3);
   (c) does not fulfil the obligations on costs and translation set out in Article 29(1) and (3);
   (d) without valid reason does not initiate proceedings as provided for in Article 23(3) or Article 26(9).

   In the case of a Union application, the decision to suspend the actions of the customs authorities shall have effect only in the Member State where such decision is taken.

Chapter III Action by the Customs Authorities

SECTION 1 Suspension of the release or detention of goods suspected of infringing an intellectual property right

Article 17 Suspension of the release or detention of the goods following the grant of an application

1. Where the customs authorities identify goods suspected of infringing an intellectual property right covered by a decision granting an application, they shall suspend the release of the goods or detain them.
2. Before suspending the release of or detaining the goods, the customs authorities may ask the holder of the decision to provide them with any relevant information with respect to the goods. The customs authorities may also provide the holder of the decision with information about the actual or

estimated quantity of goods, their actual or presumed nature and images thereof, as appropriate.

3. The customs authorities shall notify the declarant or the holder of the goods of the suspension of the release of the goods or the detention of the goods within one working day of that suspension or detention.

   Where the customs authorities opt to notify the holder of the goods and two or more persons are considered to be the holder of the goods, the customs authorities shall not be obliged to notify more than one of those persons.

   The customs authorities shall notify the holder of the decision of the suspension of the release of the goods or the detention on the same day as, or promptly after, the declarant or the holder of the goods is notified.

   The notifications shall include information on the procedure set out in Article 23.

4. The customs authorities shall inform the holder of the decision and the declarant or the holder of the goods of the actual or estimated quantity and the actual or presumed nature of the goods, including available images thereof, as appropriate, whose release has been suspended or which have been detained. The customs authorities shall also, upon request and where available to them, inform the holder of the decision of the names and addresses of the consignee, the consignor and the declarant or the holder of the goods, of the customs procedure and of the origin, provenance and destination of the goods whose release has been suspended or which have been detained.

Article 18 Suspension of the release or detention of the goods before the grant of an application

1. Where the customs authorities identify goods suspected of infringing an intellectual property right, which are not covered by a decision granting an application, they may, except for in the case of perishable goods, suspend the release of those goods or detain them.
2. Before suspending the release of or detaining the goods suspected of infringing an intellectual property right, the customs authorities may, without disclosing any information other than the actual or estimated quantity of goods, their actual or presumed nature and images thereof, as appropriate, request any person or entity potentially entitled to submit an application concerning the alleged infringement of the intellectual property rights to provide them with any relevant information.
3. The customs authorities shall notify the declarant or the holder of the goods of the suspension of the release of the goods or their detention within one working day of that suspension or detention.

   Where the customs authorities opt to notify the holder of the goods and two or more persons are considered to be the holder of the goods, the customs authorities shall not be obliged to notify more than one of those persons.

The customs authorities shall notify persons or entities entitled to submit an application concerning the alleged infringement of the intellectual property rights, of the suspension of the release of the goods or their detention on the same day as, or promptly after, the declarant or the holder of the goods is notified.

The customs authorities may consult the competent public authorities in order to identify the persons or entities entitled to submit an application.

The notifications shall include information on the procedure set out in Article 23.

4. The customs authorities shall grant the release of the goods or put an end to their detention immediately after completion of all customs formalities in the following cases:
   (a) where they have not identified any person or entity entitled to submit an application concerning the alleged infringement of intellectual property rights within one working day from the suspension of the release or the detention of the goods;
   (b) where they have not received an application in accordance with Article 5(3), or where they have rejected such an application.
5. Where an application has been granted, the customs authorities shall, upon request and where available to them, inform the holder of the decision of the names and addresses of the consignee, the consignor and the declarant or the holder of the goods, of the customs procedure and of the origin, provenance and destination of the goods whose release has been suspended or which have been detained.

Article 19 Inspection and sampling of goods whose release has been suspended or which have been detained

1. The customs authorities shall give the holder of the decision and the declarant or the holder of the goods the opportunity to inspect the goods whose release has been suspended or which have been detained.
2. The customs authorities may take samples that are representative of the goods. They may provide or send such samples to the holder of the decision, at the holder's request and strictly for the purposes of analysis and to facilitate the subsequent procedure in relation to counterfeit and pirated goods. Any analysis of those samples shall be carried out under the sole responsibility of the holder of the decision.
3. The holder of the decision shall, unless circumstances do not allow, return the samples referred to in paragraph 2 to the customs authorities on completion of the analysis, at the latest before the goods are released or their detention is ended.

Article 20 Conditions for storage

The conditions of storage of goods during a period of suspension of release or detention shall be determined by the customs authorities.

Article 21 Permitted use of certain information by the holder of the decision

Where the holder of the decision has received the information referred to in Article 17(4), Article 18(5), Article 19 or Article 26(8), he may disclose or use that information only for the following purposes:

(a) to initiate proceedings to determine whether an intellectual property right has been infringed and in the course of such proceedings;
(b) in connection with criminal investigations related to the infringement of an intellectual property right and undertaken by public authorities in the Member State where the goods are found;
(c) to initiate criminal proceedings and in the course of such proceedings;
(d) to seek compensation from the infringer or other persons;
(e) to agree with the declarant or the holder of the goods that the goods be destroyed in accordance with Article 23(1);
(f) to agree with the declarant or the holder of the goods of the amount of the guarantee referred to in point (a) of Article 24(2).

Article 22 Sharing of information and data between customs authorities

1. Without prejudice to applicable provisions on data protection in the Union and for the purpose of contributing to eliminating international trade in goods infringing intellectual property rights, the Commission and the customs authorities of the Member States may share certain data and information available to them with the relevant authorities in third countries according to the practical arrangements referred to in paragraph 3.
2. The data and information referred to in paragraph 1 shall be exchanged to swiftly enable effective enforcement against shipments of goods infringing an intellectual property right. Such data and information may relate to seizures, trends and general risk information, including on goods which are in transit through the territory of the Union and which have originated in or are destined for the territory of third countries concerned. Such data and information may include, where appropriate, the following:
   (a) nature and quantity of goods;
   (b) suspected intellectual property right infringed;
   (c) origin, provenance and destination of the goods;
   (d) information on movements of means of transport, in particular:
      (i) name of vessel or registration of means of transport;
      (ii) reference numbers of freight bill or other transport document;
      (iii) number of containers;
      (iv) weight of load;

(v) description and/or coding of goods;
(vi) reservation number;
(vii) seal number;
(viii) place of first loading;
(ix) place of final unloading;
(x) places of transhipment;
(xi) expected date of arrival at place of final unloading;

(e) information on movements of containers, in particular:
(i) container number;
(ii) container loading status;
(iii) date of movement;
(iv) type of movement (loaded, unloaded, transhipped, entered, left, etc.);
(v) name of vessel or registration of means of transport;
(vi) number of voyage/journey;
(vii) place;
(viii) freight bill or other transport document.

3. The Commission shall adopt implementing acts defining the elements of the necessary practical arrangements concerning the exchange of data and information referred to in paragraphs 1 and 2 of this Article. Those implementing acts shall be adopted in accordance with the examination procedure referred to in Article 34(3).

SECTION 2 Destruction of goods, initiation of proceedings and early release of goods

Article 23 Destruction of goods and initiation of proceedings

1. Goods suspected of infringing an intellectual property right may be destroyed under customs control, without there being any need to determine whether an intellectual property right has been infringed under the law of the Member State where the goods are found, where all of the following conditions are fulfilled:
(a) the holder of the decision has confirmed in writing to the customs authorities, within 10 working days, or three working days in the case of perishable goods, of notification of the suspension of the release or the detention of the goods, that, in his conviction, an intellectual property right has been infringed;
(b) the holder of the decision has confirmed in writing to the customs authorities, within 10 working days, or three working days in the case of perishable goods, of notification of the suspension of the release or the detention of the goods, his agreement to the destruction of the goods;
(c) the declarant or the holder of the goods has confirmed in writing to the customs authorities, within 10 working days, or three working days in the case of perishable goods, of notification of the suspension of the release or

the detention of the goods, his agreement to the destruction of the goods. Where the declarant or the holder of the goods has not confirmed his agreement to the destruction of the goods nor notified his opposition thereto to the customs authorities, within those deadlines, the customs authorities may deem the declarant or the holder of the goods to have confirmed his agreement to the destruction of those goods.

The customs authorities shall grant the release of the goods or put an end to their detention, immediately after completion of all customs formalities, where within the periods referred to in points (a) and (b) of the first subparagraph, they have not received both the written confirmation from the holder of the decision that, in his conviction, an intellectual property right has been infringed and his agreement to destruction, unless those authorities have been duly informed about the initiation of proceedings to determine whether an intellectual property right has been infringed.

2. The destruction of the goods shall be carried out under customs control and under the responsibility of the holder of the decision, unless otherwise specified in the national law of the Member State where the goods are destroyed. Samples may be taken by competent authorities prior to the destruction of the goods. Samples taken prior to destruction may be used for educational purposes.
3. Where the declarant or the holder of the goods has not confirmed his agreement to the destruction in writing and where the declarant or the holder of the goods has not been deemed to have confirmed his agreement to the destruction, in accordance with point (c) of the first subparagraph of paragraph 1 within the periods referred to therein, the customs authorities shall immediately notify the holder of the decision thereof. The holder of the decision shall, within 10 working days, or three working days in the case of perishable goods, of notification of the suspension of the release or the detention of the goods, initiate proceedings to determine whether an intellectual property right has been infringed.
4. Except in the case of perishable goods the customs authorities may extend the period referred to in paragraph 3 by a maximum of 10 working days upon a duly justified request by the holder of the decision in appropriate cases.
5. The customs authorities shall grant the release of the goods or put an end to their detention, immediately after completion of all customs formalities, where, within the periods referred to in paragraphs 3 and 4, they have not been duly informed, in accordance with paragraph 3, on the initiation of proceedings to determine whether an intellectual property right has been infringed.

Article 24 Early release of goods

1. Where the customs authorities have been notified of the initiation of proceedings to determine whether a design, patent, utility model, topography of semiconductor product or plant variety has been infringed, the declarant or the

holder of the goods may request the customs authorities to release the goods or put an end to their detention before the completion of those proceedings.

2. The customs authorities shall release the goods or put an end to their detention only where all the following conditions are fulfilled:
   (a) the declarant or the holder of the goods has provided a guarantee that is of an amount sufficient to protect the interests of the holder of the decision;
   (b) the authority competent to determine whether an intellectual property right has been infringed has not authorised precautionary measures;
   (c) all customs formalities have been completed.
3. The provision of the guarantee referred to in point (a) of paragraph 2 shall not affect the other legal remedies available to the holder of the decision.

Article 25 Goods for destruction

1. Goods to be destroyed under Article 23 or 26 shall not be:
   (a) released for free circulation, unless customs authorities, with the agreement of the holder of the decision, decide that it is necessary in the event that the goods are to be recycled or disposed of outside commercial channels, including for awareness-raising, training and educational purposes. The conditions under which the goods can be released for free circulation shall be determined by the customs authorities;
   (b) brought out of the customs territory of the Union;
   (c) exported;
   (d) re-exported;
   (e) placed under a suspensive procedure;
   (f) placed in a free zone or free warehouse.
2. The customs authorities may allow the goods referred to in paragraph 1 to be moved under customs supervision between different places within the customs territory of the Union with a view to their destruction under customs control.

Article 26 Procedure for the destruction of goods in small consignments

1. This Article shall apply to goods where all of the following conditions are fulfilled:
   (a) the goods are suspected of being counterfeit or pirated goods;
   (b) the goods are not perishable goods;
   (c) the goods are covered by a decision granting an application;
   (d) the holder of the decision has requested the use of the procedure set out in this Article in the application;
   (e) the goods are transported in small consignments.
2. When the procedure set out in this Article is applied, Article 17(3) and (4) and Article 19(2) and (3) shall not apply.

3. The customs authorities shall notify the declarant or the holder of the goods of the suspension of the release of the goods or their detention within one working day of the suspension of the release or of the detention of the goods. The notification of the suspension of the release or the detention of the goods shall include the following information:
   (a) that the customs authorities intend to destroy the goods;
   (b) the rights of the declarant or the holder of the goods under paragraphs 4, 5 and 6.
4. The declarant or the holder of the goods shall be given the opportunity to express his point of view within 10 working days of notification of the suspension of the release or the detention of the goods.
5. The goods concerned may be destroyed where, within 10 working days of notification of the suspension of the release or the detention of the goods, the declarant or the holder of the goods has confirmed to the customs authorities his agreement to the destruction of the goods.
6. Where the declarant or the holder of the goods has not confirmed his agreement to the destruction of the goods nor notified his opposition thereto to the customs authorities, within the period referred to in paragraph 5, the customs authorities may deem the declarant or the holder of the goods to have confirmed his agreement to the destruction of the goods.
7. The destruction shall be carried out under customs control. The customs authorities shall, upon request and as appropriate, provide the holder of the decision with information about the actual or estimated quantity of destroyed goods and their nature.
8. Where the declarant or the holder of the goods has not confirmed his agreement to the destruction of the goods and where the declarant or the holder of the goods has not been deemed to have confirmed such agreement, in accordance with paragraph 6, the customs authorities shall immediately notify the holder of the decision thereof and of the quantity of goods and their nature, including images thereof, where appropriate. The customs authorities shall also, upon request and where available to them, inform the holder of the decision of the names and addresses of the consignee, the consignor and the declarant or the holder of the goods, of the customs procedure and of the origin, provenance and destination of the goods whose release has been suspended or which have been detained.
9. The customs authorities shall grant the release of the goods or put an end to their detention immediately after completion of all customs formalities where they have not received information from the holder of the decision on the initiation of proceedings to determine whether an intellectual property right has been infringed within 10 working days of the notification referred to in paragraph 8.
10. The Commission shall be empowered to adopt delegated acts in accordance with Article 35 concerning the amendment of quantities in the definition of small consignments in the event that the definition is found to be impractical in the light of the need to ensure the effective operation of the

procedure set out in this Article, or where necessary in order to avoid any circumvention of this procedure as regards the composition of consignments.

Chapter IV Liability, Costs and Penalties

Article 27 Liability of the customs authorities

Without prejudice to national law, the decision granting an application shall not entitle the holder of that decision to compensation in the event that goods suspected of infringing an intellectual property right are not detected by a customs office and are released, or no action is taken to detain them.

Article 28 Liability of the holder of the decision

Where a procedure duly initiated pursuant to this Regulation is discontinued owing to an act or omission on the part of the holder of the decision, where samples taken pursuant to Article 19(2) are either not returned or are damaged and beyond use owing to an act or omission on the part of the holder of the decision, or where the goods in question are subsequently found not to infringe an intellectual property right, the holder of the decision shall be liable towards any holder of the goods or declarant, who has suffered damage in that regard, in accordance with specific applicable legislation.

Article 29 Costs

1. Where requested by the customs authorities, the holder of the decision shall reimburse the costs incurred by the customs authorities, or other parties acting on behalf of customs authorities, from the moment of detention or suspension of the release of the goods, including storage and handling of the goods, in accordance with Article 17(1), Article 18(1) and Article 19(2) and (3), and when using corrective measures such as destruction of goods in accordance with Articles 23 and 26.

   The holder of a decision to whom the suspension of release or detention of goods has been notified shall, upon request, be given information by the customs authorities on where and how those goods are being stored and on the estimated costs of storage referred to in this paragraph. The information on estimated costs may be expressed in terms of time, products, volume, weight or service depending on the circumstances of storage and the nature of the goods.
2. This Article shall be without prejudice to the right of the holder of the decision to seek compensation from the infringer or other persons in accordance with the legislation applicable.
3. The holder of a decision granting a Union application shall provide and pay for any translation required by the competent customs department or customs authorities which are to take action concerning the goods suspected of infringing an intellectual property right.

Article 30 Penalties

The Member States shall ensure that the holders of decisions comply with the obligations set out in this Regulation, including, where appropriate, by laying down provisions establishing penalties. The penalties provided for shall be effective, proportionate and dissuasive.

The Member States shall notify those provisions and any subsequent amendment affecting them to the Commission without delay.

...

§18.08 EXCERPTS OF THE UPCA

AGREEMENT ON A UNIFIED PATENT COURT

[Preamble omitted] …

PART I—GENERAL AND INSTITUTIONAL PROVISIONS

CHAPTER I—GENERAL PROVISIONS

ARTICLE 1 …

ARTICLE 2 …

ARTICLE 3 Scope of application

This Agreement shall apply to any:

(a) European patent with unitary effect;
(b) supplementary protection certificate issued for a product protected by a patent;
(c) European patent which has not yet lapsed at the date of entry into force of this Agreement or was granted after that date, without prejudice to Article 83; and
(d) European patent application which is pending at the date of entry into force of this Agreement or which is filed after that date, without prejudice to Article 83.

ARTICLE 4 Legal status

(1) The Court shall have legal personality in each Contracting Member State and shall enjoy the most extensive legal capacity accorded to legal persons under the national law of that State.
(2) The Court shall be represented by the President of the Court of Appeal who shall be elected in accordance with the Statute.

ARTICLE 5 Liability …

CHAPTER II—INSTITUTIONAL PROVISIONS

ARTICLE 6 The Court

(1) The Court shall comprise a Court of First Instance, a Court of Appeal and a Registry.
(2) The Court shall perform the functions assigned to it by this Agreement.

ARTICLE 7 The Court of First Instance

(1) The Court of First Instance shall comprise a central division as well as local and regional divisions.
(2) The central division shall have its seat in Paris, with sections in London and Munich. The cases before the central division shall be distributed in accordance with Annex II, which shall form an integral part of this Agreement.
(3) A local division shall be set up in a Contracting Member State upon its request in accordance with the Statute. A Contracting Member State hosting a local division shall designate its seat.
(4) An additional local division shall be set up in a Contracting Member State upon its request for every one hundred patent cases per calendar year that have been commenced in that Contracting Member State during three successive years prior to or subsequent to the date of entry into force of this Agreement. The number of local divisions in one Contracting Member State shall not exceed four.
(5) A regional division shall be set up for two or more Contracting Member States, upon their request in accordance with the Statute. Such Contracting Member States shall designate the seat of the division concerned. The regional division may hear cases in multiple locations.

ARTICLE 8 Composition of the panels of the Court of First Instance

(1) Any panel of the Court of First Instance shall have a multinational composition. Without prejudice to paragraph 5 of this Article and to Article 33(3)(a), it shall sit in a composition of three judges.
(2) Any panel of a local division in a Contracting Member State where, during a period of three successive years prior or subsequent to the entry into force of this Agreement, less than fifty patent cases per calendar year on average have been commenced shall sit in a composition of one legally qualified judge who is a national of the Contracting Member State hosting the local division concerned and two legally qualified judges who are not nationals of the Contracting Member State concerned and are allocated from the Pool of Judges in accordance with Article 18(3) on a case by case basis.
(3) Notwithstanding paragraph 2, any panel of a local division in a Contracting Member State where, during a period of three successive years prior or subsequent to the entry into force of this Agreement, fifty or more patent cases per calendar year on average have been commenced, shall sit in a composition of two legally qualified judges who are nationals of the Contracting Member State hosting the local division concerned and one legally qualified judge who is not a national of the Contracting Member State concerned and is allocated from the Pool of Judges in accordance with Article 18(3). Such third judge shall serve at the local division on a long term basis,

where this is necessary for the efficient functioning of divisions with a high work load.

(4) Any panel of a regional division shall sit in a composition of two legally qualified judges chosen from a regional list of judges, who shall be nationals of the Contracting Member States concerned, and one legally qualified judge who shall not be a national of the Contracting Member States concerned and who shall be allocated from the Pool of Judges in accordance with Article 18(3).

(5) Upon request by one of the parties, any panel of a local or regional division shall request the President of the Court of First Instance to allocate from the Pool of Judges in accordance with Article 18(3) an additional technically qualified judge with qualifications and experience in the field of technology concerned. Moreover, any panel of a local or regional division may, after having heard the parties, submit such request on its own initiative, where it deems this appropriate.

In cases where such a technically qualified judge is allocated, no further technically qualified judge may be allocated under Article 33(3)(a).

(6) Any panel of the central division shall sit in a composition of two legally qualified judges who are nationals of different Contracting Member States and one technically qualified judge allocated from the Pool of Judges in accordance with Article 18(3) with qualifications and experience in the field of technology concerned. However, any panel of the central division dealing with actions under Article 32(1)(i) shall sit in a composition of three legally qualified judges who are nationals of different Contracting Member States.

(7) Notwithstanding paragraphs 1 to 6 and in accordance with the Rules of Procedure, parties may agree to have their case heard by a single legally qualified judge.

(8) Any panel of the Court of First Instance shall be chaired by a legally qualified judge.

ARTICLE 9 The Court of Appeal

(1) Any panel of the Court of Appeal shall sit in a multinational composition of five judges. It shall sit in a composition of three legally qualified judges who are nationals of different Contracting Member States and two technically qualified judges with qualifications and experience in the field of technology concerned. Those technically qualified judges shall be assigned to the panel by the President of the Court of Appeal from the pool of judges in accordance with Article 18.

(2) Notwithstanding paragraph 1, a panel dealing with actions under Article 32(1)(i) shall sit in a composition of three legally qualified judges who are nationals of different Contracting Member States.

(3) Any panel of the Court of Appeal shall be chaired by a legally qualified judge.

(4) The panels of the Court of Appeal shall be set up in accordance with the Statute.
(5) The Court of Appeal shall have its seat in Luxembourg.

ARTICLE 10 The Registry

(1) A Registry shall be set up at the seat of the Court of Appeal. It shall be managed by the Registrar and perform the functions assigned to it in accordance with the Statute. Subject to conditions set out in this Agreement and the Rules of Procedure, the register kept by the Registry shall be public.
(2) Subregistries shall be set up at all divisions of the Court of First Instance.
(3) The Registry shall keep records of all cases before the Court. Upon filing, the subregistry concerned shall notify every case to the Registry.
(4) The Court shall appoint the Registrar in accordance with Article 22 of the Statute and lay down the rules governing the Registrar's service.

ARTICLE 11 Committees

...

ARTICLE 12 The Administrative Committee

...

ARTICLE 13 The Budget Committee

...

ARTICLE 14 The Advisory Committee

...

CHAPTER III—JUDGES OF THE COURT

ARTICLE 15 Eligibility criteria for the appointment of judges

...

ARTICLE 16 Appointment procedure

...

ARTICLE 17 Judicial independence and impartiality

(1) The Court, its judges and the Registrar shall enjoy judicial independence. In the performance of their duties, the judges shall not be bound by any instructions.
(2) Legally qualified judges, as well as technically qualified judges who are full-time judges of the Court, may not engage in any other occupation,

whether gainful or not, unless an exception is granted by the Administrative Committee.

(3) Notwithstanding paragraph 2, the exercise of the office of judges shall not exclude the exercise of other judicial functions at national level.

(4) The exercise of the office of technically qualified judges who are part-time judges of the Court shall not exclude the exercise of other functions provided there is no conflict of interest.

(5) In case of a conflict of interest, the judge concerned shall not take part in proceedings. Rules governing conflicts of interest are set out in the Statute.

ARTICLE 18 Pool of Judges

(1) A Pool of Judges shall be established in accordance with the Statute.

(2) The Pool of Judges shall be composed of all legally qualified judges and technically qualified judges from the Court of First Instance who are full-time or part-time judges of the Court. The Pool of Judges shall include at least one technically qualified judge per field of technology with the relevant qualifications and experience. The technically qualified judges from the Pool of Judges shall also be available to the Court of Appeal.

(3) Where so provided by this Agreement or the Statute, the judges from the Pool of Judges shall be allocated to the division concerned by the President of the Court of First Instance. The allocation of judges shall be based on their legal or technical expertise, linguistic skills and relevant experience. The allocation of judges shall guarantee the same high quality of work and the same high level of legal and technical expertise in all panels of the Court of First Instance.

ARTICLE 19 Training framework

...

CHAPTER IV—THE PRIMACY OF UNION LAW, LIABILITY AND RESPONSIBILITY OF THE CONTRACTING MEMBER STATES

ARTICLE 20 Primacy of and respect for Union law

The Court shall apply Union law in its entirety and shall respect its primacy.

ARTICLE 21 Requests for preliminary rulings

UPCA

As a court common to the Contracting Member States and as part of their judicial system, the Court shall cooperate with the Court of Justice of the European Union to ensure the correct application and uniform interpretation of Union law, as any national court, in accordance with Article 267 TFEU in particular. Decisions of the Court of Justice of the European Union shall be binding on the Court.

ARTICLE 22 Liability for damage caused by infringements of Union law

...

ARTICLE 23 Responsibility of the Contracting Member States

...

CHAPTER V—SOURCES OF LAW AND SUBSTANTIVE LAW

ARTICLE 24 Sources of law

(1) In full compliance with Article 20, when hearing a case brought before it under this Agreement, the Court shall base its decisions on:
   (a) Union law, including Regulation (EU) No 1257/2012 and Regulation (EU) No 1260/2012[1];
   (b) this Agreement;
   (c) the EPC;
   (d) other international agreements applicable to patents and binding on all the Contracting Member States; and
   (e) national law.

   Council Regulation (EU) No 1260/2012 of 17 December 2012 implementing enhanced cooperation in the area of the creation of unitary patent protection with regard to the applicable translation arrangements (OJEU L 361, 31.12.2012, p. 89) including any subsequent amendments.
(2) To the extent that the Court shall base its decisions on national law, including where relevant the law of non-contracting States, the applicable law shall be determined:
   (a) by directly applicable provisions of Union law containing private international law rules, or
   (b) in the absence of directly applicable provisions of Union law or where the latter do not apply, by international instruments containing private international law rules; or
   (c) in the absence of provisions referred to in points (a) and (b), by national provisions on private international law as determined by the Court.
(3) The law of non-contracting States shall apply when designated by application of the rules referred to in paragraph 2, in particular in relation to Articles 25 to 28, 54, 55, 64, 68 and 72.

ARTICLE 25 Right to prevent the direct use of the invention

UPCA

A patent shall confer on its proprietor the right to prevent any third party not having the proprietor's consent from the following:

(a) making, offering, placing on the market or using a product which is the subject matter of the patent, or importing or storing the product for those purposes;

(b) using a process which is the subject matter of the patent or, where the third party knows, or should have known, that the use of the process is prohibited without the consent of the patent proprietor, offering the process for use within the territory of the Contracting Member States in which that patent has effect;

(c) offering, placing on the market, using, or importing or storing for those purposes a product obtained directly by a process which is the subject matter of the patent.

ARTICLE 26 Right to prevent the indirect use of the invention

(1) A patent shall confer on its proprietor the right to prevent any third party not having the proprietor's consent from supplying or offering to supply, within the territory of the Contracting Member States in which that patent has effect, any person other than a party entitled to exploit the patented invention, with means, relating to an essential element of that invention, for putting it into effect therein, when the third party knows, or should have known, that those means are suitable and intended for putting that invention into effect.

(2) Paragraph 1 shall not apply when the means are staple commercial products, except where the third party induces the person supplied to perform any of the acts prohibited by Article 25.

(3) Persons performing the acts referred to in Article 27(a) to (e) shall not be considered to be parties entitled to exploit the invention within the meaning of paragraph 1.

ARTICLE 27 Limitations of the effects of a patent

The rights conferred by a patent shall not extend to any of the following:

(a) acts done privately and for non-commercial purposes;

(b) acts done for experimental purposes relating to the subject matter of the patented invention;

(c) the use of biological material for the purpose of breeding, or discovering and developing other plant varieties;

(d) the acts allowed pursuant to Article 13(6) of Directive 2001/82/EC[1] or Article 10(6) of Directive 2001/83/EC[2] in respect of any patent covering the product within the meaning of either of those Directives;

(e) the extemporaneous preparation by a pharmacy, for individual cases, of a medicine in accordance with a medical prescription or acts concerning the medicine so prepared;

(f) the use of the patented invention on board vessels of countries of the International Union for the Protection of Industrial Property (Paris Union) or members of the World Trade Organisation, other than those Contracting Member States in which that patent has effect, in the body of such vessel, in the machinery, tackle, gear and other accessories, when such vessels temporarily or accidentally enter the waters of a Contracting Member State in which that patent has effect, provided that the invention is used there exclusively for the needs of the vessel;

(g) the use of the patented invention in the construction or operation of aircraft or land vehicles or other means of transport of countries of the International Union for the Protection of Industrial Property (Paris Union) or members of the World Trade Organisation, other than those Contracting Member States in which that patent has effect, or of accessories to such aircraft or land vehicles, when these temporarily or accidentally enter the territory of a Contracting Member State in which that patent has effect;

(h) the acts specified in Article 27 of the Convention on International Civil Aviation of 7 December 1944, where these acts concern the aircraft of a country party to that Convention other than a Contracting Member State in which that patent has effect;

(i) the use by a farmer of the product of his harvest for propagation or multiplication by him on his own holding, provided that the plant propagating material was sold or otherwise commercialised to the farmer by or with the consent of the patent proprietor for agricultural use. The extent and the conditions for this use correspond to those under Article 14 of Regulation (EC) No. 2100/94;

(j) the use by a farmer of protected livestock for an agricultural purpose, provided that the breeding stock or other animal reproductive material were sold or otherwise commercialised to the farmer by or with the consent of the patent proprietor. Such use includes making the animal or other animal reproductive material available for the purposes of pursuing the farmer's agricultural activity, but not the sale thereof within the framework of, or for the purpose of, a commercial reproductive activity;

(k) the acts and the use of the obtained information as allowed under Articles 5 and 6 of Directive 2009/24/EC[1], in particular, by its provisions on decompilation and interoperability; and

(l) the acts allowed pursuant to Article 10 of Directive 98/44/EC[2].

ARTICLE 28 Right based on prior use of the invention

Any person, who, if a national patent had been granted in respect of an invention, would have had, in a Contracting Member State, a right based on prior use of that invention or a right of personal possession of that invention, shall enjoy, in that Contracting Member State, the same rights in respect of a patent for the same invention.

ARTICLE 29 Exhaustion of the rights conferred by a European patent

The rights conferred by a European patent shall not extend to acts concerning a product covered by that patent after that product has been placed on the market in the European Union by, or with the consent of, the patent proprietor, unless there are legitimate grounds for the patent proprietor to oppose further commercialisation of the product.

ARTICLE 30 Effects of supplementary protection certificates

A supplementary protection certificate shall confer the same rights as conferred by the patent and shall be subject to the same limitations and the same obligations.

CHAPTER VI—INTERNATIONAL JURISDICTION AND COMPETENCE

ARTICLE 31 International jurisdiction

The international jurisdiction of the Court shall be established in accordance with Regulation (EU) No 1215/2012 or, where applicable, on the basis of the Convention on jurisdiction and the recognition and enforcement of judgments in civil and commercial matters (Lugano Convention).

ARTICLE 32 Competence of the Court

(1) The Court shall have exclusive competence in respect of:
  (a) actions for actual or threatened infringements of patents and supplementary protection certificates and related defences, including counterclaims concerning licences;
  (b) actions for declarations of non-infringement of patents and supplementary protection certificates;
   Convention on jurisdiction and the recognition and enforcement of judgments in civil and commercial matters, done at Lugano on 30 October 2007, including any subsequent amendments.
  (c) actions for provisional and protective measures and injunctions;
  (d) actions for revocation of patents and for declaration of invalidity of supplementary protection certificates;
  (e) counterclaims for revocation of patents and for declaration of invalidity of supplementary protection certificates;
  (f) actions for damages or compensation derived from the provisional protection conferred by a published European patent application;
  (g) actions relating to the use of the invention prior to the granting of the patent or to the right based on prior use of the invention;
  (h) actions for compensation for licences on the basis of Article 8 of Regulation (EU) No 1257/2012; and
  (i) actions concerning decisions of the European Patent Office in carrying out the tasks referred to in Article 9 of Regulation (EU) No 1257/2012.

(2) The national courts of the Contracting Member States shall remain competent for actions relating to patents and supplementary protection certificates which do not come within the exclusive competence of the Court.

ARTICLE 33 Competence of the divisions of the Court of First Instance

(1) Without prejudice to paragraph 7 of this Article, actions referred to in Article 32(1)(a), (c), (f) and (g) shall be brought before:
   (a) the local division hosted by the Contracting Member State where the actual or threatened infringement has occurred or may occur, or the regional division in which that Contracting Member State participates; or
   (b) the local division hosted by the Contracting Member State where the defendant or, in the case of multiple defendants, one of the defendants has its residence, or principal place of business, or in the absence of residence or principal place of business, its place of business, or the regional division in which that Contracting Member State participates. An action may be brought against multiple defendants only where the defendants have a commercial relationship and where the action relates to the same alleged infringement.

   Actions referred to in Article 32(1)(h) shall be brought before the local or regional division in accordance with point (b) of the first subparagraph. UPC/en 38

   Actions against defendants having their residence, or principal place of business or, in the absence of residence or principal place of business, their place of business, outside the territory of the Contracting Member States shall be brought before the local or regional division in accordance with point (a) of the first subparagraph or before the central division.

   If the Contracting Member State concerned does not host a local division and does not participate in a regional division, actions shall be brought before the central division.

(2) If an action referred to in Article 32(1)(a), (c), (f), (g) or (h) is pending before a division of the Court of First Instance, any action referred to in Article 32(1)(a), (c), (f), (g) or (h) between the same parties on the same patent may not be brought before any other division.

   If an action referred to in Article 32(1)(a) is pending before a regional division and the infringement has occurred in the territories of three or more regional divisions, the regional division concerned shall, at the request of the defendant, refer the case to the central division.

   In case an action between the same parties on the same patent is brought before several different divisions, the division first seized shall be competent for the whole case and any division seized later shall declare the action inadmissible in accordance with the Rules of Procedure.

(3) A counterclaim for revocation as referred to in Article 32(1)(e) may be brought in the case of an action for infringement as referred to in Article 32(1)(a). The local or regional division concerned shall, after having heard the parties, have the discretion either to:

UPCA

(a) proceed with both the action for infringement and with the counterclaim for revocation and request the President of the Court of First Instance to allocate from the Pool of Judges in accordance with Article 18(3) a technically qualified judge with qualifications and experience in the field of technology concerned.
(b) refer the counterclaim for revocation for decision to the central division and suspend or proceed with the action for infringement; or
(c) with the agreement of the parties, refer the case for decision to the central division.

(4) Actions referred to in Article 32(1)(b) and (d) shall be brought before the central division. If, however, an action for infringement as referred to in Article 32(1)(a) between the same parties relating to the same patent has been brought before a local or a regional division, these actions may only be brought before the same local or regional division.
(5) If an action for revocation as referred to in Article 32(1)(d) is pending before the central division, an action for infringement as referred to in Article 32(1)(a) between the same parties relating to the same patent may be brought before any division in accordance with paragraph 1 of this Article or before the central division. The local or regional division concerned shall have the discretion to proceed in accordance with paragraph 3 of this Article.
(6) An action for declaration of non-infringement as referred to in Article 32(1)(b) pending before the central division shall be stayed once an infringement action as referred to in Article 32(1)(a) between the same parties or between the holder of an exclusive licence and the party requesting a declaration of non-infringement relating to the same patent is brought before a local or regional division within three months of the date on which the action was initiated before the central division.
(7) Parties may agree to bring actions referred to in Article 32(1)(a) to (h) before the division of their choice, including the central division.
(8) Actions referred to in Article 32(1)(d) and (e) can be brought without the applicant having to file notice of opposition with the European Patent Office.
(9) Actions referred to in Article 32(1)(i) shall be brought before the central division.
(10) A party shall inform the Court of any pending revocation, limitation or opposition proceedings before the European Patent Office, and of any request for accelerated processing before the European Patent Office. The Court may stay its proceedings when a rapid decision may be expected from the European Patent Office.

ARTICLE 34 Territorial scope of decisions

Decisions of the Court shall cover, in the case of a European patent, the territory of those Contracting Member States for which the European patent has effect.

CHAPTER VII—PATENT MEDIATION AND ARBITRATION

ARTICLE 35 Patent mediation and arbitration centre

(1) A patent mediation and arbitration centre ("the Centre") is hereby established. It shall have its seats in Ljubljana and Lisbon.
(2) The Centre shall provide facilities for mediation and arbitration of patent disputes falling within the scope of this Agreement. Article 82 shall apply mutatis mutandis to any settlement reached through the use of the facilities of the Centre, including through mediation. However, a patent may not be revoked or limited in mediation or arbitration proceedings.
(3) The Centre shall establish Mediation and Arbitration Rules.
(4) The Centre shall draw up a list of mediators and arbitrators to assist the parties in the settlement of their dispute.

PART II—FINANCIAL PROVISIONS

ARTICLE 36 Budget of the Court

...

ARTICLE 37 Financing of the Court

...

ARTICLE 38 Financing of the training framework for judges

...

ARTICLE 39 Financing of the Centre

...

PART III—ORGANISATION AND PROCEDURAL PROVISIONS

CHAPTER I—GENERAL PROVISIONS

ARTICLE 40 Statute

(1) The Statute shall lay down the details of the organisation and functioning of the Court.
(2) The Statute is annexed to this Agreement. The Statute may be amended by decision of the Administrative Committee, on the basis of a proposal of the Court or a proposal of a Contracting Member State after consultation with the Court. However, such amendments shall not contradict or alter this Agreement.

(3) The Statute shall guarantee that the functioning of the Court is organised in the most efficient and cost-effective manner and shall ensure equitable access to justice.

ARTICLE 41 Rules of Procedure

(1) The Rules of Procedure shall lay down the details of the proceedings before the Court. They shall comply with this Agreement and the Statute.

(2) The Rules of Procedure shall be adopted by the Administrative Committee on the basis of broad consultations with stakeholders. The prior opinion of the European Commission on the compatibility of the Rules of Procedure with Union law shall be requested.

The Rules of Procedure may be amended by a decision of the Administrative Committee, on the basis of a proposal from the Court and after consultation with the European Commission. However, such amendments shall not contradict or alter this Agreement or the Statute.

(3) The Rules of Procedure shall guarantee that the decisions of the Court are of the highest quality and that proceedings are organised in the most efficient and cost effective manner. They shall ensure a fair balance between the legitimate interests of all parties. They shall provide for the required level of discretion of judges without impairing the predictability of proceedings for the parties.

ARTICLE 42 Proportionality and fairness

(1) The Court shall deal with litigation in ways which are proportionate to the importance and complexity thereof.

(2) The Court shall ensure that the rules, procedures and remedies provided for in this Agreement and in the Statute are used in a fair and equitable manner and do not distort competition.

ARTICLE 43 Case management

The Court shall actively manage the cases before it in accordance with the Rules of Procedure without impairing the freedom of the parties to determine the subject-matter of, and the supporting evidence for, their case. UPC/en 49

ARTICLE 44 Electronic procedures

The Court shall make best use of electronic procedures, such as the electronic filing of submissions of the parties and stating of evidence in electronic form, as well as video conferencing, in accordance with the Rules of Procedure.

ARTICLE 45 Public proceedings

The proceedings shall be open to the public unless the Court decides to make them confidential, to the extent necessary, in the interest of one of the parties or other affected persons, or in the general interest of justice or public order.

ARTICLE 46 Legal capacity

Any natural or legal person, or any body equivalent to a legal person entitled to initiate proceedings in accordance with its national law, shall have the capacity to be a party to the proceedings before the Court. UPC/en 50.

ARTICLE 47 Parties

(1) The patent proprietor shall be entitled to bring actions before the Court.
(2) Unless the licensing agreement provides otherwise, the holder of an exclusive licence in respect of a patent shall be entitled to bring actions before the Court under the same circumstances as the patent proprietor, provided that the patent proprietor is given prior notice.
(3) The holder of a non-exclusive licence shall not be entitled to bring actions before the Court, unless the patent proprietor is given prior notice and in so far as expressly permitted by the licence agreement.
(4) In actions brought by a licence holder, the patent proprietor shall be entitled to join the action before the Court.
(5) The validity of a patent cannot be contested in an action for infringement brought by the holder of a licence where the patent proprietor does not take part in the proceedings. The party in an action for infringement wanting to contest the validity of a patent shall have to bring actions against the patent proprietor.
(6) Any other natural or legal person, or any body entitled to bring actions in accordance with its national law, who is concerned by a patent, may bring actions in accordance with the Rules of Procedure.
(7) Any natural or legal person, or any body entitled to bring actions in accordance with its national law and who is affected by a decision of the European Patent Office in carrying out the tasks referred to in Article 9 of Regulation (EU) No 1257/2012 is entitled to bring actions under Article 32(1)(i).

ARTICLE 48 Representation

(1) Parties shall be represented by lawyers authorised to practise before a court of a Contracting Member State.
(2) Parties may alternatively be represented by European Patent Attorneys who are entitled to act as professional representatives before the European Patent Office pursuant to Article 134 of the EPC and who have appropriate qualifications such as a European Patent Litigation Certificate.

(3) The requirements for qualifications pursuant to paragraph 2 shall be established by the Administrative Committee. A list of European Patent Attorneys entitled to represent parties before the Court shall be kept by the Registrar.
(4) Representatives of the parties may be assisted by patent attorneys, who shall be allowed to speak at hearings of the Court in accordance with the Rules of Procedure.
(5) Representatives of the parties shall enjoy the rights and immunities necessary for the independent exercise of their duties, including the privilege from disclosure in proceedings before the Court in respect of communications between a representative and the party or any other person, under the conditions laid down in the Rules of Procedure, unless such privilege is expressly waived by the party concerned.
(6) Representatives of the parties shall be obliged not to misrepresent cases or facts before the Court either knowingly or with good reasons to know.
(7) Representation in accordance with paragraphs 1 and 2 of this Article shall not be required in proceedings under Article 32(1)(i).

CHAPTER II—LANGUAGE OF PROCEEDINGS

ARTICLE 49 Language of proceedings at the Court of First Instance

(1) The language of proceedings before any local or regional division shall be an official European Union language which is the official language or one of the official languages of the Contracting Member State hosting the relevant division, or the official language(s) designated by Contracting Member States sharing a regional division.
(2) Notwithstanding paragraph 1, Contracting Member States may designate one or more of the official languages of the European Patent Office as the language of proceedings of their local or regional division.
(3) The parties may agree on the use of the language in which the patent was granted as the language of proceedings, subject to approval by the competent panel. If the panel does not approve their choice, the parties may request that the case be referred to the central division.
(4) With the agreement of the parties the competent panel may, on grounds of convenience and fairness, decide on the use of the language in which the patent was granted as the language of proceedings.
(5) At the request of one of the parties and after having heard the other parties and the competent panel, the President of the Court of First Instance may, on grounds of fairness and taking into account all relevant circumstances, including the position of parties, in particular the position of the defendant, decide on the use of the language in which the patent was granted as language of proceedings. In this case the President of the Court of First Instance shall assess the need for specific translation and interpretation arrangements.
(6) The language of proceedings at the central division shall be the language in which the patent concerned was granted.

ARTICLE 50 Language of proceedings at the Court of Appeal

(1) The language of proceedings before the Court of Appeal shall be the language of proceedings before the Court of First Instance.
(2) Notwithstanding paragraph 1 the parties may agree on the use of the language in which the patent was granted as the language of proceedings.
(3) In exceptional cases and to the extent deemed appropriate, the Court of Appeal may decide on another official language of a Contracting Member State as the language of proceedings for the whole or part of the proceedings, subject to agreement by the parties.

ARTICLE 51 Other language arrangements

(1) Any panel of the Court of First Instance and the Court of Appeal may, to the extent deemed appropriate, dispense with translation requirements.
(2) At the request of one of the parties, and to the extent deemed appropriate, any division of the Court of First Instance and the Court of Appeal shall provide interpretation facilities to assist the parties concerned at oral proceedings.
(3) Notwithstanding Article 49(6), in cases where an action for infringement is brought before the central division, a defendant having its residence, principal place of business or place of business in a Member State shall have the right to obtain, upon request, translations of relevant documents in the language of the Member State of residence, principal place of business or, in the absence of residence or principal place of business, place of business, in the following circumstances:
   (a) jurisdiction is entrusted to the central division in accordance with Article 33(1) third or fourth subparagraph, and
   (b) the language of proceedings at the central division is a language which is not an official language of the Member State where the defendant has its residence, principal place of business or, in the absence of residence or principal place of business, place of business, and
   (c) the defendant does not have proper knowledge of the language of the proceedings.

CHAPTER III—PROCEEDINGS BEFORE THE COURT

ARTICLE 52 Written, interim and oral procedures

(1) The proceedings before the Court shall consist of a written, an interim and an oral procedure, in accordance with the Rules of Procedure. All procedures shall be organized in a flexible and balanced manner.
(2) In the interim procedure, after the written procedure and if appropriate, the judge acting as Rapporteur, subject to a mandate of the full panel, shall be responsible for convening an interim hearing. That judge shall in particular

explore with the parties the possibility for a settlement, including through mediation, and/or arbitration, by using the facilities of the Centre referred to in Article 35.

(3) The oral procedure shall give parties the opportunity to explain properly their arguments. The Court may, with the agreement of the parties, dispense with the oral hearing.

ARTICLE 53 Means of evidence

(1) In proceedings before the Court, the means of giving or obtaining evidence shall include in particular the following:
  (a) hearing the parties;
  (b) requests for information;
  (c) production of documents;
  (d) hearing witnesses;
  (e) opinions by experts;
  (f) inspection;
  (g) comparative tests or experiments;
  (h) sworn statements in writing (affidavits).

(2) The Rules of Procedure shall govern the procedure for taking such evidence. Questioning of witnesses and experts shall be under the control of the Court and be limited to what is necessary.

ARTICLE 54 Burden of proof

Without prejudice to Article 24(2) and (3), the burden of the proof of facts shall be on the party relying on those facts.

ARTICLE 55 Reversal of burden of proof

(1) Without prejudice to Article 24(2) and (3), if the subject-matter of a patent is a process for obtaining a new product, the identical product when produced without the consent of the patent proprietor shall, in the absence of proof to the contrary, be deemed to have been obtained by the patented process.

(2) The principle set out in paragraph 1 shall also apply where there is a substantial likelihood that the identical product was made by the patented process and the patent proprietor has been unable, despite reasonable efforts, to determine the process actually used for such identical product.

(3) In the adduction of proof to the contrary, the legitimate interests of the defendant in protecting its manufacturing and trade secrets shall be taken into account.

CHAPTER IV—POWERS OF THE COURT

ARTICLE 56 The general powers of the Court

(1) The Court may impose such measures, procedures and remedies as are laid down in this Agreement and may make its orders subject to conditions, in accordance with the Rules of Procedure.
(2) The Court shall take due account of the interest of the parties and shall, before making an order, give any party the opportunity to be heard, unless this is incompatible with the effective enforcement of such order.

ARTICLE 57 Court experts

(1) Without prejudice to the possibility for the parties to produce expert evidence, the Court may at any time appoint court experts in order to provide expertise for specific aspects of the case. The Court shall provide such expert with all information necessary for the provision of the expert advice.
(2) To this end, an indicative list of experts shall be drawn up by the Court in accordance with the Rules of Procedure. That list shall be kept by the Registrar.
(3) The court experts shall guarantee independence and impartiality. Rules governing conflicts of interest applicable to judges set out in Article 7 of the Statute shall by analogy apply to court experts.
(4) Expert advice given to the Court by court experts shall be made available to the parties which shall have the possibility to comment on it.

ARTICLE 58 Protection of confidential information

To protect the trade secrets, personal data or other confidential information of a party to the proceedings or of a third party, or to prevent an abuse of evidence, the Court may order that the collection and use of evidence in proceedings before it be restricted or prohibited or that access to such evidence be restricted to specific persons.

ARTICLE 59 Order to produce evidence

(1) At the request of a party which has presented reasonably available evidence sufficient to support its claims and has, in substantiating those claims, specified evidence which lies in the control of the opposing party or a third party, the Court may order the opposing party or a third party to present such evidence, subject to the protection of confidential information. Such order shall not result in an obligation of self-incrimination.
(2) At the request of a party the Court may order, under the same conditions as specified in paragraph 1, the communication of banking, financial or commercial documents under the control of the opposing party, subject to the protection of confidential information.

ARTICLE 60 Order to preserve evidence and to inspect premises

(1) At the request of the applicant which has presented reasonably available evidence to support the claim that the patent has been infringed or is about to be infringed the Court may, even before the commencement of proceedings on the merits of the case, order prompt and effective provisional measures to preserve relevant evidence in respect of the alleged infringement, subject to the protection of confidential information.

(2) Such measures may include the detailed description, with or without the taking of samples, or the physical seizure of the infringing products, and, in appropriate cases, the materials and implements used in the production and/or distribution of those products and the documents relating thereto.

(3) The Court may, even before the commencement of proceedings on the merits of the case, at the request of the applicant who has presented evidence to support the claim that the patent has been infringed or is about to be infringed, order the inspection of premises. Such inspection of premises shall be conducted by a person appointed by the Court in accordance with the Rules of Procedure.

(4) At the inspection of the premises the applicant shall not be present itself but may be represented by an independent professional practitioner whose name has to be specified in the Court's order.

(5) Measures shall be ordered, if necessary without the other party having been heard, in particular where any delay is likely to cause irreparable harm to the proprietor of the patent, or where there is a demonstrable risk of evidence being destroyed.

(6) Where measures to preserve evidence or inspect premises are ordered without the other party in the case having been heard, the parties affected shall be given notice, without delay and at the latest immediately after the execution of the measures. A review, including a right to be heard, shall take place upon request of the parties affected with a view to deciding, within a reasonable period after the notification of the measures, whether the measures are to be modified, revoked or confirmed.

(7) The measures to preserve evidence may be subject to the lodging by the applicant of adequate security or an equivalent assurance intended to ensure compensation for any prejudice suffered by the defendant as provided for in paragraph 9.

(8) The Court shall ensure that the measures to preserve evidence are revoked or otherwise cease to have effect, at the defendant's request, without prejudice to the damages which may be claimed, if the applicant does not bring, within a period not exceeding 31 calendar days or 20 working days, whichever is the longer, action leading to a decision on the merits of the case before the Court.

(9) Where the measures to preserve evidence are revoked, or where they lapse due to any act or omission by the applicant, or where it is subsequently found that there has been no infringement or threat of infringement of the patent, the Court may order the applicant, at the defendant's request, to provide the

defendant with appropriate compensation for any damage suffered as a result of those measures.

ARTICLE 61 Freezing orders

(1) At the request of the applicant which has presented reasonably available evidence to support the claim that the patent has been infringed or is about to be infringed the Court may, even before the commencement of proceedings on the merits of the case, order a party not to remove from its jurisdiction any assets located therein, or not to deal in any assets, whether located within its jurisdiction or not.
(2) Article 60(5) to (9) shall apply by analogy to the measures referred to in this Article.

ARTICLE 62 Provisional and protective measures

(1) The Court may, by way of order, grant injunctions against an alleged infringer or against an intermediary whose services are used by the alleged infringer, intended to prevent any imminent infringement, to prohibit, on a provisional basis and subject, where appropriate, to a recurring penalty payment, the continuation of the alleged infringement or to make such continuation subject to the lodging of guarantees intended to ensure the compensation of the right holder.
(2) The Court shall have the discretion to weigh up the interests of the parties and in particular to take into account the potential harm for either of the parties resulting from the granting or the refusal of the injunction.
(3) The Court may also order the seizure or delivery up of the products suspected of infringing a patent so as to prevent their entry into, or movement, within the channels of commerce. If the applicant demonstrates circumstances likely to endanger the recovery of damages, the Court may order the precautionary seizure of the movable and immovable property of the alleged infringer, including the blocking of the bank accounts and of other assets of the alleged infringer.
(4) The Court may, in respect of the measures referred to in paragraphs 1 and 3, require the applicant to provide any reasonable evidence in order to satisfy itself with a sufficient degree of certainty that the applicant is the right holder and that the applicant's right is being infringed, or that such infringement is imminent.
(5) Article 60(5) to (9) shall apply by analogy to the measures referred to in this Article.

ARTICLE 63 Permanent injunctions

(1) Where a decision is taken finding an infringement of a patent, the Court may grant an injunction against the infringer aimed at prohibiting the continuation of the infringement. The Court may also grant such injunction against an intermediary whose services are being used by a third party to infringe a patent.
(2) Where appropriate, non-compliance with the injunction referred to in paragraph 1 shall be subject to a recurring penalty payment payable to the Court.

ARTICLE 64 Corrective measures in infringement proceedings

(1) Without prejudice to any damages due to the injured party by reason of the infringement, and without compensation of any sort, the Court may order, at the request of the applicant, that appropriate measures be taken with regard to products found to be infringing a patent and, in appropriate cases, with regard to materials and implements principally used in the creation or manufacture of those products.
(2) Such measures shall include:
   (a) a declaration of infringement;
   (b) recalling the products from the channels of commerce;
   (c) depriving the product of its infringing property;
   (d) definitively removing the products from the channels of commerce; or
   (e) the destruction of the products and/or of the materials and implements concerned.
(3) The Court shall order that those measures be carried out at the expense of the infringer, unless particular reasons are invoked for not doing so.
(4) In considering a request for corrective measures pursuant to this Article, the Court shall take into account the need for proportionality between the seriousness of the infringement and the remedies to be ordered, the willingness of the infringer to convert the materials into a non-infringing state, as well as the interests of third parties.

ARTICLE 65 Decision on the validity of a patent

(1) The Court shall decide on the validity of a patent on the basis of an action for revocation or a counterclaim for revocation.
(2) The Court may revoke a patent, either entirely or partly, only on the grounds referred to in Articles 138(1) and 139(2) of the EPC.
(3) Without prejudice to Article 138(3) of the EPC, if the grounds for revocation affect the patent only in part, the patent shall be limited by a corresponding amendment of the claims and revoked in part.
(4) To the extent that a patent has been revoked it shall be deemed not to have had, from the outset, the effects specified in Articles 64 and 67 of the EPC.

(5) Where the Court, in a final decision, revokes a patent, either entirely or partly, it shall send a copy of the decision to the European Patent Office and, with respect to a European patent, to the national patent office of any Contracting Member State concerned.

ARTICLE 66 Powers of the Court concerning decisions of the European Patent Office

(1) In actions brought under Article 32(1)(i), the Court may exercise any power entrusted on the European Patent Office in accordance with Article 9 of Regulation (EU) No 1257/2012, including the rectification of the Register for unitary patent protection.
(2) In actions brought under Article 32(1)(i) the parties shall, by way of derogation from Article 69, bear their own costs.

ARTICLE 67 Power to order the communication of information

(1) The Court may, in response to a justified and proportionate request of the applicant and in accordance with the Rules of Procedure, order an infringer to inform the applicant of:
  (a) the origin and distribution channels of the infringing products or processes;
  (b) the quantities produced, manufactured, delivered, received or ordered, as well as the price obtained for the infringing products; and
  (c) the identity of any third person involved in the production or distribution of the infringing products or in the use of the infringing process.
(2) The Court may, in accordance with the Rules of Procedure, also order any third party who:
  (a) was found in the possession of the infringing products on a commercial scale or to be using an infringing process on a commercial scale;
  (b) was found to be providing on a commercial scale services used in infringing activities; or
  (c) was indicated by the person referred to in points (a) or (b) as being involved in the production, manufacture or distribution of the infringing products or processes or in the provision of the services,

  to provide the applicant with the information referred to in paragraph 1.

ARTICLE 68 Award of damages

(1) The Court shall, at the request of the injured party, order the infringer who knowingly, or with reasonable grounds to know, engaged in a patent infringing activity, to pay the injured party damages appropriate to the harm actually suffered by that party as a result of the infringement.
(2) The injured party shall, to the extent possible, be placed in the position it would have been in if no infringement had taken place. The infringer shall not benefit from the infringement. However, damages shall not be punitive.
(3) When the Court sets the damages:
    (a) it shall take into account all appropriate aspects, such as the negative economic consequences, including lost profits, which the injured party has suffered, any unfair profits made by the infringer and, in appropriate cases, elements other than economic factors, such as the moral prejudice caused to the injured party by the infringement; or
    (b) as an alternative to point (a), it may, in appropriate cases, set the damages as a lump sum on the basis of elements such as at least the amount of the royalties or fees which would have been due if the infringer had requested authorisation to use the patent in question.
(4) Where the infringer did not knowingly, or with reasonable grounds to know, engage in the infringing activity, the Court may order the recovery of profits or the payment of compensation.

ARTICLE 69 Legal costs

(1) Reasonable and proportionate legal costs and other expenses incurred by the successful party shall, as a general rule, be borne by the unsuccessful party, unless equity requires otherwise, up to a ceiling set in accordance with the Rules of Procedure.
(2) Where a party succeeds only in part or in exceptional circumstances, the Court may order that costs be apportioned equitably or that the parties bear their own costs.
(3) A party should bear any unnecessary costs it has caused the Court or another party.
(4) At the request of the defendant, the Court may order the applicant to provide adequate security for the legal costs and other expenses incurred by the defendant which the applicant may be liable to bear, in particular in the cases referred to in Articles 59 to 62.

ARTICLE 70 Court fees

(1) Parties to proceedings before the Court shall pay court fees.
(2) Court fees shall be paid in advance, unless the Rules of Procedure provide otherwise. Any party which has not paid a prescribed court fee may be excluded from further participation in the proceedings.

ARTICLE 71 Legal aid

(1) A party who is a natural person and who is unable to meet the costs of the proceedings, either wholly or in part, may at any time apply for legal aid. The conditions for granting of legal aid shall be laid down in the Rules of Procedure.
(2) The Court shall decide whether legal aid should be granted in full or in part, or whether it should be refused, in accordance with the Rules of Procedure.
(3) On a proposal from the Court, the Administrative Committee shall set the level of legal aid and the rules on bearing the costs thereof.

ARTICLE 72 Period of limitation

Without prejudice to Article 24(2) and (3), actions relating to all forms of financial compensation may not be brought more than five years after the date on which the applicant became aware, or had reasonable grounds to become aware, of the last fact justifying the action. UPC/en 75

CHAPTER V—APPEALS

ARTICLE 73 Appeal

(1) An appeal against a decision of the Court of First Instance may be brought before the Court of Appeal by any party which has been unsuccessful, in whole or in part, in its submissions, within two months of the date of the notification of the decision.
(2) An appeal against an order of the Court of First Instance may be brought before the Court of Appeal by any party which has been unsuccessful, in whole or in part, in its submissions:
    (a) for the orders referred to in Articles 49(5), 59 to 62 and 67 within 15 calendar days of the notification of the order to the applicant;
    (b) for other orders than the orders referred to in point (a):
        (i) together with the appeal against the decision, or
        (ii) where the Court grants leave to appeal, within 15 days of the notification of the Court's decision to that effect.
(3) The appeal against a decision or an order of the Court of First Instance may be based on points of law and matters of fact.

(4) New facts and new evidence may only be introduced in accordance with the Rules of Procedure and where the submission thereof by the party concerned could not reasonably have been expected during proceedings before the Court of First Instance.

ARTICLE 74 Effects of an appeal

(1) An appeal shall not have suspensive effect unless the Court of Appeal decides otherwise at the motivated request of one of the parties. The Rules of Procedure shall guarantee that such a decision is taken without delay.
(2) Notwithstanding paragraph 1, an appeal against a decision on actions or counterclaims for revocation and on actions based on Article 32(1)(i) shall always have suspensive effect.
(3) An appeal against an order referred to in Articles 49(5), 59 to 62 or 67 shall not prevent the continuation of the main proceedings. However, the Court of First Instance shall not give a decision in the main proceedings before the decision of the Court of Appeal concerning an appealed order has been given.

ARTICLE 75 Decision on appeal and referral back

(1) If an appeal pursuant to Article 73 is well-founded, the Court of Appeal shall revoke the decision of the Court of First Instance and give a final decision. The Court of Appeal may in exceptional cases and in accordance with the Rules of Procedure refer the case back to the Court of First Instance for decision.
(2) Where a case is referred back to the Court of First Instance pursuant to paragraph 1, the Court of First Instance shall be bound by the decision of the Court of Appeal on points of law.

CHAPTER VI DECISIONS

ARTICLE 76 Basis for decisions and right to be heard

(1) The Court shall decide in accordance with the requests submitted by the parties and shall not award more than is requested.
(2) Decisions on the merits may only be based on grounds, facts and evidence, which were submitted by the parties or introduced into the procedure by an order of the Court and on which the parties have had an opportunity to present their comments.
(3) The Court shall evaluate evidence freely and independently.

ARTICLE 77 Formal requirements

(1) Decisions and orders of the Court shall be reasoned and shall be given in writing in accordance with the Rules of Procedure.
(2) Decisions and orders of the Court shall be delivered in the language of proceedings.

ARTICLE 78 Decisions of the Court and dissenting opinions

(1) Decisions and orders of the Court shall be taken by a majority of the panel, in accordance with the Statute. In case of equal votes, the vote of the presiding judge shall prevail.
(2) In exceptional circumstances, any judge of the panel may express a dissenting opinion separately from the decision of the Court.

ARTICLE 79 Settlement

The parties may, at any time in the course of proceedings, conclude their case by way of settlement, which shall be confirmed by a decision of the Court. A patent may not be revoked or limited by way of settlement.

ARTICLE 80 Publication of decisions

The Court may order, at the request of the applicant and at the expense of the infringer, appropriate measures for the dissemination of information concerning the Court's decision, including displaying the decision and publishing it in full or in part in public media. UPC/en 80

ARTICLE 81 Rehearing

(1) A request for rehearing after a final decision of the Court may exceptionally be granted by the Court of Appeal in the following circumstances:
  (a) on discovery of a fact by the party requesting the rehearing, which is of such a nature as to be a decisive factor and which, when the decision was given, was unknown to the party requesting the rehearing; such request may only be granted on the basis of an act which was held, by a final decision of a national court, to constitute a criminal offence; or
  (b) in the event of a fundamental procedural defect, in particular when a defendant who did not appear before the Court was not served with the document initiating the proceedings or an equivalent document in sufficient time and in such a way as to enable him to arrange for the defence.
(2) A request for a rehearing shall be filed within 10 years of the date of the decision but not later than two months from the date of the discovery of the new fact or of the procedural defect. Such request shall not have suspensive effect unless the Court of Appeal decides otherwise.

(3) If the request for a rehearing is well-founded, the Court of Appeal shall set aside, in whole or in part, the decision under review and re-open the proceedings for a new trial and decision, in accordance with the Rules of Procedure.

(4) Persons using patents which are the subject-matter of a decision under review and who act in good faith should be allowed to continue using such patents.

ARTICLE 82 Enforcement of decisions and orders

(1) Decisions and orders of the Court shall be enforceable in any Contracting Member State. An order for the enforcement of a decision shall be appended to the decision by the Court.

(2) Where appropriate, the enforcement of a decision may be subject to the provision of security or an equivalent assurance to ensure compensation for any damage suffered, in particular in the case of injunctions.

(3) Without prejudice to this Agreement and the Statute, enforcement procedures shall be governed by the law of the Contracting Member State where the enforcement takes place. Any decision of the Court shall be enforced under the same conditions as a decision given in the Contracting Member State where the enforcement takes place.

(4) If a party does not comply with the terms of an order of the Court, that party may be sanctioned with a recurring penalty payment payable to the Court. The individual penalty shall be proportionate to the importance of the order to be enforced and shall be without prejudice to the party's right to claim damages or security.

PART IV—TRANSITIONAL PROVISIONS

ARTICLE 83 Transitional regime

(1) During a transitional period of seven years after the date of entry into force of this Agreement, an action for infringement or for revocation of a European patent or an action for infringement or for declaration of invalidity of a supplementary protection certificate issued for a product protected by a European patent may still be brought before national courts or other competent national authorities.

(2) An action pending before a national court at the end of the transitional period shall not be affected by the expiry of this period.

(3) Unless an action has already been brought before the Court, a proprietor of or an applicant for a European patent granted or applied for prior to the end of the transitional period under paragraph 1 and, where applicable, paragraph 5, as well as a holder of a supplementary protection certificate issued for a product protected by a European patent, shall have the possibility to opt out from the exclusive competence of the Court. To this end they shall notify their

opt-out to the Registry by the latest one month before expiry of the transitional period. The opt-out shall take effect upon its entry into the register.

(4) Unless an action has already been brought before a national court, proprietors of or applicants for European patents or holders of supplementary protection certificates issued for a product protected by a European patent who made use of the opt-out in accordance with paragraph 3 shall be entitled to withdraw their opt-out at any moment. In this event they shall notify the Registry accordingly. The withdrawal of the opt-out shall take effect upon its entry into the register.

(5) Five years after the entry into force of this Agreement, the Administrative Committee shall carry out a broad consultation with the users of the patent system and a survey on the number of European patents and supplementary protection certificates issued for products protected by European patents with respect to which actions for infringement or for revocation or declaration of invalidity are still brought before the national courts pursuant to paragraph 1, the reasons for this and the implications thereof. On the basis of this consultation and an opinion of the Court, the Administrative Committee may decide to prolong the transitional period by up to seven years.

PART V—FINAL PROVISIONS

ARTICLE 84 Signature, ratification and accession

...

ARTICLE 85 Functions of the depositary

...

ARTICLE 86 Duration of the Agreement

...

ARTICLE 87 Revision

...

ARTICLE 88 Languages of the Agreement

...

ARTICLE 89 Entry into force

...

ANNEX I STATUTE OF THE UNIFIED PATENT COURT

...

ANNEX II

Distribution of cases within the central division (8): Excerpts of the RoP

§18.09 UP REGULATIONS: NO. 1257/2012 OF 17 DECEMBER 2012 IMPLEMENTING ENHANCED COOPERATION IN THE AREA OF THE CREATION OF UNITARY PATENT PROTECTION

Preamble …

CHAPTER I

GENERAL PROVISIONS

Article 1—Subject matter

1. This Regulation implements enhanced cooperation in the area of the creation of unitary patent protection, authorised by Decision 2011/167/EU.
2. This Regulation constitutes a special agreement within the meaning of Article 142 of the Convention on the Grant of European Patents of 5 October 1973, as revised on 17 December 1991 and on 29 November 2000 (hereinafter "EPC").

Article 2—Definitions

For the purposes of this Regulation, the following definitions shall apply:

(a) "Participating Member State" means a Member State which participates in enhanced cooperation in the area of the creation of unitary patent protection by virtue of Decision 2011/167/EU, or by virtue of a decision adopted in accordance with the second or third subparagraph of Article 331(1) of the TFEU, at the time the request for unitary effect as referred to in Article 9 is made;

(b) "European patent" means a patent granted by the European Patent Office (hereinafter "EPO") under the rules and procedures laid down in the EPC;

(c) "European patent with unitary effect" means a European patent which benefits from unitary effect in the participating Member States by virtue of this Regulation;

(d) "European Patent Register" means the register kept by the EPO under Article 127 of the EPC;

(e) "Register for unitary patent protection" means the register constituting part of the European Patent Register in which the unitary effect and any limitation, licence, transfer, revocation or lapse of a European patent with unitary effect are registered;

(f) "European Patent Bulletin" means the periodical publication provided for in Article 129 of the EPC.

Article 3—European patent with unitary effect

1. A European patent granted with the same set of claims in respect of all the participating Member States shall benefit from unitary effect in the participating Member States provided that its unitary effect has been registered in the Register for unitary patent protection.

A European patent granted with different sets of claims for different participating Member States shall not benefit from unitary effect.

2. A European patent with unitary effect shall have a unitary character. It shall provide uniform protection and shall have equal effect in all the participating Member States.

   It may only be limited, transferred or revoked, or lapse, in respect of all the participating Member States.

   It may be licensed in respect of the whole or part of the territories of the participating Member States.

3. The unitary effect of a European patent shall be deemed not to have arisen to the extent that the European patent has been revoked or limited.

Article 4—**Date of effect**

1. A European patent with unitary effect shall take effect in the participating Member States on the date of publication by the EPO of the mention of the grant of the European patent in the European Patent Bulletin.
2. The participating Member States shall take the necessary measures to ensure that, where the unitary effect of a European patent has been registered and extends to their territory, that European patent is deemed not to have taken effect as a national patent in their territory on the date of publication of the mention of the grant in the European Patent Bulletin.

CHAPTER II

EFFECTS OF A EUROPEAN PATENT WITH UNITARY EFFECT

Article 5—Uniform protection

1. The European patent with unitary effect shall confer on its proprietor the right to prevent any third party from committing acts against which that patent provides protection throughout the territories of the participating Member States in which it has unitary effect, subject to applicable limitations.
2. The scope of that right and its limitations shall be uniform in all participating Member States in which the patent has unitary effect.
3. The acts against which the patent provides protection referred to in paragraph 1 and the applicable limitations shall be those defined by the law applied to European patents with unitary effect in the participating Member State whose

national law is applicable to the European patent with unitary effect as an object of property in accordance with Article 7.

4. In its report referred to in Article 16(1), the Commission shall evaluate the functioning of the applicable limitations and shall, where necessary, make appropriate proposals.

Article 6—Exhaustion of the rights conferred by a European patent with unitary effect

The rights conferred by a European patent with unitary effect shall not extend to acts concerning a product covered by that patent which are carried out within the participating Member States in which that patent has unitary effect after that product has been placed on the market in the Union by, or with the consent of, the patent proprietor, unless there are legitimate grounds for the patent proprietor to oppose further commercialisation of the product.

CHAPTER III

A EUROPEAN PATENT WITH UNITARY EFFECT AS AN OBJECT OF PROPERTY

Article 7—Treating a European patent with unitary effect as a national patent

1. A European patent with unitary effect as an object of property shall be treated in its entirety and in all the participating Member States as a national patent of the participating Member State in which that patent has unitary effect and in which, according to the European Patent Register:
   (a) the applicant had his residence or principal place of business on the date of filing of the application for the European patent; or
   (b) where point (a) does not apply, the applicant had a place of business on the date of filing of the application for the European patent.
2. Where two or more persons are entered in the European Patent Register as joint applicants, point (a) of paragraph 1 shall apply to the joint applicant indicated first. Where this is not possible, point (a) of paragraph 1 shall apply to the next joint applicant indicated in the order of entry. Where point (a) of paragraph 1 does not apply to any of the joint applicants, point (b) of paragraph 1 shall apply accordingly.
3. Where no applicant had his residence, principal place of business or place of business in a participating Member State in which that patent has unitary effect for the purposes of paragraphs 1 or 2, the European patent with unitary effect as an object of property shall be treated in its entirety and in all the participating Member States as a national patent of the State where the European Patent Organisation has its headquarters in accordance with Article 6(1) of the EPC.
4. The acquisition of a right may not be dependent on any entry in a national patent register.

Article 8—Licences of right

1. The proprietor of a European patent with unitary effect may file a statement with the EPO to the effect that the proprietor is prepared to allow any person to use the invention as a licensee in return for appropriate consideration.
2. A licence obtained under this Regulation shall be treated as a contractual licence.

CHAPTER IV

INSTITUTIONAL PROVISIONS

Article 9—Administrative tasks in the framework of the European Patent Organisation

...

CHAPTER V

FINANCIAL PROVISIONS

Article 10—Principle on expenses

...

Article 11—Renewal fees

...

Article 12—Level of renewal fees

...

Article 13—Distribution

...

CHAPTER VI

FINAL PROVISIONS

Articles 13–18 ...

...

Index

R

S

www.ingramcontent.com/pod-product-compliance
Lightning Source LLC
LaVergne TN
LVHW020003031026
849161LV00023B/866
* 9 7 8 9 0 4 1 1 9 1 0 6 9 *